CW01269858

LONDON RECORD SOCIETY
PUBLICATIONS

VOLUME LII

THE LONDON DIARY OF ANTHONY HEAP
1931–1945

EDITED BY
ROBIN WOOLVEN

LONDON RECORD SOCIETY
THE BOYDELL PRESS
2017

© London Record Society 2017

All Rights Reserved. Except as permitted under current legislation
no part of this work may be photocopied, stored in a retrieval system,
published, performed in public, adapted, broadcast,
transmitted, recorded or reproduced in any form or by any means,
without the prior permission of the copyright owner

Diaries of Anthony Heap © Anthony Heap and the London Metropolitan Archives

Selections and editorial material © Robin Woolven

First published 2017

A London Record Society publication
Published by The Boydell Press
an imprint of Boydell & Brewer Ltd
PO Box 9, Woodbridge, Suffolk IP12 3DF, UK
and of Boydell & Brewer Inc.
668 Mt Hope Avenue, Rochester, NY 14620–2731, USA
website: www.boydellandbrewer.com

ISBN 978-0-900952-58-6

A CIP catalogue record for this book is available
from the British Library

The publisher has no responsibility for the continued existence or accuracy of URLs for
external or third-party internet websites referred to in this book, and does not guarantee that
any content on such websites is, or will remain, accurate or appropriate

This publication is printed on acid-free paper
Typeset by Frances Hackeson Freelance Publishing Services, Brinscall
Printed and bound in Great Britain by TJ International Ltd.

MIX
Paper from
responsible sources
FSC® C013056

CONTENTS

LIST OF ILLUSTRATIONS	vi
ACKNOWLEDGEMENTS	viii
ABBREVIATIONS	ix
MONEY AND PRICE COMPARISONS	x
INTRODUCTION	1
THE DIARY OF ANTHONY HEAP	
PART ONE: 'Flirting with Fascism', 1931–1939	23
Introduction	25
1931	29
1932	51
1933	66
1934	93
1935	121
1936	148
1937	175
1938	200
1939	228
PART TWO: 'This Battered Old Town', 1940–31 August 1945	273
1940	275
1941	340
1942	388
1943	415
1944	440
1 January to 31 August 1945	476
EPILOGUE	505
APPENDICES	
A. Principal Persons Mentioned in the Diary	511
B. Anthony Heap's Annual Culture Capture 1930–1945	513
BIBLIOGRAPHY	613
INDEX	615

ILLUSTRATIONS

MAPS

Map I	Anthony Heap's residences to 1939.	xi
Map II	Anthony Heap's residences 1940–1945.	xii
Map III	London West End theatres.	xiii
Map IV	London Cinemas.	xiv

PLATES

1. Anthony Heap's 1964 passport photograph. Photo: author at London Metropolitan Archives. xv
2. Heap with fellow Holborn Rover Scouts at Gilwell Park, 1929 Photo: from Heap's Rover Log Book courtesy of the Scout Centre. xvi
3. The building that was Peter Robinson's at Oxford Circus, W1. Photo: author. xvi
4. Heap's pocket diary entries for the 1929 General Election. Photo: author at London Metropolitan Archives. xvii
5. 139 Gray's Inn Road, WC1. Photo: author. xviii
6. 11 Penryn Street, NW1. Photo: author. xix
7. Diary entry recording Heap's father's suicide, 7 March 1933. Photo: courtesy of the London Metropolitan Archives. xx
8. 20 Harrington Square, NW1. Photo: author. xxi
9. Sinclair House, Hastings Street, WC1. Photo: author. xxi
10. Selected programmes from His Majesty's Theatre. Photo: courtesy of the London Metropolitan Archives. xxii
11. Diary entry recording the Olympia Fascist rally, 7 June 1934. Photo: courtesy of the London Metropolitan Archives. xxiii
12. Eilleen's telegram, 23 June 1940. Photo: courtesy of the London Metropolitan Archives. xxiv
13. The steps down to the crypt air raid shelter. Photo: author. xxiv
14. Entrance to the crypt below St Pancras New Church, Euston Road. Photo: author. xxv
15. Harrington Square bomb incident, 8 September 1940. Photo: Getty Images/Popperfoto. xxvi

16 The bomb-damaged Peter Robinson's, Oxford Circus, September 1940. Photo: courtesy of the Imperial War Museum – D1096. xxvi
17 The bomb-damaged John Lewis after the September 1940 raid. Photo: courtesy of the Imperial War Museum – D1093. xxvii
18 Tottenham Court Road after the land mine incident, 24 September 1940. Photo: London Fire Museum. xxviii
19 Tottenham Court Road in November 2016. Photo: author. xxviii
20 Bomb damage in Tavistock Square WC1, south side, on 15 October 1940. Photo: courtesy of Camden Local Studies and Archives Centre. xxix
21 Panorama of the damaged Theobalds Road, c.1942. Photo: courtesy of Camden Local Studies and Archives Centre. xxx
22 Queen Alexandra Mansions, Hastings Street frontage. Photo: author. xxxi
23 Rashleigh House, Thanet Street. Photo: author. xxxii
24 Heap's diaries for 1928–1941, as stored for safety in his shelter. Photo: courtesy of the London Metropolitan Archives. xxxiii
25 Whitefields Tabernacle after the V-2 incident, 26 March 1945. Photo: courtesy of Camden Local Studies and Archives Centre. xxxiii
26 Heap with his son, Anthony Charles, in 1965. Photo: author, from small print tucked inside the 1965 diary. xxxiv

The editor and publishers are grateful to all the institutions and individuals listed for permission to reproduce the materials in which they hold copyright. Every effort has been made to trace the copyright holders; apologies are offered for any omission, and the publishers will be pleased to add any necessary acknowledgement in subsequent editions.

ACKNOWLEDGEMENTS

I must acknowledge my good fortune in having had the help and advice of many people in publishing this book. In particular, I thank Dr Juliet Gardiner, whose use of Anthony Heap's diaries in her books on *The Thirties* and *Wartime Britain* first attracted my attention. I am indebted to Professor Jerry White, who listened sympathetically to my suggestion that Heap deserved a wider audience, and then advised and supported me through the task of editing fifteen years of daily entries down to a size suitable for publication by the London Record Society. I also much appreciate the assistance and advice given by Caroline Palmer and her colleagues at Boydell & Brewer, the Society's publishers, and I am grateful to my copy-editor, Dr Hester Higton, for her constructive and detailed professional comments on the text.

Much of the cost of publishing this larger than usual annual volume has been met by the financial help granted to the Society by the Camden History Society and the Marc Fitch and Isobel Thornley Funds, without whose support publication would not have been possible.

My thanks also go to Jeremy Smith and the staff at the London Metropolitan Archives, who have tolerated my many visits to Clerkenwell requiring them to repeatedly produce successive volumes of Heap's diary, and for the use of their photographs. At the Camden Local Studies and Archives Centre, Tudor Allen and his ever helpful staff of Kate Brolly, Ingrid Smits and Frances Johnson have answered my questions and produced the papers, maps and photographs requested. I also wish to thank the Friends House archivist, Lisa McQuillan, for showing me their wartime records, and the Scout Centre at Gilwell Park, who produced for me the Holborn Rover Logs written by Heap. Mr Michael Ogden kindly provided me with details of the St Pancras Church crypt. And I thank the Reference Librarians and Local Studies archivists at Westminster, and Hammersmith and Fulham, who have responded to my calls, visits and emails for Heap-related snippets in their stores.

Lastly I must thank my wife, Sonia, for her tolerance of my apparent obsession with Anthony Heap's real obsession of maintaining a daily diary for fifty-seven years.

ABBREVIATIONS

AA	Anti-Aircraft
ACIS	Associate of the Chartered Institute of Secretaries
ARP	Air Raid Precautions (later Civil Defence) – the national and local authority organisations and measures to protect the public from the effects of aerial bombardment
BBC	British Broadcasting Corporation – the radio/wireless broadcaster most listened to
BUF	British Union of Fascists
Boot's	The leading retail chemist chain, whose major branches also operated a lending library which Heap joined in 1937, when Mudie's Library closed
CIS	Chartered Institute of Secretaries
JD	Mr Doran, Heap's boss at Peter Robinson's
LCC	London County Council
LMA	London Metropolitan Archives, 40 Northampton Road, London EC1R 0HB
LPTB	London Passenger Transport Board
MR	Municipal Reform Party – until 1963 the banner under which some Conservative parties then operated in London boroughs
PR's	Peter Robinson's department store at Oxford Circus, where Heap worked 1927–1940
PWR	(Metropolitan) Police War Reserve. Heap started the training course in 1939 but was medically unfit to serve, following his peritonitis and the rupture of his stomach wall.
T C Rd	Tottenham Court Road
TNA	The National Archives, Kew
YM	*See* YMCA
YMCA	The Young Men's Christian Association, on the Great Russell Street corner of Tottenham Court Road. Heap was a paid-up member from 1928 to April 1940, regularly using its swimming pool, restaurant and library. It was also the meeting place for the Holborn Rover Group. The King George's Hall was its theatre hall on the east side of the building.

MONEY AND PRICE
COMPARISONS

Until the adoption of decimal currency in February 1971, the UK used its traditional system of the pound (£1), which was divided into twenty shillings and each shilling into twelve pence. Thus there were 240 pence to the pound and the prices were written using the symbols £, s. (shillings) and d. (pence). Some shops and institutions priced their goods (like Heap's annual CIS subscription) in guineas, each equal to 21 shillings. A sum of three and a half guineas would be written as £3.13.6 or £3/13/6.

To compare the value of goods and services recorded in Heap's diary with their approximate value in 2016, the table below uses the Bank of England figure giving the factor by which the diary price should be multiplied.[1] The Bank also notes that 'Prices fell in almost every year between 1920 and 1933.' Thereafter, inflation resumed; between 1931 and 1939 it averaged 5% annually.

Year	1931	1932	1933	1934	1935	1936	1937	1938
For 2016 value, multiply by:	62.51	64.06	65.68	65.68	65.26	64.86	62.51	61.77

Year	1939	1940	1941	1942	1943	1944	1945
For 2016 value, multiply by:	59.98	51.37	46.33	43.24	41.84	40.69	39.61

For example, Heap's dispute with a Council tenant in 1942 over her alleged non-payment of 17/4 (which Heap eventually agreed to pay himself) represented some £37.47 in 2016.

---

[1] http://www.bankofengland.co.uk/education/Pages/resources/inflationtools/calculator, consulted 31 March 2017.

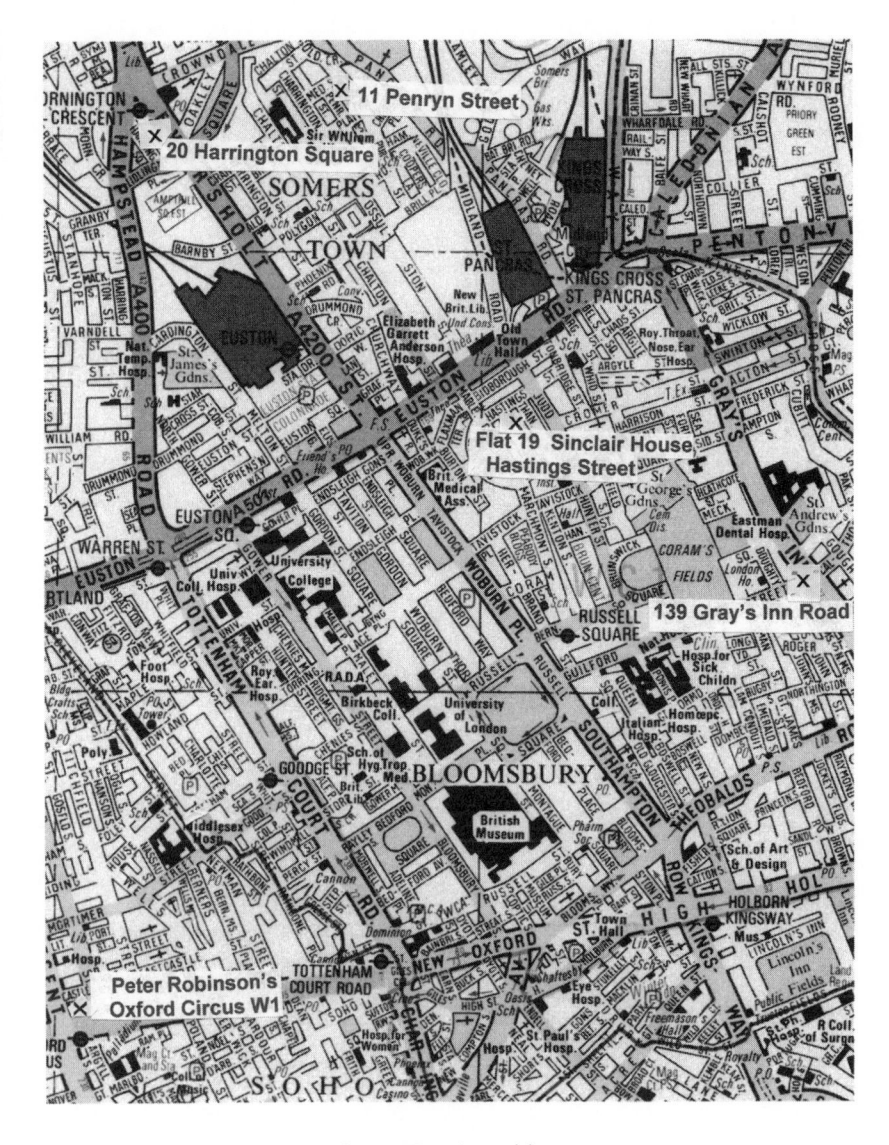

Map I: Anthony Heap's residences to 1939.

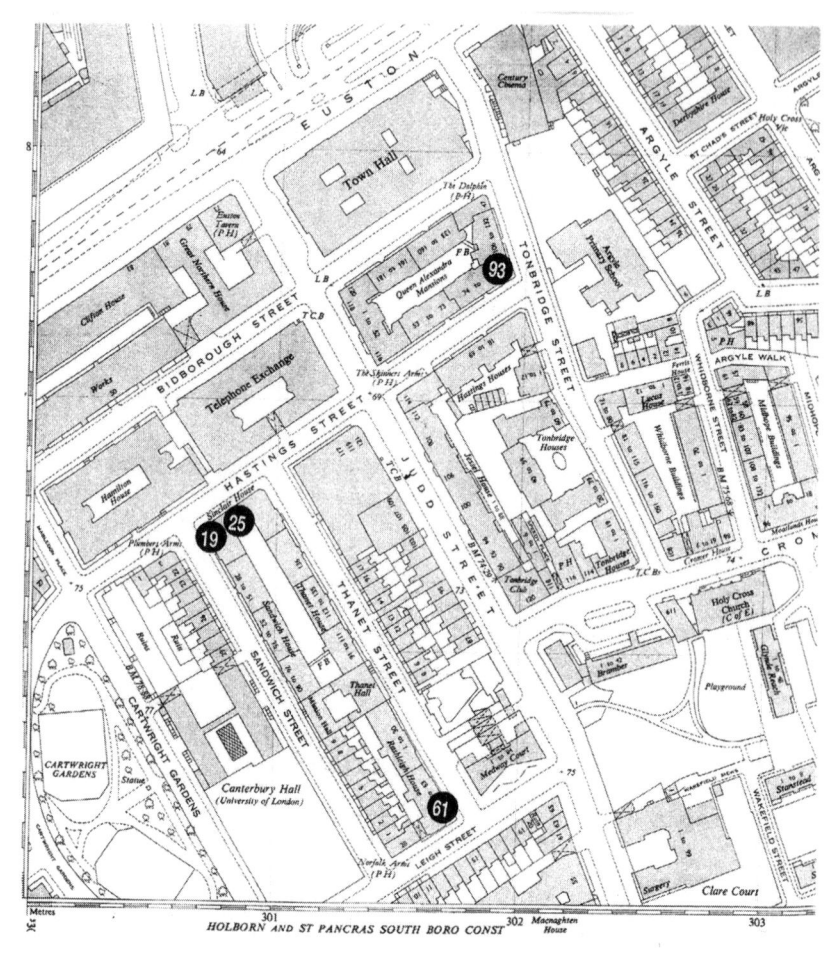

Map Two: Anthony Heap's Residences 1940-1945

19 Sandwich House, Hastings St.	15 Apr 1937 – 16 Feb 1941
25 Sandwich House, Hastings St.	16 Feb 1941 – 10 Oct 1941
93 Queen Alexandra Mansions	10 Oct 1941 – 19 Mar 1943
61 Rashleigh House, Thanet St.	19 Mar 1943 – 01 Dec 1957

Map OS TQ 3082 NW (1960)

Map II: Anthony Heap's residences 1940–1945.

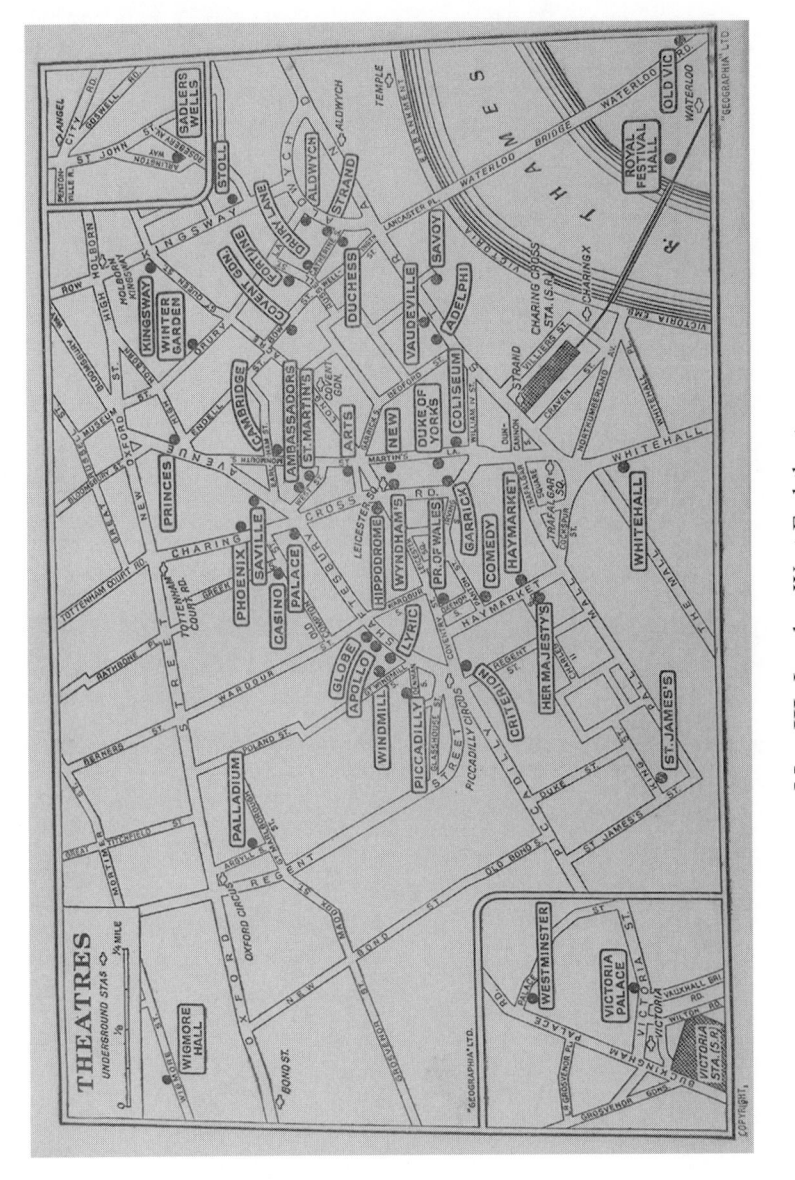

Map III: London West End theatres.

Map IV: London Cinemas.

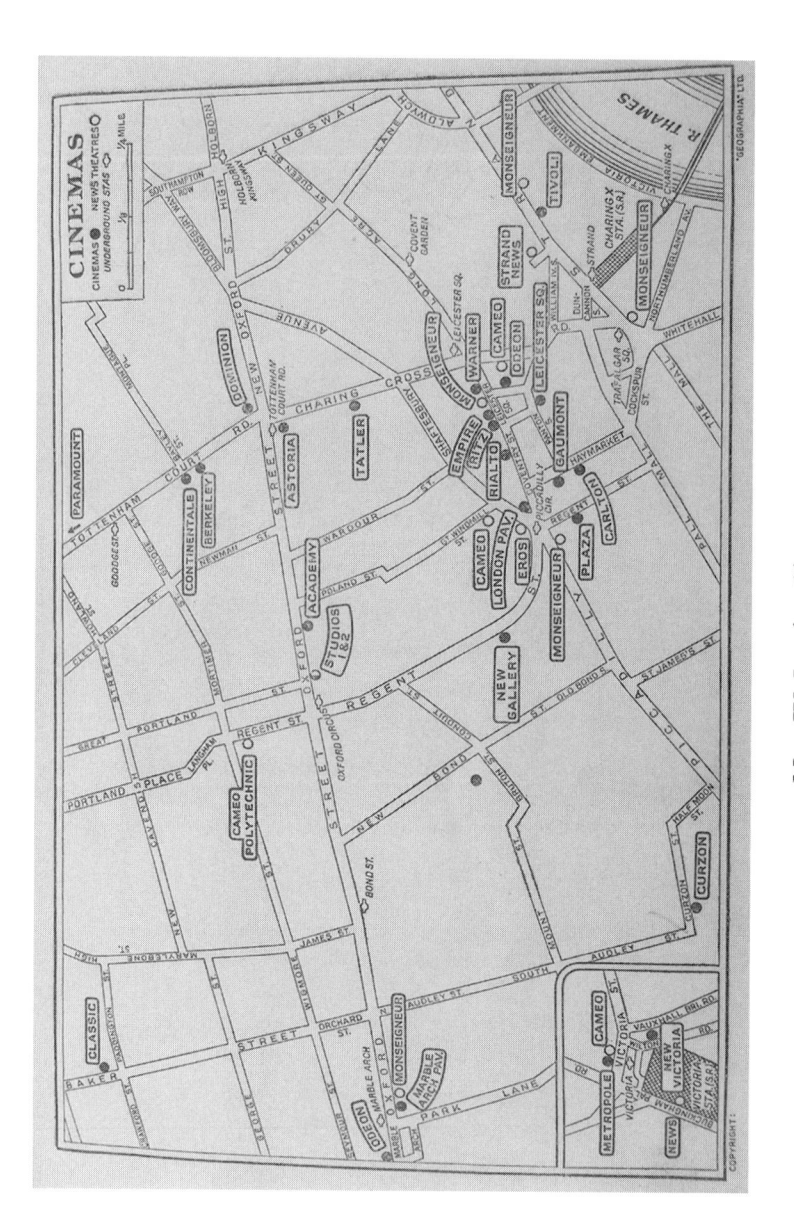

1 Anthony Heap's 1964 Visitor Passport photograph.

2 Heap (second from left) with fellow Holborn Rover Scouts at Gilwell Park (24 March 1929).

3 The building in 2015 that was Peter Robinson's on the north-east quadrant of Oxford Circus, W1 where Heap worked for 13½ years. See the bomb damage in Illustration 16 (p. xxvi).

1929 MAY—JUNE 31 & 30 Days

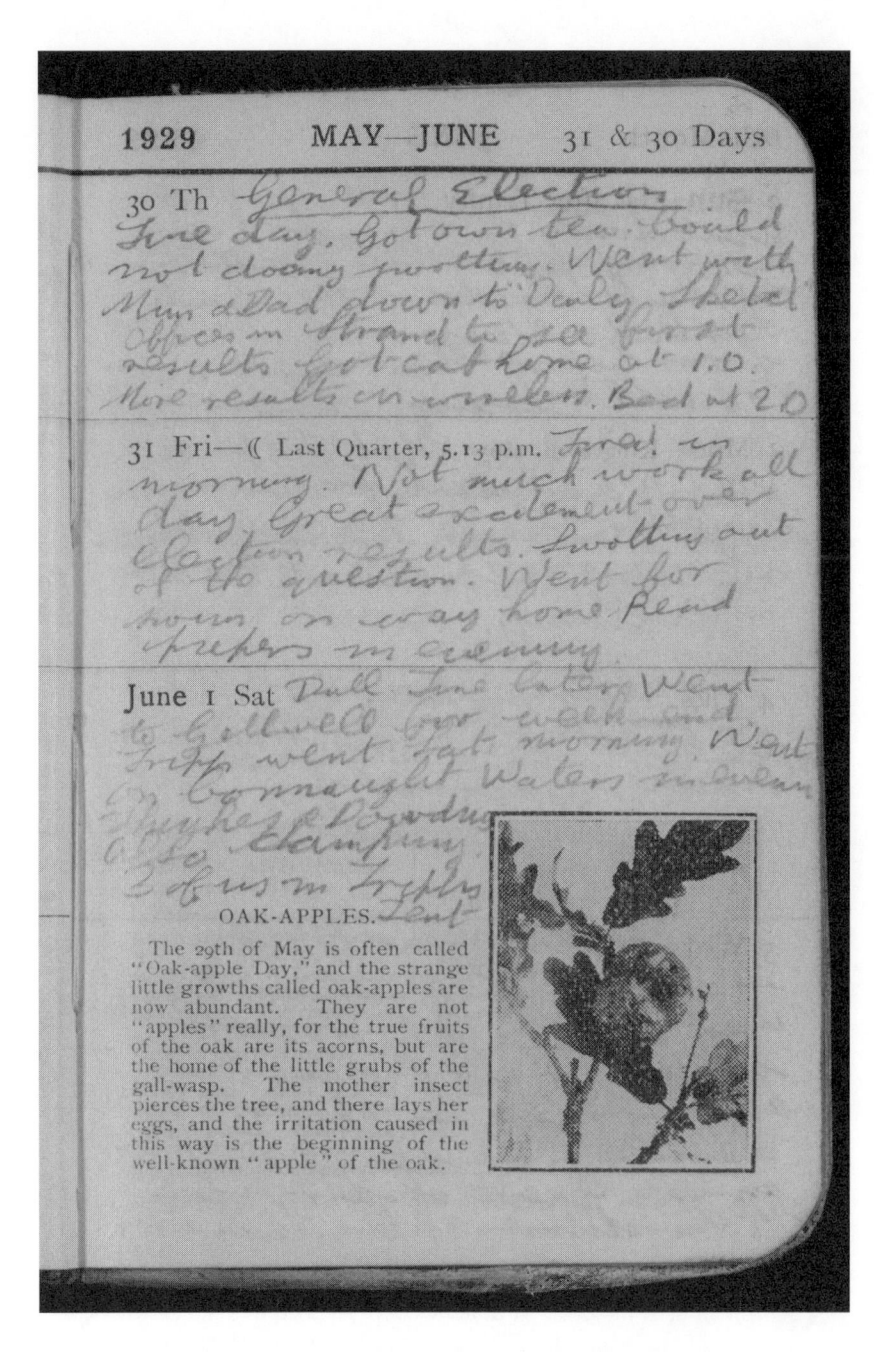

30 Th *General Election. Fine day. Got own tea. Could not doing prelims. Went with Mum & Dad down to Daily Sketch Offices in Strand to see first results. Got cab home at 1.0. More results on wireless. Bed at 2.0*

31 Fri—☾ Last Quarter, 5.13 p.m. *Fral in morning. Not much work all day. Great excitement over Election results. Swotting out of the question. Went for hour on way home. Read papers in evening.*

June 1 Sat *Pull fine later. Went to Coldwell for walk and Tripp went got morning. Went on Connaught Waters in own [?]. Hughes & [?] also clamping [?] in [?]*

OAK-APPLES.
The 29th of May is often called "Oak-apple Day," and the strange little growths called oak-apples are now abundant. They are not "apples" really, for the true fruits of the oak are its acorns, but are the home of the little grubs of the gall-wasp. The mother insect pierces the tree, and there lays her eggs, and the irritation caused in this way is the beginning of the well-known "apple" of the oak.

4 Pocket diary entries for the 1929 General Election.

5 A woman uses the cycle hire racks which in 2016 line the kerbstones outside 139 Gray's Inn Road, WC1 (centre) where the Heap family had rooms until 1932 and where Heap's father had his dental practice. Their floor is not known. CCTV now covers the entrance door and the blue plaque gives the present occupiers as the Sick Children's Trust.

6 The now gentrified town house at No 11 Penryn Street, NW1 (centre). Heap and his mother had the top floor rooms, their windows second and third from right.

10th Week   **MARCH, 1933**   3rd Month

7 TUESDAY [66—299]

The most tragic day of my life. Called into Mr Doran's private office about 11.25. Phone call for me from police. Dad had died during night. Suicide Poison. Felt ghastly. Got leave of absence & went to Hunter St Police station. Then home to Penrhyn St. Wept a bit. Called at Coroner's Court but would see no one though waited some time. At last went along to Gray's Inn Rd. Saw Dr Whyte just leaving. Mrs Stapleton there. Went in bedroom & saw Dad. Lying on side as if peacefully asleep. A sight I shall never get out of my mind.
Coroner's officer called. Took particulars. Went up to Mrs Zelgar's & phoned to Mother to come along. Upset her terribly. Undertaker called at 4.0. for body. Moments of awful tension. When it had left looked through papers etc. Found some letters I had written when five years old to him in Algeria. Baby language, infantile letters. My composure broke down then & I wept bitterly. Left at 5.0. Went home. Ate a little. Telegraphed to Uncle Fred to come to 139. Met him there at 7.15. Went up to Mrs Zelgar's. Then back & packed up some things to take so that land-lord should not seize everything as distraint for arrears. Took them home with us. Wrote to Aunt Louie in Manchester. Then at 12.30. went to bed.

7 Heap's entry recording his father's suicide — 7 March 1933.

8 Harrington Square, NW1. No 20 is the far right house, the Heaps' flat was on the top floor, the two windows (one open) top right. (2016). See Illustration 15 (p. xxvi) for the view of the terrace after the September 1940 bomb damage incident.

9 Sinclair House, Hastings Street, WC1 (2016). The windows of Flat 19 are on the fourth floor of the Hastings Street frontage (right), above the right hand Coca Cola sign next to their stuccoed Sandwich Street entrance door. In February 1941 they moved to Flat 25, on the top floor facing Hastings Street. Flat 25's windows are the pair in the centre dormer between the drainpipes (centre left). Note the railings around the roof allowing safe access to residents watching the bombing when not in their shelters.

10 Programmes for some of the shows Heap saw at His Majesty's.

7 THURSDAY [158–207]

After rushing home for a quick dinner, took Mother to Olympia for the big Black-shirt Meeting. Had to get out of bus some distance before the place owing to traffic block & red demonstrations outside. Youths distributing anti-fascist propaganda all along curb. Huge crowd trying to get in. Great crush. Managed to get in after twenty minutes or so. Seats in arena ie ground floor. Actually 6/- seats I had got free from Evening News for postcard on "Why I Like the Blackshirts". About half way back under amplifiers. Meeting began at 8.30. Half hour late. Procession of flags down centre of hall. Followed by Sir Oswald Mosley & attendants. Mounted platform. Started speech. Soon interruptions started. About 100 communists had been distributed over various parts of hall to make disturbances which they did every few minutes. All gradually got slung out but it spoilt things a good deal. One had to be chased off the roof. Towards 10.0. however Sir O. M. managed to get on without further interruption & carried on till 10.40. when the National Anthem closed the meeting. By this time the audience had thinned considerably.

(cont p 154)

11 Heap's entry for the BUF Rally at Olympia.

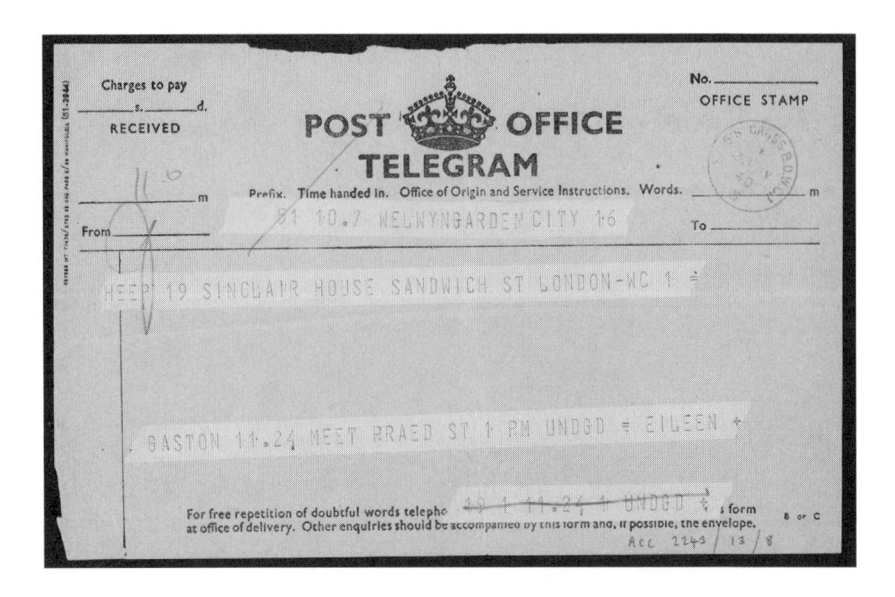

12 Eilleen's 23 June 1940 telegram changing their rendezvous as her husband was following her. Original tucked inside the 1940 diary.

13 The steps down to the church crypt that since 2002 has been used as an art gallery and is in 2016 The Crypt Gallery.

xxiv

14 The entrance to the crypt below St Pancras New Church was below the Greek revival Erechtheum at the south-eastern corner of the church. The crypt was used by Heap and his mother as their local shelter at the opening of the blitz. It was also his mother's Air Raid Wardens' Post.

15 The northern end of Harrington Square, NW1 after the bomb incident on 8 September 1940. The Heaps had lived at No 20, some 50 yards to the right of this scene. See entry for 9 September. See also Illustration 8 (p. xxi).

16 The bomb-damaged Peter Robinson's department store, Oxford Circus. Heap had been dismissed eight weeks previously but he returned to view the damage – see entry for 20 September 1940.

17 The bomb-damaged John Lewis after the 18 September 1940 raid.

18 Tottenham Court Road looking north after the fatal land mine incident – see entries for 24 and 25 September 1940. The damaged YMCA is above the Rescue Squad lorry on the corner of Great Russell Street. The damaged Blue Posts pub is off to the far left.

19 The same scene in November 2016. The Blue Posts has been replaced by a chemist's shop and the bank below the YMCA by a casino. View from outside the former Horse Shoe, Heap's favourite bar.

20 Tavistock Square, WC1, south side on 15 October 1940, now occupied by the large Tavistock Hotel. See entry for 14 October 1940. All the houses on this side of the square were damaged, including No 52, the home of Leonard and Virginia Woolf from 1924–39. No 52 was unoccupied at the time.

21 Panorama of Theobalds Road, north side, see entry for 11 May 1941. By 1942 all structures had been demolished, the sites cleared and fenced for safety, and commercial activity with street barrows had returned to New North Street (right centre) and in M. H. Buckea's restaurant on the ground floor of the surviving building (foreground with emergency replacement windows) at the Boswell Street junction.

22 Queen Alexandra Mansions, WC1 (2016). Flat 93 was on this southeast corner of the building, fourth floor, with two windows on the Hastings Street face (left) and a single window facing Tonbridge Street. The Town Hall is lower far right.

23 Rashleigh House, Thanet Street WC1 (2014) with Leigh Street on the left. The Heap's flat (No 61) was on the top floor, its two windows above the lamp post and the centre tree.

24 Heap's three pocket diaries 1928–30 and his larger diaries covering 1931–41 in an attaché case similar to that in which he packed these 14 precious volumes for storage in his air raid shelter, retrieving them six months after the blitz – see entry for 22 November 1941.

25 Whitefields Tabernacle, Tottenham Court Road, the morning after the V-2 rocket hit. See entry for 26 March 1945. Only the wide stone entrance steps remain but the badly damaged trees survived and flourish in 2017.

26 Epilogue. Twenty years after the war and after some thirteen years as a virtual single parent, this 1965 holiday photograph shows Heap relaxing with his only child, the then 16 year-old Anthony Charles on a day trip during their holiday week in Torquay.

INTRODUCTION

The London-born diarist Anthony Heap (1910–1985) was educated in Holborn and lived all his life in the neighbouring borough of St Pancras. His first job was as an accounts assistant in Peter Robinson's department store at Oxford Circus, where he worked for thirteen and a half years. His second and final job, which lasted thirty-five years, was in the Treasurer's Department of the St Pancras (later Camden) Borough Council in the Town Hall on Euston Road, just a stone's throw from each of the five small flats in which he lived for his final half-century. After his dentist father's suicide in 1933, Anthony at first shared rooms and then a small flat with his widowed mother, but when he married the country girl Marjorie Heatley (1916–1995) in October 1941, the couple rented their own small flat. Assessed as medically unfit for military service, he remained in London throughout the Second World War so that, other than annual holidays and weekend excursions to the surrounding countryside, he spent his entire life in central London.

Never more than a modestly paid cashier and book-keeper, Heap might appear to have had an unexceptional life, but outside his rather routine office and home life he achieved some distinction in two of his hobbies. Firstly, he kept a daily diary for fifty-seven years – from 1 January 1928, just eleven weeks before his eighteenth birthday, to his final entry two days before his death on 31 October 1985. Secondly, he attended as many London theatre 'first nights' as possible; between 1931 and 1984, he saw some 3,351 theatrical performances (averaging sixty-two shows a year), the vast majority as a member of the first night or preview audience. Heap wanted his diary to be read and, six weeks before his death, he made a will making 'specific bequests in regard to the ultimate disposal of my diaries'. All fifty-six volumes are held at the London Metropolitan Archives (LMA) in Clerkenwell,[1] together with a rough transcript of the diaries from May 1937 to December 1946 by the present editor.[2]

The diary of a lifelong West End 'first-nighter' would be of very limited interest to a general audience but Anthony Heap was a keen

---

[1] LMA, Accession No. 2243/1–55.
[2] LMA, Accession No. 2243/57, typescript in two large loose-leaf volumes, transcribed by Robin Woolven.

Introduction

and acute observer of people, life, politics and London life. His record of the 1930s and the wartime years are a valuable source for social historians and general readers alike. In some respects he was a typical grammar-school-educated young Londoner of the era, interested in scouting, countryside rambling, the cinema and, when he met young women who shared his interests, girls. His dissatisfaction with life and government, particularly Labour administrations, left him with many frustrations. He aspired to use his wide knowledge of literature and the theatre in a more intellectual manner than his career as a junior cashier permitted, but found no outlet for his ambitions. Earning a very basic wage, with limited business prospects during the depression and frustrated with his lot in life, he became strongly attracted to far rightwing politics in the mid–1930s.

As the diaries have been quoted by the social historians Juliet Gardiner, David Kynaston and Maureen Waller, and by the Camden local historian Martin Sheppard, this publication certainly does not claim to have 'discovered' Anthony Heap as a primary source for mid-twentieth-century London life.[3] However it is hoped that this volume, focusing on the 1930s and the wartime years, will make Heap's diary more widely available and provide a valuable resource for those wishing to know more of these two key decades in the history of modern London.

FAMILY, EDUCATION AND WORK

Heap recorded that he was born 'in London' on 13 March 1910, but no birth certificate has been found, the search doubtless not helped by his parents never having married. His father, Fred Heap (1879–1933), was a dentist who lived and worked in their rooms at 139 Gray's Inn Road, but financial problems caused him to take his own life. Heap's mother, Emily Shepherd (1881–1958), known as Mrs Heap from Anthony's birth, lived with Fred until his violent behaviour caused her and Anthony to move out in 1932. She continued to help with the dental practice until Fred's suicide but shared rooms with her son in Camden Town, after which they took a flat in an Edwardian purpose-built block on Hastings Street, off Judd Street WC1, until Anthony married in 1941. Having firm right-wing views like her son, Emily was an active member of the local Conservative Association and she unsuccessfully stood as a candidate

---

3 Juliet Gardiner, *The Thirties: An Intimate History* (London: Harper Press, 2010) (3 quotations) and *The Blitz: The British Under Attack* (London: Harper Press, 2010) (16 quotations); David Kynaston, *Austerity Britain, 1945–1951* (London: Bloomsbury, 2007) (22 quotations) and *Family Britain, 1951–1957* (London: Bloomsbury, 2009) (29 quotations); Maureen Waller, *London 1945: Life in the Debris of War* (London: John Murray, 2004) (15 quotations); Martin Sheppard, *Primrose Hill: A History* (Lancaster: Carnegie Publishing, 2013) (4 quotations).

in the borough elections in 1945 – in the same ward in which Anthony had been similarly unsuccessful in 1937.

Anthony was initially educated at Mrs Kemp's Private School, 41 Great Ormond Street,[4] before going on to the St Clement Danes Holborn Estate Grammar School in Houghton Street,[5] now the site of the London School of Economics. Intent on a career in business and commerce, in 1927 he took a job in the Finance Office of Peter Robinson's, the large department store on Oxford Circus, where he maintained ledgers, paid staff in their various departments and did occasional other duties such as shop walking during sales and delivering papers to banks and the Inland Revenue. After some years of studying by correspondence courses and cramming classes, in 1931 he passed the professional examinations to become an Associate of the Chartered Institute of Secretaries (ACIS), which he referred to as his 'degree'. In spite of his regular attendance at his work and enjoying dressing in the required black business coat, waistcoat and striped trousers of the era, his lack of advancement in business – or indeed socially – can perhaps in part be accounted for by his singular personality and his overtly expressed politics. Although he received occasional small annual increments, Heap found his junior post and routine duties boring and unsatisfying. He desperately wanted a better-paid and more interesting job outside Peter Robinson's, so he applied for many posts in other firms and organisations, in journalism and at the BBC, all without success.

Responding to the wartime downturn in trade, Peter Robinson's shed staff in 1940, and Heap was dismissed, together with his work colleague and mistress, Eilleen (her spelling). Their affair and Heap's right-wing views doubtless expedited their departure. After seven weeks of touring the employment exchanges, as the Blitz began in September 1940 Heap found a junior cashier job locally in St Pancras Town Hall, a post he retained, with limited promotions, until retirement in 1975, having become 'established' (i.e. pensionable) in 1947.

In the summer of 1941, in the course of his duties paying wartime civil defence staff at their depots, Heap met and courted the rather unstable Marjorie Heatley and they married in October that year. The couple delayed starting a family until 1949, when their only child, Anthony Charles, was born. Their life in a single-bedroomed sixth-floor flat was constrained by their limited income. Further, from the mid–1950s Marjorie's declining mental health increasingly threw all family responsibilities onto Anthony. Marjorie 'heard voices' and eventually deserted their home in 1958, living rough on the streets

---

4   The four-storey Georgian terraced house, now flats, is directly opposite the modern entrance to the Children's Hospital, which extends along the whole of the north side of Great Ormond Street.
5   The school was fee-paying but from 1922 the maximum fee was capped at £10 p.a.

Introduction

until she attacked a railway employee, whereupon she was arrested and 'sectioned' to spend time in Broadmoor Criminal Lunatic Asylum.[6] She had given police only her maiden name but, once she had been identified, Heap had her transferred to local mental hospitals, where she remained until discharged in 1972, thereafter attending daily clinics and work centres for many years.

The burden of his sick wife and his responsibilities as a virtual single parent weighed heavily upon Heap but, by working overtime and economising on expenditure, he managed to send young Anthony Charles to the private Gatehouse Montessori School and eventually onto St Marylebone Grammar School. Meanwhile Heap's widowed mother, Emily, had maintained herself by taking a series of manual, cleaning, catering and caring jobs until the war, when she became a full-time Air Raid Warden in St Pancras. As Marjorie's mental health gradually deteriorated, Emily became a very supportive grandmother.

On retiring in 1975 Heap immediately found a part-time book-keeping job working for a local businessman. Always careful with his money and concerned at the level of rent he paid, particularly when rent control became a post-war political issue, in 1971 he purchased a forty-year lease of a two-room flat in the block that he and his wife had left in 1942. At his death, he left an estate of £64,410 net.

PERSONALITY

Heap was a good-looking young man, but he was well aware that his personality was not consistently attractive, recording when he split with his girlfriend Beatrice in 1932 that he was 'now more or less my former self, selfish, self-centred, conceited, sarcastic and cynical, and a poseur. I have no one to try and please but myself and I am perfectly happy in my misogynistic state.' To those attributes must be added unpleasant recurrent outbursts of racism and anti-Semitism, views which peaked with his non-active membership of Sir Oswald Mosley's British Union of Fascists (BUF) between 1933 and 1936.[7] At his mother's request,

---

6   Near Crowthorne, Berkshire, and now known as a high-security psychiatric hospital.
7   Sir Oswald Mosley (1896–1980) was initially elected as a Conservative MP in 1918 but crossed the floor to join the Labour Party in 1924. Later that year he stood unsuccessfully against Neville Chamberlain in the General Election but he won a by-election in 1926. When Ramsay MacDonald became Prime Minister in 1929, Mosley was made Chancellor of the Duchy of Lancaster, with responsibility for proposing policies to relieve mass unemployment. However his 'revolutionary' proto-Keynesian proposals of increased public works were rejected by the party and Mosley resigned. With the support of some well-placed supporters within the establishment, he then formed his own 'New Party' but its increasingly fascist leanings – particularly Mosley's visit to Mussolini in Italy and the use of strong-arm tactics by its stewards at public meetings responding to left-wing protesters – caused many to desert the New Party, which then faded politically. Taking the more active younger contingent of the New Party with him, Mosley formed the BUF in January 1932.

in 1937 he got involved in local Municipal Reform (Conservative) politics, standing for the party in the unwinnable ward of Somers Town in that year's borough elections.

Apart from a difficult personality and extreme views, another reason for Heap's lack of worldly success might have been his unfortunate domestic circumstances. His parents' separation, the discovery of his illegitimacy and his father's suicide in 1933 resulted in enforced austerity through the economic depression of the 1930s, factors which could not have helped as Anthony entered the very slowly recovering London retail trade.

HEALTH

Anthony was always concerned with the state of his health, especially after his period in hospital 'on the danger list' in 1939. The rupture to his stomach wall, which followed his carrying heavy furniture on moving flats, and his operation for peritonitis, rendered him unfit for military service. He often resorted to patent and home medicines such as sitting with his 'feet in hot mustard water and taking two aspirin and a stiff dose of whisky in hot butter milk'. Throughout the diaries, his health and that of his immediate family is often recorded in detail, particularly when it affected his daily routine. Thus we are told of his minor ailments of aches, swellings, spots, boils, colds and upset stomachs and we are not spared his bouts of diarrhoea or his occasional 'spewing' – the latter generally brought about by evenings of heavy drinking 'with the boys'.

Heap recorded the cost of medical treatments and the full clinical details, as well as his attempts to delay his baldness by investing in various oils and clinic treatments. He also recorded the insurance cover which his family took out in the days before the 1948 National Health Service. Insurance contributed to meeting the cost of his care when he suffered his major periods of ill health in 1939; his circumcision in Bart's Hospital following a consultation with a Harley Street specialist was in part covered by his insurance company, as was his three-week peritonitis episode in the Homeopathic Hospital.

Anthony endeavoured to 'keep fit' by attending exercise classes and, almost regardless of the elements, regularly striding through the

It met with considerable public support but no electoral approval, and its drift towards intolerant anti-Semitism, particularly by activists led by 'Lord Haw Haw' (William Joyce (1906–1946)) alienated many. The BUF adopted a political 'uniform' of black shirts; their weekly paper, *The Blackshirt*, was sold on the streets and was subsequently regularly bought by Heap and many others of all ages and classes. As a result of the BUF's frequent violent confrontations with communist and socialist protesters on the streets and inside and outside political meetings, in 1936 the government brought in the Public Order Act, which banned political uniforms and required police permission for holding public marches.

Introduction

Royal Parks, Primrose Hill and Hampstead Heath. He much enjoyed the fresh air and was a regular hiker and weekend and bank holiday Youth Hosteller. In the 1930s the railway companies and London Transport encouraged visits to the surrounding countryside by offering group rates and cheap excursion tickets, opportunities which Heap seized to hike the Surrey and Chiltern Hills, Epping Forest and the South Downs. As a Rover Scout he regularly camped at Gilwell Park in Essex, at Downe Scout Centre in Kent and annually at Windsor Great Park. He was a member of several rambling and hiking clubs. Each summer his two-week holiday was usually divided between a week Youth Hostelling alone in more distant areas, such as the Cotswolds, Devon, the Lake District or Snowdonia, and a week at a seaside holiday camp, sometimes alone or with his male London friends. One of the attractions of the camps was the opportunity to meet girls, some of whom he followed up by dating for a few weeks before the acquaintance invariably faded. The other attraction was drinking with 'the lads', sometimes to excess. Drinking was not restricted to holiday times, as Heap and his group went on regular (generally fortnightly or monthly) pub crawls around the wider Fitzrovia area.

THE LONDONER

Heap was a knowledgeable Londoner who took pride in getting to know his city and its history. Although he organised and enjoyed country walks, he looked down on the provinces, abhorred the London suburbs and was always glad to get back to his urban environment. A great walker of London's streets, he often set out for a park or locality with which he was not familiar and, if he enjoyed his discovery, would return with his wife and later with his young son. There was no shortage of green spaces in Heap's neighbourhood and he regularly spent time in the local Bloomsbury squares and gardens; later, a regular walk was down to Embankment Gardens for coffee from the kiosk, then over to the South Bank's facilities following the 1951 Festival of Britain. He enjoyed observing the changing seasons in the Bloomsbury squares and in Queen Mary's Garden in nearby Regent's Park. Having walked most parts of the City and other historic areas, when he married in 1941 he took his wife on long walks to show her 'his' London. On his almost daily wartime walks during the enemy offensives in 1940–1941 and 1944–1945, often as soon as the 'all clear' was sounded, he observed and recorded in detail the still burning or collapsing buildings and other bomb damage. As his son grew up in the 1950s, the boy was similarly walked around London's sights and historic neighbourhoods.

As a young man, Heap was a regular and active member of the crowds around Piccadilly Circus who gathered to 'see in' the New

Introduction

Year, and he invariably joined in lining the streets for major public events, such as the Lord Mayor's Show, and the embankment for the Oxford and Cambridge Boat Race, or gatherings outside Buckingham Palace for national celebrations. In Rover Scout uniform he served as an usher in St Paul's Cathedral for King George V's Jubilee Thanksgiving Service and, like many thousands of others, he and his mother duly lined the streets for the funeral processions of monarchs and subsequent coronations. He had tried to witness the proclamation of George VI at St James's Palace, but was only able to reach Charing Cross to hear the loudspeaker announcements. He saw the subsequent Coronation procession in May 1937, but later that day he was knocked to the ground and punched near King's Cross so he could not tour the floodlit West End that evening.

Heap was no sportsman and throughout his life his interest in sport was limited to being a very occasional observer of a school 'Staff v Old Boys' cricket match or watching the annual Boat Race. He did, however, record the result each year of such sporting events as the Derby and Grand National horse races and the football and rugby cup finals, but his interest in international rugby and football matches did not extend beyond observing the behaviour of the supporters' postmatch celebrations. He was not a gambler, although he did join in office sweepstakes, sometimes winning a few shillings, while his gambling at cards was no more serious than gaining or losing a few pence over an evening's play at a hostel or friend's house.

POLITICS

In contrast, national and local politics were important to Heap. No liberal and, like many others in the depression years of the early 1930s, finding himself unable to improve his job prospects, this young man always held firm right-wing views. As mentioned above, he became a member of the BUF, as did many other Britons, encouraged by Lord Rothermere's *Daily Mail*.[8] Membership ranged from some of the aristocracy, through the professions and retired military people to thousands of employed and unemployed working-class men and, significantly, women. When Heap joined in 1933, the Blackshirts had between 40,000 and 50,000 members, geographically spread across the nation, all attracted by Mosley's radical employment and

---

8   Harold S. Harmsworth, 1st Viscount Rothermere (1868–1940), proprietor of Associated Newspapers Ltd, which included the *Sunday Despatch* and the (London) *Evening News*, which all supported their proprietor's 'Hurrah for the Blackshirts' campaign. Rothermere wrote the January 1934 leader under that title.

Introduction

peace-seeking policies.⁹ The historian Martin Pugh has written 'The protectionist-nationalist emphasis made an obvious appeal to frustrated Conservatives and to workers in depressed areas.'¹⁰ The BUF was anti-communist but it soon lost many members because of increasingly overt anti-Semitic policies from 1934 and the 'strong arm' methods used by its stewards at meetings that were frequently infiltrated by left-wing activists.

Anthony Heap was a non-active member of the St Pancras BUF branch and, when that faded, the Islington branch. He declined to sell their weekly newspaper on the streets and never recorded any participation in BUF activities beyond attending the occasional meeting addressed by Mosley. He greatly admired Mosley's 'manifesto' and always retained his own right-wing views.¹¹ A life-long critic of liberalism, he believed that socialists were mere apologists for, and unwitting tools of, Soviet Russia; he opposed communism in all its forms, at home and abroad.

The overriding national concern of the late 1930s was the approach of war, but this was only occasionally reported by Heap until the increasingly serious international crises broke during 1938 and as tension increased in the final months before war was declared in September 1939. All the while, memories of the losses of the Great War abounded. Heap's mother was a member of the local branch of the commemorative Ypres League and regularly attended their events, sometimes accompanied by Anthony. In the 1930s, he was always present at the Cenotaph on Remembrance Sunday and when 11 November fell on a working day, he joined Peter Robinson's staff lining the store's windows while the traffic and pedestrians below halted for the two-minute silence. Like most citizens during the interwar decades, he tended towards pacifism and certainly did not look forward to being conscripted as the call-up approached his age group.

An overt racist, on 4 October 1935, Heap had supported the Italian invasion of Abyssinia by noting: 'The war goes merrily along. Italians make steady progress and drop a few more bombs. That's the stuff to give the niggers.' He initially held pro-German views and looked askance at indications overseas that war was fast approaching, on 12 September 1938 commenting that:

> Hitler's speech this evening at conclusion of Nuremberg conference contained no important pronouncement of policy concerning

---

9 Julie V. Gottlieb, 'British Union of Fascists (act. 1932–1940)', *Oxford Dictionary of National Biography*, Oxford University Press, online edition, accessed 8 March 2015.
10 Martin Pugh, *Hurrah for the Blackshirts! Fascists and Fascism in Britain between the Wars* (London: Jonathan Cape, 2005), p. 217.
11 Oswald Mosley *The Greater Britain* (London: British Union of Fascists, 1932). See also diary entry for 8 September 1933.

Introduction

the vexed problem of the Sudeten Germans in Czecho-Slovakia which had looked like bringing the world to the brink of war.[12] The tension during the past few days has been terrific. In short a 'crisis' of the first order, though of course exaggerated considerably by the unreliable newspaper sensationalism. In any case, what concern it is of ours or why we should ally ourselves with the communist forces of France and Russia to support C-S I fail to see. To hell with Czecho-Slovakia.

The Czech question was at the centre of the Munich crisis, when Heap and his mother, like the majority of Britons, collected their gas masks from the distribution centres. On 27 September 1938 he recorded: 'Only a miracle will avert war now.' That evening the Prime Minister, Neville Chamberlain, broadcast views similar to Heap's, lamenting 'How horrible, fantastic, incredible it is that we should be digging trenches and trying on gas-masks here because of a quarrel in a faraway country between people of whom we know nothing.'[13]

Just as Heap had supported Stanley Baldwin's apparently peaceful intentions, he fully supported his successor, Neville Chamberlain, whom Heap applauded, on 30 September 1938, once the Munich crisis had died down:

And it's been largely due to one man, Chamberlain, for the decisive [role] he has played in bringing this about, he has earned the deepest gratitude of the whole world. His place in history will be a noble one. Probably no other English statesman has served the interests of his country and humanity in general so well, so thoroughly, so courageously and to better purpose. He well deserved the tremendous ovation that awaited him on his triumphant return this evening after concluding a personal no-more-war pact with Hitler, in the interests of Anglo-German friendship. A truly great man in every sense of the term.

THE THEATRE, CINEMA AND LITERATURE

Heap's lifetime hobby of theatre 'first nighting', and his many visits to cinemas and the various film societies of which he was a member, generated extensive diary entries analysing and criticising the productions he saw. There is no question that the theatre was a great lifetime interest for Heap, matched only by writing his daily diary. Theatre and cinema visits were recorded, together with his comments,

---

12   Ethnic German people living in the region of Czechoslovakia bordering Germany whose wish to become part of the latter was exploited by Hitler.
13   Chamberlain in a BBC broadcast on 27 September 1938.

Introduction

where applicable, on the published criticisms of the newspaper and magazine critics whom he regularly followed. As a result, much of the diary would probably be of little interest to readers other than theatre and film historians. His critical zenith was probably reached much later, when he attended the July 1970 preview of *Oh! Calcutta!*, his comments were broadcast on the BBC Radio *Today* programme next morning and his published reaction contributing one of the four statements of complaint that went to the Director of Public Prosecutions. The latter decided that, as 'there was very little chance of a successful prosecution for obscenity, no action was appropriate'.[14]

To save space in this volume, Heap's numerous theatre and cinema visits, together with his extensive consumption of novels and non-fiction works, have here been consigned to Appendix B, which lists the shows and films he saw each year, and where and when he saw them, together with the books he read and, if appropriate, any significant brief comment he made on the production, film or book. His lengthy criticism can be read in the original volumes in the LMA.

Heap tried to see and comment upon almost all new West End theatre productions, as well as revivals and new productions of the classics. Similarly, he tried to see and comment on most new films, whether British, American or foreign-language. He particularly liked the latest musical productions starring the debonair Jack Buchannan. His reading taste was similarly wide, for he used his various library 'wants lists' to obtain the latest works by the authors of the era, including J. B. Priestley, Hugh Walpole, Somerset Maugham, Compton Mackenzie, H. G. Wells and Arnold Bennett. Heap particularly followed the current and collected criticisms of his favourite theatre critic and novelist, James Agate. Generally reading at least one or more serious books a week, he voraciously consumed memoirs, letters, diaries and biographies, particularly of theatrical people and journalists.

Necessarily careful with his money, Heap recorded his major purchases and, as the years passed, he also recorded his annual income and savings. A proud and regular member of West End theatre gallery and pit audiences, he bought more expensive seats only on very special occasions; he similarly avoided West End cinemas, waiting until films were on general release in local cinemas. After a lifetime of first nighting, he lamented that 'The theatre, alas, is not what it used to be. And neither, I suppose, am I',[15] while his final diary entry, on 20 October 1985, recorded his criticism of that evening's opening at the Comedy Theatre of a modern production of *Camille*, which he

14 See Robin Woolven, '"A Tendency to Deprave or Corrupt in Chalk Farm?" A Camden Resident and *Oh! Calcutta!* at the Round House, July 1970', *Camden History Review*, No. 38 (2014), pp. 21–26.
15 LMA, Accession No. 2243/55, entry for 30 December 1982.

considered was 'Definitely not for the sentimental, old fashioned likes of me.'

OTHER LEISURE INTERESTS

In his twenties, Heap's other major leisure interest was Rover Scouting. Having visited France, Germany, Austria and Switzerland with his Rover Scout group in 1928, in the early 1930s he became secretary and treasurer of the Holborn Rover Group, which met in the YMCA on Tottenham Court Road. In his characteristically critical manner, from December 1927 to February 1936 he wrote five volumes of their log book, recording the group's activities of meetings, talks, social evenings and dances.[16] Then known as 'Tony', he made several attempts to reinvigorate the Holborn Rovers by forming a new patrol and urging them to invest more time and energy in Rover activities. He was a leading member of the group, which had the unique privilege of having as its leading social organiser the international choreographer and show business entrepreneur Ralph Reader, who founded the now legendary *Gang Show* at the local Scala Theatre in 1932. Heap's diary has frequent references to Reader, whose personality and activities tended to dominate the group.

Heap's early interest in camping with Scouts faded in the mid–1930s and he resigned his Rover offices in November 1936. Local politics and drinking with his friends took its place until surviving and recording the Blitz, and then his marriage, dominated.

HEAP AND WOMEN

Heap's membership of social and amateur dramatics groups, as well as of hiking clubs, in the 1930s meant that he had no problem meeting girls of his age, but he certainly had problems keeping girlfriends for more than a few weeks or months. He was generally delighted to meet and spend time with new girlfriends for a few months but their friendship never seemed to extend far beyond cinema and theatre visits, country walks and dances. Heap enjoyed his beer at such social events and this sometimes annoyed his partners if he drank too much and embarrassed them.

There were no girlfriends mentioned in the first three years of his diarising, but that changed in 1931. His group of Rover Scouts went on 'joint' Sunday hikes – the 'Co-op' hikes – with young women members of the Rangers. He was also a member of several other hiking

---

16   The log books were left to the Scout Association and may be consulted at their HQ at Gilwell Park, Chigwell.

Introduction

groups – at his workplace, at Northampton Polytechnic in Finsbury,[17] and those organised by the railway companies. But it was through the Rover Scouts that he became associated with the amateur dramatics society that met at the Polytechnic, where two of his girlfriends were members. The diary records his first girlfriend as Maud, the sister of his friend Stan Cox. He took Maud to the theatre over a two-month period in the summer of 1931, but that September he met Shelmerdine from Burnt Oak. Although Heap travelled up to Shelmerdine's home for Sunday tea to meet the family, the relationship eventually faded and there followed a period of 'freedom'. He then had an 'on and off' friendship with Beatrice from the Northampton Polytechnic Amateur Operatic Society, until she broke it off after six months in July 1932. She was followed by another member of the Drama Group, Lilian, 'a charming girl, slim, tall and very feminine, a superb voice. And not unpretty', who in 1933 'gave my life a new beauty for me and enriched it beyond words'. The friendship lasted for eight months but, once again, apparently did not extend beyond hikes, dances, film and theatre visits and the occasional late meal or coffee at the Lyons Corner House at the Oxford Street end of Tottenham Court Road.

Through the next five years Heap's meetings with young women seem to have been limited to socialising and sometimes dancing with the wives and girlfriends of his friends and fellow members of the Scout *Gang Show* and at YMCA-organised events. An encounter on a coach outing on 14 May 1937 he recorded as:

> Got acquainted with Mrs Baxter's niece Babs and we went off on our own and kept together and had a pretty good time. Much to the busy-bodied concern of all the staid prim old women, everyone except Mother and Mrs B, who rather enjoyed the joke. Transferred myself to the much livelier Baxters' coach coming home.

He invited Babs to join a hike a week later and concluded that 'I was more tight than I thought I was and thus oblivious of her facial and physical deficiencies.' After the hike he saw Babs off 'in a taxi for Chiswick, walked home and got straight into bed – still atrociously drunk'.

Heap frequently attended the annual dances of his friends' business and sporting clubs, big events held in large modern venues and, during the war, in the Royal Opera House, Covent Garden.[18] But there are very

---

17 Northampton Polytechnic, St John's Street, EC1 now City University, Northampton Square EC1.
18 Two popular and then modern venues that Heap frequented were Australia House, Strand WC2, built 1913–1918 and still the offices of the High Commissioner for Australia, and Thames House, Millbank SW1, built 1929–1930 to house ICI and Lloyd George's Liberal Party HQ, among others, but, since 1994, the headquarters of the Security Service (MI5).

Introduction

few mentions in his diary of contacts with other girls, apart from the odd game, competition or dance on his annual week at holiday camps. These relationships went nowhere beyond an occasional post-holiday drink and the inevitable end of the contact. In August 1938 he met Glynis at a Kent holiday camp and, despite spending the final two days in Kent together on the beach, they met only once back in London.

Two months before the Blitz began in 1940, a previously unreported but intense and apparently torrid affair with a married work colleague, Eilleen, took precedence in his life, but the affair ended when she opted to return to her husband and children. So it was an unhappy Heap who started his new job in the Town Hall. Once the affair had ended, he spent most nights for eight months sleeping in local public air raid shelters, before meeting and marrying Marjorie in 1941. Heap records their cautious start to married life as they first set up home in a furnished flat, then, experiencing the wartime price inflation, rationing and shortages of many things, eventually found an unfurnished flat in a cheaper block nearby. The always unstable Marjorie found it difficult to keep her series of clerical jobs but they both found relief holidaying close to her mother in Somerset. Heap particularly missed London when he was away in the country and they readily returned from their summer 1945 holiday to enjoy London's peace celebrations, before going back to Somerset for the final holiday days.

THE DIARIES

Over six decades Anthony Heap invested much time and energy in keeping his diary and he derived great pleasure from his industry. In a long entry on 20 February 1941 (see p. 347), five months into the Blitz and having just finished reading the diary of the Rev. Francis Kilvert,[19] Heap explained at length the several reasons why he undertook this 'labour of love'. The form appealed to him strongly and he believed that, by recording intelligent comments on such things, people and events as came within the scope of the diarist, it was possible to 'throw some light on the times in which one lives'. He revered both Pepys and Evelyn, but also praised the work of the modern diarists Arnold Bennett and James Agate.[20]

---

19   Francis Kilvert (1840–1879), country clergyman and diarist. The volume in question was William Plomer (ed.), *Kilvert's Diary: Selections from the Diary of Rev. Francis Kilvert, 1 January 1870–19 August 1871* (London: Jonathan Cape, 1938).
20   Samuel Pepys (1633–1703), naval official and diarist. John Evelyn (1620–1706), diarist and writer. Arnold Bennett (1876–1931), novelist and author of non-fiction works; his diaries were edited by Newman Flower and published as *The Journals of Arnold Bennett* (London: Cassell, 1932–1933). James Agate's diaries were published by Hamish Hamilton between 1935 and 1948 in nine volumes under the title *Ego*.

Introduction

Heap began keeping a diary in 1928 but the three early pocket diaries are necessarily only in note form. From 1931 he wrote in a much expanded form and continued this for the next fifty-four years. He was an acute observer of things he was passionate about, an articulate and knowledgeable recorder of society as he saw it and a competent recorder of his personal life and routine. He generally wrote in a reasonably legible hand in black or blue ink, other than on those occasions when he lacked ink, particularly when holidaying on the continent in the early 1930s, when, carrying his diary in his backpack, he used a less legible blue/violet 'indelible' pencil. The diary was mostly written up each evening although, if that proved too difficult, he would write up two or more days in retrospect, from memory or using notes made through the missing period, the latter essential during his three weeks of serious illness in August and September 1939 when he was 'on the danger list for ten days', and then recovering from surgery.

As he noted on 20 February 1941, we cannot assume that his, or any, diary is totally frank. His own certainly omits some aspects of his life as, on several occasions, characters – particularly new girlfriends – suddenly appear in the diary, no mention having previously been made of any early stages of a meeting or relationship. A small example is the sole mention, in February 1939, of 'My old flame Irene, now happily married and the proud mother of a fifteen months old boy.' Just when Irene had been his current 'flame' is not recorded, so perhaps she inflamed him before he started his diary in 1928. The most obvious example is the sudden mention of Eilleen, who first appeared in the diary on 22 July 1940 – and then only when Heap told his mother of the obviously well-developed relationship, whereupon his mother

> just won't think of E as anything but a scheming liar, of G [Gaston, her husband] as anything but an injured saint or of me as nowt but an errant child. Otherwise she attributes E's love for me to the meanest of motives and continually brings up the subject to try and induce me to give her up. Wouldn't be so bad if based on personal knowledge. But it isn't. Just spiteful malicious conjecture arising from the jealous possessiveness of mother love. As bad as PR's [Peter Robinson's], as if I don't have enough antagonism to put up with there by day without this at home in the evening as well. A hopeless situation. But I stand firm. Even if it means a definite split with Mother, I still won't give up E.

He was then aged 31 and perhaps understandably concerned to keep such a relationship from his mother – who might well have had access to his diaries when he was out of their shared flat.

Diary writing was a simple pleasure and a daily routine for Anthony Heap. On holiday he would sit on his bed or find a quiet corner of the

Introduction

Youth Hostel in which to write, while at home he had a daily routine of writing at the kitchen table until, in March 1944, he proudly recorded that he had 'bought, for £13, a dark oak bureau in a second hand shop in Chalk Farm Rd'. Three days later:

> The bureau duly arrived at 5.15 this afternoon. Tones perfectly well with the rest of the furniture – and what a joy it is to be able to sit down at a desk with diary, pen, ink, blotter, paper, eraser, with everything else one could possibly want immediately at hand instead of having to lug the whole lot out of a cupboard onto a table and put it all back afterwards.

His pleasure was completed in July 1948 by:

> Our latest acquisition – a second hand, round backed, hide seated chair for my writing desk. Bought last Saturday for £2.15.0 and duly delivered this morning. The wood being a light oak it will need to be stained to match the desk and the rest of the our dark furniture. But otherwise it's just what I wanted. Certainly a change from the hard folding kitchen chair I've had to use since we disposed of our dining room suite in March.

Heap valued and took great care of his precious diaries, packing them into an attaché case during the 1940–1941 Blitz and carrying them to the public air raid shelter with his bedding, where the diaries were stored until later retrieved once the offensive had passed. He certainly enjoyed re-reading old volumes, particularly when he had no book to read, and he then wallowed in nostalgia for the 'good old days', referring back to his comments on previous productions of a show or when comparing seasonal weather with earlier years. There was frequently a comment on his pleasant recollections of his younger days of 'freedom' when a bachelor.

Regarding the length of his daily entries, the longest in the 1930s was that on Coronation Day, 12 May 1937, when he wrote 1,172 words; the shortest was on 14 June 1938, when the single word 'Ditto' recorded another quiet day at home. His industry over half a century was considerable and, on 27 March 1952, he again referred to Kilvert, reflecting:

> How comforting it is when one wonders – as I am inclined to do at times – whether keeping a diary is worth all the time and trouble one spends on it. I think an even better explanation of the itch to record that afflicts all conscientious diarists was suggested by Kilvert when he wrote: 'Why do I keep this voluminous journal? Partly because life appears to me such a curious and wonderful thing that it seems a pity that even such a humble and uneventful life as mine should pass altogether away without

Introduction

some such record as this, and partly because I think the record may amuse and interest some who come after me.' There it is in a nutshell!

To ensure that his diaries would be available to future readers, Heap bequeathed them to the British Records Association. His Holborn Rover log books were left to the Boy Scouts Association and his large collection of theatre programmes to the Theatre Museum in Covent Garden.[21]

DIARY LOGISTICS

Heap used small (4 in × 2¾ in) pocket diaries for the first three years: a wine merchant's commercial diary in 1928, then 'Boy Scout's dairies' in 1929 and 1930. For 1931 and 1932 he moved up to using 6½ in × 4 in lined 'memo books' of 168 pages, which gave space for detailed comments and a more natural style than the pocket diaries, with their week to a small double page. A further advance was made in 1933, when he moved to using an 8 in × 5 in Letts 'page a day' desk diary. Although these larger pages made more daily space available, Heap found that he had much more to record on some days than others, so on busy days he continued his overflowing wordage onto any free space on previous pages or occasionally moved forward into the margins of the next pages. In 1938 he moved to using 8 in × 5 in bound and lined 180-page books, so that daily entries followed each other immediately, with Heap paginating the book as well as writing and underlining the day and date of each day's record.

Each December he set out to source a book for his next year's dairy, initially using Woolworth's memo books, then touring the stationery shops of the West End and the City for better books. The best supplier he found was Ryman's in the Strand, where he also bought his annual 'At a Glance' wall calendar. Problems were presented by paper shortages and wartime rationing, the initial impact of which was to limit the number of pages per book, obliging Heap to start a second volume before the end of the year from 1938 to 1940. From 1931 he always covered his diary with two layers of thick and heavy brown paper, thus protecting each volume but also providing a place to preserve – or perhaps conceal – items of sentimental value, such as press cuttings, early 1941 letters to and from Marjorie and a very few photographs. Significantly, in the covers of the 1940 diary is concealed the 23 July Post Office telegram from Eileen, changing their lunchtime lovers' rendezvous from King's Cross Station to Praed Street (i.e. Paddington

---

21 The Victoria and Albert Museum (where the Theatre Archives now reside) has no record of any Heap accessions.

Introduction

Underground), as her husband, suspicious of her frequent visits to London, was following her.

Heap had pleasant and fond memories of his past and he occasionally refers in diary entries to happenings many years before he started his diaries. Thus, on encountering a waterfall when walking in Snowdonia on 31 July 1938, he recalled: 'vaguely remember seeing when I came down here from Llandudno with Dad and Grandpa at Easter 1920', when he was ten. Similarly, on December 1938 he visited the Royal Opera House, 'in which I hadn't set foot since 1922 when it was given over to films'. Even before taking up diary writing he bought and saved the theatre programmes of the shows he saw and these doubtless account for his entries recalling earlier theatrical visits, such as that on 16 January 1931, when he reminisced about one eleven years earlier when he was two months short of his tenth birthday. He was proud of his theatrical experiences and used them when, in 1933, he 'Settled down to write the article on London in 1925 which I had written a rough of at work. Turned out to be longer than I expected it would – 1,320 words in all. Rather too long I'm afraid. Still. I'll see what can be done with it.' That article, and similar attempts at criticism which he sent to Fleet Street magazines, was professionally typed by his then girlfriend, Lilian, but was rejected by all the journals. Another example of Heap's powers of recall was after a visit to the Fitzwilliam Museum on 14 August 1938, when he recorded: 'Some excellent Augustus John portraits there and among other things Ford Madox Brown's *Last of England* which is introduced as a scene into *Nine Sharp* at the Little and a Low cartoon of the Ideal Cabinet in the *Standard* on Jan 5th 1928! What a memory!'

Such detail is of some interest, but over six decades a daily diary inevitably includes much that, three-quarters of a century later, readers might understandably consider routine or simply boring. For example, Heap was a recorder of the weather as it impacted on his daily life. It determined much of his leisure and exercise routines, such as walking to and from work or across the parks or Hampstead Heath. His spirits were invariably raised on seeing spring blossom, autumnal tints, frosty mornings or the occasional snow covering of his much loved parks[22] and Bloomsbury squares on his routes to and from work and his theatre and cinema venues. He avoided crowded tube trains and preferred, when prevented from walking by weather or longer distances, to use the buses or trams. In the 1930s he used motor coaches to reach such places as Guildford and Windsor on the outer rim of the metropolis, his local motor coach garage then being in Poland Street, W1.

---

22   Particular local favourites were the nearby Coram's Fields and St George's Gardens.

Introduction

SOURCES FOR FOOTNOTES

Unless otherwise stated, the sources used for brief biographical footnotes are the *Oxford Dictionary of National Biography* (*ODNB*), *Who's Who* or *The Times* as appropriate. Political events are invariably sourced from *The Times*, while more depth can be gained from the standard histories of the era such as the Official Civil and Military Histories and A. J. P. Taylor's *English History 1914–1945*. For wartime diplomatic and military matters *The Oxford Companion to the Second World War* (edited by I. C. B. Dear) is comprehensive, while the general wartime social scene is best covered in *The Times* (although censorship limited much information about the effects of the Blitz), Juliet Gardiner's *Wartime: Britain, 1939–1945*, her *The Blitz: The British Under Attack* and Philip Ziegler's *London at War 1939–1945*. For more information on specific wartime damage and fatalities, the three well-illustrated volumes of Winston G. Ramsey's *The Blitz Then and Now* mention most raids and major London incidents. *The London County Council Bomb Damage Maps 1939–1940* is an atlas showing the degree of damage suffered by each building in the County of London. These and similar useful sources are listed in the bibliography.

THE ANNUAL RETROSPECTS

From 1933, Heap wrote an annual 'Retrospect' of his year, in mid-December and on several separate sheets of lined foolscap paper, highlighting the major events (girlfriends, holidays, etc.) and, once this became routine, summarising his income, outgoings and savings, as well as the number of theatres and cinemas visited. In 1931 this 'retrospect' of only 75 words covered less than a single page at the end of the diary, but retrospects of subsequent years, up to and including the final one in 1980, were folded and inserted between the brown paper covers of the relevant volume. Their length grew from 680 words in 1932 to a peak of nearly 1,300 words in 1938 and varied between 1,100 and half that number during the war. Although he frequently apologised for the inevitable repetitions in these annual summaries, they do provide a useful synopsis of each of his years, his thoughts and his future plans. Thus, although the 'Retrospects' are separate sheets tucked into the covers and not written into the diaries themselves, they are an essential part of the diary and are included unedited at the end of each year.

Introduction

TRANSCRIPTION AND EDITORIAL NOTES

In his fifty-seven years of diarising, Heap wrote some two million words, making his life's work too massive ever to be published as a whole. Even this volume of nearly 250,000 words, covering fourteen and a half years, required severe editing down to a mere 27% of Heap's total words recorded in the period. Rejecting nearly three-quarters of his words has meant concentrating on extracts likely to be of greater interest to social historians, local historians and general readers, so his theatrical and film criticisms have been omitted, while the record of his daily life and work is retained. His extensive theatre- and film-going and his reading are consigned to tabulated annual 'Cultural Capture' lists in Appendix B, so that what he read or saw and where he saw it is available, while researchers can check with the original diaries should they want his detailed criticisms.

Not only have daily entries been edited but many have been omitted; where necessary, a brief note has been included summarising the events of the missing period if they were of any significance. Some idea of what Heap was doing on many of those days may often be gained by referring to the appendices listing his many theatre and cinema visits. Most daily entries have been trimmed and the punctuation adjusted to smooth the flow and retain Heap's meaning. Ellipses are only used when essential to retain meaning when cuts have been made. Other than sometimes using quotation marks, Heap did not stress proper names in his entries; for clarity, the names of publications, plays and shows, and film and book titles have been italicised in this transcription.

Only five photographs of Anthony Heap have been found, but none comes from the period of this volume. Tucked within the heavy brown paper covers of the later diaries was a passport photograph c.1955 and a print of Heap and his son, the 6 foot 2 inch-tall Anthony Charles (aged seventeen) posing on holiday at Land's End in 1965. (Heap himself was of average stature: in his 1928 diary, when he was eighteen and a half, he recorded his personal statistics as 5 feet 9½ inches tall, weight 10 stone 1 lb, size 15½-inch collar and size 8 boots.[23]) Heap's bequest of his Holborn Rover logbooks to the Scout Association includes one small photograph, dated March 1929, in which the 19 year old Heap is identified.

---

23 Metric sizes: height 1.77 metres, weight 64 kg, collar 39.4 cm; boot size 42 (continental) or 9 (American).

Introduction

THE EARLY DIARY STYLE OF 1928–1930

Heap kept a diary from 1 January 1928 and it is interesting to see how he was recording his activities and his increasingly wide range of interests just three months short of his eighteenth birthday. The following weeks of entries in the first month of January 1928 pocket diary entries show the range and note form he initially used. He started with single words, simple abbreviations or very short sentences which are reasonably easy to understand. Thus:

1 Sun Jan   Aft[ernoon] Palladium, Sullivan Company Morn Hampstead. Freezing

2 Mon   Rainy

3 Tues   Bought 18 collars. 3 Wings too large 4/9

4 Wed   [*No entry: the only instance for decades*]

5 Thur   Bought 3 new Shirts 19/6

6 Fri   Stuffy. Dull. Turns fine Midday   Floods, Gales

7 Sat   Thames o'er Banks[24]   Savoy pit – *When Knights were Bold* 2 Wing Bows 3/-

8 Sun   Hyde Park Morn. Nigger. Very fine

9 Mon   Sale starts. 6.30 till Wednesday   Gran

10 Tues   Chamber of C [Commerce] job no good. New Black Tie 2/6, Pictures *Faust*. Good Prod *Perfect Sap*.

11 Wed   Went after job BTH [Engineering firm British Thompson Houston] 10 mins late back

12 Thur   Rainy

13 Fri   Fine Morning

14 Sat   Rainy. Stayed in Afternoon. Eve *Peter Pan* Gaiety, Fair show Dull theatre, badly lit. Full House

... *then at the end of the month* ...

29 Sun Jan   Walk into City to find place. Nigger run over in Fenchurch St. Thought dead first. Recovered. Took him home.

30 Mon   Went after job. Quick interview. Bus back. Charrington Hall[25] concert S.C. Club Good. Death of Haig.

---

24   As high tide approached, the Thames had flooded the Embankment at Temple and Upper Thames Street: see *The Times*, 9 January 1928. No London deaths resulted but the 'worst storm of the winter' just a week later caused several serious injuries from collapsing houses.
25   Charrington Hall, at the northern end of Charrington Road, NW1.

Introduction

31 Tues   Book keeping

1 Wed Feb   Fusion of *Westminster Gazette* and *Daily News*. Gran

2 Thur   Rainy. Book keeping. Late

3 Fri   Haig's funeral. Liberal industrial Report

4 Sat   Dull rainy day. Stayed in afternoon, went to pictures in evening. Saw *Resurrection*.[26] Rather drawn out. Paid Old Danes subscription. Posted Sat night.

After the first two months, by March 1928, the entries were growing in length and being written in slightly more flowing English:

4th Sun Mar   Very fine. Lost Nigger on Parl. Hill in morning. Searched for hours. Found him by Highgate Pond in afternoon.

5th Mon   Went to M.R. meeting at Charrington Hall. Saw Mr Davies[27] after meeting.

6th Tues   English class.   Gran

7th Wed   Salesmanship Class. English Homework. Liberal victories at local election at St Ives and Middlesbrough.

8th Thur   Municipal elections in London. Labour gain in St Pancras. Great surprise. French in evening.

9th Fri   A little snow. Bookkeeping – 'Bills of Exchange' Case 34

10th Sat   Hampstead in afternoon with Nigger. Some snow. Garrick in evening. Saw *Tin Gods* – good play.

The trend to more detail and better formed sentences continued through 1929 and 1930, the average daily wordage quadrupling. Thus, by May–June 1929:

26 Sun May   Dull early but fine after 10.0. Went down to Chingford in morning. Training course in afternoon. Left at 7.30. Home 8.50 Plenty of sunbathing and 3 swims. Not too hot.

27 Mon   Stuffy and warm. Re-read textbook 'Company Law' in evening.

---

26   The first Italian 'talkie' film to be made.
27   Probably Councillor (later Alderman Sir) David Davies, a leading Municipal Reformer, later the Mayor of St Pancras; but there were also a father and son named Davies on the council.

Introduction

28 Tues   Cooler. Finished re-reading 'Company Law' textbook in evening

29 Wed   Met Tripp at YMCA and went for a swim. Arranged to go to Gilwell[28] at weekend. Got home 7.50. Tried to do a bit of revision after dinner from Students Notebook

30 Th   General Election. Fine day. Got own tea. Could not do any swotting. Went with Mum and Dad down to *Daily Sketch* Offices in Strand to see first results. Got cab home at 1.0. More results on wireless. Bed at 2.

31 Fri   Tired in morning. Not much work all day. Great excitement over election results.[29] Swotting out of the question. Went for swim on way home. Read papers in evening.

June 1 Sat   Dull, Fine later. Went to Gilwell for weekend. Tripp went Sat morning. Went on Connaught Water[30] in evening also. Camping, 3 of us in Tripp's tent.

The pattern of daily diary entries was thus well established by the later pocket diaries. By the end of 1930 and wanting more space each day in which to keep a more comprehensive diary, Heap moved up to a lined 200-page book. These he paginated, so each day directly followed on from the previous entry, their length now varying according not to the space available but to what he wanted to record. The first two weeks or so of the 1931 diary are transcribed unedited to show the ease with which Heap now wrote in more flowing English, reporting not just the incidents and events of his days but also his thoughts and reactions to those happenings.

---

28   Gilwell Park, the National Scouting Centre at Chingford, Essex, often spelled 'Gillwell' by Heap.
29   The General Election results were: Labour Party 288, Conservatives 260, Liberals 59 and Others 8.
30   A lake one and a half miles south-east of Gilwell.

PART ONE
FLIRTING WITH FASCISM
1931–1939

INTRODUCTION

The 1931 diary opens with Heap, aged twenty, in his fourth year of work in the Treasurer's Department of Peter Robinson's department store and living with his parents in rented rooms at 139 Gray's Inn Road. In his spare time he was working hard at correspondence courses, preparing himself for the examinations of the Chartered Institute of Secretaries. As his parents increasingly quarrelled, in February 1932 Anthony and his mother moved to rooms in Highbury, but they returned to Gray's Inn Road four months later. Harmony did not prevail and, in August 1932, Heap and his mother again moved out, this time to two rooms on the top floor of what proved to be a bug-ridden house in Somers Town, at 11 Penryn Street. In March 1933 his father's suicide was compounded by the publicity at the inquest of his mother's admission of Anthony's illegitimacy. Within a few days Heap contacted the British Union of Fascists, an association which lasted for two years.

In April 1934 Heap and his mother quarrelled with their landlord and moved to a more expensive pair of top-floor rooms at the slightly more salubrious 20 Harrington Square, with views across Mornington Crescent to the recently completed art deco Carreras Cigarette Factory. More sociable neighbours now included the Murphys on the floor below and the McLaveys in the basement.[1] Both families occasionally gave the Heaps free theatre and cinema tickets, and Bernie, the McLaveys' four-year-old son, was cared for several hours a week by Mrs Heap. The young Mrs McLavey's party-going habits caused Heap's mother some concern, she presumably feeling that Anthony should not take too close an interest in the woman. He and his mother remained in Harrington Square until 1937, when they found a small purpose-built flat in Sinclair House, Hastings Street WC1, closer to her Conservative Association friends south of Euston Road. Although retaining his interest in the far right, Heap then joined the local St Pancras Conservative Party and stood for them in the 1937 borough elections.

Earning a limited wage, Anthony continued frequenting theatre pit and galleries but found treating girlfriends to the theatre or cinema rather expensive. Nevertheless he learned to dance and attended social

---

[1] The 1936 electoral register lists Leslie and Winifred Murphy. The McLaveys (spelled several different ways in the Diary) moved often and do not appear in the electoral register.

Part One Introduction

events. He was no great romancer but he did really fall in love with two girls. After the apparently shallow relationship with Shelmerdine in 1931, he recorded straightforward but serious relationships with two other girls early in the decade. The first was Beatrice in 1932, but this faded just before his father's suicide. The sudden loss of his father was a great blow to Heap who, however, took over the much loved family dog, Nigger. Within weeks his spirits were boosted by his falling deeply in love with Lilian; that relationship ended in 1934, after which he recorded no proper girlfriend until his affair with 'Eilleen' in the summer of 1940. In the place of girls, Heap's growing interest in right-wing politics almost matched for a time his adherence to first nighting, the cinema and literature. A recurrent theme is his attempt to convert his love of and familiarity with the London theatre into a career as a critic or a journalist, as he found his retail cashier's job boring and without prospects. He wrote lengthy criticisms of the performances he saw but these details, like his extensive film criticisms and book reviews, are generally omitted from this volume.

Heap had visited Paris in 1931 with friends but throughout the decade his great interest, and much of his leisure time, was taken up with Rover Scouting, visiting Switzerland with them and eventually becoming the secretary and treasurer of the Holborn Rover Group. He also took on additional duties within the Group and across the wider London Rover organisation: he wrote up the Group log book, typed notices and a newsletter on a borrowed typewriter, reproduced copies on a machine in his bedroom and posted them; and he attended London-wide Rover committee meetings and social events. In the early 1930s he regularly went camping with fellow Rovers, and they retained the camping habit through to the opening of the war when, such was their desire for the open air life, they had to camouflage their white tents with brown paint. Regular solo and group hiking and Youth Hostelling were Heap's favourite bank holiday and summer break activity. As the decade progressed, his interest in scouting gradually declined until, in 1937, he resigned from the group and also let lapse his membership of the Central YMCA, where he had regularly taken meals, used the reading room, gymnasium and swimming pool, and attended debates and social events.

He also regularly 'pub-crawled' with his three single male drinking friends, the two Johns and Bill. Before the war they met up on Friday evenings and toured their favourite bars and clubs in and around Fitzrovia, Holborn and Hampstead, initially fortnightly, then monthly. Heap never held back on these outings but drank his fill, particularly when free drink was available; when he had paid for admission, he made sure that he drank his money's worth – a habit that annoyed girlfriends he was escorting.

Flirting with Fascism

At first sight, as with keeping his diary, Anthony Heap's theatre 'first nighting' appears somewhat intense but he greatly enjoyed both the theatre and recording his experience of the performances. Living in central London, he had many theatres within walking distance for him: close enough that he would walk to the theatre, hire a stool in the queue and often walk home for his tea before returning for the performance. He occasionally spent an hour revising a chapter of his current correspondence course, then an hour in a newsreel cinema before going on to his theatre, so he could manage several commitments in an evening, as well as taking a book to read in the intervals. All were commented on – sometimes at length – in that day's diary entry.

Late in 1939 Heap checked his diaries and discovered that he had seen 728 shows in the last twelve years, an average of just under 61 shows a year, the majority being first nights, as follows:

1928–35	1932–68	1936–77
1929–42	1933–73	1937–83
1930–50	1934–65	1938–64
1931–45	1935–70	1939–56

The visit totals listed in the 'Culture Capture' appendices may differ slightly from this table taken from his own diary entry, not least because cinemas often presented two films in one show, Heap sometimes reporting on the preferred second feature.

National and International events affecting Heap and London

Ramsay MacDonald's Labour election victory in 1929 did not impress Heap, who, in October 1931, welcomed Labour being 'wiped out everywhere' and the resulting large Conservative majority in the National Government. He naturally welcomed Stanley Baldwin's Conservative victory in November 1935, but also applauded both the Italian conquest of Abyssinia and the fascist governments in Hitler's Germany and Mussolini's Italy. The European fascist threat to the United Kingdom was not acknowledged by Heap – or by the majority of the British electorate, who generally remained opposed to rearmament until the last moment. Like most citizens of the interwar decades, he was firmly opposed to the UK getting involved in another war. Memories of the recent Great War abounded. Heap was eight when the armistice was signed and he was a regular attender at the Cenotaph on Remembrance Day, so he deprecated indications from overseas that another war was approaching. However, the September 1938 Munich crisis, with its expectation of imminent aerial bombardment, changed public attitudes in favour of preparing for war. Heap and the majority of British people nevertheless supported Chamberlain's appeasement of Hitler – a policy that at least allowed a further year of preparation for war.

Heap's diary does not comment extensively on war preparations but records how his life, holidays and leisure activities continued while London and the world waited. His reporting of the gradual militarisation of stretches of Regent's Park, Primrose Hill[2] and Hampstead Heath, as well as the slow recruitment of volunteers into the civil defence services, will be of interest to local historians. Heap remained concerned at the probability of his being conscripted into the armed services as war approached. In 1939 he hoped that his volunteering to train as a member of the Police War Reserve might save him, but it was his subsequent illness that left him medically unfit for conscription.

---

[2] See Martin Sheppard, *Primrose Hill: A History* (Lancaster: Carnegie Publishing, 2013), which uses Heap's reporting of the changes made and the diary of a soldier stationed in an anti-aircraft battery on the Hill.

1931

From 1 January Anthony Heap now wrote his diary in a larger bound memo book, allowing more detailed recording of incidents, descriptions and reflections on his life and of the world about him. For the initial fortnight only of 1931, his record is reproduced unedited to show the ease with which Heap now wrote in more flowing English. Throughout this volume his theatre-going activities, other than the occasional comment, have been consigned to the annual appendix of his cultural pursuits, to which readers should refer. In 1931, he recorded attending forty-nine theatrical performances and twenty-nine films, and reading seventeen books.

As 1931 opened, Heap was three months short of his twenty-first birthday, living at home with his parents at 139 Gray's Inn Road WC1, in his fourth year as an accounts clerk at Peter Robinson's department store at Oxford Circus and studying hard for the examinations for the Chartered Institute of Secretaries in June. Hiking and camping with the Holborn Rover Scouts, the Youth Hostel Association and several other groups enabled him to get out into the countryside.

Expanding his horizons, Heap spent the Easter weekend in Paris and had ten days over the August bank holiday with the Holborn Rover contingent at the Kandersteg International Scout Centre in Switzerland. He smoked his first cigarette in June, learned to dance in September, bought himself a dinner suit in October and 'formed a deep friendship with a most charming girl', his first serious girlfriend, Shelmerdene from Burnt Oak.

The full typescript for the year (less his detailed theatre and film criticisms) totals some 27,650 words, here cut to some 9,800 words (excluding the retrospect) – 35% of the original. So, although Heap made daily entries, this volume frequently misses many days at a time, while those that are reproduced omit the less interesting material (barring those for the first two weeks).

Thursday 1 January Having gone to bed at 12.10 a.m. after a stocious [drunken] New Year's Eve, arose at 7.35 a.m. A quick breakfast and a hurried glance through the theatre news in the papers and off to work in slight mist which soon cleared away for a bright sunny morning. At the top of Guilford St called in the International Library to buy the *Theatre World* and found the boss much displeased with his male assistant and complaining that he had to do ten times as much work. I pitied the assistant but the boss may have been right. Found enough work, what with big orders and commitments, to occupy me most of the day which has been very unusual lately. At lunchtime, walked round to Gt Titchfield St and bought a pear, 2 oranges and 2 apples for 7d, which was reasonable. At [staff] tea, our table was bombarded with sugar by some high spirited yobs at an adjoining table. In retaliating I accidently hit an ugly female on the head, much to the mirth of the company present. Walked home, dined, shaved badly with a blunt razor blade, studied hard, revising studies 1–5 'Company Law' till 11.0 To bed 11.45 but no sleep till about 12.30.

Friday 2 January A glorious, bright, sunny cold and frosty morning. Walking to work, noticed grand British Museum Avenue entirely white with frost. At lunchtime walked to the Piccadilly Theatre and booked an Upper Circle seat for Saturday week. Its number is B1 which worries me for I am always doubtful about second rows in balconies. The front row people always lean over and spoil the view. Reminiscence: 11 years ago today Fri 2/1/20, 4th visit to the Old Vic to see *Henry V* for second time. Went to YMCA to meet Jack Tripp for a swim. Met Roy Hill going in. Used to be in my patrol when I first joined in summer of 1928, but left to work in South Wales and had not seen him since. Jack did not turn up, so slightly annoyed, came home alone. Coming out met 'The Count' (Adam de Hegedus)[1] and chatted with for a quarter of an hour or so. Arriving home, found the 'Walthamstowites'[2] all there but left very soon, much to my relief. As usual on Friday evenings, did not get down to study before 9.0 p.m. Tried to read textbook section of study 7 Mercantile Law, sale of goods. Had not touched on this before and found it very difficult and had to concentrate on it. Went to bed at 11.15 but read in bed till about 12.0.

Saturday 3 January Dull, chilly and damp morning. Very displeased to learn that the new Drury Lane show, to which I intended to go tonight, has been postponed due to breakdown of scenery mechanism – upsets my arrangements. What with this and domestic strife at home arrived at work in a none too tranquil frame of mind. In the afternoon took Nigger for run round Regent's Park. Very cold, bleak and damp. Started raining so came back quick and got home 4.0. Up to Lutz[3] to get cakes, home to tea and left at 5.0 to go to Streatham Hill Theatre to see *Folly to be Wise* before it comes up to the Piccadilly next week. Got as far as Kensington, changed my mind and came back to the West End.

1 Adam de Hegedus (1906–1958) a Hungarian intellectual, journalist and author who lived in Kensington and was a 'quasi-member' of the Holborn Rovers.
2 Heap's mother's brother, Fred Shepherd, his wife, Minnie, and their children, Jack and Mary.
3 Lutz, bakery, 8 Museum Street, WC1.

1931

Walked along Strand, called in Woolworths and bought Galsworthy's *The Man of Property* (Forsyte Saga) and up to the Avenue Pavilion[4] for an hour's news-talkie. After, went down to the Apollo and saw *The Private Secretary*, the old eighties farce which like *Charlie's Aunt* and *When Knights were Bold*, is revived every Christmas. Found it mildly amusing but an old fashioned example of farce in its infancy. Had a none too good seat in the 4th row and relieved the boredom of the evening by reading my book during the long intervals. During the last act smelt something burning. Relieved to find it was not my overcoat but some chap's hat with a hole burnt through it by a cigarette end. Walked home, walked round square[5] with Mum and Dad and Nigger, supped and to bed at 12.45.

Sunday 4 January A fine brisk sunny morning. To Hampstead with Nigger, home to lunch and over to see Gran in hospital with Aunt Pop.[6] Going over Waterloo Bridge saw a small elephant being taken for a walk round. An unusual sight in London. Walked home, had tea and went over to the new Trocadero Kinema at the Elephant and Castle.[7] Arrived at 6.35 and had to stand till 8.15. Saw *Song O'My Heart*. Simple but well produced and excellent singing by John McCormack. Most magnificent place I have ever been in. Holding 5,500 people, it is the largest Kinema in Europe. Has a marvellous organ with 200 instrumental effects on it and requires some playing. Very much enjoyed a Gilbert and Sullivan selection played on it. Pipes hidden behind artistic draping. The amenities are surprising with hat racks under every seat and a special row of seats with earphones for the hard of hearing and offers of free monthly magazine and inspection of whole building and apparatus any Sunday morning. Most favourably impressed with the place and realised that it meant a revolution in entertainment. When one thinks of the drab surroundings of the neighbourhood, a place like this must be a heaven on earth to those people when all the luxury and entertainment is available for 6d to 2/4. It's a monument of enterprise. Left at 9.30, home by bus, supped and to bed at 11.40 p.m. but did not get to sleep for an hour or so, for laying [*sic*] awake thinking.

Monday 5 January Dull, very cold and frosty morning which I do not dislike. Brighter later.

Fairly uneventful day. Re-read 'Sale of Goods' in Mercantile Law textbook. Getting on very slow with it but beginning to grasp it better.

---

4 Avenue Pavilion News, 101 Shaftesbury Avenue, W1.
5 Probably Mecklenburg Square, via Doughty Street, just behind their home in Gray's Inn Road.
6 Pop Shepherd, Heap's mother's elder sister, who emigrated to America in 1931. Heap wrote her long letters every few months and they exchanged birthday and Christmas presents.
7 Recently opened in December 1930, this 3,500-seat cinema was one of the largest and finest in the country.

Part One

Went to bed at 11.15, rather earlier than usual. Rem: *Richard II* Old Vic
5/1/20

Tuesday 6 January Bright and very cold. Streets white with frost. Re-read Chapter 4 'Mercantile Law' again in evening and had a shave. To bed at 11.45. The new Sadler's Wells Theatre opens with *Twelfth Night*.

Wednesday 7 January Again bright and cold. Much disgusted with weak-minded molly-coddlers in office who are afraid of fresh air and keep closing windows. At lunchtime, went for a swim at YMCA. Got a shock when I first jumped in for the water was freezing cold. Afterwards learned that it is always like this Mondays and Wednesdays as the bath is refilled in the mornings and does not have a chance to get warmed up till the evening. Shall take care to avoid those days in future. Went to debating class in Restaurant after work. Only four of us present. Decided to abandon the class if no improvement. However we argued on 'The Nationalisation of the Coal Mines' till 8.0. As expected was amused to hear socialist propaganda and impractical idealist schemes roll out. Really a waste of time though. Rushed home by tube to get the log book and get to the Foundling[8] for the Monthly Troop Meeting by 8.30. but did not start till 9.0. Only discussed troop business. Only 16 present and was very cold. Was appointed Treasurer for the summer holiday savings fund. Does not involve much work so do not mind much. Got home at 10.40, supped on rabbit pie and hurried glance through the evening papers and to bed at 11.40. To sleep about 12.30.

Thursday 8 January At lunchtime went down to the Haymarket Theatre to try and book for the first night of *Colonel Satan* on Saturday week but no seats left. Walked back again. After work had a haircut. Joshua and Scott met me coming out and the three of us walked to YMCA intending to dine there. Unfortunately they wanted to see membership cards on the door, so much to my amazement we had to adjourn to the Beta Cafe instead. Did not enjoy dinner much. The food was not good, there was too much clatter of crockery near us and Joshua's nose bled. At 7.40 we got into the YMCA by the back way and sat in the lounge for a few minutes. Just before 8.0 we went down to the King George's Hall.[9] Mother and Aunt Pop already there. Had seats in the ninth row in a side block and were surrounded by hordes of small scouts. Was disappointed with *Cinderella* – not up to the usual standard of Roland House[10] pantos but a good performance and had excellent coffee during

8   The Foundling Hospital at Coram's Fields, next to Mecklenburg Square, WC1, was established in 1720 but relocated to Surrey in 1926, so leaving the green parkland as open space.
9   The YMCA theatre on the eastern side of the building.
10 The Roland House Scout Settlement, 29 Stepney Green, E1, established in memory of Capt. the Hon. Roland Philipps MC (1890–1916), a friend of Baden-Powell and a London scout

1931

the interval. Over at 10.50 p.m. Home, supped on tripe and onions and to bed by 11.50 p.m.

Friday 9 January On rising found that snow had fallen during night. But very thin and soon melted away and dried up. Went to Woolworth's lunchtime and bought a shaving stick of soap and ordered 25 cards. Went for swim after work – Jack could not come. Got home at 7.5 p.m. dined and settled down to write up criticism of *Cinderella* in logbook. Found it took me all the evening, so no time for study. Went to bed rather earlier than usual – 11.30 p.m. but still find it difficult to get to sleep in less than an hour.

Saturday 10 January Cold, dull day. Took Nigger for a quick run round Regent's Park early in afternoon. Very moist and misty atmosphere. Noticed trees being planted in the Outer Circle between the two parks. Lakes completely frozen over. Got back at 3.10 and went up to the YMCA. Met Cherub who showed me round the stage of the King George's Hall. Met the performers in their stage costumes and chatted with some of them in the corridor. Saw some of *Cinderella* again and liked it better than before. Stood by the side door. Could only see front of the stage with good view of the audience which contained B-P and Lord Hampton.[11] Saw stage photos taken of it. Had tea in YMCA restaurant with David Hughes whom I have not seen often lately, he poor fellow being absorbed in running a scout troop. Left at 6.50, went down to the Avenue Pavilion for an hour's news-talkies, and on to the Piccadilly Theatre to see *Folly to be Wise*. Excellent revue with Cecily Courtneidge and Nelson Keys as the stars, both being extremely versatile and working very hard. Tuneful music and clever sketches. Beautiful dresses and good chorus dancing. Has the genuine Hulbert touch – the sense of being a merry romp from start to finish. Not over till 11.20. Bus to Southampton Row, walked rest. Home 11.50. To bed at 1.0. Passed a restless night. A most full, enjoyable well-spent day.

Sunday 11 January Hampstead in morning with Nigger. Atmosphere very moist. Got home 2.10, changed and went with Aunt Pop to see Gran in hospital. Left at 3.35 leaving Aunt Pop to come on at 4.0 Got home at 4.10 and had dinner, read papers after and then wrote up further notes on *Cinderella* in log-book. Went for a walk for ½ hour but started raining. Read some of chapter 3 'Foreign Exchange'.

Monday 12 January First day of sale. Had to go shop walking on ground floor. Kept fairly busy signing bills and directing customers but very tiring. Had a man come up to me and ask a lot of details about

---

master. He was killed leading a charge on a German trench and had left his home to the East London Scouts.

11   Lord Robert Baden-Powell, the Chief Scout, was a retired lieutenant general; Lord Hampton was the President of the Hertfordshire Scouts.

the Old Vic opera. Working till 6.30 the first three days of the week. Finished reading text book study of Banking and Exchange in evening, though not very careful study. To bed about 11.45.

Tuesday 13 January Put in some good work on study notes during day. A lot of fuss in the office about bad figures in the Receiving Room Books and clearing the empty spaces in the latter. In evening re-read some of the text book section study 'Exchange'. Got on all right for an hour or so then mind started wandering again and failed to get down to it properly again. Tried to read in bed but felt so tired so gave it up as a bad job and went to sleep quickly.

Wednesday 14 January Fine, bright, crisp but very cold morning. At lunchtime I went and got the 25 visiting cards I ordered last Friday at Woolworths. After work went to the debate upstairs in the lounge, the motion being 'That we glory in the 20th century'. An interesting subject and some good speeches but had to leave at 7.45 to get to Patrol meeting in YMCA and den at 8.0 – six of us turned up, discussed various business and George Maddox talked on 'Coffee.' Came up at 9.30 and with Stan Cox went to the King George's Hall towards the end of the 2nd act of *Cinderella*. In interval went out and chatted with members of the cast. During last act Ralph Reader 'The Guv'nor' came in and sat with us.[12] Went up to the back of the hall and saw Cherub, who was looking good in full evening kit. The rest of the patrol drifted in towards the end. After the show, stayed about, chatting with Stan Cox for half an hour or so. Left at 11.10 and walked home in a slight fall of snow. Supped on a roll and butter and cheese and hot milk and to bed at 12.0

[End of unedited entries]

Friday 16 January Much milder weather lately. Did not go swimming after work as usual on Fridays but went straight home and did Test 6 'Banking and Exchange' while Mum and Dad and Aunt Pop went to the Regent. The test took me till 11.0 – much longer than I thought it would. Some wireless dance music and to bed at 11.50. Rem: Old Vic 16/1/20 *Taming of the Shrew*. Got new black suit this day last year.

Sunday 25 January Bright, sunny but very cold. Went on Co-operation hike for the first time and enjoyed it very much. 11 Rovers and only 4 Rangers. Took Premier coach from Oxford Circus to Hemel Hempstead at 9.0. Got stiff round the back of my left heel and had to limp towards

---

12 (William) Ralph Reader (1903–1982) choreographer, theatrical producer, actor, songwriter and founder of the annual Scout *Gang Show*. He was a friend of Heap and a leading member of the Holborn Rovers Group.

the end of the day. Glanced through papers, supped on prunes, rice and hot milk and to bed at 10.50. To sleep about an hour later.

Saturday 31 January Feel slightly better this morning but tooth giving a little trouble. Sore throat still the main worry but gradually got better during day. Went on a double-deck tram down the Kingsway tunnel for first time since its re-opening.[13]

Sunday 15 February Dull and rainy when I got up at 8.0 but soon left off and cleared up. Went on 'Co-op' hike in Berkshire. Left at 8.55 but only got to Waterloo just in time to get the 9.35 to Egham owing to long wait for buses. Six of us altogether, 4 Rovers and 2 Rangers. Did a long hike of 22 miles via Sunningdale, Windsor Gt Park. Tea in Old Windsor. Train back from Staines. Arr Waterloo at 9.22.

Monday 16 February Feet still very sore. Blisters under small toe each foot the chief trouble. Have to limp to walk but got to work all right. Left leg still stiff as well. Felt really 'Monday morning' as I usually do after day hikes on a Sunday. Very busy in morning with Paris orders and in afternoon with rough log book account of yesterday and writing up weekend is dreary, so not much time for study. Registry[14] shifted round after tea – much disturbance, only 7 instead of 8. Got about same amount of work as before but worrying business as might have place shifted as well. Rainy evening. Called in YMCA on way home to see if notice of hike in den yet. No luck. Put feet in hot water again and went to bed at 11.45.

Wednesday 18 February Another fall of snow on way to work, but does not lay [*sic*]. Wore grey socks with boracic powder in them so feet feel better again. Carried on Study 5 'Meetings' during day. Went to debating class in restaurant after work.

Saturday 21 February Took Nigger to Hampstead in afternoon. Very fine, clear day. Got home 4.30, shaved and changed, had tea and went to the new Tatler cinema in Charing Cross Rd for an hour. Something like the Avenue Pavilion but not half as good. Had a seat in end of front row of circle, which collapsed half way through. Left at 7.10 and walked down to Trafalgar Sq. Called in at Hippodrome to book seats for birthday. Got bus to Victoria St and went to New Horticultural Hall[15] for London Rover Ball. Stayed till 8.20 when I left to go to the Whitehall Theatre to see *Good Losers* by Michael Arlen.[16] Full of witty cynical epigrams, well suited to this beautiful little theatre in black and

---

13 Opened in 1906, the tram tunnel was closed in 1929 to have the headroom increased to 16 feet 6 inches to accommodate double-decker trams. It had reopened on 14 January.
14 The part of PR's Treasurer's Department where Heap worked.
15 Vincent Square, SW1.
16 Michael Arlen (1895–1956), Armenian-born novelist, playwright and short story writer, who wrote successfully in England, particularly in the 1920s.

Part One

white marble. Mayfair flocking there in their hundreds to applaud their Arlen. Afterwards the waiting car lines almost the whole of Whitehall. Over at 11.0. Caught bus back to Horticultural Hall. Ball still in full swing. Went round and got some impressions of the evening. Had some refreshments with 'Shelmerdine' for which charged exorbitant prices but did not worry. Over at 11.30. Met most of Holborn gathered together after. Left at 11.45. Bus to Tottenham Court Rd. Walked home from there. To bed at 12.45 but did not get to sleep for a long time.

Saturday 7 March Very cold. Wrote rough account of social last night after lunch. Went to Adam's party at 64 Abingdon Villas. Arrived at 4.15. Original tea. Only 7 there. Got a little bored. Left at 8.10, arrived at Vaudeville Theatre at 8.35 to see *The Circle* by Somerset Maugham.[17] Good revival of brilliant play.

Monday 9 March Heavy snowfall during night, 2 or 3 inches thick this morning. One or two heavy falls during day as well. Read 'Hints for Honours Candidates' just received from Metropolitan College[18] during day and went over Study 6 Company Law again. A little tired after yesterday. Wrote up log book account of Friday and Yesterday and did test 6 Company Law in evening. To bed at 11.50.

Friday 13 March 21st birthday presents – ring from Mother, gold watch and chain from Dad, gloves and £1 note from Aunt Pop – much pleased with them. Cold not gone but not worse than yesterday. Had lunch in staff restaurant for the first time for about 18 months – very raw steak. Walked round to Woolworths after and bought some ginger. No study today. Home to tea – big birthday cake – very good. Went to Hippodrome to see *Stand Up and Sing*, Jack Buchanan's new musical.[19] First rate show [*half page of criticism*] all enjoyed it very much – went to Oxford Corner House[20] after for supper – fish and chips and coffee. Got home at 12.35 and to bed very tired. Best birthday ever had.

Thursday 19 March Very warm and fine. Too warm for overcoat. Walked round to Woolworths lunchtime. Did 3 questions, Test 8 'Sec Practice' in afternoon. Temperature about 60 deg Fahrenheit. Test 8 after dinner and read a chapter on insurance. At 9.15 went up to Folk Dance Party at University of London Eastman Hall just off Farringdon

---

17 (William) Somerset Maugham (1874–1965), a very successful British novelist and playwright of the era.
18 The Metropolitan College prepared students for professional and academic examinations by correspondence courses in a range of subjects.
19 (Walter John) 'Jack' Buchanan (1891–1957), a popular Scottish debonair theatre and film actor, singer, producer and director.
20 Corner Houses were popular large, four- or five-floored café/restaurant establishments operated between 1909 and 1977 by J. Lyons in prime corner sites such as at the junction of Oxford Street and Tottenham Court Road (known as the Oxford), and on Coventry Street and The Strand. The prices charged depended on the level of sophistication of the meals and service selected by customers.

Sq. Only 20 there, very disappointing. Stayed for ¾ hour, got bored and came away. Went to bed at 11.15 and read for half an hour.

Friday 20 March Fine and warmer still, 70 deg. in shade. Revised 'Banking and Exchange'. Went for a swim by myself after work. Met Wiffles after and sundry others and chatted for ¾ hour. Also bought ticket for Elkayonians[21] concert on the 31st. Bus home, had dinner, wrote up very brief account of last night in log book, and read some unimportant chapters in *The Secretary's Manual*. To bed at 11.30.

Saturday 21 March Dull morning and cooler. Boat Race Day – to be run in afternoon. Cambridge won again by 3 lengths. Lunched with Joshua and Wiffles at YMCA and went down to Charing Cross to meet Erith Rovers. Met also Stan Cox on station. Went to Museum of Physicians and Surgeons in Lincolns Inn Fields. Very interesting and gruesome collection. Left at 4.0. Got tube from British Museum[22] to return to Shepherds Bush for *Business Efficiency Exhibition* at White City. Walked round for ¾ hour and got slightly bored. Bus back to Tottenham Court Rd. Retd to YMCA, went up to Reading Room for little while, hand wash and went into restaurant for tea. Had great shock – thought I'd lost wallet, but much relieved to find it in overcoat breast pocket. Rushed down to the Pavilion to see Cochran's *1931 Revue*. Seat at side of upper circle – almost on top of stage but could see reasonably well smart audience and Mr Cochran himself in box opposite. Very good show – to bed at 12.45. Very full day.

Monday 30 March Wrote to hotel in Paris to book rooms for Easter in morning. Revised some Book keeping in afternoon and evening. Went for a swim on way home.

Thursday 2 April Dull rainy morning. Still no appetite. Wrote up account of 'A Good Night' for the District Magazine in afternoon and posted off. Home to shave, have dinner and pack and leave at 9.30 to catch 10.10 train from St Pancras with Stan Cox and his three friends. Arr. Tilbury 11.20 and boarded boat. No berths – had to stay night on deck chairs. Got rugs but very cold and wet. Did not sleep much.

Friday 3 April (Good Friday) Arrived Dunkerque 5.30 and took 2nd class train to Paris paying excess fare. Arr. Paris 10.15 and put up at Trinité Palace Hotel in Rue Pigalle. Lunched next door for nothing owing to waiter's error on change. Cab to Rue des Pyramides to see some of Stan's friends. Walk through gardens, after to Place de la Concorde, up the Champs Elysée to the Arc de Triomphe, heavy rain, and cab back to Montmartre. After some coffee returned to the hotel till 7.0. Went to the American restaurant a few doors away for dinner. Went

21 LKO: Lord Kinnaird's Own Old Scouts Association.
22 The underground station at 133 High Holborn, which closed in September 1933 when the longer platforms at Holborn (100 yards away) were opened.

Part One

to the Casino de Paris after to see *Paris Revue* a spectacular revue. Promenaded for 10 frs. Very good view at side of front of stalls. Very interesting evening and a good show – contrast to the London theatres. Not over till 12.0. Back to hotel and bed.

Saturday 4 April Did not wake up till 10.40 or so owing to no sleep previous night. Bathed, dressed and went for a stroll round. Called back for the other three and went out for lunch. Had a job to find suitable place, eventually found a good restaurant in Montmartre and had a good lunch for 15 frs. Left at 4.30 and had tea nearby. Walked back to the hotel a long way round. At 8.0 went along to the American restaurant for dinner. On to the *Folies Bergère* revue. Exceedingly good show. Enjoyed it immensely. Went along to the Boulevard Bonne Nouvelle for a coffee after – then back to the hotel.

Sunday 5 April Got up about 11.30. Went to Gare St Lazare with Stan and called back for others. Lunched in Faubourge Montmartre. Others went to Versailles after. I booked seat at the Opera (57 frs) and walked to the Bois du Bologne. Met an English chap there and spent about 3 hours talking with him over tea in the Polaris Restaurant. Walked back with him to the Place de la Concorde and took a cab to the Gare St Lazare to change some money but the Bureau de Change closed. Cab back to hotel. Changed collar and brushed up after a sandwich, rushed off to the Opera to see *Faust*. Great show, house packed out. Had rotten seat at back of a first tier box. Much impressed by brilliance and size of the place. Had a coffee at outside cafe nearby after and walked back to the hotel. Read paper and went to sleep about 2.0.

Monday 6 April Dull and showery. Got up at 10.0. Stan and I walked along the Boulevard Bonne Nouvelle for breakfast. Another walk and cab back to Gare St Lazare to get some change. No luck again. Back to hotel. Others gone out. Joined them at lunch up in Montmartre. After lunch a climb up to Sacre Coeur and back. Went to Notre Dame in afternoon and up tower. Tea after just behind the Louvre. Cab back to hotel. Dinner at 6.0 at American restaurant, back to hotel to settle up and cab to Gare St Lazare to catch 6.56 train to Dunkerque. Other three came on later by 2nd class. Uncomfortable, dismal carriage. Boarded boat and found a place to sleep on lower deck on ground. Managed to get a little sleep.

Tuesday 7 April Got 7.10 train from Tilbury. Arrived back at St Pancras at 8.9 a.m. where Mother came to meet me. Had tea and rolls in buffet and went straight to work feeling slightly tired but not so bad as expected. Lunched down in staff restaurant. Went for a swim on way home.

Sunday 26 April Went on troop hike – only 3 of us. Motor coach from Oxford Circus to Hertford. Hike via Tewin to Knebworth. Cherub

1931

came back early. One or two heavy showers but better weather than last Sunday. Did about 16 miles. Coach back from Knebworth – Oxford Circus 7.20. Very heavy storm 7.0–7.45. Had supper, read papers, cleaned shoes and to bed at 10.30.

Sunday 3 May Went on hike with 7 chaps from office. 9.40 train from Waterloo to Leatherhead. Started raining at 11.20 and kept on for rest of day. Hiked about 12 miles and came home from Horsley at 3.0, fed up with it. Got home 4.5, changed, had tea and went to the Rialto to see the French talkie *Sous les Toits de Paris* – very good.[23] Very heavy rain all evening. Bus home from Cambridge Circus. Light supper and to bed 10.30.

Saturday 9 May Fine but chilly, warmer later. Took Nigger to Regent's Park for an hour in afternoon. Queued up at Drury Lane at 4.30. Left stool and went up to YMCA to tea at 5.0. Down to Avenue Pavilion for an hour after and rejoined queue at 7.0. Seat in 4th row of gallery. Saw Richard Tauber the £1,000 a week German tenor in *The Land of Smiles*. Very dull and boring. Grand opera but not melodramatic. Very enthusiastic reception for Tauber though indisposed and not giving his best. Mother met me coming out. Bus home, supper and to bed soon after 12.0.

Wednesday 3 June King's birthday and Derby Day. Won 6/6 in office sweepstake. Went to revision classes in Accounts (II) and Economics (I). Left at 9.15 and went on to YMCA for monthly troop meeting – Lantern lecture by Jack Houghton on 'Hiking in Kashmir' in the Social Room. Hung about talking after. Walked home. Arr 11.0. Supped and to bed.

Friday 12 June The Final CIS exam at last. Arrived at City of London College, Ropemaker St, Moorgate at 8.45 and took place in small room on 1st floor (No 694). 1st paper Accountancy 9–11. Did not do too well. Could not get BS to balance, £10 out. Took too much time over final accounts question and had to rush rest of paper. No time to do fourth question. ¼ hour break and then 'Secretarial Practice' Part 1 11.15–1.15 – pretty stiff paper and different type of questions than expected. Felt pretty despondent lunchtime. Met Mother coming out and went to lunch at Slaters. Very crowded and long wait. Back at 2.15 for 'Secretarial Practice' II – 'Meetings'. Very easy paper. Nearly all finished in well under time. Went along to Slaters for tea with Howell, a chap with a country dialect who had attended the Metropolitan College revision classes and whom I palled up with during the 2 day's ordeal. Short

---

23 A rather dark 1930 filmed musical comedy directed by René Clair, *Under the Roofs of Paris* was the first French production of the sound film era to achieve great international success. It obviously impressed Heap, who refers to it when describing the New Year celebrations of 31 December 1936.

walk round after and back at 4.45 for the last paper – Economics and extremely difficult. Could not get the gist of some of the questions. Over 6.45. Walked home with Howell who was in digs in Handel St nearby. Had dinner, revised the Students Note Book for tomorrow's subjects and went to bed at 11.30. Could not get to sleep very easily again, and woke up early next morning.

Saturday 13 June Got up at 8.0 and walked to Ropemaker St and sat in St Paul's Churchyard for ½ hour on way there. 1st paper 'Mercantile Law' 11.15–1.15. Very easy. Lunched with Howell and another fellow and walked round for a while. 'Company Law' 2.15–4.15. Fairly easy but had to rush it too much. Almost got writers' cramp. ½ hour for tea. ABC tea-shop packed out. Last paper Banking and Exchange easier than expected. Great relief when all over. Walked home with Howell, washed, changed and went down to the Gaiety to see *The Millionaire Kid*. Just got a seat at the end of a row. Pretty good show, lively and bright, good dancing and tuneful music. Feeble humour but good buffoonery. A typical Gaiety show for the 'tired businessman' or exam candidate. Walked home after, supped and to bed at 12.0.

Friday 19 June Wrote article on Ralph Reader for the troop mag. Bought wristwatch in Charing Cross Rd for 10/6. Went to gym class 7.30–8.20 and enjoyed it, sweated freely. Got home for dinner at 9.15. Went for a walk round with Mother after. Saw crowds come out of film first night at the Dominion. Bus home. To bed at 12.0. Heavy storm 5.45–6.30. Finer later.

Sunday 21 June Fine, hot sunny day. Went to Old Elkayonians reunion at Charlie Maynard's place at Knockholt. Arrived with Snowball just before 1.0. Most of them gone on hike at 12.0. Had lunch and sunbathed for 2 hours. Mucked about till 5.15 when the hikers returned and we had tea on the lawn. Had gramophone after and sat about till 8.0 when we all left to get the 8.45 train from Knockholt Station. Arr London Bridge 9.25. Bus home with Stan Cox and his sister, a charming person.[24] Cleaned shoes, light supper and to bed at 11.0. A really good day.

Wednesday 24 June Dull rain morning. Shoulder and chest still very sore, cannot go to gym class. Home to dinner and up to YMCA at 8.0. Bought a packet of De Reszke [filter tip cigarettes] and smoked first cigarette. Not so bad as expected but has to be got used to. Met Jackson and went round to the Foundling with him to rehearsal of the Holborn Rover Song for next weekend at Hatfield au lieu of monthly meeting of YMCA Rovers. Sang it 7 or 8 times. Back to the YMCA after and over to the Corner House with 8 others. Smoked another fag. Left at 11.40 and bus home.

24   Maud Cox – see entries for 26 June and subsequently.

1931

Friday 26 June Bought cigarette holder for 3d in Woolworths. Took Maud Cox to the Aldwych to see *Turkey Time*, the latest farce. Walked along Strand after to Trafalgar Square and caught bus from there to Mornington Crescent. Saw her home to Werrington St [NW1] and got tram home. Arr 12.0. Supped and to bed, very tired. A good evening.

Thursday 2 July Met Maud Cox at Marble Arch and went for a row on the Serpentine in the evening. Walked back via Piccadilly and Shaftesbury Ave etc. Arr home 11.15.

Saturday 4 July Dull and cloudy but no rain. Went to Gilwell for weekend camp. Acted as a camp warden and did some work. Arrived at teatime and messed about in evening. Camp fire pretty duff but greatly amused by remarks of group of boys in David Hughes' troop standing just behind me – Supper in hut with wireless – went round with Jim and David to see Lights Out enforced. Turned in about 12.10.

Saturday 11 July Fine day. Went to Gilwell for weekend camp with David and Bunny Kaye, Ralph Reader and 3 Knights. Arr. 4.30. Used Jim Ridley's tent. Had tea by myself, rest gone to Chingford. All went for drive down to Chingford in Ralph's car in evening. Pulled up at old fashioned pub. Back for camp-fire. Much livened up by Ralph – supped after and went over to the House – Camp Chief away – chaps in charge invited us over for a pow-wow – about dozen of us altogether. Chatted till 1.0 a.m. chiefly about shows and RH Pantos past and future. Back to camp and turned in.

Saturday 18 July Went with Jack to School Sports at the new ground in Du Cane Rd in afternoon.[25] Started raining at 2.45 and kept on all afternoon. Sports abandoned about 4.0 and prize giving got over early in the school hall. Saw all the masters, few Old Danes present, had tea and wandered round school to keep out of rain. A dismal afternoon. Left at 5.0. Tram to Wood Lane, walked to Shepherds Bush, bus to Charing Cross and tube to St James Park where met Maud at 6.0. Had tea in Lyons in Victoria St. Bus to Elephant. Tried to get in the Trocadero but packed out. Bus back to the Strand and went to the Tivoli. Saw *Dirigible*, very good film. Went in the Cafeteria a few yards down the Strand after. Then bus to Mornington Crescent. Arr. home 11.40.

Tuesday 28 July Up at 6.0 and arrived at St Pancras with Mother at 7.15. Five of us left on 2nd train at 8.0. Tilbury at 9.20. Fairly calm and arrived Dunkerque 4.15, disembarked and got train while Scots played bagpipes. Had cold dinner dished out and got 3rd train. Left at 6.30 for long journey through France. Stopped for 20 minutes at 8.25 for coffee

---

25 Heap's old school, St Clement Danes Grammar School, moved west from Holborn to Hammersmith in 1928.

etc. Tried to sleep in carriage. Got about an hour's sleep altogether. Crossed Swiss frontier at Dolle about 5.0.

Wednesday 29 July Dawned a fine day. Got out of train for a good breakfast on Berne platform at 8.15. Left 9.15. Arrived Kandersteg 10.45. Lined up and marched to site. Pitched tents and had cold lunch, bought cards, stamps etc. Walked to village and back afterwards. Turned in about 10.15.

Thursday 30 July Another fine, hot and sunny day. Got up 7.30, breakfast – went to Opening Conference in marquee in morning. Had uncomfortable seat on table. Came out 12.0, called in hotel for drinks on way back. Lunch. Went to rehearsal for pageant in afternoon – tea in marquee – drew rations for K [Knights Patrol] brew and distributed them in our small marquee. Had dinner then went to Camp Fire – very good, large number of public present. National songs and dances. Jack Best leading Scotch pipe band. Over at 10.40, back to camp and turned in.

Friday 31 July Another fine sunny day. Got browner still. Went for a walk to Oeschinensee Lake in afternoon. Very arduous, uphill climb, perspired greatly but view worth it. Back for pageant rehearsal at 6.0, drinks after. Got papers sent from home. Much elated at passing final CIS. More than expected. All went to the village in evening to dance at Hotel Victoria, stood a bottle of wine at 8 frs for exam success. Turned in about 1.0.

Sunday 2 August Parade before the Chief in afternoon.[26] Fine when started but unfortunately started pelting with rain half way to the station and kept on till we got back. Had tea in hotel near camp. Too long to wait. Started raining again at 7.0 so camp fire and pageant off. Held concert in marquee instead. We did the Rover song and the *Song Without Words*. Both fell very flat. Hastened back to the camp after to see if the tents all right. Raining harder than ever but found tents OK. Rigged up table, box stools and dining shelter. Also totem pole for flags – very good show.

Monday 3 August Cloudy but fine. Stayed in camp sunbathing till 11.30 then to the chalet and canteen and back for lunch. Lazed about till 4.0 when we went along to the village to see Shackleton in hospital. Lift down in a car. Had tea at the Adler Hotel after. Back to camp and along to the broadcasting studio by the chalet. Were to have done the Rover Song which was cut at the last minute owing to lack of time and only

26 *The Times* of 4 August 1931 carried photographs of the tented 42-acre Kandersteg International Scout Centre and of Lord Baden-Powell addressing this, the first International Rover Moot. A guest of the Swiss government, Baden-Powell had a long letter on the Moot and its prospects of encouraging international peace published in *The Times* on 21 August 1931.

did the Kandersteg Yell. To the canteen after for soup – stayed till the beginning of a film, too boring so came back to camp and turned in early (10.15).

Wednesday 5 August Got up at 5.15 a.m. for day excursion. Walked for 1½ hrs to the Blue Lake (Blausee). Stayed an hour. Walked 20 mins to Kantermand Station Train to Reichand for lunch at the Barem Hotel. Walked along to the Neisen and went up to the top of the funicular railway. Stayed up there 2 hours. When got to the bottom again storm broke out, but cleared up by the time train reached Kandersteg. Held International Tea Party at our Holborn Corner House at 6.15. At 8.15 went along to the chalet to dress for pageant. Could not keep moustache on – fixed on – very mousey. Had to wait behind Guides' chalet for 1½ hrs before London Torchlight Tattoo at end of Camp Fire was over. Pageant great success. Chief there. Over at 11.25. Back to the chalet, changed, back to camp then all to a restaurant near the camp for supper. Turned in at 1.30.

Friday 7 August All Holborn except Bob Hailes go on trip to Jungfrau. Leave at 5.30. Got up at 8.0. Breakfast. Went to the final conference in morning. Speech by Vernon Bartlett on The League of Nations.[27] Very good. Conference closed by the Chief. Rained hard from 9.30 till 11.30 – getting very muddy. Rain continued all afternoon. Cold lunch. Nothing much to do but lay in tent. Finished reading *The Silver Spoon*.[28] Got very fed up. At 4.30 walked to the chalet and had a bath. Tea in marquee after. Back to camp – went for a walk to village and back with Bob Hailes. More rain – lay in tent for ½ hr. Over to marquee for soup. Rest arrived back from the Jungfrau trip, all pleased with it for had hardly any rain, above the clouds – Jack Wilkins had injured his knee sliding down from the top. All went down to the village for supper. Had to wait long time to be served. Bad service at restaurant being a special feature of the Kandersteg. Arr back at 10.30 and went into the marquee for end of concert. Saw some good items especially the burlesque of other countries items by Hungars. Concluded at 11.45 with speech by Herbert Martin. Back to camp and to bed.

Saturday 8 August Got up at 6.30. Rush to breakfast, wash, shave, clear up and pack. Fortunately turned out a fine sunny day. Had to dress up and do pageant again for filming and official photo purposes. Rather exasperating business. Left by 2nd train at 2.0. Journey not so dull as

---

27 (Charles) Vernon Bartlett (1894–1983), journalist, prolific author and politician, was director of the London office of the League of Nations, before being appointed first as an Independent and then as Common Wealth Party MP for Bridgewater, 1938–50. The League of Nations was a major international organisation founded in 1920 at the Paris Peace Conference with the aim of maintaining world peace through collective security and disarmament. Countries not abiding by the League's wishes would suffer economic sanctions.
28 Part of John Galsworthy's *Forsyte Saga*.

feared. Cold meal served out at Berne at 4.0. Tried to sleep on floor of train during night. Got about 1½ hrs sleep.

Sunday 9 August Arrived Dunkerque 5.15. Very cold and miserable. Kept waiting about too long while a measly 'breakfast' served out. Got on 2nd boat at 6.45. Bagged berths but got chucked out again as someone else had tickets for them. Tiring, cold and depressing journey with little sleep. Arrived Tilbury 2.10 and got 2nd train at 3.0. St Pancras 4.0. Mother met me at station. Tram home, unpacked, went round the square to have photos taken, had tea, changed and went with Mother to the Avenue Pavilion in the evening. To bed at 10.15 very tired.

Wednesday 19 August Received first two lessons of Journalism course from Metropolitan College.[29] In evening went up to YMCA for *Knightlights*.[30] Committee meeting to get Sept issue ready for press. Had long argument with Fred Reilly over the amalgamation of *Our Mag* and *Knightlights*. Do not like the idea at all. Afterwards argued with Rex Barclay and one or two others on politics till 10.40 when I left and walked home. A very disconcerting evening.

Friday 28 August Bought black trilby hat for 15/- at Dunn's lunchtime. Very tight and uncomfortable but best could do. Got more used to it in evening. Met Jack at YMCA and went for a swim ... Had dinner and went to the Whitehall with Maud to see *Take a Chance* – an amusing trifle of a play. Not such a success as most of Walter Hackett's plays and a good run a doubtful proposition.[31] Still, the Whitehall is always a pleasant theatre to pass an evening at. Such sophisticated atmosphere with its ultra-modern colour scheme of black, white and green. Saw Maud home after then home myself at 11.45. Read a chapter and sleep about 1.0.

Sunday 6 September Fine and sunny but slightly chilly. Went by 9.10 Green Line coach to Windsor. Poor turn-out at camp – about 30 including a dozen Holborn Rovers. Sunbathed in morning, Rovers Own in afternoon. Sold 14 *Knightlights*. Came home with Cherub. Home 9.20, had dinner and to bed at 10.50.

Sunday 13 September Fine clear sunny day. Went on Co-op hike in Surrey. 9.17 Green Line bus from Oxford Circus to Whitehall (Caterham). Route of hike: via Blenchingly (12.0 midday drinks at the old inn), open-topped bus from Caterham – very cold. Thoroughly enjoyable day with Shelmerdene. Eight Rovers and three Rangers,

---

29   He had previously taken correspondence courses with the College for his ACIS examinations.
30   The small Rover Scout magazine for the Knights patrol at Holborn.
31   Walter C. Hackett (1876–1944), American playwright and actor who spent much of his career in England.

altogether and rather different from the usual Co-op hike. Walked with Shelmerdene to Euston after. Thence home myself, supped and to bed at 11.0.

Tuesday 15 September Went to first dancing class at Douglas Taylors in Holborn at 7.0 till 9.30. Found it difficult and requiring much perseverance. Read a little before going to bed at 11.30.

Wednesday 16 September Called at Angel's[32] on way home and bought a new dark blue double-breasted overcoat for £4.10.0. Very pleased with it. Met Shelmerdene at Holborn at 8.0. Walked along to the Tatler and up to the Corner House after. Stayed till 11.10, walked to Euston with her, then home by bus and tram and to bed at 12.0.

Saturday 19 September Fine sunny day. Went to London Rover Camp at Downe[33] by 3.30 Green Line coach from Poland St garage. Met 4 others there. Arr. Downe 5.0, pitched tents, had tea and went for a walk to Downe village and back with others. Went to camp fire at 8.30. Ralph Raeder arrived just before and put our items over for us. Fairly good show on the whole. Six of us went for a walk to Biggin Hill and back after supper. Started to rain before we got back at 12.30 and turned in. Did not sleep very well.

Tuesday 13 October Sent off advert for next month's *Secretary*.[34] Went up to dancing class in evening – fairly crowded but great shortage of men. Home at 9.45. Read a chapter of *Secretarial Practice* and to bed at 11.20.

Wednesday 21 October Started wearing overcoat to go to work. Bought evening dress accessories – short, socks, collars and tie at Meakers[35] on way home (16/-). Went to the Lyceum to see the new thriller *Suspense*, one of the most stupid, dull and boring plays I have seen for some time. Everything very inefficient, dull un-artistic scenery, bad clothed, mediocre acting and poor production. Got so fed up with it that I left after the second act, walked home and went to bed at 11.15. Had to get up at 12.0 to have toothache attended to.

Thursday 22 October Had a haircut on way home. Dined, met Shelmerdene at Holborn Hall[36] at 7.30 and went up to Sadler's Wells for Co-op party to see *The Taming of the Shrew*. Good seats in gallery. Large crowd of 30 or so. Enjoyed the play better than expected. Seen it three times before – long ago. Surprised to find it so smart and modern a theatre. Only half full though. Over 10.20. Went up to the Corner

32 Edward Angel, clothiers, 199 Shaftesbury Avenue, WC2.
33 The Downe Scout activity centre 16 miles from London, just east of Biggin Hill airfield in Kent.
34 Presumably advertising his availability for a better job.
35 Meakers, hosiers, 91 Shaftesbury Avenue, WC1.
36 The former town hall at the junction of Gray's Inn Road and Clerkenwell Road.

House after with Shelmerdene and Wiffles and his girl. Walked to Euston after. Home at 12.10. Took some time to get to sleep.

Friday 23 October Made one of my now infrequent visits to Woolworths at lunchtime and bought two dress studs. Went up to Hector Powe in Coventry St branch straight after work to be fitted for dinner suit – had it put forward from next Friday in order to be finished by next Saturday.

Wednesday 28 October General election results – Socialists being wiped out everywhere. Conservative National Government heavy gains. Final result: Cons 471, Nat Lab 13, Nat Lib 63 – Opp Lib 7, Lab 51.[37] Wrote article on hiking in afternoon for Exercise 5 of 'Journalism'.

Saturday 31 October Fine and mild. Hampstead in afternoon. After dinner, changed into dinner suit which Mother had fetched from Hector Powe's this morning – very good fit, only trousers a little too long. Had some difficulty with stiff shirt and collar. Rushed into YMCA to leave message for Cherub and met Shelmerdene at Tottenham Court Rd Tube station just after 7.0. Bus to Trafalgar Square and another along to Ludgate Circus for London Diocesan Boy Scouts Association Dance at Stationers Hall just off top of Ludgate Hill. A good dance, very dignified and formal atmosphere due to the stately and austere surroundings – stained glass windows, armorial bearings, flags, tapestries and panelling etc. Left at 11.0 and went on to the Oxford Corner House for supper. Saw Ralph with a large crowd there. Walked to Euston after. Arrived home 12.30. Could not get to sleep very quickly.

Sunday 1 November Fine, mild sunny day. Hampstead in morning. Home 1.30, changed and had lunch and went to see Gran in hospital. Left 3.45 and went up to Burnt Oak to have tea with Shelmerdene and her people. Found them much more interesting than last time. Talked for some time then went out for a long walk round with her, about two hours. Roads very deserted especially the Gt North Rd. Did not stop for supper on arriving back but went straight home by tube. Got home 10.30, had supper, cleaned shoes and went to bed at 11.30 very tired. A really good weekend.

Thursday 5 November Received formal exam certificate from CIS. Went down to Somerset House in afternoon to get some share transfers stamped – very fine day. Finished reading *Babes in the Wood*. Straight home, changed into evening kit, dined, met Shelmerdene at Russell Hotel in Woburn Place for the CUACO Club Dance (Commercial

---

37 Ramsay Macdonald continued as Prime Minster but now heading a National Government. The final allocation of seats was: Conservative 473, National Labour 13, Liberal National 35, Liberal 33 (thus National Government 554), Labour 52, Others 5.

1931

Union Insurance Co). A large crowd about 400 and quite a good dance but very hot and stuffy – perspired freely all the evening. Left at 11.45 and saw Shelmerdene to Euston and got home 12.15.

Sunday 15 November Got up at 7.30 and went to Cenotaph parade. Very large turn-out – about 4,000 though Holborn's attendance very poor. Went on troop hike after from Victoria with Cherub, Jim Figg, Reg Hatton and five others from 11th Holborn [Rover Group]. Train to Epsom for tea and train back from there to Waterloo. Lost some of party in afternoon but found them again at Epsom.

Friday 20 November Home to dinner and change and along to London Rover Social at Central Hall Westminster. Very good talk by Admiral Evans,[38] a first rate concert. The best social I have yet been to. Over at 11.0. Terrific scrum in getting out. Got home 11.35, light supper, wrote brief report of evening for magazine and went to bed at 12.50.

Saturday 21 November Called round at Fred Reilly's house on way to work to leave report. Saw his mother very distressed as her mother had died during night. Felt very sorry for them all and went on to the office – went down to Kingsway to get some forms from HM Stationery Office in morning – glorious sunny day. Home to change and lunch – Mother goes to Southampton to see Aunt Pop off to America.[39] Left at 2.0 to meet at Poland St Garage for Co-op weekend hike. Learnt that Shelmerdene was not coming till possibly tomorrow. Bitterly disappointed as she had given no reason. 2.33 bus to Guildford, another bus to Godalming for tea. Left 6.0 walked till 8.15 when we arrived at Thursley and put up at Ridgeway Farm (Youth Hostel place) for night. Settled down, had supper, sat about by fire and turned in at 11.0.

Monday 23 November Met Shelmerdene coming out of work and saw her home. Learnt that she might be affected with Tuberculosis but waiting for blood test from medical college. Supposed to retire early every night this week.

Wednesday 25 November Mother's 50th birthday. Got her to buy herself a pair of gloves as a present. Re-wrote article on 'Theatregoers' in afternoon. In evening took Mother to the Stoll to see Maurice Chevalier.

Sunday 29 November Very thick fog all day. Took Nigger for a run round Regent's Park in morning. Saw Gran in hospital in afternoon and went on to Burnt Oak to have tea with Shelmerdene. Stayed all evening, playing whist etc. Tube to King's Cross, walked round for ½ hr and got home 10.50.

---

38 Admiral Sir Edward Evans ('Evans of the Broke' in the First World War) had been Captain Scott's second-in-command on his final Antarctic expedition.
39 Pop Shepherd never returned; she died in America in 1959.

Monday 30 November Went along to see George Brook about getting a new job at lunchtime.[40] Fixed another consultation for Thursday.

Tuesday 1 December Started working till 6.30. Stayed in all evening. Drafted details of CIS exam subjects for George Brook and read two chapters of *Secretarial Practice*. To bed at 11.30.

Wednesday 2 December Revised a little 'Mercantile Law' in afternoon. In evening went to Holborn Rover Dinner at Goodies Restaurant in Store St. Sat next to Adam de H and passed a very entertaining evening. First time since [*sic*] I have seen him since his return from Berlin after a 3 month visit there. The dinner quite good for 2/6, the speeches fairly witty and the entertainment rather amusing.

Friday 4 December Walked down to Aldwych and back lunchtime to buy calendar, a diary and some Christmas cards, went for a swim on way home. A quick dinner and round to Fred Reilly's house for monthly *Knightlights* Committee. Meeting much perturbed by Jeff Cunningham's wish to write about panto instead of myself. Determined to get my own way. Got home 10.30, a short read and to bed 11.30 very tired.

Sunday 6 December Fine sunny misty day. Fresh and brisk. Hampstead in morning. Saw Gran in hospital in afternoon and went up to Burnt Oak after to tea with Shelmerdene, brothers and other relatives. Found them a decent crowd of people and enjoyed myself fairly well though not being able to play solo whist felt rather out of things. Eat, drink and smoked [*sic*] rather more than was good for me but did no harm. Got home 10.45 and to bed about 11.50.

Saturday 12 December Hampstead in afternoon. Home at 4.30, had a short rest, changed into evening clothes, had tea, left 6.50, called in YMCA for twenty minutes and met Shelmerdene at Tottenham Court Rd tube station at 7.30. Walked along to Peter Robinson's for OCCA Dance.[41] Very good dance. Party of six of us, nice atmosphere, nice surroundings, nice crowd, good band and good programme. Thoroughly enjoyed the evening. Over 11.45. Bus to Euston, got home 12.20. Took some time to get to sleep.

Saturday 19 December Worked till 6.30. A quick dinner and up to the Angel to meet Shelmerdene at 8.0. Went along to Xmas Carnival Dance at Northampton Polytechnic in St John's Rd Clerkenwell. Not a very exclusive affair. Very few men in evening dress, consequently felt rather out of place. Hall much too small for the large crowd present

---

40   George Brook, 50–51 High Holborn, WC1, presumably the forerunner of the Brook Street Bureau for clerical employment.
41   OCCA: perhaps the Old Contemptibles Army Association, a First World War veterans/commemoration group of those men who joined the British Expeditionary Force in France in late 1914.

so dancing not too enjoyable. Nevertheless a pleasant enough evening which I would have enjoyed much better in a lounge suit.

Wednesday 23 December Rushed home again after work, changed into uniform, dined and up to King George's Hall to steward. Kept 3 seats for Jack Tripp and girl and Mother – Shelmerdene (and I) selling programmes etc and stood at back during show and sold copies of songs during interval. About 20 of the crowd were there. Walked to Euston after, then home to bed at 12.45.

Saturday 26 December Hampstead in morning. Home at 1.0 p.m. changed, lunched and went out at 2.30 for a walk round West End till 3.30 when I got a train from Euston to Burnt Oak to go to Shelmerdene's house to tea and stay the evening. A dozen of us there altogether. Spent a very enjoyable evening playing various games and laughed more heartily than I have ever done before. Came home about 11.0 bringing the large 'Ever Ready' electric torch which Shelmerdene had bought me as a Christmas present. Went to bed soon after 12.0.

Sunday 27 December Hampstead in morning. Home to change and lunch. Saw Gran in hospital in afternoon and went on to Burnt Oak to tea at Shelmerdene's again. Same party there with two more. Played games again in evening and enjoyed myself just as thoroughly as yesterday. Left soon after 10.0 p.m. and got home 11.0. Thus ended Christmas which thanks to those two evenings had been a happy and memorable one for me.

Monday 28 December Back to work again after cutting myself badly while shaving with a blunt razor blade. Many business houses still closed for today. Did not feel too enthusiastic for work.

Thursday 31 December Met Shelmerdene at Holborn Hall at 7.15 and went down to the Stoll. Saw *Daddy Long Legs* and *Skippy*. Both quite good but a little too sentimental for my liking. Did not go up to Corner House as intended as she wanted to go home. So I saw her to Euston and went home myself. Get back at 11.40 and listened in till 1.0 when I went to bed and slept well.

RETROSPECT – 1931

So ends 1931, a most full, eventful and varied year.
 I passed my final C.I.S. exam after much trial and tribulation, formed a deep friendship with a most charming girl, visited Paris and Switzerland, bought a dinner suit and learned dancing, extended my knowledge of modern literature by reading as much as possible of

Part One

Michael Arlen, Galsworthy, Somerset Maugham, increased my weight to 11 stone, spent much, learned much, forgot a little and saved nothing.

New Year Resolutions:

To economise and save money once more.

To improve my dancing.

To overcome my tendency to priggishness and lose my superiority complex – as far as possible.

To get a good job and qualify myself for something better.

To leave no stone unturned to achieve success both socially and financially.

1932

Although he did not detail their disagreements, Heap's diaries reveal that his parents frequently quarrelled and, in February 1932, he and his mother moved out of the family home to rooms in Highbury. In June they returned to 139 Gray's Inn Road but the final split came in August, when Heap and his mother moved to cheap rooms in Penryn St, Camden Town. His father retained the rooms with his practice in Gray's Inn Road and the three stayed in frequent contact, with Emily continuing to help with the practice.

Heap's relationship with Shelmerdene was superseded in January by that with a new girlfriend, Beatrice, when, he later admitted, he 'knew what it was to be in love'. But it did not last the year out as Beatrice increasingly found fault with Heap's behaviour, particularly at social events, and he plainly tired of her 'moods'. Throughout the year his interest in the theatre was maintained as he made seventy-four theatre visits, but, although he made several job applications, he was unable to improve his business prospects. His daily recordings are reduced here to just 22% of his original 28,659 words and daily entries for only 17% of the year, so large gaps appear in the narrative; nevertheless, the slow evolution of his social and business life is accurately represented.

Friday 1 January Though I did not retire till 1.0 last night, did not feel at all tired today but most active. During day resolved to buy more Savings Certificates and make a definite attempt to economise and save money once more. After going to Woolworths to buy this [diary] book went for a swim on way home and met Adam de H in the [YMCA swimming] bath. Chatted with him till 7.30 and then walked home. Got caught in a shower and got fairly wet, much to my chagrin.

Saturday 2 January Went up to Hampstead in afternoon though weather very doubtful. Started to rain at 3.30 and got rather wet getting back, having no mac. Changed and had tea and went up to Tottenham Court Rd station to meet Beatrice at 6.0. Went down to the Capitol to see *Sunshine Susie*. Enjoyed the film very much – acclaimed the best English talkie yet produced and achieving a great success. Walked round Mayfair and arrived at Oxford Corner House about 10.0, an uncomfortably warm and tepid evening for walking. Stayed an hour or so, took bus to Euston then walked home. Listened in to a foreign wireless station for a while and went to bed at 1.0.

Part One

Wednesday 6 January Rainy day. Wore black suit. Had afternoon off. Left at 1.30 and went up to YMCA for half an hour. Left to go to the Whitehall and suddenly discovered wallet missing. Rushed back to the office and found in cabinet in which I keep my old office coat – had slipped out while changing it. Took tube to Trafalgar Square and arrived at theatre just in time. Came out at 5.0 and walked through the Mall in a very strong wind to the Scout Shop in Buckingham Palace Rd to get two tickets for the London Rover Ball. Walked back again and up to my barbers in Holborn to get a haircut and buy a new bottle of brilliantine. Home to dinner while a hail storm raged outside. Then up to the YMCA for the monthly troop meeting. Arriving early went into the King George's Hall to see the dress rehearsal of the Roland House Panto for half an hour. Then up to the troop meeting, which was quite well attended. Led a debate deploring the apathy towards troop hikes and rambles. Over at 10.0. Went down to the rehearsal again with Adam. Watched it till the end of the second act at 11.0. At 11.45 they decided to do the finale all over again so I left in despair and walked home, getting to bed at 12.30 fairly tired. A very full day.

Saturday 9 January Very dense fog early morning but cleared away as I went to work and turned out a very fine day. Went up to Hampstead in afternoon. Got back soon after 4.0, changed and went up to YMCA arriving at King George's Hall just after 5.0 in time for the finale of the panto matinee. The Chief Scout and Lord Hampden there. Went up to reading room for a few minutes after then down to King George's Hall for the evening performance of *Babes in the Wood*. Enjoyed it immensely, especially the songs and ensembles. Over at 10.40. Waited for Beatrice after and went over to Corner House, she being in rather a discouraging mood. Took a bus to Euston after as it was raining. Left her there and then bus and tram home myself. Turned in at 12.30 and slept badly.

Monday 11 January First day of sale. Did not have to go shopwalking as usual. Went along to Hector Powes, Coventry St branch at lunchtime for fitting of new suit. Wrote rough criticism of [Roland House] Panto in afternoon. On way home called at Post Office, withdrew £35 from Savings Bank account, took £3 and bought £32 Savings Certificates (four eight pound certificates). Stayed in evening, wrote up troop log book and read a chapter of *Angel Pavement*,[1] listened in to wireless relay from America[2] and went to bed at 11.45.

Saturday 16 January Still mild but duller than yesterday. Went up to Hampstead in afternoon. Home at 4.30, changed, had tea and went up to the YMCA at 7.0. Went down to the King George's Hall at 7.30, put

1 The 1930 novel by J. B. Priestley, set in neighbouring Finsbury.
2 An orchestral concert from New York which included the Mills Brothers, 'a Negro quartet' (*The Times*, 11 January 1932).

1932

a box of chocolates for Beatrice among presentations collection for distribution at the end of show and waited for Mother to arrive just before 8.0. Had seats in 7th row by gangway. Last night of panto – gala night. Good show, everyone in high spirits in more senses than one. Saw Beatrice after second act and heard that she had injured her ankle that afternoon. An impromptu cabaret held after the presentation with Ralph Reader as compère. Apart from Ralph, not up to expectations and fell a little flat. Over at 11.40, walked home with Mother, had a light supper and went to bed at 12.45.

Thursday 21 January At lunchtime went along to Hector Powe's for a 2nd fitting of new suit. Not satisfied with trousers so had to have a new pair made. Read novel and revised 'Meetings' in afternoon. Home to dinner and up to YMCA at 7.15. to meet Beatrice outside Dominion as arranged before I knew of Sadler's Wells postponement. She in rather low spirits mainly due to pain from sprained ankle. Went down to the Tivoli to see *The Blue Danube*. A very feeble and disappointing film redeemed only by its music.

Wednesday 27 January Went with Adam to meeting of National Crisis and Voluntary Service movement at Albert Hall.[3] Met him in YMCA restaurant at 7.10 and went along by bus. Good seats in 6th row or area specially reserved for Rovers. Heard the Prince of Wales speak and one or two others.[4] A couple of songs and the whole thing over just after 9.0. Went back to Adam's flat at Queens Gate after and discussed his new Scout play with him till about 10.45 when I left and took a bus home, getting to bed just after 12.0 and very tired. A very interesting and entertaining evening.

Tuesday 2 February On getting home, heard that Mother had arranged for us to move to Highbury at end of next week. Very pleased for the most part but naturally rather depressed at the thought of leaving the old home so, not being able to stay in for the evening, went up to the YMCA, met Adam, talked with him for half an hour and met Mother at Holborn Hall at 10.45.

Friday 5 February Got home at 6.20, dined and got ready for moving. Van called round at 7.45, loaded cases, trunks, sacks of books etc on to it and left at 8.0. Then mother and I took a taxi and followed it up to 27 Highbury Place. Arrived at same time, unloaded and unpacked

---

3 An organisation established during the Depression to encourage willing unemployed people and volunteers to take on tasks for the benefit of the community. Supported by the Prince of Wales, the Speaker of the House of Commons was its president.
4 The meeting was organised by the National Council for Social Service. The Prince took the chair and addressed the youth of Great Britain, speaking on the need for all youth organisations to combat depression and apathy. His speech was broadcast by the BBC (*The Times*, 27 January 1932).

and turned in about 12.0. Did not sleep too well which was only to be expected.

Saturday 6 February Got up at 7.0, left shave till afternoon, had a lighter breakfast than usual and left at 8.5. Took bus to the Angel and walked to work from there. Went down to the restaurant and had a snack at about 10.0. Felt a little seedy all morning. Walked all the way back to Highbury taking just over ¾ hour, which is too long to do every day. Spent the afternoon unpacking books and stacking them in a cupboard. Then had a 'bath'[5] changed into evening kit, had tea and left at 6.45. Took bus to Southampton Row and walked up to the YMCA for half an hour. Then a bus down to the Strand station to meet Beatrice at 8.0 and go to the London Rover Ball at the Horticultural Hall – a very enjoyable affair as usual but marred by Beatrice's childish behaviour in taking offence at an unintentional faux pas of mine, she assuming a very peeved air and maintaining a strong silence going home, relenting a little however when I left her at Tottenham Ct Rd station. Got home at 12.30 and turned in soon after 1.0. Naturally did not sleep well, for the evening had annoyed me considerably.

Thursday 11 February On leaving work took bus all the way home, dined quickly and hurried off to meet Beatrice at the Angel at 7.30 to go to Sadler's Wells. Found her still rather peeved over last Saturday but soon placated her. Saw *Julius Caesar* for the 6th time. Not a very good production of it, too economical. As she had a bad cold did not go on to the Corner House after, so after seeing her off at the Angel, walked home and turned in soon after 12.0.

Tuesday 16 February Went to see *Julius Caesar* at His Majesty's in the evening. Queued up for an hour and got good seat in front of gallery. Most magnificent Shakespearian production I have yet seen.[6] Though it was the 7th time I had seen this play, I was gripped from start to finish. Altogether a show not to be missed. Took bus home, supped on fish and chips and turned in at 12.15, very pleased with the evening.

Saturday 27 February Went home to lunch, changed into uniform, packed and went off to Rover Mates weekend training course at Edgware. Had difficulty in finding the Old Chandos Arms in the High St, and when I did, found the room we were staying in locked up. First session began at 8.0 (The Aims of Rovering – Cherub) followed by Leadership – J. Thurll. A break for supper than Cherub again 'The Rover and Home Life' till 12.0. The best of the lot. Took a long time turning in after. The fire kept smoking the room out and with the window open an icy blast from the north blew in. As I was under it I

---

5 With no bathroom, this probably means an 'all-over wash'.
6 Produced to the acclaim of *The Times* (9 February) by Oscar Asche, with Godfrey Tearle as Mark Anthony.

1932

kept it closed till Fred Reilly offered to change places with me, which I did. Did not sleep much however and the hard floor made my thighs ache considerably.

Sunday 28 February Got up about 8.0, had breakfast and packed kit. First session started at 10.30 after a Rovers' Own. Rather resented having to sit in this draughty smoky room while outside it was such a fine crisp day and ideal for a hike. But nevertheless an inspiring and well spent weekend. Turned in at 10.15 dead tired after last night's lack of sleep.

Saturday 5 March Went home to change and dine and went to the Northampton Polytechnic to see *Cox and Box* and *The Pirates of Penzance* in which Beatrice appeared in the chorus. Was helplessly bored for most of the evening sitting on a hard seat twelve rows back. Saw Beatrice in the interval and walked to the Angel with her afterwards in a sudden downpour of rain. Tried to persuade her to come on the hike tomorrow but without avail. Took a bus home from the Angel and went to bed at 12.0.

Wednesday 9 March After going home to dine went to Sadler's Wells meeting Beatrice at 7.30. Had seats in the back row of circle. About twenty in party. Saw a very good production of *Fruit* – Clear perfect singing. I caused much annoyance to my neighbours by smoking a cigar during the Garden scene. Beatrice got very offended over it and as we walked up to the Angel afterwards was very indignant over my inconsiderate behaviour and bad manners. Tried to console her but she was unrelenting and intimated that she did not wish to accompany me anywhere in the future, I took her at her word, left her at the station and walked home, feeling strangely elated at the termination of our friendship. After all it was the gaining of a certain form of freedom, for our association had involved much expense and a good deal of worry to me.

Sunday 13 March 22nd birthday. Celebrated in rather inauspicious manner. Called [at 139] for Nigger and took him up to Hampstead in morning. Very misty, took him back at 1.15 and went home for lunch. Saw Gran in hospital in afternoon and walked back to the Angel. Had a rotten tea and stayed at home in evening reading book and papers. Went to bed soon after 11.0.

Saturday 19 March Boat Race day. Cambridge wins again by six lengths. Took Nigger up to Hampstead in afternoon. Took him back, went down to buy new Scout hat and got home at 4.30. Had a bath and a good tea and went along to YMCA to meet Basil Green at 6.30. Tried to get in Aldwych but would not queue for standing room so went to the Rialto to see new Rene Clair film *A Nous la Liberté*. Enjoyed it immensely. One of the most brilliant and entertaining films I have seen for a long time. Went into the Coventry St Corner House after for supper. Came out at 10.50. Basil went home while I hung about Piccadilly Circus till midnight. The wildest Boat Rice Night for years especially being England v Scotland rugger match day as well.[7] Got in many scrums outside the Criterion and round Eros statue where there was a battle royal with the police just before midnight. Got a bus home and turned in about 1.15. A memorable evening.

Sunday 20 March Fine day. Went on troop hike wearing new shoes. 10.20 train from Liverpool St to Grange Hill. Only four of us. Managed to carry on till lunchtime but shoes rubbed heels so much that the skin came off so gave it up at 2.30 and came home. Got bus back to Romford from Havering and train back from there to Liverpool St. Got home 5.15, had a bath and tea and stayed in evening reading papers. Bathed heels in boracic water and went to bed at 11.15.

Friday 25 March Good Friday, a fine sunny day. Met Basil Green and Eddie Smith at Poland St Garage at 10.0 and had to wait an hour and queue for a bus to Guildford. Arrived there 12.45 and hiked across country to Thursley with a short stop for tea. Arrived at the YHA Hostel Ridgeway Farm at 7.30 and settled down. Had supper in crowded kitchen and turned in 10.30–11.0. Did not sleep too well.

Saturday 26 March. Struck south and by 10.30 reached the Devil's Punchbowl and Gibbets Hill. Stopped at an inn at Brook for lunch and coming out at 1.0, it started to rain and kept on all afternoon. At 2.0 decided to go north to Godalming to try and put up there. Arrived at 4.0 but after a fruitless search for accommodation took a bus to Guildford and had tea in the High St. Basil and I went up to the Trust House in the High St – the Angel, had an unsatisfactory and expensive dinner, met the other fellow outside and went to the Theatre Royal. Got three stalls at 1/6 each and saw one of the most pitifully bad variety shows imaginable called *A Mixed Grill* entirely performed by a dilapidated party of six. Came out at 10.30 and went to a small cosy restaurant on the top floor of a house opposite the theatre for some supper. Got back to the hotel at 11.15 and turned in.

Saturday 2 April Got an unexpected rise of 7/- week. Very pleased with it. After lunching at the YMCA went with Joshua to London Bridge Station to meet Erith Rovers for a visit to the London Fire Brigade HQ in Southwark Bridge Rd.[8]

Friday 15 April After going home to change into evening kit and dine, went to Holborn Rover dance at the Express Rooms in Charing Cross Rd. Spent a fairly pleasant evening though not entirely at ease owing

---

7 In this Calcutta Cup match, England beat Scotland 16 points to 3.
8 The headquarters did not move to the Albert Embankment until 1937.

to meeting Beatrice again. Danced with her but could find nothing to say. It was awful. Got home 12.30.

Tuesday 19 April Went and had a letter to Harrod's typed out at lunchtime. Again could not make up mind whether to phone Beatrice or not and again shirked it. Went to the Vaudeville in evening and saw *Vile Bodies* an adaption of Evelyn Waugh's novel. A bitter and witty satire on modern society and the futility of modern life. Very amusing and entertaining.

Friday 22 April Went down to the Stationery Office in Kingsway in afternoon to get copies of New Import Duties. Met Beatrice at 6.20 at TC Rd station and went over to the Corner House for tea. Made up our quarrel and became good friends once more. After a walk round went to the Victoria Hall[9] for the 3rd Holborn's Annual Concert. For the most part a pretty awful affair. Walked to Euston after, saw Beatrice off and took a bus home. Had supper and turned in 12.20.

Tuesday 26 April Went along to Harrods lunchtime for an interview but proved a waste of time as they 'grow their own office staff'.

Thursday 5 May Went down to the cashiers today and went round paying wages, mostly maintenance staff. Makes an interesting change from the usual routine. Back to office at 5.0.

Saturday 21 May. Went home to change into uniform and have tea. Went to the Foundling to do some work for the Guides Anniversary Celebrations. About 20 or so there. Messed about getting the fire going till just after the choir had started, and then with Eddie and Jasper went over to the building to sort out the books and mugs brought for the hospital. A pretty hefty job and thankful to get out of rain which got worse as the evening went on. About 9.30 got fed up with it and in order to avoid having to clear up the fire etc left with Eddie and cut out by the side entrance. Home at 10.0, supper and to bed by 11.30. Rained heavily all night.

Tuesday 24 May After going home for dinner, coming back again with Mother and spending an hour in the YMCA reading room, went up to Hyde Park for the *Daily Express* Empire Day Celebrations at 9.30. Managed to work way through the dense crowds to the side of the arena when the police gave way to the pressure of the crowd and let them swarm into the arena. As they could not clear it out, the gorgeous pageant and display planned could not take place. A great disappointment for all concerned.[10] Hung about till about 11.0, walked

---

9   Victoria Hall, on the north-east corner of Bloomsbury Square.
10 The planned pageant 'had to be abandoned owing to the size and behaviour of the crowd' (*The Times*, 25 May 1932).

back to Hyde Park Corner and took a bus home. After a cup of tea went to bed at 12.30.

Wednesday 15 June Met Beatrice at Marble Arch at 6.55 and went for a row on the Serpentine. Went on to the Hippodrome to see the new Julian Wylie show *Out of the Bottle*, rather like an adult pantomime only far funnier than any panto and full of smart dancing, clever songs and tuneful music. Enjoyed it considerably. So did she. Saw her to Euston after, then bus to Highbury and home at 12.15. Had supper and to bed 1.0.

Wednesday 22 June Met Beatrice outside the Palace at 6.50 after a hasty cup of tea and a doughnut at Woolworths, and went along to queue up at the Saville. Left stool in queue and went for a brief walk. Got good seats in amphitheatre. Saw *Tell Her the Truth* the new Bobby Howes show – the new idea of a musical comedy without a chorus. Saw Beatrice to Euston after and got home 11.50. Supper etc and to bed.

Thursday 23 June Mother met me coming out of work and we went to 139 G[ray's] I[nn] Rd for dinner. Back to Highbury at 8.30 and spent rest of evening packing ready for moving tomorrow evening. To bed at 12.0.

Friday 24 June Swim lunchtime. After taking library book back, went home to dinner and got ready for moving back to Gray's Inn Rd. Van called at 8.45 and got the stuff on. Went with it, Mother following by bus. Got there, safely unloaded stuff and unpacked some clothes. Took sacks of books down to kitchen. A harrowing and arduous evening but glad to get back to Central London again. Went to bed about 11.30 – Office shifted over to 3rd floor C Block tonight.

Sunday 26 June Fine day. Met Beatrice at 10.0 at Tottenham Ct Rd to go on Elkayonians Reunion Ramble, she being very disconsolate. Wiffles and Grace unable to come at last moment and my not bringing a rucksack owing to a misunderstanding. However as we walked up Oxford St, she decided to come, and we took a bus to Victoria from Marble Arch. Took 10.45 to Epsom and set off on a leisurely ramble. Fortunately Maud Cox and one or two other girls came along to keep Trixie [Beatrice] company otherwise she may have been even more off-handed with me than she was. What with her pretending to be irritated with some imaginary faux-pas of mine and doing all she could to annoy me, I was ill at ease most of the day and mildly disgruntled. Did about 12 miles altogether. Got back to Victoria at 9.15 and took bus to Euston Rd, Beatrice dropping her off-hand manner on the way and becoming her natural self once more, unfortunately rather late in the day till we parted amicably enough at Euston, which was fortunate. Went to bed at 11.15.

Thursday 30 June Went up to Burnt Oak in evening to dine with Trixie. Spent a very pleasant evening with her and had a good heart to heart talk. Got home 10.45 and soon to bed.

Thursday 7 July In evening went along to do some work at the SOS Society's new place in City Rd.[11] Only Jeff Birch there. Spent an hour shovelling gravel into buckets and carrying it up to front of house. Fairly heavy work which made me sweat much. As no one else turned up, both left at 9.0, I going up to YMCA where I met David in Reading Room and went down to the restaurant with him. Chatted with Cherub and some others in vestibule and then walked home. Went to bed 11.50.

Wednesday 13 July [written as *June*] Met Beatrice at 6.45 and had tea in Beta Café. She annoyed and depressed me by telling me that she might have no spare time in future owing to some mysterious new activity which she would not disclose. However passed the evening as pleasantly as could be expected and went to the Savoy to see *The Savoy Follies*, a new revue on *Co-optimists* lines.[12] Saw Trixie to Euston after and then walked home rather despondent. Of course slept badly.

Thursday 14 July [written as *June*] After dinner took some old clothes with me and went along to the new SOS house in City Rd again to do some more navvying. Five others there. Spent an arduous and perspiring hour and a half shovelling the gravel out of the back garden and carting it up to the front of the house.

Saturday 13 August On getting home, learned that Mother had been and booked two rooms at 11 Penryn St [NW1]. Went to weekend camp at Downe [Scout centre]. 3.30 bus from Poland St with Basil Green. Camped in Rovers' Field. Went for a long walk round with Jasper in evening, getting back in middle of camp fire. After supper turned in at 11.30.

Monday 15 August Up at 8.30. Very thick mist and moist atmosphere and faint drizzle. After breakfast decided to pack up and leave as the drizzle looked like continuing. Caught 12.20 coach back to Charing Cross and got home at 2.0. After changing, had a shave and some lunch and went along to the National Gallery for an hour. Then a swim and home to dinner at 6.0 Went to the Promenade Concert at Queens Hall in evening.[13] Wagner night. Very crowded as usual. Enjoyed it considerably in spite of sore feet. Stood in front, close to orchestra.

11 The SOS Society, a charitable group with its headquarters nearby at 49 Doughty Street, WC1.
12 A variety revue staged as a co-operative venture by variety and musical comedy artists including the comedian and actor/singer Stanley Holloway (1890–1982).
13 The Queen's Hall was the venue for this annual concert series until it was destroyed by enemy action in May 1941. The site is now occupied by the St George's Hotel, close to the BBC in Langham Place. That evening Sir Henry Wood conducted the BBC Symphony Orchestra.

Friday 19 August Sweltering hot again. Took Nigger up to Regent's Park for an hour after booking seat on coach to Margate and get some more oilcloth. Carried away to Penryn St and laid it in my room. Then home to lunch at 2.0. Went up to the Holborn 2nd class baths for a swim. Called at Oxford St Woolworths and home to tea and get ready for moving. Van called at 7.30. Packed our stuff. Took Tram up to Penryn St. Helped them unload and take up stuff [to the top-floor rooms]. Very arduous task, especially on such a sultry evening. Got saturated right through. Managed to straighten things out a bit by 10.30. Had some supper and turned in 11.45. My bedstead not arrived yet so slept on mattress on floor. Too hot a night for much sleep. 99 deg. in shade today. Highest record since 1911 (100 deg.).

Saturday 20 August Up at 7.30. Left at 10.0 to catch 11.0 coach from Victoria to Margate for five days holiday by myself. Arrived Margate 2.50. Put up for bed and breakfast at 51 Canterbury Rd, front room on top floor. Very dingy and old fashioned place but good enough for my purpose. Went for a swim at 4.30. Tea at Nayland Rock Café, afterwards strolling round to buy one or two things. Went up to Cliftonville in evening. Watched the Oval concert for a while and moonlight bathing in pool. Had some supper in Cliff Café and walked back to Westbrook. Turned in about 11.30.

Thursday 25 August Fine and breezy again. Sat on beach with girl friends in morning. Could not decide whether to go back this afternoon or not as intended. Thought I'd better not. Had lunch at Woolworths and went back to pack up and get ready. Settled up with landlady and went down to say goodbye to the girlfriends. Unfortunately they had not come up to expectations being rather dull and unintelligent and a trifle common. Also very disgruntled over getting sunburnt. In fact distance had lent enchantment. Got the 3.0 bus back to London arriving at Victoria at 6.20. Called at YM on the way home. Went to Rover Mates Council in evening. Got home around 12.0 and saw Mother who had worked at the Queens Hotel on Monday – but very long hours (9–11).

Friday 26 August Got up at 9.0 and made own breakfast and cleaned up after. Went up to Gas Co[mpan]y office to arrange for gas stove to be fitted. Spent afternoon emptying sacks of books and arranging them in cupboard. Went up to YM for a swim in evening. Dined in restaurant after and went down to the Playhouse.

Saturday 27 August Got up at 9.0 as gas men came to fit up stove, could not get any breakfast till 11.0. Went up to the YMCA and met David and walked to Hyde Park. Had a boat on the Serpentine for an hour. Sat and read near bandstand till 5.40 when we walked to the Coventry St Corner House for tea.

Tuesday 6 September Bought £8 more of National Savings Certificates lunchtime. Went for a swim on way home. Found Uncle Fred and family there on getting home for dinner. Left about 9.0. Read for a while after and turned in about 11.0.

Friday 30 September Paid Workroom wages in afternoon and balanced with £8 over, apparently paid to me in excess. After work went down to Meakers in Shaftesbury Avenue and bought a dress waistcoat which had taken my fancy in the window. Up to YMCA for a swim and dinner. Walked home.

Wednesday 5 October Had to start working till 6.30 again without notice. Pretext: autumn shopping. Autumn crocus would have been more sensible. However, on release dashed home, changed into uniform, had a hurried dinner and went to monthly troop meeting at YMCA. Consisted of a talk on National Savings and then AGM. Election of officers. I re-elected Keeper of Log. Went over to Corner House after and then bus home with Eddie Angel. To bed 12.40 but took some time to get to sleep.

Thursday 13 October After going home to change and dine, went to Sadler's Wells for the 'Co-op' party. Saw *Il Travatore* for the fifth time and thought it a melancholy piece of musical melodrama.

Tuesday 1 November Went to Newbold's in Sackville St lunchtime to have a new pair of spectacles made. Also to the Hippodrome to book a seat for the Christmas pantomimes. After going home to dine in evening, went with Mother to the Scala to see *The Gang's All Here*, the London Rover revue by Ralph Reader. Mostly re-hash of past Holborn Shows with some new stuff. Fairly good though the dirty and dilapidated Scala detracted somewhat from the show's merits. Duke and Duchess of York supposed to be there so fabulous prices charged for this night. Duke not there and Duchess said to be hidden at back of box, Charity, thy name is fraud. Recognised hardly anyone in audience. Mother enjoyed it immensely. However a rather inglorious evening.

Sunday 13 November Met at King Charles St at 9.15 for Cenotaph Parade. A cold grey morning and everyone well padded. Formed up on Horseguards Parade to march to Cenotaph at 9.45. Marched back round Westminster for service on parade again. Dispersed 10.35, met Mother and Jack and walked up to Charing Cross to go on hike. Only four of us. Tube to Waterloo then train to Epsom. Did a pleasant 18 mile hike over familiar ground. Back at Victoria at 8.20. Bus home, put feet in hot water and to bed at 11.0.

Wednesday 23 November Left eye rather sore. Might possibly be strain of new lenses but more likely a slight chill in it. Went along to Newbold's lunchtime to settle account of 18/-, the Prudential paying the balance of 15/- due for the glasses. After work to Swedish drill class[14] at 7.15 then patrol meeting in Rover Den. Much against my will, had to ask Adam to withdraw as he was not a Wayfarer though he had always thought so. Offended him. Did not think him capable of such pathos. As disagreeable for me as for him. At meeting thought out plan to put the patrol on the map. Decided to meet more frequently and to organise a patrol Xmas toy fund for poor kids in district. Frankly I think it a lot of baloney but it will be good fun to achieve – and achieve its purpose.

Thursday 1 December After work a light meal in Woolworth's cafeteria, fish cake and chips. Home to change into evening dress. Went to Mohicans [Rover Scout] Patrol dance at Royal Hotel, Woburn Place. Boycotted by Knights and Trojans[15] but nice crowd there. Good floor, very slippery. Formed small party with David, Bunny Kaye, Beatrice, Maud Cox and her friend Dora. Cherub came along about 11.0. First time I had seen Beatrice since July. Not changed much. Hair shorter. A little slimmer. As prudish as ever. Found it difficult to make conversation with her. Occupied herself with Bunny most of evening. But a jolly little party. Had two competitions. One for men. The gaudiest suspenders. Won it. So had to judge the girls' competition – the fairest blonde. Thought it a tie between two so someone tossed and decided it. My prize was a stick of shaving soap. Felt a bit of an ass over it all but enjoyed the momentary limelight. Did not dance a great deal. Once with Beatrice, twice with Maud, the rest with her friend Dora, a rather plump girl but a good dancer and quite sociable.

Wore white waistcoat with dinner suit for first time. Difficult to keep in place. Shirt front bulged too much. Over soon after 12.0. All walked to Euston. Four of us on to Mornington Crescent. Saw David and Dora off there. Maud home. Then home myself.

Sunday 11 December Very cold and dull 'Co-op' hike. 10.0 train from St Pancras to Luton. A large turnout. Interesting crowd. Beatrice, Maud Cox, Adam, etc. Spent morning talking with Adam. Lagged behind and got lost for about ten minutes, but Cherub came back and found us. Much relieved. A brief fall of hail about 12.0. Lunch in café in Dunstable. Scarcely a word with Beatrice, she looking more scraggy than ever. And disdainful. Tea at Hemel Hempstead. Adam left before tea served. A brief 'scene' when we sat down at the two tables. Seven of them at one – Beat, Maud, David, Cherub, Eddie etc in fact anyone interesting there. The rest at the other table. I determine to sit at table one. Complaint from Beatrice that table only laid for seven. 'Then we'll lay for eight' says I. Beatrice moves to other table. Uncomfortable look on everyone's faces. A brief silence. Then tea started. Very funny and

---

14   A vigorous form of physical exercise directed by an instructor. Heap attended Swedish drill sessions at the YMCA for years.
15   The two other Holborn Rover patrols.

very childish. Walked back to Luton in dark. Got 7.30 train back. St Pancras 8.30. Not too pleasant a day in many respects. But no regrets and no remorse. So why worry?

Saturday 17 December Changed into evening clothes and went up to YMCA and went over to YWCA Dance. I was tired and danced energetically. A gay and informal atmosphere. Dinner jackets carried unanimously. A smallish, bright hall. Hot as fury and as crowded as Hell. Collar melted. What a crowd! What a choice! Three of us went over to the Corner House after with three girls from Endsleigh House, a YWCA hostel near Euston.[16] Got home 1.10 and soon to bed. Tired but restless, the effect dancing always has on me afterwards. A grand evening.

Tuesday 20 December To Holborn lunchtime to get calendar and diary. Shopwalking again today. About same as yesterday but came up at 5.30. A relief.

Sunday 25 December A dull, slightly foggy Christmas Day. Stayed in reading papers during morning. Wrote up this diary. Went out for a short walk to Camden Town and back. A few semi-drunken young people about streets singing. Men carrying crates of beer home from pub. Sounds of vulgar voices raised in song and mournful. Pianos coming from most houses. All nausea to me. Not hungry enough for supper, I had an orange and went to bed.

Monday 26 December Lunch at home. Went to tea with Dad for an hour before going on to queue up at the Lyceum for the pantomime *The Sleeping Beauty*. Got my usual seat on the end of the front row of pit stalls. A dull show. Almost yawned my head off when the place went to sleep for 100 years towards the end of the first act. I felt like doing the same. Not enough gusto and robust humour for a Panto. All too feeble. And very plain girls in it. Some good aerobatics and lively clowning by Naughton and Gold, but that's all.[17] On the whole a long bore.

Thursday 29 December Joined Mudie's Library[18] in Kingsway lunchtime, £1.1.0 a year (fiction and non-fiction). Took out *The Star Spangled Manner* by Beverley Nichols[19] – a very amusing account of Beverley's experiences in America in 1928. Went to bed 11.20.

---

16 'For professional women and students', at 11 Endsleigh Street, WC1.
17 Charles 'Charlie' Naughton (1886–1976) and Jimmy McGonigal (1886–1967), known as Gold, were popular Scottish comedians. As members of The Crazy Gang, they were regular West End performers, particularly at the annual Royal Command Variety Performance.
18 Founded by bookseller Charles Mudie (1818–1890) in Bloomsbury in 1842, this became London's leading circulating library. It declined with the rise of publicly funded libraries: see entry for 12 July 1937 for its closure.
19 Beverley Nichols (1898–1983) was a prolific journalist and playwright, and the author of sixty books, including novels, books on gardening, six autobiographies and six successful plays.

Part One

Saturday 31 December Met Mother outside Leicester Square 8.0 and walked along to Piccadilly Circus. Crammed with people, mostly orderly. Some spasmodic shouting and cheering here and there but few attempts at singing. More people about but also more orderly than boat race nights. People in evening dress on balcony of Criterion attracting some attention. Bright lights all round. A grand place to see the New Year in. The middle of the arena. The heart of London 12.0 – 1933 enters – another ten minutes and the crowd drifts away. And so home to sup, to bed, to sleep, to hope.

RETROSPECT – 1932

A depressing, troublesome year. Much has happened but, on the whole, I have not made much progress in any direction. We have moved three times, the last one into our present home on the hottest day for 21 years (Aug 19). Domestic strife and worry has come to an end with the gaining of our independence i.e. Mother and I. My friendship with Beatrice was broken, reformed and broken again, finally and beyond repair. I am now more or less my former self, selfish, self-centred, conceited, sarcastic and cynical, and a poseur. I have no one to try and please but myself and I am perfectly happy in my misogynistic state. Not that I regretted my friendship with B. I do not grudge the money I wasted on amusing her, though perhaps it was not the worry. But it was worth the experience. I know what it is to be in love. I have realised that I am not infallible to that indefensible emotion. But now that I have, very fortunately, gained my normal state, I can look back and laugh at myself. Thank God I have my sense of humour, perverted though it may be. It has, and I hope will continue to help me overcome many bitter struggles, many nerve racking worries and several desperate crises. Next to my perfect health, my sense of humour is my most treasured possession.

So now, with the resolution that I am determined more than ever to remain a bachelor, but not as before a professional woman hater and to live my own life in my own way, let us leave this emotional analysis and get back to things more rational. My enthusiasm for the theatre is greater than ever. I have been to no fewer than 68 West End shows this year (excluding cinemas and variety shows) – a record. The theatre never fails me whatever else may. I have also developed a penchant for literature having just joined Mudie's library. There is also my Rovering. I have become a Rover Mate and Secretary and have maintained that position. I am, perhaps, slightly less popular than hitherto (if that is possible) though most of my friends are drawn from the Rovers. The theatre, literature and Rovering – these three are my main interests in life – apart from life itself, a different but human business.

My business position is no better than this time last year or any previous year for that matter. I have not been able to obtain a new job, though, I certainly only tried during the first part of the year. But it is a desperately difficult thing in the present endless depression. If, however, I can get my C.I.S. associate-ship in February, I shall try again. However disillusioned I may be, I shall look forward with hope and optimism to the future. After all, I'm not so young as I used to be and I'm not so old as I look.

But hope's not enough. Work and worry only may do it. And I'm losing my capacity for worry, and as for self-discipline. But no more of this philosophising. All that remains is the financial position. I have saved about £12 net in 1932, which is not bad considering the heavy expenses I have had to meet.

To save money, in fact, was about the only resolution I kept in 1932. The rest were either too difficult or futile. So to save money is the only resolution I will make for 1933 as it is the only one I seem capable of keeping. But this I will try and do – to be more tolerant in regard to other people's actions and opinions (which does not involve not upholding my own among them less strongly), to try and see through things and people, to try and appreciate sincerity and genuineness and distinguishing it from the false and sham, to try and avoid pettiness and triviality in all its forms. In brief to try and steady and appreciate the great comedy called Life to its fullest extent. Say I.

1933

The year 1933 proved more emotionally challenging for Heap with his father's suicide in March and his mother's consequent distress. He understandably wrote more detailed and reflective daily entries, totalling a record 47,639 words through the year, but this chapter reproduces only 24% of his original. With his father's death and its aftermath and the relationship with Beatrice having ended, Heap fortunately met a new girlfriend, Lilian, while Youth Hostelling in June. Their much more substantial relationship supported him through the rest of the year but, although he had gained his professional qualification and in spite of his efforts, he still failed to find to find a better job as the country slowly started emerging from the Depression. His interest in right-wing politics 'increased enormously' and, within days of his father's death, he enrolled as an inactive member of the British Union of Fascists – attending meetings but declining to sell the weekly Fascist newspaper on the streets. Heap's other consolation remained theatre 'first nighting' (in 1933 he attended sixty-eight performances); however, his interest in Rover Scouting started to decline.

Sunday 1 January Bright morning at start. Got up at 10.0. Light breakfast. Called for Nigger. Brought him back to see Mother then took him up to Hampstead. Noticed a man juggling with a few balls in street at Hampstead. The first time I have ever seen this form of larking. An unusual sight, somewhat naive and rather pathetic. After lunch went and saw Gran in hospital.

Monday 2 January Forgot to take lunch to work this morning, so went home lunch time for it. Called at Swan and Edgars to see some pyjamas I had fancied in window but poor stuff so did not buy. Did not get to bed till 12.15. Learned today of Bill Scott's death, one of our old office colleagues. Left fifteen months ago with consumption. Only about 21. Used to camp with him and Joshua, he being a Marylebone Rover. Always appeared healthy and normal, a really decent, good hearted fellow, an ideal friend. Then one morning 'Those whom the Gods love', I wonder.

Thursday 5 January Met Eddie at 8.10 and after seeing David went along to the Wesleyan Mission Hall, St John's Square, Clerkenwell with the remainder of our toys in a sack. Not such a difficult job as I thought it would be. Saw Sister Phipps, the Warden there and captain of their Rangers. Wanted us to come along to the children's panto at which the toys would be distributed on Jan 14th. Explained to her that most of us would be occupied with the panto racket on its last night but thought that one or two of us might manage to come along. Also she wanted a tough he-man to run an unruly boys club there. Went and had a look at them, and said I'd try and find someone but thought it a hopeless task and could not imagine any of my Rover acquaintances taking it on.

Friday 6 January Had dinner then took Mother along to the King George's Hall for second performance of the RH Panto. Very good show. Dances not by Ralph, not so energetic as usual but no worse for their naive simplicity and a lovely ballet towards the end. An altogether delightful show. Will give it a good criticism in *Young Holborn*.

Wednesday 11 January Looked in the garish 'fun fair' which now opens onto Coventry St and the Haymarket. Saw some animals in small glass cages to advertise their zoo. Small monkeys, stoats etc. A horrible revolting sight. Watched an animal walking his few inches of floor, backwards and forwards ceaselessly, going slowly mad. If I could afford to act on impulse I would have smashed the cases and let the wretched things out into Piccadilly Circus. But I could not afford it so I fled in sickening disgust. Had a cup of coffee in the new 3d and 6d cafeteria at the bottom of Shaftesbury Avenue on the corner of Piccadilly Circus. A clean smart informal place and some interesting types of characters in there. Took a distinct liking to the place. Then joined pit queue at Criterion. A vivid evening.

Thursday 12 January To YMCA by 7.20 to relieve David in charge of scouts selling chocolates. Distributed trays of stuff, made a mess up of record of stuff, copies and returns of money and stock. Could not keep any check but did not seem to matter much. Cleared everything up after the interval. Net takings £2.15.0. Afterwards went over to the Corner House with a crowd of fifteen or so of panto cast and Cherub and Bunny Kaye. A merry crowd. Beatrice also over there with Pat Moran in another small party. Heard some gossip that they are taking a more than average interest in each other. If it's true, I sympathise with Pat but she seems to like them a little mature. Such is life.

Saturday 14 January Foggy morning and afternoon. Met Joshua, Williams and Clarke at Holborn Hall at 4.30 to go along to the children's party at the Wesleyan Mission Hall, St John's Square, Clerkenwell. A rowdy disorderly affair. Nothing much to do but stand around talking to the rangers there. Joshua, in plus fours, distributed the toys (partly Wayfarers collection). Left at 6.30 and as we had had hardly any tea there, went down to the Cafeteria in Piccadilly Circus then to the last night of the RH panto. Afterwards went over to the Corner House with

Part One

a large number of the cast – about three dozen altogether. Could not find enough room so trooped out again and followed Cherub (in tails with no hat or coat) down Hanway St out into Oxford St. Nowhere else open so went back to Corner House and managed to join some tables together. Much whoopee. Came out at 1.0 and two dozen or so of us walked up to the coffee stall at Marble Arch or rather danced up there to the tune of numerous panto songs. Warned once by copper, walked down Park Lane to Hyde Park Corner (just on 2.0 by now) and walk home, buses having long since stopped and not worth a cab. Got home 2.40 and soon to bed.

Thursday 26 January Went to Gray's Inn Rd to wait for Mother and Dad to come back from News Theatre. Sat in kitchen reading book. They came in about 10.0. Stayed another hour or so while they had some supper and listened to wireless. Tram home. To bed 11.45. Exceptionally cold night.

Saturday 28 January Took Nigger to Hampstead in afternoon. Skating on ponds up there. Never seen such swarms of people at Hampstead. Took him back and had some tea at 139. Mother there as well, then change into evening clothes to go to a Holiday Fellowship Dance at Conway Hall in Red Lion Square. A dull affair altogether. Dull people, a dreary band, a monotonous programme. Nice hall though. Towards the end of evening danced with a girl who transpired to be Trevor Wignall's private secretary on the *Daily Express*.[1] Had an interesting talk about the writers on that paper and the newspaper racket in general. But on the whole a dismal evening. These dull young people.

Thursday 9 February To Sadler's Wells for Rover Ranger party. Arrived just as lights went down. Two dozen or so there. More Rangers than Rovers. The usual mob. Saw *Don Giovanni*, honestly enjoyed every minute of it. Expected to be bored with dim recollections of seeing it at the Old Vic ten years or so ago when I was too immature to appreciate the exquisitely fresh and vital melodies of Mozart. But I do wish female opera singers did not always look as ugly as sin.

Thursday 23 February An amusing incident in Oxford St opposite our windows this morning. A lorry barges into a milk tricycle van, turning it over and smashing dozens of bottles of milk over the road and pavement. A terrific crash and consternation all round. But work must go on.

Friday 3 March Took my CIS Associateship Application Form in to be signed by Mr Doran this morning. Said he'd see the Secretary with it to get a copy of the accounts and balance sheet. Brought it back at end

---

1   Trevor Wignall was a sports reporter for the *Daily Express*.

of day saying he had not been able to see the Secretary but would try again next Tuesday, being away till then.

Tuesday 7 March The most tragic day of my life. Called into Mr Doran's private office about 11.30. Phone call from the police. Dad had died during night. Suicide, poison. Felt ghastly. Got leave of absence and went to Hunter St Police station then home to Penryn St. Wept a bit. Called at Coroner's Court but could see no one though waited some time. At last went along to Gray's Inn Rd. Saw Dr Whyte just leaving.[2] Mrs Stapleton there. Went into bedroom and saw Dad lying on side as if peacefully asleep. A sight I shall never get out of my mind. Coroner's Officer called, took particulars. Went up to Mrs Zelger's [flat, at 139] and phoned to Mother to come along. Upset her terribly. Undertaker called at 4.0 for body. Moments of awful tension. When it had left, looked through papers etc. Found some letters I had written when five years old to him in Algiers. Baby language, capital letters. My composure broke down then and I wept bitterly. Left at 5.00. Went home, ate a little. Telegraphed to Uncle Fred to come to 139. Met him there at 7.15, went up to Mrs Zelger's. Then back and packed up some things to take so that landlord should not seize everything as distraint for arrears. Took them home with us. Wrote to Aunt Louie in Manchester. Then at 12.30 went to bed.

Wednesday 8 March Scarcely any sleep overnight. Went along to Gray's Inn Rd after breakfast. Beautiful morning, makes life so desirable. Uncle Fred arrived soon after and we spent the morning turning out all drawers and cupboards getting out all Dad's papers, books and all other personal belongings and taking them back to Penryn St in suitcases. Finally left at 2.0 and went home for some food. Haddock and mince pies at 3.0. Went along to PR's. Saw Mrs Somers and Mr Doran as well as [colleagues] Williams and McOrmie, all sympathetic. Also drew a week's wages due next Friday. Rejoined Mother at Mrs Zelger's after going home first and went along to 139 to wait for van from Wallis's to call at 6.0 to take all the furniture away and keep it in store for us so that Richards the landlord should not seize it as distraint for his rent due. Took about an hour. On tenterhooks all the time. However, all over at last and took cab with Mother and a few small articles back to Penryn St after having taken Dad's clothes in a bundle up to Mrs Zelger's. Came out again soon and with Nigger who must live with us now and went to Mrs Zelger's. Walk up to Holborn and back. Then tram home and so to bed at 11.30, dead tired. A good day's work.

Thursday 9 March Up at 7.30. Served with summons to inquest tomorrow. After taking Nigger for walk, went with Mother up to

---

2 The Heap family's doctor was Dr Alex Whyte of Fairlie and Whyte, 9 Mecklenburg Square, WC1.

Glaves to get black hat and scarf. Called at Dr Whyte's but out. Met Aunt Louie [AL] and Uncle Harry [UH] at Euston at 1.0. Had a snack in lounge there while Mother explained things. Then went up to Leverton's the undertakers at Mornington Crescent[3] – arranged for funeral on Saturday, UH leaving his card for the bill to be sent to him. They went on to the Strand Palace after to fix up a room till Saturday while we went home. Took Nigger for a quick run then up to Glaves again for Mother to buy a black dress, gloves and hose. Some tea in Lyons next door. Saw Dr Whyte at 4.25. Mother called to see Mrs Zelger while I went up to the YM and had a quick swim and shower. Lost 3 lbs in weight this week. Bus home. Another run for Nigger. Met AL and UH at 7.15 and went along to Henning's for some dinner. Poor food but quite pleasant anyway. Came out 9.30. Mother went on to see Mrs Salmon while I went into the YM to see Cherub. Told him everything, likewise Basil and David who walked to Euston with me after. Bus to Morn. Crescent. Met Mother taking Nigger for a run then home to bed at 12.45

Friday 10 March Up at 7.30. Breakfast. Walk with Nigger. Met AL and UH at Mornington Crescent and went along to the inquest at the Coroner's Court. I was not called for evidence, Mother was. Unnerved by the preliminary oath she made one or two injudicious revelations about Dad. Got into the papers. Saw placard in Holborn as we were going to the Prudential 'Gray's Inn Rd Dentist Suicide Verdict'. Bought *Standard* to read the whole story.[4] Set me in a furious rage – this washing of the dead's dirty linen in public. Went to Mrs Zelger's and made a bit of a scene. Was rather unkind and inconsiderate to Mother, for I had a bad attack of nerves and couldn't control my temper. Went home and did ditto. But after ten calmed down and both of us consoled each other and I resolved to take things more rationally. Went up to Camden Town and got wreath ordered in morning after registering the death. Went to K.G. Hall for stewarding *Holborn Again* while Mother went to Mrs Zelger's for evening. Did not see much of show and could not set my mind on what I did see. But relieved my gloom a little. Met Mother after and came home. A short run for Nigger and to bed at 12.30.

Saturday 11 March A bright mild glorious day. The worst possible for a funeral. Left Leverton's at 10.30. Coffin in front car, the five of us in another. Mrs Zelger came as well as UH and AL. Rushed up

---

3   Leverton's of Eversholt Street, NW1, established 1789, remains a leading Camden funeral director.
4   The 'news' that Heap's parents never married travelled beyond London: the *Yorkshire Post* of 10 March carried the report of the suicide verdict and the fact that, in her evidence, Heap's mother told the coroner 'I must speak the truth, I have been known as Mrs Heap for 23 years'.

1933

to Cemetery at Finchley at terrific speed.⁵ Service in chapel. About six other coffins as well. Dad's service, gabbled by the bearded vicar and utterly unintelligible. No sincerity. Into car again to grave. The burial. Mother wept bitterly. Into car again and home. Farewell to UH and AL and home to lunch. Took Nigger to Hampstead in afternoon while Mother left parcel for Gran at hospital. Tea at 5.30. Sorrowful reflections and hopeful talk about future with Mother as twilight fell. At 7.30 went to YM for second performance of *Holborn Again*. Saw Beatrice. Very kind and considerate about my sufferings. Tried to put my usual impartiality on show in order to write criticism of it but failed to do so. Could not enjoy it. Saw Joshua in interval and went for a walk round the block with him. Met Mother again after and came home with her. Felt terribly depressed and it took me a very long time to get to sleep.

Sunday 12 March Lunch at home at 2.0. At 3.30 left to go to Uncle Fred's new house at Forest Gate.⁶ Not being certain how to get there had four changes of buses before we arrived at Wanstead Flats. Mother left umbrella on top of bus. Took Nigger. A dull dreary district. Arrived at 98 Lorne Rd about 5.20. Stayed till 9.0. Home by train from Wanstead Park Station to Kentish Town. Tram from there. Had some supper and went to bed at 11.45.

Monday 13 March Twenty third birthday. No present or cards, not yet anyway. A fine mild day but slightly misty. Got up at 9.0. Breakfasted and took Nigger for a walk. Went with Mother to the Prudential to claim on Dad's small free Life Insurance Policy. Then to West Central Post Office to see about redirection of letters. Had lunch at YMCA at 1.45. Cherub came in soon after and sat at my table. Stayed till 2.45, last two out of restaurant. Met Ralph coming out. Went on to PR's and saw Mr Lines and Mr Doran. Arranged to start work again tomorrow. Then bus home. A cup of tea. Went through Dad's papers, cheques, bills etc. with Mother sorting them out and throwing away useless items. Went for a short walk about 9.15. Supper on getting back, fish and chips, bacon. Wrote rough criticism of *Holborn Again*. Went to bed at 11.45. So ends my tragic, vivid, frantic and extremely active week's 'holiday'. It seems an eternity since I left PR's last Friday.

Friday 17 March Dull and rather rainy again. Had a swim after work. Weight 10 st 11 lbs.

Bought a *Holborn Guardian* on way home. Very annoyed to see a report of the inquest on Dad's suicide in it as most of the Holborn Rovers buy it to see the report on *Holborn Again*. But walked home and my wrath subsided somewhat. Had dinner, stewed mutton and jam

---

5   The neighbouring cemeteries of St Pancras and Islington are in East Finchley.
6   Fred Shepherd and his family had previously been living in Walthamstow.

Part One

pudding. Felt too tired after to write to Aunt Pop as I intended. Just lazed about and went to bed early at 10.15.

Thursday 23 March Another fairly uneventful day. Decided to join British Union of Fascists – at last, talked of doing so which caused much amusement in the office about Blackshirts etc.[7]

Sunday 26 March A grand day. Too mild for overcoat. Going to get papers before breakfast saw the most ill-looking man I have ever seen in Charrington St. Shabbily but decently dressed, slight figure, small wizened and emaciated face. Probably badly weakened by illness or starvation. Mother still very upset. Cannot get Dad off her mind. The glorious weather makes it worse. Persuaded her to meet me at Marble Arch at 4.30 after I had been to see Gran. Wore my dark grey suit for third time since I bought it over a year ago. Walked to Serpentine and back. Tea in the Pavilion Café at Marble Arch.

Monday 27 March After work called at the British Union of Fascists HQ at 1 Gt George St, Westminster. A few bare rooms on the first floor. Waited in a large room overlooking Gt George St. apparently used as a gym as well, a punch ball, boxing gloves etc lying about. No furniture but few chairs. My presence forgotten so went out and was shown into a smaller room – the office. A clerk in black shirt at desk sending off circulars. Another recruit filling in forms. Another man, short and dapper in an ill-fitting D.B. waistcoat apparently in charge of things saw to me. I told him I wanted details of membership. He sold me some literature explaining the objects of movement and told me of their militant policy and strict discipline. Have to combat without weapons, communists with razors and knuckledusters at meetings. Also sell *The Blackshirt* on streets, two hours a week. These unforeseen points did not appeal to me, so I left saying I'd think it over, which is as good as saying N.B.G. [No bloody good]

Sunday 2 April Glorious day. Mild and sunny yet quite fresh. Went on PR's hike. 10.35 train from Waterloo to Sunningdale, eight of us. An excellent hike. [*page of itinerary*] Got back to Waterloo 8.50. Walked home. Food, Nigger out, cleaned clothes and shoes and to bed at 10.30.

Monday 3 April Had a haircut after work. Barber asked where Dad had got to lately. Very surprised to hear of his death. Walked home. Dined. Had some coffee. Felt very tired. Started reading Part 9 of the *Popular Educator* while Mother went to see friends.

Wednesday 5 April A lot of people in the office got rises this afternoon. I did not, nor one or two others. Annoyed at first but soon ceased to worry about it. Philosophy triumphed. After going home to dine, went along to the monthly troop meeting at YMCA. A talk by the German

7   On the British Union of Fascists (BUF), see Introduction, pp. 7–8.

scout I met yesterday evening, Fritz Bauer, on 'Hitler and Modern Germany'. Spoke remarkably well considering his talk was unprepared and in a foreign language. Very sincere too, Agreed heartily with all his views and opinions. Provoked much discussion after, first in the Drawing Room itself and then over at the Corner House. Walked back with him to Torrington Square where he is staying after buying the *Blackshirt* outside the C H. Another German fellow with us also. Left them there and walked home. A vivid stimulating evening.

Thursday 6 April As Williams was keen to see the site of the proposed open air theatre in Regent's Park, went with him there lunchtime. Allowed half an hour there and back. Underestimated distance. Twenty minutes to get there and a frantic rush back. Five minutes late. Nothing to see when we got there. A mild day too. Made me sweat. Waste of energy.

Tuesday 11 April Fine and mild. To work without overcoat today. Noticed a hole under arm of black jacket. Very annoyed, should not have worn through so soon. On getting home found CIS Recommendation form completed. Also Dad's gold watch and chain which Mother had been to get out of pawn for £10 odd. To bed at 11.30.

Wednesday 12 April Took bus to Gray's Inn Rd and called at Mrs Zelger's to bring home a bundle of Dad's clothes we had left there a month ago. Mother sold Dad's gold watch-chain today for £7.2.11.

Thursday 13 April Went to the CIS at lunchtime and lodged application forms and fees for Associateship (£6.16.6). Bought two pairs of new pants at a shop in Seymour St on way home. Walked back to Leicester Square after to meet Mother standing by the tranquil greenness of the water in the fountain opposite Buckingham Palace. Mall deserted. Very cold. No overcoat. Irritated at waiting about so tiff with Mother. Home by bus. Packed a few things for tomorrow. To bed 12.30.

Sunday 16 April Even finer and warmer than yesterday. Put oil on face for sunburn. Set off for Gibbet Hill and the Devil's Punchbowl at 9.45 with two other chaps we met at Ridgeway Farm. Lay half an hour on top of Gibbet Hill. Fine view, managed to walk up to Frensham Great Pond in afternoon. Walked back to Ridgeway farm with one of our two companions. We lost our way near end of journey and got back just after the other two. Had a cup of tea. A Rover staying there dressed my blisters for me. Supper. Large gramophone. Got talking to a charming girl. Pretty and very intelligent with a plainer and older looking companion. Went for a camp fire in corner of field after. Six of us then back to cottage and to bed.

Monday 17 April Easter Monday About 11.0 left to hike back to Guildford. Got the two girls we met last night to come with us. Oakley Common – up on the Hog's Back and along the top to Guildford. Took a particular liking to the girl friend. Her name transpired to be Norah Morris, works at Kew in a Civil Service Dept, lives at Kingston, very fond of hiking and camping and books, exceedingly healthy type. A nice voice and delightful personality. Went down to the station and saw the other three off then back to Green Line bus terminus. Had to wait an hour in long queue. Got a bus at 8.0, home at 9.45, one or two odd jobs and to bed at 12.0 A grand and glorious holiday. Has done me a world of good, physically and mentally.

Tuesday 25 April Rained a good deal. Took Nigger for a walk. Went round the north side of Pancras Rd exploring. Came across a series of dark, damp, evil smelling streets mostly occupied by colliers' depots, gas works, covered by railway bridges. A grim locality, especially at night.

Saturday 6 May Fine afternoon and evening. Went for weekend hike with Nora staying at Bentley Cottages near Peaslake, a YHA hostel. 2.25 Green Line bus to Dorking. Met her at station at 4.0. Took the road and by chance passed two YHA chaps who guessed where we were making for and put us on the right path which we would otherwise have missed. Got to Bentley at 7.45 and settled down, I in a very big shed with fifteen beds but only those two other chaps staying there. Then a high tea soon after. Sat in drawing room rest of the evening. Just gramophone, thus predicament, all rather flat. Not enough there, thus political and religious arguments till bedtime. Very nice people the wardens, Mr and Mrs England.

Sunday 7 May Did not sleep very well overnight. Rained hard all night. Much noise on roof. Got up about 8.30, left at 10.20. Set off South to Pitch Hill. Splendid view from top and got to Dorking at 5.0. Had tea in a charming shop. Refined and sedate but neither arty nor expensive. Good class customers. And plenty of *Tatler* and *Bystanders* available.[8] Saw Norah off at station after, then walked back and got Green Line bus home. Only just got a seat at back. Home 8.30. Papers, supper etc. Bed 11.0. Enjoyed every moment.

Friday 12 May Rather a fine day. My testicles felt out of sorts today. Can't tell why. Felt a trifle sore and one hung lower than the other. Rather concerned about it. Possibly nothing at all though.

Sunday 14 May After a late and light breakfast and a read of papers cleaned all the windows for Mother. Lunch at 2.0 went up to St Pancras Cemetery in afternoon with Mother to see Dad's grave. Just a mound of earth now. Mother bought some 'forget-me-nots' outside and put

---

8   *Tatler* and *Bystander* were glossy illustrated lifestyle magazines of the period which merged in 1940.

them on grave. She wept a little. Then it came over black and looked like raining hard, which it did as we came home in bus.

Monday 15 May Called to see Dr Whyte on way home about my testicles. Waited half an hour before I saw him, the waiting room filling with people meanwhile. He assured me there was nothing to worry about. A purely temporary phase, possibly due to a strain of some sort. A suspension belt might ease matters till they adjust themselves to normal again. Gratified to learn nothing much wrong. Took tram home. Had a good dinner. Stayed in evening reading Part 14 of *Popular Educator* while Mother went to see Richards about furniture trouble.[9]

Tuesday 16 May Felt easier and more normal in testicles today. Maybe the trouble was sheer auto suggestion after all. Sent off advert for the *Tax Secretary* lunchtime.

Sunday 21 May Took Nigger to Hampstead in morning. Wore new sports jacket. Rather too warm for evening wear. On the other hand too light in colour for winter wear. Very exasperating. Home to lunch at 2.0. Very good lunch, steak and mushrooms and pancakes, all perfectly cooked. Went to see Gran in afternoon. Found her very despondent and upset. Not surprising. Went to Hyde Park on leaving hospital. Listened to a much heckled communist at Marble Arch for a while. Went over and listened to band till 8.45 then walked over to Hyde Park Corner. Beautiful saplings and flowers on way there. Walked to T C Rd and bus home.

Friday 26 May Walked down to Piccadilly and caught a bus to South Kensington to go and see Adam at Manson Place, Queen's Gate. Sat for two hours in his small study in his small fourth floor flat, drinking China tea, eating coconut biscuits and smoking Turkish cigarettes and talking about all sorts of things – Holborn Rovers (the trouble over his membership status being the object of my visit), books, theatres, music, women and Ireland (from which he had recently returned). And several other minor subjects. No one I would rather spend an evening with just talking than Adam. Sheer intellectual joy. A thoroughly entertaining evening.

Monday 29 May Two females wearing trousers – according to the recent Marlene Dietrich sensational masculine fashion – appeared in the street opposite our office windows this afternoon. Caused rather a stir among the men folk thereabout. Did not seem to be quite all there. Soon disappeared.

---

[9] Mr Richards was their landlord at Gray's Inn Road. See entry for 7 March 1934 for the end of this dispute.

Part One

Wednesday 31 May Derby Day. Won by Hyperion, Lord Derby's horse at 6–1. Drew Thompson in the office sweepstake and lost 6d, that was all.

Monday 5 June Whit Monday [*on a Youth hostelling week in Surrey*] Just as scorching hot as yesterday. Set out at 10.0 for the Devil's Jumps, two or three miles westwards. Got a mile up a wrong road and walked back with an interesting old fellow who pointed out the wide extent of Lloyd George's estate at Belhurst as we passed through it. Then up to Frensham Little Pond for a swim. Met two fellows and the girl singing last night there. All joined up, swam (I wearing Harry's swimming shorts), lazed about on the banks, drank lemon squash, ate fruit and went back with them to Thursley instead of walking all the way to Guildford as we intended. To me the girl was the attraction though she was not unattached. Her name is Lilian, his Billy, the other boyfriend Jackie who turned out to be a YM member. Anyway they wanted to get back to Ridgeway for lunch as they had paid for it. So we walked back there arriving at 3.30 after calling for a drink on way back but only being able to get a milk and soda. Jackie left on his bike soon after. The remaining four of us had time together and left at 5.40 to walk over to Thursley and get the bus to Guildford. Sat with Lily on the bus and gradually got quite intimate with her, and she agreed to come to a show with me some time. Harry left us at Guildford to go back by train. We waited in queue for nearly an hour and got Green Line back at 8.6. Oxford Circus 9.35, walked up to Lyons next to Oxford Corner House and had something in the way of light refreshments. Lily walked with me along to Hampstead Rd where we got a 27 bus, she going on to Highgate, me home. Look forward to seeing her again, a charming girl, slim, tall and very feminine apart from a superb voice. And not unpretty. What will this lead to – if anything?

Wednesday 7 June Feet still sore from blisters. After going home to change into uniform went back to YMCA, dined in restaurant, up to Reading Room for a few minutes then down to the Howard Room for monthly troop meeting. A talk by a man named Patrick Sloan[10] on 'Russia Today'. Has recently returned after a long visit. Looked rather Russian and was a communist but a remarkably sane and fair one. Did not paint a gloomy picture of that controversial and mysterious phenomenon known as the Soviet and admitted failures and shortcomings while extolling the principles and ultimate blessings of the regime. Very knowledgeable and intelligent and answered questions fairly and squarely. Let us give the devil his due. I went to scoff and stayed to bray, but I don't swerve one inch from my anti-socialist nationalist opinions. On getting home found a letter from CIS

---

10 Author of *Soviet Democracy* (London: Victor Gollancz, 1937).

asking me to write to a company regarding my application for a job. Sat up late writing it out in rough.

Thursday 8 June Was considerably annoyed last night at finding my contributions to this month's *Young Holborn* very mutilated, shortened and stuck at the bottom of odd page without heading and no initials. Such is the reward of voluntary intellectual labour. But decided that it was not worth worrying about nor the individuals answered either. Just one more lesson learned. About 8.30 a small mufti-clothed missionary meeting came round the outside. Hymns and bible readings and sermons. About six to ten small kids stood round listening. About three adult heads out of windows. A poor half-witted fat head youth putting handbills containing a sentimental story under doors. That was all, very pathetic but somehow beautiful. Just faith I suppose. Had a letter typewritten lunchtime today and sent it off to Southern Area Electric Corporation.

Sunday 11 June Saw Gran in afternoon. Home via Trafalgar Square where a communist demonstration was being held. A short rest and tea at 6.15. Changed into dinner suit and off to 72 Addison Rd where Adam had invited me to a meeting of the 'Beer and Something Club' who meet every Sunday evening here at Clifford Bax's house, debate, dance etc.[11] Only other person in a dinner suit was Esmé Percy the actor and he wore a soft shirt and collar.[12] But Adam said it was usual to dress the first time so I did. A debate on the motion 'That Women Were Inefficient' was moved by Major Fitzgerald and opposed by a young woman whom Adam introduced me to when I went in but I forget names so quickly. I was called on to speak at Adam's suggestion and both shocked and amused the gathering with a few uncomplimentary remarks about women. The motion was, of course, defeated. Then the interest ended for me for, apart from Major Fitzgerald, whom I talked with after and found shared all my views on militarism, patriotism, nationalism etc they were nothing but a hollow-eyed mob of pseudo-intellectuals, as dull and uninteresting as could be, particularly the females. All young people except Fitzgerald and Bax (an American-looking aesthetic) but youth at its dreariest and most futile. The attempt to dance on a few square feet of floor was ridiculous, I tried it. The only drinks available as consolation were beer and cyder, neither to my liking. Adam neglected me the entire evening, I saw nothing of him at all later on. Left shortly before midnight, walked up Holland Park and got a bus home. Never have I been so exquisitely bored in my life, so I felt on going to bed at 1.15.

---

11   Clifford Bax (1886–1962), English author, playwright, journalist, critic and poet; younger brother of the composer Arnold Bax.
12   Saville Esmé Percy (1887–1957), English film actor.

Part One

Wednesday 14 June Wore best suit and black trilby and went along to Coleman St at lunchtime to see the Secretary of the Southern Areas Electric Corporation after phoning up and fixing the appointment. A pleasant interview without a single jarring incident. As pleasant and amiable man as ever put a nervous applicant at ease. Came away feeling that I could not have done better. But of course, nothing settled yet. Incidentally wore Rover mufti badge which I had called at YM for on way to work in morning having been left by Cherub. Mother thought it would be certain to create a favourable impression. Am inclined to agree with her, so I did.

Thursday 15 June After going home to change and dining at YMCA met Lilian Sprackton outside the Dominion and went to the Globe to see Ivor Novello's new play *Proscenium*, produced last night.[13] Seats in back row of gallery. Sweltering hot. A thunderstorm or two during evening but fine and cool when we went out during intervals. The play rather a disappointing affair, a lot of dreary sentimentalism. [*half-page of criticism*] Out at 11.20. Lilian went on to Highgate, I got out at Morn. Cres. After putting feet in warm water with potash permanganate went to bed at 12.30.

Saturday 17 June Went to camp at Downe at weekend. A gigantic crowd of scouts there (about two thousand) for the Chief Scout's visit tomorrow to open the new swimming bath. Got 3.9 train from Charing Cross.

Sunday 18 June Up at 8.0 after a reasonably good night's sleep. Wash, breakfast and shave. At 10.0 set out for the job we had been assigned of digging holes and disposing of the lots therein. Also sawed some logs and collected some wood for camp fire. Back for lunch at 1.0. Adam arrived about then and stayed the afternoon. At 2.30 marched over to the swimming pool and lined up for BP to come and perform opening ceremony at 3.30. A scout jumped in and swam a length then a general immersion into it. Hurried back to relieve Cherub and two others on incinerators but got away for a few minutes for the gathering at the Camp Fire to hear the Chief speak.[14] A lot of old buffers in mufti there and few orders of merit presented. Left 6.45 or so with five others. Train to Charing X. Home about 9.0.

Wednesday 12 July Called at YMCA after work. Found that Mother had left me an 8/6 ticket for the Heavyweight championship of Gt Britain fight at White City Stadium between Jack Doyle and Jack Peterson. So dashed home to change, back to YM for some dinner then set off by

13 (David) Ivor Davies, known as Ivor Novello (1893–1951), Welsh actor and composer of successful musicals.
14 In front of 2,500 scouts, Lord Baden-Powell opened the new camping ground for London Scouts at Downe and invited a ten-year-old Bermondsey scout to 'take the first plunge' in the new swimming pool (*The Times*, 19 June 1933).

tube to Wood Lane. Stung for dud programme in street and had to buy an official one (1/-) inside. Centre stand (the 8/6 block) almost full up when I got there. Sat at back for a while then came down and sat in front. Sat through some lengthy and tedious contests. Ringside filling up all the time with hosts of dinner suited and black trilbied backs and fur escorts evening clad. Saw Hannen Swaffer strolling about. Recognised no one else. At last at 9.45 the great fight began. [*contest described*] Suddenly the referee stopped the match and declared Doyle disqualified apparently for no reason whatsoever. All over in five minutes! The crowd furious with indignation. An obvious frame up, all a racket, easy money swindle declared the gentlemen around me. And they were not far wrong. The disappointment was too intense, 'We Want Doyle' they continued to shout, but to no purpose. At 10.30 the farce was ended and Wood Lane became a most congested area. Home by tube. An evening not without considerable interest however.

Friday 14 July Went for stroll up Regent St lunchtime. Called in the new Fascist HQ there and bought the current *Blackshirt*.

Thursday 20 July Wore grey suit and went along to Sinclair's in Cranbourne St at lunchtime to order new suit.[15] Chose blueish grey pattern at 4 gns [guineas]. Spent ½ hour in there. Rushed back to work. On leaving in evening went over to British Union of Fascists HQ in Regent's St with Williams, Harrison and McOrmie to hear talk by Sir Oswald Moseley on 'Fascism'. A basement room, packed out. Stifling hot. Sat in back row. Splendid address. Fine speaker with perfect choice of words and good delivery. An attractive and inspiring personality. A peaceful meeting. No disturbance or uproar. Enjoyed the whole thing. So did others. Went on to Rover Mates Council at Knights' Den on coming out. I was duly appointed District Rover Secretary. Discussed also Cenotaph Parade, otherwise little business.

Saturday 22 July After going home for lunch, went to DuCane Rd to see Old School Sports. Wore flannels and cricket shirt. No coat, too hot. Saw all the old masters and one or two old boys, and took part in Old Boys v Masters tug-of-war, and lost – as usual. Got free tea by going in back way. Did not pay 1/- for programme either. Left at 6.0 and went home for tea. To Rover-Ranger Social at Herbrand St Drill Hall. A good number there. Only about eight Holborn Rovers. Several Westminster people as well. A few silly games, country dancing etc finishing with a camp fire. Went out to the *Bird in Hand* behind Russell Hotel half way through. Ale. David likes the stuff when it's free, well, I don't refuse, and it does make me a little less critical of silly socials. Damn fine day.

---

15   A. Sinclair, tailor, 43 Cranbourn Street, WC2.

Sunday 23 July Very fine day. Went on Co-op Rover Ranger trip. Ten of us. Six Rovers, four Rangers. 10.9 Green Line bus to Staines. Got out two punts, 10/- each for day's hire. Only worked out at 2/- a head. Set off up river and were soon all clad only in bathing costumes and remained so all day. Thus getting in more good sunbathing. A little way up the other boat leaked a lot and had to be taken back and exchanged. When got back all set off up river past Runneymede. I paddled till lunchtime when we pulled into the north bank and ate in the boats (2.0). In afternoon went further up river to Old Windsor. Had some drinks at the lock and turned back again. I did no more paddling since lunchtime but lay in boat sunbathing. After a swim had tea outside converted bungalow opposite ferry. Two more hours and arrived back at Staines. Had difficulties to get bus back. Managed to get on a bus to Hammersmith by myself and left the others waiting. From there got a 27 bus to Morn Cres. Home at 10.20 very tired. A joyous happy day.

Wednesday 26 July Hottest day this year. After going home to change into tennis shirt and flannels and dining (fish and chips) went up to Camden Town at 7.30 to meet Lilian and go for a row on Regent's Park Lake. Very pleasant and fairly cool. Came off at 9.15 and walked to Oxford Corner House. Sat by window and [had] ices and drinks. Came out at 11.0 and took tube home. A thoroughly delightful evening. Really began to like the girl. So must go wary and be careful. Don't think I shall make the same mistake twice though. Incidentally she knows Beatrice, in Northampton Poly Operatic Society together. Coincidence!

Saturday 29 July Showery and cool. After going home to lunch and change, went to the Royal Academy Exhibition at Burlington House for which Adam had sent me a free press ticket. Very fine set of pictures and a great pleasure to view, though a more tiring pastime than wandering round picture galleries would be difficult to imagine. Decided to go to the Dominion in evening having run out of theatres.

Saturday 5 August Snatched a little lunch, grabbed pack and off to Poland St. to catch 2.33 to Guildford. Read *The Stage* on way down. Got to G at 4.10. walked down to Hindhead buses terminus and while waiting for the 4.45 had a cup of tea and cake in the adjoining cafe patronised by conductors and other waiters for buses. On getting out at Red Lion,[16] met Bill Colbourne and a party of five Jews also bound for Ridgeway Farm, so joined up with them. On getting to farm got put up in our usual ground floor in cottage. Then walked down to Hindhead, had a drink in the lounge of a hotel pub there and walked back. Supper in lounge while others went for a walk, Harry and I turned in but woken up again when they came back at 12.0. However not a bad night's sleep.

---

16   An old inn on the Portsmouth Road at Thursley.

Monday 7 August Still very hot. Max temp 88 deg. After breakfast in garden, party of six of us set out for Big Frensham Pond, Bill and Margaret by bike. Had a couple of swims there and a sunbathe and came back again for a late lunch at 3.0 by same means as we went. After lunch mucked about on lawn in front of cottage. Some played bridge, some read. Set off home at 5.50. Six of us walked over to Portsmouth road and got 6.23 bus to Guildford. Joined there by Harry and Barney on motor-bike and all had a drink together. Pint shandies. A good drink. Then parted, Bill and I to queue for Green Line coach, the rest by train. After an hour got a bus at 8.30. Decided to a camp in Cornwall with Bill for a week of holiday. Like the fellow very much, appeals strongly to me. Like those Jews. Did not take to them much at first but after a while liked them very much, a rich and spontaneous sense of humour and rather cultivated. Got to Oxford Circus at 10.0, had a waffle in Lyons and parted. To bed at 11.30. Neck very sore, head very hot so could not sleep. About 1.30 had an invasion of bugs in bed. Mother had discovered them before but had chanced it. So had to get up and go and sleep in Mother's room. Not much sleep. Bad spring.

Saturday 12 August Chilly and cloudy morning. Got better later. Went with Lilian to Thursley for weekend. Her birthday today. Don't know her age though 24–26 at a guess. Met her at Poland St and got the coach to Guildford. Looked very chic and attractive. Had some tea in a Lyons 4.0 before rushing down to get 4.45 bus to Red Lion, Thursley. Got to Ridgeway about 6.0. Full up but got fixed up all right. Lilian in Bosmark's room and I in a tent over by railway carriage. Suited me well. Comfortable bed, plenty of bedclothes. After some more tea we walked up to Hindhead, had a couple of ports in the lounge. Walked along up to Gibbet Hill. Very chilly now. Had not brought jacket. Up the valley of the Punchbowl and made back to Ridgeway. Had some supper in kitchen with crowd of others. Only bread and cheese and tea. Expected a more sumptuous meal. Dull slightly silly set of people too. Everyone self-conscious. Glad to get back to front drawing room where we waited for Dmitri to finish playing bridge to play the piano for Lilian to sing. Little time left and D either could not, or would not, play appropriate numbers. L rather disappointed.

Sunday 13 August Woke up to find dog sleeping in tent, old thing too. Rather a fine day though strong breeze made it chilly in morning. After breakfast, set out for Big Frensham Pond about 10.15. Went out of our way several times but eventually got there via the Little Pond about 12.15. Sat by it and paddled about an hour but not quite warm enough to go in bathing though we had brought our costumes. So walked back to Ridgeway but by more direct route than the way we came. Collected a lot of cones en route which Lilian had the ingenious notion of taking home to dip in gold paint and make into ornaments. Got back about 2.0 for a late cold lunch. Sat about on lawn in front of cottage after reading, dozing etc. had some tea at 5.30, packed and left to walk over to the Red Lion about 7.0. My watch had got about half an hour slow for we did not get a bus to Guildford till nearly 8.0. From there got a Green Line to Hammersmith as it was first one out. Sat separately, tiring journey, made me very sleepy. From Hammersmith went home by tube, I to Morn Cres.

Monday 14 August Kept reflecting on the damnably short duration of such exquisitely happy periods which make life worth living. The contrast makes work, a dull routine, seem almost unbearable. Oh if yesterday could go on all the week, every week all the year and so on ad infinitum. But could everlasting joy be still a joy or would it not become routine and therefore defeat its own ends? But why all this rambling despondent philosophy? Let's face it, I'm in love. So help me God.

Saturday 19 August Start holiday. Moderately fine day. So decided to go with Bill to Thursley. Also phoned Lilian but she had gone at 11.0. Changed, packed and back to Poland St Garage at 4.0. Met Bill and got 4.3 bus to Guildford. Bill bought a sleeveless shirt there and we had some tea in Lyons. Then got 6.15 bus to Red Lion, Thursley. Across fields to Ridgeway. Full up again but I managed to get us put up on a settee bed in lounge for night. Having nothing else to do we went into the tea room but could not get any to drink. Met David Haden Guest in there, son of the MP.[17] Been to Cambridge, rank Communist and looks it, a nervous wreck, obsessed with fanaticism. Argued with him for about an hour until Bill suggested we should walk up to Hindhead, which we did – the three of us. Slept fairly well. Thanks, I think, to bitter.

[*A week's holiday at Bude on the North Cornish coast*]

Saturday 26 August Fine day and much warmer. Up at 8.15. Left for Waterloo at 10.0. Mother and Nigger came with me to station and left as soon as Bill came along at 10.45. Got 11.0 train to Bude. Four of us. Played cards a good deal on journey. Read book rest of the time. Got down there just before 5.0. Met by other fellows there. About 8.30 went down to Bude again and had a few drinks at the pub and went on to the weekly dance in the Drill Hall. An amusing affair. Managed to dance quite well even though wearing hide shoes. Rather a higher percentage of good looking females than one finds in corresponding cheap London dance halls.

17 David Haden Guest (1911–1937), son of the journalist, doctor, author and politician Dr (later Lord) Leslie Haden Guest MC MP (Labour) for Southwark then North Islington. Leslie had converted to Judaism on marriage but renounced it in 1924. David was killed in the Spanish Civil War.

1933

Friday 1 September Got up to breakfast at 10.45. A dull windy morning. The four of us on dinner fatigue. Got it ready by 3.0, wrote a letter to Lilian in afternoon. Took me right up until teatime at 5.30. About 7.0 went down to The Carriers and the four of us played dominoes in the tap room. Had a good booze up being our last night. I accounted for three pints and got as drunk as ever I've been this week. Had a minor brawl with three locals on coming out but Bude's only policeman was nowhere about so no casualties took place. We all went along to the fish shop and then back to camp. Sat round a table and decided that each should hold forth on the merits and demerits of each member of the camp. A pernicious semi-comic discussion. I was chairman, spoke last. Was tactlessly frank and possibly rude about most people though more or less sober by now. Followed by a sing-song.

Saturday 2 September We were awakened by the breakfast squad at 6.45 this morning and had porridge thrust upon us. Caught the 10.40 train back to town going down to station in car. They played solo whist a good deal on the train. I finished my book. Felt very tired and fuggy. Not enough sleep last night. Train got into Waterloo at 5.0, forty minutes late. Bade farewell to the others and took bus home, on getting home, unpacked, washed and had a good tea.

Tuesday 5 September To Mudie's and back lunchtime. Got out *The Greater Britain* by Sir Oswald Mosley, a detailed analysis of the policy of The British Union of Fascists.[18]

Friday 8 September Still quite fine. Has been all week. Just mild and not too warm. Getting chillier in evening though. Went round to Fascist HQ at lunchtime and bought a *Blackshirt*. Am enjoying Mosley's *The Greater Britain*, a forceful well-written exploration of the fascist policy – a fine tonic. Kept at office till 6.15 sending off cheques.

Tuesday 19 September Took the MS of Adam's book along to Hurst and Blackett, publishers in Paternoster Row at lunchtime. Walked back via Fleet St and Covent Garden. Wrote to Adam at Nice in afternoon.

Friday 22 September Took mac to work today, so very little rain of course. Walked as far as Piccadilly Circus and back at lunchtime with McOrmie, calling in to buy the *Blackshirt* at Fascist HQ on way back. After work had a drink in the Horse Shoe[19] and took a bus up to Northampton Polytechnic. Mucked about a bit in hall while Bill and friend discussed football with others. Bill and I went up to the hiking club social. Not many there, about twenty. Had some dancing to a piano. Then about 10.0 we went up to Lyons at the Angel with a

---

18 First published in 1932, this was Mosley's manifesto for the BUF.
19 Heap's favourite bar, at 264–268 Tottenham Court Road, now Café Rouge and Garfunkel's Restaurant, next to the Dominion Theatre, across from the Oxford Corner House and close to the YMCA.

couple of girls. One Madge, Lilian's friend, the other an interesting person whom I discovered a gallery first-nighter. Therefore we got on well together. A queer girl though. Suffers from insomnia and I think inclined to be over-sexed. Or perhaps it's a case of excess of talk purging the girl.

Sunday 24 September In afternoon went over to see Gran in hospital. Went along to the National Gallery after to see one or two pictures I had read about in *London Scene* and I appreciate the pictures here much better after my study of 'Art' in the *Popular Educator*. Just a brief knowledge of the great artists through the centuries and the different schools and movements helps me considerably.

Monday 25 September After walking home to dinner in evening went along to the London Rover Council at Dennison House, Vauxhall Bridge Rd to make my debut as Holborn Secretary. Turned out to be Holborn's only representative. About 100 there. Very interesting meeting. Main business of meeting was to discuss the future of the Cenotaph Pilgrimage. Was glad that all the motions were carried as I hoped them to be, that the ceremony be continued to be held on Armistice Sunday and that no limitations on numbers be made. I spoke three times and, I think, rather effectively. A really worthwhile sort of meeting.

Thursday 28 September After walking home, getting fish on way in Euston Rd, changed, dined and went up to YMCA to meet Len Bolton at 7.45. Had arranged to show me how to do the monthly troop notices on duplicator. Got the use of the typewriter in Cherub secretary's room and so did the stuff up there instead of in Rover Den. Cut the stencil on the typewriter and then inked the duplicator, lay the stencil on it and, with the roller, turned off about 140 copies. Quite a simple job once you have got the knack of it. Using the typewriter will be the most difficult part for me. Only took about an hour and a half for the whole job.

Saturday 30 September Met Lilian outside Dominion at 6.30 and went to queue up at the Shaftesbury. Left stool in queue and went for a short walk. Got seats in front row of amphitheatre. Saw Werner Krauss, the great German actor, in *Before Sunset*. Fine tragedy. [*half-page of criticism*] Last night there was anti-Hitler uproar in gallery against Krauss, an alleged Nazi. Probably Jewish scum. Several ejected. One or two police there tonight but no sign of trouble.[20]

---

20   The stage and film actor Werner Krauss (1884–1959) was allegedly an 'unapologetic anti-Semite'. *The Times* of 29 September reported 'Uproar at a First Night', when Herr Krauss 'was interrupted at the outset by persistent shouts from the gallery and showers of leaflets'. At the next night's performance, Krauss 'got a splendid reception – uniformed police were on duty in all parts of the theatre and in the gallery plain-clothes officers sat in the audience. There were about 30 policemen in the theatre' (*The Times*, 30 September 1933).

1933

Thursday 5 October At lunchtime took the MS of Adam's book along to Grayson and Grayson, publishers in Curzon St – left it for a reading. Then walked down to the Strand. A good bit of walking in 50 minutes.

Tuesday 10 October Showery and very windy. A letter from CIS this morning asking me to write to Holbrook's Ltd at Birmingham re: my advert in *The Secretary*.[21] Did so, stating that I do not wish to leave London – so not much hope in that direction.

Friday 13 October After work went up to YM and met Bill at 6.30. Had dinner in restaurant, sat up in reading room for a while and then went up to the Northampton Polytechnic for Rambling Club social. Coming out at 10.0 met Lilian – just finished cookery classes She tried to book up for Sunday but was too late, all places gone. Disappointing. We went up to Lyons at the Angel. Found Mother in bed. Only 11.26. Why? Had got the sack from work owing to bad business. Oh hell!

Sunday 15 October Went on Northampton Polytechnic Ramble. Met King's Cross at 10.0, Bill did not turn up. Annoying and disappointing but in with others all right. Private coach took us down to Maidstone. Got off a little way outside town and hiked. Collected a lot of large apples going through an orchard just outside Longley where we had lunch at an inn. In afternoon passed the beautiful and stately Leeds Castle and from the adjoining roads caught our coach to Detling to visit a fox farm. We were given tea first and then taken round the farm by the owner-manager Commander C M Stark who extended to us his most gracious hospitality throughout our visit. About two or three hundred foxes being bred there in wire enclosures. Saw them fed with pieces of rabbit. Very interesting but the idea of keeping animals in captivity for any purpose is slightly nauseating to me.

Monday 23 October Fine mild day. Took Adam's MS to Constables, publishers, in Orange St at lunchtime. Sat in Leicester Square gardens.

Thursday 26 October On getting home in evening found Mother had been to Walkers and got a lot of furniture and books that had been in storage since March when Dad died, owing to [landlord] Richards' claim. The heavy stuff left there however. Mother had also got a job at a new club opening just off Charing Cross Rd – the Cosmopolitan.[22] Evenings 5–11. She's having some luck at last – won £2 on the horses yesterday. Starts tomorrow evening.

Tuesday 31 October Went round to Fascist HQ in Regent St at lunchtime to inquire why I had not received tickets for tonight's meeting at Kingsway Hall. Told they had all gone but after going home to dinner in evening went along on the off chance and got a seat that had been

21 Possibly a late response to that of 16 May (see above).
22 Cosmopolitan Artists Club, 35 Wardour Street, W1.

returned. Good one too. Right at the side of the platform about six yards away from it. Adam there sitting on platform. A splendid address by Sir Oswald Moseley. Immensely fiery outbursts of impassioned oratory. Very clear, outspoken and sincere. The audience was spell bound but not dumb. Responded magnificently with deafening clamours of applause. Hall packed both by audience and hordes of uniformed Blackshirts. Numerous questions after. Over at 10.30. Adam stayed behind to speak to Sir O privately. I walked home. An inspiring evening.

Saturday 4 November After going home to lunch and change went up to YM to meet Bill and Harry at 3.0 and go over to YWCA[23] for AGM of London Regional Group of YHA. Went on till 7.0 with a break for tea at 5.0. Went round to the Horse Shoe and had some drinks then back for something of a social, lone Morris dancers in ludicrous costume. A spasm of self-conscious community singing. We being a bit merry, then a feeble attempt at ballroom dancing, all very flat and at 9.0 we left with another fellow with two girls took a cab down to Bodega[24] just off Strand. All had a drink then walked up to the Haymarket Brasserie. Not a bad dive. Had spaghetti and lager. Dancing there. Came out 11.30 and dispersed. Rather heavy reckoning up – fellow and girls got off light. Walked up to T C Rd with Bill and got bus home. Some more supper and to bed at 1.20.

Tuesday 7 November After dining on spaghetti went down to see Adam at his flat in evening. Read over half of a play he had written correcting minor English grammatical errors in it. Rather an intriguing play. More a bedroom farce than anything else but with a decided continental flavour about it. Arranged to go again on Thursday to go over rest of it. A very pleasant evening. He gave me coffee and a cigar. We talked of all sorts of things books, women, Holborn Rovers and diverse personal matters. In fact to spend an evening with Adam is, to me, the height of intellectual joy.

Friday 10 November New Fascist paper out today – *The Fascist Week*, 2d. – Very good thing too.

Thursday 23 November Went up to meet Lilian outside the Dominion at 8.0. Waited and waited but she did not turn up. At last gave it up at 8.27 and took bus down to the Savoy where I had booked two seats and went in. Show had been going five minutes. Found her there in back row of amphitheatre. Explanations – she had mistaken the meeting place and waited at Leicester Square Tube, came on at 8.20 and bought a seat. So we went down to our proper seats in front row and settled down to the show.

23 Now the Bloomsbury Hotel, 16–22 Great Russell Street, WC1.
24 Bodega, 42 Glasshouse Street, W1, an Italian café/restaurant that Heap subsequently frequented.

1933

Monday 27 November Walked up to Mornington Crescent this morning to get a bus and take Cherub's typewriter back to YM. But got tired of struggling for full buses with a lot of wretched females in drab looking Macs, gave it up in disgust and had to go to work by tube. Consequently felt thick and fuggy and generally unhealthy all morning. Hell, how I hate the tube. How the poor wretches who travel by it every morning can feel fit for work god only knows! One's enough for me. Wrote to Lilian in afternoon and posted it after work.

Thursday 30 November Again woke up late – 7.50, am beginning to get expert in quick dressing and breakfast bolting in mornings. Also received my last article on '1925' from Lilian beautifully typed with three copies and a few words of round criticism as to its verbose contents. A great girl that.

Monday 4 December In passing, this would have been Dad's 55th birthday had he lived another nine months. A depressing day to start with but a merry one to finish it. Mother disclosed at breakfast that she had given notice and would cease her job at the end of the week, may make things rather awkward financially. But in evening went with Bill to dance at South Kensington. Had four beers and a very gay evening. Danced incessantly and enjoyed it most unexpectedly. Dancing usually tires me. Lilian there but stayed down in refreshment room most of time. Had one dance with her however and went home by tube with her as far as Camden Town.

Thursday 7 December Sent pantomime article off to the *Evening News* on way to work. Other '1925' article returned. Wrote out article on 'Masculine Delusions About Dress' in afternoon not having much to do.

Friday 8 December Got back '1925' article this morning from Newspaper Features Ltd. Don't think it's worth trying again unless drastically revised and shortened. In fact did so in afternoon.

Friday 15 December Very busy lunchtime. First posted off annual subscription to CIS. Then up to Stationery Shop at end of Gray's Inn Rd to buy diary and order calendar.

Wednesday 20 December Did not wake up till five past eight. Only time to dress before rushing off to work. No shave and only a few gulps of porridge for breakfast. So at lunchtime went along to the Cambridge Dining Room on Euston Rd with Harry and had a good lunch. A cheap eating house to which many chaps from the office go for. Very good food and plenty of it. Also called in at barbers – had a shave on way back. Went over to the bank in afternoon. Both ways by taxi. After work went along to meet Lilian outside the Princes at 7.30 [to *On With the Show* at the Cambridge]. A terrible show, full of cheap music hall effects and a painful attempt at humour. [*half-page of criticism*]

Boos and cries from the gallery at end which I heartedly joined in. Interrupted 'calls' and generally depressing scenes of failure.

Sunday 24 December Got up at 9.30. A chilly bleak morning. Taking Nigger with me, went up to Highgate station to meet Lilian at 11.30. Got there ¼ hour too early so walked down Holloway Rd and back. She arrived ¼ hour late having lost dog on way. Walked up Highgate Hill and over to Ken Wood. Got home a trifle late at 2.20. Had lunch and went over to see Gran in afternoon, spent evening cutting stencil on typewriter and duplicating monthly troop notices. Had supper soon after 11.0.

Monday 25 December Up at 9.0 and went along to Leicester Square station to meet Lilian at 10.30 to go along to the service at St Martins in the Fields as she suggested. She turned up late as usual. Just got into balcony. Place crowded. Poor service I thought and a feeble sermon. Got very bored. Lilian could at least practice her singing, I just had to listen to all the tripe. On coming out walked along the Mall, through St James's Park and into Park Lane and along Oxford St. Got bus to Highgate and saw her home. As we had seen Father out with [Lilian's brother] Vic, I was asked in to have some port. Met Mother, a simple old soul. Looks run down and as if she has suffered a bit in her time. Stayed almost half an hour and came away with an armful of books, borrowed a box of magazines to take home. Home to lunch at 2.0. Went up to Cemetery with Mother in afternoon. On getting home wrote out envelopes for monthly notices, stamped them and inserted notices. For rest of evening wrote up minutes of RM Council and a preface to new log book. Supper at 11.15. After a short read, went to bed at 1.0.

Tuesday 26 December After Mother had gone off to work in afternoon felt very depressed and gloomy. Wrote a retrospect of 1933 for insert at end of this year's diary. A very despondent piece of writing, took me over two hours. A futile piece of work really for it made me more gloomy still if anything. The whole trouble was, let's face it, I hunger for Lilian. I haven't been able to get her out of my mind these past few days. Will probably feel better on resuming the normal routine of things.

Sunday 31 December Northampton Poly Ramble Coach from King's Cross to Newlands Corner. A full crowd. Lilian came along. Carried her things in my rucksack. We spent most of the day together, not mixing much with the rest of the crowd. Bill and John but not Gilbert. Had a fairly good ramble. After drinks in the pub we got the bus back. King's Cross at 9.30. Saw Lilian off on tram and walked home, enjoyed the day considerably. Lilian was most affectionate and we had quite a heart to heart talk coming home on the coach. A girl in a million, that. After changing and having some supper went along to the Cosmopolitan Club as Mother asked me to see the New Year in. A stuffy and noisy place, a crowd dancing. Stayed half an hour and then came home again. Went to bed at 1.15.

RETROSPECT – 1933

A year characterised by both intense sorrow and great joy. The tragic end of Dad and the advent of Lilian – those for me were the outstanding events of 1933. The mental anguish Mother and I endured during the early part of March, consequent to poor Dad's suicide is too painful to recall. Both the sudden shock of the death itself and all the events immediately subsequent to it were terrible blows to us. But we had the satisfaction of knowing that he died nobly and friendly disposed towards us. Gradually we have recovered from the bitter tragedy and time has helped to heal our sorrows, though much less so for Mother than me. I must confess that I overcame my remorse with surprising rapidity. Even at the time I was never able to give outward manifestation to my feelings in the form of weeping. Not so Mother however. Frequently since she has had lengthy bouts of depression at the remembrance of Dad. I don't suppose she ever will quite recover from it. Not that I don't feel any the less sorrow at the recollection of Dad. But I just don't let myself think about it.

It occurs to me that this is a striking characteristic which I have unconsciously developed. I have realised that the more you think about life, the less bearable it becomes. Therefore I don't think about it too much and I try to avoid worrying about unpleasant things. But I can't help worrying about pleasant things. Such as when I fall in love. And I must confess to falling in love again. That brings me to Lilian. Ever since I first met Lilian on that enchanted Whit Monday down at Ridgeway Farm last June, my affection for her has grown increasingly deeper and sincere. I have made a pretty good effort to keep sane and sensible about her, according to my pre-conceived hedonist notions, and until recently I have succeeded fairly well. But lately I have begun to worry – the inevitable fate of every young man of very modest means deeply in love. What's it going to lead to? What exactly is her attitude to me? The uncertainty and insecurity of my present position and future prospects. These are typical thoughts which now pester my hitherto carefree mind. Maybe it's only a temporary phase. Perhaps my ability to dismiss worrying thoughts from my mind will triumph. Anything may happen. All the same a stiff will must endure, and she's a few years older than me.

As far as I've been able to judge from over seven months friendship, we are perfectly suited to one another in every respect. She appeals to me strongly, both mentally and physically. Our meetings have mostly taken the form of theatre visits, odd evenings at the Northampton Poly and the occasional walk. The time I have spent in her company has given me intense delight and I have always looked forward eagerly to my next meeting with her. Though I could never have credited it as often as not I now feel lonely and ill at ease when I go to the theatre on my own. That gives some idea of the effect she has had on me – I begin to feel troubled by loneliness. It has cost money of course, and I have little of that to spare. But it has been well worth it – far more so than ever my friendship with Beatrice was. This is the real thing. If I had plenty of money I should probably be impetuous and ask her to marry me, thereby refuting all my former resolutions to the contrary.

As it is, I haven't and must just contemplate the great obstacles of money, parents and uncertainty, both economic and emotional. Oh hell! What a life! Just feel the indescribable joy of being in love and suffer the accompanying worry and doubt – that is all I can do for the time being. Just to let fate take its playful course.

I seem to have written about all this at far greater length than I thought I could or would. Perhaps in a week or a month or a year I shall consider I have written the most sloppy and pitiful tripe herein. Perhaps to the impartial mind it is. But it is a true and sincere statement of my present feelings on the matter. That is what I am trying to set down. It is now time to leave this unduly melancholy musing on that troublesome emotion called love and get back to a resume of 1933 which is what this is supposed to be. I have also met Bill and formed a friendship with him. Not the type of fellow I usually take to. He is coarse and vulgar by temperament yet he has an air of bravado and forthright good humour about him which strongly appeals to me. He has a forceful personality for all his shortcomings and is really a modern mountebank. A rarity really. Provided you meet him on his own ground, I cannot imagine a more pleasant companion than Bill – in the male line. He has however helped me to develop a taste for beer and other intoxicating drinks. I don't think it will do me much harm. I have neither the inclination nor the money to make it a habit [*correcting* 'to carry it to excess']. But a slightly excessive amount occasionally goes a long way to putting one in a desirably merry mood. My enthusiasm for the theatre is as great as ever, having been over seventy times this year. I also formed a determination to become a dramatic critic by hook or crook and did make some efforts in that direction. Then it lapsed for a while. Then it recovered. So it goes on. It has happened like that before. But this year I have realised that I am more suited to journalism than business. Indeed for the latter I have lost all genuine interest. How I wish I had gone in for journalism at the start. I have been on the wrong track all the time.

In April I became an A.C.I.S. and have since made some unsuccessful attempts at getting another job. Not that I am really keen about it as I used to be. My situation in this direction has become very much diminished. I don't really know what to do or what I want. Here again that awful feeling of doubt and uncertainty creeps in. My position in

1933

business has not improved in the slightest degree. I have had no rise this year and prospects are no better. Something must happen soon. I am getting on in age, and, as I also remarked before, Youth's a stuff, will not endure. I am making no progress in any direction even gaining no valuable experience whatsoever. The older I get the more difficult it will become to try for anything else. What is going to happen? I have certainly in the latter part of the year made an attempt at some freelance journalism. I have written five articles. None published but I have hope for the future and mean to persevere at it. Perhaps something will come of it.

Still, it is no use meeting trouble half way. These gloomy thoughts serve no useful purpose and waste time in writing them; [rather I should] look forward to the future with hope and optimism again.

Life, besides being a great comedy, is too short to worry about. So let us enjoy it while we have the opportunity. A little more money and better prospects would certainly make it easier to enjoy but the vast majority of people might well say that. We must make the most of what we have.

Once more, to get back to the point, what else occurred last year? I became Holborn Rovers Secretary, a position which conveniently fell vacant just when I wondered just what I could do when my patrol inevitably failed. Otherwise I should most likely have joined the Fascists. I have developed the most fervent enthusiasm for Fascism in the past year and consider it to be the one hope for the future as a cure for world and international depression. I have saved scarcely any money. All I can put by goes on capital expenditure i.e. clothes, fees etc. It is as much as I can do to pay my way and have little over for pleasure and entertainment. I have read a great deal and some good books too. I have joined the Northampton Poly Rambling Club and thereby enlarged my circle of acquaintances and kept up my interest in rambling, which has ceased to be connected with Rovering to all intents and purposes. That incidentally is another characteristic of mine this year. I have got to know many more people and I think, become more sociable. That is about all of any consequence that happened in 1933, which I can think of offhand. I am not going to make any resolutions for 1934 for I know I shouldn't keep them if I do. I am going to try and do certain things, but I will not write them down. I will just try and do them.

It has taken me over two hours to write all this and I don't feel at all satisfied with the result. I have a vague irritating sort of feeling that it has been a waste of time, and that in expressing depressing thoughts at great length, I have only encouraged further depressing thoughts. Probably the only good effect has been the practice I have obtained in expressing my thoughts in writing. This time next week I may feel and think even more differently. I am merely setting down a passing phase, I hope so anyway. If not it will indicate that I am losing my sense of

Part One

humour. When I lose that I shall have real cause for despair. Likewise my perfect health. Good health and a sense of humour may they never desert me. There has not been much trace of the 'great joy' hinted at in my opening sentence in these lines. But it has existed all the same and on this cheerful note I will finish.

Thank God I met Lilian. She has given life a new beauty for me and enriched it beyond words.

So enter 1934.

1934

Heap 'began the year with a hopeless infatuation for Lilian' and, in mid-January, he broached the subject of marriage. This was not accepted and, although the relationship continued for some months, it cooled and 'lapsed towards the autumn months after some 15 months'. Although his former girlfriend Beatrice occasionally appeared at social events, Heap now considered himself 'carefree and untrammelled' and determined to live a bachelor life. In the interests of economy, he spent more weekends at home with his mother, whose irregular employment and bouts of stomach trouble (probably the symptoms of cancer) put her in hospital for some weeks. Heap learned to look after himself but, disheartened by the landlord and his bug-infested rooms in Penryn St, he and his mother moved in May to more expensive rooms looking over the green of Harrington Square to the art deco Carreras Cigarette Factory on Hampstead Road.

By writing a winning letter to the London Evening News *explaining 'Why I like the Blackshirts', Heap won tickets and took his mother to the famous – or rather notorious but well-recorded – June rally at Olympia addressed by Sir Oswald Mosley. Heap's theatre- and cinema-going and his reading intensified over the next two years as his interest in Rover Scouting continued to wane. Only 34% of his daily entries are reproduced here, the whole a mere 26% of his original 45,268 words written through the year.*

Monday 1 January [*After seeing in the New Year at the Cosmopolitan Club*] Walked home, dined and finished article (650 words complete). Had a short read after then went to bed. Rather foggy. Felt rather tired after tramping all day yesterday and going to bed at 1.30 and in none too good spirits. Trouble is I began the New Year by suddenly realising I'm deeply in love, and that emotion tends to make for blues as well bliss. Anyway it did so today. 'Sic transit gloria.'[1]

Wednesday 3 January Had to go down to the Cashiers this afternoon and count out money to pay maintenance staff wages tomorrow. After work took Harry along to YM, dashed home to change into uniform, came back at 7.0 and took him down to restaurant. Afterwards waited for Lilian to arrive at 8.15 and went round to Rover Social in Howard

---

1   'Thus passes the glory.'

Room. A riotous evening's fun got up by Ralph [Reader]. All sorts of games and comic stunts. Large crowd there. Refreshments in Reception Room at 9.15. Afterwards got let in for very embarrassing game. Involved being gradually made to undress till I had only my shorts on. Damned nuisance having dirty vest on. Shouldn't have been so keen on offering to go out with a few others while the game was disclosed. After that was dressed up in newspaper to resemble a Scotchman. All the best of fun however. Finished up with songs round the piano and at 11.0 went home. Think L enjoyed it, except for the rough and tumble and not knowing the songs sung. [Lilian] looked beautiful in a charming blue frock. I get more infatuated with her every time. She's adorable. Home by tube after leaving Harry on platform. To bed at 12.15.

Tuesday 9 January Wrote after a job in the *Telegraph* this afternoon. First time I have done that for a long time.

Wednesday 10 January Very slack in office so wrote an article on 'The Theatre Queue Racket' – 700 words long. Mother came to see me lunchtime and told me about a new job offered her. Went over the road and had a drink together.

Thursday 11 January Went along to the YM to meet Lilian and go onto King George's Hall to see first night performance of *Puss in Boots*, this year's RH Panto. Was very disappointed and annoyed in interval when Lilian told me she couldn't come to beano on Sat. owing to more attractive engagement with some fellow down from Hull for week, going to mess up our sketch as well. Still, I don't blame her. Very disappointing but can't be helped. Must make the best of it.

Monday 15 January Wrote in reply to advert in *Telegraph* today. Office job offered requiring £50 investment. Then thought better of it and tore it up. Can't afford to risk two thirds of my worldly fortune.

Tuesday 16 January Mother told me at breakfast about a snack bar on New Oxford St for sale very cheap. Thought we might take it on between us. Good idea, a risk but worth it. Went along to see it at lunchtime. A small but well-appointed place. To discuss it with agents on Thursday. Met Lilian at 8.20 and went over to Corner House, having run out of theatres for the moment. Talked a great deal about future. Confessed my love towards her and expressed the hope that I could afford to offer her marriage in the near future. Took her rather by surprise, learned two surprising things about her (a) That she is 30, thought she was 26 or 27. (b) That she has over £500. She protested the difference in age between us but I think that is only a pretext to hide her indecision. Anyway just left her to consider the possibility. Must just try and make money and hope for the best. It's all very difficult.

Walked home and looked at snack bar (Incidentally she encouraged me in my idea of starting in this line and offered to lend me £25!) and then walked along to Mornington Crescent under her umbrella. Saw her into tube than walked home. To bed 1.0. Won't get much sleep tonight I can see.

Thursday 18 January After work met Mother and went up to see Sumnuiks, the property agent, about that snack bar in New Oxford St we think of taking. Looked over the shop again and discussed expenses in office. Left decision over till tomorrow evening.

Friday 19 January Up to Holborn for a haircut then along to meet Mother about snack bar proposition. Decided to abandon the idea. Expense too heavy, too great a risk on such little capital. Not sorry really. Some anxiety off my mind anyway.

Saturday 20 January Went up to Northampton Poly in afternoon for Rambling Club AGM. Back to KGH [King George's Hall] for last night of Panto. Sat with Claude and friend in third row from back. All went out in interval and had a few more drinks taking Fatty Baines with us as well. And slipped out for a couple near the end of show. So Bill and I got more demonstrative as the evening went on. At the 'prize giving' at the end we were about the only people keeping up continuous applause. Then went round to the stage door and waited for the cast to come out – Bunny and Trixie (laden with gifts). On coming out a crowd of us walked up to Marble Arch and went in new all night Corner House. Trixie kept with me most of the time and seemed to pay a certain amount of affection towards me which, I must confess, I found very agreeable. On leaving at 2.30 walked up Edgware Rd to St Johns Wood where Bill and Laurence Nelson and myself turned off eastwards. Very tiring. Got in just before 4.0 and went straight to bed. What an evening!

Sunday 28 January Northampton Poly hike in Chilterns. Coach was just leaving at 10.15 when Lilian rushed up just in time. A near thing. So she sat with me in front. Started walking from West Wycombe, lots of mud, lunch at The Plough Inn. [*page of walk itinerary*] Lilian very affectionate in coach on way home. Charming. King's Cross 10.0. Saw Lilian off on train and walked home, very tired.

Tuesday 30 January Roland House Panto Ball at Grosvenor Hall. Harry came home with me to change into evening kit. Mother left dinner for us and a bottle of port. Got there about 8.15.

Went straight into bar for drinks. After half an hour or so went up to ballroom. A fair number there, not many I know though. A stiff and starchy crowd. Dull, so went out and found a pub at end of street. Better than G H bar where no draught bitter which I prefer. On getting back things much better. The more interesting and brighter people arrived in the meantime. Had a couple of dances, went up to pub again with Harry and Fatty. Was rather tight by this time. Ralph there tight also, wearing DB [double-breasted] dinner jacket and turn down collar, American style. Introduced Bill to him. A lot of drunken talk and joshing. Very funny and merry. Up to ballroom. Dances, one with Trixie, very cold and dull a companion. Not enough to drink apparently. Home at 12.50. Thick head but not aching. A good evening.

Friday 2 February Two disconcerting ailments today. A nasty boil coming up at back of neck. First one for two and a half years. May be due to alcoholic excess Tuesday and constipation since. Also a couple of small hard swellings made penis slightly painful to press. No idea what this can be. Must go to doctor's if they don't go down in a few days.

Sunday 4 February Dull morning but no rain. Very cold. To Highgate with Nigger to meet Lilian. Came along ten minutes with [her brother] Vic. Usual walk over Hampstead to Jack Straw's Castle for drinks. Had to stand three drinks 1/10½. An annoying and needless expense. But can't be helped. Must fall in with these social customs. Walked back again to Hampstead Ponds and had three more drinks i.e. one each at top of Highgate Hill. Made us slightly late. Tram down to Holloway Rd. Left L & V near here and walked down to Nag's Head. Two glasses of beer blunts edge of appetite, coincidently felt drowsy and blown out in afternoon.

Monday 5 February To Mudie's lunchtime. Got Vernon Bartlett's *Nazi Germany Explained*.[2] Started reading it at tea and found it exceedingly interesting and well written. The man has an explicit style and a sense of the dramatic in international politics.

Wednesday 7 February Paper full of Paris riots today. Mob rebels against corrupt government. Police and Army fire on them. Many deaths and injuries. Would love to be over there. The French have such a perfect sense of the dramatic in public life and express themselves with picturesque force.[3] Afraid my Rovering days are nearing an end. Used to get a minor thrill out of troop meetings. Now they bore me desperately, I'm getting past it. Will probably leave and throw in my lot with the Fascists soon.

Saturday 10 February Peculiar weather. Rather dull. Also faint missling [*sic*] rain at time. Hampstead with Nigger [then] home for tea. Changed into evening kit. Bus down to Strand station to meet Lilian. Called for two drinks at Horse Shoe on way. Bus round to Victoria St for Horticultural Hall, Vincent Sq. London Rover Ball. L came up

2   See entry for 7 August 1931, n. 28.
3   Communist and other 'anti-Fascist' riots caused the government of Édouard Daladier to resign. A new 'Government of Truce' was formed by Gaston Doumergue next day.

1934

beautifully dressed in blue. Had a dance or two. Went out for a couple more drinks with Wiffles after much searching for a pub. Another dance or two. Harry and Vic arrived late about 9.0. Went out to pub again with them. Three more drinks and a cigar. Was rather tight on getting back. Made rather an ass of myself and I'm afraid annoyed Lilian. Justifiably so I must confess for I was certainly very neglectful and inconsiderate towards her. Didn't dance much latter part of evening. Just fooled about with Harry. Over 11.30. Party of us went up to Oxford Corner House. Talk and general atmosphere rather restrained at times. Out at 12.50. Three of us tried to get on 29 bus. L and I got on top, Vic left off as conductor had said full up. Actually six or seven empty seats on top. A minor catastrophe as he had key and L would have to knock up people at home which she didn't relish. However it was no use my going up there and not being able to get back so I got off at M Cres. and came home. To bed 3.0. A rather unfortunate evening altogether.

Sunday 11 February Had tea and read papers and book. Washed up some things. Wrote a letter to Lilian apologising for last night. Wrote up troop log book and then diary.

Tuesday 13 February Phoned Lilian this morning. Found her in an agreeable and conciliatory mood much to my relief and arranged to take her to theatre on Thursday.

Wednesday 14 February Made a list of Dad's dental books and one or two others we thought of trying to sell. Don't think there's much hope of doing so. They're all out of date.

Thursday 15 February On getting home found Sick Notice from hospital saying Gran is on danger list. Mother coming in shortly after much perturbed by it went out immediately to hospital to try and see her. Fears Gran may die any minute. Ought to have gone with her I suppose. Instead went to bed at 10.30. Will I sleep? I wonder.

Saturday 17 February Lambeth Hospital in afternoon to see Gran. Had lunch at Lyons at Westminster. Gran not so bad, could talk all right. Stayed half an hour. [To His Majesty's.] Second night of *Conversation Piece*, Noel Coward's new play,[4] Cochran's production of course. Disappointed with it.

Sunday 18 February Northampton Poly Ramble. Coach full except for three not turning up. Harry came as a visitor getting on at Tooting. Lilian and Vic came. Went down to Hog's Back district in Surrey. [*half-page of itinerary*] Walked with L. But at lunch got damnably annoyed with a fellow named Frank Storey who would persist in taking trivial liberties with L. Thought it put me in a slightly ridiculous

---

4 (Sir) Noel Coward (1899–1973), extremely successful, witty and polished theatre playwright, composer, singer, director, film actor and cabaret performer; knighted in 1969.

position. Consequently put my back up all afternoon and I was slightly reserved towards L and a trifle unpleasant to others. Tea was almost equally unpleasant and hardly a word spoken between L and I walking back to coach after. However we sat together coming home and cordial relations were more or less restored. Don't really know whether she had been upset or not by my attitude and whether she had even noticed anything amiss. A silly petty thing to worry about really and probably arising from quite unintentional motives of good humour. But there you are. It's little things like that which irritate me. Can't help it. Spoilt the day (rather a sombre one in any case). But mustn't let my sense of humour fail again like that. It's absurd. Let's forget it.

Thursday 22 February Mother had two complimentary stalls for first night at the Alhambra tonight given her yesterday. Passed them on to me. Phoned up L asking her to come. Said she wasn't sure. Someone else had asked her to go out this evening. A doubt though. Asked me to phone up later. Dejection! Phoned up just before 6.0, she could come. Raptures of delight! (well perhaps not quite but something along that line). *Julius Caesar* – disappointing production.

Wednesday 28 February Caught in heavy snowfall going to work. Got rather wet. Snow did not lay. Home to dinner by bus. Took L to the Saville. *Here's How*, a new musical comedy. Damned fine show I thought. A most tasteful and clever production and extraordinary good dancing. George Robey at the top of his form.[5] [*page of criticism*] I thoroughly enjoyed it.

Friday 2 March Went along to *Great Days*, Ralph's troop show at the Christchurch Hall, Herbrand St. Round to the pub again during interval and got fairly tight. Stayed till after closing time and went back to the hall at 10.15. Saw Ralph and others after and went round to Bogey's Bar with Bill and the fellows. Coming out wanted to make water badly so had to rush round to Tavistock Sq and use railings. Walked home with Claude.

Sunday 4 March Lunch 2.30. Saw Gran in afternoon. Much better after her recent relapse. Walked back. Came by Trafalgar Sq. Hunger marchers demonstration there. Red banners, large crowds, cohorts of mounted police but no disorder. All very orderly and futile. Impresses some.[6]

Wednesday 7 March Mother at home for evening. Had learned that furniture of 139 sold by auction last November without her hearing of it. Very upset about it. At 7.45 walked along to back of British Museum

5 (Sir) George Robey (1869–1954), English comedian and musical hall performer.
6 The Prime Minister, Ramsay MacDonald, had claimed earlier in the year that 'the hunger march from the provinces was arranged for "purely political purposes"' (*The Times*, 24 January 1934).

to find first clue of Treasure Hunt which constitutes this month's troop meeting. Found it in syrup tin. [*Other clues followed up*], skipping the next two clues. Sicilian Avenue and Dickens House – next along to finishing place – a coffee stall opposite Rowton House.[7] No one else there so walked home. Very tired after three hours continuous walking.

Thursday 8 March LCC Elections today. Went round with Mother to vote before going to work in morning. Election scenes last night – bands of kids marching round streets banging tin cans, singing a song, carrying Labour bills. Three people round on Liberal platform – blaring, the MR candidates talking through loudspeaker from van at next street corner.[8] Hecklers no chance against that. Mother been out all day canvassing for election, comes in to get dinner ready, goes out again after.

Tuesday 13 March 24th Birthday. Wretched day too. No cards or presents, not yet anyway, apart from clothes. Went along at lunchtime and ordered a new suit. Special offer of suits at 55/- owing to purchase of stock of woollen ones going out of business at large discount. Chose a dark grey worsted. Bed at 11.0. Birthdays aren't what they were. Haven't had a reasonably decent one since my 21st.

Wednesday 14 March More rain. Pelting on way home. Had to go by bus. Went along to Queen Mary's Hall, YWCA. Debate on 'Propaganda in the Theatre' under the auspices of the Left Theatre, an organisation to promote bolshie [Bolshevik] propaganda through the medium of the theatre. Full of half-baked neurotic fantastic looking pseudo-intellectuals. Middle class hypocrites who attempted to justify the existence of pamphlets about the 'working class' of which they knew nothing. Motion ably proposed by Herbert Griffith. But St John Ervine[9] in opposing it gave them more than they bargained for. Told them the truth about their stupid ideas but in a thoroughly witty discerning good-natured [way]. Motion carried of course.

Friday 16 March A new paper called the *Clarion* out today.[10] Bought a copy. Mostly bolshie propaganda and pretty dull at that. Piffle. Threw it away.

---

7 Rowton House, 1 King's Cross Road, WC1, a hostel for working men. Now refurbished as the King's Cross Holiday Inn.
8 The Municipal Reform (Conservative) Party held both St Pancras South East and South West but the Labour Party – led by Herbert Morrison – took control of the LCC with 80 councillors and aldermen to the 64 of the Conservatives. Labour retained control of the LCC until its replacement by the larger Greater London Council in 1965.
9 St John Ervine (1883–1971), Ulster-born author, writer, critic and dramatist; biographer of Carson and Shaw and one-time director of the Abbey Theatre; became increasingly anti-(Irish) nationalist and pro-Unionist.
10 *The Clarion* was founded in 1891 as a socialist newspaper. With similar socialist aims, *The New Clarion* was launched in 1932. This was presumably yet another relaunch.

Part One

Saturday 17 March An unexpectedly fine day. Numerous sporting dashes – Boat Race – Cup semi-finals. England v Scotland rugger match,[11] Sandown Races, oh, everything. Cambridge wins boat race again by 4½ lengths in record time for 11th time in succession. An earthquake may safely be prognosticated for the year Oxford wins again! Went along to Piccadilly Circus after. Riotous scenes. Got in numerous rough houses though could not enjoy them to the full for fear of getting spectacles in pocket broken or toe caps of shoes bashed in as I have done hitherto. Did not fare too well in this respect this time either. At 12.30 retreat from this fray while still raging and walked home, buses being full. Supper and to bed 2.0.

Wednesday 21 March On getting home in evening found Mother in. Had lost her job again. Unfortunate of course but can't be helped. No need for undue worry I don't think. And she certainly doesn't appear to indicate it.

Monday 26 March On getting home found Mother just off to work. Had got back her job at the [Cosmopolitan] Club. Very gratifying news. After dinner (eggs and bacon and apple pies), washed up and settled down to cut stencil for monthly troop notices on typewriter for rest of evening.

Tuesday 27 March As usual lately, a fine day after a dull opening. Got a rise of 5/- a week today. Most of office did. Also I can do with it too. May be able to save a bit now.

Friday 30 March Started out on Easter tramp with Harry in Berks, Bucks and Oxon. staying overnight at youth hostels. 9.42 coach from Oxford Circus to High Wycombe. Left gloves on bus but retrieved them at coach station.

[*Easter weekend walking in the Chilterns*]

Monday 2 April A poor night's sleep. Had an uncomfortable bed shared by Harry. Shared a cold water shower, packed and went over to hostel for breakfast. Afterwards cleared bowels for first time since Friday morning. Left at 10.0 and walked towards Penn via Forty Green to High Wycombe. Just had time for some tea in Lyons before getting 6.0 bus back to London. Great scrum to get on it, there being no queue but got on the auxiliary run with the Green Line coach alright. Oxford Circus 8.42. To bed at 11.30 after pricking blisters.

Thursday 5 April After a good night's sleep felt quite fit again today except for slight diarrhoea, appetite regained. I went over to the Old Vic with Harry in evening. Found Lilian in queue on arriving. Both

---

11 England beat Scotland 6–3 at Twickenham.

greatly surprised. Totally unexpected call that. However it didn't make any difference. Saw *Macbeth*.

Wednesday 11 April Went along to Drury Lane from work to meet Lilian. Waited quarter of an hour. No sign of her. She came along about 7.25 having had to work late at office. Still, we got in all right seats on left corner of gallery. Saw *Three Sisters*, the latest spectacular musical comedy by Oscar Hammerstein and Jerome Kern. [*page of criticism*] A show, in brief, that moves the mark.

Thursday 12 April Electric light being installed at home. Workmen in yesterday and today. Not finished yet. Went along to see Adam in evening. Took back magazine he lent me to write to editor for short story he had translated. Spent evening talking about all sorts of things including politics. Gave me coffee, not much to my taste I must confess but acceptable as a gesture of hospitality. Very hot and stuffy in his small study. Stove full on and no window open. Poor Adam was slightly depressed. Black outlook abroad. His [Hungarian] paper might go bust or he lose his job. Told me journalism not worth worrying about if you can help it. Maybe he's right.

Saturday 14 April Very mild, cloudy sort of day. London invaded by Scotsmen down for England v Scotland soccer match.[12] Met Lilian 1.15 and gave her library book she wanted to borrow. Then home by tube. Stayed in afternoon then as weather seemed doubtful and listened in to wireless which Mother had fixed up in morning. Electric light installation completed. Walked along Coventry St. Streets swarming with Scotsmen, mostly drunk. Went in fun fair off Coventry St. Witnessed a lively rough house in there. A free fight between toughs and uniformed janitor stopped by public. Very good fun. Bugs about again in bedroom.

Monday 16 April Asked JD for time off on Wednesday this afternoon. Said he was glad to hear I was still in the scout movement. Charming. A bad night last night. Not much sleep. Bugs staged a big 'come back'. Had to get up and change rooms. Then mouse obliged with further distinction. Hope for better conditions tonight.

Tuesday 17 April Dined, washed up and went up to our local cinema at Mornington Crescent.[13] Quite good seat for 1/-. A bit of a bug hutch (though apparently not such a one as my bedroom). First time I've been in there.

Wednesday 18 April Cool and showery. Took uniform in case and left it at YM on way to work. Got off at 5.30 and went off to the Albert

---

12 At Wembley, England beat Scotland by three goals to nil.
13 The Camden Hippodrome, 1a Camden High Street, NW1. Now a music club venue and Grade II listed.

Part One

Hall to attend the big scout display. No need to have got there so early as nothing to do till 7.30 and precious little then. Stewarding badly organised. Posted myself with four others in a gangway of the arena. Showed a few people to seats thus assisting the venerable old gentlemen in pre-historic dress clothes directing people at the entrance. A charming old man, big white beard, looked like a benevolent and less saturnine Bernard Shaw. Ralph to show other people to box and to entrance. Full house, a few people in evening clothes. When display started at 8.0 went down and sat with other stewards in vacant seats in third row. Most efficient yet scarcely interesting. Not to me anyway. So left at 9.30.

Thursday 19 April Straight home to dinner. Bedrooms being fumigated today to get rid of bugs. Door sealed up. Can only use front room. Will have to sleep in there tonight.

Friday 20 April On getting up this morning went in to where sulphur gas had been [used] to fumigate room. A most strong and foul stench immediately assailed me. My clothes which had been left in the wardrobe all reeked of it which annoyed me like hell all day. Clothes in drawer affected in like manner. Wonder if the smell will wear off them at all. It had not by the time I got home in the evening. Bedroom unfit to sleep in for time being. That shocking smell still prevalent and walls in an awful state again after last night. Will have to be distempered and papered again and front room may have to go through the same process, and hell, I'm sick of the whole business. The havoc a few bugs can cause!

Saturday 21 April Mother told me this morning [of trouble] with the landlord over Nigger and dilapidations caused by fumigating. Decided that we had to move very soon and look around for somewhere else. A great worry. Seem to be continually moving, though won't really be sorry to leave Penryn St provided we can get somewhere suitable and reasonably cheap. Decided to give the theatre a miss this week. Been overdoing it a bit lately and nothing I particularly want to see for the moment.

Monday 23 April Big Fascist meeting at Albert Hall last night. Much prominence given it in *Daily Mail* and *Evening News* today.[14] Would I had gone to it. After work called at YM for Cherub's typewriter and took back home. Dined and washed up. Cut stencil on typewriter for monthly troop notices and duplicated about 40 copies.

14   Lord Rothermere, the proprietor of both papers, was a Mosley supporter. *The Times* (23 May) reported that he spoke uninterrupted for 90 minutes, claiming that 'The Blackshirts had done something in less than two years to light a flame. The way to avoid excesses was for the people to adopt Fascism. The proceedings were ended with the singing of the Fascist anthem and the National Anthem.'

1934

Friday 27 April We've found a new flat at last. On calling at YM, found note from Mother telling me to call at 20 Harrington Square to see 3rd (top) floor flat. So went along there and saw it. Very pleased with it. 2 large rooms and use of bathroom on ground floor. Gas but [wire] can be run up from electric downstairs for radio. Splendid outlook both sides and first rate position. A good class house in a good class square. Had wanted 20/- for it but Mother had got it for 18/- a week. A brief chat with Mrs Soleby[15] the landlady. An optician's widow. Fat and very pleasant and genial. Fond of fresh air. No objection to dog. Told me about last occupant of flat – a young journalist with wayward but likeable habits, who had left to get married, foolish fellow. Paid £1 deposit, said we should probably move in at the end of next week and came home feeling very pleased with things.

Monday 30 April After work went along to Straker's[16] and ordered some visiting cards with our new address and then on round to YM for dinner. Then on to Mrs Zelger's in Gray's Inn Rd to collect two suitcases she is holding for us for moving stuff to our new flat. On getting home got busy filling them with ornaments, china, photo frames, a few books and papers and the odds and ends and walked them round to Harrington Sq. With two cases full twice, dumping the stuff in a cupboard round there. The first time not so bad but the second relay was almost beyond a joke as regards weight. I simply staggered along with them, stopping about ten times as my wrists feeling the strain badly. But got there alright and unpacked the stuff in the dark. Took pictures down and did a little more packing before going to bed at 11.45, fagged out.

Tuesday 1 May Sensation at Opera last night, Sir Thomas Beecham rebuked audience and told them to stop talking. Papers full of it today.[17] Had some amusement about it at office. Something to be said for both sides. After a dull cold morning turned very fine and warm in afternoon just like yesterday. Far too warm for overcoat and moving home. After dinner filled two suitcases and went up to Harrington Square. Mother had laid down lino during day. Put spare paper under it and shoved books, papers and theatre programmes and other stuff I had brought up in cupboard. Then while Mother went back, I took bus up to YM, NW Area Rover Mates Conference in Drawing Room. Think I have strained myself a bit carrying those suit cases full up to top of the Sq. Nothing serious though.

Thursday 3 May Everything packed up ready for moving tomorrow morning. Sat and ate fish out of paper as table not being available

---

15 This is the spelling in the diary but the St Pancras electoral register gives Gladys Soleberg.
16 Straker's, stationers, 49–55 Ludgate Hill, EC2.
17 At Covent Garden the season opened with *Fidelio*. *The Times* (1 May) commented that the 'exasperated conductor had to shout "stop talking" while the overture was in progress'.

Part One

and Nigger finished it off. Then took wireless set up to Harrington, was detained for at least ten minutes talking to Mrs Soleby, or rather she talked to me and how that woman can talk! Then went up to the Dominion. Home by bus and after packing away my final odds and ends to bed at 1.0 for the last time in Penryn St. From tomorrow our abode will be 20 Harrington Square. May it be a happier and more permanent sojourn.

Friday 4 May Got up a little earlier to do final packing and left Mother at it when I went to work at 8.20. Carriers to call at 10.0. Home at 8.45 i.e. Harrington Square. Things have been moved in quite alright and laid out and arranged in fairly good order. Nigger very excited to see it. Spent the rest of evening unpacking suits etc. hanging them in wardrobe. Had got rather creased through faulty folding. No time for much else. Went to bed at 11.30 feeling dog tired.

Saturday 5 May Spent afternoon sorting out books papers and various miscellaneous junk and filling cupboard therewith. Then went round and paid final rent payment to Elliott,[18] got laundry etc and came back and had tea.

Monday 7 May Find that it takes me 49 minutes to walk to and from work which is 6 minutes less than Penryn St and about the same time as it used to take from Gray's Inn Rd.

Thursday 10 May After going home to dinner went up to Sadler's Wells in evening with Lilian. Special extension season after Shakespeare open season.

Tuesday 15 May Phoned up Trixie this afternoon about that dance I promised to take her to while under the influence of alcohol.[19] She said she didn't think it right to go out with a fellow she didn't care tuppence for, which suited me as it will save me money and I shall probably have a much better time. I admire her frankness if not her style. So that's off. Finished varnishing edge of floor in my bedroom. Washed up.

Wednesday 16 May Struck on a couple of ideas for articles today. Hope to write them in near future. On getting home found Nigger sitting on pavement outside. Mrs Soleby, on step talking. Said he'd been out since 10.0 and wouldn't come in despite everyone's efforts to induce him to enter. Of course, came in excitedly when I came home. Rather odd.

Saturday 19 May Whitsun and Ridgeway Farm. Weather so so. Dull and cloudy but no rain. Consistently so over whole holiday. After dashing home to lunch and change, met Bill at Oxford Circus at 2.10

18   Their Penryn St landlord.
19   Possibly back on 30 January.

and caught coach to Guildford, thence bus to Thursley. Made a nice merry little party. All went up to the Huts at Hindhead for the evening, but not to sleep for a rough house developed from my playfully pulling the covers from under the double bed. Blankets, pillows, boots, rug, anything and everything was used until eventually our high spirits were exhausted. Settled down for the night but slept badly. Only about two hours sleep altogether.

Monday 21 May Frank up to his usual audacious flirting again regardless of swains who as it happened were not nearly so high spirited as the girls. One of them really beautiful. I could scarcely keep my eyes off her. And I caught a sly glance or two in return. Oh that she had not been accompanied. But you never know. Frank got the other's phone number and there is a possibility of their coming on Poly ramble next Sunday. So there's hope still. Bid farewell to our two girlfriends of the weekend and the four of us adjourned to a pub for final drinks and game of darts. But one game led to several and one round of drinks to many more as well as those accruing from games of darts. So by the time we had finished with a committee meeting as to future plans and arrangements we did not emerge till 9.35 all pretty well sozzled. Queued up for Green Line Bus. Long queue, had to wait an hour. Gilbert left to go by train. Bill amused queue a good deal with drunken jests to passers-by. Also passengers on coach. Oxford Circus 11.30. Home 12.15 by now quite sober. Nothing to eat. Bed 1.30.

Thursday 24 May Note from Frank this morning saying the two girls we met on coach last Monday are coming on Poly ramble on Sunday and that he had booked me up and Bill. Decided to go. Gilbert may be the fly in the ointment, but we shall see. After going home to dinner met Lilian at Leicester Square station and went to the Haymarket. Went to Honey Dew cafeteria after for coffee. Last time I shall see her for four weeks as she goes on holiday on June 2.

Friday 25 May Another letter from Frank Storey this evening. Awful writing, difficult to decipher. Apparently those two 'b—' females (Frank's expression) are not coming on Sunday after all. So he's cancelling my booking too. May be more difficult about payment despite cancellation if unable to fill place. Will phone him in morning. Ah, consternation, this game is women, are they really worth the bother they cause? I sincerely doubt it – yet we go on letting them make fools of us. Such is life.

Monday 28 May Almost forget, wrote and posted to *Evening News* before going to bed on 'Why I like the Blackshirts' hoping to get two free tickets for Olympia meeting on June 7.

Tuesday 29 May Straight home to dinner after work. Letter from Lilian giving me two addresses to write to her on her cruise – Lisbon and Casablanca.

Thursday 31 May After dinner and washing up spent rest of evening writing two letters to Lilian to reach her at Lisbon and Casablanca when she gets ashore at these places on her cruise. Wrote rather long letters as I usually do and I think quite good efforts considering the powers of invention that have to be brought into play in writing to someone on a cruise before they've even started on it, for the letters have to be posted before 6.0 on Saturday to get there in time. Absurd, of course, but there you are.

Thursday 7 June After rushing home for a quick dinner, took Mother to Olympia for the big Blackshirt meeting. Had to get out of bus some distance from the place owing to traffic block and red demonstrations outside. Youths distributing anti-fascist propaganda all along curb. Huge crowd trying to get in. Great crush. Managed to get in after twenty minutes or so. Seats in arena i.e. ground floor. Actually 5/- seats I got free from *Evening News* for postcard on 'Why I like the Blackshirts.' About half way back under amplifiers. Meeting began at 8.30, half hour late. Procession of flags down hall. Followed by Sir Oswald Mosley [and] attendants, mounted platform, started speech. Soon interruptions started, about 100 communists had been distributed over parts of hall to make disturbances which they did every few minutes. All gradually got slung out but it spoilt things good deal. One had to be chased off the roof. Towards 10.0 however Sir O.M. managed to get on without further interruption and carried on till 10.50 when the National Anthem closed the meeting. By this time the audience had thinned considerably. Though a triumph for the Blackshirt spirit, I was disappointed from the public's point of view. Reds still outside on coming out. Home by bus and tube. Light supper. Bed 12.50.

Friday 8 June Rather tired today. Press full of last night's riots at Olympia. Mostly exaggerated of course.[20]

Sunday 10 June Upset Mother when I disclosed that I had substituted a *Theatre World* cover portrait in an old picture frame containing an Indian painting of a pot of flowers on rice paper and broken a corner of the wretched thing in doing so. Didn't dream the thing had any value either sentimental or monetary. Not sure now what it is. Women in a peevish temper are so incoherent and vague. Still it didn't affect it much.

---

20   *The Times* of 8 May carried a report, 'Sir O. Mosley at Olympia: Interruptions and Ejections', and a longer column, 'Fascists at Olympia: Sir O. Mosley on a New Order', the latter detailing the leader's speech. There appears to be no conflict between Heap's brief account and the newspaper reports of the event and incidents observed.

Wednesday 13 June A busy lunch hour. Then to Mudie's to change book. Got out *B.U.F. –Oswald Mosley and British Fascism* by James Denman. A study of the modern movement outlining the career of Sir Oswald Moseley and the growth of fascism. Real good stuff.

Saturday 16 June Took Nigger to Regent's Park in afternoon. Ground very parched and dry due to drought. Trees yellowing slightly too. Water shortage may develop if it becomes more acute. Economy strongly advised. Home to tea at 5.15. Washed up after. Read *B.U.F.* book for a couple of hours. A most enlightening exposition of the development of political thought and the failure of social democracy and the triumphal advent of the new dynamic creed of Fascism, outlining in the process the adventurous and noble career of Sir Oswald Mosley. A grand book. Incidentally received membership card and badge from the B.U.F. this evening.

Sunday 24 June After read of papers decided to clean windows. While cleaning my bedroom window it jammed and trying to get it loose again smashed one of the panes of glass, which is just one great big b—y nuisance. The expense and trouble of getting a new pane put in – Oh hell! After a cold lunch, in more senses than one, Mother, already feeling 'run down', considerably upset by incident, went over to Tooting to see Gran in hospital. Had been moved to a first floor ward since I was last there. Seemed quite well and cheerful. Left 4.30.

Friday 29 June Dug out and read through log of Austrian Tyrol Hike four years ago, which I had promised to lend Harry to read. Also relevant snaps. Still makes good reading – that log. I'm sure I could write better then than I can now. And I had the glorious enthusiasm and self-assurance of youth then, before disillusionment and apathy supplanted them. How like a senile cynic I talk or is it still the self-assurance of youth? I don't know. What's it matter anyway?

Saturday 30 June To the office in flannels and sports coat for first time this morning. After rushing home for a quick lunch, to Oxford Circus for 2.20 bus to Guildford for weekend at Ridgeway Farm. Claude, Alec and Trixie came along. Bus Guildford to Thursley. C, A and myself in cottage upstairs, Trixie in railway carriage which she didn't like. Then into the Public Bar to play darts. Beer flowed freely, by the time we came out I was gorgeously drunk. Felt great. Rolled home. Some supper in kitchen. Think I was rather amusing, being obviously tight.

Sunday 1 July After a fairish night got up at 8.0 with a slightly thick head. Shaved, washed and dressed and came over to join others. Trixie came back from church, into breakfast. Margaret had my eggs and bacon which I didn't fancy. Just had roll and marmalade. At 10.30 we went to Frensham Pond for a swim. Gilbert and Frank still in bed when we went [to] Frensham Little Pond at 11.35. Rotten swimming.

Low water owing to drought. Lot of mud and reeds. Sunbathed after on bank. Some ragging and larking about among others in the course of which Trixie had her clothes hidden and hurt her legs by falling out of a bramble bush, got peeved and went off in a huff. I followed to placate her and merely got rudely snubbed for my pain which forced me to assume a somewhat cold attitude towards her for the rest of the day. Always some damned silly trivial nonsense when women are included in a party. Had tea. Frank entertained us by trying his Petruchio [amorous] stuff on Margaret, much to my amusement and the others' disgust. The sort of fellow who would do Trixie good. Left 6.30. Walk to Highfield. 6.50 bus to Guildford thence straight on to Green Line to Oxford Circus 9.30.

Friday 6 July Paper seller in Charing X Rd carefully explained final Test match score as I bought paper.[21] Do I look as if I'm interested in such a topic or does he tell everyone who buys a paper off him the same? An understandable yet strange phenomenon, this test match mania. Cockney wit, poorly dressed cockney sitting on doorstep with a kid in pram, Nigger makes water against pram – 'Alright, it doesn't need oiling.' Rather tickled me.

Saturday 7 July Fine and hot, a pleasant breeze. Regent's Park with Nigger in afternoon. A pleasant snooze under shady tree. Cricket matches including an all-women one. Played pretty well. Good crowd of onlookers. Some applause. Home at 4.45. Teatime dance music continually interrupted by accounts of Test match and tennis. Only about ten minutes dance music altogether. Utterly ridiculous pandering to sport.

Sunday 8 July To Tooting Bec Hospital with Mother in afternoon to see Gran. Sat on bridge-way with her. Stayed nearly an hour. Home at 5.0. Went up to Hyde Park in evening. Speakers at Marble Arch. Bonar Thompson not quite at his best but very good. Smaller crowd than usual too. Apart from BT, usual gang of anti-fascist and red riffraff round 'Charlie' [another orator]. Walk back along Oxford St. Four sideshows (a) Phrenologist – debonair handsome screen villain featured (b) man trying to get out of straight jacket (c) Henry Garrard numerologist, mauve cloak and skull cap over lounge suit. (d) fortune teller with one hand. Also Blackshirt meeting, usual sort of Irish and communist scum howling and yelping. Bus home from Oxford Circus. Supper. Bed 11.20.

Thursday 19 July Bought a sample cabinet of 100 cigarettes at Rothman's lunchtime. Hadn't got any cigarette cases included in offer (6/3) but

---

21   This third test match at Old Trafford was drawn, England having declared at 637 and Australia having avoided the follow-on. The draw left the series at one match all with two matches to follow. Australia won the series by taking the final match.

would put one by for me when they come in. A quick rush home for dinner then down to Leicester Square station to meet Lilian at 7.50. Went to Wyndham's.

Wednesday 25 July Walked home, first taking a walk up Camden Town High St to see some flannel trousers. Paused outside shop window. Tout (Jew of course) came up to me and lured me inside. Offered me a best quality pair of light grey flannels at 12/6 for 10/-. I quibbled about width, shade, length etc and nearly slipped through the wily salesman's fingers several times until at last, in exasperation, knocked them down another bob and on his offering to have the width narrowed 1½ in, I clinched the deal at 9/-. A good twenty minutes hard bargaining, with satisfactory result. But these Jews certainly know their salesmanship – and how!

Sunday 29 July Up at 9.30. Tea and toast. Hot bath downstairs. First time I've used it. Dressed, got papers, read them. An early lunch at 12.0. Then off to Paddington. Mother and Nigger came to see me off. Shower on the way there. Met McOrmie. Caught 1.0 train to Stratford on Avon. Changed at Leamington Spa. Pouring hard with rain, overcast sky. Gloomy prospects. Train from Leamington Spa to Stratford the smallest I've ever seen. Arrived Stratford 3.30. Made for Shottery, a mile away. Got very wet getting there. Left our kits in a shed at hostel and went back to Stratford. Tea in Rosebud Tea Rooms in Church St, then walked around the town. Nothing to do at all. A short walk and to bed at 10.0.

[*there followed a week of Youth Hostelling and walking the Cotswolds*]

Monday 6 August After breakfast [back in Stratford] with our German [Youth Hostelling] friends, left Shottery hostel for last time at 10.0 and took our kits over to station to leave them in luggage room. Down to Memorial Theatre locality.[22] Sat about an hour. Place swarming with trippers of a very plebeian variety, probably from nearby commercial centres. Girls in shorts (hideous fashion) and accompanying yobs. Ruin the place. Rubbish left everywhere. About midday suddenly decided to flash a bob and look over the theatre. Went round with a guide. Extraordinarily interesting, especially mechanism at top of theatre. Girders supporting roof of auditorium, top of drop curtains etc. Fine view from top roof. Also went over adjoining picture gallery and library (only part of old building hut destroyed by fire). A fine collection, some striking pictures. The 5.46 train home. After changing at Leamington had to stand in the corridor all the way to Paddington. Arr 8.5. Home at 8.30. Unpacking etc. Bed 12.30 after Nigger had returned.

22 The Memorial Theatre, Stratford, opened in 1932.

Tuesday 7 August Paggioli's[23] for dinner then onto the Islington branch of the BUF at Holloway. Had had a note sent to me while away asking for me to attend a meeting at this branch. So went along to what it had been about. Apparently to notify members of closing of St Pancras branch and its temporary affiliation to Islington branch. Officers in charge (in mufti) took some particulars down recording my visit and enquiring to pass on to some superior officer and I left.

Friday 10 August After going home to dinner went to the YM to meet McOrmie and our two German friends whom we met at Stratford on Avon to show them round the West End. They turned up ¼ hour late at 8.15. Set off down Charing Cross Rd and Shaftesbury Avenue to Piccadilly Circus. They were more impressed and astounded by our voluminous and intricate traffic system. We hurried round to the Cameo for an hour's news and features, films, comedies. Went round to Coventry St Corner House, 2nd floor. Not very full. Orchestra. One drink each, nothing to eat. I had lager. Talked for an hour and a quarter mostly about Fascism. Herse a charming and interesting talker. Doesn't understand England very well. Ginger mainly frivolous in rather a boorish manner. Wojold asked to have exchange addresses, promises to write, then I saw them down tube. Bus home.

Saturday 11 August About 8.0 went for a stroll round West End. Or rather a brisk strenuous walk. Home 9.15. Took Nigger round to get fish. Greenshirt meeting round by [Mornington] Crescent.[24] A feeble affair.

Sunday 19 August Shortly before 6.0 set out to walk to Marble Arch. Became acquainted with the district lying between Portland Place and Edgware Rd for the first time. Have never made the close exploration of it and its merits. Quite dignified streets and squares full of fine houses. Many charmingly picturesque and rarely two alike. All with an individuality of its own. Also for the first time stumbled on the Wallace Collection quietly nestling in Manchester Square. Must take further walks round this way.

Wednesday 22 August A spot of bother with the Green Band (anti-Fascist) scum opposite our windows on Oxford St this afternoon. Exchange of rude gestures etc. Till three of the rats came over to see JD. Fortunately he was at tea and they went away. JD was quite amused however when he heard about it.

---

23 Pietro Poggioli, 5 Charlotte Street, W1.
24 In 1935 Green Shirt (anti-fascist) supporters clashed with Communist and Fascist groups and were linked to a small number of incidents in which green-painted bricks were thrown through the windows of 11 Downing Street. The Public Order Act (1936) banned the wearing of political uniforms in a public place or a public meeting.

1934

Thursday 23 August Post mortem on the Green Band incident yesterday this afternoon. Holford came over to see JD about it. Was called into office and interrogated, then acquitted with a caution. What a childishly contemptible business! Met Lilian at Leicester Square station at 7.50. Went along to the Garrick and saw *West End Scandals*, a non-stop revue. Self-styled 'London's Moulin Rouge'. It wasn't quite that but who cares? Certainly met the simple hearty audience that packed the place. A crude but more or less effective show by those who have never been nearer Paris than Southend it might be considered daring – and so it was!

Sunday 26 August Up at 8.15. Fine day. Got papers. Breakfast. Read papers. At 10.30 left for Victoria replete with Bergen [rucksack]. Got there in twenty minutes. Met McOrmie by indicator and got 11.15 to Maidstone East. Arr 12.37 and set out to walk to Charing Youth Hostel. Discovered I'd lost my key as we approached it. Damned nuisance. Left kit at hostel and went for a short walk up a hill overlooking the Weald of Kent, South Downs in the distance. Wonderful extensive view. Back to hostel, wash, some supper. Poor and inadequate.

[*holiday week Youth Hostelling in Kent*]

Sunday 2 September Got to Maidstone at 4.45. A large number of Blackshirts about selling papers. Bought paper off one. Told me they'd come down from London for the day. Tried to get in Lyons but full up. Seemed the only place open in town. Eventually discovered small snack bar up by station. Tea and cake. 4.45 train from Maidstone East. Only one stop. Arrived Victoria 6.50. A fairly good week's holiday. Walked about 100 miles in 6 days. Good going. Weather could have been better but didn't inconvenience us much. Total cost £10.8.6.

Monday 3 September Woken about 2.0 by Mother. Had been trouble at the club – she'd brought back the old lady proprietress to sleep for the night. Had to let her have my room while I slept on the floor in front room. Still, didn't matter. Slept alright. Wrote four letters. To Lilian, Bill, Jim and editor of *Blackshirt*. Mother brought the old lady back again about 10.15.

Wednesday 5 September Noticed in office today that the Green Band (anti-Fascist) scum opposite had cleared off. So good riddance!

Sunday 9 September A cup of tea at 3.30 and then up to Hyde Park for Fascist rally. Got there 4.40. Big crowds waiting to see trouble that didn't happen and big anti-fascist demonstration organised as well. Their processions arrived from 4.30 onwards and formed in a corner of the park near Marble Arch. Fascists arrived about 5.45 and marched into the big oval space already cordoned round by the police. Speeches from six carts therein. Couldn't hear anything. Mobs of filthy cockney and Yiddish scum howling foul insults and abuse at them. Their futile yappings of vacant men. But the lash they hoped for didn't come off. Sir Oswald spoke for a short while and then they all marched off, escorted by police, as peacefully as they had come. The scum also gradually drifted away. The whole thing had only lasted an hour or so but it had proved a comparative triumph for the Blackshirts.[25] Went over and listened to Bonar Thompson after.[26] Some of the frustrated reds tried to heckle him but soon realised they'd come to the wrong place for it.

Wednesday 19 September Rather disturbed today about Mother. Had talked about writing to Aunt Pop to come over and live with me in case the worse [*sic*] should happen. Though her fears appear to be quite groundless, I shall be glad when this anxiety is over. Wire in meter had been disconnected so no electric light, but after dinner went round to phone up Electric Supplies and Repair Co and a man came round and put it right shortly after.

Friday 21 September Walked home. Greeted with news that Mother goes into hospital tomorrow. Didn't expect to so soon. Spent evening making preparations and arrangements.

Saturday 22 September Mother went into hospital this morning. Will now have to fend for myself for a time. Should be a valuable experience but the shorter the better. Inclined to be very expensive business.

Sunday 23 September Up at 9.0. Got papers, had breakfast. Read papers for a short while after. Then cleared up and set about preparing lunch. Cooked steak and potatoes and beans. Made fairly good job of it. After went along to the National Temperance Hospital[27] to see Mother. Was in fairly good spirits. A bright pleasant place. Uncle Fred and Aunt Minnie came along with Jack and Mary – who had to wait outside. Broke visit to dash back and get Mother a couple of books and some biscuits. Afterwards Fred and family came back to tea. Left just after 6.0. Spent evening addressing envelopes for monthly notices, wrote a letter to Lilian and went round to post it.

Tuesday 25 September Didn't wake up till 7.30 this morning. An even greater scramble with breakfast sandwiches but only five minutes late. Swedish drill after work. Collected Cherub's typewriter after and on my way home, called in hospital to hear how Mother was. Told she was quite all right. No definite news about the operation yet. Cooked some steak for dinner. Turned out to be too underdone when I ate it. Washed up after. Also washed shirt, socks and vest. Oh to have lived in

25 *The Times* (10 September) reported 'The Fascist demonstration and the Anti-Fascist counter-demonstration passed off without any serious disturbance of the peace.'
26 The well-read Thompson was Heap's favourite Speakers' Corner orator.
27 A short distance south along Hampstead Road, NW1.

those gay, carefree halcyon years just before the war! There is certainly cause to envy the middle-aged people of today. They've experienced something which went out of the world in 1914, never to return, we can only imagine it.

Wednesday 26 September A letter from Mother this morning, said she was under anaesthetic two hours on Monday for an inspection. Feels better now. Also a charming sympathetic letter from Lilian. Mrs Soleby had been to see Mother this afternoon. Said she was in good spirits. Mrs Zelger went also. Wrote a letter to Mother and went out to post it with papers for Aunt Pop. Back to dinner. Washed up after. Then typed up Monthly Notices on stencil and duplicated a hundred notices.

Friday 28 September After work went to see Mother in hospital (6.30–7.30). Took her a bottle of lavender water from Woolworths which she wanted very much. Having operation next Monday. Was very disappointed when she had returned, it was only an examination on Monday. Had thought it was the operation itself. She tried to be cheerful but it obviously wasn't easy for her. Looked a little thinner and weaker, possibility due to lack of food and sleep as well as worry.

Saturday 29 September Found Nigger rather strange when I got home lunchtime. Not at all frisky as he usually is when I came in. Moved stiffly and slowly and shivered a little. Evidently something happened to him while he was out this morning but I can't make out what.

Monday 1 October Mother underwent operation. Called at hospital on way home. Was told she was getting on quite satisfactory but was not allowed to see her. So came home, had a meal, took Nigger out and got some shopping. Came back, washed up, wrote a letter to Mother and at 10.0 went round to hospital again to inquire. Heard she was getting on as well as could be expected, which seemed very vague indefinite unsatisfactory information. So left my letter and came home again.

Wednesday 3 October Mrs S [Soleby] had seen Mother today. Said she looked much better and was fairly bright though still suffering pain. After changing into uniform and disposing of a quick meal, dashed off to YM for monthly meeting. Firstly AGM. Was reappointed to all my present offices and in addition was appointed treasurer in succession to Len Bolton who had suggested that the post of Sec. and Tres. be combined. This was agreed to. After, over to Corner House. Hot milk, cheery company etc. etc. Bus home. Bed 12.30.

Friday 5 October A quite uneventful day. Saw Mother in hospital after work. Making gradual improvement but still in pain. Has to lie quite still in same position. But quite bright and cheerful.

Part One

Saturday 6 October Another dull rainy day. From work at 1.0 went up to Wallace Collection[28] which I had never visited before. Some really fine pictures there particularly of the eighteenth century French and Italian schools. From there walked to the Victoria and Albert Museum to see theatrical exhibits I remembered seeing seven years ago. Now alas removed. Only a few uninteresting designs for costumes remain.

Sunday 7 October After lunch went along to see Mother. Had only just come to from anaesthetic, having had radium taken out after being in stomach for a week. Felt faint and in great pain and did not feel like talking much. A great shame. They should have done it earlier to give her a chance to recover in time.

Tuesday 9 October Ironed shirt and collar. Radio – sensational murder of King Alexander of Jugo Slavia and M Barthou, French Foreign Minister on the former's landing at Marseilles this afternoon. A horrible crime. Anarchist fanatic of course.[29]

Friday 12 October Had to pay workrooms in afternoon. Was 3d short on balancing, so paid it out of my own pocket to save any trouble or displeasure. Went on to hospital to see Mother after work. Looked and felt much better. Had been eating and sleeping well and little pain lately. But had expected to come out soon and very disappointed when told that she had to have X-ray treatment (whatever that may be) and go under a different doctor. Still, to all for the good I suppose. Shopping after, then home. Three annoyances (1) Broke an egg putting bag on table. (2) accidentally jerked electric light switch fitting out of the wall and couldn't replace it properly (though light not affected fortunately) (3) bill for rent of stove and fire 3/8, totally unexpected turn of expense.

Saturday 20 October Harry came to tea at 5.30 prior to going to *Gang Show 1934* at Scala. We met Bill at 7.15. After four drinks each went round to the Scala. Seat in third row of upper circle. Saw the first half through. Good show, according to pattern. Walked round to pub in interval, had four or five more drinks and got properly blotto. Tarried in pub till turned out at closing time. Back to Scala, saw hardly anything of second half. After the show went round back stage, more drinks round there in bar then upstairs, champagne with Ralph and a few members of cast. Left the theatre about 12.10, to Corner House with Bill and Harry.

Wednesday 24 October Cherub mildly reprimanded me after about Saturday night. Apparently I had been unduly familiar with Koko

---

28 In Manchester Square, north of Oxford Street.
29 *The Times* (10 October) carried a half-page of reports from Marseilles on the assassination, and a brief report that the new King Peter, still at Sandroid School in Surrey, was being given increased police protection.

1934

backstage at the Scala.[30] Which only confirms my recently formed notion of Koko as a stodgy-minded self-important prig. Who cares anyway?

Friday 26 October Sent off two month's [*sic*] BUF subscription. After work to hospital, Harry had given me grapes to take. An unexpected and generous gesture. Mother getting on fine. Started X-ray treatment today. Glad to be having something done at last. Afterwards did some shopping. Took it home then up to Northampton Poly to pay annual subscription. Back at 9.0. Mother's insurance agent called to see me and give me Mother's sickness benefit to date (£1.15.0). A needy looking and rather illiterate young man in plus-fours. However he seemed to be doing his best and I'm sure he's persistently going to try and get me to take out an endowment policy. But I just can't develop enthusiasm for insurance of any sort.

Monday 29 October A letter from Mother saying she won't be out of hospital till Wednesday or Thursday now. Wrote a reply and took Nigger round to post it before going to bed at 11.0.

Thursday 1 November Mother looked ill again. Had overdone it today. Been all the way to Tooting and back with Fred and Minnie to see Gran who wasn't too bad after all. A good dinner of tripe and onions, after which Mother went to bed at 9.0 while I did washing up, ironed shirt etc. and went to bed at 10.45.

Sunday 11 November A fairly fine day. Up at 9.15, got papers, breakfast. Cenotaph service on radio. Two minutes silence standing at window with Mother and Nigger. Went over to Forest Gate in afternoon to see Fred and Minnie. Had tea and spent the evening there. Played whist etc. A PC friend of Fred's came in for a little while off his beat.

Saturday 17 November After a good lunch and washing up, went shopping with Mother. Changed and waited for Harry to come along for tea. Went along to the Scala to see LPTB Players in *The Desert Story*. A couple of drinks each on the way. Round to the pub with others in interval. Stood at back most of second part. Went back stage after greetings. Long winded speeches, greetings from Lilian, off to a party with other principals. Six of us went up to the Horse Shoe. Pints of beer, sandwiches, pseudo-Hungarian orchestra playing. Lengthy futile argument with a man in uniform there. At 12.0 went over to Corner House, sat talking over coffee till 1.15. Delightful atmosphere of good fellowship prevalent. Bed at 2.0.

Sunday 18 November Had just got up at 10.45 when Uncle Fred arrived, had received notification of Gran's death from Tooting hospital. Poor

---

30   The entry for 11 November 1936 states that 'Koko' succeeded 'Tiny' as the District Commissioner of Holborn Rover Scouts.

old Gran! Death is always sad but in her case it must be accounted a blessed relief. 85 years old and in an advanced state of senile decay. No, it wasn't too soon.

Friday 23 November Mother had come in at 10.30. Had been with Fred and Minnie to Gran's funeral at Charlton today. Said she'd been surprisingly free from pain – for this relief much thanks – Hamlet I.i.

Sunday 25 November Mother's 53rd birthday. Up at 10.0. After breakfast and a read of papers, set off for a walk round Chelsea which I had never explored. A bus to Westminster. Many people about. Stands erected for view of Royal wedding occasion on Thursday. Looked in Abbey and then walked along Millbank to Chelsea Bridge, went over, through Battersea Park. Back over Royal Albert Bridge, along Cheyne Walk, through to King's Rd and back to Sloane Square and through Belgravia to Victoria for bus home. Pleasant walk though mist to appreciate scenery – views along river.

Monday 26 November After going home to dinner took Mother round West End to see streets decorated for Royal Wedding on Thursday. Many other sightseers about, Trafalgar Square – Pall Mall – St James's St – Bond St (best display here: Floral decorations across road all the way along and brilliant displays in shops. Swarming with people. Crowd outside the Embassy Club). Back along Piccadilly – Leicester Square up Charing Cross Rd – bus home. Not much to see really. Practically no floodlighting and few flags and paper chains here and there. May be better later in week.

Thursday 29 November Wedding of Prince George [Duke of Kent] and Princess Marina at Westminster Abbey this morning. A great occasion. The climax of a gay festive week. After work met Mother outside the Dominion and went for a walk around the West End. Huge crowds around streets. Gala atmosphere. Flags and decorations everywhere, but practically no boistering. Most impressive night, the torches on iron stands burning outside many clubs in St James's St and Pall Mall.

Friday 30 November Home to dinner. Tube to Sloane Square. Called at HQ BUF in King's Rd to fix up a speaker for monthly troop meeting Wednesday week. Went to Central Hall Westminster for London Rover Social. Very large crowd. A drab talk by a man named Smythe, leader of a Mount Everest expedition last year.[31] After interval Ralph and the Gangsters gave an hour's show. The potent mixture as before.

---

31 Following the failure of his colleagues Lawrence Wager and Percy Wyn-Harris to reach the summit without supplementary oxygen, F. S. Smythe (1900–1949) himself reached 28,120 feet (8,570 metres) alone before turning back.

1934

Tuesday 4 December Road menders outside in Oxford St today with electric drill. Rather a din though working men of toil never seem without an odd element of humour to me.

Monday 10 December Got away from work at 5.30 and, meeting Mother, went round to dental clinic at Margaret St Hospital to have four teeth out by gas. Must have been under for about quarter of an hour but felt nothing till I came to. Cost 5/-. Home by tube. Mother made me bread and milk. Sat and listened to wireless in evening. Teeth continued to bleed a little and ached a good deal.

Wednesday 12 December Caught in rain on way to work. Had to run most of way. Damned nuisance. Gums still very stiff and swollen. After work, home to dinner then to YMCA for monthly troop meeting. A chap named Auton came along from the BUF HQ to talk on Fascism (fixed up by me). A very short man, slightly reminiscent of Napoleon in build and features. Proved to be a first class speaker and answered the rather obtuse questions of Charlie Maynard and others. The whole thing lasted from 9.10 to 10.50 and the interest of all was maintained throughout. A distinct success. Corner House after.

Tuesday 25 December Left at 11.15 to spend Christmas with Uncle Fred and family at Forest Gate. Soon out there just after 12.0. Had a drink and lounged about till dinner at 2.15. Fairly good conventional fare. King's speech on radio at 3.0. In afternoon sat in front parlour till about 5.0 when a PC friend of Fred's brought his family round to spend the evening with us. Pleasant people named Mathews. Very simple and affable. A type that I usually suppose designated 'homely' (Horrible term). However we soon filed back into the back room for tea during which one got the impression of being overrun with kids (female). Awful to do. After that back to the parlour for rest of evening. Sat round and talked, listed to radio (occasionally), drank a good deal of beer, told a short story and generally upheld the festive spirit of the occasion. Supper at 12.0. Bed soon after (sleeping with Jack).

Thursday 27 December Up at 10.0. During and after breakfast we were provided with a humorous interlude by a Mr Lamb, the next door neighbour. The sort of convincingly 'funny man' who drops in for a moment and stays an hour, erstwhile [sic] drinking a whisky and giving a comic monologue. Oh! Those funny men. Intended to go for another walk this morning but it started pouring with rain so we had to stay in and read the papers. At 3.45 set out to come home again. Bus took much longer than it did coming. Got home about 5.0. Nigger in, safe and sound after two and a half days outside.

Monday 31 December Rain early morning but cleared up for a fairly fine day. Very slack in office. Then on to Drury Lane where Mother had been keeping a stool in the queue for me since 5.15. Huge crowd there.

Part One

Just got seats in 7th row. *Cinderella* – Julian Wylie's last production.[32] Working on it when he died three weeks ago. A beautifully conceived and tasteful production notable for its lovely dresses and scenery and the dazzling blends of gorgeous colours there. [*half-page of criticism*] On coming out at 11.15 walked through to Piccadilly Circus to see the New Year in at 12.0. Big noisy crowds there. An authentic festive air prevailing. Home by tube from Leicester Square. Some supper and to bed at 1.50.

RETROSPECT – 1934

A drab depressing sort of year, relieved only by infrequent brief spasms of pleasurable jollification.

Its outstanding features have been (a) first and foremost Mother's illness which has greatly overshadowed the latter months and if it is possible to single out two others from a mass of diverse happenings then (b) the end of my attachment to Lilian and (c) our moving to Harrington Square.

Early in September, Mother lost her job and soon after, as a result of constant pain in stomach and back and sleepless nights, went to be examined at hospital. A form of cancer was diagnosed and she went in for five and a half weeks for treatment. During this period, of course, I had to fend for myself and so had a foretaste of a real bachelor's existence. It certainly has its disadvantages but on the whole I didn't find it too incompatible and come to two conclusions. Firstly that even under present circumstances, it is eminently more desirable than a state of married bliss. And secondly that the desirability of the bachelor state increases in direct proportion with the income available for its maintenance. On the last day of October, Mother came home as a semi-invalid and out-patient of the hospital for treatment. But some slight improvement is noticeable lately and she is now taking things easy and hopes for some sort of cure. Yes, the last four months of 1934 have been trying and sad in the Heap ménage. Though the only immediate hardship at its close is slight financial stringency following Mother's loss of job. The coming year will I feel sure bring things to a head in one form or other.

I began the year with a hopeless infatuation for Lilian, which however soon cooled off to a more rational attitude. I continued to take her to theatres regularly but as the year went by I came to realise it becoming a mere habit rather than a spontaneous pleasure such as it had been originally and early in October, mother's illness and the constant need for economy, provided me with good reason as well as a

---

32   The producer, the impresario Julian Wylie (1878–1934), was described as the 'King of Pantomime'.

1934

suitable opportunity to break off the attachment altogether. There was no awkward explanation or row or some or anything of that sort. Things just lapsed. After fifteen months duration, that chapter was closed. I shall continue to treasure most happy memories of my friendship with Lilian, particularly those associated with the earliest phases, and shall be for ever grateful to her for them. But the episode is now dead. Let it remain so.

And so I am now my own happy unattached me once more. My attitude to life is, as ever it essentially was, cynical, sceptical and critical. My enthusiasm for the theatre and literature has been continued and is still as intensive as ever. My other interests also have been kept up with some degree of success. In spite of some criticism and waning interest on my part, I have retained my secretaryship of the Holborn Rovers and indeed, been appointed treasurer as well. My interest in fascism, on the other hand, has increased enormously and I have enrolled as a non-active member of the B.U.F. I have not done nearly as much hiking as I intended to do. Three or four Poly rambles and a couple of similar weekends and that's about all. This has been due mainly to (a) laziness and lack of interest (b) consideration of expense and (c) lack of opportunity. These latter two have assumed great importance since September as it is now almost imperative that I spend Sundays at home with Mother. And very pleasant Sundays at home they usually are too. On the other hand this was remedied to a certain extent by a holiday consisting of two weeks holiday in Warwickshire and Kent in the course of which we covered about 180 miles altogether. Digressing on other matters, I have almost overlooked my third most important event of the year. The removal of our abode early in May from Penryn St to Harrington Square, was, apart from the necessity of it following upon a row with the landlord, a good move despite the higher rent involved. We changed two rather small rather bug-infested rooms with a drab miserable outlook for two large, clean, light and airy ones with bright, green and spacious outlook in much more compatible surroundings and a more convenient position. The internal conveniences are perhaps not all they ought to be, that's only a question of getting used to it.

One thing is certain. These new surroundings and the introduction of the radio into our home, consequent upon the electric light installation, have done a great deal to mitigate the depression and melancholy which might otherwise have arisen. The trying experiences of this autumn would have been well-nigh intolerable in Penryn St.

My business and social position have not improved in the least degree. I am still in the same job with the same lack of prospects, which I must confess I have done practically nothing to improve. Only I don't see what I really can do to advance them. Yet here again, there has been a small compensation in the form of a 5/- a week increase in salary.

Part One

My attempts at freelance journalism a year ago have not been continued despite endless resolutions to do so. A touch of laziness and an appalling lack of good ideas for articles might, I think, account for this shortcoming. As was the case a year ago however, the great dream of my life is still to become a dramatic critic. If only I could comprehend the right way to bring about its fulfilment!

As regards money, I have managed to save £5 in the course of the year, and, am at the moment worth, in all, approximately £82, which is I suppose if not even a small fortune, then at least, a useful sum to have by for stormy weather. My total annual expenditure – apart from household expenses, and pocket money continues to be in the region of £20. I have kept the same friends as I had a year ago, Bill and Harry being about the closest and most reliable. Others, such as Adam, Gilbert, Jim etc, I would place in a more general category. Gran died in November at the age of 85. This must have been, for her, a blessed release from a prolonged dotage and for such we must be thankful. It was the writing of Finis to a chapter that had long been completed. As has occurred in each summary in the past few years, I have come to realise that, while achieving practically nothing in the material sense, so much has happened that must inevitably tend to mould my character and influence my outlook and understanding of life, in other words, I feel that at the end of each year I have added something new and valuable to the rich experience of life. I have in the past year, retained my good health and regained my sense of humour which I feel sure I must have lost when I wrote that gloomy epistle Retrospect 1933, which I remember, depressed me for days after. Then, of course, I was very much in love. Now that irksome burden has once more been lifted from my spirit which soars forth carefree and untrammelled to whatever the Gods have in store for me. At the present time I have far greater cause for melancholy than I had a year ago. Yet I am not. Possessed of the aforementioned two attributes I am coming more and more to appreciate the soundness of that philosophy which discounts worry by taking life as it is and as it comes. And so upon this cheerful optimistic note I will end this discourse and declare this year of disgrace 1934, closed.

1935

In yet another year lacking advancement in his employment prospects, Heap finally acknowledged that he had no chance of getting as job as a journalist and a very limited chance of a better job in his chosen business line. Having ended his relationship with Lilian, he further diminished his social prospects in 1935 by failing to find another girlfriend, as his weekly nights out with his drinking friends played a more important part of his social routine. He recorded support for Italian Fascism but let his membership of the BUF lapse. His interest in Rover Scouting further flagged as well, but he greatly enjoyed serving as an usher at King George V's Silver Jubilee Thanksgiving Service at St Paul's Cathedral, and he proudly toured London's Jubilee decorations. His rather routine diarising is here reduced to only 27% of his original 41,500 words and entries are included for only 30% of the days.

Tuesday 1 January After celebrating New Year's Eve at the Drury Lane Pantomime and Piccadilly Circus and eventually getting to bed at 2.0 a.m., oddly enough didn't feel in the least tired during today. The New Year has begun just as the old year squelched out in continual rain. It fell most of today and looks like carrying on the bad work. About 9.30 went downstairs with Mother to Mrs Pan's basement flat[1] where a party of lodgers was being held. Seven of us down there altogether. A few drinks and sandwiches knocking around and some attempt at dancing to the radiogram. Atmosphere mildly merry but I was actually bored, by 11.0 so tired of it that I gave up and went to bed, leaving Mother down there.

Wednesday 2 January After a quick dinner went along to the YM for the Holborn Rover New Year Party in the Howard Room. A large crowd of Rovers and girlfriends about 70 strong. Ralph ran the show and arranged some quite funny games and pastimes for our jollification. There was also half an hour or so's refreshment in the Reception Room – of which I did not partake – at the absurd charge of 9d. It was rather a good evening in its way, but I didn't really enjoy it. This sort of childish fun appeals to me less and less nowadays. It seems to require a very simple and immature mentality to fully enter into it and that, alas, I don't seem to possess.

---

[1] Mrs Pan was a new resident at 20 Harrington Square.

Part One

Tuesday 8 January An office sensation this morning – Old Dan Walker, the 72 year old office veteran, died yesterday evening after collapsing with a stroke at St Pancras in the morning on his way to work. Old Dan who looked like lasting for ever.

Wednesday 9 January Read Noel Coward's *The Vortex* in *Play Parade*. Reading it in cold print at the present makes it seem almost incredible that it shocked when staged in those too too frightfully emancipated days of ten years ago.[2] Almost but not quite 'Autre temps, autre moeurs'! For despite its highly emotional exhibitionism, it does seem rather tame and artificial today. Still, interesting … interesting

Monday 14 January Had two more teeth out by gas this evening round at the clinic in Margaret St. Mother came with me. They also probed into the gum where I had one [of] the teeth extracted a month ago, to get what both they and I believed to be a bit of a tooth left in. Alas, only turned out to be the socket! Will shortly have to arrange to have a plate made now.

Tuesday 15 January Heard the result of the long-awaited Saar Plebiscite on the radio early this morning – a 90% poll for Germany.[3] Gums still bleeding a little today and jaw a trifle swollen, but no pain.

Saturday 19 January In afternoon went up to the Northampton Poly for Ramblers Club AGM. The usual crowd of dull facetious bores there and Gilbert. Didn't start till 4.0. Had arranged to meet Jim there and go onto Panto in evening but he didn't turn up, so when the meeting finished at 5.30 went along to try and find his abode round Essex Rd. Walked practically the whole length of that lengthy road but couldn't find Albany Cottages so came back to the Angel and had some tea in the Corner House there. Thence onto the Horse Shoe where I met Bill and we had some drinks before we went to the KGH [King George's Hall] for the last night of *Jack and Jill*. Jim's seat was, of course, wasted. Joshua and fiancée next to us. Jim Ridley and boyfriend in front. Went back to the Horse Shoe in interval accompanied by Jim Ridley and stayed there about an hour, jointly hitting on two young couples we fell in with there and getting just ever so highly drunk. However we got back in time for the finale and 'prize giving' and went round to stage entrance after. But the usual last night festive spirit was obviously lacking this year. Everyone was very sober and seemed resolved on going straight home. So we sheared off too and in preference to the Corner House went over to Mac's Snack Bar in Charing Cross Rd. A

---

2 When the play opened in 1924 at the Everyman, Hampstead, Noel Coward was the producer and took the lead role of a young repressed homosexual man addicted to cocaine.

3 Under the 1919 Versailles Treaty, the Saarland had been put under the control of the League of Nations for fifteen years. The internationally monitored plebiscite was for its people to decide whether the Saar should now retain its independence or return to being part of Germany. The 90.3% vote in favour of Germany was a boost for Hitler.

low dive but much more interesting than the garish artificiality of the CH, and better service and food. To bed at 1.30.

Monday 21 January Much talk and discussion in office today about joining Territorials.[4] Home to dinner then on to the Prince Edward with Mother to see the trade show of Jack Buchanan's new film *Brewster's Millions* for which Murphys had given us two tickets.[5]

Wednesday 23 January Dined, addressed and stamped envelopes for monthly notices in evening. A fellow called round at about 8.30 to inform me that the Blackshirts had opened a local branch again and would be glad to see me along there. I said I'd call in soon and we left it at that.

Saturday 9 February Met Bill at the Horse Shoe at 7.30 and after one or two drinks went round to the dance at the YWCA. Fell in with a party we know there. Maud Bilt present attraction, four other females and another fellow. A very tame starchy parochial sort of affair. I was thankful when the interval came and after attending the refreshment fiesta in the cafeteria we were able to slip round to the Horse Shoe again. There we got talking to some fellows about Shakespeare, Dickens, America, the Empire and such other things as men will talk on over their cups. Bill and other bloke got bored with this and went back, there was no drawing me away from this genial intelligent exchange of views to a dull dance so I stayed till we were turned out at 11.0. On getting back, a couple of dances and it was over. Mac's Snack Bar with Bill after. Bus home.

Friday 15 February Before coming home after work made several purchases of P.O.s [postal orders] for the Easter bookings at Youth Hostels – (Have decided as usual to do the hike with Harry – Surrey and Sussex this time) – Stamps, envelopes, bay rum, spectacles case, matches, razor blades, shaving soap and bang went seven and sixpence. After dinner, addressed and stamped envelopes for monthly Rover notices.

Saturday 16 February Went along to the Horse Shoe at 7.30 to meet Bill, Gilbert and Frank. In Popular Bar for an hour then took a cab to the Horticultural Hall for Caistor Holiday Camp Annual Dance (CHC being one of Bill's present enthusiasms). A huge very plebeian crowd there. Quite gay and lively really but totally lacking in any sense of elegance or refinement. In plain words 'leery' was the predominant element. Had one or two dances, which I didn't much enjoy, and one

---

4   The dearth of recruits for the Territorial Army was a current topic of letters to *The Times*, particularly as the London regiments were to be designated as the capital's anti-aircraft force.

5   This is the first of sixteen recorded gifts from the Murphys of cinema tickets, mostly for trade showings.

or two drinks at the well patronised bar counter, which I did. No, I don't think CHC would be quite my idea of an ideal holiday. Just a question of personality and temperament. Coming out at 12.0 we walked through to Victoria St, stood chewing the rag for some time and then walked along to Westminster and had coffee and pies at the Coffee stall opposite *Boadicea*'s statue. Trekked over Westminster Bridge to Waterloo and left Frank to wait for his train. Back over Waterloo Bridge, bid farewell to Bill and Gilbert (who had missed his last train and had to go home with Bill) and walked home. Got to bed at 2.0.

Wednesday 20 February Unusually slack day at the office. Spent a good deal of the afternoon drafting the monthly troop notice. After going home to dinner, went to the Dominion to meet Lilian, whom I hadn't seen for three or four months. Tried unsuccessfully to get into first night at the Globe so went along to the St Martin's to see *The Man from Yesterday*.

Friday 22 February Spent an hour or so cleaning out the duplicator. A filthy inky job. Gets the fingers into a devil of a mess.

Tuesday 26 February Swedish drill after work. On getting home, found everyone greatly distressed over the death of Mrs Pan's dog this afternoon from pneumonia while Mother was looking after it for her. Just as we had finished dinner, Mrs P came up to fetch it. She was terribly distraught, poor soul.

Saturday 2 March Saw Shakespeare's *Henry IV (Part 1)*, star George Robey as Falstaff. And very finely he acquits himself. [*half-page of criticism*] Heavy and ponderous, for all its excellent cast. Bill was constantly dozing off and I must confess I found it three parts boredom myself. Extremely annoyed to find I'd lost programme on getting home.

Wednesday 13 March Twenty fifth birthday. Not a particularly jubilant occasion. After going home to dinner in evening, took Mother to the Comedy to see *Mrs Nobby Clark*, Marie Ney's new actress/manager venture.[6] A mildly depressing experience. The evening's disappointment a little allayed by the humorous ejaculations and guffaws of three jocular cloth-capped cockneys behind who had obviously come to the wrong play.

Tuesday 19 March Swedish drill after work. On getting home tried on mac-cape which Mother had bought for me at Caledonian Market for 4/6. Fitted well. A good bargain.

Sunday 24 March Glorious day. Far too warm for an overcoat. Went to Petticoat Lane (Middlesex St) in morning. First time I remember

---

6 Marie Ney (1885–1981), English stage and film actress.

having visited this notorious street market.[7] A huge conglomeration of junk, mostly clothes and toilet preparations though there were items of practically every conceivable kind of merchandise to be found somewhere or other. All Yiddish hawkers of course. Crowds of cockneys and cosmopolites thronging the street and clustering round various stalls. A very live and active place altogether. Only purchased two ties at a shilling apiece myself. Tram home from Moorgate. Lunch at 2.30. Took Nigger to Regent's Park in afternoon. Crowds of people there too. The fine weather is bringing 'em out now. Buds on trees now beginning to shoot out. Beautifully soft, clear fresh atmosphere. Got first good view I've had from top of Primrose Hill. Home to tea at 5.30.

Wednesday 27 March Getting a terrific amount of work to get through every day in the office now. Scarcely a minute's time to spare. Evening: cut stencil and duplicated monthly troop notices. Got into usual filthy exasperated state. They came out in a hopelessly indistinct condition again. I felt like throwing the whole b—y thing out of the window. In any case I vowed never to attempt them again on this archaic apparatus and to avail myself of Hugh Carter's offer to do them on his machine in Maidstone. So farewell to Ink and Inc. To bed at 11.45.

Thursday 28 March Notified of 5/- a week rise this afternoon, which brings me up to £3 a week. Will certainly come in useful. Straight home after work.

Friday 29 March Evening: Party for Mrs Soleby's nephew, Jack, down from Manchester for a brief stay in Mrs Pan's room down in the basement. A very funny affair which would demand the eternal sympathetic pen of a Priestley to do it full descriptive justice. It was just too ludicrous for any words of mine. For my own part I spent three hours or so down there talking theatre, films and books with the guest of honour, whom I found to share my enthusiasm for those arts. The rest of the company present amused themselves as best they could, leaving us to our mutually agreeable preoccupations. However, poor Jack eventually departed about 12.30 and we came up.

Monday 1 April To Mudie's lunchtime to get James Agate's Autobiography *Ego* which I left reservation card for ten days ago.[8] Had to take *Three Englishmen* back after only reading about a sixth of it. Read first three chapters of *Ego* – Grand stuff. Can't resist continually dipping into the latter part of the book which is in the form of a diary (period 1932–34) and naturally more engrossing than the earlier chapters. But I shall enjoy every page of the book. That much I do know already.

---

7 The traditional Sunday market in the Middlesex Street neighbourhood at the eastern end of the City.
8 James Agate (1877–1947), diarist and Heap's favourite theatre critic.

Thursday 4 April Still very cold and frequent rain. Excitement this afternoon, McOrmie punched Savage on nose, much to our delight. A lot of blood about on the floor. S blubbed to JD rather than hit Ginger and went off to hospital. We await developments.

Friday 5 April The upshot of yesterday's office fracas was that Savage, absent today, transpired to have his nose broken and is now in hospital and is to have it reset whereas poor Ginger McOrmie got the sack this afternoon. A very unfortunate affair on both sides, but sympathy is largely with Ginger. Altogether a bloody shame and damned hard on Ginger, a decent fellow for all his little snobbish tendencies. I shall miss him in the office.

Saturday 6 April Boat Race this afternoon. Cambridge won by 4½ lengths. To the St James's with Bill in evening. Side of front row of gallery. Up to Piccadilly Circus after. Home by tube.

Tuesday 9 April After work went along to the Third Annual Camping and Open Air Exhibition at the Imperial Institute at South Kensington.[9] Walked there through Hyde Park. Very forsaken, hardly a soul in there. Yet it was fine striding through in the dusk scenting the faint fresh smell of the newly drenched grass and foliage. Went primarily to hear Tiny Chamberlain talk in the Cinema Hall on Lightweight Camping. One of the mighty series of shows organised by *Rover World*. A good talk and demonstration as far as it went, which wasn't far. Followed by film of Kantersteg Rover Moot which I had attended in 1931. Quite good. Nothing of much interest to me in exhibition itself. Met Trixie with one of the 3rd Rovers after and accompanied them as far as Oxford Corner House.

Wednesday 10 April On getting home took Nigger round to P.O. to get stamps and to shoe repairers to collect re-soled shoes (1/9, excessive charge).

Sunday 14 April In evening went for a walk with Mother to see the seating stands and other erections in preparation for the Jubilee procession in Charing Cross Rd, The Mall, St James's and Green Park, Belgrave Square, Piccadilly and so home. Stands the whole length of the Mall, Constitution Hill and Piccadilly as far as the Ritz. Many streets such as the Strand, Piccadilly, St James's St etc lined with long narrow striped poles surmounted with axe-heads. An ingenious idea. Looks most impressive.

Friday 19 April Set off on Easter Hike. 9.54 coach from Oxford Circus to Reigate where I met Harry at 11.20. Went south a little, started to rain 12.30, eastwards along the Pilgrim's Way [*page of itinerary*] to the

---

9   On Exhibition Road, it became the *Commonwealth Institute* and is planned to be (2016) the *Design Museum*.

1935

Godstone Youth Hostel about 5.0, bagged bed, washed etc and went for a stroll round Godstone village. Dinner in kitchen at 8.0. Good English fare.

[*Easter weekend solo hike in Surrey Hills*]

Monday 22 April Up and early breakfast at 8.0 and away by 8.40, set out west but struck the wrong road early. By 1.30 we had got no further than an inn on the main road, we had to get all the way back to Reigate. [*page of itinerary*] Arrived at 5.45 very tired and foot sore after about 26 miles. Got 5.55 coach home. Did about 70 miles altogether. Approx total cost, fare, food, everything 17/-. Got home about 7.30. Found a letter from Cherub asking if I'd like to do duty at St Paul's for Thanksgiving Service on May 6. Accepted with alacrity.

Wednesday 24 April After dinner cleaned windows till it got dark soon after eight. Drafted letter to Sir Alfred Beit applying for a job.[10] Spot of radio then took Nigger out and posted troop notices. To bed 11.15.

Thursday 25 April During the lunch hour took the letter for Sir Alfred Beit over to a bureau in Oxford St to be typed. Said they'd do it in two or three minutes. Waited. Typing interrupted by (a) five minute conversation on phone (b) six minutes interview with a caller. Result – my letter not completed in time and I had to tear back to work and leave it till tomorrow. Such abominable inefficiency always rankles considerably with me.

Saturday 27 April Cup Final day. Sheffield Wednesday beat [West] Bromwich Albion 4–2. Which means I've won a few bob in the office sweepstake in which I drew that result. Don't know exactly how much yet. Took Nigger round Regent's Park for an hour. Getting home found letter from Cherub informing me of his engagement and imminent leave taking to work in the West Country. Both terrific bombshells to Holborn Rovering. Then went over to Elephant [and Castle] to buy sports jacket and flannel trousers at Hurlock's in Walworth Rd[11] – 16/6 to 9/11 respectively. Very good value.

Sunday 28 April After tea went for a walk round West End with Mother to see latest preparations and decorations for Jubilee – Oxford St, Bond St, Coventry St, Trafalgar Square to T C Rd and bus home. Selfridges looks as if it will be the best display of the lot when completed. Crowds

10 Sir Alfred Lane Beit (1903–94), 2nd Bt, philanthropist and art collector who inherited his wealthy uncle's South African interests. He was Heap's Unionist MP for St Pancras South East 1931–45: see subsequent entries showing Beit's activities and hospitality in the constituency and at his home in Kensington Park Gardens.
11 Wm Hurlock's, linen drapers, 60–68 Walworth Rd, SE1.

Part One

flocking the streets, several of which are decorated with garlands and flags now.

Monday 29 April Won 8/- in the office Cup Final sweep. Comes in very useful this week. New edict this season, doors shut on late-comers till end of first act. One of [Sir Thomas] Beecham's bitter pills. Will be awkward in the case of *Das Rhinegold* [*sic*] in which there is no interval at all. Oxford St outside PR's being bedecked with festoons and bunting today.

Tuesday 30 April Started wearing summer underwear today. Purchased the *Silver Daily Mail* on way to work. A souvenir of the Jubilee but not worth 1/-.

Thursday 2 May Reply from Mrs Bernard this morning. Ridgeway [Youth Hostel] booked up for Whitsun two months ago. Offers to billet me at a nearby house and farm. Wrote to Bill on proposition. Evening: Took Mother to the Strand to see *1066 and All That* – adaption of the famous book.[12] A coarse history of England with music: That is to say a sense of burlesques of historical moments in revue form. [*page of criticism*] It was all so damnably tame.

Friday 3 May Fine and warmer today but still just sufficiently chilly for an overcoat. Letter from Trixie telling me of her engagement and denying certain false gossip circulating in Holborn concerning the identity of her fiancé. An amusing and rather charming letter. So typically Trixie.

Sunday 5 May Very warm today. Almost sultry. Evening: walked round sightseeing with Mother. Mainly the route of the procession tomorrow. Bus to Ludgate Circus – up to and in St Paul's – Fleet St – Strand – Whitehall – Horseguards Parade – and St James's Park – Green Park – Piccadilly – Leicester Square and home from there by tube. Multitude of sightseers parading the streets making progress very slow. London almost more miserable under a plethora of flags, bunting festooning the other decorations. Most of the shops along route boarded up to prevent windows getting broken. Saw little floodlighting, most of it starts tomorrow but the fairy lights all along both sides of Piccadilly and St James's St give a very lovely effect and London has suddenly become a dream-like place overnight. Bed at 11.30.

Monday 6 May After an almost sleepless night due to continual sounds of revelry, up to 6.15 into uniform, a good breakfast and away to St Paul's to help distribute the service papers for the Jubilee Thanksgiving

---

12   W. C. Sellar and R. J. Yateman, *1066 and All That: A Memorable History of England, Comprising All the Parts You Can Remember, Including 103 Good Things, 5 Bad Kings and 2 Genuine Dates* (London: Methuen & Co, 1980). First appeared in *Punch* magazine, then as a book in 1930.

1935

Service. Mother came with me as far as churchyard and eventually saw the procession from a window in Fleet St. Entered the Cathedral at 8.20. Eleven other Holborn Rovers there and about four dozen others. Was allocated to my two rows about half way down the side (North Nave B to be exact) and awaited arrivals. Got terribly cold, should have had more on under shirt. By about 10.30 all seat holders assembled. A magnificent array of pomp and splendour. Men in glittering uniforms and court attire far outshone the women in sartorial display. Procession began to arrive. Prime Minister, Cabinet etc. Finally the King and Queen and royal family at 11.30. The Queen looked superbly regal. The King very happy and benevolent. Service lasted an hour or so. Archbishop of Canterbury's address very dull.[13] The miserable drone of his voice the last word of tedium. At 12.30 the royal procession passed up the aisle once more back to the West door and into their carriages and back to the Palace by direct route. Was within about six yards of the aisle and had a fine view of everything. An impressive and unique experience. Left at 1.0 with Jim Ridley and Laurence Nelson and managed to work our way through the huge pile of swells standing on the steps waiting for their cars. Was very warm out in contrast to the cathedral interior. Couldn't have been a finer day – beginnings of a heat wave. Home to a late lunch at 2.30. Dozed and read papers till tea at 5.30. Radio till 8.25. Good speech by the King at 8.0. At 9.0 set out with Mother to see the floodlighting and general events. Started from Baker St. Huge crowd outside Selfridges' – one of the best displays in London. Encountered Gordon Selfridge himself unrecognised in the crowd. Went through Hyde Park to Hyde Park Corner – down to Buckingham Palace. Huge bonfire in the Park – down to Buckingham Palace. Cheering mob outside it hoping to get King out on balcony – through St James Park beautifully lit up – Horseguards Parade an exquisite sight floodlit there – met Cherub in Parliament St sightseeing on eve of departure – saw green-lit Banqueting Hall – up Whitehall and tube home from Charing Cross. Supper and bed at 1.45.

Tuesday 7 May Not so warm today. Bought six papers this morning for Jubilee procession news and pictures. Found myself in three pictures (same shot) of St Paul's Thanksgiving Service. Taken from upper balcony looking up the aisle.[14] Evening: straight home dinner, wrote up troop log book – a couple of pages on yesterday morning and several newspaper cuttings of past two days' events, news and pictures. Took Nigger out, bed 11.15.

13 Cosmo Gordon Lang (1864–1945), Archbishop of Canterbury 1928–42, was unlikely to impress Heap as Lang later denounced the Italian invasion of Abyssinia, condemned anti-Semitism and supported the later appeasement policy. He also took an 'uncharitable' strong moral tone against Edward VIII during the abdication crisis.
14 Both the *Daily Express* and the *Daily Mail* published long shots showing hundreds of worshipers, making individual identification virtually impossible.

Part One

Wednesday 8 May In evening went along to the Bedford Kinema in the [Camden] High St with Mother to see *Royal Cavalcade*, the one and only full-length Jubilee film.[15] A swift comprehensive panorama of events, episodes and features of the past twenty five years with special emphasis on the part played by the King in them and ingeniously linked together by the circulation of a 1912 penny. A whole galaxy of famous stars made brief fleeting appearances. A splendid film altogether, just the thing for the occasion. Home to bed at 11.30.

Thursday 9 May Ginger McOrmie came along to PR's today. Went for a walk and a drink with him lunchtime. Has just started work at a car hiring business in Harrow Rd – looks after the accounts. Doing fairly well but has to put in a good deal of overtime. Evening: dashed home and changed into evening kit and rushed along to the Shaftesbury Hotel to join Mother at the S.E. St Pancras Conservative Association (Woman's Section, Ward 8) Jubilee Dinner. Went along mainly for the purpose of meeting and having a few words with Sir Alfred Beit who was in the chair. Which was duly accomplished. About seventy there, mostly middle aged and elderly women. A mere handful of men. A fair dinner, a few dry speeches after and some songs by an enormous fat woman. Followed after an interval by dancing till 12.0. Not a great success owing to scarcity of men. Went over to Mortimer's twice with Mother. Had met Mortimer in street before going in this evening, but not in there when we called over later. Home by tube after with other members. To bed 2.15.

Friday 10 May Swim after work, home to dinner. Radio till 9.30 *From the Royal Diary*, musical marches from shows the King has seen over the last 25 years. Good feature. Then went round to the West End to see floodlighting and illuminations again. All traffic still stopped. Places like Piccadilly Circus and Regent St seem very odd without it. Just a babble of voices. Didn't see much more than Monday night. Usual multitudes cheering at Palace. Pall Mall, usually a very subdued street, brilliantly lit. But was very cold walking about without overcoat and was glad to get down tube and home. Bed 12.0.

Saturday 11 May Home to tea then back to the Alhambra to meet Bill at 7.15, [and] a couple of drinks at the Queens. Went over to the Queens in the interval and had a job to get back. Door shut so had to go round to front entrance and up Upper Gallery back stairs. On coming out went along to Piccadilly Circus. A night of great jubilation in the West End. Swarms of sightseers and merry makers along main streets. Went in three pubs just off the Circus and on coming out of Bodega's at 12.0 went and danced and generally joined in the High Jinks around the

---

15 A compilation of newsreel footage and re-enacted sequences to commemorate the twenty-five-year reign, its many stars including George Robey and Harry Tate as themselves. The film was also shown at four West End and many local cinemas.

'centre of the world'. Finished up in Trafalgar Square at 1.0. Bid Bill farewell and walked home. To bed at 2.0.

Sunday 12 May Regent's Park with Nigger for an hour before lunch at 2.15. Afternoon: Went to Hyde Park with Mother for *Daily Express* Jubilee Thanksgiving Service. About a hundred thousand people there.[16] Somewhat dull and uninspired. Mostly hymn singing, still the idea was good and I daresay most people there were satisfied.

Monday 27 May Got an extra job bunged onto me at work – clearing money out of phone boxes after tea and counting it up on the morrow. Evening: Took Mother to the *Tower of London Pageant and Tattoo*.[17] Held in the Moat – vast arena erected around it. Had good seats at the side looking across the Moat. The vast auditorium only about half full. A bad night, weather looked very dubious before it started at 9.0 but held off. The whole show very well done. Excellent surroundings and perfect setting for the presentation of the numerous historical episodes and military display. They seem to have spared no effort or expense to make it a great success. Good lighting effects, fine colourful costumes and a gigantic host of performers. Lilian [Heap's ex-girlfriend] appeared as Queen Elizabeth in one of the episodes. Got very cold sitting watching it, even in overcoat, but well worth seeing. A grand experience.

Monday 17 June One of those days of which one is conscious of laboriously 'getting through'. A slow lazy but not unpleasant process. Straight home after work. In evening listened to first cut of *The Yeoman of the Guard* from Sadler's Wells on radio and addressed envelopes for monthly notices. Took Nigger out and went to bed early at 10.45.

Sunday 23 June Heat wave continues. Went on *Rover World* Thames Cruise to Clacton and back. Mother came with me to Mark Lane station[18] to see us off from Tower Pier on the *Crested Eagle* at 10.0. About 1,100 of us all together, 82 from Holborn. A marvellous turnout and a perfect day for it. The only thing to do was laze about and sunbathe, which I did, or join in the *Gang Show* choruses, which I didn't. Arrived at Clacton about 2.40 and after some speech making and other palaver were allowed on shore for an hour or so. Walked for twenty minutes or so around town. Thought it very tame and suburban and altogether uninteresting and came back to the pier which is crammed with various fun fairs and side shows and a swimming pool. Couldn't get in this and went without a bathe and dallied about for four hours till 6.0 when we embarked and started back. A few left behind, including about ten

---

16   On this, the first of their four tours of London, the King and Queen drove through Hyde Park 'in an open landau, drawn by four bay horses' (*The Times*, 13 May 1935).
17   The *Pageant* ran from 25 May to 8 June.
18   Replaced by Tower Hill station in 1967.

Part One

Holborn blokes, who had to follow back on a later boat. Return journey not much more exciting than the outbound one, just lounged about and either stared at the sea or river bank. Last half hour the best. The river took on a truly romantic glow in the setting sun as we approached Tower Bridge. Got off at 8.45. Could only eat gooseberry tart and custard for supper, poor appetite. Terribly sunburnt. Is going to cause discomfort. To bed at 11.0.

Wednesday 26 June Rather fresher and cooler today. An ideal day for walking. Sunburn has passed the sore stage and developed into a tingling sensation. After dinner at home, went along to the Lanes Club again to see some all-in wrestling.[19] Usual five contests. On the whole not such good fighting as last week. Fewer displays of skill and speed and one pair very badly matched. One thing struck me tonight was the way in which the crowd instinctively gives voice to its hostility to any sign of foul play even though it is within the rules. They're very quick on the uptake.

Sunday 30 June Up at 7.30 and at 9.30, set out for Victoria to go on Southern Ramble with Bill and Gilbert. On arriving there, discovered that I had mistaken the station, the train actually starting from Waterloo. So made a frantic dash there only to arrive a few moments too late. So came home again and took Mother and Nigger up to Hampstead with our attaché case full of sandwiches, fruit, lemonade etc. for lunch. Sat on the grass over by Ken Wood and spent afternoon there. Tube to Waterloo to meet Southern Ramble train returning. Met Bill off the train and went round to a pub in Waterloo Rd to console him with beer. Thence walked over the bridge and along to Charing Cross where we got a bus up to Oxford Corner House and dived therein for coffee. Argued about all sorts of things including a vague fantastic idea of Gilbert's about making his way round the world, a notion to which, of course, Bill heartily concurred. On coming out, parted and wended our ways home.

Thursday 4 July Went round paying maintenance staff wages most of day. Hot, tiring work. Vest and shirt constantly saturated with sweat. Balanced alright on finishing. After work went along to Baker St Station, met Bill there and took a tram up to Wembley where Gilbert joined us and went along to the recently built Empire swimming stadium.[20] Paid 1/- to go in and 6d to hire a pair of trunks and 2d for a towel. A colossal place, cafe and dancing in an upper hall overlooking actual swimming pool. Stayed in bath about three quarters of an hour and got very chilly standing about when not swimming. Came out and went up to the bar cafe section. Had a drink or two then for two hours or so stood or sat

19 The Lanes Club, King Street, off Baker Street, W1. Heap's first visit was a week earlier, when he had found all-in wrestling 'a grand, thrilling, exciting sport, to watch anyway'.
20 The pool was opened in July 1934.

about doing nothing in particular getting thoroughly bored with the whole thing. I dislike the style and atmosphere of this sort of place. This is, in fact, not my notion of an entertaining evening. Far too vast and cold and bare for all its would be impressive magnitude. Stark and superficial in an obviously unattractive way. In short, suburban youth's idea of glamorous glittering gorgeous. They're welcome to it. Left 11.5 and got tram back to Baker St.

Monday 8 July First day of PR's sale. Went shop-walking, as usual ground floor beat. Terribly fatiguing job, both mentally and physically. I get thoroughly sick of it within the first hour. Observed a queer looking individual walking through shop and inspecting ladies stockings. Then elderly man, Panama hat, Eton collar and bow, grey flannel jacket and shorts, black woollen stockings covering knees and jumper adorned with buckles! Otherwise he looked quite sane. Why he was thus attired God knows and he only knows I suppose.

Sunday 14 July Up at 9.30. Still very hot but contrived to spend the day in some degree of cool comfort clad in cricket shirt and flannels, went up to Hampstead with Mother and Nigger and taking our lunch in our attaché case, found a couple of deck chairs in a nice shady spot and spent the afternoon up there. A very pleasant way of spending a fine Sunday in summer, providing one finds a not too crowded spot and, withal, very economical. Came home tea-time when Hampstead begins to get unpleasantly crowded though, as may be expected, the plebeian populace which bring about this dire effect do not go too far afield and totally ignore the most beautiful parts of the heath. But how freely they scatter their paper about! One would think they came up specially for that purpose. Light supper, to bed at 11.15.

Monday 22 July Started leaving off work at 6.0 once more. Very slack in the office just now. The afternoons drag out terribly. Am much disconcerted by certain small hard ridges which have lately formed in the joints of my penis and have now become very painful to touch. The trouble is I can't draw the foreskin back to see what the trouble is. Don't know whether to go to the doctor's or not. Horrible thoughts of circumcision and suchlike revolting operations now morbidly occupy my mind. The very thought of any surgical manipulation on myself especially in that part of my anatomy fill me with the greatest horror and nausea.

Wednesday 24 July On getting home this evening found that Mother had started off on a new job with the Child Welfare Section, Public Health Dept of the St Pancras Council. Have to go and look after mothers during childbirth and tend to the children (former issue) if any, of same. So had to get my own dinner ready and do washing up for first time for many months.

Part One

Friday 26 July Very busy day. Spent most of the morning paying workroom wages. Plenty of work to dispose of in afternoon too. Swim after work. Have taken to wearing a swimming helmet to keep the water from my hair and ears. It occurs to me that my thinning hair lately may be due to getting water in it too frequently. And it is just as well to keep it out of the ears in any case, the possibility of deafness and all that.

Friday 2 August A frenziedly busy day in office, well-nigh rushed off my feet. Had to go paying workroom wages both morning and afternoon and then a double portion of normal work on top of that. And somehow I did it.

Saturday 3 August Went up to spend the weekend at Bill's place in Ilford. Or rather the nights there and the days watching Bill play cricket. Went to office in flannels and sports coat in morning and met Bill at 1.15 outside Horse Shoe. Tube to Liverpool St, train to Ilford, bus to Goodmayes Park where Bill was playing in afternoon. Seemed to run into acquaintances of Bill on the way and have a drink with them. Lasted till 8.0. Very urban surroundings. Good crowd of spectators. Dull and overcast most of the time, got very chilly sitting in a deck chair all the time. Had some more to eat and sat up playing dominoes. Was about five pence up at the end, when, leaning back in chair, I slipped right over on to the floor and banged head on wall in falling. Damned funny incident. Slept on floor of dining room with [fellow guest] Andrews.

Sunday 4 August Got away about 11.15. Bid Andrews farewell and then, Bill being late, made a frantic dash by two coaches to get to the sports ground of Bill's sports club at Harold Park (about six miles away, half way between Romford and Brentford). Just about did it. Excellent lunch for 1/6 at a cafe down on the main road and a brief tea on the ground. Left at 8.0 and went up to The Bull, a mile up the road on the way to Brentford. Played darts with the locals in the public bar. Lost some games, won others. Left at 10.0, a bus back to the bungalow. Slept in Bill's bed tonight.

Monday 5 August A much better night. More comfortable. Bill had slept on dining room floor that time as originally intended. Up at 9.0. Bill cooked breakfast, his other [half] being out on another call. Left at 11.15 again and took coach along to Gidea Park sports ground. Watched game in morning. Rather slow and tame. Finished 7.30. Had a drink or two in clubhouse after and then got the bus back towards Ilford. Two more drinks with Bill then got a bus back to Ilford station and train back to Liverpool St. Tube home from there. To bed at 12.30. A very good weekend, quite enjoyed it. Total cost about 19/-.

1935

Tuesday 6 August Didn't sleep too well again so somewhat tired today and ever so slightly liverish. Felt in an oddly morose mood. Was inclined to give Mother the benefit of it when I got home after a swim at YM. Shouldn't have let that happen. She wasn't in a too jubilant mood herself. And with more reason for it than myself, heavens knows! Bed soon after 11.0.

Friday 16 August Met Bill after work, went round to Paggioli's for some dinner. Then went round corner to Marquis of Granby[21] for a couple of drinks intending to go on to a music hall or something. But the two drinks multiplied themselves – we got talking with members of the bizarre Bohemian congregation which foregathers there and eventually stayed all evening. A most interesting little tavern, full of cosmopolitan misfits. Predominant tone definitely pseudo-literary and journalistic. We drank an excessive amount of lager and bought a few drinks for amusing sponges who apparently make a habit of accepting drinks ad lib from strangers and giving in exchange diverting informative egoistic talk. An admirable arrangement providing their personality is up to the standard of the drink. It was tonight. Some of the types to be encountered here are simply amazing, an education in the fantastic. Feeling a trifle inebriated, walked home by devious route after trying to combat its effect, with little success.

Sunday 18 August Set off on five day tramp in the Chilterns. 10.15 Green Line coach from Baker St to Dunstable. Walked across Dunstable Down and down along road. [*page of itinerary*] Evening walked over to Youth Hostel 2 miles north of Hemel Hempstead.

[*First week of annual holiday spent hostelling solo in Chilterns*]

Thursday 22 August Up at 7.30 and after a good breakfast (not bacon and eggs thank God, but grapefruit and kipper), set out from Henley at 10.15 on last lap to Maidenhead. Managed to cut across country and dodge the main road most of the way. Only about eight miles so had time for good long rests. Via Cockpole Green, [*walk itinerary*] into Maidenhead. Learned when I got there that Green Line service doesn't run there now. So had to take a bus to Slough and get a Green Line from there back to Trafalgar Square. Got home 6.30. Reflections on ramble: enjoyed my first experience of lone hike far better than anticipated. Own company and free will most congenial. Very fortunate with weather. Ever hot and fine and fresh to the eye. Ideal weather to be out of London. Discovered two good and two mediocre hostels. Henley exceptionally good, meriting many re-visits. Feet not good,

---

21   Marquis of Granby, 2 Rathbone Street, W1, a Bohemian pub.

very nearly detracted from enjoyment. Feel infinitely better for the fresh air anyway.

[*Second holiday week spent with his mother at Margate*]

Saturday 24 August Went to Margate for a week with Mother. Also decided to take Nigger with us at the last moment. Got the 12.5 train from Victoria, was as foul a day as it was possible to imagine. Rained practically all day. However, arrived at Margate at 3.0 and after wandering around for an hour trying to get accommodation at various places – including Baird's in Westbrook Rd where we stayed in '28 – eventually got fixed up at 94 Canterbury Rd some little way up Westbrook. Good comfortable quarters. A front basement bed-sitting room for Mother (also for meals, there being no other lodgers thank goodness) and a top back room for myself. No objection to dog. Quite satisfactory and reasonable. Had some tea. Took Nigger out for walk along sea front. Some fried fish at 7.0. Leaving Nigger indoors walked up to Cliftonville and round Dreamland. Rain left off. Back about 10.0. All out again for some Horlicks. Back and to bed at 11.0.

Saturday 31 August. The end of an imperfect week. And it was at least consistent. Dull, cool and cloudy with occasional hint of rain. Spent the morning walking about. Along the front, to the end of the pier and back up the High Street. Called at Marine Pavilion for six copies of photographs taken therein on Thursday and ordered yesterday and, on going back for lunch at 1.0, despatched one to both Aunt Pop and Cherub. After lunch settled up and went along to the station. Caught the 2.4 train back to Victoria. Very crowded but comfortable enough in our carriage, home at 4.40, afterwards went shopping with Mother up the High St. Came back and listened to radio for rest of evening. Supper and to bed 11.30. So, in effect, ends my holiday. A rather unsatisfactory one in one way, yet I certainly feel all the better for the change of air and the exercise. The first few days were perfect but the last week has been so uncongenial as regards weather that it would seem to be a waste of money (for it cost about £7.10.0 for the two of us). Still, it might conceivably have been worse and the exhilaration of the ozone laden air is always some compensation for shortcomings.

Monday 2 September Back to work – and plenty of it thanks to the absence of September holidaymakers. Walked down to Charing Cross station to get new Southern Rambler leaflet. Blackshirt meeting in Adelphi theatre across the road. Also attracts large crowd. Several police about and a few hostile pamphleteers but no disturbances.

Tuesday 3 September Had a haircut lunchtime. Hair doesn't seem to be getting any thicker on the crown and is still receding on one side of my temples. The tonics of Vaseline and Harlene will have to do better than this. A swim after work plus shampoo and shower bath. Walking home, Jim Ridley pulled up in his car by me in Hampstead Road. After dinner Mrs Beattie called round to see Mother about a new flat she thought would suit us better than our present abode, up Kentish Town somewhere. We thought not. After, I wrote two letters. One to Joshua, gently and diplomatically requesting the payment of £3 – the sum he agreed to compromise that four year old debt of his on the transference of my six guinea Metropolitan College fee to his account.[22]

Monday 9 September Overwhelmed with work at office. Endeavouring to wade through it. JD away all week. Mother started on another job today – or 'case' as they call it. Maternity and child welfare business – same as the brief job she had about six weeks ago. Doesn't like this one so much.

Monday 16 September With return of people from holiday, the office work got back to normal again today and I was able to take things easier. Straight home after work. Spent evening on second lesson of shorthand from *Popular Educator*. Find it an exceedingly difficult subject to master and not in the least absorbing. Still I shall persevere at it now.

Wednesday 18 September Received a note from Josh Reynolds this morning enclosing cheque for the three quid he had owed me for some considerable time. So long in fact I'd almost given up hope of ever getting it. Cashed it at PR's during the morning. On the strength of this sent off for a supply of address printed stationery to the tune of 6/- lunchtime. Wrote after job in *Telegraph* in afternoon at £200 a year. After dinner went along to [Rover] GEC meeting at YM in evening. Poor attendance and air of futility until, Tiny being absent, Bunny flared up into a heated condemnation of the hopeless state of affairs the Association has got into through Tiny's [failing] to devote sufficient time to things or find suitable leader. Charlie Maynard tried to defend Tiny's position and a stormy argument ensued. A damned good rumpus in the making. I only hope the AGM will be ditto on this major one. It certainly helped to make this the first GEC Meeting at which I haven't been bored stiff.

Sunday 22 September Started sleeping on settee bedstead in front room last night letting Mother sleep in my bed while she is so crocked up.

Wednesday 25 September Remarkable the way everyone in the office has suddenly become concerned about my falling hair. Not a day passes without a comment or a joke from someone or other. It's getting sickening.

---

22   There is no earlier reference to Heap transferring any correspondence course or fee.

Thursday 26 September Mother called away in middle of night to attend to childbirth prior to the usual fortnight's attendance on mother and other children (if any). So what with getting to bed late and intermittent sleep, didn't have too good a night and felt tired most of the day. Also had to get own breakfast and prepare sandwiches.

Monday 30 September After going home to dinner went to London Rover Council Meeting at Victoria in evening. Very large attendance, sat with Tiny. A good deal of important business on agenda such as the adoption of a new policy and organisation for London Rovering. But the item that acquired the most significance was the last one – to wit the form of service to be held after the Cenotaph Pilgrimage. The Committee at the instigation of some damned Jew on it had recommended a non-specifically Christian form so that our Jewish brethren and other religious oddities might take part in it without questions as to conscience etc. The question was hotly discussed and defeated and a lot of bad feeling and bigotry was displayed, such as only religion can bring about. All the old dogmatic bunk about religious toleration of Jews and an example to the world was jabbered forth and much other nonsense. Until someone moved an amendment not to have a service at all after. Put to the vote this was carried by 37 to 35 and then 43 to 35, Tiny and I voting in favour.

Tuesday 1 October Electric light had fused. Had to use gas for light but they soon came round and put it right.

Wednesday 2 October Monthly troop meeting in YM Oak Room in evening. Feeble attendance, fourteen all told. Ralph's first night at the Hippodrome accounted for it to some extent. AGM first at which I was again elected to all my present offices with not a murmur of dissent. Then a talk from Mr Toynbee of the Workers Educational Association[23] entitled 'Can Democracy Survive?' Dull and involved. Informative to a certain degree but imparted in an ineffective spiritless style. Rather in keeping with the whole meeting which was an utter wash-out. Tiny drives Eddie Angel and myself home after. Sit in car in Harrington Square for about 20 minutes discussing Italian air question.

Thursday 3 October Italian–Abyssinian War started today with the Italian invasion.[24] Placards this evening 'War! 1,700 Italian Casualties', 'Italians bomb women and children', 'Abyssinians claim victory at Adawa' etc etc. Things are looking up!

23 Not the historian Arnold Toynbee (1889–1975) but probably Hugh S. Toynbee, in 1935 Vice Chairman of the WEA's London District and, after the war, Chairman of the WEA's Trade Union Committee (WEA Archives at London Metropolitan University).
24 In the Second Italian–Abyssinian War, Italian ground and air forces extended the Italian Empire by invading and occupying Emperor Haile Selassie's Abyssinia. The League of Nations, deciding that Italy was the aggressor, very slowly imposed economic sanctions on Italy but crucially these did not include oil imports.

1935

Friday 4 October The war goes merrily along. Italians make steady progress and drop a few more bombs. That's the stuff to give the niggers.

Monday 7 October A quiet industrious day. Didn't feel so tired as expected. Plenty of work to get through in office. And in evening, after dinner and radio, carried on with shorthand self-tuition. To bed early at 10.30. Latest development in Ital-Abyssinian War – Italians capture and occupy Adowa – the worst to come yet though – The League sleeps on.

Tuesday 8 October The war continues to be the subject of discussion and argument in the office. I am all for Italy in the dispute and hope she gives the niggers hell. Everyone else of course, focusing their feeble unimaginative progressive minds on the correct conventional and commonplace lines of thought are teeming with ludicrous self-righteous indignation against Italy, the deep double-dyed 'villain of the piece'. The childish and costive [constipated or slow] outlook of the British public on such questions is incredibly stupid and short-sighted – the result no doubt of the decadent mentality wrought by an effete democracy and parliamentarianism. Italy is showing a fine example of national pride and strength of character to the world. May she sweep all before her.

Wednesday 9 October All quiet on the Abyssinian front. The League thinks about sanctions.

Friday 11 October The League yesterday decided to apply 'sanctions' – a silly word merely meaning economic warfare – against Italy. Britain represented by the buffoon Eden[25] well to the fore of course. Now sending arms to the Niggers. That of course will stop the war! What a sorry pass England has come to!

Monday 14 October Humdrum sort of day. Perfect contrast to yesterday. Had a huge amount of work to get through in office and nearly did it. Mother late home in evening from new 'home help' job up Kentish Town, started yesterday. Fish and chips plus peaches and cream for dinner.

Tuesday 15 October Glowing criticism of first night of *Gang Show 1935* in today's *Morning Post* and *Evening News*, *Times* also good but more deferential and punctilious in keeping with its general tone.[26] The rest of the 'Popular Press' have not realised, of course, that this annual show is 'News'.

---

25 Anthony Eden (1897–1977), Under-Secretary of State for Foreign Affairs.
26 *The Times* (1 October) did not name Ralph Reader but applauded the 'outwardly amateur performance' and suggested that the 'Holborn Rover who is responsible for lyrics, the music and indeed the whole production, must have had professional experience.'

Part One

Thursday 17 October Took Mother to see *The Gang Show of 1935* at the Scala. The whole thing done by Ralph Reader. [*page of admiring criticism*] Ralph came on towards the end. Ear splitting reception, richly deserved. Bus home from Euston Rd. To bed 12.30.

Friday 25 October Parliament dissolved today prior to General Election on Nov. 14. National Government out a year before its time, to force the issue on sanctions and support of the League and so shelve the most important issues of home affairs and of unemployment, which of course does not lend itself to such vote-catching stunts. They will, of course, get in on that socialist policy and stay in till they can wisely pinch another item from the socialists' programme, put it forward in another catch-penny election as their own and forestall the reds again. Christ! What a racket!

Saturday 26 October Before coming home intended to walk to the Scout Shop to obtain last two issues of *Rover World* but in Charlotte St ran into Adam which inevitably led to lengthy discourse and delay. As we walked very slowly along TC Rd and into Warren St I learned among other things (a) That he had just got back from Brussels (b) Wasn't feeling in good health – liver trouble (c) Thought of going into pot-holing business (d) Didn't know what to do about Holborn Rovers (e) Decided that the English lower class is hopeless.[27] Afternoon went up High St with Mother to help carry shopping back then took Nigger to Regent's Park for an hour and got back to tea just after 5.0. Evening: Mother went off to Ypres League concert[28] while I spent one of my ever so rare Saturday evenings at home, there being nothing worth seeing in the theatre I haven't seen. Spent some time clearing out my cupboard in a futile attempt to rearrange things. Got into a hopeless mess, gave it up and finally put everything back as it was before.

Sunday 28 October Spent most of the evening carefully filling in an application for employment form sent to me by the Frigidaire Co. to whom I wrote last Friday. Took Nigger out. To bed 10.45.

Tuesday 30 October Local Association AGM at YM Oak Room in evening. Fairly large turnout. George Edwards in chair. Koko also present. Only one thing of any importance happened – Bunny's resignation. Expected for some time as a result of long extended temperamental clashes with Tiny. A tremendous pity. He was above all else an amusing and colourful personality such as is all too rare

---

27 Adam did not mention that he was now a British citizen. The Home Office copy of his Naturalisation Certificate, dated 1 August 1935, shows that 'Adam Martin de Hegedus de Lapos, known as Adam de Hegedus' was born on 14 December 1906 in Kolosovar, Hungary, his occupation was 'Journalist, literary critic and literary translator' and he was living at 14 Manson Place, Queen's Gate, South Kensington, SW7 (TNA, HO334/138/6048).

28 Heap's mother was a member of the League, founded in 1920 as a Great War veterans' and remembrance society.

in Holborn Scouting. Who will replace him, Lord only knows. Won't be an easy task. Like the Rover leadership and most other executive offices in Holborn will just be allowed to lapse I suppose. Can't blame Bunny. Things have reached a hopeless pass. Would do the same myself for two pins. Still, I shall be very sorry to lose his friendship, if it comes to that. However it was accepted complacently and just left to a committee to solve the problem. How like an executive committee!

Thursday 31 October Went along to the City lunchtime to meet Bunny Kaye who took me to a silverware dealers just off Cannon St to order Cherub's present. He gets stuff at trade price from them. We chose a silver plated tray and left it to be suitably inscribed by next Wednesday. Bunny, who was by the way silk hatted a la Stock Exchange, then stood me a drink, had a last moan about Holborn Scouting, walked back to the tube with me (in pouring rain) and bade me farewell. Wonder if I shall ever see him again. Melancholy thought.

Wednesday 6 November Went along to the City lunchtime to collect Cherub's wedding gift. On getting it home in the evening and unpacking it discovered that the bloody fool who engraved it had got the wrong date on it. Nov 1st instead of the 27th. This sort of thing is unpardonable, the engraving had cost 27/6 out of £3.9.6 the total cost. However I had to take it along to the troop meeting in evening to present it to Cherub who had stayed in London till tonight especially for this prior to returning to Bristol at midnight. It had to be taken back and put right. So, Tiny only came in for a few minutes so I had to make the presentation and say a few words. After an interval he had to say a few words. He also said a few words on his new work which he has been doing for six months.

Monday 11 November Stood at office windows for two minutes silence. Oxford Circus crammed full of people. In afternoon had to shift my position in office to other end of desk, up by the draughty window. Despite formal reasons given – psychological effect of changes around and suchlike humbug – I know it was only done to inconvenience and humiliate me. Just as I am kept in my tuppenny halfpenny office boy's job for the same reasons – and a stubborn refusal to ass-crawl on my part. It did however make me desperately determined to get out of this bloody place as soon as possible and at whatever cost. So home and went to bed feeling utterly sick both physically and mentally. Christ, what a day!

Wednesday 13 November Met Bill after work and went round to Poggioli's for some dinner. Alarmed to hear that he is taking up his affair with Peggy (girl met on Southern Rambles) seriously. Even thinking of becoming engaged. Would be a tragedy, we must do our utmost to rescue him. Then round to Scala. London Transport Players production of *The Show Boat*. A vile business altogether. We decided

Part One

to cut our losses and clear off. Whereupon Rico took us round to the Malaya Club[29] just off Tottenham Court Rd where we quaffed beer, played darts and listened to Rico singing till the place closed at 11.0. Returned to Scala, went back stage, hasty greetings to Lilian and then off again.

Thursday 14 November General Election Polling Day. Went round with Mother and Nigger to vote for Mitcheson, local National Conservative candidate,[30] before going to work. Lunchtime: Went along to an unemployment bureau in City to get details but didn't like the look of it so came away. Also called at Petty & Co in Haymarket [who] charge 5% of 1st year's salary as commission. An exorbitant fee. 2% is quite adequate. Gave out election results till 1.0 but found it tame sitting listening to them and left at 11.30. Bus home, more results on radio.

Friday 15 November Election results through all day. Beit, Mitcheson and Fraser all got in for St Pancras boroughs [constituencies]. National Government likely to get 260 majority over Labour.[31]

Tuesday 19 November After dinner wrote three letters to members of the CIS Council asking for a job. Took Nigger round to post them. Bed at 11.0.

Saturday 23 November After tea changed into dinner suit and went along to meet Ron at Horse Shoe at 7.0. A couple of drinks then strolled down to Bush House for Southern Ramble Dance, calling at the Sir John Falstaff in Drury Lane on way. Huge crowd at the dance, not a great deal of room. Bill came along with his Peggy. Spent most of the time by the bar-counter with Ron and some others drinking and talking. Had quite a good time, the sort of dance I enjoy. To bed 1.15.

Tuesday 26 November After dinner and Mother had gone out, the local Prudential Insurance agent called to see me. Tried to sell me an endowment policy and offered as bait the possibility of my getting a job as an agent when armed with such a policy. Now I just don't want an insurance policy of any sort and an insurance agent is about the last job in the world I'd be any good at. Yet I listened to their glib tale for half an hour only finally got rid of them by signing some damned un-obligatory proposal form and promising to give them a decision by the end of the week. Which will, of course, be negative, always so much easier for me to convey by letter than orally. I can never bring myself to be so downright rude and hurt anyone's feelings and that seems to be the only way to dispose of insurance agents.

29 The Malaya Social Club, 27 Stephen Street, W1.
30 (Sir) George Gibson Mitcheson (1883–1955), MP for St Pancras South West, 1931–45; knighted 1936.
31 The final result was Conservatives 432, Liberal 20, Labour 154, Independent Labour 4, Communist 1, Others 4.

1935

Wednesday 27 November Inadvertently left my spectacles at home in morning. Found it too painful working without them so walked all the way home and back for them during lunch hour. Exasperation in excelsis.

Friday 29 November On way home I purchased a hair restoring outfit. Cost me 7/6. Sufficient for a month. Extravagant but I'm determined to get my hair thick again at all costs.

Saturday 30 November After lunch wrote up troop log book. Went along to Horse Shoe to meet Bill and Ron at 6.30. Bill immediately excused himself and dashed off to take his beloved Peggy to the theatre. So Ron and I went along to Hammersmith on our own to see Enrico[32] singing at the Hammersmith Palace. A foul night, terrific downpour of rain. On getting off the bus at the Broadway dashed into a pseudo-Tudor pub for a drink and then hurried along King St to the theatre, a real shake-down of a place, one time variety place, now third-rate films with three or four turns. Went round to Enrico's dismal dressing room and chatted while he changed into dress clothes. Not doing too well by all accounts. Scrawled in white on mirror 'Enrico de Sula in the act of casting pearls etc etc'. However we went round the front to see him appear. Was utterly hopeless. Voice didn't carry. Couldn't hear a word he sang. Badly needed a microphone. Did three songs. Lukewarm applause. Turn that followed even viler still, then another ... But we couldn't stand it any longer, so came out and after a couple of drinks in adjoining pub, went back to the dressing room and came back to the West End with Enrico and his manager Tony who appears to be as much on his beam ends as Rico. Another drink then along to the Soho cafe for a final coffee. Bus home with Ron.

Friday 6 December To Holborn lunchtime. Called at shop at top of Gray's Inn Rd where I annually order my special red-bordered 'at a glance' calendar. Bought a new diary for 1936 and ordered calendar and pocket diary.

Saturday 21 December Went to lunch up at Gt Portland St with Montague and Power who, like several others in office, go there every day. Very cheap, roast beef and two veg: 8d, Pudding 3d, Beer 3½d. Good at the price.

Sunday 22 December Very cold and wintery but fine otherwise. Got up at 10.40. After breakfast and *Sunday Times*, took Nigger up to Hampstead. A good part of the heath covered by heavy ground frost. Made a rather lovely effect. Buildings which usually seem white somehow show up cream or dull yellow in contrast to the pure glistening white of snow or frost. Ponds partly frozen over by thin ice. A wan wistful sun did

---

32   A friend of Ron's.

its best to shine through the frosty faint mist. All this and the fresh exhilarating air made it a glorious day for brisk walking.

Tuesday 24 December Had to go paying most of day. Took Mother to Drury Lane in evening. went straight along there after work. First night of new pantomime *Jack and the Beanstalk*, produced by Ralph. Plenty of lavish spectacle. [*page of criticism*] Reception good but not rapturous. Whether it is worthy to supersede the successful *Glamorous Night* is a dubious point.

Wednesday 25 December Up at 9.30. A fairly bright and not over cold day. Set out about 12.0 with Mother and Nigger to spend the day at Forest Gate chez Shepherd. Fred on duty 2–10 but kept dropping in during that time nevertheless.[33] After dinner at 2.15 listened to King's Speech on radio. Then took Nigger and Mary for a walk to the other side of Wanstead Flats and back. Sat by fire for a while till the Mathews family arrived just before tea at 6.0. Spent evening in front parlour sitting round fire drinking, listening to the radio occasionally but more often to the kids squabbling and generally making themselves objectionable and watching Jack making a perfect hog of himself. I felt thoroughly bored and quite out of my element and was mighty glad when after a late supper the Mathews departed and I was able to get to bed about 2 a.m.

Thursday 26 December Got up about 10.45 and after breakfast took Nigger for a walk over Wanstead Flats and through the Park. Mary and her friend insisted on coming with us but after a while Mary, like the horrible spoilt and perverse little wretch she really is, left us and went back on her own on the plea that I had teased her! So I sent the equally precious friend of hers back after her and Nigger and I had a good walk after lunch. In the afternoon went along to Seven Sisters station to meet Bill at 4.30. He came along with his beloved Peggy and we walked back to his place. His brother and wife are staying there. Everyone except the old girl seemed to have colds or bad feet or something or other and not feeling up to much. However we had one or two gramophone records spun to liven things up and after tea went along to Bill's social club at the end of the road. The women also insisted on coming with us. Nothing doing there at all. Bare modern architecture sort of place, had a few drinks and games of darts and went back to Bill's place again. Played cards till about 10.30 and then came back to Forest Gate. Everyone round at the mother's place this evening. Got there just in time for supper, afterwards came back to Lorne Rd and turned in about 2.0 again.

---

33 Fred Shepherd was a serving Metropolitan Police Constable (information courtesy of the archivist at the Metropolitan Police Heritage Centre).

1935

Friday 27 December Up at 9.0 and after breakfast came home. Bus terribly slow through East End and City. Got home at 11.45. Changed clothes and had a read till lunch at 1.15.

Tuesday 31 December Getting home in evening found Mother had had all her remaining natural teeth out this morning. Consequently didn't feel too jubilant. After dinner went along to the YMCA to attend GEC Meeting and, finding everything either booked or darkened, I assumed that everyone else had had sense enough to forget all about it and so emerged from the deserted morgue-like YM and walked home. Read book and listened to radio till shortly after 12.0. So to bed. And thus passed out 1935.

RETROSPECT – 1935

According to the science of numerology, 1935 is – or rather was – one of my destiny years. That is to say some important significant event in my life, likely to affect the whole of my future existence, should have befallen one in the course of the year. In actual effect however, this has been a most singularly static year for me. Looking back, I cannot readily call to mind any outstanding feature of it. There was none of the emotional chaos or tense anxiety which characterised '33 and '34. My social and financial position, my friends, my interest in philosophy and general outlook have, all, except in minor aspects, remained unchanged. We haven't even moved our abode again. So much for numerology! It may, however, be interesting to review these minor points of change. They possibly indicate tendencies. Mother, after last year's serious illness, has fortunately continued to steadily progress to recovery and, at least to all outward appearances, has kept in moderately good health. Whether it is more apparent than real I don't really know. She keeps up a bold front anyway. That is all one can judge by.

I am still stuck in the same dull job with the same appalling lack of prospects. There was, of course, the usual consolation of a 5/- a week rise but that compensated for neither, and I am now desperately determined to get out of it and obtain a better job somewhere else. And towards the end of the year, I have at last renewed my long delayed efforts in that direction. I now also have at long last – more or less abandoned the notion of going in for journalism, freelance or otherwise. Though this is not to say that I would not do so given the opportunity and dramatic criticism still appeals to me as the ideal occupation. But it seems to me that I must face up to the fact that in the circumstances i.e. taking into consideration my age, experience, qualifications etc, there is not the least hope of my getting any opening in London journalism.

Part One

Not that the prospects in the business world are much more rosy. But I do at least stand a better chance there. So let's get to it.

My financial position is fairly satisfactory despite the slightness of the improvement. I finish the year worth, in cash, approximately £92, an increase of £10 on last year, made up partly by £5 of savings and the rest interest. That is the total of money I have invested in Savings Certificates and P.O. Savings Bank with interest to date. I also carry forward a surplus of £3 to meet current expenditure.

I find it increasingly difficult to save money owing to the continual encroachments of expenditure on personal requirements and pleasures on my inadequate income. Still I do manage to keep just on the right side and that is really all that matters. My interests and activities have undergone the least change of all. The theatre and secondly literature continue to be my ruling passions. Rambling I also remain keen on, though I haven't done so much as I should have liked. Incidentally during one week of my summer holiday I discovered the delights of lone rambling. That was one of my very few new experiences this year. My interest in Fascism has practically ceased altogether, since I resigned my non-active membership of the B.U.F. early in the year.[34] Likewise I have lost most of my enthusiasm for Rovering though I have remained Holborn Rover Secretary and Treasurer largely on sufferance and, I suppose for purely sentimental reasons, now that Cherub has left us and got married, even those reasons for carrying on don't really exist any longer. I doubt if I shall stick it for another year.

Though my friends have remained the same, my relations with them have changed to a certain degree. Bill has continued to be my best and most intimate friend, but now that he has badly fallen for a damned girl and even looks like going the way of all flesh, I shall probably lose him eventually. Still, he may get over it. I fervently hope so. I should be sorry to lose Bill's friendship. On the other hand, Ron, whom I only met this year and is well past that sort of thing, tends to make up for Bill's present deficiency. Even if more subdued than Bill, he's a good hearted, carefree, happy-go-lucky type and I like him immensely. We are the best of friends. I'm afraid that, owing to temperamental differences, Harry and myself have drifted apart a little. I had come to find his somewhat prosaic, prim, unimaginative and very conventional outlook and mentality very trying and tame and his furtive bewildered expression and silly little mannerisms rather irritate me. It's not his fault really. I suppose the influence of Norbury's stilted suburban life is too much for him. Only it doesn't coordinate very well with my own mental make-up and perfect harmony in that direction seems to me essential for real intimate friendship. I can't say that I get on

---

34 There is no record of his resignation from the BUF, the only indication of his loss of interest being his non-committal response to the BUF member who called on him on 23 January to tell him of the re-opening of the local branch.

exceptionally well with Gilbert either, though for different reasons, I never feel quite at ease in his company. I don't know why. It may even be my own fault. Yet I just don't. And he can become a most crushing bore sometimes, such as when he will persist in talking shop with Bill. Still he is not too bad in his way and in any case, he never was exactly a close friend of either Bill or myself. So in the general category of friends he remains. Likewise does Adam, of whom I have seen rather less than usual this year. My health has remained as excellent and unimpaired as ever, though a considerable falling of hair has given new cause for some anxiety and aroused fears of premature baldness. It has been brought about, I think, by allowing my scalp to remain dry and ill-nourished for too long and getting too much water on my hair. But whatever the cause, I am determined to spare no trouble or expense to return it to its former thick abundance. Yet I suppose that when all's said and done, the foremost impression of 1935, which will remain in my memory above all others, will be the Jubilee celebrations in May – attending the St Paul's Thanksgiving Service, the flag, flower-festooned and bunting bedecked streets, the floodlighting and other hectic glamorous nights – and all the rest of the revelry and pageantry which marked that memorable occasion. These were not however, strictly personal phenomena. They were the common experience of practically everyone who had the good fortune to live in the most glorious city in the world in 1935. It was that sort of year.

1936

Unsuccessful at improving his business prospects by finding a better job, lacking a girlfriend, approaching his twenty-sixth birthday and still living with his mother in rooms in Camden Town, Heap nevertheless entered 1936 in a slightly more optimistic mood. In an attempt to adopt a more mature image, he started smoking a pipe. This did not always agree with his stomach, particularly as he was drinking more, and more frequently, with his friends. But his record seventy-seven theatre visits in 1936, together with keeping his diary, hiking with friends and sometimes solo, and regular 'nights out with boys', kept Heap occupied through a personally generally uneventful year. A significant diary event was the death of George V in January, when Heap queued twice to file past the catafalque before witnessing the funeral procession. His support for the monarchy was, however, severely tested by King Edward VIII's affair with Mrs Simpson but the abdication crisis showed Heap's admiration for the statesmanship of the Prime Minister, Stanley Baldwin. Faith in the monarchy was quickly restored in December with the proclamation of King George VI, and the prospect of a coronation cheered Heap at the end of a not particularly enjoyable 1936. Only 25% of his 46,000 words are given below, but his activities during the lengthy gaps may easily be identified in the busy 'Cultural Capture' appendix.

Wednesday 1 January The New Year opened just as the old year finished – raining. And it seems like lasting too. For first time in weeks had just enough work to keep me going all day in office. Home to dinner then along to the YMCA for Holborn Rover New Year Party in the Howard Room. Much the same as two previous ones at the beginning of '34 and '35. A mixed crowd of about sixty or seventy Rovers and girlfriends – games – refreshments in Reception Room – Ralph at piano – songs to end with. Would all of course have been impossible without Ralph to run it. As it is these parties make the Rover meetings in the year worth going to, apart from collecting money for refreshments.

Thursday 2 January Called at YMCA on way home to settle about refreshments last night. They insisted that we had eighty at 9d each served out. I maintained that it couldn't have been more than sixty so we compromised at seventy, which then leaves a balance of 12/- to be taken out of funds to make up the balance over cash collected.

1936

Wednesday 15 January Phoned Ron and learned (a) that Ron's father had died and (b) that the Bill – Peggy romance was shattered! Very glad to hear of the latter anyway. After dinner at home, went to the Phoenix to see the second batch of Noel Coward playlets in *Tonight at 8.30*. Even better than the first. [*page of criticism*] This will be the show for months to come with the probable exception of the Cochran opus – the [recently married] Duke and Duchess of Kent in stalls caused much excitement, also James Agate in a box.[1] Saw his fur coat emerge after.

Monday 20 January After dinner sat listening to radio. Was announced early in evening that the King's strength was fading still further after his long illness. Then at 9.38 came the announcement of a bulletin issued at 9.25 to the effect that the King's life was passing peacefully away. Thereupon all stations closed down till 10.0 and again at further intervals of a quarter of an hour until a further bulletin was issued – the final fatal news "Le roi et mort. Vive le roi!" Though it hadn't yet come to that when I went to bed at 10.30. Thus with the end of the reign of George V ends a drama in five acts – pre-war prosperity – war – post-war chaos – depression – revival. No other reign has seen such vicissitudes. What the future holds, God only knows. Edward VIII now occupies the stage and all eyes are focussed on him, but to reiterate a line "It isn't 'arf funny without the King".

Tuesday 21 January The King died at five minutes before midnight last night. A solemn and mournful day despite its bright sunniness. The demeanour of everyone conveyed a great personal loss. For such it is. All theatres and cinemas closed for today. The body to be brought to London on Thursday to lie in state. Funeral to take place on Tuesday. Burial at Windsor. No radio today either, except an inspired little address by the Premier at 9.30.

Wednesday 22 January Edward VIII proclaimed King at St James's and in the City today. Mourning has now become practically universal. A man without a black tie or a woman without a black hat is scarcely to be seen now. All except one or two theatres and all cinemas reopened today despite prospects of poor business. A revised and curtailed programme of music only was relayed and [the BBC] closed at 10.0.

Thursday 23 January A busy crowded lunch hour. First down to Mudie's to change book. The beginnings of a crowd already lining Kingsway curbs to watch King George's coffin pass by this afternoon on its way to Westminster from Sandringham.

Saturday 25 January Walked to Westminster to try and see the Lying in State of King George in Westminster Hall. Open to the public for four days. Walked along Millbank and eventually found the end of the queue

---

1 See entry for 1 April 1935.

about a mile and a half mile away on Vauxhall Bridge! Joined on the tail and moved along at a snail's pace towards the ultimate Mecca. That was at 8.5. By 10.0 when the Hall was due to close, I was at Lambeth Bridge but an extension must have been granted for we continued to move on. Then, to put the lid on it, it started raining heavily. I stuck it for a while then until about 10.45. I heard a policeman say it would be another hour before we got in. I hesitated no longer and made a dash along to Whitehall for a bus home before I got thoroughly soaked. Supper and to bed at 12.30. A wasted evening, still, an experience.

Sunday 26 January Up at 8.0 and after a quick breakfast and a glance at papers went along to Waterloo to go on the Southern Ramble. But as neither Bill nor Ron turned up before the train left at 10.3, I didn't go on it and in a fit of pique walked all the way home again. As an alternative went and had another shot at trying to get into Westminster Hall. Joined the queue at 12.0 over the Embankment. Took 1½ hours to reach Vauxhall Bridge where I started last night and 5½ hours to reach Westminster Hall. Quickly passed through in about three minutes filing past the catafalque on both sides three abreast. A solemn and simple yet intensely majestic sight and certainly a memorable experience. Thousands still arriving to join three mile queue when I came out at 5.30 and got bus home. A good dinner awaiting me, which I instantly consumed, and a cup of tea about an hour later. Waked home from Waterloo for second time today. A light supper and to bed at 10.45.

Tuesday 28 January Up at 4.30 to go down early to get a good position to see the Funeral Procession of King George on its way from Westminster to Paddington, en route to burial at Windsor. Got down to Trafalgar Square by 6.0 and walked along part of the route, the Mall, up St James's and into Piccadilly. Still dark. Crowds three and four deep already lining pavements. Took up good position on north side of Piccadilly just by Down St under some scaffolding of new building just as it started to rain at 6.30. Left off after an hour. Dawn came and with it ever more crowds swarming down roadway. Also considerable amount of traffic trying to get along. Soon all came to a standstill and a chaotic muddle set in. Traffic couldn't move. Pedestrians either couldn't, or more likely wouldn't. And this lasted an hour, until some infantry made a clearing down the centre and got the traffic out of it. Left the pedestrians on both sides however about fifteen people deep in front of us on pavement. Outrageously bad organisation. So, thanks to the London Police force, I saw practically nothing of the procession when it came along about 10.30 despite my early morning diligence.[2]

2   Under the headline 'Record Crowds in London', *The Times* of 29 January reported that '80,000 people arrived at Hyde Park Corner Station ... The crowds in the streets near Hyde Park Corner and Green Park became so dense that passengers arriving at these stations found it difficult to leave them, and the police consequently gave instructions for them to be closed.'

Only by standing on tip toe in my cramped position could I get a glimpse of military or naval headgear. Also a peep at the coffin on the gun carriage. Couldn't see any royal mourners, home or foreign, whatsoever. A bitter humiliating disappointment. Came home after in high dudgeon. After lunch at home, went down again and strolled round the Mall and St James's Park during afternoon. A few crowds round the palace awaiting return of King Edward and Queen [Mother, Mary] back from Windsor. Bus home from Westminster. Tea at 5.30. I stayed in evening reading. Bed at 10.0.

Wednesday 29 January Colder and less unsettled. Fine pictures and description of Royal funeral in the morning papers. The *Mail* easily the best, both in size and content. Took Mother to the Tatler in evening to see the GB [Gaumont British] film of the Funeral scenes. A good piece of work. Also several other shorts of varying interest. Best of the bunch a humorous and very droll discourse by Robert Benchley, celebrated New York dramatic critic[3] and his funniest one 'How to Sleep'. A unique piece of fooling. Got home in time to hear end of Peterson–Harvey fight on radio. Peterson just won on points.[4] To bed at 11.15.

Wednesday 5 February Monthly District Rover meeting at YMCA. Held a discussion on 'What I expect to get out of Rovering.' I spoke for ten minutes or so in it. Then one or two others followed by lengthy discourse from Tiny and general discussion. A gloomy business. Deviated into a revelation of what everyone had expected to get out of Rovering and hadn't, it seemed more like an inquest on Holborn Rovering with Tiny [more] as the coroner than anything else. Someone asked if the log book had been sent at the end of the meeting. It hadn't so I read it. On finishing some muddle headed fool started carping as to the nature and relevance of its contents. I explained the obvious to the best of my ability and patience and Tiny himself abruptly closed the meeting before that meandered into a discussion. And that is Rovering. Thank the Lord there is at least some talk of discontinuing these miserable meetings.

Tuesday 11 February The weather is definitely in the news now. 'Bitterest Day of the Winter' the placards declare it to be this evening. Certainly didn't go above freezing point at any time. Seems like lasting some little time too. Went to Swedish drill after work. Plenty of good strenuous stuff to warm one up. Weight after 10 st 9 lbs. Walked home. Pondered over Easter hike again and more or less decided to abandon the South Downs trip in favour of the Berkshire Downs, theformer

---

3 Robert Benchley (1889–1945), American humourist.
4 Jack Peterson thus retained the British Heavyweight Championship.

being amply covered this spring by Sunday Southern [Railway Company-promoted] Ramble.

Wednesday 12 February After work, dashed home, changed into evening suit, had a quick snack and went along to the Horse Shoe to meet Bill, Ron and Leslie and go to the Southern Ramble Dance at Victoria Hall. Got to the Hall just in time for one dance before the interval. Went into the bar and had more drinks and gradually got pretty well sozzled. Didn't dance much and didn't like the Hall a great deal, so obviously what it is – a formal uninspirable uncongenial dance hall. Preferred Bush House much more to this, general opinion seemed to be otherwise. Round to the Soho Cafe with Ron for a final quick coffee before bus home.

Friday 14 February After dinner, washed up then wrote off to book up at Hostel at Easter. Have decided to go to Berkshire or Wiltshire Downs, starting and finishing at Newbury. [*paragraph of planned itinerary*] I'm totally unfamiliar with this bit of the country. To bed at 11.0.

Monday 17 February Fog early but fine and clear later. Office sensation – Reeve got fired. Given a week's notice but left immediately. Reason presumed to be general inefficiency though I believe there was much more to it than that. A pity the oldest of my contemporaries (early 1929 vintage) he was a bit of a simpleton but a good fellow for all that. The only thing is 'Who goes next?' It looks ominous.

Tuesday 18 February The real truth behind the Reeve sensation leaked out today. It transpires that for some time past he had disposed of unwanted or inconvenient credit notes and return dockets by putting them down the WC, thereby causing it to flood. Takes all Saturday to put right and led to their discovery. Really fine example of course for poor old Russ. He couldn't foresee that. And probably the best place for them anyway. Straight home to dinner. Wrote after a job in the *Telegraph*, then along to the 11th Den at St Andrews Rectory, Holborn for Rover Mates Council. A very satisfactory meeting, seven of us present. New and more congenial surroundings. Tea and biscuits on the house. Decided to discontinue monthly district meetings inter alia monthly notices a lot of bother and trouble for there will now be no need to keep up log book either. Only intend to write up account of RM Councils and issue every three or four months to RMs.

Sunday 1 March A broadcast speech by the King at 4.0 this afternoon. Very short in length and conveyed very little. Didn't really seem worthwhile.

Thursday 5 March Straight home after work, changed into evening dress and went along to the Horse Shoe to meet Bill and Ron and go along to the Rowland House Panto Ball at the Grosvenor Hotel

1936

(postponed from Jan 28th). Spent most of the time down in the bar with Ron. Danced very little. Trixie was there – one of the few remnants of the old gang present. Had the night off from her fiancée. Is getting married this summer. Being more or less in the same lonely boat she spent most of the evening with us. Bill attached himself to some other damsel and left with her shortly before the end. Trixie came along to Soho with Ron and myself after, only just got the last train in the nick of time.[5] Bus home and in to bed at 1.30.

Tuesday 10 March A good deal of discussion in office on the possibilities of war following Germany's occupation of the Rhineland forbidden military zone and France's demand for reprisals.[6] Situation is certainly serious but all possible outcomes of it are only guesswork yet. Anything might happen in the next week or two.

Friday 13 March My 26th birthday and as usually happens about as dull and unmemorable a day as one could possibly imagine. Still, suppose the celebration is really tomorrow night.

Saturday 14 March Took Mother to the Vaudeville to see the new Charlot revue *The Town Talks*.

Tuesday 17 March Radio news: Germany accepts invitation to League Council meeting in London on Thursday. Thus some relief in international situation which is still very delicate.

Sunday 29 March In afternoon accompanied Mother to Charlton Cemetery primarily to see that Gran's name etc. had been properly inscribed on the newly cleaned Solloway family tombstone. A melancholy tram ride through South London and a long walk to and from the cemetery. Not without interest however. Came back via Blackwall Tunnel and Poplar. Have never been through tunnel before, a remarkable phenomenon really. Must have been a great feat to accomplish.[7]

Wednesday 1 April Practically everyone else in the office but me got a pay rise today. Not that I care much, it only makes me realise more forcibly that I've got to get out of the damned place pretty soon or die in the attempt.

Friday 3 April Went onto the doctor's to see about my rib trouble. Whyte examined me, seemed rather baffled and called in his colleague who was apparently, more expert in this sort of thing. Also seemed a bit mystified. Said it was extremely rare phenomenon and proceeded

---

5   This is the final diary mention of Trixie/Beatrice.
6   With Allied troops having withdrawn from the Rhineland in 1930, Hitler's reoccupation of the territory violated the terms of the Versailles and Locarno Treaties.
7   Originally constructed in 1897 and until 1967 a single bore, the 4,400-foot (1340-metre) tunnel connects Poplar with the Greenwich peninsula.

Part One

to prod me all over erstwhile [*sic*] conversing with Whyte in obscure medical jargon. Began to get rather apprehensive about it i.e. broke out into a sweat – which made me feel even worse still. However they eventually finished. Whyte gave me a prescription for some stuff to rub into it, told me there was nothing to worry about and to call again in ten days.

Saturday 4 April Fine and bright but cold and windy with it. Boat Race in morning, Cambridge won yet again for 13th year in succession, by 5 lengths. Scotland v England match at Wembley in afternoon. A draw 1–1. Thousands of Scotsmen invaded London for the day. The streets swarmed with Tam O'Shanters. Spent the evening round the West End with Bill, Ron and four other chaps – assembled at the Horse Shoe from 7.30 onwards and went on to the Malaya about 8.15. Poor old John [Hobson] got very sozzled. Had a job to get him away when we all left with Monty at 10.30 and an even greater job as we moved further west. Tried Colombo's[8] but too crowded so walked down to Piccadilly Circus and tried the Haymarket and Criterion Brasseries as well as the Corner House but couldn't get in any. Eventually Monty led us back up to the Cafe Blue in Compton St. And there with sober coffee we finished a pretty good evening. I only spent about three shillings altogether which was good value.

Monday 6 April Straight home after work. Dined and went to Paddington station to inquire about trains to Newbury on Friday. A delightfully dilapidated shambling old station, typically late Victorian. The newly constructed Post Office, Boots shop etc along Platform 1 look completely out of place – a sort of reluctant concession to modernity. But the small musty little enquiry office is still perfectly in character. A prim antiquated old lady sits perched on a stool at one end of the counter with a timetable in front to her and pertly disposes of a queue of half a dozen inquirers one by one. The alacrity and precision with which she dispenses time tabular information is a joy to watch – if one dared to spend more than the minimum time possible in the enquiry office. Somehow those formidable pince nez would forbid such a waste of valuable time. And rightly so, this is Paddington.

Friday 10 April Set off on lone four day youth hostelling Easter hike in Berkshire on 9.10 train from Paddington to Newbury.

[*Easter weekend solo hike in the Chilterns*]

Monday 13 April Return trek to Newbury. Had some tea and caught 5.12 train to Paddington. Had to change and wait about half an hour at Reading. Got to Paddington at 7.0 and got bus home. Despite the

8   Joseph Colombo's, 7 Great Titchfield Street, W1.

shortcomings of weather and feet, had been a darned good Easter tramp which I enjoyed to the full. Lovely inns, hilly country full of good walks with magnificent views and the weather could have been much worse. It could have rained instead of occasional snow, could have been much better hostels. And as for my feet, they always pack up in any case.

Monday 20 April Rainy and cold. Forgot to take spectacles to work, consequently had some strained eyes all day. Felt hellish. Called in to see Dr Whyte on way home. Said there was nothing more could be done about my fibrous trouble except rubbing it with ointment. Nothing really to worry about, just carry on in the normal way, including vigorous exercise etc.

Tuesday 21 April Dull, cold rainy evening. Budget Day. Income Tax up 3d and increased duty on rest, mainly to meet increased expenditure on defence. On the other hand, extra reliefs for married family men – no consolation for over-taxed bachelors however.

Wednesday 29 April Saw my old friend and ex-colleague Ginger McOrmie again today. Hadn't seen him since about a year ago, shortly after he left PR's. About to start a new job in an insurance office. Is also being sued by Savage for damages for the broken nose he gave him. Also told us that Reeve, who left ignominiously two months back, is working at Vickers Armstrong at Weybridge making armaments. And so on, was glad to see him again and doing well. Shall probably see more of him now he has more time to spare.

Wednesday 6 May Mother got a new job at a women's residential club in Cavendish Square. Hours 7.30–3.30.

Monday 11 May The new boil on my neck causing me considerable discomfort. Also a similar sort of eruption on my left hand. Something wrong with my blood sans doubt. Note en passant: Mother already given up the new job she got last Thursday in order to start looking after the four years old offspring of the basement dwellers[9] while they go to work during day.

Wednesday 13 May Boil on left hand has caused considerable swelling and inflammation around it. Had to have hand bound up today. Exceedingly painful, especially when holding arm straight down to side. Have to keep it in upward or horizontal position. Called at doctor on way home about it. Told me to keep putting iodine on it and gave me a prescription for a bottle of iron tonic for the blood together [with] some dressing for my hand.

---

9   Young Bernie McLavey, who features in years to come.

Friday 15 May Walked to work with arm in sling but discarded it on getting there. But still have to keep forearm horizontal so couldn't do any paying of wages today. Called at doctor's after work and had look at boil on hand – squeezed out. Fortunately it had spread enough to have this done without cutting. Had it tightly re-bandaged and caught a tram home.

Tuesday 19 May Walked home, dined on eggs and spinach, a food I have hitherto loathed but am now compelled to take for my blood. Did not seem too bad after all. This is my fourth meatless day in succession. Have Bernie up with me for the early part of the evening most days of the week (Mother looking after him during the day. A vital, exuberant and altogether loveable little bundle of juvenile joie de vivre).

Saturday 30 May A wet unpromising start to Whitsun but had cleared up a bit by the time I had dashed home, changed, had lunch, and set off on a weekend hike on the North Downs. Caught 2.42 coach from Baker St to Godstone. Arrived there at 4.15.

[*Whitsun weekend solo hike around the North Downs*]

Monday 1 June A walk over to the view point before breakfast for one final glimpse of that magnificent vista of South Eastern England. Got the 6.39 coach back from Sevenoaks. Got off at Horse Guards Avenue and took bus home. Home at 8.30. Supper. Wrote up three days' diary. Bed 11.35.

Tuesday 16 June To Mudie's lunchtime and got out *On An English Screen* by James Agate, first published in 1924. Not having much work to do in the office and JD being away on holiday, I started reading [in] the afternoon. I avidly read one essay after another and soon came to realise that I would not be able to put the book down until I had devoured the whole lot. I read it during tea, I read it after tea, after dinner and on through the evening until, at 10.45, I finally came to the last of 222 pages and 42 essays every one of which radiate in no lukewarm manner the shrewd sense of humour and witty warm-hearted personality of their author. Never before as far as I can remember have I read a full length book in a day, let alone half a day perhaps never – or rather very rarely have I encountered a book so appealing or entertaining to induce me to perform such a feat. Anyway, there it is.

Saturday 20 June Swelteringly hot. Temps hitting the high spots. Up to 84 today. After lunch a short read and an early tea went up to Kentish Town station to catch the 5.5 evening train to Southend (2/- return). Packed out, almost unbearably hot and stuffy. Got down there just before 7.0, made straight for the front and walked along to Westcliffe and back by the upper promenade. Then went to the end of the pier and back on the electric railway. Still having time to spare before meeting Bill at the pier entrance at 9.0, walked along to the Kursaal and back. Waited half an hour for Bill but he didn't turn up so went along to the Kursaal for a quick look around before getting the return train at 10.30. Took just over two hours getting back. Faster going, otherwise not a bad trip. Shouldn't care to stay at Southend. Back at Kentish Town at 12.35 and walked home from there. Bed 1.40.

Sunday 21 June After tea at 4.45 decided to go to Kew Gardens and Richmond for the evening. So went up to Camden Town station and got a train to Kew. Very convenient, only takes half an hour and costs but 11d return to Richmond. On getting out at Kew made straight up to the Gardens and strode sharply round them covering as much ground as possible. A delightful spot but requires adequate time for a leisurely canter round it to be appreciated properly. Had only been in the train ten minutes when the storm broke. Fortunately at Camden Town I could get a bus almost from door to door. After pelting down with tremendous gusto for two hours the rain at last slackened off at 10.30. Some storm!

Sunday 28 June After dinner went up to Camden Town to get a train to Richmond. Strode through the main street thereof, ascended Richmond Hill (for the first time) and past the Star and Garter and into Richmond Park. Made a thorough tour and inspection round the park also in which I had ne'er set foot before today. Very charming spot, two lakes, roaming deer, band, everything, and a very pleasant towpath. 9.50 train back to Camden Town. Home 10.50.

Friday 3 July Bus home and had dinner then went down to have a talk with Mrs Soleby's nephew Jack, down from Manchester for a few weeks. An entertaining and vivacious fellow with an enthusiasm for the theatre almost as great as my own and, to a lower degree, of films and books. A chap after my own heart. We whiled away two hours with such shop talk.

Saturday 4 July After lunch went with Mother to the Mansion House with a party of the Ypres League. Didn't see a great deal: the board meeting room, the tiny court room, a couple of drawing rooms. C'est tout. Bought a new ash walking stick.[10]

Sunday 12 July Took Nigger up to Hampstead in morning. Would have taken Bernie too but he was laid up a bit queer for the day. Was about to board a bus coming back when the conductor refused to let Nigger on, on the grounds that he had a lot of trouble with dogs. I was naturally most indignant but appeared that there is no remedy in such a

---

10 Heap used a walking stick when hiking and when he had blistered feet but he has not previously mentioned carrying it on social nights. He does occasionally mention it in later entries.

Part One

matter for the conductor is allowed to use his discretion regarding dogs and his decision is final. Still, only twice before in Nigger's nine years have I had similar set back and oddly enough coming back by tram on both occasions. In the first instance it was wet and the conductor feared that Nigger would jump up and dirty the curly covered seats. In the other there were several dogs on top already and the conductor was apprehensive as to the possibility of a dog fight.

Wednesday 15 July Made one or two house purchases at PR's this morning. Four 1/3 Van Heusen collars less discount 4/2, a 27/6 Rolls Razor[11] for 22/11, and ordered a 4/6 Ordnance Survey map of Lakeland. Also bought 5/- P.O. for *Gang Show* tickets. A veritable small orgy of spending.

Thursday 16 July Went along to Sinclair's in Cranbourne St lunchtime and ordered a new suit. Chose a dark grey material with a slight tinge of blue. Normally costs 5½ guineas but he offered to let me have it for 4½. An attempt on the life of the King was made today as he drove along Constitution Hill to the Palace after attending a military function in Hyde Park. Mother was there with Bernie a few yards from where the would-be assassin levelled a revolver at the King and was jumped on from horseback by a special constable who it transpired to be Tony Dick, the husband of Aunt Minnie's sister, therefore a distant relative of ours.[12] After the incident occurred, Mother dashed over and phoned the *Evening Standard* about it. Got £3.2.0 for the story. A good morning's work all round.

Sunday 19 July An accursed day. I lost about the most valuable thing I possessed – the small gold signet ring which Mother gave me for my 21st birthday. I had worn and treasured it ever since. It must have slipped off my finger in Regent's Park this morning when I took Bernie and Nigger for a walk there. I thought I felt it slip off over by the lake but after searching the close-cut grass in vain thought it had just been imagination and had left it at home. However when we did get home that hope proved to be in vain. So I dashed back again and searched that spot thoroughly, without avail. Reported the loss to the keeper on duty and came home again for a late lunch, after which Mother

11 An expensive proprietary brand of safety razor, the solid blade of which was honed on a strip within the carrying case.
12 *The Times* headline of 17 July was 'Alarming Incident in Royal Procession'. The half page report by two *Times* correspondents and their photographer, who were present on Constitution Hill as the King, at the head of the Brigade of Guards, approached Buckingham Palace, did not mention Special Constable Dick. He was later named, with a photograph, when he gave evidence when George McMahon, an Irishman with a grudge against the police, was sentenced to twelve months' hard labour for 'producing a revolver near the King with the intent to alarm his Majesty' (*Daily Telegraph*, 15 September 1936). TNA, MI5 file KV2/1505 and Metropolitan Police file MEPO3/1713 show McMahon to have been a intelligence nuisance who claimed that he had been in a plot with German officials. He had approached the Italian Consulate alleging a similar plot in May 1936.

went back with me to search, calling at Albany St Police Station to report it on the way. Still it didn't come to light and at last we gave up and came home to tea. Felt utterly wretched and miserable for it was irreplaceable, its sentimental value being far greater than its monetary value. Mother tried to console me by promising to get me another one to replace it. A lovely sentiment on her part even though a replacement could not be the same as the one I've lost. A tragic business, unless by a miracle someone brings it to a happy ending by finding it and taking it to the Police Station. What hopes!

Saturday 1 August After lunch went down to Bravington's at King's Cross and bought a new signet ring for my left hand small finger to replace the one I lost. Chose a 9ct. solid gold one at 17/6. Have to leave it to be reduced a few sizes (my finger being so exceptionally slender) and have an initial engraved. Didn't get a better class ring as Mother also proposes to replace the lost ring (which of course she originally gave me) by having Dad's diamond dress shirt stud set in an 18 ct gold ring for my third finger and making me a present of it for my next birthday.

Monday 3 August Took Nigger up to Hampstead. Usual bank holiday fair on up there. But though it was impossible to escape the din of it all over Hampstead, we did manage to get away from the crowds now and again. Not that I dislike fairs as fairs, only I didn't go up there with the purpose of attending this one, but to enjoy 1½ hours brisk walk over the heath, which I did. So what! Walked up to Marble Arch in evening. Spent some time enjoying with amused delight the raucous disorder prevailing at a meeting where an anarchist was not very successfully endeavouring to extol the glories of Soviet Russia. It is a rare sight to see a communist heckled.

Tuesday 4 August After dinner took Bernie and Nigger up to Regent's Park for the evening. Climbed to the top of Primrose Hill and got the most enchanting view over London I have ever seen. Everything stood forth in such a clear rich mellow glow as the rays of the setting sun boldly defined the distinctive beauty of the whole vista. And far away in the distance, as if floating on the horizon there was an ethereal looking Crystal Palace. A lovely, unforgettable sight.[13]

Wednesday 5 August Called in Bravington's on way home for the new signet ring I left last Saturday to be inscribed and made smaller. Now fits my small finger perfectly and looks très chic. Amazingly cheap at the price (17/6).

---

13   Heap's enjoyment of the sight of Crystal Palace on the horizon is particularly poignant as he missed seeing it destroyed by fire four months later – see 1 December below.

Part One

Saturday 8 August Got off from work at 12.30. Dashing home, changed, had lunch and accompanied by Mother and Bernie went along to Paddington to catch the 2.10 train to Stratford on Avon. Got talking on the train to a very interesting fellow, Mal Davies by name, just down from Oxford. Talked on literature, art and the theatre and all manner of things. He wanted to renew the acquaintance in London later. I was to be invited to the Overseas Club[14] and down to his place near Folkestone. So we exchanged names and addresses and he went on to Wales. I got out to change at Leamington Spa. Eventually got to Stratford on Avon at 4.50. Had hoped to get a bus down to Mickleton [Youth Hostel] but learned that there wasn't one till 9.0 so after getting some tea, set out to walk it. Some nine miles or so.

[Nine nights of youth hostelling, solo walking the Cotswolds, including a night at the home of his old Rover friend 'Cherub' at Tuffley, south of Gloucester]

Monday 17 August [Caught] The 1.37 from Gloucester to Stratford-on-Avon, bringing with me a box of flowers from the [Cherub's] garden in my pack. Arrived Stratford 3.25 and having a couple of hours to spare, went and had a look at Shakespeare's Birthplace. Had some tea then caught the 5.46 back to London, arrived Paddington 8.15 and got a bus home. Found Mother with head bandaged and eye bunged up. Considerable pain, Pitiful business. 'Bout time her health gave her a break. Had supper, unpacked and went to bed at 11.30. So ended a thoroughly good holiday. Have enjoyed it to the full.

Friday 21 August After breakfast and papers went round to Lyons Head Office at Cadby Hall where I had obtained an appointment with the Chief Accountant.[15] Huge offices mainly staffed by girls. Had to wait about for some time. Couldn't offer me anything definite but might have something in a semi-supervisory secretarial capacity in a few weeks. So much for that.

Saturday 22 August Fine and warm. Went down to finish my fortnight's holiday with a weekend at Joshua Reynolds's place at Westfield. Caught the 10.10 train from Charing Cross to Hastings. Arrived just before 12.0 and walked down to the front and went up the West Cliff to Hastings Castle, bus to Rye, two-hour looking around there, got to Joshua's at 9.0, whole family looking well. Supper and to bed 12.30.

Sunday 23 August Left soon after 6.0 and caught a bus into Hastings, Josh coming with me to spend the evening there. Strolled up to the end

14 St James's Street, SW1.
15 At 66 Hammersmith Road, W14, Cadby Hall was the J. Lyons & Co. Ltd headquarters and their huge food factory. The site was cleared in 1983.

of the pier and back then left them to cut up to the station and catch the 7.50 train back to London. Very packed, lucky to get a seat (in a 1st class compartment at no extra cost) so came home in comfort. Arrived Charing Cross 9.50 and got bus home. This ends my fortnight's release from the yoke of PR's. Haven't done so badly really. Made good use of it and had reasonably good weather. No, nothing to complain about at all.

Tuesday 25 August Had a bilious attack during the night. Had to get up three times to be sick. Apparently due to eating rather unripe apples I had brought home from Joshua's. So didn't get much sleep and naturally felt pretty foul when I got up in the morning. Could scarcely touch my breakfast however went to work just the same and soon felt all the better for having done so, occupies both the mind and body, felt practically normal by afternoon.

Thursday 27 August Went along to Keith Prowse's [clerical employment agency] offices in Bond St lunchtime, filled up a form and had an interview. Nothing definite resulted, just a suggestion of further negotiation should a vacancy in the offices arise.

Friday 28 August Took my recently purchased Rolls Razor to pieces to see how it worked. Want to start using it next week. Found the handle wouldn't fit onto the blade. A damned nuisance. Will take it back tomorrow to be put right.

Sunday 30 August Up at 7.15 and cleaned the windows before breakfast. Up to Hampstead for the day taking picnic luncheon in attaché case with us – Mother, Bernie, Nigger and self. Set out at 11.30. About half an hour's walk the other end to a pleasant spot over near Ken Wood. Got a couple of deck chairs and settled down for the afternoon. Fine warm day. Hot in sun but very cool in shade owing to a fresh breeze prevailing. Stayed up there till late afternoon and got home at 6.15.

Tuesday 1 September Went along to the City in lunch hour to keep an appointment with Powell Duffryn Associated Collieries Ltd on Gt Tower St. Had an interview with one of the officials. Took down some further details re: experience etc. Couldn't offer me a definite job but would keep my name and particulars in mind should anything crop up in the future. Which I suppose is as good news as I can hope for from writing up to firms on the off chance. After, wrote a couple of chance job letters and spent rest of evening revising some 'Secretarial Practice' from my old study notes. It's going to be a bit of a job to pick it up again after five years procrastination, but I must try and be prepared for the possibility of finding a new job.

Part One

Saturday 19 September After tea went up to the Britannia Cinema[16] to see H G Wells' *Things to Come*. A most colossal and sensational film. A veritable masterpiece [*page of criticism*].

Sunday 27 September Couldn't go out in morning so helped Mother get the room ready for the painters coming in to do the place up this week. Ceiling to be whitewashed and the walls repapered, consequently had to move everything away from them. This involved emptying the bookcase and my special cupboard and loading them again. All of which of course will have to be done again when they're finished. The devil of a job.

Saturday 3 October Decorators finished papering the walls this morning so spent afternoon helping Mother get the place straight again. The floors had to be washed, the furniture dusted and replaced in original position. Also broke off to get some shopping in middle of it. A strenuous and trying task but eventually managed to get things in some sort of order by the time we had tea at 6.0. After, shaved with my new Rolls Razor for the first time. Made a bit of a mess of it, face very sore after, apparently takes time getting used to it. Then changed into decent suit and went along to the Horse Shoe to meet Bill, Ron, John, Harry and Les and proceed thence round to the YMCA for the Ramblers Association Dance. A so-so sort of dance, I detest the hall, there's no bar attached to it but otherwise it wasn't too bad. I did actually dance once or twice. It ended at 11.0. Into Horse Shoe again for a final beer and sandwich and round to Soho for coffee with Ron and John.

[*Surprisingly, Heap made no mention of the famous Sunday 4 October 'Battle of Cable Street' in the East End, when Sir Oswald Mosley paraded over 2,000 uniformed BUF marchers but, at the request of the Metropolitan Police Commissioner, agreed to abandon his march owing to the presence of strong communist, anarchist and Jewish crowds who fought the 6,000 police present and erected barricades to oppose the Fascist marchers. Many injuries and arrests resulted. Although Heap retained his Fascist views (see 1936 Retrospect below), he had not mentioned British Fascism since 9 September 1934.*]

Wednesday 7 October A considerable bus strike broke out in London today. But not so great that one would have noticed the difference without having to read the papers. It only makes me realise what a colossal undertaking London Transport is when 1,600 busmen on strike and a mere twenty or so bus routes affected can make such little difference.

---

16   At 211 Camden High Street, NW1.

1936

Sunday 18 October Up at 7.30 to go on auto ramble with Bill's Portelet Rambling Club[17] down Hindhead way, for which I composed the notices thereof. Coach left Charing Cross at 10.0. 35 of us [for walk and tea]. Then up to the pub at Thursley for drinks and darts before getting coach home. Called at another pub just this side of Guildford on way back. A good long half way halt, nearly an hour, which we made full use of. And so to the last lap, which brought us back to Charing Cross at 10.15.

Saturday 24 October In evening went along to the Horse Shoe to meet Bill, Ron, John and go along to the East End to see something of Limehouse and the Docks. As it happened we saw precious little of either. Took a bus to West India Docks intending to go straight to the notorious late Charlie Brown's pub The Blue Posts now carried on by his son.[18] But Ron, thinking he knew the way when he didn't, led us right along East India Dock Rd to the entrance of the Blackwall Tunnel whence we made our way back through some back streets (calling at a couple of pubs en route) to West India Dock Rd and eventually reaching journey's end. Was well worth visiting. By then the others had had enough so we walked up the main road and got a bus to the West End without going into Limehouse proper. Had a final drink at the Malaya and went down to the Corner House Brasserie for supper. Parted outside at 12.30 and got bus home. Bed at 2.0. Not a bad evening but there's only one thorough way of exploring London and that is by day and alone. Which I intend to do very soon.

Thursday 29 October Have been badly constipated all the week since cutting out Epsom Salts. A dose of syrup of figs this morning broke the spell however. Walked home. After dinner calculated my financial position. At the end of the year my total investment in Savings Certificates and Savings Bank with interest to date will amount to £100.8.1½. Which represents, I suppose, something of a minor achievement. One could, of course, if need be live on such a sum for a year without doing a stroke of work. Not sumptuously by any means, but just adequately. However, may that never befall me! One or two rainy days would be quite enough.

Wednesday 4 November Wrote to Tiny Chamberlain resigning my position as Secretary and Treasurer of the Holborn Rovers, which have obviously ceased as an active body and [so] it will not make much difference [without] the interest or enthusiasm from me.

Friday 6 November Received a reply from Tiny this morning re my resignation. Was very pleasant and reasonable about it and even invited

17 The group was formed around those who had met at the Portelet Bay holiday camp in Jersey.
18 At 73–75 West India Dock Road, E14. The new landlord was Charles William Brown.

Part One

me to dinner one evening. After dinner wrote two letters, one to the District Association Secretary and the other to the London Rover Secretary re. resignation. According to Tiny, I shall have to hand over all the books, papers, cash and other junk related to the late lamented Holborn Rovers to the former. May he have plenty of room for them to clutter up!

Saturday 7 November Instead of going to theatre in evening decided to stay in and write the lengthy letter due to Aunt Pop which I pen every four months. After getting some coals for Mother, started on it at 7.0 and continued till 8.30 when I went down to see Bernie. Doctor called in late tonight diagnosed scarlet fever. Don't know whether he'll have to go away or stay at home yet.

Wednesday 11 November Two minutes silence duly held at 11.0. All stood at windows as usual. Cold bleak morning. Remarkable example of the herd instinct, the way everyone rushes along to crowd together in some spacious spot such as the Royal Exchange, Piccadilly Circus or Oxford Circus. There were thousands crammed into the latter. Silence seemed to last much longer than usual. Don't suppose it actually did. Straight home to dinner. In evening packed all the Holborn Rover stuff into a suitcase and took it along to Coram Fields HQ, newly built in a corner of the old Foundling site, and handed everything, cash and all to Mason, the district secretary, for disposal in due course as Koko thinks fit. Koko, I gathered, has succeeded Tiny as DC [District Commissioner]. I have now of course rid myself of any responsibility regarding Holborn Rovers and automatically severed my connection with Rovering altogether. Except in the unlikely event of an Old Scouts Association being formed in Holborn, which I would probably join. On getting home wrote a couple of letters to Koko and London Rovers Sec. to clear things up.

Monday 16 November Mother not too well – fell down stairs and sprained her ankle and injured herself generally.

Tuesday 17 November Mother in a bad way. Did herself considerable harm in that fall yesterday. Was up vomiting all night, and was too weak to get about today. Had to lay on the bed, in great pain nearly all day. It was with the greatest reluctance that I dashed off to work this morning. It's awful having to leave her like that unattended all day, though I don't suppose I could do much if I stayed at home. And she won't have the doctor in either being so certain of being right by tomorrow. I only wish to God she could be! But why such things have to happen at all is beyond comprehension even when life is considered a meaningless joke. To the Horse Shoe to meet Bill and to go around trying to fix up somewhere for the Portelet Ramble Club dance just before Christmas. In other words, we pub-crawled. Bed in front room at 12.0.

Friday 20 November Mother still bed-ridden and very much the same. Had doctor in this afternoon to look at her but didn't seem to convey much idea of what exactly is wrong with her, don't suppose he really knows. Dashed home after work to change into evening dress, bolt a snack and hurry along to the Horse Shoe to meet Bill and the rest of the crowd and go on to the Southern Ramblers Dance at Victoria Hall, Bloomsbury Square. Don't like the place much, far too ultra-modern for my old-fashioned taste. But it was a merry, beery and boisterous evening, at least as far as our little coterie was concerned. In other words I got thoroughly sozzled and so enjoyed the evening very much which I wouldn't have done otherwise. Into my bed at about 1.15 and slept perfectly.

Sunday 22 November Had a late breakfast in the back room where Mother has to stay in bed and therefore warmer and cosier. Took the armchair in there, used a couple of chairs as a table and what couldn't go on there went on the floor and on top of a chest of drawers. A decidedly messy business but quite good fun for once or twice in a while. Did the same for lunch also very late, about 3.0 after having taken Nigger for an hour's run around Regent's Park and Primrose Hill.

Wednesday 25 November Had an insurance agent in to see me at the office this morning. About the sixth pest of this variety I've had to dispose of. An unpleasant task as they all seem such decent fellows. Still, it's my own fault really for I never can remember to avoid the elementary error of telling them I'm not insured already. I shan't forget in future however. My lesson is learned.

Saturday 28 November Mother worse than ever, throat and ears in very bad condition but won't stay in bed. It's becoming pitiful. Went and did most of the shopping for her this afternoon then took Nigger up to Regent's Park for a run around. On the way there a down and out on the pretext of enquiring Nigger's breed cadged a fag off me saying he was absolutely 'futtered'. A new colloquial expression to me. Still, I never mind being asked for fags. Money's another matter though I never could understand a hungry man's craving for cigarettes. Smoking is the last thing in the world I feel like when hungry.

Tuesday 1 December The Crystal Palace, all but two towers, burned down last night. I read it in the paper this morning. For that grand old gigantic glass edifice always had a warm spot in my heart. It had a most impressive grandeur and majesty and somehow stood for all that was great and glorious in the Victorian age. Though I actually only went there twice, I can easily recall offhand the exact dates. Thurs 22 Aug 1929 when I went with a party of foreign scouts from Empress Hall to see the fireworks – and also Easter Monday 21 April 1930 when I went on my own to snoop around. It was also a lively landmark from all over London and many miles around, and I shall sorely miss it in the view from Parliament Hill and Primrose Hill on clear days. Strangely enough it was so beautifully clear and moonlit last night that I had a strong inclination to go for a walk across Hampstead and Parliament Hill which I have never done at night. Would to God had I obeyed that uncanny intuition. I should then have seen the tragic but awe inspiring sight of the tremendous blaze away over South London. Even if I had heard of it on the radio in the 9.0 news as everyone else seems to have done, I should have gone up there like a shot. But no, I was determined to miss as well as lament its passing evermore. We shall never see its like again.

Thursday 3 December The cat was out of the bag with a vengeance this morning. The press revealed for the first time what the American papers have been screaming for the past two or three months – that the King intends to marry the twice divorced American Mrs Simpson. A crisis has arisen as the Cabinet rightly opposes the scandalous match. For it would not only make the King appear cheap and contemptuous in the eyes of the whole country but depress our trade and lower the country's prestige enormously as far as the rest of the world is concerned. In fact he's made a complete and utter fool of himself and there only seems to be two courses open to him. Either he can abandon the absurd notion of marriage altogether and, if he likes, retain Mrs S as his mistress, which she undoubtedly is already, and if he'd had a grain of sense, he'd have remained in that position without all the furore. In which case no one would have known anything about it and not cared two hoots if they did. Or else he can go through with it and in doing so proving himself unfitted to rule, be forced to abdicate in favour of his brother. No other alternative seems feasible. An ugly kettle of fish altogether.

Friday 4 December The constitutional crisis continues without any sign of solution yet. The King apparently hoped to get away with a morganatic marriage but the Government are firmly resolved against any such measure and clearly affirm that Mrs S (who today flew to France) would, if the King married, be a fully-fledged Queen. And though this only clears the air to a minor degree, it might prove very effective in forcing the King's hand one way or t'other. Meanwhile the whole country continues to discuss it and everywhere one goes one hears arguments for and against the King having his own way. Not for a very long time has there been a topic of such universal controversy. The whole town's agog with it.

Saturday 5 December It is now a clear fight to a finish between King and Parliament with no possibility of compromise on either side. Unfortunately the popular press, in order to appeal to the loose thinking sentimental mob, is veering round in support of the King and GBS [George Bernard Shaw] in a damnably witty parable *The King, the*

1936

Constitution and the Lady provides them in today's *Standard* with the most effective broadside they could wish for.[19]

Monday 7 December No change in King v Government situation. The former is still dithering about trying to make up his mind while the popular press now press for morganatic marriage which the Government has firmly set itself against. And of course the usual number of scatter-brained imbeciles continue to write to left-wing newspapers and make silly little demonstrations in Downing St and outside the Palace in favour of the King.[20]

Tuesday 8 December 'End of the Crisis' blithely announces the *Express* today. This on the strength of Mrs S's offer to withdraw from the match. Offer is the operative word which is in effect anything but a solution to the difficulty. It merely amounts to challenging the King 'Desert me now if you dare'. And he, no doubt will be duped into falling for this sham heroism and become more obstinate still. End of crisis be damned. It's hardly begun yet.

Wednesday 9 December The royal scandal is now beginning to fizzle out in rumour and denials of various sorts and after an incessant week of it everyone is getting thoroughly sick of the whole business, including the endless photos of Mrs S in every edition of every paper and it looks like going on ad infinitum. Mr Baldwin, the Dukes of York and Kent and the King's lawyer[21] rush hither and thither twixt London and Fort Belvedere, continual conferences, interviews and cabinet meetings take place and no one is any the wiser. Would to goodness he'd make up his mind and put an end to the whole damned silly business.

Thursday 10 December History was made today. The crisis at last reached the most dramatic as it possibly could – the King abdicated in favour of the Duke of York. This was, I think, the most thrilling and exciting news I've ever experienced. It had no other reaction on me whatever. No sorrow or regret and certainly no sympathy for the King for how can anyone other than muddle headed sentimentalists sympathise with a man who can so lightly abandon his great heritage and fail so dismally in his duty to his people for the sake of a commonplace cow like Mrs Simpson, especially after having gone out of his way to gain immense popularity and behaving like an impetuous schoolboy, he's

19 Shaw's parable that evening featured a new forty-year-old king and a Mrs Daisy Bell, who 'as she was an American she had been married twice before and was therefore likely to make an excellent wife for a king who had never been married at all'.
20 'A small crowd gathered in Downing St yesterday [and] as Mr Baldwin drove away he was given a rousing cheer' (*The Times*, 8 December 1936).
21 Walter Monckton (1891–1965), the first person to be knighted by Edward VIII, was the King's legal advisor during the abdication crisis, having been Attorney General to the Duchy of Cornwall from 1932. After the war he became a Conservative MP and Minister of Labour. He was Eden's Minister of Defence and was the only member of that cabinet to oppose Eden's Suez policy in 1956.

let the country down badly and cost it many millions in lost trade. Still the worst disgrace of all i.e. Mrs S becoming Queen has, thank Heaven, been avoided thanks to Mr Baldwin who alone emerges from this sorry business with honour and esteem. The speech in the Commons after the abdication was first announced this afternoon was magnificent. He'll go down in history as the saviour of his country on more than one occasion. A truly great man.

Friday 11 December Second thoughts on the King's abdication convince me that it is the best thing that could possibly have happened. For he has never been really suited to the position neither in temperament or outlook despite immense popularity – or perhaps because of it. He rather seemed to have made himself too popular by half. After all, dignified and gracious bearing and demeanour are the first essentials of Kingship and in this respect this is totally lacking, though it mattered little when he was Prince of Wales. On the other hand his brother, the Duke of York, who succeeds him as George VI fulfils these qualities admirably and will therefore, I think, make an infinitely better King. If he errs, it is only on the right side of quietness and reserve. The only possible snag is his wife who (now Queen Elizabeth) has shown an unfortunate tendency to play to the gallery in similar lines to Edward. Still, the new responsibility will perhaps correct that tendency somewhat.

Saturday 12 December Final reflection a propos the change of King – By an odd coincidence King George died exactly three weeks from the beginning of the year while King Edward has abdicated exactly three weeks from the end of it – We have thus had three Kings in one year for the second time in our history – 1483 was the last time (Edward IV, Edward V and Richard III). Went down to see and hear the Proclamation of George VI read this afternoon. Couldn't get anywhere near St James's however so went along to Trafalgar Square and heard it there through the loudspeakers as it was read at Charing Cross, and saw the procession as it came through from the Mall and passed across to the Strand on its way to Temple Bar and the Royal Exchange. Dense crowds all along the route. A very impressive business despite the glum gloom of the afternoon for it was very dull and a faint drizzle fell throughout. Walked up Charing Cross Rd after and bought a 2/6 pipe. Have decided to have another shot at a pipe even though my first attempt at one four years ago was far from successful which was probably due to it being a Woolworth's pipe and my inability to fill it properly. I fancy I should do better this time with a better quality article and ready-made easy-fill tobacco. Should not give up cigarettes altogether but a pipe is certainly preferable sometimes e.g. pub-crawling, fishing etc. Besides it goes much better with beer and is decidedly more masculine.

1936

Sunday 13 December Wrote a retrospect of the past year which I always do every year as an appendix to my diary. Had nearly finished when, at 5.30, Fred and the family arrived. Must have left a few minutes before the arrival of Mother who got home about five minutes later. Proceeded to Victoria to meet the Ramblers' train. Ron and the rest of the lads had been out and Bill came along to see us also. Stood in the buffet drinking, pipe smoking and talking till 10.0. Didn't feel good when I got home. Slightly sick, believe the pipe's upsetting my stomach in fact, will soon get used to it I expect.

Saturday 19 December Washed up and after, changed and at 7.0 went along to the Green Man in Berwick St for the Portelet Rambling Club annual concert. Turned out to be quite a good merry evening though it was very slow starting and fizzled out at the end. The dinner didn't actually start till 8.40, about fifty there altogether. A simple three course dinner, rapidly and efficiently served. My ten minute speech after, proposing the health of the Chairman (Bill), went off very well and proved to be of such a surprising nature as to take the wind out of Bill's sails when he had to reply. The number of congratulations I received on it afterwards became almost embarrassing. After Bill had spoken, as it was getting on, the rest of the toasts were dispensed with and we all adjourned to the bar downstairs while the tables were cleared away. Didn't really have a great deal to drink though what I did have was very mixed – two glasses of sherry before dinner, three of wine during dinner, two of whisky and soda and two of Bass after. Finished things up with some very rough and ready rag-tag dancing followed by concertina upstairs by Bill. I spent most of the time down in the bar. About thirty of us trooped along to the Oxford Corner House. Couldn't get in of course so march back down Oxford St singing most of the way and Ron took us to the Venetian Club in Kingly St. A pokey little underground night club, stuffy, dimly lit and horribly respectable really in spite of its pretensions to a furtive sort of pseudo wickedness. A bar, a few tables and chairs and a two man dance band and a few square feet of dance floor. And of course ridiculously expensive and after a few glasses of beer, which was diluted to tastelessness at that, we all cleared off after twenty minutes. Some went home, the rest of us to Coventry St Corner House where we finally finished up at 1.0. Walked home with Ron. Bed at 2.15.

Monday 21 December Next to nothing to record of today. Took Nigger round to P.O. to post some Christmas cards. Took special care he didn't escape. He did so last night when Mother took him round there and she had to sit up till 5.30 this morning waiting for him to come back. But he got away just the same for all my precautions. Completely vanished as soon as I let him off the lead within a few yards of the door as we came home. This so enraged me that I decided to sit up myself tonight, wait for him to return and give him a sound thrashing when he did so.

Stayed up till 12.0 listening to a half hour *Round London at Night* radio feature. Got Mother to go to bed in my room and I sat in the front room till 1.15 reading book. This turned my trusting to luck, wondering if I went to sleep or not or hear him when he did so.

Tuesday 22 December Nigger returned at 3.45 this morning. Didn't get any sleep prior to that, or much after either – just a sort of nightmarish semi-consciousness most of the time. So naturally felt pretty tired this morning. Took Nigger round to post last two Christmas cards – to Bill and Ron but did not let him off lead so we shall both have some sleep tonight. Bed early at 10.35.

Thursday 24 December A very hectic evening. Had arranged to meet Bill and Ron at the Horse Shoe at 7.30 to discuss the next Portelet Ramble and quietly celebrate Christmas. So after going home to dinner and getting some coal for Mother; duly went along there and arrived at exactly at 7.30. No one about. Had a drink, began to get impatient and waited outside. At 8.40 Ron turned up with the excuse that he he'd been buying a turkey or something of that sort. He gives me a cigar, we order drinks and wait for Bill with diminishing hope of him coming. Until at 9.0 in walks John Bodle with three or four other Portelet blokes and announces that Bill is following on from some pub in Down St where they'd been celebrating since early evening. They'd left him arguing with someone. And about twenty minutes later he did arrive, more drunk than I've ever seen him before. He was in fact mad drunk and got worse as the evening went on. He sang and shouted at the top of his voice everywhere we went, accosted everyone we came across. We went on to the Malaya until it got too hot for us. They wouldn't let him into the Corner House so we took a cab to Bodega's in Glasshouse St (all pubs having an extension till 12.0) and while we were there tending one of our party sick in the convenience, he went off apparently under the impression we'd all left too. And that's the last we saw of him. Lord knows what happened to him after that.

Friday 25 December Up at 10.0. Fine but slightly foggy. Rather in keeping with that melancholy gloom which is to me a characteristic of Christmas. We stayed at home this year instead of going to Forest Gate as we have done for the past two years. This of course proved much more expensive for us and gave Mother considerably more work as regards shopping and cooking. But all the same I find it infinitely preferable to stay at home quietly with a good book and the radio to staying with relatives and having to reluctantly participate in ghastly parties with a lot of screeching kids sprawling all over the place. Dinner at 2.40. Excellent turkey and pudding. Sat by fire in afternoon listening to a very good concert from Hastings on the radio. Wrote a lengthy letter to Bunny Kaye who, writing to acknowledge my Christmas card,

1936

asked me to write for him one of my normal long screeds and gave him all the news to date.

Saturday 26 December Dull murky fog with slight drizzle. After a late breakfast and an early light lunch went to the Coliseum in afternoon to see Prince Littler's pantomime *Cinderella*. Stood at back of Upper Circle for 3/- and was lucky to get that (all balcony being reserved for today). Enjoyed it tremendously. This decidedly a cut above the ordinary. It had a fey, delicate dream-like quality about it and was exquisitely mounted with a discriminating eye for beautiful colour effects and splendidly produced with an originality at once pleasing and effective. Looked after Bernie again in evening while they went to a party.

Sunday 27 December Bet McLavey half a dollar that *Chu Chin Chow* finished at His Majesty's in 1921. He swearing that he saw it there in '22. *The Era* answers to correspondents is to decide who's right.[22] Went with him up to the Albany St barracks this morning, an HQ of the Military Police. Being ex-Navy he habituates the barracks every Sunday morning and at least one night a week. Called for his brother-in-law at a block of flats nearby – where I made the fatal mistake of starting off with a glass of port, somehow picked up another and so to the mess-room. Here drank five beers, which was the extent of the round, chatted with various soldiers and so to the local pub in Albany St where I consumed three more and assiduously talked to the friend about the company secretarial racket which he's in – promised to see what he could do for me if he comes across anything. Out at 2.0 and home to a whisky downstairs which combined with the port prelude made me so sick that I couldn't touch any lunch. Lay on bed instead and slept all afternoon. Up at 5.30 to tea with cold turkey. No head but very liverish. Took Nigger out and then went down to look after Bernie once more with Mother [who] went out with the Macs. They came home at 11.0, up to supper and bed at 12.0. So ends the Christmas holiday which I have unexpectedly enjoyed in quiet but unusual fashion. I brought home a book and was expecting to finish it – I haven't read a word!

Thursday 31 December Took Nigger out then at 9.20 off with Mother and Mrs M to celebrate New Year's Eve. Called for the latter's mother-in-law up at the flats and adjourned to the local pub in Albany St. Turned out to be a bit too much of a hen party there but the exceedingly hospitable publican who dispensed free cigars and drinks all round was adequate compensation for that. I've never come across anything like it before. Left at 11.20 and got a bus down to Piccadilly Circus but had to get out half way down Regent's St and walk the rest. Started to faintly drizzle but nothing much. Got in a terrific crush around the Eros statue.

---

22 Heap was correct, as the show ended at the theatre in 1921 after a record 2,238 performances.

Part One

It was much worse than Boat Race night. As soon as it turned 12.0, fought our way out of it and stood for a while by the Pavilion corner of Shaftesbury Avenue up which we eventually ambled. Saw it was impossible to get a bus home from Cambridge Circus so walked down to Trafalgar Square to try there. Stood awhile at the corner of Bear St watching couples dancing in that narrow street to the accompaniment of an accordion. This was as near as anything to the Parisian scene that I've ever seen in London. It was 'Sous les toits de Paris' as the life. But the marvel of it was the police didn't attempt to stop it. They just kept discretely absent. When we got to Trafalgar Square saw it was just as impossible to get a bus there, so took a taxi home. A befitting end to this quaint evening which befittingly ended a quaint year. To bed at 2.0.

RETROSPECT – 1936

After recently glancing through Retrospect 1935, I can't for the life of me see in what way I can sum up 1936 without reiterating practically all of its predecessor all over again. For if such a thing is conceivable 1936 has for me, been an even more static and uneventful year than the last one. Neither my social or financial position nor interests, friends, outlook or philosophy have altered in any but the most minor aspects. And though it was a near thing, neither have we moved again yet.

Mother in spite of occasional spasms of un-disguisable pain and discomfort and one unfortunate relapse in the direction of scarlet fever which badly affected her ear, continues to at least appear to be in moderately good health. There have been no very serious relapses and there still appears to be some hope that she may eventually regain complete normal health. For which I am truly thankful. It would be a grim year for me when I have to record otherwise. I am still stuck in the same dull job with the same appalling lack of prospects. And, ignoring the meagre compensation of an unexpected 3/- rise, I am still just as desperately determined to get out of it and continue to make spasmodic efforts in that direction. Yet the rut is a damnably comfortable one to endure.

On the other hand I still hanker after journalism – or to be more precise, dramatic criticism – regardless of the extremely remote prospects of ever getting an opening of any sort in London journalism, and so continue to dully and generally waver between the two conflicting ambitions. And thus get nowhere. My financial position i.e. my total savings has been improved to the extent of a further £10, comprising £7 actual saving during the year and £3 interest and so finish the year worth approximately £102. The acquiring of over £100 does, I suppose, signify a definite landmark in my saving career such as it is.

The theatre, literature and rambling – in that order – continue to be my ruling passions and I have made further successful experiments in

1936

the lone variety of the third. As regards the first and second, I have probably seen more plays and read more books this year than ever before. My doubts as to whether I should stay Rovering for another year have been fulfilled. Not that there was really anything left to do whether I had wanted to or not, though I won't have done so in any case. But no meetings have been held for eight months and neither having seen or heard from anyone during that period, I finally sent in my formal resignation as secretary and treasurer of the Holborn Rovers towards the end of the year. It wasn't only that I didn't see the point of continuing to be an official of a virtually non-existent movement and defunct body, though that was reason enough in itself. I had, in fact, lost all interest in and enthusiasm for the movement. That, so far as I could see, was neither the movement's fault nor mine. One just inevitably grows out of it. It was grand fun while it lasted. Now it's finished, it's best to finish it properly. That's what I've done.

My friends have, to all intents and purposes, remained the same. Bill continues to be my best and most intimate friend and even he has to go and repeat himself by falling badly for another damned girl. But as he has unexpectedly got over his last fit of love, there is no reason to suppose he should not make a similar recovery in this case. I shall therefore express no further concern over his spiritual welfare though this sort of thing is decidedly disconcerting while it lasts.

We have likewise continued to see a good deal of Ron and we remain consistently good friends. We have also acquired one or two new semi-friends semi-acquaintances in the course of our rambling activities and all meet together at frequent intervals. All good sports and the best of fellows.

My final and long overdue break with Harry occurred early in the year and from then until he left PR's in November (and not even then) we never spoke one word more to each other. How it came about I don't quite know but I certainly know why it did. Our temperaments and tastes and dispositions were so violently opposed that continual clashes and an eventual split were inevitable. How our friendship lasted as long as it did (some four years) is a mystery I shall never comprehend. In time we got so sick of one another and so obviously got on one another's nerves that it was just a case of waiting for an opportunity to part company and go our different ways without any unpleasantness or ill-feeling. So when it came we took it. There was no row, no misgivings and no regrets. It just happened in the best way possible and to the best possible advantage. So be it.

Gilbert has faded out altogether. We haven't seen or heard of him at all this year. Neither have I seen Adam since the early part of the year.

If I digress at such length on my friends it is only because they are of such tremendous importance to me in making for a certain degree of content and happiness. After health and wealth, friendship is, I consider, the most important and essential thing in a man's life.

Part One

I cannot help thinking how much more gloomy and depressing life would be for me were it not for my friendship with Bill and Ron and the convivial evenings and occasional Sundays we spend together. For these are definitely something to look forward to and they make life a tolerable joke and if it is only a tragic meaningless one. No, the importance of friendship cannot be overestimated. I refer of course solely to male friendship. Friendship with the other sex, platonic or otherwise, is a totally different matter and a source of endless worry, jealousy, envy, distrust and countless other petty reactions. But that's got nothing to do with it. My health remains consistently good and my hair continues to fall out. However I now worry much less about this than I did and endeavour to meet the malady in the only reasonable way – philosophically.

Apart from King George's death three weeks from the beginning of the year and King Edward's abdication three weeks from the end of it, there have been no events of public importance to give one outstanding memories to harness to the past year. The two events specified, giving us three kings in one year, was [sic] of course very memorable and important in its way but not in the sense that last year there was the Jubilee and next year there will be the Coronation. This year there was nothing of that nature. It can only be summed up as a quiet year of sluggish stagnation. And I can't honestly say that I haven't enjoyed it as such. I could, after all, have been so much worse off in many respects. Or on the other hand, so much better. So what?

1937

In spite of an occasional murmur of interest in women, 1937 was another year of 'drifting' for Heap. The domestic highlight for him and his mother was their April move from Camden Town to a flat in Hastings Street, WC1, just south of Euston Road, as Emily wished to live closer to her friends in the local Conservative Association, while Heap, happy to return to Central London and wishing to please his mother, joined the local Municipal Reform (Conservative) Party. There he volunteered to become Assistant Ward Secretary, hoping that he would meet leading councillors who might help him get a better job. He stood for the party in the November borough council elections but, in the strongly socialist ward of Somers Town, he and his fellow right-wing candidates predictably lost. Although he made a record eighty-three visits to the theatre, this was not a particularly eventful year for him, other than his delight at the coronation celebrations and decorations in May – this in spite of being assaulted on coronation evening. Again annoyed by getting a very restricted view of the procession when it passed him in the Haymarket, he blamed 'the usual inefficiency on these occasions of the police'. Of the 49,600 words he wrote in 1937, only the more interesting and relevant 23% are included below.

Sunday 3 January Went with McLavey up to the Albany Street barracks again this morning. As we went downstairs we saw Mrs Soleby sitting at her desk writing. Looked like an old Buddha sitting there – I thought this a ludicrously funny comment. Had five drinks at the barracks and two more in the pub after. But felt little the worse for it on getting home, instead of being sick and laying up for the afternoon as I was, and did, last week after a good dinner and a book. Due I suppose to the fact that I didn't smoke a pipe today. I've given it a three week trial and found it didn't agree with me. I'm not meant for a pipe. A moderate game is cigarettes and a very occasional cigar is as much as I need or want as regards smoking. It's not even a habit with me. Neither is drinking for that matter. Which makes both all the more enjoyable and desirable when I do partake.

Monday 4 January Have got a nasty boil coming up on neck. Thought I'd had enough last Spring to last me some time. Also another singular and rather painful lump just behind the right ear. Must be out of condition. Very cross at discovering I hadn't got a clean pair of [long] pants to put on tomorrow. I'd left my other pair off three months [ago] and they hadn't gone to the laundry yet. So in a fit of pique I washed them myself though they won't of course be dry by the morning. Will have to wear a short pair for a day.

Tuesday 5 January Started wearing a completely new outfit of clothes. New suit, shirt, collar and shoes, and even a clean set of underwear to go with them.

Thursday 7 January Went with Mother, Mrs M [McLavey] and Bernie to Bertram Mills Circus at Olympia.[1] Despite bolting a quick dinner of tripe and onions first, got there late owing to a slow bus going a roundabout route. The place was absolutely packed. This was in fact an entirely new experience for me, never having been to a circus in my life before. And I don't think I shall ever go again unless, as was the case tonight, we get taken with free tickets. It's certainly the sort of thing I would never pay to see. Not that it wasn't good in its way because most of the acts were amazingly clever and some really brilliant. Besides, Mills Circus is renowned as one of the best, if not the best in the world. Had boil treated – it's at last beginning to break – before turning in at 12.45.

Friday 8 January Went with Mother and Mrs M to look at a flat up in Chester Mews[2] in the evening – a dingy pokey little hole over a small lock up garage wherein Mappin and Webb[3] keep a couple of cars. Had the key to get into this and found our way up some steep narrow stairs to see by the light of a candle. Three small cramped rooms, one with no window at all and one with a mere slit and the other looking out onto the miserable mews. The whole flat would have gone into our top front room in Harrington Square. And for this they wanted 16/- a week. They ought to pay more than that to anyone who is willing to be in such a hovel.

Sunday 31 January We were awakened at 4.0 a.m. by Bernie coming up the stairs in his pyjamas declaring he'd woken up and found both parents missing. Mother put him into bed with me where he stayed for the rest of the night and went down to investigate. It transpired that Mrs M had gone off at 10.0 p.m. in spite of Mr M imploring her not to while he, like a mug, had thereupon started fretting himself to death over her, having gone in search, which seemed to occupy him most of the night. She eventually returned at 6.0 this morning, supposedly from some all-night party. A pretty kettle of fish forsooth. However a rapid reconciliation seems to have been made though whether it will last is

1   The annual appearance of this leading circus company at Olympia was well patronised by public and royalty.
2   Between Chester Terrace and Albany Street, NW1.
3   Now owned by Asprey's, Mappin & Webb were a leading firm of high-quality silversmiths and cutlery manufacturers.

dubious. The man's an utter fool really. He doesn't attempt to keep her in hand properly and so gets all he asks for.

Tuesday 2 February Accompanied Mother and Mrs M to the first night of Cochrane Coronation Revue *Home and Beauty* at the Adelphi. Cab home again after. Hadn't been in a few minutes when screams from the bottom of the house sent us rushing down to find that Mr M had assaulted Mrs M as the result of some infidelity of hers. Spent ten minutes or so trying to restore some sort of order and came up. A reparation is bound to follow. Bed at 1.15.

Wednesday 3 February Scarcely a wink of sleep during the night. My mind was a whirlwind of self-inflicted torment. And having scarcely any work to do in the office there was nothing whatever to counteract it. Even as I write this it sounds incredible yet it's perfectly true. The fact that it seriously affected my appetite was ample proof of that. I may have got over it by tomorrow, which was what I said of the McLavey domestic upheaval last night and, well, nothing happened. Both at home today. He's out of work and she feigned indisposition as a result of the blow she received. There again, a solution is awaited.

Thursday 4 February Mother went to hospital today for periodic examination and overhaul. Was passed OK for yet another four months active service at 20 Harrington Square.

Saturday 6 February Went to the Portelet Reunion and Dance at Portman Rooms[4] in evening. Got fairly drunk, scarcely danced at all and didn't enjoy it a scrap. My mind was far too occupied with other matters. As I left this evening before 7.0, ran into Mrs M a little way along, coming home with some shopping and not having seen her since that fatal Tuesday night, naturally stopped and spoke to her. Whereupon Mother appears at the window and starts shouting some nonsense about the possibility of my being late. She must of course have had some petty-minded suspicion at the back of her mind in watching me go out at all from the window for she never dreams of doing so in the ordinary way at this time of the year. Anyway the incident so annoyed and incensed me as to ruin the evening for me with a bad attack of nerves (which wouldn't have taken much doing in any case) and when I got home at 12.30 gave full vent to my feelings on the matter.[5] There followed a very unpleasant altercation at the end of which Mother went to bed while I, in a fit of pique, went out again and walked as far as Charing Cross Rd and took a bus back, thus getting to bed at 2.0. I'd have given anything to prevent things turning out the way they have

---

4   At 59 Baker Street, W1.
5   One obvious explanation of Heap's turmoil and his reaction to his mother's suspicion at his contact with the reportedly flighty Mrs McLavey is that he had perhaps taken a fancy to Mrs McLavey which his mother had detected.

done, both with the McLavey family and our own and also the various other relations. It has all come to a sorry pass indeed. But it can't be helped. I am determined to use my own judgement and discrimination as regards my relations, other people, male or female, married or single and cannot continue to allow even Mother to try and wilfully influence me in this respect, however well-intentioned she may be. I must be my own master.

Friday 12 February At loggerheads with Mother again. Not on speaking terms. Relieved the high tension to a certain extent by going to the Horse Shoe and getting drunk with the boys. Went primarily to meet Bill but it turned out he was working late and couldn't get along. He did drop in for a moment about 10.0 but his beloved Lilian was waiting outside for him, so he might just as well not have come in.

Saturday 13 February Ecstatic reconciliation with Mother. Had one final furious row after tea at the end of which, overcome with remorse, I broke down and wept like hell. Sobbed violently for ten minutes or so, was duly soothed by Mother and lo and behold the relief was incredible. The stress and the strain was all over, the depression that had weighed me down for the past eleven days had lifted and my spirits soared again free and happy. Thank God I still have the capacity to weep when my pent up emotions can no longer stand the storm. Things are now of course where they were and perhaps all the better for the experience.

Sunday 14 February The monthly Portelet Ramble led by me. A dull and misty day. Got off the coach and started walking about a mile north of Westerham [Kent]. [*page of itinerary*] Had a few drinks first then several more at the Half Way House at Farnborough on the way back. I kept entirely to Bottled Bass and naturally got rather tight. In fact I felt absolutely glorious and up to anything. This jubilant mood suddenly took a highly amorous turn with the result that after flirting most assiduously with a certain well developed wench named Josephine, even to the extent of cutting out the callow competition who was supposed to be accompanying her, I myself accompanied her home to Earls Court on getting to Charing Cross. Something like a day!

Monday 22 February Went into a Milk Bar for the first time (they've sprung up all over town during the past few months) and had a hot orange milk shake. Cost 4d. Not worth it, less than half a pint of milk actually. And I detest the stuff anyway.

Wednesday 24 February A second milk bar incursion lunchtime. Got much better measure with a hot apricot shake this time. Perhaps it was diluted though.

1937

Thursday 4 March After dinner finished reading [John Gunther's] *Inside Europe*, very good book in its way although that way is not the sort I very much care for. It was recommended to me by someone a few months ago for its impartiality. Actually it's about as impartial as *The Daily Worker* or *The Blackshirt*. A marked left-wing bias is obviously present all the way through. While Stalin and his associates and anything in Russia is lauded to the skies (the section on Russia is artfully kept to last), Hitler and Mussolini and all their followers are portrayed as deep double-dyed villains of various hues and descriptions, a menace to the peace of the world and that sort of the *News Chronicle* brand of communistic clap trap. It almost leads one to suppose that the *Chicago Daily News*, of which the author has been foreign correspondent for some years, is the American counterpart of that most despicable of English journals. It is above all eminently readable. But this varied and highly flavoured dish needs to be taken with a very large pinch of salt to neutralise the red pepper used in its preparation.

Saturday 6 March The McLaveys got a week's notice to quit this morning. Had recently moved up to the ground floor at a considerably increased rent which, in view of accumulation of debt and prolonged spell of unemployment, they are unable to manage. Shall be really sorry to see Bernie go. The place won't be the same without him. I've become tremendously attached to the kid during the past ten months in which Mother has been looking after him.

Friday 12 March Received Aunt Pop's usual birthday present of six dollars this morning.[6] Must write to her again very shortly. Went on to the Horse Shoe after to see Bill and the rest of the crowd. Tried to get a bus home but hopeless. All packed so went by tube. Likewise packed, but tube trains can somehow always be packed and fractious.

Saturday 13 March Passed my 27th birthday quietly at home. Did intend to take Mother to a theatre this evening but as there were no new plays on worth seeing that I hadn't seen already, didn't go anywhere – or celebrate in any way whatever. Spent all the afternoon and early evening writing a letter to Aunt Pop. Wrote eight full pages in all and thus disposing that obligation for another four months.

Wednesday 17 March Won 6/5 on bet, office sweepstake on the Lincoln. Drew Laureate II which came in second. Believe it's the first time I've ever won anything in an actual sweepstake. Home after work to change into evening clothes, then down to Australia House for Montague Burton's (the tailors) dance which John Bell asked us along to. Presumably held tonight in celebration of St Patrick's Day. Why, I don't know. A rather poorish affair really. A most astonishing plain,

---

6 Pop Shepherd annually sent Heap $5 or $6 for his birthday (the latter worth 30/- as at that time £1 was the equivalent of $4.85).

uniformly unprepossessing crowd of people, scarcely any of whom seemed to have any idea of how to dress even. Didn't notice a single man, woman, fellow or girl in the place with a really striking or distinguished appearance. Was also surprised to see scarcely any Jews present. Everything was as drab as could be. Likewise the hall, which was in fact exactly what one would expect to find under Australia House! Got to bed to 2.0.

Wednesday 24 March For the first time since 1928 and for the second since 1913, Oxford won the Boat Race by three lengths. As has been my wont for about ten years past, went down to Piccadilly Circus late in the evening expecting to see some really riotous Mafeking as a result of the phenomenal achievement. Actually it was just about the dullest and tamest Boat Race Night I remember, even for these days of spineless milksop undergraduates, not to mention the modern lack of high spirited fun and virile guts. Apart from the spasmodic shout and a few extra police and bystanders around, there was nothing to indicate that anything had happened at all today. Certainly not the least suspicion of a rough house anywhere and I've always contrived to get in one hitherto. Disgusted, came away. Eros must weep for shame!

Thursday 25 March The McLaveys moved today, though not far. Went into a glorified milk bar outfit in Tottenham Court Rd and thence bus home. Pelted with rain all evening and was still hard at it when I turned in at 1.00. A cheerful prospect for Easter!

Monday 5 April Met Mother lunchtime to go to look at a flat in a block just off Judd St, fourth floor. Smallish front room, large dark back room and kitchen. Rent only 12/6 a week. Seemed a very favourable proposition and decided to take it. On getting home in the evening however, found Mother sobbing away and horribly miserable altogether. Had discovered that one of the conditions of tenancy prohibited dogs. Which automatically puts the kybosh on it for although Mother has set her heart on going there, I just won't give him [Nigger] up under any circumstances and will in no case refuse to submit to such a stupid Grundyesque regulation. It is a pity but it can't be helped.

Tuesday 6 April Thought over the new flat proposition during the day and came to the conclusion that as Mother has set her heart on it, if we can manage to have Nigger looked after properly somewhere although it would still be a wrench – we might have it after all. On getting home, found Mother had forestalled me by burning our boats behind and confirming the flat at 19 Sinclair House leaving the problem of Nigger to be solved as best can be. Was just off to see Mrs Baxter and ask her advice. Came back while I was running Nigger round square and said Mrs B had agreed to look after him as well as her own dog, which she keeps against the regulations in the adjoining Queen

Alexandra Mansions.7 So that settles that. Don't know how it will work out, but it is a relief anyway. Will move about the middle of next week so ending nearly three years living at 20 Harrington Square. Had decided to move for various reasons – high rent out of proportion to value of room considering inconveniences and lack of amenities – the tax on Mother's strength and health caused by having to climb six flights of stairs several times a day (though on the fourth floor, the new place has a lift) – and very important, the lack of privacy and continual interference of Mrs S in one's affairs, too much of the school mistress – in short, the disadvantages of not having one's own front door. Against that can be set the fact that I shall very much miss the outlook over Harrington Square from our front rooms and the lofty tree which overhangs my bedroom window at the back – the outlook being the important one in favour of Harrington Square, and the placing of Nigger elsewhere. But on the whole the pros in favour of moving easily outweigh the contras.

Sunday 11 April A tiring arduous day, our last Sunday in Harrington Square. In afternoon went along to new flat with Mother to see if it was now ready for occupation, taking with us a suitcase and attaché case full of stuff out of my cupboard – diaries, theatre programmes and papers of various kinds to secure in a cupboard there. Home again to tea. Spent evening taking up all the oilcloth and carpets ready to be sent on in advance. Then took up two suitcases full of stuff – mostly [theatre] programmes to leave in flat.

Monday 12 April Called at Straker's on way home to collect new cards printed. Just after dinner some St Pancras Rovers called round armed with a trek cart to take some of our junk away for their bazaar (old books, Bernie's toys etc). The gallant fellows also agreed to take our rolls of oilcloth round to Sandwich St for us, their own destination only being the next turning.8 So went round with them, saw the oilcloth duly dumped up in the new flat and came home again to fill a suitcase with paper and return again to lay down the lino, after, of course, spreading the papers underneath. Awkwardly shaped rooms, especially round the corner. Had to cut off several chunks off lino to fit it around properly.

Tuesday 13 April Spent entire evening packing up ready for moving Thursday afternoon. Filled four big boxes, which the removal contractors left today, with books and another with china and ornaments. Packed into a trunk various odds and ends [from] various drawers. Bunged all the old clothes and surplus junk into Bergen and kit bag. Finally took down the two big over-mantles in the front room and practically

---

7 The large apartment block on Judd Street behind the new town hall. When Heap married in 1941 he initially rented a flat there; in 1971, he purchased a small flat in Queen Alexandra Mansions.
8 Presumably in the Cartwright Gardens/Leigh Street area.

everything is now ready for removal, though how the hell they'll ever lift those boxes full of books, let alone get them down three floors, God only knows!

Thursday 15 April Left Harrington Square this morning for the last time and went home in evening to Sinclair House for first time. Takes eighteen minutes to walk from PR's and a much more pleasant route. The moving had been accomplished this afternoon. Spent the evening sorting things out a bit and getting the place into some sort of order. Though the two most exacting jobs, filling the bookcase and my cupboard, had perforce to be left till Saturday. Went around the corner to the Baxters' flat in Queen Alexandra's Mansions about 9.0 to see Nigger and take him out for a short walk. Old Baxter there on his own looking after him and his own dog, a yapping little Pekinese. They seem to get on alright together though he must miss us even more than we do him. Was a job to keep him back when I left him.

Friday 16 April Home by bus to Euston. After dinner, put in an hour arranging the books in the bookcase in exactly the same position as they were before, 'assisted' by Bernie, who was parked with us all the evening. Went round to Baxter and took Nigger out for a walk soon after nine. Then on to the Horse Shoe to see the lads whom I found engaged in a serious argument about morality and convention.

Saturday 17 April Had tea and went down the Lyceum to see the *Gang Show* film. Opened there on Tuesday amid much fanfare of publicity and the personal patronage of the Duke and Duchess of Gloucester. Received the plaudits of the critics and was generally held to have made film history. All well and good. Tonight, when I went in. I found the place absolutely empty except for the first six rows of stalls at 1/6 which were absolutely full – obviously of Rover Scouts in mufti. Around the back row wherein sat the attendant until yet another customer should require showing to one of the thousands of empty seats. Really amazing. They may be able to pack the Scala a fortnight every year and turn £3,000 away from the box office but it's apparently got no pull on the 'film going public' whatever. They just aren't interested in 'boy scout shows' and Ralph Reader's name means nothing to them yet, though it may later, for this is his first starring film and he comes out of it pretty well. He really can act after a fashion and his breezy personality suits the screen, and vice versa. His emergence as a star was in fact the film's chief interest to me. Though apart from that, the *Gang Show* has been very well adapted to film production by Herbert Wilcox. It merely consists of a few numbers from the first two shows strung together by the thread of a slender plot, but it certainly does

1937

make a grand entertainment and recaptures a good deal of the spirit of the original. C'est la vie, especially round about Wardour St.[9]

Wednesday 21 April Started working till 6.30 for three months, a week earlier than usual. Probably PR's idea of a coronation treat, for the staff a week's extra overtime. After dinner took Bernie home for Mother and then went with her round to the Conservative Club in Argyle St for a meeting of the local ward committee. This because she seemed to think I'd meet some useful men to know there. Actually there was only Sperni there who mattered.[10] The rest were mostly old women haggling over some minor tuppenny halfpenny notes that won't make that make much difference to anyone. Just as I expected the thing to be. In short I just sat in a dismal depressing room and a lot of dreary people, ground down by a few Edwardian portraits, listened to a lot of drivel and got really bored. The only palliative being the free round of drinks on the Chairman [Councillor] Evans. And the dithering about after! It was just like one of the more exasperating old Rover meetings, only much worse. Heaven preserve me from this sort of thing in my dotage!

Saturday 1 May No buses in London today. All busmen came out on strike at midnight last night. Result of refusal of shorter hours which are already ridiculously short anyway. All negotiations had failed. Now, to make any settlement unlikely, 'an inquiry' is to be held and much good may it do either side. In my case, the strike doesn't really have much effect in inconveniencing the public while the tubes and trains are still running.[11] If they came out, well it would be a vastly different matter, especially in view of the imminence of the Coronation – and they weren't really missed on the streets today for with thousands of charabancs bringing northerners down for the Cup Final, as well as more cars, the traffic was just as congested as ever.[12]

Thursday 6 May Went round to the floodlit St Pancras Church.[13] Looks fine, took Nigger with me. Is beginning to spend as much time with us as the Baxters regardless of the ban on animals.

---

[9] Wardour Street was the centre of the British film industry. On 9 April, *The Times* announced that the Duke and Duchess of Gloucester would 'graciously attend the World Premier' on 13 April.

[10] A family friend of the Heaps, the local ward councillor John Sperni became mayor of St Pancras in November. He was a leading member of London's Italian community and was later arrested and interned between 1940 and 1942 as an undesirable enemy alien. See Robin Woolven, 'The Fall of John Sperni, Mayor of St Pancras 1937–1938', *Camden History Review*, 35 (2011), pp. 9–14.

[11] *The Times* (3 May) reported 'Heavy demand on tubes and taxis' as the Court of Inquiry opened that day. The strikers returned to work on 28 May.

[12] In front of 93,495 people, including the King and Queen, Sunderland beat Preston North End 3–1.

[13] The new St Pancras Church on Euston Road was floodlit for the Coronation. The Heaps used the church crypt as their local public air raid shelter once the Blitz started.

Sunday 9 May Rained all morning and afternoon. I set out for a long walk to see the rest of the coronation route. Not too pleasant walking, atmosphere damp and humid with a thick mist hovering about. Got very hot and sweaty. Hit route at Oxford Circus and went down Oxford St to Marble Arch. Dense crowds and solid traffic block all the way along. Selfridges the great attraction. A wonderful display, undoubtedly the best individual show in London – though not quite complete yet. Still a lot of scaffolding up. Selfridges [spending] £25,000 on it. Said to be after a Knighthood. Deserves it. Besides the part would suit him.[14] Went on past Marble Arch along East Carriage Drive to Hyde Park Corner, down Constitution Hill to the Palace, along the Mall to Trafalgar Square, Pall Mall, St James's St, Piccadilly, Regent's St and so back to Oxford Circus thence home. A remarkable spectacle, every bit of it. Have now been over entire six mile route.

Wednesday 12 May Coronation Day Up at 3.30 a.m. to go down and take up position on procession route with Mother. Though still dark, lamps being extinguished on Russell Square as we walked through it at 4.0 on our way to Trafalgar Square. Too crowded already there (being the only point on the route which the procession passed twice, both going and coming from the Abbey) so walked along a little way and took up our stand on what seemed a favourable view point at the bottom of the Haymarket. Here was a prospect of seeing the procession come up Cockspur St and pass into Pall Mall. And there we stood for ten hours. Mercifully the rain held off till the early afternoon though even then it caught the cavalcade on most of its journey. Cold and misty in the early morning, dull and warmer later, never bright at any time. As time went on we began to see the weakness of our position standing thirty or forty deep behind us in the Haymarket, the crowd kept moving us forward as pressure increased behind with the result that we in the front were continually crushed and cramped to an almost unpleasant degree. Women fainted by the dozen (or feigned fainting), ambulance men wading in to bring them out and so make the crowd worse. But what was even worse than this was the way the police, with their usual inefficiency on these occasions, allowed people to come and stand in front of the barriers just in front of us at the last minute. Thus although they were only two deep in front of us when we arrived, they were three or four deep when the procession came along. Thanks to this sort of thing I scarcely saw anything of George V's funeral procession after waiting five hours. And thanks again to the wonderful way the police manage these things, I saw positively damn all of George VI's coronation procession today, either of the

---

14   The American-born (Harry) Gordon Selfridge (1858–1947) was a very successful retailer but, following his wife's death in 1918, he spent his fortune on women and ran up a large tax debt. He became a British subject in 1937 but was not knighted and resigned from the Selfridge board in 1940.

section of troops which came by about 1.30 or the second main section escorting the carriages and coronation coach. I did get a glimpse of the mounted participants and even a glimpse of the King, fleeting as it was, or it may have been the Queen, by standing on tip toe and straining every muscle in my body to do it, but for the rest I just saw carriages with no view of their occupants at all. It was all most maddening. Very disappointed with things. I was glad when it was all over and we could get away, especially as it had started raining soon after 2.0 and a succession of heavy showers for the rest of the day. Must have spoilt things considerably. Walked home and, as soon as I got indoors, I flopped on to the bed and slept for two hours.

Got up at 6.15 and had tea, went out and bought papers, had dinner and listened to the King's speech on the wireless at 9.0, went round to Baxter's for me to take Nigger out while Mother stayed and chatted, intending to go up West to see the floodlighting after. But fate decided otherwise. For while running Nigger round I was beset upon by four hooligans outside a pub in Cromer St[15] for no reason whatsoever and without warning, given a terrific punch in the left eye and another in the right jaw and sent sprawling in the road and had been flung over and before I could recover from the surprise and collect my senses, found myself hurtled into Judd St by a few onlookers and advised to take my dog home as quickly as possible and mind any further consequences. Which I duly did, rushing back to Baxter's and out again making a terrific noise, thereafter to go to police etc. However Mother and Mrs B followed me out and with the added inducements of some of the aforesaid onlookers, persuaded me to return to the Baxter's to repair the damage. By this time I managed to collect my senses and remembered that there was nothing else for it but to lump it. So sat round at Baxter's and had my eye bathed, dressed and drank some port and smoked a cigar. By a coincidence an old woman, a friend of Mrs B's, called to see her and recounted how she was set upon by two ruffians some time ago, robbed and seriously injured. So we seem to have come to a 'tough' neighbourhood. For all these years I never believed such things happened on London streets. Now I know. An experience anyway. A minor consolation. By the time we left Baxter's it was too late to go up West (about 10.45) and raining hard. So it was just as well we hadn't gone. Came home and went to bed as soon as possible. Total injuries: a painful swelling over left eye (somehow missed a 'black' one), a lump on forehead and a very slightly stiff right jaw. And a slightly dirty mac, which, fortunately can be remedied more quickly than the other mishap, is that a lucky getaway? Or is it? The end of a perfect (Coronation) day!

---

15 Cromer Street runs between Gray's Inn Road and Judd Street, in the King's Cross neighbourhood.

Thursday 13 May Eye half closed up and very painful all day. And jaw so stiff I could scarcely eat anything for the jolts it gave me, just had to nibble. Called at doctor's on the way home to be reassured that neither are really severe or require special treatment. Just a question of time healing with the aid of hot fermentation. After pecking at some dinner went along to the City to see the floodlighting there on the Tower, Tower Bridge, Bank, Exchange, Mansion House (these three very well done), Guildhall, Bow Church, St Paul's (very poor) and down past Ludgate Circus to Fleet St and Embankment. Some grand displays along here, HMS President moored alongside Somerset House, Savoy, the imitation bonfire on top of Shell Mex House, and further along, Big Ben and the green-hued County Hall across the water. Had intended to only do the City this evening but having reached Charing Cross decided I might as well cut up Northumberland Avenue and get just a view of the West End sights as well – the National Gallery and St Martin's, Horse Guards Parade, Buckingham Palace (in the distance), the flaming torches and brilliant illumination of Pall Mall. Saw cars drawing up for reception at the German Embassy in Carlton House Terrace. So up Lower Regent St and across Piccadilly Circus, through Shaftesbury Avenue and Bloomsbury and home. Walked for three hours at a fairy quick pace so must have covered about ten miles this evening. And it was worth it too, despite the strain on my eye of the constant floodlighting. Wouldn't have missed it for anything. Hot fermentation on my eye and jaw before bed at 12.30.

Friday 14 May Eye much easier. No pain whatever, but jaw still very uncomfortable for eating purposes. In evening went to Windsor with Mother on Conservative Club charabanc outing. As guests of Sperni, didn't cost us anything, apart from drinks. Five coaches in all. Set out at 7.30 and did the journey in 1¼ hours. Pretty dullish crowd in our coach, mostly old women. Got acquainted with Mrs Baxter's niece Babs and we went off on our own and kept together and had a pretty good time. Much to the busy-bodied concern of all the staid prim old women, everyone except Mother and Mrs B, who rather enjoyed the joke. Transferred myself to the much livelier Baxters' coach coming home. Stopped half way at the Osterley road house for half an hour or so and danced on a very cramped floor. Very uncomfortable. Got quite funny in the circumstances. Saw the floodlit Selfridges on way home. A magnificent sight. Got back to Argyle Square at 12.45. Quite a good outing, better than I expected. Thanks to all, never mind. Bed 2.15.

Saturday 15 May Was awakened by the strains of a dance band playing down in the west yard[16] for the children's Coronation tea party. Bernie down there, staying with us over the weekend. The place remarkably

---

16   The three conjoined blocks of flats fronting Hastings, Sandwich and Thanet Streets each had a large central atrium.

well decorated. Pity weren't a warmer day. Still, the rain kept off. Went to the G.B. Movietone News Theatre in Shaftesbury Avenue to see the Coronation films, three shorts lasting forty minutes with one of the Abbey ceremony, one of the procession and a technicolour feature mostly devoted to the procession. All very well done. Also saw a short retrospect of the King's life and a Walt Disney thing, both of which I'd seen before. Walked round to see the floodlighting after. Went up Regent St and along to Selfridges to get a better and more complete view of it than I did last night. Dense crowds all along Oxford St. Took half an hour to get past Selfridges which is indeed an absolutely staggering sight. A wonderful vision of loveliness and splendour in its rich colour and artistic design. Thence down Park Lane and Constitution Hill to Buckingham Palace. Not a very large crowd outside, all seemed to be in St James's Park. Took me another half hour getting across the bridge. Looked around Westminster, got the view along the Embankment from the Bridge, came back round Horse Guards Parade, up along Pall Mall (all beautifully lit up), up St James's St, along Piccadilly to the Circus, up Shaftesbury Avenue and so home. Must have walked nearly ten miles this evening. Still I have the satisfaction of knowing that there's nothing in the way of decorations or floodlighting worth seeing in the City or the West End I haven't seen. Band still at it in the courtyard when I got home – dancing in progress. They certainly did [well].

Thursday 20 May Mother came over faint in street today. Just managed to get to McLavey flat before passing out. Rested some time and came home in taxi leaving Nigger there. Felt a bit better by evening however.

Friday 21 May Talked on the phone to Bill lunchtime, was both grieved and horrified to learn that he was about to commit himself to a life sentence – in other words that he was to be married to Lilian in a month's time. Bill, whom I had always looked upon as an incorrigible bachelor as myself! Thus do I lose my best friend of four years standing. A blow but I suppose I shall recover.

Saturday 22 May Took Nigger and Bernie to Regent's Park in afternoon. Army still in occupation there but gradually evacuating.[17]

Monday 24 May Empire Day celebrations down in courtyard this evening. Kids marching round following the Irishman who plays the bagpipes. All to be given a present each.

Tuesday 25 May Went over and took Nigger for half an hour's walk around the Bloomsbury squares which are to be seen in their loveliest aspect of serene stateliness in the twilight of a warm summer evening. I'm convinced that a good Bloomsbury square is the most desirable

---

17 Regent's Park was traditionally used to accommodate troops under canvas and their heavy vehicles during such events as coronations and victory parades.

place to live in London. I used to regard Mayfair as that criterion but now I'm not so sure. The place seems to be getting modernised and commercialised out of all recognition while Bloomsbury does make a commendable attempt to retain its elegance and spacious Georgian characteristics.

Thursday 27 May The 27th and last day of bus strike. All start again tomorrow. And they've gained absolutely nothing by it. The 7½ hour day is still as much a cherished dream as ever. On the other hand everyone has lost heavily, the men a loss in wages, the unions in strike pay and the LPTB in fares. And, to add a tone of poetic justice to it, they now propose to close a number of lines to a certain extent so several of them will probably be fired. Still, it hasn't affected me in the slightest degree. I could have gone on doing without them indefinitely. So, I believe, have most people discovered.[18]

Saturday 5 June In course of evening strolled with Mother round to Brunswick Square to see the end house which collapsed last night. Was occupied by the actress May Blane and family.[19] She was actually in it at the time but miraculously escaped somehow. A continual stream of sightseers at the barrier across the road to see it. Curiosity's a powerful force.

Thursday 10 June Evening: home to change into evening clothes to go with Mother to the S.E. St Pancras Conservative Association at the Royal Hotel, Woburn Place. Tremendous crowd there, anything between five hundred and a thousand. About half in dress, half not. But nearly all looking more or less dowdy, or 'homely' would be the polite description. I did manage to consume quite a lot of whisky in the course of the evening and I also had an occasional dance, as my saturated underclothes and shirt (soft fortunately) and even suit bore ample evidence by the end of the proceedings at midnight. However it wasn't at all a bad affair really. And it must have cost Beit[20] a pretty penny too, the whole stock of the bar was completely cleared out before the end.

Monday 14 June After work went round and met Bill in Wardour St and presented him with his (or rather my) wedding present. Good intelligent beery talk such as I have oft engaged in.

18   The possibility of the busmen continuing an unofficial strike was dismissed by Ernest Bevin, General Secretary of the Transport and General Workers' Union.
19   Heap here appears confused, as *The Times* of 5 June reported that the four-storey collapsed house was that of the stage and film actress Mary Clare (Absalom) (1892–1970), who was in the house at the time with her daughter and three other women. Cracks appeared in the walls as the neighbouring building was being demolished. Mary Clare was able to appear at the St Martin's Theatre that evening, in a play that Heap did not record as having seen. Her husband, Lionel Mawhood, had died in August 1935. The actress whom Heap named was May Blane (1910–1959).
20   The local Conservative MP (see note for 24 April 1935).

1937

Thursday 17 June Nigger in a bad way, suddenly lost the use of his hind legs while out with Mother last night. Must be paralysed or something. Can't walk at all. Most alarming. In evening went to see the Military Tattoo at Rushmore Arena, Aldershot with Mother and Bernie. Met the McLaveys (who gave us the tickets) down there. First time I've ever seen it and unless on future occasions I'm given a seat at the best and most elevated stand and obtain a swifter means of transport than we had tonight, it will probably be the last. For the seats we had tonight were in the most absurd position possible for seeing the displays properly – within about two yards of the edge of the area, on a level with it, and right round the side by the performers' entrance. It was exactly like seeing a play from the wings of a stage. It was all a wonderful spectacle and efficiently arranged and produced. Yet the whole thing is altogether too vast and vague to be entirely satisfactory and effective, a deficit which I've found attaches to all shows and displays of that kind. In retrospect one feels glad of the experience but rather dubious as to whether a mere two hour prospect of such a nature was worth five dreary hours in a coach and one dusty hour on foot. Still, it could have been worse.

Saturday 26 June After an early tea went up to Camden Town to take the evening excursion train to Southend (1/6). Due out at 5.20 but was twelve minutes late starting and getting there at 7.13. Arriving at Southend went straight down to the front and walked along past Thorpe Bay. Back to the station to get the train home. Was likewise late starting and even later getting back to Camden Town (2.0). But it was worth it, a very pleasant evening.

Wednesday 30 June Nearly joined the 'Imps'! (Junior Imperial League[21]) but got home too late from Swedish drill to go along to the Charrington Hall to do so. Suppose I shall have to do so next week though willy nilly. Which means that I'm not doing so on my own accord (not being politically minded to that extent) but really in order to please Mother.

Saturday 3 July After lunch went over to the new Town Hall on Euston Rd.[22] Open to the public yesterday and today after Thursday's official opening which Mother attended. A wonderfully well-appointed building in which its plain unprepossessing exterior gives little idea. Took an hour to go all round the place conducted round in parties of twenty or so with different guides for each floor. Very well and efficiently arranged. No obsequious cadging for tips or anything of that nature. The bright and cheerful yet decent colour schemes are the most striking

---

21   The forerunners of the Young Conservatives.
22   Opposite St Pancras station; from 1964 the London Borough of Camden Town Hall. See Robin Woolven, 'Camden's Vestry and Town Halls: Vestries, Councils and Ratepayers', *Camden History Review*, 39 (2015), pp. 8–15. The major offices moved to Pancras Square during the King's Cross development.

feature of the internal decoration which is, of course, decidedly modern in design – yet not overdone. Saw everything, basement kitchens and electrical plant, offices of every description, committee rooms, the Mayor's suite (including bathroom!) and most impressive of all, the elegantly arranged and decorative council chamber and the large and impressive assembly hall. Have never enjoyed going round such a place of interest quite so much. It was a revelation to me.[23]

Wednesday 7 July Actually went along to the Charrington Hall this evening and joined the 'Imps'. And from what I saw of them this evening joining is about as much as my particular interest in the organisation will extend to. As I expected, they are all of a much younger age than me, mostly in their late 'teens and therefore of a totally different mentality and disposition. But what I didn't so much expect was the poor type of person in it. There wasn't more than half a dozen of the fifty or so there with any evidence of good breeding in them – the rest were just a rough crowd of lairy [cunning] boys and girls. Not that I'm such a smart one to despise or look down upon them for that, for the same type of youth forms a large proportion of the Scout movement and kindred organisations which they would do better to join. But they are best left to themselves where people like me are concerned, for I just don't fit in and couldn't do so under any circumstances. My age, temperament, outlook are all against it. There is no appeal whatsoever to my intellect here and certainly none to my sense of good fun. A more dreary evening I never endured in my Rovering days at their lowest ebb. Starting over half an hour late, the main part of the evening was devoted to a lot of silly and very unfunny impromptu speeches in which various people were supposed to be certain notabilities and had to explain why they shouldn't be dropped out of an overloaded balloon and lost to the world. All conducted in a half-hearted chaotic manner with continual rowdy interruptions. This was followed by a brief weak tea drinking interlude. This was followed by some rough and rowdy rag-time dancing in the course of which I thankfully and unobtrusively silently strode away. I may give it one more trial when Bert comes along to speak in a fortnight's time and after that the August vacation will probably enable me to fade out unobserved. I'll do a lot to please Mother and to a certain extent the Baxters but to keep up this sort of thing is, I fear, rather too great a strain on my better nature.

Monday 12 July Was startled to read in paper this evening that, after unsuccessful attempts to reorganise the business and keep it going, Mudie's [lending library] had at last closed down.[24] This was all the

23   Heap was to work in the Town Hall for thirty-five years from 1940, sleeping there on duty one night in four from 1941 to 1945.
24   In its leader of 12 July, *The Times* described Mudie's as 'a famous institution' and reported that a court order had closed the ninety-five-year-old firm.

more surprising in that I was only there last Friday and no indication whatsoever was given of this then. A very sad business altogether. Have belonged to it for four and a half years now and for an annual subscription of a guinea have borrowed some forty or fifty books – mostly good, new and expensive – each year which is really good value. I shall now miss that lunchtime and afternoon walk down to Kingsway to which I have become so accustomed. But there is also a disconcerting side to all this – my subscription for this year has still six months to run. Must therefore go along tomorrow and make some inquiries and take my book back with me.

Tuesday 13 July Went along to Mudie's depot in Southwark St [SE1] lunchtime and took my book back. Seemed rather surprised I didn't want to keep it as it appears that most subscribers are doing, in view of the fact that owing to the assets being inadequate to pay off the creditors and debenture holders, no unexpired subscriptions will be returned. I might have done the same had I a decent book out but as luck would have it I hadn't. So there's nothing else for it but to lump it and to look around for a new library. Went and got particulars of The Times Book Club, but they are more expensive than Mudie's are.

Wednesday 14 July Very warm again and more sunny. Decided not to join another library for two or three months (am considering Smith's and Boots as well as The Times) and in the meantime take the opportunity to read a few of the classics which fill our bookcase at home.

Friday 30 July Went round to meet Bill after work and had a few drinks. Confided to me strictly, entre nous, that Lilian was expecting an event about next January, hence the real reason for the sudden premature marriage. He always would take chances on that sort of thing. A wonder to me that it never happened to him before.

Monday 9 August On getting home from work found Mother talking to friends of hers from QA Mansions who had come over to bring the sad news of poor old Baxter's death over the weekend. Was about 78 though he didn't seem so old. Had been on his own for last two or three weeks, Mrs Baxter being on holiday in America. Just collapsed on the floor with heart failure and the continual barking of the dog led to the discovery. He cut a somewhat pathetic and ridiculous figure, but for all that he was very decent, well-meaning and kindly at heart.

Sunday 15 August Bright and sunny but very cool. Up at 6.30 to see Mother and Bernie off to Margate on 8.45 coach from King's Cross, Mrs M went with them just for the day. Should be fun with the 'mob' at Margate and Mother will have her hands full with Nigger as well. After coach had gone came home again, read paper, had some coffee and then off at 11.10, round to Euston to get the 12.0 train to Windermere. Train packed. Just managed to get a seat in the Pullman, on back to

Part One

front. Two incidents on journey – woman smashed glass lamp shade with tennis racket and man discovered he'd lost his wallet with £3.10 in. Otherwise a quiet uneventful journey. Walked the two miles or so up to the hostel, High Corn Castle, in course of which right heel which got rubbed off by these new shoes, chafed ominously. Got to hostel at 8.30. Up to bed at 10.0 after a lovely view of L[ake] Windermere moonlit a la mode.

[*A fortnight's walking in the Lake District, where his swollen ankle and blistered heel eventually required daily medical attention*]

Wednesday 25 August Got away at last. Rose early, washed and packed quickly, put on my stiff shoes, had breakfast before anyone else and was driven down to the doctors at 8.15 by some local lad before he went to work. Having an hour or so to wait, thereby, amused myself by perusing a huge volume containing the complete bound edition of the *Illustrated London News* for 1883, especially the dramatic criticisms of G.A.S. (presumably George Augustus Sala, but what initials). But apart from these what illustrations, what postures, what sentiment. However after seeing doctor for third and last time and received final dressing and benediction at his hands (a very decent chap – he only charged me 5/- for three visits) and the assurance that my foot was definitely improving though I'd got to go easy on it for a while – got a car to Ambleside. To Windermere station to get the 11.25 to Lancaster. Train to Preston, where I had some tea in buffet and changed there for Blackpool. Arrived 6.35. The place crammed with people – everywhere seemed full up. At last got fixed up at 24 Adelaide St with bed and breakfast at 4/6 a night, a bit more than I intended to pay but quite a nice place, within a hundred yards of the Tower and sea front and right bang at the centre of everything. So can't grumble especially as that was on knock down from 5/6.

Saturday 28 August Yet another perfect day. Went for a walk on the beach before breakfast. Everyone glumly floating around in their best clothes waiting for the homebound trains. Got into Euston 35 minutes late at 11.10. Mother, Bernie and Nigger there to meet me. Home to supper, unpacking and bed.

Sunday 29 August Total cost of holiday including bookings sent off in June and even postage thereon – almost exactly £7, and it was worth it.

Friday 17 September Had a chat with [Bill] at the door of his work in the course of which I gleaned that he is not to have an heir apparent yet after all owing to a fortunate miscarriage on Lilian's part. They are therefore saving like hell and are determined on having a good time for a year or two before settling down. A lucky break for Bill. Called at Williams' in Charing Cross Rd to buy a bowler hat. After Bill had left [the Horse Shoe] and Bill R [Redfern] had also faded out, all went up darting at the Malaya. To bed at 12.30 mildly and congenially sozzled.

Friday 1 October Went along to Boots in Regent St lunchtime and joined the library.[25] Took out a Class A subscription for three months (6/6). It's only 17/6 for a year (equivalent to what I paid 21/- at Mudie's) but this will take me to the end of this year and give me a chance to give it a good trial before definitely deciding to become a permanent subscriber. First impression highly favourable. A busy and bustling library and much more prepossessing looking assistants than Mudie's ever had.

Monday 11 October On getting home learned that Dale, Conservative agent for St Pancras, had called and seen Mother with a view to my being nominated as a candidate for Ward 6 – a hopelessly red Somers Town locality, in the forthcoming borough elections – all expenses paid. Mother gleefully acquiesced of course, and I'm supposed to go and see Dale tomorrow night. So help me God.

Tuesday 12 October Duly went round and saw Dale at Charrington Hall after dinner. Signed the nomination papers, had a brief chat and came away with a stack of deliveries for Sinclair House. Then went up to join Mother at Mrs Beattie's in Oakley Square. Had to have some supper which I didn't want – tinned salmon, grapes, coffee and two glasses of very sweet white wine – the latter excepted. Mrs B held forth at some length on various epics – odes in her family history – singular habit peculiar to people – particularly women – on whom a very little alcohol reacts exceptionally quickly and effectively.

Wednesday 13 October Went up to Charrington Hall again in evening for a meeting of the candidates of the three S.E. St Pancras wards. About twenty of us. Lasted about an hour or so. Some vastly amusing skirmishes [Councillors] Bulsom as the meeting's fiery trumpet and Davies as chairman and one or two others. Otherwise all that was decided was to concentrate on canvassing, send a loudspeaker van round the streets and hold no indoor meetings. Spoke with other fellow Ward 6 conspirators after and intended to meet next Tuesday. Walked home with one of them, White the journalist, evening institute tutor. An amusing cove, a touch of Dickens about him, from which he does in fact give recitals.

Saturday 16 October Did two shows in one evening. First to the Palace for the first house of *Take It Easy* which was taken off shortly after its disastrous first night, overhauled, revised, recast and re-produced again last night. Left before it was over and went on to the Globe to see *Blondie White*.

---

25 Boot's Chemist and Lending Library, 182 Regent Street, W1.

Monday 18 October First fog of season descended heavily and took us unawares today. Became a real 'pea souper' by evening. With Mother round to Argyle Square for a Ward 8 Committee Meeting. Made my debut as Assist. Sec. by reading the minutes I'd written and then resigned myself to an hour or more of thorough boredom, listening to Dale giving an outline of the Borough Council Election campaign and various people allotted streets to canvass, which was all that happened. No agenda, no minutes to take down. Nothing to do at all but yawn my head off – or nearly.

Tuesday 19 October To Charrington Hall after dinner for meeting of Ward 6 candidates. Only three of us out of six turned up so couldn't do much. Just took one or two lists of electors each for canvass (Mother's going to do mine) and came away.

Thursday 21 October Home to change and on to the Shaftesbury Hotel in evening for Ward 8 Committee Dinner and Dance. The usual stodgy affair these things invariably turn out to be with about 5–1 preponderance of old women. But with the aid of a half bottle of hock and five bottles of Bass, I somehow managed to have quite a good time. Sat at the top table for the dinner which was fairly good. The long succession of back-patting speeches not so good. And the atmosphere stifling. Did very little dancing in the ensuing two hours attempt at frivolity. Spent most of the time drinking, first with one party then another. Over at midnight.

Tuesday 26 October Mother having finished off my canvassing for me today, we both went along to Charrington Hall this evening and took the books back to Dale, took three more small books for canvassing and came down again, Mother going on to Ward 8 Committee rooms and I home.

Friday 29 October To the Horse Shoe to meet Bill. Finished up in a dive down Villiers St called The Shades under Charing Cross Hotel where some poor seedy down-at-heel artist fellow sketched profile pen portraits of us at a tanner a time. Quite well done though they bore but the faintest resemblance to us.

Saturday 30 October Suddenly occurred to me today that the fellow who did the sketch of us last night might be the same fellow that did one of me in bowler hat and winged collar outside the Horse and Groom round Lincolns Inn Fields ten years ago. Naturally I could not rest content until I dug out the old one – which took me a good half hour's ransacking of cupboards – and there, sure enough, was the same signature at the bottom – D. Cotter 1927. A most odd coincidence.

[End of Acc. 2243/10/1]

1937

Monday 1 November Borough Council elections. Rained heavily all morning and well into the afternoon. Apart from going along to vote for the Ward 8 Municipal Reformers, didn't take part in the electioneering in the evening though polling went on till 9.0, not even in Ward 6 where I'm a candidate. For one thing I didn't really see what possible use it would be if I did go along and potter around, and for another thing I felt damned tired. So I just stayed in and read a book while Mother went out and continued to endeavour to rout out apathetic voters. But there surely never was a voter more apathetic than I was as a candidate.

Tuesday 2 November Much excitement over the opening for inspection of Littlewood's store on the opposite side of Oxford St this afternoon.[26] Mother (who started a week or two of afternoons at W.H Smith's depot today) waiting for me to go round to the Town Hall where they were still holding re-counts for some of the wards. Had been at it all day and no St Pancras results published yet. As expected, we didn't get in Ward 6, couldn't get hold of the figures.[27] Ward 3 was also won by the Socialists but not Ward 8. So Sperni gets in all right and becomes Mayor. Went home to have some dinner and returned. Not finding it so exciting as Mother seems to do, came home and again took Nigger out.[28]

Thursday 4 November Went straight from work to the first night at the Saville. Encountered Lilian Sprackton whom I used to knock around with three or four years ago, coming out after. Exchanged a few brief words before she dashed off to go backstage and see some girl in the show who used to be in the [London] Transport Players. So much for that.

Thursday 11 November The two minutes' silence once more and as usual spent standing at the windows gazing down at the crowd in Oxford Circus. At the Cenotaph ceremony this year the silence was broken by some lunatic dashing out to within a few yards of the King shouting some gibberish about 'No More War'. Though when you come to think of it, it is rather a wonder that this sort of thing has not happened before. It is, after all, only a somewhat audacious form of communistic publicity and they will stop at nothing to give it effect. We also viewed from the windows early in the afternoon the spectacle of a man stretched out dead on the pavement below just outside our premises, awaiting the arrival of the ambulance. Heart failure. It looked

26 203–211 Oxford Street, W1.
27 'The St Pancras result was a close one and there was much recounting of votes' (*The Times*, 3 November 1937). The results were that the Municipal Reformers took 33 seats to Labour's 27. As predicted, in Ward 6 Labour took all six seats with 73% of the votes. Heap gained 632 votes and was third of the six MR candidates. In his local Ward 8, MR took all nine seats (Blackmore, Davies, Chambers, Evans, Fincham (mayor), Mrs Stone, Seear, Watts and Sperni).
28 Nigger had presumably moved permanently to the Heap flat on the death of Mr Baxter.

most oddly pathetic to see a large piece of paper covering his face with his hat placed on top of it to stop the wind blowing it off.

Friday 12 November Onto the Horse Shoe to meet Bill Redfern, John Bell and John Hobson and discuss with them my proposition to make our future rambles all-male affairs. For they were all dead set against it right from the start of the argument, which went on for about an hour and a half. Still there was more satisfaction from having the matter thrashed out – the air cleared in that respect and my own views and attitudes made quite clear. Though they didn't seem to quite understand my ideas on the question and thought they would only be temporary anyway. I shall of course continue to attend the rambles every three weeks and, while continuing to notify some of the females, even lead some if they want me to. But, at the same time, I shall make no conscious effort to depart from my present attitudes towards the feminine element unless I feel inclined to do so. ...

Sunday 28 November Portelet ramble in Ashdown Forest district of North Sussex. Couldn't have picked on a more perfect day for it. Went by the 9.50 Southern Rambler train from Victoria to Forest Row [*itinerary*]. Then caught] the 8.30 train which we had special permission to return by instead of the official Southern Rambler by paying 2d extra. All bundled into a couple of first class compartments coming back but were too crowded to enjoy the comfort thereof. The town immersed in a murky yellow fog which played the deuce with my cough. A strenuous but thoroughly top hole day.

Thursday 16 December Evening, to the Conservative Club, Argyle Square with Mother for Christmas party. The usual crowd of dowdy old women with a mere handful of men. Actually more of an amateur concert than a party. The atmosphere pretty deadly till Mother contrived to liven things up with her comic songs and grotesque caperings in the vein of Nellie Wallace and Lily Morris,[29] after which the proceedings went with more of a swing and actually almost became abandoned towards the end. But it wasn't really my sort of fun and I couldn't enter into the spirit of it, simply because I don't fit into such a thing – only when I'm drunk, which I wasn't.

Friday 24 December First night of Prince Littler's pantomime *Cinderella* at the Princes. Somewhat disappointed to find this was merely a 'revival' for I saw practically exactly the same production last year.[30] I still consider this the loveliest and most exquisite pantomime I've ever seen, but to produce the same pantomime two years running

29   (Eleanor) 'Nellie' Wallace (1870–1948) and Lily Morris (1882–1952) were leading music hall singers and comedic actors whose songs ('Three Cheers for the Red, White and Blue' and 'Don't Have Any More, Mrs Moore' respectively) were widely sung.
30   See entry for 26 December 1936, at the Coliseum.

in the West End without making it quite clear that the second is merely a revival isn't quite playing the game.

Saturday 25 December The most unseasonable Christmas Day I can remember. Very mild with a dense, murky, misty fog during the day into the night. Spent the day at home on our own. Only Christmas present I received was a pair of bedroom slippers from Mother though she received any number of presents, mainly edible and drinkable items, from her friends. Too bad to go out for a walk in morning so just did one or two odd jobs for Mother and sat by the fire with book. Consequently didn't have a very good appetite when we had dinner at 3.15 just after the King's speech – but managed to put up a fairly good show all the same.

Friday 31 December Burton's New Year's Eve dance at Australia House in evening. After going home to eat and change, got to the Horse Shoe at 7.30 to meet Ron. All trooped over to the pub and stayed there nearly an hour before going into the dance and made several lengthy return visits before they shut just after 12.0. Some of us were actually in there when the old year merged into the new. Had a very riotous and hilarious evening, drank copiously, smoked two cigars and had the same number of dances. Over at 1.0. Looked in to see Mother for final half hour of Primrose League Dance at St Pancras Town Hall which went on till 2.0, seemed pretty flat by then.[31]

RETROSPECT – 1937

Yet another year of aimless drifting, differing in no considerable degree from its predecessor.

Such being the case, there is really no purpose to be served in reiterating the greater part of last year's retrospect. At least, not in any detail. The briefest summary will serve.

Thus: Mother's health has remained fair to changeable with no serious relapses and my own merely fair to fine. I am still stuck in the same dull dead-end job at the same mediocre wage, with as poor prospects as ever, have made no further attempts to get out of it and still regularly and ineffectually aspire to become a dramatic critic in the sweet bye and bye.

Except for the accrual of about £3 interest on my savings my financial position remains exactly the same for I haven't saved anything at all this year. I am therefore now worth approximately £105.

The theatre, literature, rambling and I suppose drinking with all that it involves, continue to be my ruling passion and I believe I may add

---

31   Founded in 1883 'to uphold and support God, Queen and Country and the Conservative cause', the Primrose League transformed the Conservative party by achieving a working-class majority among its membership.

without exaggeration that I have seen more plays, read more books, walked more miles and drunk more beer than in any year hitherto. My friends have remained essentially the same. I have lost no old ones and gained no new ones. Not even Bill's sudden, unexpected untimely and – as it subsequently turned out, unnecessarily premature marriage affected our friendship to any great extent. For during a considerable period prior to his marriage in June I had seen him no more frequently than once every three or four weeks, which is about as often as I see him now.

But for all Bill's assertion to the contrary, I can't help reflecting what a misguided and unwise step it was for a fellow of Bill's erratic temperament to take and that ultimately he is bound to regret it. Still, that's his funeral. As long as I can continue to count Bill as my friend, I am content. Which likewise goes for Ron too. The rest of the Portelet crowd fill in as an agreeable and attractive circle of friends on a less intimate level.

In what respects then, has 1937 been at all noteworthy? What deviations from my daily course of existence call for special comment? I can think of but two. One is the fact that after three years at Harrington Square we have moved again, and, to outweigh the small disadvantage of having to give up a rather pleasant outlook for a somewhat less attractive one we have gained the considerable advantage of a cheaper and more reasonable rent, and all the amenities of a self-contained flat including the privacy attendant upon the possession of one's own front door. We got used to the change remarkably quickly and Harrington Square has rapidly become but a memory. The other noteworthy phenomenon is a direct result of our moving to Sinclair House, which is in Ward 8 of South East St Pancras, the centre of Mother's erstwhile political activities and in close proximity to the abode of several of her partisan friends. She has therefore not only resumed an active part in the affairs of the Conservative Association but also induced me to join it and do likewise. I have thus become Assistant Secretary to the Ward 8 Committee and unsuccessfully contested the borough council election as a Municipal Reform candidate in the hopeless Somers Town district of Ward 6, partly to please Mother and partly with an eye to the vague prospect of getting a better job through acquaintance with some of the more affluent male leading lights. In a way, this rather takes the place of Rovering as a spare time activity. But not being essentially politically minded (what political sympathies I have are still with the Fascists) or feeling not quite in my element in an organisation of which the personnel chiefly consists of frowsy old women, I cannot bring myself to become really enthusiastic about it all. Still I suppose I shall have to give it a fair trial.

And that is about all of any consequence that has happened this year. I had expected the Coronation celebrations to overshadow all other memories of '37 as the Jubilee did those of '35, but somehow it

1937

failed to do so even in so otherwise comparatively a quiet year [*sic*]. For various reasons the Coronation and all appertaining to it, was, at least as far as I was concerned a mild disappointment and in particular no pleasant or striking memories adhere thereto.

Neither an eventful nor yet completely uneventful year either. A year without heights or depths, light or shadow. A year of endless drifting ...

1938

Anthony Heap's 1938 was initially dominated by his grief at the loss, in February, of his beloved dog, Nigger, and he found himself unable to walk the parks and Hampstead Heath without 'the dearest friend I've ever had'. Six months later he and his mother tried replacing Nigger, but the first puppy was returned as it proved to be a bitch, and the second developed distemper and was put down within days of arriving. Resolved never to keep a dog again, Heap eventually found his grief supplanted by his – and the national – concern at the imminence of war with Germany, peaking during the September 'Munich' crisis. His admiration for Chamberlain's 'adroit' appeasing statesmanship is clearly recorded, as is his distaste for the reaction to the crisis of the 'vacuous whining and carping of left-wingers and John Bullish German haters'.

With his far right-wing beliefs recharged, Heap continued his secretarial duties on his local Conservative ward. He and his mother collected their gas masks during the crisis and, like their fellow Londoners, were greatly relieved when war did not break out. However, with air raid shelter trenches having been dug in the local parks and an anti-aircraft defence site having been established atop Heap's beloved Primrose Hill, war clouds increasingly threatened. The crisis contributed to the fall in his annual theatre-going to 'only' sixty-four visits. Socially, he continued his regular drinking evenings with his old friends and he enjoyed a solo summer walking week in Snowdonia. A second week at a holiday camp produced a brief flirtation, after which he considered pursuing the girl – but their sole subsequent meeting was unsuccessful and he again accepted that he would avoid marriage. The threat of another war gets greater emphasis in the diary but Heap's original 48,000 words have been edited down to 25% of his original.

Sunday 2 January Portelet ramble round Westerham – Ide Hill – Crockham Hill district of Kent. An all-male party. Wasn't arranged as such but it just so happened that no females turned up. Perhaps just as well. [*hike itinerary*] One of the best rambles we've had for some time. And I'm convinced that it was due more to the all-male attendance than anything else. Quite a different atmosphere altogether. No restraining or disturbing influences and good fellowship abounding. Would it were ever so!

1938

Monday 10 January After dinner went up to King George's Hall to hear Captain von Rintelin[1] talk on 'Secret Service in Wartime' in the regular Monday night lecture series. Obviously a special attraction as the place was packed long before he was due to start. Came in in dress clothes and occasionally sipping some pink liquid, talked for over two hours with no questions after or 'chairman's' formal thanks – the curtain just came down as he walked off amid tremendous applause. A novel and welcome sort of ending. A good, lively and entertaining talk even if slightly too long – no talk should really last longer than an hour and a half. I was sufficiently intrigued by his discourse and general personality to buy a 6d copy of his book *The Dark Invader* on coming out.[2]

Friday 21 January Usual Friday night gathering at the Horse Shoe. Bill Redfern highly elated having just passed some Architects Association examination and thereby being entitled to add – as far as I can remember – ARIBA after his name. Insisted on buying all the drinks for the entire evening. A noble and befitting gesture on Bill's part which was duly appreciated and taken full advantage of by all.

Wednesday 2 February. Nigger has gone. Where, God only knows. We can only hope he'll send him back to us. He slipped out about 9.0 last night and hasn't come back. Mother searched the streets and went to the Police Station today but with no result. He may be dead, lost or stolen. That's the damnable part about it, not knowing what's happened to him. Though it does leave some slight hope that he's alive and may somehow get back – for a day or two anyway. All this made me feel so wretched and despondent that after dinner this evening I broke down and wept bitterly at the prospect of never seeing him again, the dearest little friend I've ever had, or even knowing his fate. Naturally no mood in which to go to the theatre but unfortunately I'd booked for the new Herbert Farjeon revue at the Little, so had to go.[3] Luckily it was a show calculated to drive away gloom.

Thursday 3 February Still no trace of Nigger. Mother went to Battersea Dogs Home[4] with Mrs Baxter today and enquired at more police stations but to no avail, [and] Bow Dogs Home where they are mostly

---

1 Franz von Rintelin (1878–1949), a German naval intelligence officer who worked in the then neutral United States during the First World War, published his story as *The Dark Invader* (1933) and *The Return of the Dark Invader* (1935). The latter included an explanation of German anti-Semitism and von Rintelin's criticism of the UK in sending him to America for trial, where he served five years in prison for his acts of sabotage. Feeling that these were not properly acknowledged in post-war Germany, he appealed to the Reichstag. Both books were later banned by the Nazis (*The Times*, 22 December 1937).
2 Presumably the *Penguin* edition, published in September 1936.
3 Herbert Farjeon (1887–1945), leading West End theatre manager, playwright, revue performer, lyricist and songwriter – including, in 1927, 'I've danced with a man, who's danced with a girl, who's danced with the Prince of Wales'.
4 The leading home for abandoned and lost dogs, founded in 1860.

sent from this district – a very remote likelihood [to] see if he's for sale at Caledonian Market or Club Row.⁵ We're also having a few notices offering £2 reward for his return posted in shop windows. Just can't give up hope of losing him altogether, though as each day passes it will, alas, become more remote. Poor little fellow! To think that we should part after all these years. Went for a long walk round this evening to try and tire myself out and ensure a good night's sleep which I haven't had since Monday. Felt too restless and depressed sitting indoors. It's knocked Mother up pretty badly too. She hasn't been so ill for a long time.

Friday 4 February At last we know the worst. Nigger is dead. He was run over round at Cartwright Gardens on the night he slipped out, Tuesday. A dustman found his body in the early morning and flung it on to his cart. Either the man didn't know he should have taken it to a police station or he didn't trouble. Thus it was quite by chance that we found out at all. Mother happened to ask him if he'd seen Nigger around, showed him his photo and the man asserted that it was Nigger; he'd found him dead on the ground beyond any doubt. Thus the dear little fellow went out of our lives. In a way it was something of a relief to know that he was dead after the anxiety we'd suffered during the last three days, lest any worse fate had befallen him. We do at least know what happened to him which is a shade better than endless uncertainty, even though it means the end of all hope of our seeing him again. But he deserved a better end. [*four more pages on losing Nigger*] I learned the tragic news on arriving home in the evening. I certainly couldn't restrain my tears altogether but fortunately Mrs Harrison being there to keep Mother company did help to cheer us up a little and after few minutes I managed to buck up, eat some dinner and listen to the *Gang Show*⁶ on the wireless and betake myself up to the Horse Shoe to see the lads. Wished I hadn't really for I just couldn't feel other than gloomy and depressed in the circumstances and must have made a poor drinking companion. I didn't even feel like drinking much and so didn't. My mind was elsewhere and so was my heart. No, I shouldn't have gone.

Sunday 6 February Portelet ramble to Herts. Almost perfect day for it. Fine and dry and just right temperature. Fifteen of us out, six fellows and nine girls. Excursion train to Rickmansworth. There by 11.0. [*walk itinerary*] A very enjoyable day's walk. Voted a great success by all. The cheapest Portelet Ramble I've ever been on. The whole thing including everything cost me no more than 5/-. I naturally couldn't

---

5   A dog market in Spitalfields, E1.
6   This was not listed as such in *The Times* Broadcasting listings, but *Ralph Reader's Revue* was listed for 8.15–9 p.m. on the next day on the BBC Regional programme.

1938

quite shake off my misery but I'm sure it couldn't have been more worthwhile.

Thursday 10 February Annual General Meeting of Ward 8 at the Club in evening. Left Bernie at home in bed on his own while we went. He's becoming quite reconciled to it now. A rather more lively and businesslike meeting than usual. Mrs White and myself remaining Sec. and Assist. Sec. and five new committee members – all men – appointed.

Tuesday 15 February Went along to the House of Commons in evening. Had got a ticket for the Members' Gallery from Mrs Harris. The House sitting late, debating the Housing Finance Bill. Had quite a good seat in second row. Just in front of me an odd looking fish, blue collar, black bow, long hair, beard and something on the crown of his head that looked like a schoolboy's cap without the peak. A bare sprinkling of a dozen or two dozen on each side till about 10.0 when the opposition benches suddenly filled up and were occupied by about eighty members. Recognised a few of the Labour stars – [Herbert] Morrison stroking his head with a pencil, Cripps, Clynes, Silkin, Ellen Wilkinson and Greenwood but only Sir Kingsley Wood, Minister of Health, on the government side. I sat there listening to the debate for two and a half hours. The only two speeches to attract any attention were some illiterate tub-thumper 'representing' Stoke on Trent who trotted out all the old dogmas and clichés about overcrowding in the working class dwellings (seventeen families in one room etc)[7] and Morrison, who though he spoke pretty well, went on for so long that I got sick of the sound of his voice, and after he'd been at it for half an hour, left and came home. A valuable and well worthwhile experience which reaffirmed my already unfavourable opinion of (Parliamentary) government.

Saturday 19 February Went to the Jubilee (Jersey) Holiday camp dance at Thames House in evening.[8] Bill Redfern went there for his holiday last year. Met him, Les, John Hobson and Ron in the Horse Shoe at 7.0. Ron, not knowing it was to be an all-male affair, brought along some female Malaya Club acquaintance of his, much to his embarrassment, though he did make the best of a bad job. After a drink, walked along T C Rd and looked over the new Darts Club just opened near Stephen St. Ron saved our face by being a member there, whereupon we all trooped out and proceeded to Thames House on the corner of Lambeth Bridge and Millbank, a most draughty spot. Soon filled up to eventually

---

7   This detail is not recorded in *Hansard* but, in a twenty-eight-minute speech ending at 9 p.m., Mr Ellis Smith (Stoke-on-Trent) quoted his local medical officer of Heath reporting that 'In 737 cases there are three, four, five, six, or even seven families living in one house, although these are not legally overcrowded' (*HC Deb*, 15 February 1938, vol. 331, cc. 1727–1837).

8   Thames House, Millbank SW1, built 1929–30, housed ICI and Lloyd George's Liberal Party HQ among others; since 1994 it has been home to the Security Service (MI5).

become the usual crowded, congested, rowdy, boisterous affair these holiday camp dances more usually are. Though this was rather a cut above the average of its type. A very good place actually, nicely laid out with two bars and a balcony, not too big and not too garishly modern. Had one or two drinks to start with but soon tired of it and spent the rest of the evening in the bar. Over at 12.0. A terrific scrum in the cloakroom after to get hats and coats, two attendants to about a hundred blokes in a very small room. The black hole of Calcutta wasn't in it. Walked along to Westminster to get a bus home and was in by 12.50. Beer is certainly not having the effect on me it used to. By the time I got home I felt as well-nigh sober as makes no difference. Either beer is not what it was or I'm not. And I can't believe beer has deteriorated to that extent, so it must be me!

Sunday 20 February Didn't get up till 11.0 and after breakfast and papers went out at 11.5 for a good long walk as far as Lambeth Palace and back by a different route. Saw the crowds gathering on Downing St on return route to watch the ministers arriving for the first of today's three special cabinet meetings. A state of crisis is reported to have arisen over the deadlock between the Premier and Eden and their supporters on the Italian loan scheme. Eden said to have already resigned the Foreign Secretaryship by some papers but no official confirmation yet. In addition to this, Hitler's eagerly awaited speech this afternoon following his Austrian coup, served to make it a most alarming day of political sensations. Though the radio news this evening rather gave the lie to the various newspaper scares propagated throughout the day by revealing no world-shocking pronouncements in Hitler's speech and no news whatever concerning the results of the cabinet meetings. Were possibly being officially withheld for a while. Stop Press: Announced on radio at 11.0 that Eden had resigned.[9] So that is that.

Monday 21 February Statements and explanation by Premier and Eden in the house this afternoon. Considerable sympathy for Eden expressed by the illiterate, the ignorant, the yobs and yahoos [and] left-wing dupes in general but Chamberlain, like Baldwin during the Abdication crisis, has I think the weight of sound authoritative public opinion behind him. He's certainly gone up in my estimation for this bold stand against the mischievous policy of anti-fascists and his determination to bring about a better understanding with Italy and Germany.

---

9   Alerted by his staff, the Foreign Secretary, Anthony Eden, returned from holiday in southern France to find that the Prime Minister, Neville Chamberlain, was determined to take personal control of foreign policy, particularly in Anglo-American and Anglo–Italian relations, thus exposing Eden's policy differences with the majority of the Cabinet. Churchill described Eden's resignation as 'one strong young figure standing up against long, dismal, drawling tides of drift and surrender, of wrong measurements and feeble impulses. Now he is gone' (quoted in *The Spectator*, 3 April 1976, p. 5). Lord Halifax took Eden's place, but Eden was to return as Churchill's Foreign Secretary in 1940.

Saturday 26 February Spent an hour wandering round the British Museum in afternoon.

Sunday 27 February Led Portelet Ramble in Surrey. Eleven of us out – six fellows, five girls. Caught 10.0 train from Waterloo to Horley. Apart from the slight lapse in the weather, a most excellent and enjoyable day's walk in every respect.

Thursday 3 March Mother to the hospital again to see specialist. They now want her to go inside to examine her under anaesthetic. She naturally doesn't want to go as it would mean her having to give up Bernie and generally mess things up all round. A most vexing business. Can't make up her mind what to do about it. She is indeed in a very bad way.

Sunday 6 March Walked to Hyde Park and back in morning. On the way saw Mayor Sperni, with corporation of course, emerging from Whitefield's Tabernacle on T C Rd after some civic service there. Had no sooner got to Marble Arch than I ran into Adam, who I see, alas, all too rarely since the break-up of the Holborn Rovers. Looked very spic and span in a smart new lounge suit, black Homburg and elegantly rolled umbrella. He is now at work on a novel and intends to devote himself to travel books entirely.[10]

Sunday 13 March Spent my 28th birthday quietly and pleasantly at home. Walked round Hyde Park and Kensington Gardens in morning. Home to a divine lunch of chicken, plum tart and cream. Also opened a bottle of white wine we'd kept since Christmas. Great hullabaloo in papers today over Hitler's annexation of Austria to Germany.[11] Seething indignation, protests galore. As if it had anything to do with or mattered to us.

Thursday 17 March Mother to the hospital again. Had X-ray photograph taken on Monday and seems to be making satisfactory progress. Not nearly so much pain now and no vomiting. Hasn't got to go again for three weeks anyway. So it doesn't look as if she'll have to go in after all.

Saturday 26 March Mother went by coach with party to Tilbury to see Mrs Baxter and Mrs Harris off on a six months cruise. Got up a bit earlier myself to see the coach off at 7.45. Was quite a beano by all accounts.

---

10 *The Struggle with Angels* (1956) was Adam de Hegedus' only novel. It followed the seven travel and autobiographical books published between 1937 and 1951.
11 The Anschluss, Hitler's invasion and annexation of Austria into the German Third Reich on 12 March, brought another European war a step closer, but it appears not to have unduly bothered Heap.

Part One

Tuesday 29 March After dinner, washed and put Bernie to bed before going round to the Conservative Club to join Mother there and attend a meeting of the Entertainments Committee in a small room upstairs. Fifteen of us. More bickering and futile argument than actual business done – as usual. On getting home at 10.0, wrote up minutes and an account of the Mayor seeing Mrs B[axter] and Mrs H[arris] off at Tilbury last Saturday, from data supplied by Mother, for the *St Pancras Gazette*.

Saturday 2 April Was notified of 4/- a week rise this morning. To start next Thursday. Must try and make this a definite clear weekly saving – apart from the 10/- a week I already put by for current yearly expenditure. Holiday list round yesterday. Put down for first and fourth weeks in August. Present intention – a week's hiking probably in North Wales and a less strenuous week somewhere on the South Coast, possibly at a holiday camp. Listened to the Boat Race on the wireless after lunch. Oxford won by two lengths. One of the best races for years. Very close thing all the way. Had supper and went back to West End an hour or so later to see the Boat Race Night excitement – if any. Actually there was a fair amount, far more than last year – but I have known them to be somewhat wilder. Stayed an hour in Piccadilly Circus where Eros was cautiously boarded up and then caught a bus home.

Sunday 3 April Walked down to the Embankment via Lincolns Inn Fields and back before lunch. Passing through Houghton St found that the greater part of the old school buildings have been pulled down and supplanted by a huge block of offices.[12] Only a fragment of the old building now remains.

Tuesday 5 April Started wearing new black jacket, vest and stripes to work. New shirt, collar and tie as well.

Friday 8 April To Boots lunchtime. Again no books on my [wants] list available. Spotted Agate's *Ego* which I read exactly three years ago; started leafing through it again and decided that it could easily take another re-reading now, especially the diary part of it. So away I came with it. Up to the Horse Shoe to meet Ron and the two Johns. Then who should turn up but that tiresome and boring pseudo-funny man Bob with his woman who, wearing a perpetual gum-displaying grin, is just one degree more exasperating than he is – if that's possible. The two Johns followed Ron up to the Malaya and I came home having made up my mind that under no circumstances will I go up to that damned place again. I loathe the obnoxious crowd that gets up there and the whole atmosphere of the place is so drab, depressing and altogether

---

12   The London School of Economics was built on the former site of Heap's school, St Clement Danes Grammar School.

nauseating that I can't for the life of me understand how I've stuck it for so long. Never again, ever.

[*Easter spent on solo day trips: on Good Friday to the South Downs, visiting Oxford on Sunday and revisiting the South Downs on Easter Monday*]

Friday 29 April To the Horse Shoe after dinner to meet Bill at 7.30. Has at last left home and set up house – or rather a ground floor flat – with Lilian at Thornton Heath. Very pleased with himself and once more tried (vainly) to impress on me the advantages of living in the suburbs. Didn't go into the Horse Shoe straight away but took him over to the Blue Posts for an hour.[13] He agreed that it was infinitely preferable to the H.S. Just our sort of pub in fact. Finished the evening 'doing' a couple of pubs in Soho. A long evening's drinking. Had rather too much really as evidenced by the fact that I didn't feel up to writing this diary before turning in. Always a sure test.

Friday 6 May Mayor Sperni's reception – Dinner – Dance at Holborn Restaurant in evening.[14] A terrific event. About five hundred guests including the Mayor of London and Sheriffs, the three St Pancras MPs, diverse other metropolitan mayors, all the St Pancras councillors and aldermen and a number of eminent people from various 'walks of life' and a very passé star for the reception in rather small stuffy music halls, old Kate Carney.[15] Must have cost him a few hundred quid. Nearly all the men in tails, a few in uniform, a small minority (including me!) in dinner jackets (I even descended to soft shirt and collar in view of mildness of weather) and an even smaller minority in lounge suits. Sherry, cocktails, gossip and so up to dinner in the King's Hall. A lofty imposing place. Which was more than could be said for the dinner. The inevitable uninspired hors d'oeuvre – soup, salmon – chicken – ice – coffee sequence served in the most minute portions I've ever seen, with a niggardly glass or two of mediocre wine. The only satisfactory thing was the cigar at the end.

A military string band and three turns to regale us during the pseudo-sumptuous repast! Two singers putting over the usual hackneyed stuff and a confounded accordionist, who played in the darkened hall with a coloured limelight on him (a cheap cinematic effect) and finally walked round the hall, stopped behind the Mayoress and played 'When Irish Eyes are Smiling', she being partly Irish of course. This, for some reason or other, made her start weeping and the spectacle became so

---

13   6 Tottenham Court Road, opposite the Horse Shoe. Destroyed by a bomb in September 1940.
14   218 High Holborn, WC1.
15   Kate Carney (1869–1950), then aged sixty-nine, was a London music hall comedian and singer of popular Irish and Cockney songs.

embarrassing that I just could not watch it.[16] Everyone else, however, just wallowed in it and, I suppose, thought it pathetically 'sweet.' And what a story for the *St Pancras Gazette*. Four speeches after, all commendably brief and to the point. Best was Mitcheson, SW St Pancras MP, who spoke first proposing the health of the Mayor. Beit, and chairman of Steam Navigation, his [Sperni's] one-time employer when a deck boy, followed up in similar hues and Sperni replied to the three. Bouquets all round. This took till 10.0 – an hour later than schedule – when we all drifted out while they cleared the hall for dancing till midnight. Spent the rest of the evening in the company of John Sperni, the Mayor's eldest son, and an old school friend of mine, and his very charming wife.[17] Haven't seen him since we left school eleven or so years ago. Still just as exuberant and vivacious as ever though rather slimmer. Seemed to have had more to drink than he is accustomed to, whereas I never came within a mile of getting tight the whole evening, there was no chance of that. We did have a couple more drinks during the dance – in which we didn't participate once – but even these (scotch and gin and lime) were so meagre that they didn't amount to half a mouthful. We talked a lot in those two hours or rather he did, and found we still had a lot in common including an adherence to Fascism and a hearty detestation of the Jews. He further discoursed on school-day reminiscences and the advantage of joining a Masonic lodge, though I surmised that most of his talk was also just talk and nothing more. Still, a most amusing and likeable cove whom I was glad to meet again. The evening was over all too soon at 12.0. In bed by 1.15. A good evening really in spite of the short rations. 'Tis pity he's [Sperni senior] a teetotaller for he doesn't know what we're missing!

Sunday 8 May Another day's tramp on the South Downs, around the Arun valley this time. Did about 22 miles altogether today and got quite sunburnt. Boots still hurt a bit round the tops but I'm gradually breaking them in alright. A top hole day in every way.

Sunday 15 May Did the fourth and last of my walking tours of the South Downs by covering the western ridge to the south of Midhurst. And yet another perfect day for it. Did about 18 miles altogether. No trouble whatever with feet today. The new boots must be broken in at last.

Saturday 21 May Before going to the theatre in evening went along to the Tatler to see the much talked of new March of Time film *Inside*

16 Mayor Sperni lived a complicated family life. He did not marry the Irishwoman who was his Mayoress in 1938 (Miss Annie Challis, the mother of five of his seven children) until 1945, after his release from internment.
17 John Sperni Junior continued to express extreme Fascist views. He left London for Rome with most of his family (but not Sperni senior) with the Italian Ambassador soon after Italy entered the war in 1940 and, known as 'The Italian Haw Haw', later broadcast on Rome Radio.

Nazi Germany.¹⁸ An atrociously biased film obviously taken under false pretences by Americans without disclosing their intention of adding a commentary to it which grossly distorts the implication of everything shown on the screen into a blatant, vicious and insidious anti-Nazi propaganda. An utterly disgusting business, calculated to appeal to the lowest instincts and the meanest mentalities, in which object it doubtless succeeds. The rest of the programme on a correspondingly putrid, if not such a pernicious level. Never have I begrudged a tanner more than I did to savour this garbage.

Sunday 22 May Only five of us turning up for the Portelet ramble fixed for today. John Bell, myself and three of the girls, the others decided to join up with the Excels¹⁹ who were also out on the 10.20 LNER Ramblers' excursion from Marylebone to Gt Missenden. [*two pages of itinerary*] Back at Marylebone at 8.55.

Tuesday 24 May With Mother to the AGM of the St Pancras Conservative Association at Charrington Hall in evening. Dull and unexciting evening with no fireworks. Beit came along and gave a short and rather commonplace talk on the government and its foreign policy. Endless verbal back slapping and soft soap. I got so sick of the tiresome monotony of this empty flattery and so especially sick of hearing about the 'Imps' who were present at the back that I felt like doing something drastic from sheer boredom. Walked home with a crowd of about ten others. Why, I can't imagine.

Saturday 4 June After an early tea went up to explore Harrow on the Hill in the evening. Went by tube to Edgware and walked over from there. Went along to the King's Head – a very select and expensive sort of place – and had a lager in the German Beer Garden. Why 'German' I can't imagine. It's certainly a garden and since one drinks beer in it, I suppose it might claim to be a beer garden but it bears about as much resemblance to a German biergarten as a black pudding does to a German sausage. Thus I explored Harrow. I don't think I shall trouble to go there again.

Monday 6 June Whit Monday Decided to have another lazy day. Went for half an hour's walk before lunch and spent the afternoon at home reading, browsing over the 22 page long [piece] I wrote on the Rover hike in the Tyrol we did eight years ago.

Tuesday 7 June Had a haircut after work before coming home. Monthly Ward 8 Committee Meeting round at Argyle Square in evening. Poor

18 *The Times* (29 April) reported that this sixteen-minute film 'was staggering in its force and power, the commentary and whole balance of the film is tilted against the doctrine of Nazism, stressing the suppression of liberty'. The film is available on YouTube, https://www.youtube.com/watch?v=Wb__OIUCaRM (last accessed 10 April 2017).
19 The Excelsior branch of the Southern Ramblers Group.

attendance of about twenty or so. Not much business to dispose of. A fairly good talk by Councillor Newbery on the potentially depressing and vexing, but very topical, topic of ARP.[20] With a brisk and lively practical demonstration of the use of the gas mask. All much more bright and interesting than I expected.

Sunday 12 June The 'Swan Song' of the Portelet Ramblers. Only four of us turned up – the last remnants – Bill R, the two Johns and myself. We decided to call it a day, not bother about notifying anyone else in future and go on with the Excels – which we shall probably continue to do on future occasions. 10.15 train from Waterloo landed us at Milford at 11.7. One of the most gruelling and stiffest walks I've ever experienced. But we did it all right and raced into Milford station with just a couple of minutes to spare. With our shirts and vests wringing wet with perspiration we collapsed into our seats on the train, completely exhausted. What a walk! We walked further in that last hour than we had done in the whole morning and afternoon and it was ostensibly the hardest piece of work I'd done for months.

Monday 13 June Quiet evening at home, seeing Bernie to bed and reading.

Tuesday 14 June Ditto. [*Heap's shortest ever diary entry*]

Friday 24 June To the Horse Shoe to meet John Hobson. John Bell, newly appointed to the manager-ship of Burton's new branch at Southgate, turned up late and joined us after we'd adjourned to the Marquis [of Granby]. Stayed there till closing time.

Sunday 26 June Went down to Thornton Heath to spend the day at Bill's new abode. Bus from Charing Cross to Green Lane where he met me at 10.5 and escorted me up to 'Comely Bank' the usual little uniform semi-detached villa. Lilian didn't strike me as looking either as healthy or attractive as when I last saw her over a year ago. The lunch itself was completely cold, meat, boiled potatoes, salad, cherries, cream – everything. Washed down by cold water in cold cups. I may be looking a gift horse.

---

20 Councillor Charles Allen Newbery became Chairman of the St Pancras ARP Committee and later Borough ARP Officer. In 1945 he assembled reports from the heads of the twenty-two St Pancras ARP services on the work of their departments, published as *Wartime St Pancras: A London Borough Defends Itself* (London: Camden History Society, 2006). This is the first mention in the diary of the increasingly important topic of Air Raid Precautions, the measures being taken to protect the public from aerial bombardment. The Home Office had set up its small ARP Department in April 1935, which issued a circular to local authorities in July requesting them to recruit and train volunteers for the ARP services, but no greater publicity was politically possible until after the 1935 General Election. These measures were made compulsory by the ARP Act of December 1937, which gave exchequer grants for authorised local authority ARP expenditure.

1938

Sunday 3 July 'Did' Salisbury and Stonehenge. Took the 9.38 Southern Ramblers train from Waterloo to Amesbury. [*three pages of itinerary*] Wonderful value for 8/9 return.

Tuesday 5 July Very showery and most unseasonably chilly. Monthly Ward 8 committee meeting in evening. Talk by young Councillor Conway, Jewish Imps chief, on 'General Political Survey'. All it really amounted to was three cheers for a few minor achievements of the government and a lot of clap trap about preserving democracy against dictatorship, presumably for lack of any major achievements to credit the government of this wonderful democracy with. When it came to questions I lost my temper a little and started to ask a question; deviated into a pro-Fascist speech until I was quite justly called to order by the chairman. Beside, I wasn't expressing myself too well. I never can on the spur of the moment, in any case it wasn't really worth getting het up about shallow twaddle of this sort.

Saturday 9 July Wrote to Alderman Fincham[21] enclosing particulars of qualifications, experience which he asked me to send him when he spoke to me at the meeting on Tuesday. Mrs Butler had written to him from abroad explaining about my wanting a better job. So he's going to see what he can do.

Tuesday 12 July Went round to see John Sperni [Junior] in evening about coming to the old School sports on Saturday. Was told he was away on a job somewhere and his wife away for the day as well. So came home again and later strolled round with Mother to see the new Sperni père ménage in Doughty St [No 8], only two of the daughters at home.

Sunday 17 July A grand day's walk in the Chilterns with Bill and the two Johns. But they joined with the Excels so, when we arrived at Princes Risborough at 11.20, I set off on my own not fancying the Excel much today. [*two pages of walk itinerary, including tea near Chequers*]

Tuesday 19 July Fournier, an office colleague of some ten years and also a near neighbour of mine, gave in his notice today. Is joining the Fire Brigade after recently serving as an amateur fireman with the ARP Scheme. Offers better pay and more congenial occupation to him so naturally has no qualms in quitting PR's, especially as he is getting married soon. A bit of a philistine but quite a nice sort of fellow really.

Saturday 23 July Went to the Open Air Theatre in evening to see Aristophanes' *Lysistrata*. The ancient Greek version of the anti-war satire proved to be no better than its modern counterpart. Worse, if anything in its puerile coyness. [*page of criticism*]

---

21 R. F. W. Fincham, member of the Municipal Reform Party, Mayor of St Pancras 1936–1937.

Part One

Saturday 30 July Dashed home after work, changed, had a good lunch and then round to Euston to catch the 2.40 to Llanrwst, changing at Llandudno Junction. Mother came to see me off. Found my reserved corner seat easily enough and settled down for the six hour journey. Round about Chester rain became imminent and along the North Wales coast 'My heart leapt up when I beheld a rainbow in the sky'[22] or if it didn't quite do that in true Wordsworth fashion, it tried its best. But instead of clearing up after this the weather got worse and by the time the local train got to Llanrwst it was teeming with rain. Got pretty wet walking the mile or so to the hostel through the village, over the Inigo Jones designed bridge to Gwydir Castle and then a steep zigzag path up from the road to the hostel – a large spacious nicely situated house – once a dower house to the Castle. Thought I'd be too late for a meal so had some sandwiches on train just before I got to Llanrwst. Made bed, washed and wrote up diary in dining room, the small inadequate common room being packed to suffocation. Bed at 10.50.

Monday 1 August Got away at 9.0 and climbed up past Llyn Idwal over the pass, walked along to Nant Peris and got the bus into Llanberis where I walked up to the hostel and dumped my pack till the evening. As it was only 1.0 and a fairly clear day thought I might do Snowdon in the afternoon while there was a good chance of getting a decent view from the top (which doesn't, I believe, happen often) though I already decided to do it either tomorrow or Wednesday. Encountered the Seears[23] just about to ascend by the mountain railway but I didn't feel inclined to accompany them by this route especially when the charge is as much as 8/- return and 5/- up. So made my way up the long, tedious Llanberis path. After going a about a mile and a half however it became evident that it wasn't worth going any further for it had come over cloudy and the summit was obscured by some stationary cloud which was obviously going to stay the afternoon. So slowly down again and went round to the waterfalls at the bottom of the path. I couldn't take my eyes off them for fully ten minutes. Had some tea at Snowdon station before going to the hostel about a mile to the north. Wrote some postcards before dinner and after it spent an hour washing up a colossal pile of washing up and then off the rest of the evening writing to Mother. Bed 10.0.

[*a further week in Snowdonia and Chester*]

Monday 8 August I decided that I'd seen quite sufficient of Chester on a day like this and silently plodded back to the station to catch the 4.18 home to London. Got to Euston at 8.20, about half an hour

---

22 The opening of Wordsworth's nine-line poem of 1802.
23 Elderly dentist and St Pancras councillor in Heap's Ward 8.

late. Mother and Bernie to meet me. Thus ends a grand and glorious nine day's holiday. One of the best I've ever had. I just can't imagine how it could have been bettered – superb scenery, exhilarating air, wonderful weather (for the most part) and well behaved feet. Also quite inexpensive really – about £4.15.0 inclusive of everything. I came back feeling as fit as can be. And the beauty of it is I've still another week's holiday to come shortly. I am well contented, and 'indeed to goodness' I am.

Sunday 14 August A day in and around Cambridge. Got there at 12.35 and going up to the University at the other end of town, went round many of the colleges (i.e. from the grounds) as I could find. Didn't seem to me either as extensive or imposing as Oxford. On the other hand, Oxford has nothing to compare with the sylvan loveliness of the 'Backs' at Cambridge. The Cam is in fact the real glory of Cambridge. It somehow sets the whole tone of the place as well as that of the flat surrounding meadow lands through which it passes. Spent about three hours wandering round the University quarter including lunch by the river and a look at the Fitzwilliam Museum art galleries. Some excellent Augustus John portraits there and, among other things, Ford Madox Brown's *Last of England* which is introduced as a scene into *Nine Sharp* at the Little, and a Low cartoon of the Ideal Cabinet in the *Standard* on Jan 5th 1928! What a memory. Had a final glimpse of the University and the Backs by twilight as I passed into the town to catch the return train at 9.30. Five minutes late, got into Liverpool St at 11.0. Home in twenty minutes, supper and to bed by 12.45. A delightful day.

Monday 15 August Back to my usual work again and, after last week, very welcome too. At home in evening reading and listening to the Wagner Prom on radio. The creditors having discovered their hide out at Primrose Hill, the Maclaveys moved again today to Camden Town High St. A vagabond family if ever there was one. Pathetic, funny and scandalous all at one and the same time.

Tuesday 16 August Was deprived of my glasses for the afternoon. Leaving them on the radiator while I was working just before lunch, someone accidentally plonked a big book on top of them and broke one of the sidepieces. Luckily it wasn't the lenses. Very apologetic about it, offered to pay for the repair. So straightaway took them round to the opticians and collected them in the evening. Cost 2/6, which seems fairly reasonable. Actually my eyes didn't feel so bad working without them as I expected.

Saturday 20 August Went to work in sports jacket and flannels, got off at 12.30 and went straight down to Charing Cross to catch the 1.15 to Walmer. Mother came to see me off and brought my case with stick and lunch which I ate as soon as train started moving. Arrived Walmer at 3.55, along to the Camp at Kingsdown.

Part One

[A week at the Kingsdown Holiday Camp in Kent]

Saturday 27 August Have spent practically the whole of the last two days in the company of a Welsh girl called Glynis with whom I became acquainted at the dance on Wednesday night. A delightful personality, gay, vivacious, charming and blessed with a melodiously attractive voice. We have got on wonderfully well together and enjoyed each other's company to the full. I've never been so much at ease in any woman's company before though it nevertheless gave rise to the inevitable disturbing emotions which have always arisen whenever I've become particularly fond of anyone of the opposite sex. I've never yet experienced a great affection for anyone without feeling absurdly miserable at the same time. Though in this case the liking is more generally mutual than ever happened with me before. I do feel that at last I've met someone who does really care for me in no small or uncertain degree and well that is rather a big moment in one's life. Whether it'll just pass over as a brief holiday flirtation or develop into anything more, I can't yet foresee. And after all, our friendship though deep enough has only been of the shortest duration so far. Still, it's all very disturbing. I record all this emotional reaction stuff here only by reason of the fact that my getting to know G and going round with her added to the enjoyment of the week at Kingsdown considerably. I don't think I'd have ever been able to enter into a glorious carefree spirit of the camp otherwise. It has indeed been a wonderful week far exceeding my expectations. And perfect weather nearly all the time. No wonder they all go 'back to Kingsdown' year after year. There's something about the place that gets you. It's certainly got me. And as we come to the last day – the wistful, melancholy regretful day of parting. Even the weather seemed to feel the sadness of the occasion for it was inclined to be dull and oppressive – certainly not as fine as the last few days. Having disposed of packing etc. before breakfast, had a last round of putting with G immediately after same (incidentally she lives, works at North Middlesex Golf Club – what memories of the mid-twenties does that place conjure up!), then down to the beach for the last of our blissfully happy hours together thereon before early lunch at 12.30. Likewise the cliffs after lunch, the whine of ships' hooters out at sea adding the requisite finishing touch of pathos to the occasion. And so after a last long lingering look around the camp did we wend our way down to the house with our luggage and clamber onto the private bus for Walmer Station to catch the 4.30 back to London. Got into Charing Cross just after 7.0, about half an hour late. Mother there to meet me. Bid au revoir to G and so out to the homebound bus.

[New volume, Acc. 2243/12/1, started 1 September]

1938

Sunday 4 September At last, seven months after the passing of Nigger, we decide to have another dog. Nay, more than that, we actually went and bought one in Club Row this morning.[24] We had been looking round for a good hour before we finally alighted on 'Bob' for such we have decided to call him. A mongrel fox terrier about two months old, roughly fifty–fifty black and white with a dash of brown on face and backside, we spotted him in a basket with eight or ten others for sale. They wanted 12/6 for him. Mother held out that it [was] too dear until we got him for the odd price of 11/-. I went prepared to pay 10/- anyway. So we acquired Bob. If he gives us half the joy and happiness Nigger gave us, he will be worth his cost a hundredfold. Not really being allowed to keep dogs here, he'll have to be kept quiet as quiet and inconspicuous as possible in any case. Still, he'll be worth the trouble of bringing up and looking after, I think. And, thank heaven, I'll be able to go up to Hampstead and Regent's Park again now. No more Sat aft. and Sun morn. blues!

Tuesday 6 September Not being able to leave the pup at home, Mother brought him round with her and of all the cursed things that happen to spoil our peace of mind, it's not a dog but a bitch. This really damnable. It was sold to us as a dog and not being able to judge from the undeveloped state we naturally assumed that it was so. Now we're in a real dilemma. It will have to be taken to an expert to make absolutely certain what it is and if it is a bitch will then have to be disposed of somehow – taken back to Club Row and exchanged or sold or exchanged elsewhere or something for I just won't have a bitch under any circumstances. The fact that even in two days we've grown so fond of it will make it hard to part with it and the longer we keep it the harder twill be. But unless it is a dog, go it must. What damned rotten luck we do have.

Saturday 10 September Went up to Finchley in evening to see my Kingsdown acquaintance Glynis. Met her at Tally Ho Corner and went round to see fete in Finsbury Park, Friern Barnet. Exhausted its interest in half an hour or so and went along to the Orange Tree for a couple of drinks. Finally took the bus to Muswell Hill and walked through to and around Alexandra Palace. Fascinating view of the 'lights' of London therefrom. Not a very successful evening. I somehow knew it wouldn't be. I don't quite know why I embarked on it really. Perhaps because I don't like to drop such an acquisition, recalling as it does much happy memories, too abruptly. Though it's always the wisest policy in the long run. These holiday flirtations should end with the holiday. One sees people in a different light after. It's never quite the same thing. The spirit and the atmosphere of the seaside are lacking. She's a good

---

24   The animal market in Shoreditch, E2. It closed in 1982.

sort and it was good while it lasted but, well, it was just destined not to last long. So be it.

Monday 12 September Hitler's speech this evening at conclusion of Nuremberg conference contained no important pronouncement of policy concerning the vexed problem of the Sudeten Germans in Czecho-Slovakia which had looked like bringing the world to the brink of war.[25] The tension during the past few days has been terrific. In short a 'crisis' of the first order though of course exaggerated considerably by the unreliable newspaper sensationalism. In any case, what concern it is of ours or why we should ally ourselves with the communist forces of France and Russia to support C-S I fail to see. To hell with Czecho-Slovakia![26]

Saturday 17 September Have got the new [male fox terrier] pup. Mother went up to the Caledonian Market and selected him yesterday. Cost 10/-, off which they allowed 7/6 for the bitch in part exchange. So net extra cost 2/6. Like the other one a mongrel fox terrier about six to eight weeks old, black and white with a dash of brown but rather more black than white and not unlike Nigger. Ran into Turner, ex-office colleague at PR's on Marchmont St on way home. Left seven weeks ago to join the Fire Brigade. Still training in Southwark and studying hard to get through tests. Unaccustomed hard work but he likes it and it doesn't take long to get into the regular service when, apparently, it's an easy life. Well, I wish him luck.

Thursday 22 September A lull in the crisis is now evident while Chamberlain has further talks with Hitler in Germany on Sudeten territory problem. Has abated somewhat since the Czechs accepted the British–French peace plan whereby the Sudeten lands were to be given back to Germany and the new frontier guaranteed. Now however the demands of Hungary and Poland for the return of their minority areas in C-S have arisen to complicate the issue and the Czech government has fallen. Still, Chamberlain and Hitler will probably fathom it out satisfactorily and avert war in spite of vacuous whining and carping of left-wingers and John Bullish German haters. I don't know which are the most despicable of the two.

Sunday 25 September A dull damp morning but cleared up later in day. Lay in till 1.0. A short stroll before lunch at 2.30. Read book in afternoon and in evening walked to Marble Arch and heard Bonar Thompson discuss the crisis (now as grave as ever, Hitler having issued a six day

---

25   Although he had previously reported and reflected on the conflicts in China, Abyssinia and Spain, this is his is Heap's first direct mention of a possible war with Germany.

26   This was not an uncommon reaction. In a BBC National Channel broadcast on 27 September, the Prime Minster lamented: 'How horrible, fantastic, incredible it is that we should be digging trenches and trying on gas-masks here because of a quarrel in a faraway country between people of whom we know nothing.'

ultimatum to the Czechs to 'evacuate Sudetenland or else') means war, in a characteristically cynical and light hearted fashion to counteract the gloom and tensions of these grim depressing days. Still, much may happen in six days. And whatever the outcome it's certain anyway to be an exciting week. The sort of excitement perhaps we could well do without, but nevertheless exciting. Home at 8.30. No fresh news of any importance on radio. Supper, a short read. So, Pepys-like, to bed.

Monday 26 September Went round to the Town Hall with Mother in the evening to see the *St Pancras through the Ages* exhibition, opened there today. Mostly photographs and prints of various descriptions. Nothing of very great interest. A dull and silly little play about Dickens performed on the stage. Half an hour just about covered everything worth seeing. A long queue waiting outside front entrance to be fitted with gas masks. The war scare grows apace. Nobody talks about anything but war, war, war. All the old, blind, ignorant, vicious, stupid, prejudice against Germany is being worked up again to fever pitch. Even the schools are ready for movement to the country by the end of the week, so certain does it seem. Millions of Englishmen, women and children are to be slaughtered to bolster up international communism, backed by Jewish finance, which is all the Czech-Franco-Russian alliance amounts to. We've got to stand by France and fight her wars for her again, help Russia to attain its unthinkable domination of Europe. And all the mugs fall for it – a similar illusion in 1914 (in both senses). It makes one feel utterly ashamed of my country, this crass criminal murderous stupidity.

Tuesday 27 September Nothing seems more certain than a European war now. Neither the Czechs or the Germans will give way, giving little hope of peace. Only a miracle will avert war now. That being so we took the precautionary measure of going round to the Mary Ward Settlement in the teeming rain to obtain our gas masks.[27] Took Bernie as well. A long queue even there but within a few minutes we were feeding into the theatre hall where about two dozen fitters were in attendance and a demonstrator addressed us from the platform. All surprisingly speedy and efficient. Came home and put B to bed while Mother went out. I see in the evening papers that they are appealing for volunteers for auxiliary fire brigades and special constabulary, for both of which I'm eligible regards age. I might consider one of these if it will serve as an exemption from the fighting forces. For I would refuse to fight (if the mass murder of modern warfare can be termed such) for a cause I didn't believe in and against a nation I admired and

---

27 Established by the Victorian novelist Mrs Humphry (Mary) Ward to provide social services to the urban poor and to campaign for social justice and equality, the art deco Mary Ward Settlement, built on land donated by the Duke of Bedford at 5 Tavistock Place, was ideal for fitting and distributing the government-funded respirators.

respected, sympathised with and in fact in a war for which we had not the slightest justification in entering. But the above mentioned services are on a different footing. Purely defensive and of some use to the community. Dangerous too perhaps, but not so much as the battlefields and in my case better than prison or the firing squad, the only other alternatives.

Wednesday 28 September A day of hope lights up the horizon at the eleventh hour. Hitler has invited Chamberlain, Mussolini and Deladier to Munich tomorrow to make a final offer of seeking a satisfactory solution of the problem without resort to war. It's too early to say yet but it looks as if the miracle might happen yet if this conference attains its object. I'm inclined to think it's more about Mussolini working behind the scenes. He hasn't seemed too keen on going to war against France and Britain although pledged to support Germany. And he's more clever than he's ever given credit for. Chamberlain's efforts however should not be underestimated. He has worked and is continuing to work for peace as no other statesman has ever done before so practically or tirelessly. If he succeeds he'll be the saviour of Europe as well as Britain. The heartening news spread round the world like wildfire late this afternoon when it was given out unexpectedly on the radio. We could hardly believe down at tea where I first heard it. In fact many were downright incredulous. Just another rumour – but on coming out of work it was in the papers. The relief was intense. It was in such a mood then that I hied me to the Palladium [*to see* The Crazy Gang]. Excellent. Home to supper at 9.15, lapped up the news on radio and went to bed fairly early, tired and hopefully happy.

Thursday 29 September The big four duly gathered together at Munich and had three meetings in the course of the day. No statement regarding any decision thereat has, however, yet been issued. So the world continues to wait on tenterhooks, hoping for the best. Walking home through the Bloomsbury squares was struck by the strong smell of earth emanating from the digging of air raid shelters, a drive which is being feverishly carried on day and night all over London in any open space available.[28] Despite today's lull in the anxiety, there's been no slackening of Air Raid Precautions. Perhaps it's just as well to be prepared for the worst.

Friday 30 September The miracle has happened! Late last night the four powers at last reached an agreement and so averted the world war that would have meant practically the end of civilisation. So sanity prevailed and Europe breathes freely again. As I beheld the placards this morning bearing the one magic word 'Peace' my heart leapt for joy. I

---

28   In St Pancras, air raid trench shelters with an eventual capacity for 17,000 were dug in the public squares, Regent's Park, Primrose Hill and Parliament Hill. Commercial premises had their basements strengthened as additional public shelters.

heaved a sigh of overwhelming relief. And it's been largely due to one man, Chamberlain, for the decisive [role] he has played in bringing this about, he has earned the deepest gratitude of the whole world. His place in history will be a noble one. Probably no other English statesman has served the interests of his country and humanity in general so well, so thoroughly, so courageously and to better purpose. He well deserved the tremendous ovation that awaited him on his triumphant return this evening after concluding a personal no-more-war pact with Hitler, in the interests of Anglo-German friendship.[29] A truly great man in every sense of the term. Met Bill outside the Horse Shoe at 7.15, went over to the Blue Posts for half an hour then to the Bird in Hand where we engaged in darts playing and the two Johns joined us soon after 8.30. This was the time Bill said he must definitely leave for home, having been out every night this week on ARP work. Actually he left at 9.35. We stayed on for a little time then walked up to the Robin Hood to see the lads up there.[30] We're all going to their firm's do tomorrow, for which I am duly roped in and sold a ticket. Might as well go as there's nothing much to see in the way of plays, three of this week's first nights having been postponed till next week.

Saturday 1 October In accordance with Munich Pact, German troops marched into the Sudetenland today to begin Germany's token occupation of certain areas. The bulk of the territory is to be occupied and policed by British troops pending its gradual transference to Germany and evacuation of the Czechs, who accepted the proposals without demur.[31] Poland appears to be causing trouble now about the small Polish minority in C.S. but it's not likely to come to much, I don't think. After doing the washing up I lay on the bed for an hour in the afternoon before going along to the Robin Hood in evening to meet the boys and proceed to the Wheelers Sports Club dance over the Victoria Coach Station. Six of us. Joined by some more of their friends there including Phil and Kath Smart, Phil an ex-Holborn Rover acquaintance who used to be in the Roland House Panto. Had one dance with [Kath] and then spent the rest of the evening down in the bar which like the dance hall was very small, chic, intimate and delightedly overcrowded. We all got gloriously drunk. Rolling out at midnight someone dropped the key of his car down a drain and borrowed my stick to see how deep it was but what use that knowledge was to him I couldn't quite see. Got bus home from Victoria, the lads bellowing bawdy songs all the way. Got to bed at 1.30 or rather 12.30 for summer time ends this morning.

29 Neville Chamberlain arrived back at Heston Airport that evening and proudly showed the waiting crowds and photographers his 'piece of paper' detailing the agreement that he and Hitler had signed.
30 The Robin Hood, 281 High Holborn, WC1.
31 The War Office was reported to be drawing up operation orders for British troops and members of the British Legion, together with French troops and ex-servicemen, to take over policing (*The Times*, 1 October 1938).

Friday 21 October A hell of an evening. The dog was in a dreadful state, vomiting and emptying his bowels every few minutes and then rushing round like mad. Couldn't leave him unwatched for five minutes. Seems perfectly hopeless. Looks as if we've been 'sold a pup' for the second time. What luck we do have!

Saturday 22 October Had to have the pup done away with. Mother, after being kept up all night again nursing it, took it along to the dispensary this morning where it was at once put out of its misery for good. Twice bitten, once shy. Not really worth the worry and trouble involved, especially for Mother – not to mention the official ban on dogs here. So I decided that I'll have to get used to going up to Hampstead on my own and went along to Regent's Park as a 'try out' in the afternoon, which was blessed with glorious weather. Wasn't nearly so dejected as I expected. Went over to Primrose Hill to find not only unsightly Air Raid trenches dug all around the lower part[32] but the entire summit fenced off and all the trees cut down. Asked policeman the why and wherefore of it. He told me that anti-aircraft guns had been placed up there during the crisis week and since removed. Meanwhile the public are deprived of a splendid viewpoint and the beauty of the hill marred by ugly tree stumps. This stupid useless desecration of the beauty of London's open spaces everywhere so infuriated me that I almost kept the inevitable thoughts of Nigger out of my mind, but not quite. I could still see him trotting along a few feet in front of me many a time.

Sunday 6 November Went to Regent's Park in the afternoon. More ground at the top of Primrose Hill being fenced off, provisionally for ARP purposes.[33] Apparently this enclosure, which is higher and more elaborate, will when complete supersede the present one. Thus leaving the south fringe of actual summit with its sundial and fine view over London open to the public again. Well thank heavens for small mercies anyway!

Thursday 10 November Listened to symphony concert on radio. Also to Premier's speech from the Lord Mayor's Banquet at Guildhall. The customary discussion of the Government's foreign policy, which of course, has far more significance this year than usual. A splendid speech on his favourite theme on Peace, goodwill and conciliation – the blessed trinity!

Friday 11 November Armistice day. Twenty years after – and every country in the world preparing for another war by piling up armaments as fast as they can. What a world! Mother out selling poppies. Started

---

32 Just inside the park, by the Gymnasium, opposite Albert Terrace and the end of Fitzroy Road.

33 See Martin Sheppard, *Primrose Hill: A History* (Lancaster: Carnegie, 2013), ch. 12, 'The Impact of War', where Heap is quoted.

about 5.0 in the [previous] evening, and with two hour breaks finished in the afternoon. Did a roaring trade. Saw Bill in the evening, in the Blue Posts. A good argument between the two Johns and the R H [Robin Hood] boys and myself about the latest outbreak of anti-Jew riots in Germany and Jews in general. Most of the R H boys being as pro-Fascist and anti-Jewish as I am. A most gratifying evening.

Sunday 13 November At last after nine months, I went up to Hampstead once again this morning by the new trolley buses[34] which have now supplemented the old trams, my first attempt to get used to Hampstead without Nigger. The new enclosure at the top of Primrose Hill now completed and the temporary one removed. I hope to goodness they're going to paint it green or do something to eradicate the unsightly stark newness of its light coloured wood and so make it conform with its surroundings.

Saturday 19 November Unlike last Saturday, a perfect afternoon for Hampstead to which I duly went and had a good two hour walk. An inevitable touch of melancholy about it, the sight of every dog of reminding me of Nigger as did much else besides. Hampstead will never be quite the same to me without him but it is ever lovely to behold and wonder o'er and thank heaven the ARP vandals have left it entirely alone. No it wasn't as hard to get used to on my own as I expected.

Friday 25 November Mother's 57th birthday. Treated her to a ticket to the Conservative Christmas Party at Earls Court on Dec 6th as a present.

Thursday 1 December Ward 8 Annual Dinner at Shaftesbury Hotel[35] in evening. Went to the unnecessary trouble of getting half an hour off in order to leave work at 6.0, dash home, change and be at the Shaftesbury on time for the reception (6.45–7.15). At 7.45 dinner was served at last and we trooped in. Sat near end of top table between Mrs White and the elderly lounge suited reporter from the *St Pancras Chronicle* who, much to my surprise, didn't have shorthand and scribbled down the speeches in some sort of longhand. Mother on the other side of him just round corner. Dinner pretty good and the better part of a bottle of St Julian I had with it even better. Speeches rather prosaic and matter of fact. Not a glimmer of wit or sparkle in any of them and so long that I couldn't wait till they'd finished before slipping out to make water. Beit [MP] did his famous 'dropping in' act in which he stays for half an hour to say a few words before dashing back to the House. An old gag but it still goes down well. I was mentioned in despatches

---

34 The replacement of trams by trolleybuses was started in October 1935 and continued until June 1940, when war intervened.
35 At 65 Shaftesbury Avenue, W1.

Part One

thrice. Sperni replying to the toast made a bad faux pas erroneously referring to me in eulogistic terms as Secretary and making no mention of Mrs W at all. [Councillor] Seear gave me a verbal pat on the back on my current capacity of Assistant Secretary and Goddard spoke of my 'witty' minutes. I liked this best of all – the more so as it was the most unexpected tribute of the three. But they were all most gratifying and I must confess my vanity was tickled immensely. Mother also had no end of praise lavished on her as did several others besides. The dance wasn't too great a success. I had three or four dances but the small floor was rarely filled except for such inane caperings as the Lambeth Walk and Palais Glide.[36] The adjoining lounge with its improvised bar seemed far more popular. I had four light ales in there on top of the two over at Mortimer's and the claret at dinner. So by 12.0 when it finished I could hardly have claimed to be strictly sober. Got taken home in Sperni's car. Bed at 1.0, whacked. Total cost of evening including 6/6 ticket was 16/4.

Friday 2 December Rather weary and almost dead beat by the evening. Stayed in, wrote up last night in here and read a little, while Mother went up for gas chamber test ARP course.[37]

Saturday 3 December Hampstead in afternoon. Noticed several small patches of ground on the other side of Spaniards Rd fenced off, presumably to let the grass grow on it again.[38] Also a couple of public seats placed in view points and endowed to the memory of someone or other. A far better form of memorial I think than the most elaborate tombstone.

Wednesday 7 December Monthly Ward 8 Meeting at the Club. Read my draft of the Annual Report which was duly approved. A short talk by Sir Alfred Beit on recent proceedings in Parliament relating to the National Register and Colonies, followed by the business part of the meeting. Subtly pro-Jewish and anti-fascist in tone as might have been expected of the wealthy but undistinguished scion of a non-Aryan family. Sperni however making his reappearance at these meetings after his term of office as mayor, did make a good attempt to counterbalance things on the pro-fascist side in his vigorous, buoyant vote of thanks.

Saturday 10 December After dashing home to tea and changing, got to the Robin Hood at 6.0 to meet John Hobson and some of the other

---

36 Two popular 'romping' sequence dances of the late 1930s, for couples or groups in a line abreast performing the easy sequence. See C. Madge and T. Harrison, *Britain by Mass Observation* (London: Muller, 1937), ch. 5, 'Doing the Lambeth Walk'. 'The Walk' was included in the Victoria Palace musical that Heap saw on 18 December 1937.
37 She was concerned about the fit of her gas mask. In November 1939 she volunteered as an Air Raid Warden, which also involved a gas test.
38 Sites from which sand was dug to fill sandbags during the crisis.

lads. Thence five travelled up to Muswell Hill[39] by tube and bus, the rest by car with cigar and presents (our contribution to latter being 2/3 each). All the others there when we arrived except John Bell who came on later. Twelve fellows, five girls altogether. Nice flat, well furnished. A first rate party thanks largely to Phil's ingenious ideas in the way of fun and games. He kept things going at top pitch all the evening and we all had a really hectic time of it. All the beer you could possibly want, draught on tap for the other lads, bottled pale ale for me. About 2.0 things began to slow down a little and one or two started falling to sleep. The advent of tea and coffee and birthday cake at 2.30 revived the party spirit a bit but by 3.0 general exhaustion point had been reached, and about 4.0 we all departed in three car loads. Fortunately two of them were bound for King's Cross district which suited me perfectly and so I was duly deposited at the corner of Caledonian Rd at 4.25 a.m. Five minutes' walk and I was home, and fifteen minutes later I was in bed, dead beat. I haven't laughed so much for a long time. I certainly haven't been to many parties in my life but this one was easily the best I've struck so far.

Wednesday 21 December Snowed all day while the temp went up a little to round about 28 deg. The main streets a sea of slush tonight, snow three or four inches deep in the quieter ones. Accidentally tore the seat of my trousers on edge of office radiator this afternoon. Borrowed an unfinished pair from tailoring Dept to wear while I had them mended round in the workroom. Made an excellent job of it. Stitched the four inch gash almost invisibly and it cost me but 6d.

Saturday 24 December After going home to dinner went to Drury Lane in evening to see *Babes in the Wood*. Rather an inadequate sort of pantomime in many respects, especially in regard to story and humour and even production. [*page of criticism*] A disappointing affair altogether, a long way behind the Lane standard.

Sunday 25 December A real 'white' Christmas at last – the first for eleven years – with full Christmas card effects. Called for Bernie in morning and took him up to Hampstead. Snow between six inches and a foot deep in most parts. A good deal of tobogganing on the slopes and some skiing but no skating on the ponds. Apparently it's not safe enough while the temperature continues merely to hover round freezing (32 deg. was today's average). Came over slightly foggy now and again but it was a joyous jaunt which the Imp [Bernie] enjoyed as much as I did and gave us both the appropriate appetite for the disposal of Christmas dinner. Thus lunch at 3.0. Washed up, walk at 8.15. Contrary to expectations heard very few sounds of usual revelry by night, indeed from one house in Woburn Square I heard instead the

---

39 The home of his camping friends Phil and Kath Smart.

industrious sounds of a typewriter in action issuing forth into the still night. To bed at 12.0. As quiet and congenial Christmas Day as most I've spent.

Saturday 31 December To the Robin Hood at 8.0 to meet John Hobson and the R.H. [Robin Hood] boys together with their various womenfolk. About two dozen of us altogether. Enough to fill three cars and two taxis anyway when we set out from the R.H. at 8.45 for Albany St Barracks to see the Old Year out and the New one in at the Sergeants' [Mess] Dance there. A jolly informal, free and easy affair. A huge dance hall with one end partitioned off for a bar which was surrounded by completely black walls which gave the place a singularly eerie and somewhat grim wartime atmosphere. But there were two other bars apart from this one and it was quite a miniature pub-crawl going round from one to the other, in which fashion, needless to say, we spent most of the evening. All the drinks astoundingly cheap at each of them. Danced but once in the whole evening. At the striking of the midnight hour we duly celebrated the advent of 1939 in the customary fashion with Auld Lang Syne followed by an orgy of handshakes, kisses, hugs and embraces all round. Finished at 1.0 when we piled into cars and cabs again and went up to someone's house at Tollington Park.[40] All crowded into a small and rather dismal sitting-cum-drawing-cum-dining room and sprawled around drinking bottled beer and singing raucously. A few scraps of dry bread and cheese and cake all appeared on the scene but they were quite uneatable really. After about an hour things reached saturation point and everyone started drifting off. One or two including John H decided to stay the night there. I got a lift home in a Streatham-bound car as far as St Pancras Church and got in at 3.30. About the best New Year's Eve I've ever spent.

RETROSPECT – 1938

Two things happened in 1938 to make it the most eventful year for me since '34. Nigger's tragic death cast a gloom over the early part of the year, which not even the freakably fine early spring weather could dispel. It took me a long time to recover from the grip of this sorrowful bereavement, as a result of which Mother had a serious relapse, but fortunately recovered just as she was about to go into hospital again.

After seven months we decided to have another dog and bought a puppy which turned out to be a bitch. We got rid of it and tried again. The second one contracted chronic distemper so it went too. Being apparently destined not to have another dog, we gave it up as a bad job. I then willed myself into going up to Hampstead and Regents Park on a

---

40 Islington, N4.

1938

weekend – on my own. It was rather miserable at first but I persevered and soon got into it. The memory of Nigger will abide with me for ever but time has healed our sorrow.

The crisis was, strictly speaking, a matter of national rather than individual concern, but in so far as it brought it to the very brink of a world war, it was a time of deep personal anxiety for everyone, myself included. Only a miracle in the form of Chamberlain's adroit statesmanship saved us from the catastrophe. Being by nature a bit of a pessimist I was cast into the depths of despair and despondency for some days – especially as my sympathies were entirely with our potential foe, Germany. It looked like being the end of things – and it very nearly was. The subsequent relief as the storm passed over was equally overwhelming and intense.

But that momentous week left a profound and everlasting impression behind it. No one who lived through it will ever forget it. It also served to make me more contemptuous than ever of the shallow, vicious, hate mongering mob mentality that democracy fosters and thrives on, and more convinced than ever that Fascism is the most effective and beneficial form of government ever conceived. Nevertheless for Mother's sake I have carried on my prosaic Assistant Secretarial duties in the Conservative Association with as much aplomb as possible.

However, 1938 wasn't all gloom and depression by any means. There were offsets on the brighter side of things. There was, for instance, the most enjoyable two week's holiday I've had for years. My nine day tramp in the mountains of North Wales was sheer delight from start to finish. While my second week at Kingsdown Holiday Camp was equally enjoyable both as a complete contrast and as an entirely new experience; arising out of the latter was the brief holiday flirtation I indulged in. Fortunately with the sudden change of background and on getting back, I fell out of love again as quickly as I'd fallen into it.

At 28, I remain as determined as ever to avoid the pitfalls of undue affection for the opposite sex to shun the very thought of marriage like the plague (which it really is) and to enjoy the freedom, the peace of mind and the untrammelled joys of bachelor existence to the very end.

But my holiday experiences don't exhaust the year's more pleasant memories. I did quite a lot of rambling during the spring and summer months – more than I'd done for some time past. I thoroughly explored the glories of the South Downs. I visited many places of historic interest I had long wanted to see such as Oxford, Cambridge, Salisbury, Stonehenge and Chester, not to mention Snowdon and the castles of Caernarvon and Conway. The Portelet Rambling Club at last expired and I went out on my own on these day trips and enjoyed my solo carefree pre-rambles immensely. My increasing delights in these lone walks abroad was indeed one of the most significant phenomena of 1938.

Part One

Though my main interests have remained materially the same they have undergone a slight modification. Thus I have not been to the theatre this year quite so often nor read quite so many books as I have in recent years. Nearly but not quite. The reason being that I have endeavoured to be more discriminating in my choice of plays and so avoid wasting time and money on utter duds – and incidentally enjoy those I did see all the more. And whenever I've got hold of a really good book, I've taken my time over reading it and so savoured its goodness to the full. In like manner I haven't gone in for heavy drinking so fervently as hitherto, but carefully selected the appropriate occasion for more occasional and more enjoyable indulgence. As regards walking however, I can't honestly say that I haven't walked as much as usual because I have a damned side [*sic*] more, and I think am all the better for it.

My friends haven't altered much as though the ties tend to become a trifle slacker. I have continued to see Bill every month or so but he is obviously becoming more and more domesticated and has succumbed to that appalling practice of rushing off home in the middle of an evening for fear of trouble from the wife. I don't suppose our friendship will ever lapse entirely but it's far from being what it was. Ron migrated to Southampton in the spring and then disappeared completely, since when he has neither been seen or heard of. Whether we shall ever see him again I don't know. I hope so, for with all his faults and shortcomings, I liked him very much. My two most constant companions are now the two Johns, but they would scarcely be termed close friends.

Instead, then, of developing friendships or fostering new ones, I have tended to become increasingly introspective and diary conscious. Perhaps my most besetting folly these days is making too much of a conscious effort instead of a mere hobby of diary keeping. For instance, I spend far too much time sitting up late at night writing detailed criticisms of plays (thus getting correspondingly less sleep) and worrying generally about what I'm going to write in it (which is no doubt partly due to nerves). But there it is. I just can't help it. After all, it's my only means of self-expression and I must have an outlet for that at all costs.

A small rise in wages in April enabled me to start saving again – apart from the 10/- a week I put by for capital expenditure in the course of the year. Only in a small way it's true, at the rate of 4/- a week or £10 a year but definitely a clear saving. With this and accrued interest, I finish the year the richer by £10 and so am now worth £115, plus £10 for clothes etc in the capital expenditure a/c.

In fact about the only thing that hasn't changed in the least but remained solidly static this year have been my job, my prospects, and my ambitions – or lack of them. And I'm beginning to doubt whether they ever will change. Let it be recorded, however, that in a sudden fit of inspiration, I did make a brief abortive attempt at freelance journalism early in the year, which alas, was nipped in the bud by the grief of Nigger's untimely death and came to nought [sic].

Yes, it's certainly been an eventful and a rather turbulent year. A year of varying and conflicting moods and emotions, with some sense of drama about it. 1938 was vivid, real and altogether unforgettable.

1939

Following his approval of Chamberlain's appeasement of Hitler, the right-wing Heap was disturbed by the continuing rise in international tension as Germany at first threatened, then occupied, more of Eastern Central Europe. As London made increasing preparations for war, he eventually decided to make his personal contribution to the Air Raid Precautions Service, by volunteering for the Metropolitan Police War Reserve, not least in the hope that this might stop him from being conscripted. He started the weekly training sessions while his mother volunteered then trained as a St Pancras Air Raid Warden. But approaching war does not monopolise the diary, as it is only mentioned when significant international incidents occur, and Heap otherwise 'carries on', maintaining his routine theatre and cinema visits and regular nights out with his friends. His health, however, now played a very significant role in his life: not his circumcision on May Day but his severe stomach pains while on an August week at a holiday camp. This required him to undergo emergency surgery on his return to London and he remained in hospital until war was declared on 3 September and the hospitals were cleared of patients that evening. He returned to work after a short convalescence and settled down to an uneventful but exciting routine through the first months of what was, for civilians in London, a 'Phoney War' with no immediate military activity directly affecting them.[1] Understandably, Heap's daily diarising increased with the imminence and subsequent outbreak of war and he wrote a record 48,500 words through the year, of which nearly 45% are reproduced here.

Sunday 1 January Got up at 11.00 feeling as fit as a fiddle without any 'hangover' whatever from last night's fiesta.

---

[1] The phrase 'Phoney War' was coined by an American newspaper to describe the prolonged period of military inactivity (other than some naval actions) which followed the declaration of war. The naval actions had no direct effect on the civilian population, 'whose mood of determination to meet an immediate attack soon changed to boredom, bewilderment and resentment at the disruption of the blackout, rationing, and the evacuation of children' (I. C. B. Dear (ed.), *Oxford Companion to the Second World War* (Oxford: Oxford University Press, 1995), p. 691).

1939

Monday 2 January Have changed my morning paper from the [*Daily*] *Express* to the *Mail*. The theatres don't advertise in the D.E. and the D.E. won't print criticisms of new plays or any theatrical news whatsoever. A paper incomplete in that respect, however excellent otherwise, is no use to me at all. The *Mail* possesses most of the general characteristics of the D.E. and gives the theatre its proper due. And I certainly like its attitude of reasoned goodwill towards foreign countries. I must however continue to get the D.E. on Thursdays and Saturdays as well in order to read Agate.[2]

Tuesday 3 January Annual General Meeting of Ward 8 at the Club. A tussle between Seear and Sperni for the chairmanship.[3] A most unfair one too for Seear had arranged an obvious frame-up to get himself elected instead of leaving it to the meeting to nominate a temporary chairman to conduct the election. Sperni himself proposed Seear and Mother proposed Sperni, whereupon John Evans gave one of the most bad mannered and ill-tempered displays of unfair bias (against Sperni) that could possibly disgrace the role of chairman. Everything he could do to turn the election in Seear's favour he did do, even to the extent of trying to eliminate any discussion in favour of Sperni whatsoever. This naturally caused considerable ill feeling and several protests. A ballot eventually took place and Seear was re-elected by 22 votes to 17. A great disappointment for the Sperni faction, including myself. I was made Joint Secretary with Mrs White, which is I suppose a sort of lift up from Assistant Sec. Most of the old committee was re-elected en bloc and, there being no time for Sperni's talk after, stayed an hour after listening to Sperni talking about the Jews to a circle of listeners, which reminded me strongly of Gilwell's monologue.[4]

Wednesday 11 January Finished reading *England, Their England*,[5] mildly amusing on the funny side of the English as seen by a Scotsman – a great deal of innocent fun at the expense of our national cults and institutions such as bibulous journalists, cricket, golf, the League of Nations, highbrow Sunday drama, weekend country house parties, general elections, fox hunting and so on and so forth.

---

2   Heap greatly admired the prolific critic James Agate, who, although primarily a respected drama critic, novelist, essayist and playwright, wrote on other topics and produced nine volumes of autobiography – the *Ego* series.

3   The Municipal Reform councillor Seear (and two other councillors) later gave evidence against Sperni to Special Branch officers investigating the unpopular Sperni's business and political background when he appealed against his continued internment as an undesirable enemy alien to the (MI5) Advisory Committee (Italian). While in Brixton prison, Sperni was known as 'Mr Mayor' to his fellow prisoner Sir Oswald Mosley and the staff, Sperni having welcomed Mosley to speak at St Pancras Town Hall. See TNA, KV/1745 and KV/1746.

4   Presumably one of the sixteen long monologues written by Ralph Reader and still available from the Scout Association at Gilwell for performance by Scouts and Guides.

5   A 1933 comic novel by A. G. Macdonell (1895–1841), satirising English rural life and featuring a village cricket match.

Part One

Saturday 14 January Went to last night of Roland House Pantomime *Sleeping Beauty* at King George's Hall with the Johns and R.H. gang. Very poor stuff, even after making all possible allowances. Crude and shoddy, dull beyond belief. It occurs to me however that the acute boredom I suffered in watching it might have been attributed to either (a) the fact that I was half tight before seeing it and therefore incapable of appreciating its better qualities, if any (b) the possibility that I may have become more critically detached regarding these shows since I last saw one (three years ago) or (c) the plain fact that it really was a rotten show by any standards of judgement. Drove round to Cheffie's[6] whither the rest had already repaired for supper. Egg and chips and tea all round. An amusing evening even though it seemed to finish up all wrong.

Saturday 21 January After disposing of a few odd jobs, had a sudden impulse to drop into the British Museum for half an hour. Nostalgia of boyhood twenty years ago. Neither of the two old lecturers I used to go round with there now, presumably dead.

Sunday 29 January Bitterly cold. Went down to Norbury to spend the day at Bill's place. Arrived about 12.30 and ran the whole gastronomic gamut of lunch, tea and supper. No other guests, just me. In the afternoon Bill took me for a 'walk' around Croydon Airport. A fourpenny bus ride each way and when we got there, just stood about in an icy wind for half an hour watching aeroplanes taking off and landing. This absolutely fascinated Bill but merely left me cold. No, I didn't particularly enjoy the 'walk.' Spent the evening playing cards for small stakes. Still, it was a pleasant enough day, if unexpectedly quiet and sober.

Monday 30 January On getting home found a note from Seear asking me to go over and see him. A lot of fuss about the notice for the next meeting, which I'd dared to draft in a different and more attractive way from the stereotyped one used hitherto by Mrs White, and without consulting either of them. As I insisted on my notice however, he agreed to decide which should be used. If mine is not used though, and I don't think it will be, Mother and Mrs Baxter intend to create a hullabaloo about it at the meeting. Came back and regained my composure of mind by listening to Beethoven's 1st Symphony on radio, surely one of the loveliest things in the whole of his works. Then a report of Hitler's eagerly awaited speech on the 6th anniversary of the Nazi regime. Significant.[7]

---

6   Café/restaurant at 68 Millman Street, WC1.
7   In fact, *The Times* (31 January) considered it significant that Hitler did *not* make an anniversary speech, although there were celebrations and torch-lit marches in Berlin. The headline noted 'Herr Hitler's Silence' and reported Dr Goebbels' speech to the youth of Germany, exhorting them 'to work, learn, fight and be strong'.

1939

Friday 3 February Foggy. Bernie no longer staying with us now. Mother started work today on a temporary job round at the Mary Ward Settlement in Tavistock Place, tending to invalid school children. Hours 8 till 3 and reasonably good pay. If only she could get it permanently 'twould suit her down to the ground.

Tuesday 7 February Cut the monthly Ward 8 meeting entirely and went to the Roland House Panto Dance. Three years since I last went. Arrived there around 8.30 in a downpour of rain. My old flame Irene also came along.[8] Now happily married and the proud mother of a fifteen months old boy. A grand evening which I wouldn't have missed for anything, least of all a lousy meeting.

Sunday 12 February Had only just got back at 8.45 when who should call but old Ron – about the last person I expected to see. Hadn't heard from him for about two months or seen him for eight months. Not being able to stick the provinces any longer, he has at last chucked up his job at Northampton and come down to live in London once more. Took him out for a drink (or rather four as it turned out). I suggested the Museum Tavern in Gt Russell St, so we walked up there. Oddly enough the only other time I'd been in there was exactly three years ago this very night, when I dropped in with 'Trixi' on our way from the Horse Shoe. Talked about our various experiences since we last met till closing time when we walked up Gower St and parted in Euston Rd. Well, it's certainly good to see old Ron again.

Tuesday 14 February Swedish drill after work. Home to dinner at 7.45. On my own for the evening, Mother having gone to see Mrs Zelger. Spent an hour or so reading through my diary for the early part of 1931 over which phase I happen to be in the throes of one of my nostalgic sentimental reminiscence complexes just now. Eight years ago! How incredibly young and innocent I was still! What a wonderfully simple and straightforward world it all seemed! The things that have happened since then!

Thursday 16 February Met Mother in Oxford Circus. Went to a cocktail party given by Sir Alfred Beit at his house, 15 Kensington Palace Gardens.[9] Took us about three quarters of an hour to get there by bus and on foot. A magnificent mansion lavishly but tastefully decorated and furnished and absolutely chock full of old masters. About two or three dozen other people there, all St Pancras Conservatives of various degrees and denominations. I gather he does this sort of thing regularly to keep his supporters enthusiastic, all arranged by [his agent] Dale of course. Drank no end of cocktails and sherry and finished up on

---

8   No previous reference to this 'old flame' is obvious in the diaries.
9   Known as 'Millionaires Row', this luxury gated complex has for years been occupied by embassies and some of London's wealthiest residents; see note for entry for 24 April 1935.

whisky. Don't think I've ever got so tipsy in so short a time before – less than an hour it took me. Mother went on to an Ypres League supper at the Bedford Head[10] whither she induced the Barrows and the Bakers to accompany her. So Baker drove us all there in his car. I left them and came home to eat Irish stew though I couldn't actually face it for at least an hour so injudiciously had I indulged my alcoholic appetite. However I got it down eventually – wasn't even sick after it.

Sunday 5 March Hampstead in morning. Rather windy but quite fine and mild. St Paul's now clearly visible from Parliament Hill, a sure indication of the advent of Spring. Cleaned windows and read papers in afternoon while Mother went to confirmation of younger Sperni offspring, followed by tea at the Bonnington.[11] Came back much impressed by the catholic ceremonies, the stately demeanour of the bishop and the antiquity of St Ethelred's Church where it all took place.[12] Evening – book – walk – radio – supper – book.

Tuesday 7 March Monthly Ward 8 Meeting at club in evening. The question of the joint role and our respective duties being on the agenda had to come up for discussion, but it was all glossed over quite amicably and we are now very much 'as it were' – as it were. Evan Evans gave a talk on 'Electricity'. Dull as could be. Just read out an endless series of voluminous figures from his papers. But mercifully brief. Somewhat comic interlude after when we attempted to distribute stocks of *Londoner* newspapers for delivery.[13] Many more left behind than taken away and can't wonder at it. Wouldn't catch me delivering papers for nothing.

Saturday 11 March Aunt Pop's usual birthday present – five dollars – arrived this morning with accompanying card and letter. So, as it was raining for the third Saturday in succession, spent the afternoon writing my periodical letter to Aunt Pop – 7½ pages in 2½ hours.

Monday 13 March My 29th birthday. Celebrated my reaching this last outpost of the twenties (wistful thought) in the most modest fashion imaginable, by going along to the King George's Hall in evening to hear a lantern lecture on 'London, Quaint and Curious' by Herbert Banyard, a London taxi driver. A most excellent lecture. Yes, I've spent far duller birthdays than this before now. Lumbago slightly easier today but still in evidence. To bed earlyish again with hot water bottle and flannel.

---

10   Pub at 40 Maiden Lane, WC1.
11   Hotel at 92 Southampton Row, WC1.
12   One of the oldest Roman Catholic churches in England, at 14 Ely Place, EC1.
13   The *Londoner* was the newspaper of the (Conservative) London Municipal Society from 1948. It had previously been the *Ratepayer*, so *Londoner* may well have been its popular name. See Ken Young, *Local Politics and the Rise of Party: The London Municipal Society and the Conservative Intervention in Local Elections, 1894–1963* (Leicester: Leicester University Press, 1975), p. 195.

1939

Saturday 18 March A terrific hullabaloo over Hitler's annexation of Czecho-Slovakia on Wednesday and alleged designs on Rumania.[14] Chamberlain makes speech of denunciation, notes of protest fly around, Ambassadors are withdrawn, tension and anxiety abound everywhere and the old war clouds gather on the horizon once more. What a life!

Sunday 19 March Hampstead in morning, very bleak and gloomy. Kept trying to rain but held off. Hardly anyone about. Over near the Spaniards Road noticed four small lorries pulled up by the side of the track with aerials on top and three or four men wearing earphones sitting in each of them. Can't imagine what they were doing though in these days of course one naturally suspects something sinister. Was quite surprised not to hear newsboys coming round the streets every few minutes today as they usually do on crisis Sundays, trying to cash in with every little tit bit of alarmist news on a credulous public. A strangely quiet day in fact.

Monday 20 March The prospects of continued peace in Europe not looking too rosy again, decided I'd better join the Auxiliary Fire Brigade or something like that before they get filled and the ranks close up, in which case I'd be left out in the cold and conscripted. So went round to Euston Rd Fire Station in evening to enrol. They asked me if I'd filled in the form on National Service Handbook.[15] I hadn't, having forgotten about all that, so I was given a form and a booklet and came away to fill in the one and peruse the other. Did both as soon as I got home then suddenly changed my mind and thought I'd sooner join the Police War Reserve which involved less arduous training and seems a more attractive proposition altogether.[16] However, decided to sleep on it and decide tomorrow and having a bit of a cold, went to bed forthwith or almost forthwith.

---

14   On 15 March Hitler had threatened the Czech President with an air attack on Prague unless his army capitulated. The Czechs were quickly crushed and, the following day, Hitler went to Prague and proclaimed the German Protectorate of Bohemia and Moravia, which they had invaded on 15 March. A European war thus moved several steps closer.
15   Copies of the Home Office booklet 'National Service' – dated January 1939, signed by the Lord Privy Seal, Sir John Anderson, and with an introductory 'Call to National Service' from the Prime Minister, Neville Chamberlain – had been delivered to all households appealing for volunteers. Heap has made no mention of receiving his copy.
16   The booklet explained: 'The Police War Reserve consists of persons who would serve only in the event of war, when their duties would be the same as those of the regular police. At present this auxiliary service is confined to the Metropolitan and City of London Police Forces.
     Applicants should be men of 25 to 55 years of age, of sound physique and health and good character. Some men between 20 and 25 are also wanted.
     Recruits receive not less than 20 hours training during the first year and 12 hours in subsequent years without pay. When serving in war time members of this reserve would be paid and receive free medical treatment, compensation being payable in respect of death or disablement in the course of duty. Applications should be made to any police station within the London area.'

Tuesday 21 March Decided to delay decision on joining the police reserve for a few days. Will probably go along next Monday if I decide to join.

Thursday 23 March Took Mother to first night of Ivor Novello's new Drury Lane show *The Dancing Years*, a glittering glamorous show, well up to standard of *Glamorous Night*, his first and greatest Lane success. The only jarring note was struck by an unnecessary and quite irrelevant little scene at the end which was not only an incredibly crude, artless and blatant piece of anti-Nazi propaganda but worse still an anti-climax.[17] Without that unfortunate little scene it would have been absolute perfection.

Saturday 25 March Very cold with varied showers of snow, hail and rain. Regent's Park and Primrose Hill in afternoon. The top of the latter looking more presentable now that the construction of the anti-aircraft 'pill boxes' has been completed and most of the fencing removed.

Friday 31 March Evening met the two Johns at the Horse Shoe at 8.45. Had three drinks a head there then walked round to the Camden[18] and had five more apiece. At the end of the fourth round I retired to the closet and heartedly spewed. The tomato sauce with the spaghetti I'd had for dinner had reacted on the beer with these dire consequences. But oddly enough and contrary to all expectations I didn't feel the least bit put out by it and returned to dispose of a final drink as if nothing had happened. We meant to finish up at the Robin Hood whither we haven't been for a month now. But somehow we got no further than the Camden. Maybe it was the singularly attractive barmaid there with whom we got into jocular conversation. Maybe that's why we went there at all. Maybe – anyway it was the Camden we emerged from at closing time and parted outside.

Saturday 1 April A moist clammy sort of day. Cambridge won the Boat Race by four lengths – a walkover. Walked round Regent's Park and Primrose Hill in afternoon. Walked up to Piccadilly Circus after to see the Boat Race revelry. Actually there was precious little. Very tame and unexciting. Too many police about moving the crowds on. One of the dullest Boat Race nights I remember, and I've seen at least a dozen now.

Monday 3 April Went along to Gray's Inn Road Police Station in evening to join the Police War Reserve. Filled in application form, and a signed undertaking to serve full time on pay in the event of war and do the necessary period of training etc. and left them to be

---

17 *The Times* (24 April) stated: 'Mr Novello proceeds after the interval to show the shadows closing in on Vienna, sentiment replaces gaiety. A place once alive with song and laughter is now dead.'
18 At 18 Store Street, now the College Arms.

forwarded to the Ministry of Labour. If they pass my application, then I go up for medical test and, if I pass that, then I start training – one hour a week either Monday or Tuesday with minimum of 20 hours first year, 10 hours subsequent years. Had a chat about the service with the sergeant in charge, a most pleasant and agreeable fellow and left feeling quite pleased with myself. Well, I had to do something about National Service if [I] didn't want to be conscripted when war comes although or even before that, and what with this new pact with Poland against Germany and all the rest of the European turnout lately it seems to be getting more inevitable again every week.[19] And if it does come, the police seems to be a more attractive proposition than any of the fighting services or even the fire brigade. I've no doubts about passing the M of L alright. The only snag is will the doctor pass my eyesight which is, of course, good enough for all general purposes but not perfect. Well, we shall see.

Tuesday 4 April Monthly Ward 8 Meeting at Club in evening. Hardly any business. Mrs Baxter's talk on her travels in the dominions last year filled up the evening. Very adequately too. A most lively and animated address as was to be expected – and well-illustrated with a screen full of pictures and tables full of souvenirs, most of which she gave away after. I clicked for a wood cigarette case, one of those novelty ones which as they slide open, springs underneath the cigarettes pop them out. But the funny part of it was that this souvenir from Australia bore underneath the designation 'Made in Japan'!

Wednesday 5 April After dinner wrote up an account of last night's talk in the Minutes Book. Then during the greater part of this, wrote a further story fit for the *St Pancras Gazette*. Don't suppose half of it will ever get printed – if any at all.[20]

Thursday 6 April My application to join the Police War Reserve passed by the Ministry of Labour. Go up for medical examination next week. Quiet evening at home. And so we come to the Easter break at last. Not before it's needed either after the strain and stress of these winter months. Hope to get out into the country for a tramp each day if the weather is reasonably good. Doesn't look too hopeful at the moment. But then it rarely does just before Easter though it usually turns out alright.

Friday 7 April Good Friday – and so it was! Rather cloudy most of the day and a bit chilly but otherwise not at all bad. Went for a tramp on my beloved South Downs. Looking as lovely and friendly and green

---

19 According to *The Times* (1 April), on 31 March, the Prime Minister had announced that Britain had given Poland '"an assurance of all support in his power" if Poland's independence were clearly threatened'. The same page reported an appeal by the War Minister, Mr Hore-Belisha, for 250,000 recruits for the Territorial Army.
20 It was printed: see entry for 15 April below.

as ever. If only there hadn't been an endless series of confounded aeroplanes flying low overhead all day to mar their usual peace and tranquillity 'twould have been perfect. [*page of itinerary*] Caught the earlier of the two trains back at 7.25 and got to London Bridge at 9.30. Supper of scallops, bacon and chips and the news that Italy had invaded Albania which will be made the pretext for a new crisis by our worthy government.[21] What a relief it is to get away from all this for a day or two. How remote it all seems in these gentle and peaceful climes – or would be but for the damned planes.

Saturday 8 April Went down to Dorking by Green Line for a walk round the Leith Hill district. I haven't been down that way for three years now. Besides, one can always get lost in the bewildering hinterland – I did so three times today. Long tiresome journey down. Wished I'd gone by train. [*two pages of itinerary*] Got a coach back almost at once and was home at 9.30, bed 11.30.

Sunday 9 April Even finer and warmer and sunnier than it was yesterday. Unfortunately my heels were still too sore for any long distance walking so instead of getting out into the country again and making full use of such a lovely day, had to rest up, more or less waste it. Went up to Hampstead in afternoon not to walk but to sit in a deck chair on Parliament Hill and later over by Ken Wood and read book – quite pleasant despite the swarm of people up there.

Monday 10 April Easter Monday Went for a tramp down Epsom Downs and Box Hill way – easily the finest stretch of country within a short distance from London. Got the 10.43 from Waterloo. Home bound train packed, had to stand most of the way. So ends yet another Easter Holiday and as refreshing and enjoyable a one as any I've yet had.

Tuesday 11 April Far too warm for thick vests, long pants and overcoat. Bought some short pants on way home. Had the greatest difficulty in getting a couple of pairs with ordinary tops. Tried three shops before I came across one that stocked any other than those horribly uncomfortable things with elastic tops that seem to be generally worn nowadays. Before going to bed contrived to wash myself all over in the kitchen. An awkward business but had to be done in view of medical inspection tomorrow evening.

Wednesday 12 April Got off half an hour earlier from work and went round to Cavendish Court in Wigmore St to be examined by doctor for Police Reserve. A very brief sort of examination. All over in about five minutes, perhaps less. Passed alright on everything – physique, heart, teeth, tongue – even eyesight.

---

21   Italian troops landed at four points on the Albanian coast. Germany announced that 'it would neither understand or approve' of any action by other powers (*The Times*, 8 April 1939).

Thursday 13 April Played Ludo with Bernie while Mother went to an ARP meeting. Notification of acceptance for Police War Reserve with details of training classes etc just to hand. Mondays 6.30–7.30. Tuesdays 7.30– 8.30. Which means Tuesdays for me for some time to come thanks to the 6.30 closing. Must start next week.

Friday 14 April Alarming rumours going round this afternoon to the effect that everyone's salary was to be reduced to a maximum of £3 a week and each job assessed at that or a lower value regardless of age etc – take it or leave it. All of which, if true, will be just too bad. It's quite feasible with all the former executives gradually being weeded out in favour of a new clique and several old retainers reduced to servile jobs on a mere pittance. There's something rotten in the state of PR's. Went to the Camden, finished up at the Robin Hood.

Saturday 15 April This week's *St Pancras Gazette* to hand. My account of Mrs Baxter's talk actually got printed word for word as I wrote it, with only the last paragraph lopped off! Astonishing. Hampstead in afternoon. Wrote after a *Telegraph* job I noticed this morning.

Monday 17 April Cold enough for overcoat again. Lost the phone money collecting, a job which jointly with Power I've been doing for the last four years. Being taken over by Cashier's Dept. to whom of course it rightly belongs. Not sorry to lose it really. Got more work than I can properly cope with now without that.

Tuesday 18 April Went up to Gray's Inn Rd Police Station for first War Reserve instruction class 7.30–8.30. About three dozen of us sitting round three walls of a big room with the instructor and a blackboard full of notes occupying most of fourth. Given small police note books. Filled six pages of mine. Quite an interesting and instructive lecture. The sergeant in charge of them certainly knows his job. And has a grim sense of humour withal. Was measured for uniform after, though I wouldn't get it till called up for active service. This made me even later than I expected to be getting to Ward 8 Entertainments Committee meeting at the club. Was there in time for most of it anyway.

Friday 21 April Called on Dr Whyte after work to ask him whether I needed circumcision or not – a problem which has been disturbing my peace of mind somewhat of late. He examined my penis and advised me to have it done. As to ways and means he could recommend me to a Harley St consultant who would charge me a small fee of a guinea or so, take me under his wing in Bart's or St Paul's Hospital and get a good man to do it.[22] Otherwise going to an ordinary hospital it would probably mean staying on a waiting list for months before getting in.

---

22 Barts: The Royal Hospital of St Bartholomew, Smithfield, EC1; St Paul's Hospital, 24 Endell Street, Covent Garden.

Part One

Finally he advised me to think it over and let him know if I decided on the former. So I guess that's what it'll have to be. Will be mighty glad when it's over and done with. Am certainly not looking forward to it. Went up to the Horse Shoe. At about the third beer, an unpleasant sickly feeling in my throat suddenly made me realise that I'd unwittingly had tomato sauce with my boiled skate at dinner. Tomato sauce being the fatal prelude to beer for me. So straightaway went on scotch and stayed on it till closing time, thus avoiding any unpleasant consequences.

Monday 24 April Having decided to go through with the circumcision business as Dr Whyte advised, called to see him again after work and got the name and address and phone number of the Harley St consultant I'm to go and see.

Tuesday 25 April Phoned Harley St consultant and made appointment for Thursday afternoon. Will have to get time off. To Gray's Inn Rd Police Station in evening for second instruction class – aircraft and official secrets. Also given small printed book, duties etc to read, mark, learn etc, badge next week. Holiday lists round. Put down for last week in July (22–24) when I shall probably do a walking tour of the Peak District and second week in August (5–12) when I go with the two Johns and Bill Redfern to a holiday camp – Brean Sands, Somerset being the likeliest at present. At the moment however the prospects of our all still being at PR's throughout the summer to take our holidays at all, are still looked upon as somewhat dubious.

Wednesday 26 April Quiet evening at home studying Police War Reserve Handbook. Conscription for all men aged 20 announced today, 6 months full time training followed by 3½ years in Territorials. A foolish move which still only serves to intensify the ill feeling already existing in Europe. Carried out of course at the instigation of France, not to mention our own war mongers.

Thursday 27 April Got an hour off from work in afternoon and went to 61 Harley St for consultation with Dr Hume at 4.0.[23] Most opulent consulting room tastefully furnished and decorated in the most up to date manner. Even the waiting room had copies of the latest glossy magazines on the table including the *Theatre World* – about the last journal I ever thought to find in a doctor's waiting room. The consultation was brief, business-like, reassuring and very much to the point. I explained my trouble, was duly examined and found wanting of circumcision. Was given a choice of St Bartholomew's Hospital or St Anthony's, Dollis Hill, I chose the former. Would go in on a Sunday in one of Dr H's beds to be operated on by him on the Monday and come out Thursday. Perfect. Then came the slight shock – to wit the

---

23   John Basil Hume MB BS FRCS (1893–1974), of 61 Harley Street, a 'Practical Surgeon' at Bart's and later a deputy Vice-Chancellor of London University.

fee – three guineas. I said I hadn't expected it to be as much as that. He asked me what Dr Whyte had said it would be. I said a guinea. He then suddenly recalled that I'd mentioned belonging to the HSA[24] and that seemed to clinch the matter. So a guinea it was. Phew! Having a good part of my hour's leave still in hand, had some tea in Lyons before going back to work.

Friday 28 April Hitler's long awaited speech before the Reichstag in reply to Roosevelt's peace proposition took place at noon today. As expected it was most illuminating, conciliatory and non-committal. In the words of Jerome Kern's most fascinating ditties 'He didn't say Yes. He didn't say No. He didn't say Stay. He didn't say Go'.[25] On getting home found a card summoning me to Bart's Hospital on Sunday. Very short notice and at least a week before I expected it. Must try and fix it at work in morning. Still, the sooner it's over and done with the better as far as I'm concerned.

Saturday 29 April Got a week off from work alright. So I go in tomorrow. Cup Final Day, Portsmouth beat Wolverhampton 4–1.

Sunday 30 April After lunch went along to Bart's arriving at 2.30. Had to wait till visitors departed at 3.30 before settling in, Mother staying till then. Had tea, undressed, bathed, opened bowels, sat around gas stove chatting to other inmates including oldest inhabitants (some tough cases among these) and finally got into bed at 7.30. The ward is called Waring and is situated on ground floor of new surgical block. Big, airy, holds 22 beds but not very light. Hemmed in by tall buildings all around including back of GPO on one side. Would sooner have been higher up. Still, I won't be in long enough to worry much about that. Hardly slept a wink all night. Felt cold at first so had blanket doubled. Then too hot. Not being able to get up had to call for bed pan at 2.0 for a second purge. Then to crown everything, after I at last dozed off, was woken at 5.0 for an enema – yet another clear out. So came the dawn.

Monday 1 May Breakfast at 6.0 followed by washing (in bed), armada of cleaners, paper sellers and a barber to shave round penis in preparation for operation this afternoon. Hot milk at 9.0, lemonade at 10.30 – my last food or drink today. Lay waiting all the afternoon to be called for. Chief surgeon Sir Girling Ball came round about 3.0 with some students to study his more interesting – complicated cases.[26] Then the

---

24 Probably Health (or Hospital) Savings Account: private health insurance.
25 At a press conference on 14 April and in letters to Hitler and Mussolini, President Roosevelt had sought a ten- to twenty-five-year moratorium on them invading thirty-one European and Middle Eastern countries and colonies. But in his 28 April speech to the Reichstag, Hitler denounced both the Anglo-German Naval Agreement and the Treaty of Non-Aggression with Poland, so the world took another step towards a European war.
26 Sir (William) Girling Ball FRCS (1881–1945), Dean of Bart's Medical School and of the Medical Faculty of the Senate of London University.

fun began. Had to wait while the two fellows in the next two beds to me were called for and disposed of, and what an eternity of time it seemed to take! Struck me how oddly a green overall affair worn by one of the students wheeling the trolley looked more appropriate to a carnival or fancy dress ball than a hospital. At last, after being injected with a needle in arm and being rendered duly drowsy they came for me at 5.0 and was wheeled away through a network of passages to the theatre, given ether in out-chamber and was completely unconscious before being wheeled into the theatre itself. As I went under I vividly recalled how exactly similar it felt to when I last had a tooth out and was conscious of thinking precisely the same subconscious thoughts as then. Thus was I circumcised. When I came to after passing through various hazy transitional stages I was back in bed (where, I later learned, I had been for at least an hour). It was 6.30 and Mother had just arrived to see me. Wasn't fully conscious. Still a sort of drunken daze. Not a bit like the dentist's anaesthetic from which I never have any after effects. Penis hurting a bit but not terribly. Given some tea to drink which I instantly brought up again intact! However I managed to talk to Mother for half an hour in a vague dilatory sort of way. Brought me some fruit and eggs which are only collected immediately afterwards, and some fags as we are allowed to smoke for two hours in the morning and evening. As soon as she'd gone I slipped off into a blissful long-needed sleep from which I awoke at 1.15 a.m. from then till breakfast got about an hour's sleep all told. A May Day I shall certainly never forget.

Tuesday 2 May Felt considerably better this morning. Effects of ether completely worn off and no pain apparent apart from the natural soreness. The relief and gratification at having the operation over and done with and nothing to do now but to wait for it to gradually heal up was grand to experience. And felt even better still after being shaved in morning. Otherwise the day passed away in the usual hospital routine with the regular succession of meals, examinations etc. and on to sleep in fits and starts.

Friday 5 May After a final bath and dressing, donned my clothes, bid farewell to all my fellow unfortunates (much more so than I), had a last word with the charming old sister, went out to join Mother who came to fetch me home, called in Steward's office and got discharge paper and so left Bart's at 11.15 having acquired one more experience. A most interesting and enlightening experience too. At last I know what it is like to go into hospital and have an operation. One learns quite a lot about life in hospitals – and about hospitals. The only adverse impressions of my sojourn were (a) the fact that I scarcely, at any time, felt quite warm enough (b) the food seemed neither quite plentiful enough or of sufficient variety. Apart from these I have nothing but the utmost admiration and praise for hospitals and particularly the staff who carry out the most splendid and difficult work under the most trying and unattractive conditions. A propos nurses in their places, I was told that the majority of them belong to good families, are of independent means, get paid next to nothing and do this work just for the love of it. I don't deny the possibility of this but I find it mighty hard to believe.[27] On the whole it's been quite a pleasant and restful little break from the routine of the daily toil. At the same time I'm not sorry it's all over. In a week's time my penis should have properly healed up and then I should feel less sorry still. Meanwhile I must bathe myself and dress it every day. On getting home, Mother went off to work while I settled down to write up the events of this journal since Sunday. Had smoked haddock and a cup of tea at 2.30 followed by a shave and a read. A pair of kippers encore tea about 6.15, another read then to the Horse Shoe at 9.0 to meet the two Johns. Told them all about it – much to their amusement of course. Went from there down to the Marquis of Granby in Cambridge Circus. Went easy on the beer and only had four in the whole evening.

Saturday 6 May After breakfast in bed got up at 11.0. strolled or rather hobbled (for I can't walk naturally yet) round to Boots at King's Cross and bought Vaseline, boracic powder. Also changed library book while I was there and got Somerset Maugham's *Christmas Holiday*. Came back and bathed and re-dressed penis before lunch. Sat in Regent's Park and chatted to an old lady about the perilous state of the world today. We agreed on quite a lot of things. To Wyndham's in evening.

Monday 8 May Back to work. A hell of a lot of it too. In a chaotic state.

Tuesday 9 May Managed to get work up a bit more straight. Still far too much of it though. Police War Reserve class in evening. Presented with badge. Not healing up particularly quickly. Back to Vaseline again.

Wednesday 10 May Learned that I'm to receive full pay for absence last week. A bit of luck really. Wasn't altogether sure of it.

Friday 12 May Met Bill in evening. First time in over two months. Had rather a bad break lately, [his wife] having given birth to a stillborn child, she convalescing in the country so he is on his own for a week or two. And obviously making the most of his brief spell of freedom. Spent the rest of the evening there drinking steadily and getting oiled, Bill likewise. On getting home made the fatal mistake of trying to eat some more supper. Only a few mouthfuls sufficed to make me sick. Still it only happens once in a while.

---

27   Helen Day, Matron of Bart's from 1927, wrote that 'Most [nurses] selected were from middle-class but not academic backgrounds, university women would not do well as nurses.' She particularly wanted to see trained nurses better paid, in order to encourage them to remain in the profession and seek promotion. Information from Kate Jarman, Bart's Deputy Archivist.

Part One

Tuesday 16 May Police War Reserve class in evening. First of four first aid lectures. Fairly instructive and interesting despite the special instructor being vocally handicapped through having had all his teeth out recently. Also issued with two further handbooks – *An Elementary Course of First Aid* and *War Duty Hints*.

Wednesday 17 May Evening at home studying map of Peak District in conjunction with YHA Regional Handbook trying to plan out a route for my week's walking tour at the end of July and at same time listening to Beethoven's Seventh and Eighth symphonies conducted by Toscanini from Queen's Hall.[28]

Saturday 20 May Left off bandage for first time today. A certain amount of discomfort when walking but am gradually getting used to it. Up to Hampstead in evening. Handel's 'Music for the Royal Fireworks' played in its natural and something like its original setting, over by Ken Wood, followed by grand firework display. Part of London Musical Festival. The music and fireworks equally enchanting. Thousands of people there, a queue at least a quarter of a mile long waiting for buses over at Parliament Hill terminus after, walked down to Kentish Town and got one there. Home at 11.15. Supper and to bed an hour later.

Tuesday 23 May As warm a day as we've had this year as yet – 74 deg. in shade this afternoon. Police War Reserve class in evening. More First Aid – fractures and all that.

Sunday 28 May A day's tramp in the unfamiliar country of East Herts. A quiet peaceful unspoilt district of gentle hills, much meadowland and charming little river valleys. 10.44 train from Liverpool St to Stansted St Margarets. [*two pages of walking itinerary*] Home at 9.40. Supper. Feet in warm water, slightly sore. Face likewise from sunburn.

Monday 29 May Whit Monday. As fine as could be. Spent the day exploring the country between Tring and Wendover. Went by the 11.15 Rambler's train from Euston to Tring. [*two pages of walk itinerary*] Return train packed to suffocation by the time it had stopped at Berkhamsted. Like Easter this year, this has been the finest Whitsun for six years, and I'm certain I haven't enjoyed one as much since '33.

Tuesday 30 May My old friend and one time office colleague 'Joshua' Reynolds came into see us this afternoon, proudly carrying his one year old daughter. Has given up the shop down at Westfield and got a job at Siemens's works at Woolwich,[29] living at Bexley Heath. Looking

---

28 Arturo Toscanini (1867–1975), Italian conductor with exacting standards. This, the fourth Toscanini concert of the London Music Festival, was broadcast on the BBC National Station.

29 Originally a German industrial company, Siemens had several factories in the UK, including a cable plant in Woolwich. The shares of their English company were confiscated by the British Government in 1914 but contact was re-established in 1929.

1939

rather more careworn and thinner than he used to, but that's only to be expected. Police First Aid class in evening. The blood system, bleeding and all that.

Wednesday 31 May Met another old office colleague, Fournier. Now married and living up at Hampstead. Just passed out of his probationary period in Fire Brigade and stationed at Clerkenwell. Enjoying life immensely.

Saturday 3 June To camp with Phil and Kath near Tylers Causeway 1 mile south of Little Berkhamsted, 4 miles north east of Potters Bar and 19 miles from London. Called for them at 5.0 and went up by bus. A delightful site miles away from anywhere of any consequence, fairly high (about 400 ft), a commanding and fine extensive view. Only the three of us on Phil's site this weekend – he usually has quite a crowd to occupy the six tents he leaves standing all the week but the R H [Robin Hood] boys were present in full force on their site nearby. After evening meal went down to a pub. Stayed till closing time at 10.30 and all drove back in a couple of cars. Turned in as soon as we reached camp but – as I expected – didn't sleep too well – thighs kept getting sore despite the straw paillasse Phil had provided me with. Still, I did doze off now and again, that was something.

Sunday 4 June Sunbathed a bit during and after breakfast until about 10.0 when I put on a shirt. Just as well I did for I would now have been in agony with sunburn otherwise. As it was I got my face, forearms and ankles pretty well baked. Lazed about rest of morning except for game of quoits at which I didn't exactly excel. Home at 11.0. Still, I enjoyed the weekend – my first real camping experience for six years – immensely. This is just the sort of camp I like – nice quiet secluded country, good company, good food, not too much work and all the amenities the combination of perfect host and adept handyman such as Phil can provide me, with tables, stools etc. How different from the camping I used to do – not that that too wasn't enjoyable in its way. But here one has only to [take] the lightest of kits – no grand tent, primus cooking apparatus, cutlery or crockery – Phil provides all these. And what one does take can be left there if need be. Camping without tears in fact. It suits me down to the ground!

Monday 5 June Didn't feel either as tired or as stiff or sore as I expected to feel today. Went straight from work to PWR class, not being able to go on Tuesday this week.

Saturday 10 June To weekend camp again with Phil and Co. Took the 2.50 train from King's Cross to Cuffley and walked over from there. Quite a pleasant walk of about 2½ miles, mostly footpath and uphill. A bit of a sweat in such a sweltering hot afternoon as this. Did it in exactly ¾ hour. All walked back together. Innumerable anti-aircraft

Part One

searchlights being tried out in the fields all round as we wended our way along Sandy Lane. A rather striking scene.

Sunday 11 June Very little opportunity for sun bathing anyway. Not too bad on the whole, but indifferent. Stayed in camp all morning till about 12.30 when Phil, Charlie and myself strolled up to the R&C [Rose & Crown] and had a couple of drinks and a game of darts. Caught the 8.56 back to King's Cross and was home by 9.45. Just right.

Tuesday 13 June Police W.R. class in evening. Lecture on war gasses. Started on them late owing to preliminary palaver on the War Reserve Social Club we are going to form and the general meeting thereon next Tuesday at the Macnaghten Section House in Judd St.[30] Walked home after, saw our Territorials from Handel St Drill Hall being drilled on Foundling Ground and the artillery replete with guns round the dead end side of Brunswick Square. Have also noticed similar drilling on Tavistock Square sometimes as I come home from work. Why must they make a public spectacle of this depressing and unsavoury business. Surely there is enough accommodation indoors for them. But perhaps the powers that be don't think the public are quite war-minded enough even yet. So the prospective heroes who are going to die for democracy, and so make the world safe for Jewry and businessmen, must needs be paraded before the vulgar gaze. What a world we live in!

Saturday 17 June Camped the weekend with Phil and Kath once more. Only the three of us this time. His other guests called off at the last minute. Went off by 2.39 train to Cuffley same as last week and walked over from there. Arrived and had tea almost straightaway. Played Kath a game of badminton (my first ever) and helped Phil cut the long grass around the site till it was time for us to stroll over to Newgate St and join the R.H. [Robin Hood] crowd at the Crown. Actually we met them on the way over. Spent the best part of the evening there, knocking back several rounds of drinks, playing darts, singing round the piano and talking politics, to the campsite of some strangers we'd met in the pub – and had a campfire. The piece de resistance was Charlie's solo rendering of 'Vienna City of Dreams' both in English and German. He was really good. Was well past midnight before the fire burnt out and we at last dispersed. Walked back to our own camp and turned in forthwith.

Sunday 18 June Up at 8.30 after usual scrappy night's sleep. Though I did fare a little better than the last Saturday night. Perhaps by the end of the season I may be sufficiently hardened to it to get a full night's sleep in camp. Or I may not! Didn't bother to go over to the Crown as we usually do Sunday afternoon. So we stayed in camp, speedily cleaned up, broke camp and walked over to Cuffley to catch the 8.56

---

30   Actually in Compton Place, WC1, built in 1936: see TNA, MEPO9/106.

back. Home 9.45. Disposed of a good supper, glanced at papers and wearily clambered into bed at 12.15.

Tuesday 20 June Terrific thunder and lightning storm early in afternoon. After dashing home and bolting down dinner in ten minutes, went round to Macnaghten House in evening for general meeting of the Police War Reserve to form a social club. Instruction classes as well to be held at this spacious newly built section house in future, which suits me fine being just round the corner. About ninety there, lasted two hours. Elected various officers as a committee, formulated some rules [and] other preliminary matters. Everything went as smoothly as could be expected. No difficulty or disruption whatever. How different from the meetings I'm used to in Ward 8 with the endless haggling and back biting and general bad feeling that prevails at them. But then there are no women attached to this that makes all the difference. Looks like being a great success once we get going. On getting home, drafted a brief account of Ward 8 outing to Hastings on Sunday (which of course I didn't attend) for the *St Pancras Gazette*. An awkward job trying to make something 'I was not of' but Mother had left some rough notes for me with the inscription 'Try and muck about with this'. The result was a model of brevity, if not exactly 'the soul of wit'!

Thursday 22 June Did think of going to see *Pericles* at [Regent's Park] Open Air Theatre this evening but wasn't quite warm or fine enough so stayed in and wrote periodic letter to Aunt Pop instead. Not really due for a fortnight or so yet but thought I might as well get it over and done with. Finished at 11.30 – covering nine pages.

Saturday 24 June Camp. Eight of us in Phil's camp this weekend and only three in the other. More often it's the other way about. So except for sleeping, the lonesome three came over and joined us. Weather much the same as last weekend. Overcast and cool with rain continually threatening but fortunately not materialising. Over to the Crown for the evening. Went on draught bitter for a change and got fairly well oiled as did most of the others. Rolled back to camp along the road singing lustily – and before turning in gave final vent to our high spirits by slinging stools across at each other's tents, two of them getting ripped in the process. Good job it didn't rain in the night or the water would have passed through the splits. Phil, of course, took it all in good part (he was one of the slingers anyway), patched the big one up in the morning and took the small one home to mend.

Sunday 25 June Up at 8.30 after the best night's sleep I've yet had in camp – four or five hours. Spent the entire day lounging and larking about in camp. Left at 7.25 and caught the 8.26 from Cuffley. Home at 9.20. Supper, papers and to bed at 11.30.

Monday 26 June Only some six weeks ago I was swearing never to go to an amateur show again, yet here was I sitting in the theatre of the City Literary Institute watching the Peel Players[31] perform some obscure little comedy called *Till Further Orders*. As the cast was composed almost entirely of the weekend crowd however I couldn't very well have dodged it. Still it didn't turn out to be so dire an evening as I expected. Went round and saw them all after and came away with Phil and Kath. Walked up to TC Rd and got on their bus as far as Euston Rd where I changed onto another one home. Bed 12.15.

Tuesday 27 June Weather becomes a shade more seasonable at last. Brighter and warmer. Police Reserve class round at Macnaghten House in evening. Fitted with our [service-pattern] gas masks and instructed in their use. Told us the same masks are also issued to the fighting services and fire brigades as well, and are the finest in the world, costing as they do about 15/- each to make, which no other country can afford to spend on them. Cheery reflection!

Thursday 29 June Mother starts a new job at Town Hall – clerical work in connection with ARP. Probably only temporary but well paid. Continuing with her small job with Mary Ward School as well.[32] Not home in time to get dinner ready in evening, so had it at YM before coming home.

Friday 30 June Home to dinner at 9.0 then to the Camden at 10.0 to meet the Johns. John Bell just bought a car in which we shall go up to Brean Sands in August instead of by train. Assuming of course that we are not at war by then over the Danzig bother – which seems more than likely at this moment.[33] Anyway, if we're not plunged into war within the next month or two to protect Jewish communist interests in Poland and elsewhere, it wouldn't be for our 'national' government's lack of trying!

Saturday 1 July Camp. Only five of us on Saturday but considerably augmented on the Sunday. The weather as erratic and exasperating as ever. Brilliant sunshine as we walked over from Cuffley in the afternoon. Walked over to the Crown. Didn't get there till nearly 9.30 so we had barely an hour to slake our thirsts and exercise our powers on the dart

---

31 An amateur dramatics group.
32 See entry for 3 February above.
33 The 1919 Versailles Peace Conference had re-established the state of Poland, and assured its access to the Baltic Sea by creating the 'Free City of Danzig' (Gdansk), overseen by the League of Nations, with a 'corridor' along the Vistula estuary, which was formerly part of western Prussia. But the Poles wanted it as part of Poland and the 90% of the population of Danzig who were German-speaking wanted it to become part of Germany. Hitler used the issue of the city's status as the pretext for attacking Poland. He had explained to German military officials in May 1939 that his real goal was obtaining *Lebensraum* ('living space') for Germany, and isolating the Poles from their Western allies.

1939

board. Still we did pretty well. A really tip-top pianist strumming away, also added to the gaiety of the thing.

Sunday 2 July Cool, cloudy and generally unsettled. Hardly any sun but also no rain despite one or two attempts at it. Didn't get up till 9.0. Breakfast, preparing and clearing up, shaving etc till about 12.30 when Charlie drove us over to the Crown for a few drinks. 'Broke' camp at 7.35 and came back by the 8.26 from Cuffley. Indoors at 9.15. Bed 11.0.

Tuesday 4 July Dinner at YM before coming home. Round to the club for Ward 8 Committee meeting in evening. Bigger and more representative attendance than usual. Business mainly electing people for this and that. Rest trivial.

Friday 7 July On getting home for dinner at 9.0 found a hand delivered note from Ron, who has apparently blown into town out of the blue again saying he was meeting the two Johns at the Horse Shoe at 8.30. Would I blow along? So after bolting down my dinner, I did and arrived there at 9.40 to find no one present. No sign of Ron, he is a most elusive and unreliable sort of blighter.

Saturday 8 July In camp, seated round the table in the big tent munching biscuits and cheese they tried – unsuccessfully – to initiate me into the mysteries of Solo Whist. Until they all fell off to sleep leaving Fred and myself to argue about Fascism till 1.0 when we too succumbed to the spell of Morpheus.

Monday 10 July For first time in umpteen years did not have to go shopwalking for first day of the sale. Blessed relief! Went straight into King's Cross Police Station after work for try-out of our service respirators in gas-filled room in the yard at the back. Went in ten at a time and stayed in about five minutes. On coming out took off our respirators and sniffed some sample bottles of gases to distinguish their smells. And that was all. In and out in half an hour. I was home by 7.40.

Friday 14 July After dashing home to change, met Bill at the Horse Shoe at 7.30. Got talking firstly about my camp gear which he wanted to borrow for his holiday early in September, secondly about our old friend Gilbert Mason. Racked our brains trying to think how we would get in touch with him again. At which point who should roll in but Ron – the old reprobate himself. Just started work as an armaments inspector at Woolwich Arsenal and about to settle down in London again. Close on his heels came the two Johns, and as was inevitable with Ron being present, we soon drifted up to the New Malaya[34] to spend the rest of the evening on the dart board there. Played various games at 1d a time and lost every one – into bed at 12.0 – a lively and eventful evening.

---

34   Presumably a refurbished Malaya Social Club, 27 Stephen Street, W1.

Part One

Saturday 15 July Decided to forget about my provisional date to go along to the old school sports this afternoon and went to camp at usual time. Only five of us this week, Stan Garrard and his wife (Phil's sister) and self. None of the RH [Robin Hood] crowd camping on the other site. At least they didn't show up at the Crown in the evening so we assumed they weren't down. Was most uncommonly quiet in there all evening in fact. So we stayed there till closing time. On getting back sat talking about holiday making abroad with Stan for half an hour or so (like Bert Petry he's very enamoured with Belgium seaside resorts) before turning in. And for a change I really felt like it.

Sunday 16 July Strolled up to the Rose and Crown for a drink before lunch. Spent the afternoon playing rings, badminton (a hopeless proposition in this incessant wind which always seems to prevail down here) and cards. While Phil, 'Prince of Handymen', made two solid wooden stools and went off to the wood and started on the construction of a wooden dresser. He is unquestionably a real genius at this sort of thing, a modern Robinson Crusoe in fact. Brought shoes, shorts and towel back with me as, with holidays intervening, I won't be camping again for a month or so. 11.0 p.m. Mother just back from Mosley's rally at Earls Court. Went with the Spernis. Apparently a stupendous success with a colossal attendance and will the press make mention of it tomorrow? Not bloody likely.[35]

Tuesday 18 July After dinner at the YM went to Police Reserve class at Macnaghten House. Brief lecture on traffic duties by young Inspector Hayes, our usual instructor Sergeant Prizeman presumably being away. Got tapped for a bob – first month's subscription to the new social club – and was given a membership card. The first 'do' – smoking concert at White Hart, Holborn[36] takes place next Tuesday – when, of course, I'm away.

Friday 21 July After dinner went along to the Horse Shoe at 10.0 to meet the Johns. Had just gone round to the Malaya so followed them up. Ron there too. Played three games of darts and had three drinks. Learned that John Bell can't get Saturday evening off when we go to Brean Sands which means we will have to wait till early Sunday morning before we set out and so waste half a day. A bit of a nuisance but can't be helped. Will still save the train fare anyway, and twenty-five bob's not to be sneezed at by any means. Sounds of revelry by night up at the club this evening. Piano and saxophone accompanied

---

35 Sir Oswald Mosley spoke for 'almost two hours' at this Britain First rally to a 'fairly well filled hall that holds 30,000 people'. He said that the demonstration was for peace and warned those clamouring for war that 'A million Britons shall not die in your Jews' quarrel' (*The Times*, 17 July 1939).
36 White Hart: either 126–128 Theobalds Road or 39 High Holborn.

1939

by a lot of screeching and caterwauling – and occasionally singing.[37] Out at 10.55, walked home – by some strange miracle it wasn't raining – and to bed at 11.50.

Saturday 22 July Set out on my first week's holiday – a walking tour of the Peak District. Went by the 2.30 train from St Pancras to Matlock; Mother coming over to see me off. Left five minutes late. Not particularly full. My booked seat was actually quite unnecessary. Observed en route: the abundance of air raid shelters in the suburban borders of Leicester: A *Times* placard 'Premier Flying to see Hitler'[38] stuck on the side of a truck just outside Derby. Arriving at Matlock at 5.40.

[*Eight days youth hostelling in the Derbyshire Peak District*]

Sunday 30 July After a night of continual rain with a thunderstorm thrown in for make weight – turned out pretty fair if a trifle unsettled today for my last lap. Fully absorb my last grand Peak District panorama before descending the footpath down to Matlock and tea at the Crown Hotel – about the only place open in the whole town before catching the 5.59 to Derby and there changing onto the express to St Pancras. In dead on time, 9.28. Mother there to meet me. Had a good dinner on getting indoors, unpacked, glanced at the papers etc. Bed at 12.0. This ends my first week's holiday this year. It fully came up to my expectations in all respects. The weather could have been a little finer towards the end of the week but over the whole week even that was far better than I expected. The hostels were variable yet taken all round, of a reasonably good standard. I assure you that there are things in Derbyshire as noble as in Greece or Switzerland wrote Byron. Well, I can't actually vouch for the former comparison but in the latter respect I'm inclined to agree with the noble Lord. Total cost of trip £3.15.0. About the finest holiday value I've ever known.

Monday 31 July The sort of day which makes returning to work quite pleasant. Agreeably surprised to find that my work had been kept up straight without any exasperating accumulation of arrears and queries.

[*From 1 August in Acc. 2243/13/1*]

Tuesday 1 August Dined at the YM and went to the Police War Reserve class in evening. Some preliminary palaver on the social club – apparently the smoking concert last week was a great success, financially or otherwise – followed by lecture on the reporting of street

---

37 No major national or local events warranting celebrations are obvious. The second test match against the West Indies was to start at Old Trafford the next day.
38 Presumably reporting Chamberlain's two September 1938 flights to Germany.

accidents. Then had to wait about till the thunderstorm raging outside eased up a bit and I could cut and dash home round the corner.

Friday 4 August And still it teems down as heavily and relentlessly as ever. The cause of it, St Swithin's with a vengeance. Weight down to exactly 11 stone. Must have lost three or four pounds last week. Went on to the Robin Hood for the first time in several weeks. Only Alby there. Rest away. Round to Cheffie's in Charlie's car where we sat for nigh on two hours drinking tea and holding an argument on the value, merits and demerits of money. A welcome change from politics, anyway.

Saturday 5 August Up to Hampstead in afternoon. The fair already well under way and raucous strains of the music over most of the Heath. Reminded me that I hadn't been up there since Whit Saturday when similar sights and sounds assailed – or rather intrigued my senses. Atmosphere beautifully clear and fresh. To bed at 10.15 having to be up at the crack of dawn tomorrow to set out with the Johns in John Bell's car to Brean Sands Holiday Camp in Somerset for the second week of my holiday. It irks me to have to waste half a day by waiting till tomorrow, especially such an all too rare fine half day, but JB must work till 9.0 this evening.

Sunday 6 August Up at 5.0. The Johns called for me with the car sharp on 6.30 and by 7.0 we were well out of London along the Great West Road. A smooth straight run with only two brief stops as far as Bath which we passed through about 11.0. Thereafter, the road was neither so smooth nor so straight but full of ups and downs and twists and turns over the Somerset hills towards Burnham and on round along the coast to Brean Sands. Was 12.40 before we drove in and introduced ourselves. Just had time to register as members of the club, have a drink or two and dump our mattresses in the chalets before lunch. The Johns share one chalet and I the next one with another bloke, whom I have just met. I gather he detests London and is passionately devoted to golf and is named Bill Smith. Had no time for further converse as he had to rush off to join his ladylove waiting for him. So I don't suppose I shall see much of him down here anyway. Still, an amiable individual. A boozy evening in the bar. Emerged occasionally to participate in the social, the fun fair and the dance which followed one another in rapid succession. But for the most part it was bar, bar, glorious bar. Got very friendly with the management, who doubtless recognise us as the bar's best potential customers for the week!

Monday 7 August Held the election of this week's King Kong and Queen of Brean in the morning. And who should click for the former honour but John Hobson. They certainly couldn't have made a better choice. The very life and soul of any party is our John. He could make anything go – even the dullest gathering. Was duly crowned this afternoon with full honours – which only consisted of buckets of lather and water slung over him first. Would have gone in for a swim if the tide hadn't been such a deuce of way out.

[*The week continued with the campers enjoying themselves, not least by spending time in the camp bar. On the last day of the holiday Heap's stomach pains became acute.*]

Saturday 12 August Felt ghastly. Stomach started aching as soon as I got into bed this morning – thus giving me practically no sleep and kept on all day today. No appetite, feeling alternately blown out and empty. Packed and vacated our chalet by 10.0 and wandered round all the morning, all dressed up and nowhere to go. Left immediately after lunch and returned to London by road, the same route as we came. Called at Bath for half an hour to look around. Took the waters in the Pump Room and inspected the Roman Baths. A fine old town beautifully arranged. The absolute quintessence of eighteenth century stylishness, elegance and grace. Stopped at Marlborough for tea. At Reading called at a chemists for some stomach mixture so exasperatingly prolonged is my pain becoming. Got home just after 9.0, unpacked. Tried to eat something but couldn't. Drank a glass of hot milk and immediately brought it up, so gave up and went to bed. This week's holiday doesn't seem to have done one much good. Don't feel half as fit as when I went despite the healthy tan the sun has given me. What with poor food, too many late nights, too much beer and the terribly relaxing soporific air of Brean, my system has been overtaxed and a stomach disorder results. Have enjoyed the week in some ways but on the whole Brean Sands has proved most disappointing. Never again!

Sunday 13 August Took a short stroll before lunch – likewise scanty – and afterwards slowly made my way up to Parliament Hill to doze in deckchair for an hour. Then my stomach pain – which later today had gently concentrated itself on the right side – came on really bad and spread right over again. So came home again as quickly as I could which, bent up with pain as I was, wasn't very quickly. Had a cup of tea, a dose of stomach medicine and two doses of castor oil, spewed twice, and then at last managed to relieve myself properly, which eased up the pain considerably. Mother wanted to take me to the doctor or the hospital when some of the most agonising pain occurred but we decided to leave it as things calmed down, at least for tonight. Am almost convinced now that it's nothing more than acute wind and flatulence and must endeavour to keep bowels open at all costs. Will also eat or drink nothing but slowly sipped milk for a while. What to do. Never had anything as bad as this before. A lesson well learned.

Part One

[*The significant gap before Heap was able to write up his diary daily is explained in the next entry.*]

Monday 14 August–Sunday 3 September For the first time since I started keeping a diary many long years ago, circumstances have prevented me from keeping up the daily chronicle of my life activities and impressions. For one thing I have not been capable of writing a diary or anything else, and even if I had been, a daily record would merely have resulted in a dull repetition. In other words, for the first time in my life I have been seriously ill and undergone a spell in hospital compared with which my previous brief experience of those institutions was trifling.

Briefly the facts are these. On the morning of Monday 14 August, instead of going back to work as I intended to, I went, still doubled up with pain, and called on Dr Cutner at his surgery.[39] After sitting for an hour in his stifling waiting room, I at last saw him. Swiftly examining my stomach, he calmly informed me that unless I was immediately operated on within an hour or two my chances of survival would be somewhat slender – which was reassuring to say the least of it! Apparently I had peritonitis, the most complicated and dangerous form of appendicitis, whereby the appendix has become perforated. And I thought it was only wind!

So round to the Homeopathic Hospital in Gt Ormond St I was rushed in Dr C's car, put straight to bed, examined by the house surgeon and duly carved up by an eminent West End specialist, Dr Power. And a very good job he made of it too by all accounts, I certainly didn't have any pain of any sort afterwards and made a good and speedy recovery. But it was rough going all the same. For two weeks I laid there in that second floor ward in a most absurdly cramped position, semi-sitting, semi-lying about with pillows heaped up against a back rest, a rubber ring under my backside and a bolster under my legs – all this to enable the puss to drain off my stomach. At first I had a rubber tube but this was taken out after two or three days. I had to exist solely on fluids for not a morsel of food was I allowed. It was sheer torture to watch the others eating at meal times, unappetising food though it was sometimes (as I subsequently discovered). Food in fact occupied most of my waking thoughts, it became almost an obsession. I, day by day, dreamed of all the things to eat that I'm particularly fond of – steak and chips, spaghetti, toasted cheese, hors d'oeuvres, apple pudding, pancakes, jam roll – what varieties of gastronomic bliss! Never did I appreciate food so much as when I had to go without any for a fortnight. But that wasn't the only vexation. During the first week when I lay with a temperature and had to have frequent applications by

---

39   At 9 Mecklenburg Square, WC1.

1939

the young medics in my arm to make me keep still and fitfully asleep in brief spells of half an hour or so, a heat wave occurred to add to my discomfort. Mother came in and sat beside me for long periods day and night. I was generally in a bad way.

The second week brought some improvements. My temperature settled down and I began to sleep better. Still on fluids I was able to pass on from fruit drinks, of which I got heartily sick in more ways than one, onto milk and tea. I began to take interest in things again, to read the papers and books. The latter were indeed my one consolation. I read four altogether in my three weeks inside, Compton Mackenzie, John Gielgud's autobiography, *The Pickwick Papers* which I had long meant to read but somehow never had the opportunity. And what solace it was in these deranged days to be transported back into a world that was serene and sane and humane.

So at last came the third week and more improvements. My stitches had been taken out and my name removed from the danger list after ten days. The puss had also ceased to be drawn off and I was allowed to start eating again. Milk puddings, which I heartedly detest, and I was soon on a more attractive light diet including chicken, fresh eggs etc. Then, at the end of the third week, outside events took a hand in things. For a fortnight a state of crisis over German–Polish Danzig – a Polish Corridor dispute that had daily grown more acute and war scares had been ceaselessly present.[40] All negotiations for a peaceful settlement having failed, things at last came to a climax in the early hours of Friday Sept. 1st when Germany invaded Poland and thus precipitated another World War. Britain and France bound by treaty to defend Poland sent ultimatums to Hitler to withdraw his troops from Poland. No reply being sent by 11.0 on the morning of Sunday 3rd Sept. we were from that hour at war with Germany. And France from the expiration of her time-limit of 5.0 pm. Italy, instead of supporting her ally Germany, remained unexpectedly neutral – yet another instance of Mussolini's acute statesmanship.

Thus ended a period of doubts and hopes and fears and tension such as would have disturbed the peace of mind and composure of the most urbane and complacent of beings. And to have to lay completely helpless and immobile while all these momentous events were afoot while the greatest thing that happened in my lifetime was taking place, while history was being made, the streets of London was [*sic*] utterly damnable. A hospital was the last place I wanted to be in at a time like this. How I longed to be out and about to see the changing aspects of the streets where all the big buildings and shop fronts were being sandbagged and barricaded up, to study the crowds and sense the abnormal atmosphere which inevitably prevails at times like these. Particularly did I long to be out and around in the West

---

40 See entry for 30 June and accompanying note.

End on the night of the first big black-out – Sept 1st – when I heard that the multitude of searchlights in the sky made a most fascinating eerie night (and, as if to foreshadow the imminent catastrophe, one of the fiercest thunderstorms in living recollection occurred). But there it was, my only contact with the outside world was through the wireless and newspapers and my several visitors which, apart from Mother, included Bill, Phil, the two Johns, Ron Jenkins from PR's (which by the way sent Mother my pay for the first two weeks), Fred and Minnie, Mr & Mrs Sperni and Mrs Zelger.

At 11.15 on that fateful morning of Sept 3rd we listened to the Prime Minister's speech to the nation announcing the declaration of war on a loudspeaker specially brought in for us. Five minutes after he'd finished the air raid alarms went off, whereupon we were all pushed into the middle of the ward and given gas masks to put on. No one seemed to know whether this was a real raid or an ARP stunt. Actually it was false alarm occasioned by a single unidentified plane crossing the channel.

Still, it was apparently enough to put the wind up the hospital authorities. For us, in the afternoon during the visitors period after Mother had just gone and Fred and Minnie were with me, the house doctors came round to decide who to send home and who to evacuate.[41] Actually those who could be sent home had already been sent home earlier in the week and there were now but a few dozen left in the entire hospital. All the other hospitals however had evacuated their cases requiring treatment on Friday when all the schoolchildren were evacuated as well and most of the Homeopathic staff had gone [evacuated] to Watford thus leaving the hospital free for air raid casualties. Despite this however, I had been told I would stop there war or no war and I resigned myself to that. Now at the last moment they had changed their minds and decided to clear the place completely of patients at once. Given the choice of going home or to the base hospital at Watford and having to decide on the spur of the moment, I plumped for home not realising as Mother afterwards [said] that she would have to be on duty eight or more hours a day patrolling the streets as an Air Raid Warden (her new job) and so not able to look after me sufficiently during the day.

But the die was cast and there was no retreat. Fred and Minnie dashed off to let Mother know and at 7.0 a car came to fetch me and take me home, dressed solely in pyjamas, dressing gown and slippers. An unforeseen snag the other end was the three flights of stairs at Sinclair House, for not being able to get up till the next day, I wasn't able to walk yet. However the problem was resolved by Mother fetching the

---

41 On the declaration of a state of emergency, all hospitals except mental hospitals were instructed to send home all patients considered not to be in urgent need of treatment (*Statement on the Emergency Hospitals Scheme*, Cmd 6061, para 25, July 1939).

caretaker and another man who carried me up in a chair – by lift to the 4th Floor and down a flight to the 3rd. So straight into bed, a light supper and to sleep from which I was rudely awakened by air raid sirens and the sound of people scurrying down the stairs at 2.30. If I could have walked we'd have gone down as well, but as I couldn't we just stayed put. Actually nothing happened and at 3.0 the all clear signal went off so presumably it was another false alarm.

Thus after three weeks have I come out of hospital – but at least a week earlier than I would have done in the normal way. According to the memorandum I have from the hospital to Dr Cutner, I have got to stay in bed most of the day for another ten days yet – a rather over-cautious estimate of the rate of my recovery I'm inclined to think – and be visited by either the doctor or the district nurse to do my dressing once a day. But I'm not really sorry I decided to come home. For although Mother's out for a bit, she can call in at frequent intervals and I shall be able to get about on my legs, when necessary, in no time now. And I can have decent well-cooked food now and, within reasonable limits, anything I like. What is more I am certain I can cure myself quicker and more surely at this stage than the hospital with their strict adherence to routine and precedence could.

And now what of the future, for the war means that I come out of hospital to an entirely different state of things to when I went in. Till I get properly fit again of course, I can do precious little and it's not worth worrying over much till then. How long it will take I don't know. A fortnight or possibly more. Then I shall have to report for service in the Police War Reserve. What I shall do if and when I'm conscripted I don't know for all classes from [ages] 18 to 40 will be called up eventually. Then again it's no good worrying about that till it actually happens and it's just possible it might not. Won't be for some time yet anyway I should think. I don't suppose I shall be going back to PR's again anyhow. Wonder if they'll carry on now. Must go along and see what's happening there when I can get out. But enough of these ruminations. The worst has happened. The war came, at a somewhat inconvenient time for me, it's true but one must make the best of a bad job. It is not even a scrap of use musing over the why and wherefore, rights and wrongs, the cause and effect of all that's led up to it at this time of day. It's best not to have opinions during a war, they're likely to land one in trouble. No, all I've got to worry about now is getting as fit as I can as quickly as I can.

Monday 4 September So once again I resume my daily chronicle. And with what satisfaction and gratifications do I set pen to paper and open up my never failing outlet for self-expression again! It eases my mind immeasurably! Had breakfast in bed at 8.0 and stayed in bed till 11.0 when I got up and sat in the front room writing up some account of the last three weeks in this diary till 3.0, which of course was very naughty of me, against all the rules and regulations. Mother came home at 4.0 and cooked the dinner. One thing I miss now I'm home again is the radio for our old worn-out set won't give any results on the new wavelength the B.B.C. has now adopted.[42] Looks like we'll have to invest in a new radio. All theatres, cinemas and other places of entertainment have had to close down until further notice. Just on the threshold of the autumn season too when dozens of new productions were in rehearsal. This is the unkindest cut of all and it brings the war home to me more acutely than anything else, except perhaps for the air raid warnings. Seems as if books will have to be my sole recreation for some time now. After dinner – chump chops, mashed potatoes, French beans, rice pudding and raspberries – my first square meal for weeks – dozed for an hour or so. A cup of tea at 6.30 then read till 9.30 when I got up again and sat in the front room and had supper. Managed by pure chance to get a faint reception on the radio – just audible so it can serve for the news after all. This and gramophone records are practically all that is broadcast now. For the news, the radio set is so indispensable or, oddly enough, the records provide much better entertainment than the ordinary programmes did on the whole. Back to bed and sleep at 11.15.

Tuesday 5 September A peaceful night. No air raid alarms, not even false ones. Very little progress either way on the war yet. Poles still holding back the German attack just inside the Polish frontier but no engagements between German and Anglo-French forces yet. German U-boat has sunk the liner *Athenia* in Atlantic – great indignation over this though many passengers and crew were saved. And last night the RAF flew over Germany and dropped a million leaflets without, apparently, being engaged by German fighting planes or anti-aircraft guns. And that's about all. After breakfast and papers got up at 12.0, sat at kitchen table and had a shave and then in front room for three hours, where I sat and studied Police War Reserve Handbook then started on *Nicholas Nickleby*. Got up at 9.15 and sat in front room. Filled in Income Tax return which has been waiting here three weeks for me and had supper. Back to bed at 11.30.

Wednesday 6 September Was woken at 6.45 by air raid sirens. Quickly donning my shoes, trousers and overcoat (in which I now keep [Post Office Savings] bank book, money, gold watch, and other valuables in case of anything that should happen to the flat) we went down to the flat of some people Mother knows on the first floor. One or two other upper floor residents taking shelter there as well. Very congenial and hospitable woman made tea for us all and everyone cheerful and friendly. There's nothing like an air raid for getting to know one's neighbours,

---

42 The BBC switched to lower-power transmissions on other wavelengths to prevent the Luftwaffe homing into the powerful main London transmitters.

or any common danger for that matter. Stayed down there for over two hours before the all clear signals went at 9.0. Nothing happened at all as far as England was concerned. Later transpired that some enemy planes were sighted off the East coast but after some lengthy fighting they were driven off. On getting back to bed had breakfast and stayed there most of the morning and afternoon, alternately reading and dozing and getting up for a few minutes only when necessary. Had a good lunch at 2.30 – chump chops, mashed and baked beans, pineapple and cream. No fish whatever has been obtainable this week. Had a cup of tea then sat on the settee, feet on a chair, reading *Nicholas Nickleby* which I'm not progressing with very fast. Devoted rest of the evening to radio (such as it is) and supper – fish and chips. Supplies have come through at last. Back to bed at 11.0.

Thursday 7 September Dr Cutner at last blew in this morning about 10.0 – a few minutes after Mother had gone on duty. In a tearing hurry as usual. After looking at the wound, said the best thing I could do now was to get out in the fresh air as much as possible. This in spite of the hospital note about ten days in bed. Actually I completely forgot to give him the note till he'd gone. Made out a prescription for spirit and medicine and a certificate and then dashed off. So after a leisurely shave and a short read, dressed and slowly walked over to the Commercial in Euston Rd for lunch.[43] Getting quite sound on my legs now but body needs considerable building up again, still it's grand to be able to get out at last, even if for only a short duration. Apart from an occasional sandbagged or boarded-up shops and buildings the streets look very much the same. Otherwise the only apparent indication of the war are the barrage balloons dotted all over the sky (a most picturesque sight), the blue or black steel helmets of the police and air raid wardens (Mother wears one) and the square cardboard boxes containing gas masks which everyone carries either in their hand or over the shoulder on string. I carry mine in an old haversack slung round me. Damned nuisance having to lug these things around perpetually but it's not worth the risk of going out without one. After supper and before going to bed changed dressing as usual, applying spirit to wound for first time and swapped big elastic bandage for smaller one with adhesive tape.

Saturday 9 September After lunch with Mother at the Commercial went up to Hampstead in afternoon and sat on deck chairs on Parliament Hill idly gazing upon the metropolis sprawled out below. Was quite surprised not to find an anti-aircraft battery at the top of the hill. Hampstead completely unchanged – and no sign of air raid shelters anywhere. Took a bus down to Oxford St. Called in YMCA, not much shelter

---

43 Not identified, but there were at least thirteen cafés, restaurants and dining or refreshment rooms listed on Euston Road. Heap's 'Commercial' was destroyed by bombing on 18 September 1940.

there either. Learned swimming bath is to remain open but no gym classes. Tea in Lyons in Oxford St then set out for a short tour of the West End to see what it looks like now. Bus to Westminster – walked through St James's and Green Parks up to Piccadilly, bus home from Circus. Streets not nearly so crowded as usual though parks pretty full. Good many soldiers in uniform about. Scarlet coated Horse Guards in Whitehall replaced by khaki clad infantry. Innumerable police reservists in blue steel helmets and with arm band – not issued with uniforms yet. One or two very short and weedy specimens among them. The closed theatres, still wistfully (or is it optimistically) displaying their bills outside, wear a forlorn and dejected air, as indeed does the whole entertainment starved West End. For what after all is the West End without its theatres, cinemas and revelry by night – its very life blood. At the present moment it is like a salad without dressing on, an egg without salt, or strawberries sans cream. In short, NBG [no bloody good]. How long this sorry state of affairs will last is still uncertain. Some cinemas and theatres in the provinces and outer suburbs are now being allowed to re-open but as regards central London the powers that be are still adamant.

Sunday 10 September Have now been at war for a week and not a single air raid yet, only three false alarms. As for the progress of the war, Hitler has easily won the first round on points, for the Germans have advanced into Poland on all sides and the fall of Warsaw seems imminent. While the Western Front still seems to remain more or less All Quiet. Mother was out on duty. Up to Hampstead in afternoon, my observation yesterday to the effect that Hampstead was completely 'unsheltered' was somewhat inaccurate. I decidedly hadn't seen enough of it. For today I found deep sand-quarrying [for filling sandbags] being quarried out over areas on both sides of the Spaniards. I thought Hampstead would sooner or later have to be spoilt or desecrated somehow for war purposes. The notion that its beautiful expanse would be left unmarred was, indeed, too good to be true.

Monday 11 September Went up to Gray's Inn Rd Police station to find out how I stood regarding the War Reserve. Found that all the business of the station had been transferred to Macnaghten House so came back and went there. Saw Sergeant Prizeman very harried and preoccupied. Advised me to go up and see Inspector Hayes – wasn't in. Would I call back at 4.0 and saw him. Told me they were now full up with no vacancies. Hadn't been able to keep my place open as they had to get up to full strength with active men. Up till this morning when the last batch were sworn in they would have organised it. Now it was too late. Gave me an option on the first vacancy or resignation which might occur within a week or two, or might not in which case I'd have to resign myself. And that was the best they could do for me. So we left it at that. Now I'm damned if I know what to do. Whether to go and try to get my job back at PR's and resign from the reserve if I do. Or whether to see if I can carry on with it till the Police do need me. Or whether to just wait and do nothing for a while and see if anything turns up. It's a damnable dilemma. Dispelled the depression which started to settle over me in the evening by going out and taking a stroll round the West End to see what blacked out London looked like. By bus as far as the Dominion and from there did the familiar round of theatre land – Charing X Rd, Shaftesbury Avenue, Piccadilly Circus, Leicester Square, Trafalgar Square, Strand and then bus home from Wellington St. Not a complete black out for the green and red traffic signals and the dimmed lights of cars and buses provide a certain amount of light but effective enough to make nocturnal London appear strangely unreal and unfamiliar. With an air of mystery and intrigue about it all. The black outlines of many buildings, silhouetted against the starry sky reveal an unexpected beauty in their symmetrical design obscured hitherto as they have been by the blatant glare of neon lights. While away from the traffic of the main thoroughfares, the secluded back streets somehow suggest the quiet repose and serenity of eighteenth century London by night. One almost expects to see torrid laden linkboys or sedan chairs to appear round the corner any moment.[44] Yes, there is an exciting and disturbing coolness of an eerie and almost ethereal quality about the darkened streets of central London now and frequent flakes of what appeared to be lightning enhanced their effects considerably. A fair number of people about except in the vicinity of the Strand which was practically deserted. The evening a welcome change from the eternal book and radio evenings.

Tuesday 12 September A cold cheerless day. Went along in the morning to PR's to see how things stood there. The first remark of nearly everyone I saw was 'had a pretty rough time haven't you?' Called in staff office Scheele not there. Up with Massey and likely to be there rest of morning. So said I'd call in again in afternoon and went up to the office to see J.D. Likewise with Massey. Only a fraction of the former staff left – less than half anyway. All the rest called up for national or military service. As a result most of the work is about two weeks behind. Stood around chatting to all and sundry for about half an hour and then left. Went along to Boots[45] to change book then to the Stationery Office in Kingsway to get a copy of the Reserved Occupations Schedule. Of all the grades of office staff specified therein, I don't come under any of them. So presumably I'm unreserved. Scheele still not available so I decided to return on Thursday provided the doctor will pass me as fit enough. Which solves my problem for the time being. Now I suppose the Police will send for me in a day or two and put me in another

---

44 At night before street lighting, linkboys carried a flaming torch to light the way for pedestrians.

45 Chemist and Lending Library at 288–290 Euston Road.

quandary. Went up to try and see J.D again but just missed him. Hung around an hour waiting for him to come back but he didn't so after collecting some further money due at Cashier's left a message for him. Called at Dr Cutner's surgery to find out the best time to see him and at insurance agent's abode in Argyle Square before returning home. The latter called to hand over sick benefit while I was out, leaving card. Wasn't in of course but found out when he would be tomorrow which was something. Home just after 6.0. Had some tea and settled down for a quiet evening at home, mostly reading.

Wednesday 13 September Called on Dr Cutner at surgery in morning. Said he had about one minute to spare and he certainly gave me no more. Without bothering to examine me at all, passed me as fit for work and made out the necessary certificates with a final tonic prescription. And that was that. After lunch at the Commercial went round to try and see the insurance agent again. Not of course in so left a message for him and came home. Had some coffee and a brief rest; then took bus up to Regent's Park and walked over to Primrose Hill. Most of the north side of it fenced off and occupied by anti-aircraft units and their camps over the grass at the top of the hill. Started to rain on way back. Fine spell seems to have properly broken up now. Home at 3.40 and had some tea. Spent evening reading and clearing up one or two odd jobs. Mother came in feeling not too well so went to bed early while I cooked supper. Turned in, fairly early night 10.30. So ends my last day at large.

Thursday 14 September Went back to work after five and a half weeks absence, including a week's holiday at the start. Everyone seemingly glad to have me back. Both Scheele and J.D. expressing considerable concern that I didn't overdo things and strongly advising me to take it very easy for a while. A most gratifying welcome. Certainly plenty to do. And so very few left to do it. Gave what general assistance I could on costs and selling figures which were several days behind, taking care not to overwork myself – by special request. Had lunch downstairs in the restaurant for the first time in about seven years – steak and chips and syrup pudding. Not too bad.

Still acting on the advice of Messrs Scheele and Doran, went home at 5.0. Will continue to do so for a few days. Insurance agent called about 6.30 and paid me two weeks benefits etc. The other two weeks to come next week. Sergeant Prizeman having called to offer me War Reserve job this morning just after I'd left for work, went round to Macnaghten House in evening. Prizeman having gone off duty saw Inspector Hayes and explained that I would not be really fit for police work for two or three months, so would have to decline. He told me in that case would I be willing to resign as a full member of the Reserve and enrol instead for part time voluntary service, mostly inside clerical work, such as would occur after heavy raids. This seemed to suit me perfectly so I agreed to do that. Inquiring how conscription would be applied in the Police force, he showed me the letter from the Home Office to the effect that exemption would only apply to the regular force and not to the special constabulary or War Reserve. So I'm just as well off out of it as I would be in it in that case. In fact had I known that at the time I don't suppose I would have joined at all. Nor would many others methinks. Still I don't mind some form of inside work in my spare time and he was really so nice about it that I could hardly refuse anyway. Incidentally he told me they'd never take me in the army with my belly. Well that's some consolation. Perhaps my peritonitis will turn out to be a blessing in disguise after all. So having settled that problem or rather having it settled for me, and got me out of my quandary in the most satisfactory manner, came home again and listened to the radio for an hour. Then round to the fish shop with Mother to get something for supper. No fish available but had sausages in batter and chips so got some of them. Not at all bad either. Streets are as black as hell. No moon or stars or light of any sort. Bed 10.45.

Friday 15 September The ban has been lifted – all theatres and cinemas throughout the country allowed to reopen from today provided they close by 10 p.m. except in the West End, and here's the snag – when 6 p.m. is the curfew hour. Not so good for the theatres, as it will mean matinees only and in most cases the running expenses would hardly make it worthwhile to try and carry on under these conditions. Still, we shall see. A weekly Saturday afternoon visit to the theatre will be better than nothing. Waded through a lengthy and complicated book of instructions in theory to try and help Mother get some idea of her task in her forthcoming job as a National Register enumerator.[46] Made me dog tired. So much so that I went to be as early as 10.15.

Saturday 16 September Had just finished having a tub down in afternoon when Phil called. Said he'd been round two or three times in the last week and no one in every time. Gave him some tea and chatted for a couple of hours about the war and our mutual friends and things in general. Asked me if I'd like to come along with them, but I had to regretfully decline. So asked me to come to Muswell Hill to a small party on Tuesday evening instead, which invitation I gleefully accepted. One of the nicest fellows I've ever known. Went to Colombo's after and had an excellent spaghetti and coffee. Haven't been there for over three years. Not so uncomfortably crowded as it used to be. Walked home, clear starry night. Bed by 12.50.

---

46 The National Registration Act 1939 was an emergency measure which established a National Register, effective from 29 September. Enumerators visited each household and issued national identity cards, which people were required to produce on demand, or present to a police station within forty-eight hours. See entries for 30 June 1940 and 20 July 1941, when Heap was required to show his card.

Part One

Sunday 17 September Up to Hampstead in afternoon, sat on Parliament Hill and read book. Everything in fact, seems to indicate that Parliament Hill is about to share the fate of Primrose Hill as an anti-aircraft site. By next week I shall expect to find it all fenced off and all. Radio news not very reassuring, Russia now invading Poland as well looks like what is technically known as a 'carve up.'

Monday 18 September The German and Russian forces converged in Poland this evening and now occupy between them practically the whole of the country. Warsaw hopefully still holds out but the government has fled into Rumania along with hordes of refugees and Poland is to all intents and purposes no more. So the sooner we face up to the fact that we've backed a loser, cut our losses and call it a day the better for everyone concerned, particularly us. But will we? Not bloody likely. Not while there's a chance to throw a few million lives away for those nice inspiring ideals, liberty and democracy. And of course slaughter a few million Germans to make them realise what they're missing by giving those two wonderful illusions the go-by. We must smash Hitler even if civilisations get smashed as well in the process of attempting it. Lord, what fools these mortals be. And English fools the biggest of the lot.

Tuesday 19 September Tired of carrying gas mask about in rather bulky and inelegant haversack. Mother got me a black soft leather container to try. Also a small torch for use in street at night. Also a wide length of elastic to make into a supporting belt for my stomach which, since my operation, bulges and sags in a decidedly ugly and uncomfortable fashion. Whether this will serve the purpose of a surgical belt which is what I really need is possibly open to doubt, but it's worth trying if only for the fact that it's considerably less expensive.

Thursday 21 September Mother not taking on job as National Register enumerator after all. Has taken all the stuff back. Too much to tackle – carrying on as ARP warden instead. Went up to Golders Green Hippodrome[47] in evening to see the Gielgud revival of *The Importance of Being Ernest*. My first play in fact for exactly two months. What a genuine joy, house packed but balcony closed, this being the only theatre within reasonable distance of central London allowed to keep open till 10.0 and easily get-at-able by tube – it looks like becoming London's No 1 wartime theatre.

Friday 22 September To the Horse Shoe in evening to meet the Johns. Went onto the Robin Hood. Phil and Kath there as well as the usual crowd. I stayed on till 11.0 with the others. Took the bus to Euston and

---

47 The 3,000-seat theatre/music hall, famous for presenting pre- and post-West End productions.

1939

called down the vaults of [New] St Pancras Church[48] for Mother on the way home. Was on duty down there. Waited for her to knock off at 12.0 so walked home together. Lights mysteriously went out soon after we got in. So after a light supper, I pen this by candlelight. Got to bed at 1.0.

Saturday 23 September [At PR's] Spent half the morning packing everything up prior to being moved down to the main building basement over the weekend. So we're going to be turfed out of our light airy third-floor down to the artificially lit airless basement after eighteen months talk about it. Am certainly not looking forward to the change, it's bound to tell on one's health, short of anything else. Saw a newsreel with the inevitable silly interviews with some rather illiterate survivors from the [HMS] Courageous[49] and the ARP film entitled *Do It Now* which purported to instruct the public on what was general knowledge three weeks ago. Still, they all had their amusing moments.

Monday 25 September Our first day down in the dungeon.[50] Fully as foul as I expected. Glaring electric light, no fresh air, and bad ventilation. Must try and make the best of a bad job however, for jobs are rightly scarce now cannon fodder being the only vocation in great demand for men. Even a job under these conditions and precarious as it is just now is better than nothing.

Wednesday 27 September Went up to Muswell Hill for another convivial evening Chez Phil. Walked down Pentonville Rd to King's Cross and came home. A brilliant moonlit night. A joy to be out walking in it. The sort of night blackouts were made for – or ought to have been.

Thursday 28 September War Emergency Budget introduced yesterday, a real snorter. Income tax up from 5/6 to 7/6 with smaller allowances and increased taxation on beer, whisky, tobacco and sugar. Thus a pint of beer, a sip of whisky, twenty cigarettes and a pound of sugar will all cost a penny more. The effect of all these drastic increases will be, of course, to completely paralyse industry and trade, which are already surely stricken as it is, and bring about further unemployment. Perhaps, now the past bill is presented, the nation will begin to wonder whether the luxury of trying to 'smash Hitlerism' is really worth the cost.

Friday 29 September To the Horse Shoe at 9.0 to see the Johns. Found three of the Brean Sands crowd there as well, John Bell having got them along. I went to the Robin Hood, argued with Phil about the latest

---

48 The crypt was used as the ARP post for the area and as an air raid shelter by the Heaps once the Blitz began in September 1940.
49 The first British warship to be sunk in the war, the aircraft carrier was torpedoed by a German U-boat off western Ireland on 17 September, with the loss of over 500 lives.
50 The basement of Peter Robinson's.

turn of the war – the new German–Russian mutual understanding[51] while the rest of the crowd sang. Was just about to turn out at 11.0 when I suddenly realised that I'd left my gas mask on the table at the Horse Shoe. Dashed back there and inquired but they hadn't got it. So can only assume that either it was pinched for the sake of the black case it was in, or one of the Johns brought it away with them. Damned nuisance if it has gone west, though we have a spare medium size one at home that would serve till another large one was obtainable.

Saturday 30 September John Hobson, coming straight from night work, brought my gas mask round this morning while I was shaving. Stout fellow!

Sunday 1 October Observed that gas masks are definitely out of fashion. Presumably tired of carrying them around for nothing, people now leave them at home. Whereas during the first few days of the war not one person in ten was to be seen without one, now there is scarcely more than that ratio with them. Still, I think I'll continue to take mine around for a while.

Friday 6 October Started wearing winter underwear – long pants and all that. Also thicker and tighter elastic body belt to keep my stomach in. To the Horse Shoe to meet the Johns and Ron. From there walked round to the Wheatsheaf[52] before going up to the Malaya, finally slid off on my own to the Robin Hood to see Phil and the rest of the lads. Gus and Bert there in naval uniform celebrating their last day's leave in the midst of a large family gathering.

Sunday 8 October Hampstead in morning. Some minor military manoeuvres being carried out on Parliament Hill. After lunch took bus to Hyde Park to see what sort of a mess they've made of it there. Was surprised to find that apart from an anti-aircraft base and some trenches, it hasn't been spoilt very much. And Kensington Gardens, which are of course much lovelier in every way, has been left almost entirely alone. Amazing!

Wednesday 11 October First night of the new Palladium production *The Little Dog Laughed*, a bright, broad boisterous bizarre, blatant and blazing show with its naïve conglomerations of uniforms, union jacks, martial music and all the rest of the paraphernalia on which war fever finds its glorious expression. When Bud Flanagan got Ivor Novello and Beatrice Lillie[53] to come up from the front row of the stalls onto the stage and sing one of his chorus songs with him, the response took on

---

51. A treaty of mutual non-belligerence signed on 23 August.
52. At 25 Rathbone Place, W1.
53. Bud Flanagan (1896–1968), leading music hall comedian; Ivor Novello (1893–1951), Welsh actor and composer of successful musicals; Bea Lillie (1894–1989), leading comedy actress.

ecstatic proportions. Blackout or no blackout, this show is so assured of success that only a bomb could possible bring its run to an end.

Monday 16 October The first air raid on the British Isles during the present war took place this afternoon – in Scotland, around Edinburgh and the Firth of Forth region. Only minor damage and casualties and damage to shipping however, most of the bombs falling in the water. The raiders were driven off and two or three brought down. Have decided to take a six month course of hair restoring treatment with the Fredk. Godfrey Institute of Matlock. Sent off diagnosis form and fee (33/-) today. This is my last desperate stand against premature baldness, for my hair has been falling out for four or five years past and is now as thin and lifeless as can be and I already look almost bald at the back. Should this fail then I shall resign myself to my hairless fate without further ado. But I think it's worth trying the remedy for which so much is claimed first. There may be something in it.

Thursday 19 October Received my instructions and equipment for first month's treatment from Renew Hair Institute. This involves hydropathic treatment with pomade application and massage every morning and evening and a few neck ones thrown in as a makeshift. Am glad that at least I don't belong to any of the 'three' types – rheumatic or arid – for whom dietic advice is also included. Quite enough to get on with without that.

Sunday 22 October Went for a good fifteen mile walk in Herts with Phil. Must be fairly fit again for I felt no strain whatsoever after it. Was grand to get out into the country again. Spent the evening playing various games of cards, most of the games new to me. Had real beginner's luck and won three games of cards – in cash value about 1/3. Came home by bus. A delightful evening rounded off a perfect day perfectly.

Thursday 26 October Trouble with spectacles. One of the tortoiseshell rims has snapped apart, loosening the lens which thus easily slips out. Repairing it would necessitate entirely new frames. As however, I've had these spectacles for exactly seven years, I might as well have my eyes tested again for new ones.

Saturday 28 October Spent the greater part of the afternoon and evening writing my lengthy periodical letter to Aunt Pop. Started at 3.0 and with a break for tea finished 9.30 filling both sides of six full size sheets of notepaper. The longest letter I've ever written.

Sunday 29 October In afternoon went down to Thornton Heath to have tea with Bill & Lillian. Both of them in the Auxiliary Fire Service now, he as an acting sub-officer, she on Watch Room duties. So they're not doing too badly between them. Live in the station five days a week and only two at home.

Monday 30 October False air raid alarm this morning about 10.0. All went down to the sub-basement, stood there for four or five minutes until the all clear signal went off and then came up again. Too brief an interlude to be even amusing.

Tuesday 31 October During lunch hour went along to Newbold's, the opticians who made my present spectacles under Dr Turley's prescription seven years ago. Enquired about treatment under the National Eye Service Scheme and learned that I first have to go to panel doctor, get a certificate to the effect that my eyes need retesting, send it to the insurance society and take the resultant form along to the optician.

Friday 3 November Dinner at the YM. Back to Horse Shoe to meet the Johns. Left to keep a date with Phil at the Robin Hood. Frank, the Guvnor, invited us all to a bit of a party upstairs after closing time, sat around for two hours drinking, singing and fooling about in general. I rendered an eleven year old parody on Hannen Swaffer[54] to the tune of *Old Man River*, which since I first put it over at a party up at Phil's place some months ago, seems to have become recognised as my party piece.

Saturday 4 November Went round to the Homeopathic in the afternoon to see Dr Cutner. Also Dr Power who operated on me. Both had a look at my stomach and seemed very satisfied with the way it's healed up. Asked Cutner what the chances were of my passing a medical examination if called up? He asked me if I wanted to pass. I said no, not particularly. In that case he could certify that I was still defective in all sorts of ways and liable to all sorts of possible troubles. Should I have any difficulty in that direction, I was to go and see him about it and he'd see what he could do for me. A most gratifying suggestion.

Sunday 5 November Hampstead in morning and Regent's Park and Primrose Hill in afternoon. Noticed that the ARP trenches in the latter vicinity have been reinforced with concrete, covered over and made to look much less unsightly. This was being done to trenches in parks and squares all over London. Can it be that the authorities have at last tumbled to the fact that open trenches with piles of earth alongside are not only not particularly safe but also something in the way of the nature of an eyesore. Incredible!

Wednesday 8 November [King] Leopold of Belgium and [Queen] Wilhelmina of Holland, alarmed at the possibility of a German invasion of their countries, offer to mediate between Germany and the Allies. Stand about as much chance of success as a revival of *Journey's End*

---

54 Frederick Hannen Swaffer (1879–1962), socialist journalist, drama critic, editor and spiritualist.

would at the moment.⁵⁵ And yet the war gets duller and duller every week, with the war correspondents at their wits end to find something to write about. But it's a crazy world – and an even crazier war.

Saturday 11 November This was once Armistice Day. But now that the same stupid slaughter has started all over again, the commemoration has of course ceased to have any significance, except perhaps an ironic one. Poppies are still sold – Mother after all-night duty spent the morning selling them, but there is no longer two minutes silence or any Cenotaph ceremony. Such things are conveniently forgotten. If the sheep paused two minutes to think, they might not be coaxed to the slaughter so easily.

Monday 20 November A good deal of ships sinking by German mines over the weekend, otherwise the war is still proceeding very quietly with practically no activity on the Western front or in the air.

Thursday 23 November The installation of flood gates and other ARP works having been completed, the central London tube stations are now all opening again as usual.⁵⁶

Saturday 25 November Mother's 58th birthday. Went to Alby's wedding at St John's Church, Red Lion Square. Same old vicar and sexton still there and neither looking a day older. Can't say I was impressed by it. The vicar just stood mumbling away in the normal expressionless monotonous clerical manner for about a quarter of an hour. A mere recital ritual like all church ceremonies. Reception upstairs at the Robin Hood after. About thirty guests who well filled Frank's spacious drawing room. Started at 4.0 and went on all evening. A good deal of singing of course, they even found time for dancing. Aye, it was a grand do. Unfortunately I drank far too much and by the end of the evening was hors de combat. Whether this was due to the fatal error of mixing my drinks, the beer was interspersed with a fair levelling of whisky and once with a gin and lime – or to the fact that since my operation I can't take it so well as I used to I don't know, possibly both. But I was without doubt in a very bad way. Just conscious enough to hear talk but so physically helpless that I decided the best thing to do was to keep my eyes and mouth shut, except for occasionally vomiting, [and] affect complete unconsciousness. And thus I was brought home by Phil, Charlie giving us a lift in his car. As soon as Mother came in shortly after, they'd helped her undress me and put me into bed. The rest was blessed oblivion – the end of perfect day.

---

55 R. C. Sherriff's 1927 'war play', set entirely in a Western Front trench.
56 The Tube lines beneath the Thames in particular were fitted with steel doors to prevent flooding if the tunnels were damaged by enemy action: see www.britishpathe.com/video/raid-proof-tubes/query/Tube (last accessed 11 April 2017).

Sunday 26 November Got up at 11.0 feeling very much 'the morning after the night before' like. Stomach uninjured thank goodness. Walked to the Robin Hood and back in evening to collect gas mask and stick left behind last night. Back at 9.15 in time to hear Chamberlain talking about the war on the radio.

Monday 27 November Got an extended lunch hour to go and have my eyes tested by Willoughby Cahill at 42 Charles St, Mayfair. Ward 8 Conservative Committee apparently intend to resume operations again for a meeting has been called for tomorrow evening – the first since the outbreak of war. This lapse has given me a long hoped for chance to gracefully fade out of the dreary picture and I don't intend to lose it now, so am sending in my resignation as joint secretary on the grounds that 'I see no useful purpose to be served in pursuing any party political activities whatsoever until the war is over.' That should do the trick I think. Only one of my reasons really and not even the most important, but good enough for that decrepit crew of cretins.

Friday 1 December Down to Newbold's after work to get new spectacles. They fitted perfectly at last. Total cost £1.14.0, of which I pay 17/6 and the Prudential 16/6, which isn't too bad. Tonight's news sensation – the Russian invasion of Finland proceeds apace. And the 22s are called up.[57] Oh let us be joyful! Met the Johns at the Horse Shoe at 8.0. We took a bus up Holborn way and went to the Mitre.[58] Rather disappointing. Actually we didn't finish there but after one round, went over to the Green Parrot,[59] where the lights fused and took about fifteen minutes to fix, made an old year resolution never to set foot in any of these pokey little clubs again. I prefer to do my drinking in good honest pubs.

Sunday 24 December Checking up on the number of times I've been to the theatre during the last twelve years, I find my yearly visits work out thus:

1928–35	1932–68	1936–77
1929–42	1933–73	1937–83
1930–50	1934–65	1938–64
1931–45	1935–70	1939–56

Making 728 in all, which with my innumerable visits to the Old Vic and various other theatres prior to 1928 when I first started keeping a proper record, must, I feel sure bring my score to date up to the

---

57 Men were called up (conscripted) for the armed forces by yearly age groups.
58 At 68 St Martin's Lane, WC2.
59 The Green Parrot Club (later 'Sid's Club') occupied the large vaulted basement below the corner premises at 38 Alfred Place and 19–21 Store Street, WC2; for many years, this building was Sidoli's Restaurant, but opened as a Co-operative Food shop in 2016. The entrance to the club was via a set of iron steps, now the fire escape for the basement, which is still owned and used by the City of London (and the Co-operative).

thousand mark. And I'm not yet thirty. Surely a record of which any inveterate play goer might feel proud. I certainly do.

Monday 25 December There is nothing very noticeably different about the first Christmas of the war. Trade has been as brisk as ever at this time of the year with plentiful supplies of everything and the holiday is being celebrated in much the same festive way as usual. In fact one is apt to forget that there is a war on at all, so strangely static is it. I don't suppose there has ever been a war in history in which so little has happened in the first four months. Mother has bought me a woollen dressing gown for Christmas. The first one I've ever possessed, having made do with a white bath-wrap up till now. This is alright for the summer (such as we get), but somewhat inadequate for the winter when the d.g. will come in very useful. A bit on the long side but I daresay it can be changed for a size smaller. Had our Christmas dinner at 3.0 – roast duck, apple sauce, potatoes, cauliflower and Christmas pudding and a glass of port – accompanied by the King's Empire broadcast. A hesitating speech, uninspired and uninspiring. Am getting dreadfully cynical about these things lately.

Tuesday 26 December Went to the Coliseum to see *Cinderella*, the West End's only pantomime this year and a pretty poor one at that. Incidentally, all the West End theatres, bar three, have now reopened. Theatre land is itself again.

Friday 29 December Bought a new bowler at Horne Bros sale. Went along to the Horse Shoe at 8.0 to meet the Johns. John Hobson accompanied by one of his girl-friends, a petite and pleasant little person. Went over to the Blue Posts and then round to the Bricklayers Arms. They up to the Green Parrot and I went on to the Robin Hood. Walked home through the moonlit and still slushy streets and got to bed by 11.50.

Saturday 30 December In evening went to a dance up at Haringey with the Johns. The dance was a public one and at a place called the Palm Bal on Green Lanes which, needless to say, had no affinity to the Gallic but an unsavoury savour of Cockneydom in its most unattractive guise. And worst of all, there was no bar there thus necessitating excursion to a nearby gin palace, a most uncomfortable crowded place to say the best of it. I danced once in the evening. Quite enough too. A disappointing evening on the whole but it had its compensations.

Sunday 31 December As soon as Mother went on duty at 4.0, went over to tea with the Bolins, the people in the opposite flat. He is a fellow member of the YM though I've never come into contact with him there and like me is fond of hiking and beer. A very pleasant couple. Left at 6.30 to go up to Muswell Hill and spend the evening at Phil's. Saw the New Year in, in the most quiet and sober fashion and left at

12.30. Walked as far as Archway Rd then got a couple of buses down to King's Cross. Home at 1.30. So ended 1939. And good riddance too.

RETROSPECT – 1939

Whatever else this fateful year may have been, it was certainly not uneventful, either for me personally or the world at large. On the contrary it was full of incident and in a way very exciting. True, a good deal of it was the sort of excitement one would rather do without. Nevertheless it was exciting.

I suppose my foremost personal memory of 1939 in years to come will be of the two operations I underwent in it – one very minor one, circumcision – and one very major one, peritonitis. In the latter case, I came within an inch, or rather a few hours, of losing my life, so suddenly and unexpectedly did the illness beset me. Fortunately the perforated appendix was taken in time, the operation was successful and I made a good and speedy recovery. But it was a mighty near thing and an experience I wouldn't care to repeat. Never having had a real illness in my life before and always enjoying perfect health, this relapse left me physically deflated and unable to indulge in my accustomed physical exercises for some months, except for walking. Still, I really ought to think myself lucky to be alive.

On top of all this came the outbreak of war. This proved to be not nearly as terrifying a business – at least as far as London was concerned – as we expected it to be. No air raids took place and the black out, on moonlit nights made us realise for the first time how beautiful nocturnal London can be. All disconcerting enough however.

Had it not been for the peritonitis, I should now most likely have been serving in the Police War Reserve which I joined early in the year and had completed four months training when called up for service. But being then unfit for such duty I had no option but to resign and carry on with my job at PR's, thankful enough that that was still available. And even more thankful now that I realise how monotonous and incomprehensible police work would have been for me. Should I be exempted as unfit if and when I'm called up for military service, my spot of bother may yet prove to be a blessing in disguise.

Yet there were some happier features for which I shall also remember 1939, the year in which I reached the last outpost of the twenties. I started camping again after a break of six years and enjoyed a succession of truly delightful weekends as one of the guests of Phil and Kath at their camp in a remote corner of Hertfordshire. Until a succession of holidays, hospital and hostilities brought them to an abrupt end for me, I went on some very pleasurable rambles solitary or otherwise. I discovered the varied and manifold charms of the Peak district during one of my busy two weeks' holiday and on the other had a second though not so enjoyable experience of a holiday camp, culminating in the appendix trouble as soon as I got home. Seems as if I can't get away from that whatever I dwell on. It dominated 1939 for me. even the war took second place to it.

In some ways my life and habits have remained very static. My job and prospects for instance. Apparently not even a war can change them. Except that the former was rendered even more incompatible than hitherto by the office being moved from the third floor down to the basement. I went, of course, to the theatre a good many times, though thanks to the early wartime closing restrictions, not so often as I probably would have done under normal conditions, there being simply none or fewer open to go to for several weeks. On the other hand I read rather more books than usual, albeit I remain a slow reader. And I also saw a few more films than is my wont in the course of a year.

I have assiduously kept up the same friendships – Bill, the two Johns and Ron who once more appeared on the scene and is still on it – and also acquired or rather developed a few new ones, notably that of Phil and Kath, one of the most charming and tolerant pair of sophisticates it has ever been my good fortune to know. They have given me many happy weekends and evenings during the past year.

I retain a liking for beer and occasional convivial evenings of tipsy exuberance. At the same time I have undoubtedly been more moderate in my imbibings over the past year as a whole, than in many previous ones. Partly from choice, partly from necessity.

Money? I finished the year with just over £140, some £15 more than I started it with. As however this really represents a reserve to provide my wardrobe with a much needed replenishing (though in these uncertain times of drastic economies and rising prices it doesn't follow that it will get it) my financial position can scarcely be said to have improved much. Still, it's a tidy sum to have by.

And that was 1939 – in some ways so very ordinary, in other way [sic] so very extraordinary. But the latter aspect undoubtedly predominated. For me it was essentially a trying troublesome year – a disturbing year of doleful destiny. And at the end of it, with the war gradually gathering momentum, the immediate outlook is more uncertain and gloomy than I've ever known it in my life before.

What 1940 holds in store I hardly dare speculate upon. 1939 was quite enough to be getting on with. I'll leave it at that.

PART TWO

THIS BATTERED OLD TOWN:
1940–August 1945

Heap was correct in concluding that 'the war was gradually gathering momentum' but it was not for another nine months, in September 1940, that London came under heavy and frequent air attack. Once the enemy onslaught opened, he duly recorded his experiences and the effects of the successive bombardments. This part charts his life in these daily wartime entries until the end of August 1945, the final month of the war.

1940

For Heap, 1940 proved his most emotional and stressful year since his father's suicide in 1933. Not only did he lose his job in July but also he lost his greatest love to date – the previously unmentioned mistress Eilleen, a married woman with two small children. Two of her letters were tucked into the covers of his diary and these are quoted where appropriate, although, as only one is dated, their exact chronology is uncertain.

More significantly the 'Blitz' – the German air offensive on London – opened in earnest on Saturday 7 September. Nine days later, Heap started work in the Borough Treasurer's Department in St Pancras Town Hall, just three minutes from home. But by that date, responding to numerous air raid warnings, he and his mother had adopted a semi-troglodytic existence by sleeping most nights in public air raid shelters. As soon as the 'all clear' signal was sounded, Heap left the shelter to tour his neighbourhood before work, observing and recording the raid damage and those incidents still in progress. He often extended his tours further afield to the West End and, at weekends, to the City and beyond. He also took advantage of his time out around the borough on council business to observe and record recent bomb damage.

Before and throughout the Blitz, Heap tried to live as normal a life as was permitted by wartime conditions; he still went weekend camping and took walking holidays. The significance and interest of the year warrants including 59% of his original 50,600 transcribed words; after the beginning of the Blitz, very few days are omitted.

Monday 1 January Had the day [off work] in lieu of an extra day at Christmas. After lunch went off for a walk around Regent's Park and across Primrose Hill on which I saw the Polish Ambassador Count Raczynski[1] and his spouse taking what they doubtless term their 'constitutional.' Have noticed them nearly every time I've been around those parts lately. Presumably since Poland no longer exists except in

---

[1] Count Edward Raczynski (1892–1993) was the Polish Ambassador in London who signed the 25 August 1939 treaty in which Britain guaranteed assistance to Poland against German aggression. He later became Foreign Minister of the Polish Government-in-Exile. He died in London.

the imagination of democratic diplomats, the little count has little else to do these days but take 'constitutionals.'

Tuesday 2 January Royal Proclamation issued today calling up all men between the ages of 18 and 28. Though actually the registration of the various groups will be spread over the year. So it seems they'll not be after me for at least another year yet. Mother being on evening duty means dinner at the YM for rest of the week.

Friday 5 January After dinner at home went along to the Horse Shoe at 8.0 and met the Johns. Ron also turned up a bit later. Ambled round the Bricklayers Arms (or the Bricklayers Rest as the boys call it) and then to the Wheatsheaf. Finished up at the Fitzroy[2] after which they went up to the Green Parrot and I on to the Robin Hood. Phil and Charlie and the rest of the gang there. Bus home. Bed at 12.0.

Saturday 6 January The first major political sensation of the war has occurred with the resignation of Hore-Belisha as War Minister following serious clashes with the generals. The left wing press is of course all het up over the affair, hinting that it has been brought about by social bias rather than political differences and demanding a full dress investigation and explanation of the facts. The real trouble lies, I think, in his attempts to 'democratise' the army by drastic and sweeping reforms, for nothing lends itself less to democratic reform than the army. This with his Jewish flair for attracting an incessant blaze of limelight and publicity on himself and his ostentatiously flamboyant personality has made him too popular by half. The same thing happened to Edward VIII, though in a different way. Such men are dangerous. Fortunately they ride unerringly to their inevitable fall. I should dearly love to see Churchill ride to his now. 'Twas a mighty pity he ever recovered from his first one in the last war.[3] Oliver Stanley takes over the War ministry. Possibly not so brilliant but a much more reliable man for the job I should imagine. While Sir John Reith becomes head of the Ministry of Information, an appointment which seems to meet with universal approval.[4] The MoI badly needs pulling together. Its incompetence and hush hush policy has been a standing joke ever since the war started. Having run out of theatres for the moment and no outstanding films

---

2 The Fitzroy Tavern, 16 Charlotte Street, W1, was the famous regular watering hole of writers (including the poet Dylan Thomas), artists and, doubtless aided by its proximity to the BBC, leading performers and authors. See the landlord's daughter Sally Fiber's *The Fitzroy* (Lewes: Temple House Books, 1995).

3 Having masterminded the disastrous Gallipoli campaign, Churchill resigned in November 1915 and joined a regiment on the Western Front.

4 Sir John Reith (1889–1971) was a British broadcasting executive who established the tradition of independent public service broadcasting in the United Kingdom. In 1938, he was appointed chairman of Imperial Airways by Chamberlain, then Minister of Information in 1940, but Churchill briefly moved him to Transport and then to become Minister of Works with a peerage. After two years, he was replaced, whereupon, unfulfilled, he served for two years in the Royal Naval Volunteer Reserve.

1940

showing locally, decided to spend one of my rare Saturday evenings at home. In other words an armchair by the fire. Best place too, these nights.

Monday 8 January Bought 100 Saving Certificates of the latest issue at 15/- each which becomes 20/6 in ten years, equivalent to compound interest at the rate of £3.3.5 per cent per annum. Made up the £75 purchase price by means of (a) cooking my £20 worth of Saving Certificates of the 3rd issue purchased in 1926 and now realising £33.6.8 (b) withdrawing £30 from my P.O. Savings Bank account and (c) making up the balance by £11.13.4 with ready cash saved during the last year. Have just calculated the total interest I have earned on my savings since I first started my P.O Savings Bank account in 1922 and find that it amounts to no less than £35.2.0 (£8.13.8 on my P.O. a/c and £26.8.4 on Savings Certificates) which represents exactly a quarter of my total savings at the moment £140.9.8. Nice work. Rationing started today – ¾ lb sugar ¼ lb ham or bacon and ¼ lb butter each a week. Meat rationing later.

Sunday 14 January Very cold and very foggy. Temp 33 deg. Under these conditions neither Hampstead nor Regent's Park seemed very attractive propositions. But have to get out and exercise or I feel rotten all day so took a long triangular walk round with the Strand as the base line and the Law Courts and Trafalgar Square as its two angles. A good proportion of soldiers among such few pedestrians as there are about the streets. In Trafalgar Square a group of Canadians asked me where British Colombia House was. I hadn't the least idea. Alternatively did I know the whereabouts of the George the SEVENTH memorial? I wasn't sure whether they meant George V or Edward VII but on either case I didn't know so had to confess equal ignorance thereto. And I thought I knew my London! At that moment an aged flower seller appeared on the scene and doubtless in the expectation of a tip relieved me of my embarrassing questioners. Though I don't suppose she could direct them any better than I could. And I doubt even more if she got a tip. Passing the Duke of York's Theatre, observed that it has got play bills of a cheap melodrama which was on just before the war, displayed outside.[5] Appalling neglect! This, together with the Playhouse and the Haymarket are the only three theatres which haven't reopened since the war started. The only important cinemas still closed are the Tivoli and the Regency. The Carlton kept them company until very recently but has now opened up again. The base of Nelson's Column is now covered with four-sided National Savings advertisements. While nearby Charles I's statue is completely boarded up as a precaution against an attack. Presumably this is the only statue in London deemed worth trying to save.

---

5   The main West End theatres are shown on Map 3, p. xiii.

Wednesday 17 January In addition to a mild touch of diarrhoea – (I never can spell that damned word) had the symptoms of a chill hanging about my system all day, apparently uncertain whether to come or go. In order to persuade it in the latter direction, I went to bed at 9.30 after putting feet in hot water and making hot milk – for I had scarcely any appetite for dinner on getting home at 8.0, and I'd lay ten to one on its being shaken off by morning.

Thursday 18 January I won last night's bet with myself for the chill was completely routed by this morning and appetite regained. Still felt a bit drowsy though and am not quite sure that the diarrhoea's entirely disappeared. So intense and prolonged has been the cold spell, which has all Europe in its grip, that our water pipes froze overnight. Consequently had to heat the water out of the hot water bottle for shaving, dispense with washing and have hot milk in lieu of tea for breakfast. Later we obtained a supply from the flat opposite.

Friday 19 January Our water supply resumed work again this afternoon. Not that there is any noticeable drop in temperature. Must have taken pity on us. Met the Johns at the Horse Shoe soon thence to the Bricklayers Arms. Left them at 10.15 and went to the Robin Hood. Home by bus but 'twas such a magnificent moonlit night that I wished I'd walked.

Saturday 20 January Temperature well below freezing point again. And once more our water supply froze overnight. This morning taps were connected to the mains pipes under the pavement so people could go out into the street and get supplies, almost like people drawing water from the village pump. Bought an extra pair of striped trousers in Burton's sale for 10/6.

Sunday 21 January Went down to Thornton Heath in afternoon to have tea with Bill and Lilian, both still in the AFS [Auxiliary Fire Service]. Took nearly two hours to get there. Waited twenty minutes in the freezing gloom of Whitehall waiting for a 159 bus, before I learned from a 59 conductor that they only run from Streatham Common on Sundays. Arrived at that desolate spot I stood in an icy hurricane for a full half hour waiting for that same accursed bus before another conductor enlightened me to the fact that they started from the opposite corner a little way up the road. Thus, after duly blasting the heath of Thornton for its awkward inaccessibility, I at last arrived at journey's end round about 5.30. After tea spent the evening chatting about one thing or another and listening to the radio. Heard, for the first time, the famous 'Lord Haw Haw' (as his detractors call him) who nightly broadcasts from Germany in English.[6] We can't of course get him

6   William Joyce (1906–1946), alias Lord Haw Haw, was born in America and brought up in Ireland. A member of the British Union of Fascists in the 1930s, he left for Germany in

on our set – we're lucky enough to get London clearly now. He has the most attractive cultured voice and the most suave subtle style of talk imaginable. Everybody listens to him nowadays not only because he's a joy to listen to but also because they realise that for all the propaganda entailed, he gives out more truth and facts about what's really happening both here and abroad than we get in our own stilted censored news. If only our own announcers were half as good as the redoubtable Haw Haw! Got home easier than I got there, though even so, I didn't get in till 11.40.

Thursday 25 January Just as I got into bed about 12.15, a water pipe burst on the landing just outside my bedroom window and made a hell of a row as it poured along the passage and down the stairs.[7] Kept me awake nearly an hour. One of my oldest colleagues, Cook, gave in his notice today after 22 years' service with PR's. When Carroll was called up for anti-aircraft duties last August, he took over his work, which mainly consists of supervising all the registers, and all being well, I succeed him in the job. Had a long talk with Doran, about this. He was very favourable to the idea and promised to try and get me a rise to go with it if he could. Still, I shall be sorry to see old Cookie go.

Sunday 28 January News about the severe cold snap in the middle of the month has just been released by the censor and appears for the first time in today's papers. Apparently it was the coldest spell this century, since 1894 in fact. It's certainly hit the theatres badly. I noticed that only sixteen West End theatres are now open – less than half the total number which were nearly all open at the beginning of the year And out of this month's eight new productions, only three have survived. Not that the other five really deserve to do so, but they might have stood a better chance under more favourable weather conditions. After falling all night, left off snowing this morning leaving a layer of a few inches thickness. Putting on my hiking boots, four pullovers, sports jacket, woollen scarf and mac, went up to Hampstead in morning and had a good plod over the thickly covered heath. A good deal of tobogganing in progress on Parliament Hill and over near Spaniards Rd even some skiing here and there. As usual, scarcely anything worth listening to on radio.

Monday 29 January Walking to work this morning seemed like ploughing through the wastes of Siberia, so thick was the snow and so piled up the drifts. Walking home in evening too for that matter

---

September 1939 and broadcast pro-German propaganda throughout the war. In 1940 he had audiences of millions and his unmistakable English accent was much mocked. Captured and tried in 1945, he was unrepentant, and was executed on 3 January 1946. See Peter Martland, *Lord Haw Haw: The English Voice of Nazi Germany* (Richmond: The National Archives, 2003).

7   The flats in this purpose-built block are accessed by external landings on the inside of the complex overlooking the central courtyard.

for it hadn't melted at all. Wore my nailed hiking boots with trousers bottoms tucked up and took my ordinary shoes with me to change into as soon as I got to work. Everyone arrived about an hour late, all forms of transport having been thrown into complete chaos by the severe weather conditions and in many instances brought to a complete standstill.

Sunday 4 February The big thaw sets in with a rise of about 10 deg in the temperature. Hampstead this morning was just one vast sea of melting snow and ice which, together with a slight drizzle and a damp clammy mist, made it even worse than yesterday for walking. Never seen it so completely deserted.

Monday 5 February Took over Cook's old job which, what with the yearly figures one thing and another, is likely to keep one very busy indeed for a week or two. Am also carrying on with my own erstwhile job for a day or two until they get someone else in to take it over. As a compensation however we started knocking off at 5.30 again today, which just enables me to get home in the dim twilight without having either to grope my way in the dark or use a torch.

Wednesday 7 February A dizzy day at the office. Management clamouring for end of year figures, which despite a whole day of chasing everyone around, could not be got out owing to invoices being held up. The maintenance men come in and start substituting our old high bench desks with tables so that they can take them away and cut the legs down. The hell of a day.

Friday 9 February By a superhuman effort and going without tea, I at last got the totals out this afternoon. Phew, what a week!

Saturday 10 February Up at Hampstead in afternoon. All the ponds frozen over. On the lower slopes of Parliament Hill on the southern side and on the way towards Ken Wood were several men digging up the turf. Thought at first that they were starting to make air raid shelters but on closer inspection and direct inquiries discovered they were to be allotments.[8] In some cases whole families were working on them but the majority were lone diggers, presumably unemployed. So this is the latest scheme for spoiling the beauty of Hampstead and no doubt many another open space, for which purpose the war provides the vandals with so many ingenious excuses. And sure enough, on the way home, I noticed on the placard of a local weekly rag, 'War Allotments on Primrose Hill' – as if that hadn't been desecrated enough already with the anti-aircraft base and air raid shelters! How the remaining small

---

8   As part of the 'Dig for Victory' campaign, large areas of parks and open spaces in St Pancras were given over to allotments for the growing of vegetables – most significantly, several large areas of Parliament Hill (and eventually Primrose Hill) not used by the military or for air raid shelters.

area of untouched and unenclosed grassland must have worried the powers that be. How best could it be defiled? Ah, allotments. A real inspiration offering unlimited scope for besmirching the few remaining beauty spots of London. And so patriotic to 'Dig For Victory' and All That. Such are the ways and means of wartime London.

Sunday 11 February A touch of spring in the air, even though still very cold. In fact 'twas such a bright clear blue day and so exhilarating did I find 'the champagne air of February' up at Hampstead in the morning that I went out again in the afternoon to enjoy a further draught – to Primrose Hill. Couldn't find any trace of the allotments there – apparently they haven't actually been allocated yet – except in the local rag. There was however an ARP demonstration taking place outside some houses in Primrose Hill Rd, watched by a crowd of a hundred or so people. One or two casualties were lying about on the pavement and a few tin-hatted men standing on the balcony of a house replete with ladder, a few more standing about the roadway and a fat Jewish looking individual howling explanatory notes to the crowd through a megaphone about what was supposed to be happening. So far as I could see, nothing was happening. Le ARP s'amuse!

Friday 23 February Called at the tailors on way home and ordered a new suit of black jacket and vest and striped trousers. Didn't actually need it for a few months yet but I thought I'd better get it while the getting's good and prices are still fairly reasonable. And as it happed my apprehensions were well founded for they only had a small amount of cloth in stock and were having the utmost difficulty in getting new supplies. My wardrobe is now sufficiently equipped for one or two years if need be.

Saturday 24 February The calling up of men for the forces is being speeded up considerably now that they can absorb them more quickly. A different age group registers every month and by June even the 27s will have registered. A new proclamation will then be issued calling up the next few groups – 28 and over in the late summer or autumn. Which means that I shall probably be called up before the end of the year. I don't like the sound of things at all. The clocks are advanced an hour tonight when 'summer time' starts, two months earlier than it normally would.

Sunday 25 February Swarms of people about up at Hampstead in morning enjoying the first day of 'summer time' with its promise of seasonal joys to come. Also to Regent's Park and Primrose Hill in afternoon. Went even further than usual on this latter jaunt and strolled up to and around the heights of Swiss Cottage, a locality I've always found singularly attractive with its air of bright, clean freshness.

Tuesday 27 February Before settling down to read my book this evening, the fancy took me to calculate how many books I'd read during the last few years. Turning out my lists and totting up the entries therein I find that from 1933 to 1939, both years included, I've read 286 books – an average of 41 a year or one every nine days or so. [9] This would appear to suggest that I'm not quite so serious a book reader as I am a play-goer, though not very far behind in that respect.

Thursday 29 February Bought two new pairs of long pants for next winter. In pursuance of my present policy of anticipating clothing requirements as much as possible cognisant rising prices.

Saturday 2 March Met John Hobson and Ron at the Angel[10] at 7.30, waited for over an hour for John Bell to arrive before going on to an AFS [Auxiliary Fire Service] dance in some miserable elementary school situated in a dismal street off City Rd. One of John H's pals connected with it. About the last place in London one would think of going to for a dance. And it was too! A wretched affair altogether. Cheap and nasty and ill-favoured beyond belief. And such a grimly depressing atmosphere about it all. We stood for a while in the improvised classroom bar and drank a beer or two while an octoroon[11] was entertaining the ghastly nondescript crowd in the adjoining improvised classroom dance hall. He played a ukulele, sang, told jokes and made the most hideous row imaginable. Our endurance at an end, Ron and I fled at 10.0, took a bus to Tottenham Court Rd, had a drink in the Marquis, packed to suffocation, another at the Malaya and finished up at the Green Parrot where the Johns rejoined us and [where] we stayed till about 2.0 drinking whisky and listening to some records. Thus was I induced to break my resolution not to go to these clubs again. Still, resolutions are made to be broken now and again and I have at least kept it for three months. And even the club was more tolerable after that horrible abomination of a dance. Had quite an enjoyable time up there actually. As we left John Hobson, more than a little drunk, stumbled down the dark stairs and crashed on his nose, causing it to bleed profusely. Helped him along TC Rd till we could find a taxi and sent him home with it with John Bell who, after spewing all over the roadway, wasn't in much better condition himself. Whereupon Ron and I complimenting ourselves on our apparently greater staying power, had some coffee in a snack bar and walked up as far as Euston Rd where we parted and made our respective ways home. Bed at 3.0.

---

9   Heap kept lists of books read and shows and films seen on loose sheets of paper; most were discarded but a few remain in the covers of diary volumes. The totals in Appendix 2 (pp. 513–611) may not always tally with the totals counted using his diary entries.

10   The historic site (and underground station) at the junction of Islington High Street and Pentonville Road, N1.

11.   Person of mixed race; literally, one-eighth black.

Sunday 3 March The war has been on exactly six months today – and yet it hasn't really started yet. The strangest war in history. Incidentally the Boat Race was run yesterday – not over the usual course but at Henley for the first time in a century or more.[12] Cambridge won as usual. Went with Mother over to East Ham in afternoon to see Fred and Minnie and Jack (Mary's been evacuated) at their new house in Shakespeare Crescent. Went by bus and came home by train, a long dreary journey either way. Forlorn, God forsaken place backing onto railway junction and a hell of a way from station or bus route. Not the sort of place we're likely to go more than once in a very long while. Nothing much to talk about except the war and who wants to talk about that bore?

Monday 4 March Received my usual birthday present of five dollars with a card from Aunt Pop this morning – six days in advance. Wrote my reply letter in evening, not so long as usual. Only took me two hours and covered but four and a half pages. Very little to write about in these times.

Tuesday 5 March Went to first night of *Beggar's Opera* revival [at] the Haymarket.[13] When I saw yet another revival of it at the same theatre ten years ago, I was bored to death with the thing. The same thing happened tonight. Had the utmost difficulty in getting a programme as one usually does on first nights at this theatre unless arriving early. One surely goes to forget the damned war for a while.

Friday 8 March Went along to the Horse Shoe at 8.15 to meet the Johns. Waited till 8.45 when Ron turned up. Surprised at their non-appearance we assumed that John H had broken his nose on Saturday night [2 March] and was in hospital having it re-set or something like that, but after calling at the Rising Sun[14] and the Fitzroy, we decided to try the Malaya as a last resort and there they both were as large as life – as of course they naturally would be.

Saturday 9 March Came home to change before going up for tea with Ron at Belsize Park. 'High Tea' the mainstay of which was welsh rabbit. Sat round large table with the other boarders, all very informal, in sweaters, dressing gowns and suchlike garments. These included Jack White, a band leader,[15] about to take over from Joe Loss at the Astoria, his brother who doesn't bear the faintest resemblance to him and plays

---

12. The first Boat Race was run at Henley in 1829.
13. John Gay's 1728 satirical ballad opera.
14. At 46 Tottenham Court Road.
15. (Eugene Joseph) Jack White took over the family band on his father's death in 1930; Tom White was the drummer. The popular band played at the leading dance halls, recorded for Parlophone Records and broadcast regularly, including 309 editions of *Music While You Work*. Both brothers were called up in 1941. See http://turnipnet.com/mom/jackwhite.htm (last accessed 12 December 2015).

the saxophone, and their crooner, a frail diminutives girl of fifteen with her head hopelessly turned by being a 'discovery.' Afterwards we went over and spent an hour or so in a couple of the locals on Haverstock Hill before drifting down West. All went to finish up at the Parrot. Stayed there talking and drinking till nigh on three in the morning, though I was as sober as a judge when I left. And so hungry that I couldn't drink any more. If that is not a sure sign of sufficiency I don't know what is. However was too late to eat on getting home so went straight to bed.

Sunday 10 March Hyde Park and Kensington Gardens in afternoon. Crowds of people about. Except for men in uniform, didn't notice a single gas mask being carried. Meetings at Marble Arch in full swing, but the greatest draw of all was the set of four newly placed anti-aircraft guns nearby.

Monday 11 March Was notified of a 5/- a week rise. About time too. And even so, I get nothing like what Cookie and Carnell my predecessors earned, or at least drew. Meat rationing starts today, 1/10d worth of meat each a week. This doesn't include however game, poultry, oxtail, liver, tripe and suchlike 'offal.'

Wednesday 13 March My thirtieth birthday. A definite landmark midway between youth and middle age. Yet I can't say I feel any great emotion or awe at the significance of the occasion. Only a mild sense of satisfaction at reaching intact even such an immature age as thirty in these precarious times when lives are wantonly destroyed and sacrificed by the million for the sake of futile causes. After three and a half months of bitter fighting, the Russo-Finnish war came to an end today. The gallant though rather foolhardy resistance against overwhelming odds has at last broken down and they've been compelled to accept Peace terms with much heavier concessions than were demanded of them in the first place. In other words, they've gained nothing by their resistance and lost a hell of a lot.[16] Now of course, Russia is free to help Germany against us.

Friday 15 March Pub-crawled with Ron and the Johns Horse Shoe – Fitzroy – Marquis – finishing up at the Parrot till gone 12.0, walked home.

Saturday 16 March Did two theatres in evening. After tea went to first night of Ronald Frankau's review *Beyond Compere* at the Duchess.[17]

16 Having fought for four months, Finland's army was overwhelmed by a million Soviet soldiers with superior artillery, so they reluctantly agreed to a Soviet naval base in Western Karelia, and the cession of the province to the USSR.
17 Ronald Frankau (1894–1951) was a music hall and radio comedian who adopted an upper-class accent when presenting his saucy jokes, in contrast to the Liverpudlian accent of his radio partner, Tommy Handley, when they broadcast as 'Mr Murgatroyd and Mr Winterbottom'.

Coming out soon after 8.0, dropped into the Aldwych to see *Nap Hand* – a complete waste of an evening. I must keep all my difficulties and problems for solution while watching farces. A delightful discovery!

Friday 22 March Good Friday. Equipped with sandwiches and fruit, took a train from Waterloo down to Leatherhead and did one of my favourite walks over Leatherhead Downs. A delightful walk especially in the spring and not too long! Good to get right away from everything to do with the war. Once away from Waterloo and its swarm of soldiers, there were no visible signs of it anywhere. Doesn't seem to have affected the countryside much, thank heavens.

Saturday 23 March Hampstead in morning. The Easter fair[18] in full swing despite the war and the necessity of closing down at 7.0 p.m. and subduing the organ music and the roundabouts in case it should be mistaken as an air raid siren.

Wednesday 24 March Went on a ramble in Herts with Phil, Charlie, Stan, Fred and their respective spouses. Started out from Muswell Hill about 9.30 and got a train from Wood Green to Hatfield. [*itinerary around the outskirts of Welwyn Garden City*]

Thursday 4 April On my way to the theatre this evening witnessed a very odd incident in Seven Dials. In the middle of the road was an elderly man raving. Had flung his coat down and stood in his shirt sleeves shouting in meaningless jargon at passers-by in general while a crowd of amused spectators stood around the kerbs watching him. Not a policeman in sight of course. Was he mad drunk or just plain mad I wonder. We shall never know.

Saturday 6 April. Not an uncommon sight in London streets now is women in uniform accompanied by men in mufti – this would have been inconceivable in the last war. Meant to have a sleep in the afternoon to make up for the week's late nights but was too fine out to stay in so went to Regent's Park and contented myself with half an hour on the bed after tea. Up to Belsize Park and met Ron at 8.0 had two in the George and one in the Haverstock before going down west. Called in the Fitzroy then went up to the Parrot. Very crowded. Turned us all out at 12.0, expected a raid, so home to supper and bed.

Sunday 7 April Hampstead in morning with one George, an ARP colleague of Mother's. Like me he is thirty, works in office (shipping) is an ACIS and none the better off for it. Unlike me he talks with a broad Scots accent. An engaging cove.

---

18   The traditional bank holiday fairs held on the lower heath were very popular and large London crowds (generally including Heap) traditionally frequented 'Appy 'Ampstead.

Tuesday 9 April The war at last looks like beginning in real earnest with the German invasion of Denmark and Norway to 'take them under their protection following the laying of mines by the Allies along the Norwegian coast.' The former was of course an overnight walkover but Norway is putting up some resistance and the Allies, of course, promise 'full support.' Here we have the government's long awaited opportunity to sacrifice the lives of Britain's young manhood without stint. The more the merrier – for the armament makers. Now, more than ever with me it will be a case of eating, drinking and getting all the damned fun I can out of such uncertain span of life now left to me – for the morrow we get maimed, mutilated or murdered for the glory of democracy and all else that's rotten in the state of England today. So be it.

Sunday 14 April Hyde Park in afternoon. Ran, or rather walked into my old friend Adam de Hegedus by the orators' corner at Marble Arch. Hadn't seen him for two years and oddly enough, it was on the very same spot on a Sunday.[19] He looked just the same as ever, immaculately dressed, elegant and polished whereas I, as usual on a Sunday, was clad in my oldest and dirtiest clothes. Which made me feel a trifle embarrassed as we strolled round the park, talking of this and that, mainly about money and operations. He had also had one recently – going all the way to Buda Pest to have his tonsils out! Apparently he's still the London correspondent for the Hungarian paper *Magyrsing* and still hoping to get another book published. I left him at Knightsbridge, he to take a bus back to Queen's Gate where he now resides, while I strolled through Green Park and St James's Park before going home to tea. I ought to keep in touch with Adam. He's one of the most interesting talkers I've ever known.

Monday 15 April Straight from work to the Old Vic which reopened tonight for first time since the war started, with John Gielgud as *King Lear*. Over very late. No buses so walked over Waterloo Bridge.

Friday 19 April Mother went and bought a new radio today, second-hand Phillips make at £3.10.0, less 15/- for our old set, a bargain. Met the Johns and Ron at the Horse Shoe in evening. Went round to the Fitzroy, the Marquis and then up to the Parrot where we played darts and talked to all and sundry till past midnight. Bed at 1.30.

Saturday 20 April Stayed in afternoon and had early tea before going to the Empire to see *Gone With the Wind*.[20] Adapted from the thousand page best seller, this has been universally hailed as the greatest film ever. But what a film! Though we've had a copy of the book for two

---

19 See entry for 6 March 1938.
20 Margaret Mitchell's 1936 novel set in the American Civil War and Reconstruction era. The 1939 film, starring Clark Gable and Vivien Leigh, was then the highest-grossing film ever.

or three years, I've never felt inclined to tackle it. After seeing the film I feel like doing so even less. It made one that weary.

Sunday 21 April One effect of the war in Scandinavia and the consequent curtailment of the supply of wood pulp for paper manufacture has been a considerable reduction in the size of newspapers. Most of them are now half their former size. This is especially noticeable with a paper like the *Sunday Times* whose feature writers are severely rationed. James Agate[21] for instance who used to spread himself over two columns is now compressed into barely one third of that length – and the others in proportion. That, to an ardent play goer and a lover of the arts in general, is what I call real hardship.

Tuesday 23 April Started wearing new shirt and black jacket, vest and stripes. St George and Shakespeare took second place today. Increasingly heavier burdens on the taxpayer to pay for this wretched war. Letter post up to 2½d and post card rate up to 2d. Beer up 1d a pint, whisky 1/9 a bottle, tobacco 3d an ounce (3d on a packet of cigarettes) and matches ½d a box. Income tax up a further 6d to 7/6. And there won't be a murmur of dissatisfaction from the poor bloody British Public. After all, it's to save liberty and democracy etc. Bah!

Monday 29 April The morning newspapers have now ceased to display plays owing to the acute paper shortage. The evening papers still have the houses. Sent back the Income Tax return. Can't claim for Mother this time as a dependent relative. Her income's too high.

Tuesday 30 April Went along to the YM after work for the last time and had a shower bath. My membership expires today and have decided not to renew it. A bit of a break for I've belonged to it for 12 years but it's just not worth £2 a year now that I can't use the gym or swimming bath since my operation. So had my last shower, took my last reading – 11st 1lb, brought my gym kit home and thus ended my apprenticeship of the YMCA.

Saturday 4 May Started camping again with Phil and Kath up at the old site near Tyler's Causeway. Glorious weather all weekend, blue sky and warm sunshine. Got 2.38 train from King's Cross to Cuffley and arrived at camp about 4.30. Sunbathed till past 6.0 when Phil and Kath at last arrived, we had tea forthwith and after daubing brown paint on the tents to camouflage them, walked over to The Crown in Newgate St. Didn't get there till gone 9.0. Had four or five drinks a head and cheese and pickles and played darts. Out at closing time 10.30 and back to camp. Starry night. A lot of searchlights at times. Didn't sleep very well even though very tired. Felt too cold for one thing and having no straw to fill paillasse with, the ground was too hard for another.

21 James Agate (1877–1947), diarist and Heap's favourite theatre critic.

Part Two

[*Heap spent a further eight weekends camping at Cuffley until his final visit on 3 August, after which his holidays and the war intervened. These weekends are not included below except when wartime preparations are mentioned.*]

Monday 6 May Our attempts to stop the German invasion of Norway has ended in complete fiasco with an ignominious withdrawal.[22] The government getting more than they bargained for in this war. Five years ago today was the Jubilee of George V.[23] What a contrast between London then and now.

Thursday 9 May New proclamation issued today calling up 28–36 age groups. One group each week is [called] at present. Which means that I shall have to register about August. Cheerful prospect. Widespread revolt against the government is afoot over the failure of the Norway campaign. Only escaped a vote of censure last night by the skin of their teeth, in other words a majority of 81. Looks as if Chamberlain will resign shortly. In any case there's bound to be widespread change.

Friday 10 May Chamberlain resigns and Churchill becomes Premier with a new coalition government.[24] At the same time the war rears up in real earnest with the invasion of Holland and Belgium and the bombing of various French and Belgian towns by Germany today. New ARP instructions are given out on the radio[25] and everyone, apprehensive about the possibility of invasion and air raids, begins to carry their gas masks again for the first time since the start of the war. Furthermore the Whitsun bank holiday due to fall on Monday has been cancelled. Whether we open or not at PR's had not been decided by the time we left this evening. However, these alarming developments didn't deter me from attending the first night of the revival at the Garrick of *By Pigeon Post*, a spy play.

Monday 13 May Have almost cut out smoking altogether once the price of cigarettes went up to the exorbitant price of 1/5 for 20. Though I was never more than a very light smoker, now I'm classed as a negligible rather than submit to this imposition.

---

22 For the Norwegian Campaign, see I. C. B. Dear, *The Oxford Companion to the Second World War* (Oxford: Oxford University Press, 1995), pp. 773–774, 821–823.
23 Heap had been a steward at the Silver Jubilee service at St Paul's Cathedral (see entry for 6 May 1935).
24 The coalition included Chamberlain as Lord President, Kingsley Wood at the Treasury, and the Labour Party leaders Attlee (Deputy Premier) and Morrison (Supply). Sir John Anderson retained his responsibility for ARP.
25 These Home Office 'general announcements' included advice on reporting parachutists (who might be in civilian clothes), on what to do in an air raid, on always carrying gas masks and an identity label, on fighting fires and on lighting restrictions and not using the telephone except for very urgent messages (*The Times*, 11 May).

1940

Tuesday 14 May. The Germans continue to sweep all before them. They have already driven a wedge into Holland whence the Queen and government have fled to London, penetrated well into Belgium and are now attempting to break through the Maginot Line at its weakest point near Sedan which has been evacuated.[26] Soon no doubt our King and government will be fleeing to New York to govern the country from there!

Wednesday 15 May The Dutch army surrendered to the Germans last night after but four days fighting. Exit Holland.

Thursday 16 May Butter, sugar and bacon ration to be reduced still further – butter to ¼ lb a week instead of ½ lb and sugar to ½ lb instead of ¾ lb – compulsory slimming in fact.

Friday 17 May A big landslide is taking place in theatre-land. More than half the shows now on announce 'last week' or 'last two weeks' and new productions are being shelved for the time being. Which means that by the week after next only about ten theatres will be open, a terrible state of affairs. Met the Johns at the Horse Shoe at 8.30, thence to the White Hart in Windmill St, the Fitzroy and the Malaya and finally the Green Parrot. Completely empty. The pitch had apparently been cleared by a [presumably police] raid which took place last Friday at 11.45.

Saturday 18 May Had an air raid drill [at PR's] at 9.0. All went down to the new gas-proof shelters in the sub-basement which have taken about six months to complete, stood there about five minutes and came up again. Very tame.

Monday 20 May The Germans continue to sweep all before them, the greater part of Belgium is now in their hands and their 'bulge' into France where they broke through the Maginot Line grows daily wider. Now is the time for all the clichés 'Backs to the wall,' 'Conquer or die' etc. etc. to be trotted out for our beguilement, and sure enough, they are.

Wednesday 22 May The government now announces dictatorial powers and proposes to mobilise the country's wealth and property and manpower ad lib.[27] Can they have realised at last that a dictatorship is the only way of getting anything done?

---

26 Stretching from Luxembourg to the Swiss frontier, this defensive string of deeply buried concrete forts spaced at 5-kilometre intervals, and separated by casements with machine and anti-tank guns, was intended to deter a direct German assault on France. The Germans in fact advanced through Belgium; when the Line was ordered to cease resistance on 25 June, only one fort had fallen and that owing to the asphyxiation of the occupants.
27 The Bill 'conferring complete power of control over persons and property for the prosecution of the war' was given swift passage through both Houses of Parliament (*The Times*, 23 May).

Thursday 23 May The Germans have at last reached the coast of France. Fighting in the streets of Boulogne this afternoon. That should just about clinch it. The Allies' number is up!

Friday 24 May Sir Oswald Mosley and his leading associates in the British Union of Fascists were arrested last night and put in Brixton jail.[28] Thus is the great democratic sham exposed for what it's worth. In other words our pro-Jewish, pro-communist government knows the game is up and their last mean, vicious, desperate act of revenge before the Germans come here and kick the skunks out, assuming they haven't scuttled to America before that happens, which is much more likely. No action will be taken against the communists of course, especially as we are now slobbering over and pandering to Russia once more. Every conceivable excuse no matter how ludicrous is found for Russia's invasion of Poland and Finland. Russia can do no wrong. Nor can the dear comrades here. But poor Mosley has to pay the price of real patriotism. I'm downright ashamed to be an Englishman today.

Tuesday 28 May Was called up to the staff office this morning to see Scheele, staff manager, and Massey, financial director. Apparently the police for some inexplicable reason had been in enquiring after Mother's political activities. What this has to do with them I can't imagine. Nor apparently could they. However I was cross examined thereon as well as on my own political views about which some malicious tale bearing swine in the firm had obviously been supplying information. Also what I proposed to do when called up. But right from the start they were prejudiced against me and determined not to give me a chance to say a word in my defence. I was accused of not being frank, holding things back and when I did endeavour to be frank I was disbelieved and virtually called a liar. In any case Massey's bullying tone and third degree methods put my back up very soon and I was naturally on my guard. Though not sufficiently to realise they were asking me several questions that they had no right to ask and which I should have refused to answer. However I succeeded in exhausting Massey's patience and was summarily dismissed from his august presence. Whether from the firm or not I don't yet know. I shouldn't like to bet on my remaining much longer anyway. Even if I do, it won't be exactly pleasant for me, but perhaps PR's staff itself won't be there much longer, the way things are going. I sincerely hope not. I register for military service on June 22nd, much sooner than I expected. And today King Leopold of the Belgians surrendered to the Germans against the advice of his government who, of course, want to go on needlessly sacrificing lives

---

28   The government had strengthened Defence Regulation 18B to include the detention of 'members of organisations which have had contact with the enemy, and may be used for purposes prejudicial to nation security' (*The Times*, 24 May). Heap's friend Councillor Sperni was arrested three months later and was in a neighbouring cell to Mosley in Brixton prison.

in a hopeless fight. Oh the howls of self-righteous indignation that rent the air. Traitor! Coward, Scoundrel etc. Yet in spite of all this I carried out my intention of going to the first night of *The Peaceful Inn* at the Duke of York's.

Wednesday 29 May Mother came up to see Massey and Scheele this morning about yesterday's to do. Apparently they were quite amiable and reassuring towards her intimating that the significance of the thing had been exaggerated and that we need worry about it no further. I can only assume that I rubbed them up the wrong way, but then I'm never very adept at adapting myself to different people. I appoint the same attitude to everyone, often alas to my detriment. Went over to The Old Vic in evening.

Sunday 2 June Walked to Marble Arch after tea, took a short turn around the park, observed the newly dug lines of four to five feet deep trenches with the mounds of earth piled neatly alongside – and then walked home again. Got in just in time to hear the doleful 9.0 news mainly about the last withdrawals of the BEF from Belgium.[29]

Tuesday 4 June Big air raid in Paris last night by 250 planes. Dropped 1,000 bombs and killed 254 people and wounded 650. In retaliation the French today bombed Munich. Surely London cannot escape much longer.

Friday 7 June Wholesale sackings going on at PR's; business is almost at a standstill and the old firm is foundering on the rocks. I can't honestly say I'm sorry, their treatment of the staff in general doesn't inspire much sympathy. Pub-crawled with John Bell in the evening, John Hobson being away at Brean Sands for the week. Had a vulgar postcard therefrom the other morning. Why he should go to that lousy dump again I can't imagine. No accounting for taste.

Monday 10 June Italy declared war on the Allies and so come into conflict on the order of Germany today. Now the fat is in the fire.

Tuesday 11 June Italian cafes and shops in Soho and smashed up last night when the police started rounding up Italians for internment.[30] German bakers' shops suffered a similar fate at the beginning of the last war. The childish, loutish and altogether inexcusable behaviour never ceased to appeal to a large section of the English public. The

---

29 The British Expeditionary Force under Lord Gort had been sent to France in September 1939 to support France. Having met fierce opposition from the superior invading German forces, the BEF carried out a fighting withdrawal through Belgium and north-western France until some 338,226 Allied troops were evacuated from the beaches around Dunkirk between 26 May and 3 June. See Dear, *Oxford Companion to the Second World War*, pp. 312–313.
30 'There were anti-Italian demonstrations in parts of Soho. In pitched battles between Greeks and Italians, bottles were thrown and a policeman injured. The windows of several restaurants were smashed' (*The Times*, 11 June).

Part Two

more harmless, guiltless and defenceless the victim, the greater the incentive to vent their spleen on them. Foreigners, alas, haven't such a monopoly of cowardice as our press would have us believe.

Thursday 14 June The Germans entered Paris this morning, the French having withdrawn therefrom to save it being completely ruined. At no time during the last war did they attain such a sweeping measure of success as this. Called on Dr Cutner in evening to see how I stood medically in view of my imminent calling up. Both he and his partner Dr Crawford examined my stomach to see how the operation had healed up and observed that it was still in such a condition as to render one unfit for active service or anything but Grade III or sedentary duties. Finally Dr Crawford, who is in an army medical board and was likely to carry more weight in the matter, wrote me out a certificate to hand in when called up for examination. Exit AH [Anthony Heap] emitting a huge sigh of relief.

Sunday 16 June All the place names have now been removed from station platforms so that unless one is familiar with a station, it is apt to be difficult to discover when one's destination is reached. The object of course is to counteract the possible invasion by paratroopers by making it difficult for them to find their way about. For the same reason all sign posts and other indications of localities have been removed.

Monday 17 June The French Army decided to give up the fight this morning and sued for an armistice from the Germans. Britain, like its government, blandly and stupidly pig-headed to the last, instead of having the sense to do likewise while the country is still intact, carries on the hopeless futile struggle alone against overwhelming odds until we are completely and utterly annihilated. I can see no other possible fate for us now if we carry on the war. It makes me most horribly depressed. False optimism never was a strong rout of mine. Evening at home. Read a book to try and take my mind off things. It didn't quite succeed.

Wednesday 19 June Air raid by 100 planes on East coast area last night. 12 killed and a few more injured, some houses wrecked. A mere prologue. Germany and Italy have settled the conditions on which they'll constitute the French request for an armistice but apparently intend to take their time over arranging for a discussion thereof. Meanwhile the fighting in France continues.

Friday 21 June Hitler, with a superb sense of drama, elects to receive the French envoys and hand them the armistice terms in the very same railway carriage in the Forest of Compiegne where Foch humiliated the German envoys and forced them to accept the French armistice terms on Nov 11, 1918. Fatherland thou art avenged! Met the Johns at the

Horse Shoe in evening and pub-crawled round the northern province of Soho which we have made our own.

Saturday 22 June Went up to the Penton St Labour Exchange[31] after lunch to register for military service in the 1910 class. Consequently had to wait for the next train to Cuffley an hour later and so didn't get to camp till 5.30.

Sunday 23 June France at last agreeing to accept Germany's still un-revealed terms (as if they had any option!) has signed an armistice and now hasten to conclude one with Italy so that hostilities can finally cease. So much for our wonderful ally who swore to accept no 'separate' peace. Presumably the entente will now be somewhat 'un-cordiale.' Met Adam de Hegedus, chatted with him for an hour or so. Or rather he chatted and I listened. He always has such infinitely more interesting things to tell me than I have to tell him. I could listen to him for hours. Home at 9.20 just in time to hear the ever gloomy news on radio.

Monday 24 June The armistice terms at last revealed today involve a complete surrender by the French government, the disbandment of the army, navy and air force, the handing over of all war equipment and the occupation of Northern and Western France. The armistice with Italy signed this evening mainly involves the demilitarisation of all home and colonial border areas. So exit the lion of France, its tail very much between its legs.

Tuesday 25 June Was rudely roused from my midsummer night's dreaming at 1.0 a.m. this morning by the moaning of air raid sirens. Hastily donning slippers, flannels, sports jacket, dressing gown and pocketing such odds and ends as watch, wallet, loose change etc. I made my way down to the underground shelter leading out of the courtyard while Mother went round to the ARP Post under St Pancras Church. In company with some few dozen other residents, sat on wooden bench for three hours. Heard neither bomb explosions nor gunfire. Tried unsuccessfully to doze and felt intensely piqued such a boring and unnecessary waste of good sleep did it seem. At last at 3.55 the all clear signals sounded and we ascended into the dawn. This was the first air raid alarm London had since the first week of the war. The experience was sufficiently rare to be to be novel. A novelty which will I fear soon be worn away by the friction of regularity. Felt a trifle weary at work today as indeed did most people.

Thursday 27 June These are dire days for theatre-goers. The very time, when entertainment is most needed there is none to be had. Or precious little anyway with but ten theatres left open. First nights are

---

31 Barnsbury, Islington, N1.

now a thing of the past. There hasn't been one for three weeks and no new productions whatever are planned. So I must now perforce spend practically every evening doing nought [*sic*] but sitting at home reading as I did again tonight. A pleasurable pastime taken in moderation but apt to get very monotonous if too frequently indulged in.

Friday 28 June Russia marches into Rumania and annexes the province of Bessarabia without a murmur of disapproval from anyone – not even Rumania and certainly not Great Britain. The newspaper leaders barely mention it and those that do, discreetly gloss it over as no concern of ours. Russian aggression apparently never is – only the German variety is made our sole concern. In any case when Russia grabs large slabs of other countries it isn't really aggression at all. Oh dear no! It is just benevolent protection. As if those soulful, stainless high minded communists could do any wrong! Blasphemous thought! Pub-crawled with the Johns in the evening.

Sunday 30 June [*after camping weekend*] Going home in the evening encountered a few militants and some doddering old men with rifles (local defence volunteers) playing at soldiers by stopping everyone on the road at Tyler's Causeway and asking to see their identity card.[32] Fortunately I'd remembered to transfer mine from my wallet to sports jacket pocket yesterday and so duly produced it. Otherwise I'd doubtless have been detained as a suspected German spy.

Tuesday 2 July War Minister Eden announced in the Commons today that all men up to and including 27½ except a few special categories had now been called up for service. This is utter nonsense. Neither Alby nor Alf, who both registered with the 27s on May 25th have even had their medicals yet. Neither of the Johns, both 26 have yet been called up, while there are fellows of 24 and 25 at work still at large. Why, I can't imagine.

Tuesday 9 July Two small sidelights on the war: 1d bus and tube fares raised to 1½d, tea to be rationed at the rate of 2 oz. a week. Walking and coffee drinking should thereby regain their lost popularity. Went up to Southgate in the evening to see the Johns.

Wednesday 10 July It is now estimated that the war is now costing the country £9½ millions a day. Even heavier taxation still threatened in the near future to meet it. A criminal waste of wealth.

Thursday 11 July These are deadly monotonous days in the dull and airless underground dungeon which serves as an office, for there is

---

32 On 14 May the Minister for War, Anthony Eden, had broadcast a call for men between seventeen and sixty-five to volunteer to join the Local Defence Volunteers (renamed the Home Guard on 22 July) to protect coastal areas and important national assets. Eventually 1.5 million men volunteered.

hardly a scrap of work for anyone. One just sits pretending to work but actually merely watching the clock go round. A most depressing and irksome state of affairs.

Thursday 18 July Went to the first night of *Women Aren't Angels*, the new farce for Robertson Hare at the Strand.[33] Suffice it to say that the antics and drolleries of the said old latest pair of clowns have never been more furiously funny. Incidentally this is the first theatre I'd been to for six weeks.

Friday 19 July As equally distressing day as yesterday.[34] Eilleen came up again lunchtime. We went to Regent's Park and I broke down again. The afternoon was dreadful. Decided to get my holiday as soon as possible to get out of the place and also, if possible, get my day off Tuesday as my day off in lieu of Whitsun still due. She may come up for the day then. Couldn't eat my dinner on getting home and, unable to keep it from her any longer, told Mother all about it, absolutely everything. Fortunately she took it well, more than I expected, was reasonably sympathetic despite apprehension as to the consequences and anxious to meet Eilleen. Having 'got it off my chest' felt better and went along to the Horse Shoe and caught the Johns just as they were about to leave at 9.30, went up to the Green Parrot for the first time for many weeks. John H now married an Old Flame, Joan, up there only too anxious to be re-lit.

Monday 22 July Had a violent row with Mother about E after dinner. Was a fatal mistake to tell her anything about it at all. She just won't think of E as anything but a scheming liar, of G[35] as anything but an injured saint or of me as nowt but an errant child. Otherwise she attributes E's love for me to the meanest of motives and continually brings up the subject to try and induce me to give her up. Wouldn't be so bad if based on personal knowledge, but it isn't. Just spiteful malicious conjecture arising from the jealous possessiveness of mother love. As bad as PR's, as if I don't have enough antagonism to put up with there by day without this at home in the evening as well. A hopeless situation. But I stand firm. Even if it means a definite split with Mother, I still won't give up E. Ended the row by slamming out of the place taking a bus up to Parliament Hill, having a good two hour walk over the heath. Soothed my nerves and made me pleasantly tired. I needed that walk.

---

33   Robertson Hare (1891–1979) was a comedy actor who made his name in the Aldwych and Ben Travers farces.
34   The previous day's entry made no mention of any distress or of the previously unmentioned Eilleen, with whom (according to the 1940 Retrospect) Heap had been having an affair since 'the Spring'.
35   Eilleen's husband, Gaston, the father of her children.

Part Two

Tuesday 23 July Had a day off in lieu of Whit Monday still due to me. Spent it with E who came up for the day, ostensibly to look for a job. At the last moment G decided to come with her but after sending me a warning telegram changing the rendezvous[36] she managed to shake him off at King's Cross and make her way to Praed St where I met her at 1.0. Had a couple of drinks and some sandwiches in a pub then took a bus to Kew Gardens, thus fulfilling one of our early dreams. For on our first lunchtime walks we had often longed to go to Kew Gardens for the afternoon. Instead of back to PR's dungeon. It was glorious there especially when after a dull morning the sky at last cleared and the sun came out. Had tea in the gardens and came back to the West End and going up to Hampstead for the evening. It was all perfect, a lovely day we shall all treasure in our memory.

Wednesday 24 July Back to the dungeon and the inevitable sense of gloom and desolation which the place now casts over me. Chief effect of yesterday's budget: Income Tax up 1/- to 8/8, cigarettes up 1d to 1/6 for 20, beer up 1d a pint, cinema prices to be raised soon and purchase tax will raise the prices of clothes and various semi-luxuries. And that's how we're winning the war – if we only knew it!

24 July   72 Handside Lane

The worst happened – after our perfect day, Gaston was waiting for me last night, and I was put through the third degree stunt, only a little worse than usual until I told him I would scream the place down if he touched me. Even then he wouldn't let me go to sleep, but kept pulling the bed clothes off me and demanding to know where the rubber cap was, who had I been out with, where had I gone etc, until I was nearly as angry as he is!

I am going to Hitchin tomorrow. If I can sneak out and see about a separation. I can't hold out much longer.

I was offered a job out at De Havilland's today £2.5.0 but I want something better than that so shall go on trying a bit longer. Tony, darling, don't think badly of me but I'm going to cry off on Friday – I can't come. I'm literally scared stiff of Gaston. If you can forgive me, will you try and come down one evening next week?

My love is yours always, and may Kew live forever,

Ever yours, Eilleen

---

36   See p. xxiv.

1940

Thursday 25 July Just the reverse of yesterday. A disturbing letter from E ref the aftermath of Tuesday[37] and having nothing to do in the dungeon all day but ponder over it served to set me back in the depths of despair and despondency again. And then, to crown it, I must needs go to the first night of a horrible and puerile little bedroom farce called *High Temperature* at the Duke of York's. It was agonising. Incredible that some people can laugh at such stuff. Fortunately I missed most of the last act phoning E at a friend's. She'd landed a job up in Welwyn today, starting next week and was going to see a solicitor about a separation or divorce tomorrow but too scared of G to see me tomorrow night. Have got to watch our steps very carefully now.

Friday 26 July Was given the sack with a week's wages in lieu of notice, leaving tomorrow. This together with my wages for this week and two weeks holiday which I was due to start tomorrow leave me with a month's money in hand. Usual reason given – reduction in staff. Thus ends my 13½ years at PR's. Wasn't at all downcast or even resentful. Quite the reverse, I dreaded going back after my holiday. The place has been quite intolerable for me since E left. Best thing that could have happened really. Now I'm free to do something. In fact I've damned well got to do something that I should have done many years ago if I'd more gumption and go to it. If only they'd hurry up with that damned 'medical' then I'd know where I stood. I managed to get up to Welwyn Garden City in evening to see E. Went to her friend's house and talked over the situation with them. We decided that she'd have to go ahead with separation proceedings at once, leave G as quickly as possible and take the children with her and live at her parents. Seemed the best solution of the problem for the time being, albeit a temporary and unsatisfactory one. There being no means of getting back from there after about 9 p.m. had to stay the night at a guest house nearby. B & B 5/6d. Didn't enjoy it at all.

Friday 27 July Caught the 7.20 up in the morning and got back in time to change before going to PR's for the last time. Drew my last money, got my insurance cards, cleared my desk, bid my last farewells and shook the lousy dust off my feet for ever. Had lunch on my own over at the Commercial after weathering a hail-storm getting there. Walked to Regent's Park and back in the afternoon breathing in the very fresh air and dozing in the sunshine. Spent the evening with John in the Rising Sun. After two heavy skirmishes this week over E, am now reconciled with Mother – pro tem at any rate. I think she'll see reason and realise she's wrong in time in spite of her highly developed possessive maternal instinct.

---

37   See above.

Part Two

Monday 29 July Up late and to the Labour Exchange to find out if by any chance my not having to be called up for a medical was due to my being in a reserved occupation. Discovered this was so. So in the afternoon went to Laurie's, the leading City employment agency to see if they could get me anything. Told me that it was difficult now at my age but in view of my ACIS degree, they might be able to do something for me. So came away with form to fill in and return. Rather anxious about E. Was to have started work today but when I phoned the firm in afternoon was told that no one of that name worked there at all. Thinking something must have happened, tried to phone the friend in the evening but got no reply each time. A very disturbing day. P.S. Learned on phoning next day that she had started work but under maiden name.

Tuesday 30 July Regent's Park in afternoon and up to the Garden City in evening and spent the night with E. An ecstatic and very sleepless night. Discreetly left at 5.0 and wandered in Shepherd's Wood[38] till it was time to get the train back to town. L'amour impropre!

Wednesday 31 July Spent about two hours at the Penton St Labour Exchange registering for work. An involved and exasperating business involving lengthy waits, being passed from one place to another, giving the same details to different clerks and then getting no real satisfaction in the end. Precious few clerical jobs at this exchange, a vast dingy depressing place filled with labourers, mostly elderly. Wrong district. Will have to get transferred to the Snow Hill one which feeds the City. In my case I don't hold much hope of getting a suitable job through the exchange at all. This first experience of their workings didn't impress me favourably at all. Heart-breaking places. Put in an hour in Regent's Park before tea and to please Mother an hour in the public gallery of the Borough Council meeting over at the Town Hall after it.[39] Very dull apart from some occasional fireworks from Sperni. The normal manifestations of the petty jealousies and hatreds.

No 72, W G C
[undated] Wednesday

Dear Grumble Guts,

Thank you for a very long letter! You really are a very tiring person –what would it benefit either of us if you came down? I should lose my remotest hope of a separation – plus both the

---

38   Probably Sheppardspark Wood, a tract of ancient woodland to the north-west of Welwyn.
39   St Pancras Town Hall, Judd Street, had opened in 1936 and was just 300 yards from the Heaps' flat.

1940

kids – which you know I value very much – also I really can't hear you speak when you write a letter.

Meantime, regain your appetite, get more sleep.

I wired Donald[40] this morning asking him to write today and ask me over for Sunday evening, so all being well I should see you on Friday, catching the 7 pm train as you suggest.

I am cleaning No 72 at the weekend. I don't want to go before the summons is served on Gaston otherwise he will probably spend Friday following me around.

Tony darling, you are an awful clot and everything is difficult here, but, remember, I haven't broken faith with you and I do not think I shall in the remaining few days left.

After doing what I have done I feel almost entitled to resent you saying I shall be eating out of his hand – but no doubt lack of sleep is having its effect.

Please don't say any more beastly things, otherwise, I might crack up and really do as you suggest. It is not easy living under this strain, at this end either.

Hoping to see you in a better temper on Friday,

Yours, Eilleen

[*Acc. 2243/14 opens here.*]

Thursday 1 August A very typical day in my present precarious existence – up at 10.30. After breakfast in bed, to the Snow Hill Exchange. Vastly superior to the Barnsbury chamber of horrors. Less crowded, less depressing and much more business-like. They do at least take an intelligent interest in one, even though they had nothing to offer at present. I was advised to get a form of application for government work from Barnsbury and after lunch over at the Commercial, this I duly did. The rest of the afternoon I spent reclining on Parliament Hill enjoying the delights of warm sunshine and fresh breezes. Exquisite day. To the Apollo in evening.

Friday 2 August To Snow Hill, not so much in the hope of getting anything as to keep them familiar with my requirements, which alas was all I succeeded in doing. To Barnsbury to lodge my application for government work. To the CIS to fill in an application form there and be put on the appointments register. To the Horse Shoe for a drink with the Johns before going to meet E and blissfully round off the day up at Hampstead again. And so to bed at 1.0.

Monday 5 August Today's bank holiday was cancelled weeks ago on account of the war. Occupied the morning with a fruitless journey to

---

40 An unidentified but presumably obliging friend.

Part Two

Snow Hill and an expedition to Gibbs, my usual barber in Wells St. for a haircut.[41] Long waits at both. Went up to Hampstead with Mother in afternoon. The fair in full swing with people everywhere. Found as quiet and uncrowded spot as possible and dozed in deckchairs. Stayed in evening reading book, until about 9.0 when I received another disquieting letter from E. Whereupon went out for a long walk to ruminate upon it, came back and wrote an equally disquieting letter in reply. Peace of mind is practically an own-sustained state with me these days.

Tuesday 6 August Got so tired of waiting at the end of a long immobile queue to enquire about vacancies at the Snow Hill this morning that I came away without seeing anyone. In any case they've never got anything for me. My being of military age and lack of any really useful experience are dead against me. A hopeless business.

Thursday 8 August Was summoned to Barnsbury Rd this morning about my application for government work. All they wanted me for was to know how I stood regarding liability for military service. I told them so far as I know and that was that. In evening for lack of anything better to do and to escape the ennui and boredom of sitting at home, I went to the Stoll.[42] It passed the evening away agreeably enough.

Monday 12 August The beginning of yet another wearisome week of aimless time-killing. This incessant worry and mental strain isn't doing me any good at all. Something's got to happen soon or I'll be cracking up completely. Didn't go out till the afternoon and then went up to Hampstead for two or three hours. That place is a godsend.

Monday [*typed, undated*]   23 Beechfield Rd, WGC

Tony dear,

I can't manage the early part of the week to get to London, but I'm still trying to arrange something for the latter part of the week. If I am still not able to arrange anything, come and see me on Saturday at the usual time, and I will ask Bella to take the nippers over Old Welwyn for the afternoon.

It's a glorious day here, and it would be lovely in the woods again, and it stays put until Saturday.

Everything is still very depressing, but the only ray of luke-warm sunshine at the moment is the fact that Mrs Stone has suggested that if I am unable to get anything fixed up by the end

---

41 Wells Street, W1, north of Oxford Street, had been on Heap's daily walking route to and from Peter Robinson's.
42 In Portugal Street, off Kingsway, WC2; renamed the Royalty in 1960, and rebuilt as the Peacock Theatre in 1996.

of a fortnight, I can still stay with her, shifting her lads around a bit. It will be pretty bloody, but anything is better than going back to No 72.

Yours rather depressed, but bearing up, Eilleen

Tuesday 13 August Waited at Snow Hill for an hour this morning to enquire after vacancies and then gave it up as a bad job. Went up to Southgate in evening and saw the Johns. From the Rising Sun walked over to Broomfield Park, watched some 'broomstick army'[43] manoeuvres for a few minutes.

[*letter in pencil, undated and may well be earlier*]

72 Handside Lane

Tuesday

Tony darling,

The official came again on Saturday evening and still pressed for a reconciliation, and as I was still adamant about it, he said leave it until Thursday and write to him my decision. Today I received a letter from Hatfield advising me to get in touch with a Solicitor to have facts presented correctly. This I did at 1.30 am today and he is very certain that I have not got a leg to stand on and that Hatfield will not grant a separation on the evidence that I have. He knows Gaston and during our conversation referred to him as being a bit queer!
 However he is coming to see Gaston tonight in an endeavour to get him to sign an agreement to separate, giving me the custody of the children. The Solicitor said there is no power in the law to make me live with Gaston, or to make me return to him if I do leave him but the insuperable obstacle is of course the nippers.
 If Gaston refuses to sign and refuses to give up his children, I don't know what course to follow. I am beginning to feel rather a little hunted animal. I have the hounds of fate at my heels and the three [options] open to me – living with you and giving up the nippers which will mean a large slice of my heart gone. Living with Gaston, whom I hate and keeping the nippers – by losing you my dear – if only a light would shine on me like St Paul, but of course it won't.
 Tony darling, I am very unhappy and I think very selfish – I want you and the children and it seems that I can't have both.

43 The Home Guard.

Part Two

Without being prejudiced by your own feelings, write to me and try to clear the air. I feel in such a hopeless jumble and so think tonight I shall have a damn good cry.

Yours very miserably, Eilleen xxxxx

[*in ink*] PS Send to Champ at Brockswood Lane

[*Another brief undated letter from Eilleen includes* 'It looks as if it will be Goodbye until after the 16th – but I will see if I can find a way.']

Wednesday 14 August Snow Hill in morning, Barnsbury Rd and Regent's Park in afternoon. Heard from E to the effect that the separation proceedings have broken down, her solicitor advising her that she hasn't a leg to stand on as regards sufficient evidence. So she now has no alternative but to take the law into her own hands and leave G forthwith and have the children looked after elsewhere. About time too. What's been transpiring up in Welwyn lately has been causing me no end of worry and anxiety. The sooner she gets away from that irksome fiend the better.

Thursday 15 August Left my Mack behind in the theatre last night. Remembered it when I'd walked as far as Cambridge Circus and dashed back. Went into the completely empty theatre, retrieved it and came out without seeing a soul. Regent's Park and P.H. [Primrose Hill] in morning and Hampstead in afternoon. In evening went to the Dominion. Had just got in when, at 7.20 an air raid warning was announced. The place was packed but as far as I could see no more than about two dozen people left the theatre. The programme continued and, after about twenty minutes, the all clear was announced. You could 'feel' the tension relax.

Friday 16 August Two more air raid warnings today. The first at 12.20 when I was in the middle of Regent's Park. Made over towards Baker St and after a few minutes came across a shelter just by the lake. Went down it and stayed there until the all clear signal went off half an hour later. The second alarm sounded at 5.0. I'd just got back from Hampstead and was about to have tea. Went down to the shelter but nothing happened, the enemy again got tired of it after twenty minutes and [I] came up for a late tea. The all clear went off at 6.5. I'd just had a shampoo and was about to have a tub down which I forthwith did. Met E in evening. Has now moved in with her friend R, the maid looking after the children at her own house. Went to the Horse Shoe first, spent half an hour or so there with the Johns then up to Hampstead. Wanted her to come camping with us for the weekend but she wouldn't risk it. This rather upset me and caused me to behave somewhat erratically for the rest of the evening. Nerve strain, I suppose.

Saturday 17 August Took a coach up to W.G.C. and spent the afternoon with E. Walked up round Welwyn and Digswell, a lovely day and a lovely walk. And needless to add we had a lovely rest. Completely dispelled the depression which had settled on me last night. Back by coach again. Had to stand nearly all the way but made the journey surprisingly quickly – 52 minutes.

Monday 19 August Up to the Barnsbury Rd Exchange in morning to claim unemployment benefit, this being my first actual week on the dole. Only took me about an hour which is comparatively quick for a labour exchange. I now have to 'sign on' Wednesday and Friday afternoons. How I loathe having to go up to that revolting place. Every one wearing a cap and choker and the smell of unwashed bodies and dirty clothes savouring strongly of a second-class public baths. Feeling more depressed than ever at not having anything to do and little prospect of getting anything to do, pottered about at home in afternoon. Made some cigarettes on my patent Rizla machine – an economy device whereby I can make cigarettes at the rate of 10 for 5d instead of the current rate. Wrote letters to (a) the exchange querying the likelihood of my application for government work and (b) The Town Clerk over at the [St Pancras] Town Hall as to possibility of getting a job in the council offices.

Tuesday 20 August Letter writing most of the morning. Another evening at home reading. Am trying by this means to economise a little for I've been spending far more than I can afford in my present circumstances lately. But it's hard going and makes one so despondent and dejected that I doubt if it's really worth it, especially on a dismal wet evening like this one. I seem completely enveloped in gloom.

Wednesday 21 August After signing on at the Exchange this afternoon, was offered a job in a builder's office at 70/- a week plus overtime whereby one could bring it up to £5 a week. But it was in the Midlands (exact place unspecified) which I was given the option of doing without prejudice having no experience of building trade. I refuse to leave London unless I'm absolutely compelled to. Saw E in the evening. Came down late and went back late. Went up to Hampstead as usual. Very cold and squally, although fortunately the rain kept off.

Thursday 22 August Had a letter from the Laurie's asking me to call at Taylor Walker's brewery in Limehouse about a vacancy there. So went along there in the morning and found it tucked away in the middle of a network of greying slum streets. Saw the chief accountant, a lean, elderly, dour looking man, who somehow gave me the impression that he never drank a glass of beer in his life. The job was that of an ordinary sales ledger clerk, not reserved, therefore no use whatever to me, and vice-versa I was of no use to them. So we both cursed Laurie's after wasting our time and I came away at least thankful that I wasn't going to work in a foul, dismal, god-forsaken hole like Limehouse. Heaven preserve me from the East End.

Friday 23 August After being woken by the drone of a plane hovering about overhead somewhere, the sound of distant gunfire. The air raid alarms went off at 3.30 a.m. this morning. Threw on some clothes and went down to shelter. But nothing further happened and at 3.55 the all clear sounded, whereupon we went up and resumed our slumbers. It subsequently transpired that most of the damage was done at Edmonton where a cinema and a few shops and houses were wrecked.[44]

Saturday 24 August Three air raids today, the first from 8.20 till 9.10 [a.m.] during which I went down to the shelter. The second alarm sounded at 3.40 [p.m.] when I was up at Hampstead. Made down to a street surface shelter near the Bull and Bush[45] but got tired with hanging about in there after half an hour or so and walked back over Parliament Hill and got a bus home. Though hundreds of people continued to sit or walk unconcernedly over Hampstead, the streets were deserted. The all clear went off at 4.45 as we passed through Kentish Town. The third occurred late in the evening. I had been with John Hobson up to the Odeon in Upper St, Islington. Went onto the Green Parrot where we saw Ron and arranged to go down for a walk tomorrow. Left about 11.15 and was walking home when the sirens went off. Speedily covered the rest of the route but instead of going down to the shelter, hung about in the courtyard at the entrance of it. Everyone said there had been rounds of gunfire and an explosion a few minutes before the alarm was given but I hadn't heard a thing. After some time a plane could be heard overhead and then the whining noise of a bomb dropping. Soon the sky was lit up with the reflection of a blaze from a fire in an easterly direction. One or two of us went up to the roof to see it and what a fascinating sight it was too. About two miles away over in the City somewhere the flames were soaring up well above the skyline of the house tops. Must have been a big factory or a warehouse full of inflammable stuff. Fire engines were making their way towards it from all directions. The sound of planes overhead returning, we reluctantly descended but nothing further happened till the all clear was given out at 1.20.[46]

---

44   The Luftwaffe were concentrating their attack on airfields to destroy RAF fighters. The first significant attack near central London was that on Croydon airfield on 15 August, when 62 people died and 131 were seriously injured. The raid on Edmonton destroyed the Alcazar cinema and several properties on Fore Street, but there were no fatalities. See Robin Woolven, 'The Middlesex Bomb Damage Maps 1940–1945', *London Topographical Review*, vol. 30 (2010), pp. 143–144.
45   In North End Way, NW3.
46   The main German targets on 24 August were Fighter Command airfields such as North Weald, but many parts of southern and western England were also raided. Some 'indiscriminate' raiding on the City (Fore Street, EC2) and other areas by a single raider

1940

Sunday 25 August After a fierce and really quite unnecessary row with Mother over E, got to Waterloo late this morning to meet John H and missed the train to Leatherhead we intended to catch. Got the 11.12 to Oxshott instead and walked down to Bookham from there to Epsom, though every pub and every street in every town down this way is packed with Canadian soldiers who, with their cocksure arrogance, tend to make themselves a nuisance and spoil every place they frequent.[47]

Monday 26 August Had a further raid alarm last night though only of short duration – went down to the shelter and read my book. And even after the all clear sounded enemy raiders could still be heard overhead. Most people actually started going down to the shelter again but no further alarm was given. It subsequently transpired that it was this, post-alarm raid that did most of the damage somewhere in the suburbs. The big fire on Saturday night was in a big warehouse in Fore St. Two more today. The first in the afternoon and like its immediate predecessor comparatively brief. The second alarm was of a record duration – for this war at any rate – and I should imaging for the last as well, over six hours. After staying in reading till 9.0 I had gone out for a stroll round and was walking back when at 9.30 the sirens went off. As a matter of fact I was in exactly the same spot in Tavistock Place as I was last Saturday night when the alarm caught me walking home. So made home at the double, dashed up and got my valuables (wallet and bankbook chiefly) and went down to the shelter. And what a hell of a time it was! Occasionally a plane could be heard passing over and searchlights swept the sky but none seemed able to find anything, so much cloud was there about, coming over in small relays at regular intervals, not with the object of doing much damage (for no bombs could be heard dropping or fires discernible), but rather of keeping the population up all night and adversely affecting its morale and staying power through lack of sleep.

Tuesday 27 August Went up again with E in the evening and was over the heath when the air raid alarm went off at exactly the same time as last night – 9.30. Walked across to the bus terminus in the hope of getting a trolley bus back but none were running so we had to walk all the way back home to King's Cross. Fortunately we made it in comfortable time for E to get the train home, for they were still running, air raid or no air raid. The all clear went at 11.50 soon after I'd come in. A mildly adventurous and exciting evening even though all we saw or heard of the raid were a few searchlights and the occasional drone of a plane flying over – but we could have done without that walk!

killed nine Londoners. Churchill authorised RAF Bomber Command to retaliate by raiding Berlin the following night.

47   The three Canadian infantry brigades that had arrived in the UK by December 1939 were based in the greater Aldershot area for training. There was also a Canadian Red Cross hospital at Taplow, Berkshire.

Part Two

Wednesday 28 August Had replies to job application letters from both the Borough Council and the BBC this morning. Went over to the Town Hall straight away and saw McKeer.[48] The departments he sent me to see were expecting one or two vacancies during the next week or so and thought they'd be able to fit me into one of them provided the reserved age for council employees isn't raised again above 30. And fortunately they didn't ask me too many searching and awkward questions as to my experience and seemed to think I'd be very suitable for the job. I only hope I get it as it would suit me down to the ground, even if the salary isn't more than I was getting at PR's. Phoned the BBC after that and made an appointment for tomorrow at 4.0. Had to pay one of my twice weekly visits to the Exchange in afternoon. Was sent round to the vacancies section after signing where they answered verbally my five days old letter about the government work application. Just told me I was 'in the pool' whatever that might be, and would have to wait till 'something turned up.' Offered me a temporary job dealing with Income Tax forms. I politely declined and went to Regent's Park to recline on the grass for the rest of the afternoon. About 10.30 tonight's alert was a record, exactly seven hours. Stuck it down there till 3.30 when I came up for something to eat. London had lost another night's sleep.

Thursday 29 August These all-night raids are apt to disorganise meal times considerably. Today for instance, laying in as late as possible, I had breakfast in bed at 11.30. This was followed by lunch at 2.30 though I hadn't really sufficient appetite for it by then. Finally a late 'high tea' at 6.45. Supper must now perforce be a matter of sandwiches which one can take down to eat in the shelter, which I am still trying to reconcile myself to for long periods. It's extremely difficult. Although it has an immediate effect of making one feel suddenly and strangely drowsy, I can never get comfortable enough either to concentrate on a book or doze off to sleep. I therefore keep wandering out to the steps to glean anything to be heard or seen and there hardly ever is. Until I get tired of standing about and begin to feel cold, for it is damned chilly there nights – then go back for a further spell of uncomfortable bench squatting. Such is life in August 1940. Nothing came of the BBC application. Went along for my interview this afternoon at some office of theirs in Bolsover St but as soon as they told me I'd have to be prepared to go to their evacuated [base] in the Midlands if they could give me anything,[49] I had to frankly admit that I wasn't prepared to leave London and let the matter lapse. So the Town Hall is now my sole hope of salvation. Walking through Berwick St (the land of the

---

48 W. F. McKeer, Principal Assistant in the Town Clerk's office, was made Chief Clerk in December 1940 (St Pancras Council Minutes, 1941, p. 18).
49 Much of the BBC moved to several sites away from London, particularly Wood Norton Hall near Evesham, Worcestershire.

waving palms) this afternoon I noticed that practically every shop was to let.[50] These were all formerly chiefly Jewish shops into which they cajoled customers from the pavements. So the war's put pay [*sic*] to that little racket – one of the very few beneficial results therefrom. The Fritzes have disappointed us tonight, up to the moment of writing anyway, which is 11.30. For the first time in a week I go to bed at normal time.

Friday 30 August Nothing happened all night but they made up for it today. We've had three alarms so far – at 11.45 when I'd just got up and started to shave – 3.15 when I was in the Exchange about to draw my first week's 'dole' and 4.35 when I was in Regent's Park. They lasted ¾, ¼ and 1¼ hours respectively. On each occasion I made for the nearest shelter, and stayed there till the all clear. I had met the Johns at the Horse Shoe at 8.30, had one there and we were just about to go over to the Sussex when at 9.10 the sirens went off for the fourth time today. They decided to go up to the Parrot but, not relishing that, I walked as far as the door with them and then carried on home. Planes seemed to be overhead all the way with searchlights from all directions trying to pick them out. I hadn't intended going up to the Parrot in any case. I'm tired of the artificiality and neurotic gaiety so prevalent these days. A few silly little shop girls and air force boys monopolise the place and turn it into a kindergarten. During a raid with everyone showing how devil-may-care and light hearted they can be it could be a damned sight worse. The raid turned out to be another all-night affair. Stayed down the shelter most of the time, lying flat on a form with a cushion for pillow, trying unsuccessfully to sleep.

Saturday 31 August Six raids today, the third just after 10 which lasted an hour. I had had an early lunch during one of the intervals and was in a train just leaving King's Cross for Welwyn Garden City to spend the afternoon with E when it started. Proceeded very slowly and cautiously, got in half an hour late at 2.10. hadn't heard the all clear go ten minutes before. Every man in the train was trying to sleep. No wonder! Walked through the woods up to Digswell and had tea in the garden of Trust House near Welwyn station. Then round to Old Welwyn to collect the kids from the maid who can no longer keep them there and take them down to one of E's mates in W.G.C. who has agreed to have them for the next fortnight provided E sleeps there with them every night, such a short duration and then some recurring problem of what to do with the kids will crop up again. The only solution seems to be for E to get an unfurnished flat, take some furniture and have them with her there. But it will be extremely difficult to do that on £20 a week and keep the maid too even if G lets her have sufficient furniture. We sat gloomily

50   Berwick Street, W1, was a largely Jewish market: see Judith R. Walkowitz, *Nights Out: Life in Cosmopolitan London* (New Haven, CT and London: Yale University Press, 2012), ch. 5.

discussing these difficulties over tea and bread and cheese after the kids had been put to bed – for the maid being away for the night we had the place to ourselves – until past 8.0 when I had to dash off to catch the 8.27 back to town. I needn't have dashed for it came in fifteen minutes late – due no doubt to the raid alarm which had prevailed from 6.0 till 7.20. People now quite reluctant to leave the shelter having settled down there for the night.

Sunday 1 September Had just settled down in bed last night when the confounded siren went off again – the seventh time in twenty four hours. This was just before 1.0. The all clear was given at 4.0. Three hours lying flat on a form in the shelter. Hell! I was up in Hampstead during the second one, never seem to go up there now without alarm going off while I'm on the heath. I walked back over Parliament Hill and caught a bus and, sure enough, the all clear sounded as we went through Kentish Town – an exact repetition of my experience of last Saturday. Ken Wood is still closed, the bomb hasn't gone off yet. It surely never will now. Not even the longest delayed action bomb could explode after a week. Apart from the perpetual raid alarms, I dare say the bulk of the population are spending the day trying to make up for lost sleep throughout the week.

Monday 2 September An alarm just after 3.0 this morning. The next at 4.35 [p.m.] when I was up at Hampstead again. Two separate plane formations of about a dozen each passed right overhead, coming from the north and passing straight over London, one about an hour after the other. As they dropped no bombs and weren't intercepted I presume they were our own planes, probably from Hendon. On the top of Parliament Hill were about a hundred people sitting in rows of deck chairs arranged like an open air auditorium facing London. An admirable vantage point to watch any air battles or bomb dropping which might occur over the town. But none too safe from falling shrapnel or machine gunning. The all clear went just as I got home at 5.50. Night alarm duly went off at 10.30. Lasted till 3.0. Down in the shelter the whole time.

Thursday 5 September The alarms go off three times a day with so much regularity that they hardly seem worth mentioning. They have become part of our daily lives. Waited for today's first (10.0 to 10.55) to blow over before going to Regent's Park for the morning. Another scorching hot day. Was delightful laying in the shade of a tree on Primrose Hill and enjoying the gentle breeze which wafted over. Sat on Parliament Hill reading book in afternoon. Too hot for walking. An alarm sounded as soon as I got there just after 3.0 and last till 4.30 when I came home. Heard an occasional plane or two pass over but for the most part I forgot all about it, so absorbed was I in my book. As happened last night, I'd just got home and had supper when the evening alarm went off at 9.20. Stayed down in the shelter till about 1.0 when I got sick of it so, all being quiet, came up for a lay on the bed in my clothes instead. Dozed off in fits and starts till 4.50 when the all clear sounded at last, making a record 7½ hours.

Friday 6 September Only twenty five minutes after the all clear at 4.50 this morning the damned alarm sounded again just to add a fourth half hour and make it a round figure of eight. I was greeted by the siren on rising at 10.0 this morning. At first I took it as a warning then realised it was the all clear. I hadn't heard it go off over an hour before. I've rarely slept as soundly as that before. Stayed in evening reading. The alarm went at 8.55 just as I was starting on my supper. Waited till I'd finished it before going down to the shelter. A couple of flares were seen above King's Cross station and two local [barrage] balloons set on fire but didn't hear bombs dropped anywhere near, all clear at 11.15, thankfully to bed but, alas, with small hopes of an undisturbed night.

Saturday 7 September My apprehensions last night were only too soon realised, for the alarm was off again only twenty minutes later at 11.0, all clear at 1.0. Still, they did give us a good rest after that. No alarm today until 6.0 p.m. lasted half an hour. Went up to Welwyn Garden City and spent the afternoon and evening with E. Walked through the woods to Digswell, had tea at a Trust House and back through the woods to the Garden City and back with her to her sister's place where she's still abiding with the kids. Came home on the 8.27. At Hatfield a warning was given out and the train lights turned off, there being no blinds in the compartment. A little further on saw the blaze of a big fire lighting up the sky in the direction of London. Didn't realise it was as far away as the centre of London till the train got nearer, and then the big dimensions and wide extent of the fire became more apparent. As soon as we got into King's Cross I dashed round home up to the roof to get a good view. It was over in the City in exactly the same direction as the last big blaze a fortnight ago and, I should imagine, about the same distance away. Some more big warehouses probably. Rumour has it that St Katherine's and the Surrey Commercial docks were the chief seat of the conflagration but I await more official confirmation before believing it. I went up on the roof again three hours later. The fires were still burning just as fiercely and seem to have spread over a wider area. A further big one had started on the south somewhere. Bombs could be heard dropping continually some near, some far off. Undoubtedly the worst raid central London has had so far this war. The all clear didn't go off till 4.45 – a new record 8¼ hours.[51]

51 This was 'Black Saturday', the opening of the predicted 'Blitz' on London with heavy raids on Becton Gas Works and the London Docks. Unless required to amplify Heap's narrative, individual raids will not be noted. Readers are referred to the standard works for raid and damage details, particularly the well-illustrated Winston G. Ramsey, *The Blitz Then and Now*, 3 vols (London: Battle of Britain Prints International, 1987–1990). The degree of damage

Sunday 8 September Rumour was right, for once. Most of the fires were along the docks and Thames-side warehouses and were apparently started by the early evening raid.[52] Five hundred bombers took part in the raid and so far it is estimated that last night's casualties amount to four hundred dead and three times that number injured. Several casualties occurred on Friday night when bombs were dropped on the Elephant and Castle district after the all clear had been given. A store and a variety theatre were hit during the second raid last night but I don't know where they were yet. Today's follow-up came at 12.20 [p.m.] and lasted till 1.20. The evening alarm went at 8.0 as I got home. Gets earlier every night. Seeing a glow in the sky, I went up to the roof as soon as it was dark. A big blaze still going on in the direction of the City. Whether it was last night's still going on or whether it was a fresh blaze I'm not sure. I should hardly think the dock fires could have kept burning all the time however big they were. In any case even if they were so, fresh fires had obviously been started in other directions – one particularly big one over towards the Angel way. Didn't stay there long for planes were passing overhead constantly. It was a particularly hectic night with guns firing and bombs dropping in the immediate vicinity with characteristic frequency. Apart for dashing up for a few moments to get some supper, I stayed down the shelter the whole time. The lights went out about 4.0 – turned off at the main – but came on again shortly before the all clear at 5.30. Yet another record – 9½ hours.

Monday 9 September Terrific havoc caused in Central London by last night's raid. Three hospitals and two museums hit, any number of fires caused, buildings galore knocked down and a large number of time bombs scattered about. I heard of all sorts of places near us that were supposed to have been bombed but on walking round it was the usual pack of false rumours. With one exception, Harrington Square where we used to live at No 20 and there something had definitely happened. It was difficult to see the full extent of the damage for the three sides of it including Hampstead Road and Lidlington Place were roped off and buses diverted around Mornington Crescent. I could see however

---

    suffered by individual properties across the London Administrative County is recorded on the originally hand-coloured maps reproduced in Ann Saunders (ed.), *The London County Council Bomb Damage Maps 1939–1945*, with introduction by Robin Woolven (London: London Topographical Society, 2005), and Laurence Ward, *The London County Council Bomb Damage Maps, 1939–1945* (London: Thames & Hudson, 2015).

52 In this early phase of the Blitz, the German raids were on specific and easily identified targets such as riverside docks and (Becton) gas works. Once the defensive forces were strengthened, the bombers were forced to bomb from much higher altitudes, accuracy suffered, attacking individual targets was less easy and, without specific targets, attacks became 'terror raids' as the bombs were released on general areas rather than pin-point targets. The impression that hospitals, schools and churches were specific targets was encouraged by the Ministry of Information, who approved photographs of damage to such targets for release to home and foreign media. Very few photographs showing damage to identifiable targets were seen in the press within a month of those attacks.

that two houses on the north side of the square a few doors away from No 20 had been completely demolished. A bomb had dropped in the roadway and blown a bus up against them. The bus was still there standing lengthways against the ruins. Furthermore the roofs had been blown off two houses on the corner of Lidlington Place and thirteen houses in Eversholt St which backs on the damaged side of the square. And of course many windows in the other houses and even the Carreras factory were broken by the blast.[53] Most of the square's inhabitants had been down the shelter escaped injury but one or two people had been killed and they were still trying to get out someone buried in the basement under the debris. A terrible to do. The volume of gas in our stove very slight today. Presumably some of the borough's supply is being transferred to other districts where the mains have been hit.

Standing down in the passage during a tea time raid, I heard that Tussaud's Cinema had caught a packet last night so, as soon as the all clear went at 6.25, I dashed along to see. And by gosh it had too. Only the front of it in Marylebone Rd and the proscenium were left standing. The rest was completely demolished as were some buildings behind it as well. The wall of Chiltern Court was badly damaged and not a single window in any building in the vicinity remained intact. Huge crowds thronged along Marylebone Rd to see the ruins. It was one of the sights of London today. Alarm at 8.35, went round to St Pancras Church crypt with Mother but didn't like it there much so came home and went down to our shelter. Not so hectic as last night. Less gunfire and fewer explosions could be heard. But several big fires were started, which I observed from the roof. All clear at 5.40. Bed at 6.0.

Tuesday 10 September Spent the entire afternoon going round sightseeing in the raid devastation areas, though we didn't realise it, they struck much nearer home last night. Doubtless they were trying to hit the powerful Foundling searchlight, for most of the damage was done around it.[54] A bad mess has been made of some houses and a pub in Argyle St which is scarcely a stone's throw from us, and they are still trying to extricate bodies from the ruins this afternoon. Two houses comprising a nurses' hostel in Mecklenburg Square had been knocked down, craters were burning in Guilford St and some damage had been done to the Children's Homeopathic Hospital in Gt Ormond St. From there I went further afield to see some more of the havoc wrought by Sunday night's raid, in which 284 were killed and some

---

53 The Carreras factory, also known as the Arcadia cigarette factory, lay along the western side of Harrington Square. It had two bronze cats outside the main door, 'Black Cat' being a popular Carreras brand.
54 On Coram's Fields, Brunswick Square, WC1.

1,400 injured. Holborn was easily the worst of the lot.[55] Most of the centre of it between Chancery Lane and Red Lion St was laid waste, some buildings partly damaged, others completely demolished by both explosives and fire. Our old haunt, the Robin Hood was among the latter. Whether [the landlord] Frank and his family escaped I don't know. They wouldn't have stood much chance if they'd been anywhere on the premises, even in the cellars. In Neal St, Covent Garden, just behind one of Odham's new buildings, a block of tenement flats had been brought down. The occupiers – at least those still living – were being accommodated in the Shaftesbury Hotel. All over London today were lorries full of homeless families being transported to temporary accommodation. Then to the City where several fires had been caused in the vicinity of St Paul's and the Guildhall. Couldn't see much here however as most of the damage had occurred in narrow back streets and the whole district had been roped off. I did however see some fires still smouldering in and around Cheapside. Coming home in a 63 bus from Smithfield, was diverted round Gray's Inn Road to King's Cross. Going back to find out why, discovered that two small houses at the bottom of Frederick St had been slightly damaged but were in such danger of collapse that the whole of the considerable King's Cross Rd traffic had to be diverted in case the vibration knocked them down. By far the most deadly and destructive damage has been done in the dockland areas which I haven't yet seen. Whole streets have been demolished there and hundreds of families rendered homeless. Only two theatres kept open last night – the Coliseum and Criterion. The West End and local cinemas kept open but did hardly any business. Tonight's raid lasted from 8.15 till 4.35. Didn't sound if anything dropped very close, though you never can tell. A few fires started – one very close, not much further than Gray's Inn Rd so far as I could judge from the roof.

Tuesday [*undated*]   23 Beechfield Rd WGC

Tony darling,

Thank you for writing and of course I understand how you feel – but I still feel so darn miserable that every night right now I cry myself to sleep – I don't know how long it will last but I think very soon I shall definitely go away.

    Today I heard that Gaston intends letting No 72 furnished – and you know that a fair proportion of the stuff there is mine. Tried to get hold of the Solicitor but he is away for 3 days and his partner will not be here until tomorrow afternoon. Can't come

---

55 In fact, Holborn was only one of the worst-hit boroughs; there can be no reliable 'league table' of casualties, bomb tonnage or properties destroyed or damaged as the boroughs were of vastly different areas and populations.

1940

down on Saturday – the usual monthly curse has arrived – and anyway I am quite sure that this time I should spend the whole time weeping on your shoulder. Tony, if I could try terribly hard to get a small house would you pay any instalment on some furniture I should want?

Please think very seriously about it because I am very frightened all the same, you will do something that you may regret later.

Don't come on Saturday – I couldn't bear to see you – and I feel I can face up to general bloodiness of everything if I am alone.

Thank you again for writing, it was a tonic to hear from you, and I really think I shall become religious and pray for your safety each night.

Yours always, Eilleen

Wednesday 11 September The Commercial where we usually go for lunch was closed today owing to shortages of gas for cooking. Went into Lyons at King's Cross to see what I could get there. Nothing hot whatever, either food or drink, so I had to be content with cold pie, potato salad and milk. Bloody awful! The second of today's alarms (the first was a very brief one at 12.0) caught me in the Exchange. Had to wait over at the shelter well over an hour before the all clear went and they reopened. Their object seemed to be to cause more fires in the City [and] 'East End' and so light up London for tonight's raid. Coming down Pentonville Rd after, passed many scenes – fire engines rushing up in that direction. Another brief alarm half an hour later just as I got home and a nine hour spell tonight 8.35 till 5.35. Very warm reception from anti-aircraft batteries. Fierce and heavy gunfire could be heard the whole time.[56]

Thursday 12 September Went over to Town Hall this evening and saw McKeer again about the job there I was half promised a fortnight ago. Said there were still no vacancies in the dept. he had in mind [owing] to the present staff still waiting to be called up. But he sent me round to see the Deputy Borough Treasurer and within five minutes I'd got a job. Asked me no questions as to my work at PR's – the letter I'd originally sent in was enough. Was even rather apologetic about offering me such a low paid job – £3.7.0 a week to start – but the prospects of advancement are reasonably good – the reason for the

---

56   The noise of anti-aircraft guns increased after the 9 September raids as the batteries were ordered to boost public morale and 'find some more effective answer to the Hun. Every gun was to fire every round. Guns were to go to the approximate elevation and fire' (General Sir Frederick Pile (Commander-in-Chief, Anti-Aircraft Command 1939–1945), *Ack-Ack: Britain's Defence against Air Attack during the Second World War* (London: Harrap, 1949), pp. 151–152.

vacancy is because they wanted to push someone else up – and it is at least a job and reserved at 30. In fact I'm mighty thankful to get it for I'm certain I'd never get one anywhere else now. Seven weeks out of work has been quite enough for me. I start on Monday. Hours 9 till 5, Saturday 9 till 1. The work is something to do with rating. I only hope I get away with it. A very lucky break. Now I must get in all the sleep I can before Monday for if the nightly fireworks display keeps going, I certainly will not get much after.

Walked round the West End and saw some of Tuesday night's damage in afternoon. Some buildings destroyed at corner of Kingsway and Remnant St. The Strand roped off from Southampton St, Maiden Lane, Henrietta St closed waiting for a time bomb to explode. One had already done so at the top of Bedford St. The top part of Shaftesbury Avenue was likewise closed for the same reason. Some damage had been done to buildings in Regent St opposite Austin Reed's and also to the north end of Burlington Arcade. And that was about all. But nothing in Central London can compare with the Holborn catastrophe for extensive damage. Today's first alarm didn't go off till 4.40. It lasted an hour, I spent it writing cards and letters to various people apprising them of my good fortune. Tonight's alarm didn't go off until about an hour later than usual – 9.15. However the all clear didn't sound till 5.45 so there wasn't much in it. The anti-aircraft barrage was exceedingly active again throughout the night and doubtless proving as effective as last night. Bed at 6.15.

Friday 13 September Had both the longest and shortest daylight raids so far. The longest lasted from 9.50 to 1.55 and followed on from 7.30 to 8.00. I had hoped to sleep throughout the morning and I tried to do so despite the raid but it was impossible with planes flying over, guns firing and bombs dropping every now and then. The shortest came in the afternoon at 4.0 and lasted for about ten minutes. I was up at the [Labour] Exchange which was besieged by hundreds – the darned place having been shut all morning during the raid. Tried to catch an hour or two of sleep after tea. Hopeless! Bombs dropped in Euston Road near the station today and burst a water main, also in Buckingham Palace and Charing Cross. Tonight 8½ hours from 9.0 till 5.30. Gunnery very noisy.

Saturday 14 September Went to the Exchange in the morning to sign off i.e. get my cards and draw my last dole instalment. Thank heaven I shan't see that horrible place again, I hope, anyway. Went up to Welwyn and spent the afternoon with E walking through the woods to Digswell for tea and back. Caught the 5.47 home. Today's fourth alarm started as we got to Finsbury Park about 6.20. At King's Cross the station was cleared and everyone ushered down the underground shelter as the raiders were passing right overhead. Stayed there for minutes until they cleared off for a bit and dashed home. Two further alarms though no sound of planes, guns or bombs or either. Then a strange unbroken silence until past midnight. A mystifying departure from routine.

Sunday 15 September We didn't quite get away with a peaceful night. After the guns had been firing and planes hovering overhead for about half an hour the sirens went off again at 1.15 [a.m.]. Still even so it was a comparatively brief spell for the all clear was given out at 3.0 and we weren't disturbed again until 12 noon today, thus enabling us to get a fairly decent and long overdue sleep. Went up to Muswell Hill as soon as I'd finished and saw Phil and Kath. Left early while it was still light even though another alarm had started about 7.0, but the all clear went after half an hour as I walked down to Wood Green tube and got a train to King's Cross. Some of the platforms, especially Caledonian Rd, were packed with families sheltering for the night. I didn't know they allowed that on the tube now.[57] However peace did not reign for long, for today's fourth alarm sounded just as I got home at 8.10 and the guns were soon in action. Had supper and lay on the bed fully dressed for two or three hours but the incessant heavy gunfire drove me down to the shelter where I stayed till 4.30.

Monday 16 September Started work in the Borough Treasurer's office over at the Town Hall. Wages, superannuation and all that. Large office on ground floor, light and airy accommodating about a dozen of us, congenial atmosphere here to work in, everyone being very affable with a complete absence of petty rules or regulations and red tape. In fact a complete contrast to PR's. The work itself simple and easy so far – such as I did today for what with endlessly retreating to the basement every time the air raid warning went, it amounted to about two hours altogether. There were three alarms during the morning and one which lasted the whole afternoon from 2.10 to 6.0. I'd come home and had tea by then, I've certainly started work at the right time. It's money for jam for most wage-earners these days. Tried to sleep for a couple of hours before the siren curfew sounded at 8.10 but couldn't. Lasted as usual till 5.30 with about an hour's interval from 2.40 till 3.45. Got sick of settling down in the shelter so came up at 1.30 and went to bed. Got about four hours sleep, all told.

Tuesday 17 September Actually did about five hours work today, so infrequent were the alarms – two in the morning from 8 till 10 and in afternoon one from 3 till 4.30. We carry on working now until we hear bombs or gunfire. The West End was heavily bombed last night and the Tate Gallery and Law Courts have been hit in recent raids. Also I've no time now to get around and see what London looks like – what's left

---

57   Although the relevant Cabinet sub-committee did not recognise the 'opening of the tubes' until 21 September (TNA, CAB75/3), there had been a slow acquiescence by the authorities to the public taking shelter in Tube stations.

of it! Went with Mother round to the crypt of St Pancras Church for tonight's 8 till 6, with a pillow, a cushion and some blankets.

Wednesday 18 September Had so many raids today that I lost count of them. Hardly anyone takes the slightest notice of daylight raids. One just carries on in the ordinary way and forgets all about them till the all clear goes. Bourne & Hollingsworth, John Lewis and D H Evans [Oxford St department stores] all had direct hits in last night's raid. I went along to see the damage after work. Apart from broken windows, B&H didn't look very bad from the outside though it is supposed to have suffered badly. Couldn't get anywhere near the other two for Oxford St was closed from Oxford Circus onwards and they were still trying to put out the fire at Lewis's caused by an oil bomb. JL's was the worst damaged of the three and Evans next door, the least. Roadway between BH and JL had a lucky escape. Perhaps one was meant for these? On way back also saw wreckage of bomb dropped between Rathbone Place and Newman St. In each direction north, south, east and west bombs have now been dropped within a quarter mile of Sinclair House [his flat]. If I was at all superstitious I suppose I should now become a wood-trekker.[58] A horribly apprehensive night. As soon as the siren sounded at 7.45 went round to the crypt again. About an hour later came a terrific explosion outside. A magnetic mine dropped by parachute had landed outside St Pancras Goods Yard on Euston Rd and wrecked every building within reach. I was terrified in case Sinclair House, only 150 yards away had been affected. Fortunately it hadn't. Not even a window broken, though nearly every window in the vicinity had gone including the Town Hall's, Queen Alexandra Mansions and even the shop downstairs in Hastings St and as far away as Leigh St. When the all clear went at 5.30 we came back along Euston Rd before they stopped and picked a way through the debris by the dim light of dawn. A pitiful scene of havoc, desolation. If this goes on much longer, London will be laid waste completely.

Thursday 19 September Chaos and consternation in the Town Hall this morning. All the windows smashed and dust and fallen plaster from the walls everywhere. A tame bird escaped from its cage flew into our office and stayed for some time before flying off again to seek more comfortable quarters. Couldn't even get started on my work for at least two hours till the mess had been cleared up a bit. Even then the prevailing weather was hardly conducive to work under those conditions for it was a cold and wet and windy and utterly wretched sort of day. In fact it became so intolerable that we shifted down[stairs].

---

58 Probably a reference to seeking refuge by nightly 'trekking' off to the woods or suburbs as practised by some East Enders in 1917 and by many in Merseyside, Coventry, Hull, Plymouth, Southampton and Portsmouth. See the official histories: T. H. O'Brien, *Civil Defence* (London: HMSO, 1955), pp. 10, 427–430; R. M. Titmuss, *Problems of Social Policy* (London: HMSO, 1950), pp. 306–309.

Not that it was much warmer down there. When we left at 5.0 the windows were being boarded up, which now means that we shall be deprived of daylight and fresh air and have to work by artificial light. I thought I'd got away from that when I left PR's. I hope it is only a temporary measure. I now lunch down in the canteen every day where an excellent well cooked meal is obtainable for 1/8. The Commercial went west last night. Bombs were dropped locally on the Hampstead Rd, Gordon St, Euston Square and an unexploded magnetic mine is perched on the top of a house in Harrington Square. An unlucky spot that. Round to the crypt for the 8 till 6 night raid. Managed to get some sleep

Friday 20 September PR's has copped a packet after all. Having missed it in the Oxford St stores Blitz of Tuesday night, they came by that way again and made sure of it the night after. Nothing positive in the *Mail* this morning. I dashed along to see it after lunch. No buses were going along Oxford St at all and had to walk up to the Circus which was completely roped off. The bomb had fallen right on the Circus corner of PR's and knocked down a bit of every floor into a pile of stone debris in the roadway. Every window was, of course, shattered and no doubt the internal damage is considerable though the main building was still intact and put the burners out of action for some time. Possibly for ever for it would cost a pretty penny to repair the damage and, judging by the way they were faring even before I left, it's very unlikely they could afford it. Therefore a lucky break for me when I was fired from there eight weeks ago. The Gt Portland St and Gt Titchfield St area was also shut awaiting the explosion of a time bomb. Also bombed recently: Selfridges, County Hall, Inner Temple, Wallace Collection, British Museum (slight damage). Down in the crypt from 8.0 p.m. till 5.30 a.m. I now spend at the most two hours a night in my bed before getting up at 7.50. Which with the three or four hours I sleep I contrive to get laying on the table in the crypt give me as much slumber as anyone can reasonably expect these nights.

Saturday 21 September Went up to see E in afternoon. As luck would have it she hadn't been able to get anyone to look after the kids so had to bring them along with her. Our walking through the woods and it being an unexpectedly glorious afternoon only added to the worry as the continuation of the love making, or any of the manifestation of affection, was of course out of the question. Terribly depressing and harassing. Fate is dead against us at the moment for not only is E's maid leaving her in a week's time but her cousin is unable to accommodate her much longer. And the Garden City being full of evacuees, there's not a flat or a house to be had in the place. Her only hope now is to get the separation settled at once and try to get a house possibly. In fact they have now definitely reached a crisis. Came home on the 5.47. Air raid warning about 6.15 as we went through Barnet. They seem to make a point of starting early Saturday – gala night presumably – then the nightly full length performance from 8.15 till 4.45.

Sunday 22 September A still damp and melancholy day. Didn't go out till the late afternoon when I took a walk round the West End and saw some of the latest air raid havoc. Mayfair has been badly hit, any number of buildings between Piccadilly and Oxford St have been raised to the ground. Had a good look at John Lewis's for the first time – a ghastly scene. PR's is also in worse way than I thought it was for I noticed today that the back was badly crumbling as well. The Langham Hotel has also been hit and buildings in Foley St and Gt Portland St too. You can't go far in Central London now without coming across wreckage of some sort. Incidentally, with one short interval at 4.0, an air raid warning lasted nearly the whole afternoon from 2.0 till 6.0.

Monday 23 September Shampoo and tub down after tea then to the crypt from 7.45 till 6.20. The clergy having appropriated our usual corner, we had to move round into one of the passages, where I slept on the floor. Not nearly as good. A dusty filthy hole with far too much loud talk in the vicinity. And the air was foul. I don't relish trying that again.

Tuesday 24 September A hell of a lot of damage done in Kentish Town last night by incendiary bombs. Every time anyone in the office goes out wage paying or rent collecting, they come back having witnessed some fresh scene of devastation. The daylight raids tend to slacken off as the night time ones get more prolonged. We rarely get more than one or at the most two during the day now. University College on Gower Street and Oetzmann's in Hampstead Rd[59] were set on fire during the night raid (3.0 till 5.30). I dashed up to see them, both still blazing fiercely. At the UC it had started at an out building and had just spread to the dome. The orange glow of the flames set against the rich blue sky at daybreak made a fascinating sight. But then there's a horrible fascination in watching any fire providing it involves no personal loss. The one at Oetzmann's which had likewise been raging all night was more smoke than flames and another fire was just starting at Maple's depository over the way. Walked up to the other end of T.C. Rd which was thick with smoke to see the damage done by a magnetic mine which had dropped along by the Blue Posts opposite the YMCA. It was considerable and extensive. A small fire was burning there too. As I came back, the Maple's fire spread to the Euston Rd frontage and looked like lasting a good while. Home at 7.30. No time for any more sleep but shave and washed.

Wednesday 25 September Heard that the Queen's Theatre had been hit by a bomb last night. Went along to see it in evening. It had – very much so. The bomb had apparently gone clean through the front corner

---

59   A major furniture retailer, 67–87 Hampstead Road, NW1.

1940

in Shaftesbury Avenue. This is the first theatre to be hit so far (not counting Tussaud's Cinema). Another bomb had completely demolished the famous old church opposite – St Anne's, Soho. Others had fallen outside Endell St schools opposite the Princes [theatre], in Russell Square just opposite the Imperial [hotel], on a house in Brunswick Square and on a church in Wakefield St. Saw all these on my way back as well as large sections of Bloomsbury roped off awaiting the explosion of time bombs. More damage to life and property must have been caused in the last month than in the whole of the raids on London during the last war.[60] I now hear that large numbers of YMCA members who were sitting in the reading room overlooking T C Rd last night were killed from the blast of the mine from the building opposite. Also people who were killed in the Blue Posts which was still open (it was just before 10.0). A ghastly business. Crypt 8.0 till 6.0. Slept on camp bed for a while then on the floor. Over-slept the all clear by half an hour. No local incidents.

Thursday 26 September An upsetting day. Couldn't get lunch at the Town Hall, the canteen being now confined to ARP personnel and others unable to leave the building. So came home to munch bread and cheese and found a distressing letter from E [*not found*] who [is] unable to find any new accommodation whatsoever in Welwyn G.C. Looks like having no alternative but to go back to G. On top of this had to work late on wage sheets till 6.15. There was nothing I felt less like doing this afternoon. But I did it to the bitter end. Went along to the shelter under the Royal Hotel[61] tonight instead of the crypt and slept on the floor. Slightly more pleasant than the crypt even if not quite so safe. Less dark and dirty and stuffy anyway. Two alarm periods 8.00 till 4.0 and 5.0 till 6.0. Waited for the second to end before coming home.

Friday 27 September Lunch at home today – stew. Four daylight raids. Bombs dropped in central London during the first. Round again to the Royal all-night session (8.15–6.0). Slept well.

Saturday 28 September A terrible blow – Eilleen has decided to give me up and go back to Gaston. I arranged to go up and see her [but] she phoned me telling me not to come as apparently a bomb had dropped opposite their house in Handside Lane [WGC] and, on going along yesterday morning to see the damage, she suddenly felt that she ought

60 During the First World War, 670 civilians were killed by German bombing in the Metropolitan Police District (H. A. Jones, *The War in the Air: Being the Story of the Part Played in the Great War by the Royal Air Force, Vol. 5* (Oxford: Clarendon Press, 1935), Appendix 2). By 30 September 1940, 5,940 civilians had been killed in the London region; by 2 December, of the estimated 790,224 houses in the London Region, 32,160 had been destroyed and 466,765 were damaged but considered repairable (TNA, HO186/952; Churchill Archive, Churchill College, Cambridge, Papers of Kenneth Parker CB, Deputy Chief Administrative Officer of the London Civil Defence Region 1939–1945).
61 Bedford Way, WC1.

to go back to G after all. I just couldn't understand this and implored her to see me once more to explain properly. She wouldn't so I went up to Welwyn straight from work to try and call on her nevertheless. I had to see both her and G together. She'd confessed everything. This was the first time I'd met him. It was a painful scene. There was the forgiving husband, the repentant wife and the thwarted lover. None of us could talk freely. I wanted to speak to her alone but he obviously couldn't trust her either. That is why I can't believe she's doing this for any other reason than for the sake of the children – and obviously what she thinks is best for me and all of us in the circumstances. In other words in telling me she no longer loves me but G all the time, she is forcing herself to lie. He has somehow cast his spell over her again with devastating success. Yes it was a forced and artificial conversation and served no purpose whatsoever. In the end I just had to give in and with a bitter parting shot at her which I bitterly regret after [I] left. I dashed down to the station wanting to get out of Welwyn as quickly as possible but of course had to hang about for an hour waiting for a slow train back. I managed to wait until I got home before breaking down and weeping then I wept like hell. I'm afraid this will knock me up for some time. It's such a sudden and unexpected and altogether cruel blow. I shall get over it in time though never I think completely. I've loved her as I have never loved anyone before and doubtless will again and, what's more, I'm certain she still feels the same about me. I shall always treasure the memory of our love which alternated between the heights of ecstasy and owing to stress and anxiety over the difficulties and complications involved – the depths of despair. And there alas it ends. There's nothing more I can do but accept my fate with as good grace as possible and suffer in silence.

Under the Royal from 8.15 till 6.0. Didn't sleep much and didn't expect to.

Sunday 29 September Instead of going to bed on getting home as I would normally do, stayed up and had a very early breakfast and spent the entire morning writing a long letter to Eileen in which I said all the things I couldn't say yesterday. It was a relief to get it all off my chest and pouring out my aching heart on paper did not ease the pain a bit. Went up to see Phil in Muswell Hill in afternoon but they weren't in. So went to see John Hobson instead. Hadn't seen him for a month (Incidentally I haven't had a drink for a month either). He's now working days instead of nights in the P.O. and still expecting to be called up any minute. Meanwhile he's taking everything with his customary carefree happy-go-lucky manner. A constantly cheerful companion. Noticed a queue outside Mornington Crescent station waiting to go down the tube for shelter tonight at 2.0 p.m. Every station is crammed full at night long before the warning goes. Also saw some of the damage up Kentish Town. The High St is in a very bad way. Holloway and

1940

Islington looked pretty unhealthy too as I passed through Highgate to the Angel. Home to tea at 5.30. Royal 8.0 till 6.0. Slept well.

Monday 30 September A cold gloomy day in keeping with my spirits. I feel utterly wretched. Thoughts and memories of Eilleen haunt me all day long. I shall never be able to get back where I was before I knew her. And the fact that not a single recreation distraction is now available to me doesn't help matters. Not that they would necessarily alleviate my misery if they were, but they might to a small extent. I have never known such a grim and hopeless outlook. Four daylight raids before the nightly one from 7.45 till 6.0. Strolled round after tea and saw some more of the local damage – Guilford St hit for third time – at corner of Millman St, Harrison St and Regent Square. No end to it.

Tuesday 1 October Took another evening stroll and discovered further damage – in Red Lion St at corner of Sandland St and at Bedford Row end of Hand Court. Three corners completely demolished. Royal 8.0 till 5.30.

Wednesday 2 October I hear today that The Old Bull and Bush (and Golders Green Station) were bombed last night. This affects one more than any other raid catastrophe so far. It had such memories for me. Eilleen and I almost invariably called in there for a drink and usually for a snack with it every time we went to Hampstead. A lovely old pub with a splendid atmosphere it had a very tender spot in my heart. Alas that we should never call there any more should the opportunity ever [arise] again. It becomes a sadder world every day. Workmen still necessary about the empty window frames. Office still bitterly cold. Evenings as well as days now follow a monotonous routine. Tea, 30 to 45 minute stroll round. Go up to Royal about 7.0 walking up and down outside waiting for the alarm then down for the night. Turn in about 9.30 after an hour's radio. Wake up around 3.0 to hear loud snoring. After that sleep on and off till 6.0. When the all clear sounds packing up and home. Tonight it was 7.45 till 6.20. Raining in the morning.

Thursday 3 October Initiated into a new job this morning. Went round in a wooden car-come-van with an office colleague, Walen a District Warden at the various ARP posts. Some eight or nine calls in all, our first being the crypt of St Pancras Church where I pay Mother! I'm to take over from Walen and do this job every week. A bit of a break even on such a wet and miserable morning as today was. Anything's preferable to that ice house of an office these days. Was frozen stiff working out wage sheets in afternoon. Finished our round at Malet St First Aid Post or rather in the pub over the road with one of the men therefrom. He had some gruesome stories to tell of raid casualties. The most unenviable job imaginable. This was the first drink I'd had for five weeks. We left the Town Hall at 9.40 and got back at 11.55. Tonight's alarms were from 8.0 till 9.50 and 10.0 till 2.10. This is the

Part Two

shortest night spell for weeks. However we all stayed down the shelter sleeping till 5.30. Incidentally there are far more foreigners down there than English. Mostly Norwegian refugees.[62] It's quite rare to hear one's own language spoken.

Friday 4 October About the longest daylight raid on record, 12.45 till 5.35 then off again at 6.0. Bombs dropped on Hampstead Rd and on Covent Garden in the afternoon. Spent most of the day working down in the [Town Hall] basement. Was impossible to do so in the office so perishing cold was it with the windows open. Phoned E after work to try and reason with her but it was impossible. She hadn't yet had my letter and wouldn't then promise to read it when she did get it and kept up an obviously false air of callous indifference throughout. I can understand her attitude. She is determined to burn her boats behind her and break off our relationship for once and for all. There's a lot to be said for it but it's terribly hard on me. The 6.0 alarm lasted half an hour or so. The next soon after at 7.0 as we were going round to the Royal. Didn't hear the all clear at 4.0. Woke at 6.0 and home. Have to lug all our blankets and pillows backwards and forwards now instead of leaving them there as we have hitherto.

Saturday 5 October I now have lunch every day at the Swiss Café in Euston Rd. Not a bad meal for 1/3d except that the puddings are always over-baked. Went up to Muswell Hill in afternoon to try and see Phil and retrieve my sleeping bag but drew a blank again. Both out. Left a note and came home. Saw the Stanhope St damage on the way home, two or three houses demolished at the Mornington Crescent end. They seem determined to get Carreras factory which is now being used for armaments manufacture. Royal from 7.20.

Sunday 6 October Walked over Hampstead in morning, a good deal of damage even over there. Parliament Hill [tram and bus] terminus in ruins. A block of flats by Whitestone Pond hit and several houses opposite Bull and Bush as well as Golders Hill House wrecked. The B&B itself, contrary to the rumour during the week was only slightly damaged, namely broken windows, certainly not beyond repair. Three bombs here and there over the heath. Went down to Golders Green and got a bus up to Muswell Hill, saw Phil and retrieved my camping things at last. Came home via Golders Green and Hampstead again in order to see damage at Belsize Park. Very slight, what I could see of it. Home to lunch at 2.0. A wet afternoon and evening. Wrote letters to Cookie and Norah, a girl at Manchester whom I formed an attachment with at Brean Sands over a year ago and kept up a regular correspondence ever

---

62   By the end of 1940, just over 30,000 civilians from Belgium, France, Poland, Holland and other countries had been arrived in the UK, in addition to 20,000 Channel Islanders and 10,500 Gibraltarians (Titmuss, *Problems of Social Policy*, pp. 246–247).

since.[63] If only she were in London instead of Manchester she might prove a great consolation to me just now – quite an attractive girl and only twenty one. Today's alarms were most irregular – a very brief evening one from 8.20 to 8.40 and then nothing all night till 5.40 to 6.30. The first peaceful night for over a month. Nevertheless we stayed down the shelter all night.

Monday 7 October Today's press explanation of last night's aerial inactivity – gales prevented them from taking off. Went to two blocks of council flats up Kentish Town way, sat in the caretaker's den for an hour or so at each took the rent and entered up the books. Banked the money immediately after. A tricky job at first but not difficult, one gets accustomed to it. Would be twice as simple if it weren't for the arrears. Didn't get home to lunch till 2.0. Back in office at 2.30. They are actually putting some glass into the window frames and have already completed half of them. Glorious day out. Complete contrast to yesterday. Went up and saw the Chancery Lane damage in evening. About the worst I've seen so far. Six huge blocks of buildings including the London Safe Deposit completely demolished, only a few jagged remnants of walls standing here and there. The top half of the Woolworth Building in Holborn Bars also damaged. Common sites. Right along Holborn for first time since those first bombs were dropped there a month ago. Tonight's alarm lasted from 7.20 p.m. until 7.0 a.m. a further new record. In the course of it a bomb fell at the corner of Sandwich St and Leigh St making a crater in the pavement, knocking in a few shop fronts. Little further damage. A near thing. No electric light when we got home.

Tuesday 8 October Two bombs in Shaftesbury Avenue overnight. Went along and saw the results lunchtime. One had fallen on the fire station opposite the Palace [Theatre], the other by the Saville Theatre. Realised for the first time that the top of Shaftesbury Avenue is lined with trees a la boulevard. Further damage done in Holborn this morning when bombs fell during the rush hour. One hit a bus and killed several passengers. Went up there in the evening. Damage was between Henekeys[64] and Gray's Inn Rd this time. Manzoni's restaurant[65] in adjacent building demolished. The remains of the bus had been removed. Local hits last night also included Chamberlain House where a bomb dropped on the shelter in the courtyard and Handel St drill hall on which a bomb fell through the centre and left the exterior undamaged. Royal 7.15–6.30.

Wednesday 9 October Deserted the Royal for shelter tonight and tried the crypt of St Pancras church again, Mother having found a place where we can sleep on some forms and leave our stuff down there. No

63 Norah Morris: see Appendix 1.
64 Wine merchants, 22–23 High Holborn.
65 At 12 High Holborn.

good at all. The air so foul that one could hardly breath [*sic*], but the place packed to suffocation. We go back to the Royal tonight.

Thursday 10 October Paid Wardens in morning. Different round to last week's in Primrose Hill, Chalk Farm, East Camden Town Division 2. Went round by car with Capt. Walen. Bomb in Cromer St, just off Gray's Inn Rd last night. Several casualties in pub on which it fell and two Wardens on patrol killed outside.[66] The corner of the Bedford Head Hotel in TC Rd also knocked down. And another corner building in New Oxford St opposite Imhof's.[67] Saw the first lunchtime, the other in the evening. Back to Royal for night. Much better, except for snorers who invariably wake me up and keep one awake for some time. But you can get them everywhere.

Friday 11 October Paid the road sweepers etc. of the NW district up at the Chalk Farm depot in afternoon. There by cab, back by bus. The cab driver had a white beard and would have looked more at home on a Hansom cab. Walked round to Guilford Place in the evening where some of the old Queen Anne houses had been completely demolished in last night's raid. Guilford St must be about the unluckiest street in London. Six hits so far. Won't be much more of it left to hit soon. St Paul's hit recently and the high altar smashed. Damage not beyond repair though – even a hole in roof. Royal 7.15 till 6.15 even though the all clear went at 3.0. Slept soundly.

Saturday 12 October Spent the afternoon doing an extensive sight-seeing tour of the recent raid damage. Took the bus to Blackfriars and started from the damaged building. Went up and into St Paul's. The broken masonry was still piled in front of the hole in the altar and the sun streamed through the hole in the roof. On the whole the damage remarkably limited. Then down Ludgate Hill and along Fleet St. At Temple Bar turned into the Temple and had a look around there. A pitiful sight to see the havoc brought on to this lovely and secluded old spot. It's many years since I wandered round there, used to haunt it during my school holidays when I was about nine years old. Proceeded along the Strand where a bomb had landed by St Clement Danes and hard on Montreal Place alongside Bush House. I walked up into Covent Garden. A crater in the roadway where Wellington St runs into Bow St – houses demolished in Endell St and Maiden Lane. Back to the Strand to Trafalgar Square and into Whitehall where two minor hits had been scored. Saw the damage done to the House of Lords by the Richard I statue (only the sword has been bent on this) then got a bus up to Piccadilly Circus in order to come back via Soho where on Thursday night a bomb wrecked the corner of Greek St and Old Compton St

---

66   The St Pancras 'Role of Honour' gives just Warden Walter Dunne among the twenty-nine killed in a parachute mine incident on Prospect Terrace, Cromer Street.
67   Television dealers, 112–116 New Oxford Street.

and buildings in Charing Cross Rd opposite Foyles. The whole area around Cambridge Circus on the north side is in a terrible state now. Practically every street is blocked with debris which the Army Pioneer Corps have now been detailed to clear away.[68] Next week 5,000 of them start work all over London. Home to tea at 5.30. Night alarm slackening off. Tonight though it started at 7.15 and was over by 2.10. Stayed on at the R[oyal] till 5.30.

Sunday 13 October Instead of going to bed on getting home this morning had an early breakfast followed by tub-down and shampoo. Then to Hampstead for a brisk walk over the heath before lunch. Hyde Park in afternoon. Bus there and walked back. From Marble Arch strolled along Park Lane to Hyde Park Corner where a bomb had almost demolished 145 Piccadilly, the house in which the King and Queen used to live when Duke and Duchess of York.[69] Then right along the Serpentine to Kensington Gardens Pond and back to Marble Arch. A beautiful afternoon and sunny. Crowds of people everywhere. During the afternoon two alarms, the raiders could be seen at a great height leaving a trail of white exhaust smoke in their wake. A good way out though, I should imagine. Home to tea at 5.30. Tonight's alarm 7.5, exactly 11 hours.

Monday 14 October Collected Flaxman Terrace rents, all plain sailing. Balanced easily. Only snag about the job is the awkward hours – normally 12 till 1.30 which means I don't get lunch till 2.0. On Mondays I have it at home, Monday being Mother's day off. On the other days I now go down to the canteen where they managed to fit me in due to the fact that I couldn't get a pass. A close shave at the Royal tonight. A bomb dropped a few yards away on corner of Tavistock Square and Bedford Way demolishing houses in both. Gave us a scare though all that happened in the shelter was more dust falling off the ceiling. On getting home at 6.45 went out to discover where the other bombs had fallen in the locality for we'd heard several others during the night. Found it was mostly up Tottenham Court Rd way. Windmill St, Ridgemount Gardens, Bedford Square and Russell Square had all had hits, the latter two only small ones in the centre. Several fires around this area too. Some minor damage on York House, the other side of Sandwich St but couldn't make out exactly what happened, from AA

---

68 By 23 September, just two weeks into the offensive, such was the effect of the destruction that 1,800 roads in the London region had been blocked by debris, an estimated 3 million tons of rubble had built up and needed to be removed, and 24,000 people were in rest and feeding centres across the region. Sir Warren Fisher was appointed as a Special Commissioner to deal with debris clearance and quickly obtained from the War Office the services of Pioneer Corps and Royal Engineers to tackle the clearance and repair tasks. Heap's comment on 28 November (see below) refers to their success. See Robin Woolven, 'London's Debris Clearance and Repair Organisation 1939–45', in M. Clapson and P. Larkham (eds), *The Blitz and Its Legacy* (Farnham: Ashgate, 2013), pp. 61–72.
69 Now occupied by the InterContinental London Park Lane Hotel.

shell burst most likely. Spent a whole hour on the tour getting back at 7.45.

Tuesday 15 October Saw some more of last night's damage in evening. London Pavilion burnt out inside but nothing visible outside. St James's Church in Piccadilly partly demolished. The Fifty Shilling Tailors building opposite burnt down. Likewise a building in St James's Square. The Carlton Club in Pall Mall stopped a direct hit. Also Carlton House Terrace on the corner of the Duke of York's Steps opposite the former German Embassy.[70] A gala night. Got very close to the Royal again tonight. Land mine supposed to have got Woburn Court at top of Bernard St but presumably didn't explode for although all roped off, we couldn't see anything wrong with it on going round at dawn.

Wednesday 16 October No gas at all this morning so ergo had to wash in cold water and had cold breakfast. Horrible. No water in the taps by the afternoon though managed to get some from the tap in the basement at tea time.[71] Eight land mines dropped in St Pancras last night, four still unexploded. The others fell (a) on the signal box of St Pancras station which was shut today – this went off after the all clear this morning. (b) Somewhere up Camden Town (c) in Cromer St (d) on Prospect Terrace. Saw the results of the last two lunchtime, extensive damage. Down in the Royal shelter, a comparatively quiet night on the central western front.

Thursday 17 October Called at Boots on way back from paying in Wardens Division 2 and changed book. Nothing on my list available. Did ¾ hour overtime on wage sheets, leaving at 5.45. Several bombs dropped on Kentish Town during a raid this afternoon. Another fairly quiet night. Exactly 12 hours between warning and all clear 6.50 p.m.–6.50 a.m.

Friday 18 October Paid wages at Bangor Wharf up at Camden Town in afternoon. Some £600 odd. Deserted the Royal and started going to a new night shelter, opened for the first time tonight. Basement under the Friends House, Quakers' building in Euston Rd. Holds 50 but only ten there for the first night. Will doubtless fill up later. More spacious and lighter than the R[oyal] and due to be fitted with bunks soon. And, best of all, we can leave our bedding there.

Saturday 19 October Eighteen at Friends House for second night, business picking up.

---

70 Nos. 6–9 Carlton House Terrace, now the home of the Royal Society.
71 Water supply was restricted across north London for a short period owing to a bomb having broken the three huge underground pipes carrying the New River supply in Enfield at 9.15 p.m. on 15 October (LMA, Enfield Incident Log, MCC/CD/WAR/01/005).

Sunday 20 October Some minor near hits last night including the back of Mary Ward Settlement on [5–7] Tavistock Place and Euston Station. Walked to Regent's Park in morning, bus back to King's Cross to meet John Hobson at 12.30 and bid him farewell before he reports at Brighton on Tuesday to join the Royal Artillery. John Bell also came along for a little while. Had three pints in the Euston Tavern[72] and a final half pint and a scotch. So goes one of my few friends and one of the best, I shall miss John and his cheerful camaraderie too. Still no gas. Have to do such cooking as we can on a Valor heater stove. Had to forgo potatoes to go with boiled rabbit for lunch. Lucky to get that. Water very spasmodic too. Five raid alarms during the day. Only had an average of 1½ or so recently. Wrote to E in afternoon. A letter I've had on my mind for the past week or two. It had to be written. More bombs dropped within a stone's throw of the Friends House. Three very close together on the north side of Gordon Square, one demolishing a house, and a fourth further on Tavistock Square. Otherwise a peaceful night!

Monday 21 October Collected Flaxman Terrace rents again in morning erstwhile [*sic*] a raider hovered around overhead. Got short on balancing. This and paying District 2 Wardens on Thursdays are two of my regular jobs. In the shelter this evening, comparatively quiet night till about 4.0. Three more games of chess in the evening, won two, getting into my stride again.

Tuesday 22 October The only major local incident last night was up in Eversholt St where an outsize bomb fell in the roadway making a deep crater and even penetrating down to the Mornington Crescent to Euston tube line, so they say. Boots again lunchtime, still nothing on my list available. Turned to the fiction shelves for a change and picked on *Scoop* by Evelyn Waugh, one of the 'bright young men' of the decade whom we hear little of these days.[73] All clear very early tonight, round about 12.0 or 1.0 or something like that. Didn't hear it anyway. Never do down in the FH shelter, or the alarm, but can hear guns and bombs well enough. Nothing about tonight though.

Wednesday 23 October Saw the Eversholt St crater lunchtime, about 30 ft deep. Didn't go down to the tube but burst a water main which flooded it. Finished *Scoop* in the shelter, far-fetched satire on newspapers. It bored me.

Thursday 24 October Everything went awry with the Wardens' pay round this morning. Waiting for cashier to come in and open safe, got away half an hour late. After being further delayed in Euston Rd traffic

---

72   The Euston Tavern at 73–75 Euston Road (in 2016 'O'Neill's Kings Cross Irish Pub'), at the Judd Street junction, was the local pub for the Town Hall across Judd Street.
73   (Arthur) Evelyn Waugh (1903–1966), English novelist, journalist and travel writer; convert to Roman Catholicism; best known for his satirical *Decline and Fall* (1928) and his *Sword of Honour* trilogy (1952–1961).

block, our car gave out in Hampstead Rd through lack of petrol. The horse died under us as Capt. Walen put it. Which made us at least an hour late getting round to the 'troops' for we had to walk to ARP HQ in Camden High Street[74] and phone for another car and wait and then round to the first post in Parkway to await its arrival. Sullen protests and threats of protest to the 'Chief' all round. Quite understandable for after being on duty for twelve hours all night most of the poor blighters have to wait on from 8.0 till we arrive for their money. The system's all wrong. Took set of chessmen and board along to shelter tonight and played with a young French doctor. It must be over twelve years since I last played chess yet I picked it up again in no time – actually won one of the three games we played. A wonderful absorbing game, one becomes quite oblivious to the passing of time – or anything else for that matter. The least boring evening I've had for many weeks past.

Friday 25 October Paid pensions at Inverness St depot in early afternoon. Cold, uncomfortable job, open shed, low table, no seat, ought to have better arrangements than that.

Saturday 26 October Lunch at the ABC. Still no gas supply ergo nothing hot but tea. Had to be content with a measly bit of ham and salad, roll and butter and a cup of tea – 1/6½ d. Not half the value of the Town Hall's hot electricity-cooked 1/3 lunch in it. Disgusting. Buses of all colours and shapes on the London streets now. Brought in from the provinces to supplement the LPTB buses on the busier routes. Bomb in Blackfriars Bridge Rd yesterday morning hit five trams held up by traffic lights during rush hour. Many casualties. Summertime is to be extended throughout the winter. No chess tonight as my fellow player not there. Whist instead.

Sunday 27 October Wrote to Norah in the morning. Then a short stroll before an early lunch at 12.30. A long afternoon walk around the West End as far as Hyde Park and back. Saw a lot more air raid damage notably in Leicester Square, Grosvenor Square, Savile Row and Brewer St. This last hit on shopping thoroughfare adjoining Berwick Market occurred only yesterday. Also another hit behind the Saville Theatre, the fourth on this [spot], one on Generos restaurant in New Compton St. Drury Lane Theatre too only just missed a bomb which fell in Catherine St and slightly damaged the back of the Strand Theatre as well as the corner building opposite. But I couldn't discover which are the other two theatres, apart from the Queens, alleged to have been bombed. Played chess to so late an hour tonight that they had to turn the lights out on us, every one having turned in, whereupon we returned to the corridor and finished the game out there. I was playing with a young French dentist, the friend of my other opponent, and they spent

74 At 72–76 Camden High Street (in 2015 the Argos store).

about ten minutes arguing in French over every move. What with this, and wondering when I would be able to get some sleep, I was unable to concentrate in the end and lost the game.

Monday 28 October A new phase of the war – Italy invades Greece which thereby becomes yet another of our worthless allies.

Thursday 31 October The Wardens pay went off better this morning though still a bit late owing to the car bringing Walen along to the Town Hall again conking out through lack of petrol and his having to get another. Still the moans were much less vehement. Time sheets down late this afternoon so couldn't finish wage sheets by 5.0. Brought them home with me for which labour I shall claim an hour's overtime – a practice generally adopted in the office since the blackout time has got so much earlier. Actually I did them down in the shelter.

Tuesday 5 November Yet another new job – paying out refugees' pocket money up at the Working Men's College in Crowndale Rd. Under 17 they get 6d and over 17 the princely sum of 1/6 per week. They each produce an identity card and an interpreter sits beside me to deal with any queries. About a hundred of them came along – varied nationalities, French, Belgian, Poles, Dutch, even Maltese. An instructive experience.

E's friend P phoned me this afternoon to tell me that she hadn't been able to pass on either of the letters for E I'd sent her, for the for the simple reason that E hadn't come near her since she went back to G. In fact after I'd phoned E a month ago and told her I'd sent a letter to P for her, she'd actually been callous enough to send G into P for it, though of course, this so disgusts one that I can no longer feel any real regret or sorrow at the ending of our liaison. As if it wasn't enough to betray me to G without betraying P who has been such a good and helpful friend to her as well. I feel strongly urged to phone E for the last time and tell her just what I think of her. But I suppose it's not worth even that especially when it costs 7d to do so. An incredible woman! However this is definitely the finish.

Thursday 7 November Capt Walen having been appointed deputy superintendent at Malet Place First Aid Depot, had a new district warden with me on my pay round this morning, Blane, a young ex-post warden. Also Cawthorne from HQ, to show him the round. For once in a while it was a fine morning and the car had enough petrol in it! Put in an hour's overtime finishing off the wages sheets down in the shelter again.

Friday 8 November St Pancras station hit again last night. The variety of provincial buses on the streets now suggests a new spotting game adding how many towns or districts painted on the routes thereof I can collect. Childish perhaps but I've known many a more childish pastime of a similar nature practiced [*sic*] by adults.

Saturday 9 November I have nothing whatever to do except sit at home or wander around the streets of Hampstead on my own – which only makes me feel all the more melancholy, lonely and depressed. I'd much sooner be working and have no days off at all than this. Bomb dropped at back of King's Cross station this morning. No warning, several casualties.

Sunday 10 November Mother has broken the thermos flask in which we take our cocoa at night. This is a minor catastrophe as they are unobtainable now. Six bombs in Gt Titchfield St, all nicely spaced out every hundred yards or so. Dickens' wine shop in Oxford St completely demolished. Also Rymans the stationers on the corner of Gt Portland St opposite PR's and the fourth bomb on the Dolcis building on Oxford St which broke every window in PR's eastern block opposite. I'm afraid I've no sympathy at all for the old firm in their present plight. For the way they treated their staff in general and E and myself in particular, I consider they deserve all they get. Neville Chamberlain, the now derided champion of peace died today, a broken disappointed man. But whatever the bellicose little upstarts in power today may think of him, history cannot but judge him as a fine statesman and a great gentleman. No raids today until the evening. Some people like to link this with Chamberlain's death as a mark of respect.

Monday 11 November A good deal of aerial activity during the day despite it turning extremely wet again. 140 planes in mass attack on London this morning. I didn't hear or see anything of them though. Played one or two simple games of cards in evening but read most of the time.

Thursday 14 November The last general election was held five years ago today. The main issue the sanctions against Italy over the Abyssinian invasion. Both parties were for them, the only difference being the Conservatives urged rearmament as well but the Socialists were still against it. The whole thing was a farce of course and a perfect example of the muddle headed ineffectuality of democratic government. Did my usual Thursday night's hour's overtime in the shelter.

Friday 15 November Terrific raid on Coventry last night. Cathedral among buildings destroyed and a thousand casualties. Revealed in tonight's paper that Drury Lane was one of the theatres hit in 'recent' raids. I also heard earlier in the week that the Cambridge was another theatrical casualty. The secrets that are leaking out! At D.L. the bomb went through the roof, gallery, upper and dress circles to explode in the pit. The stage and the historic part of the building backstage were left undamaged. A quiet evening reading in the shelter.

1940

Sunday 17 November Another stroll round the West End in afternoon. Saw some more of Friday night's damage, principally at the Savoy Hotel and Hampton's furniture store on the corner of Trafalgar Square which had been completely burnt out. Minor damage to National Gallery, Suffolk Place and Dunn's shop next to Strand Palace Hotel. On way back I noticed the building next to the Homeopathic Nurses' Home in Great Ormond St had been completely demolished. When this happened I don't know. Someone at Drury Lane has a sense of humour. For outside the entrance has been placed the 'Pit Full' boards. So it is – of debris!

Monday 18 November The evenings in the shelter get duller and duller. All games, cards, darts have lapsed. No gramophone, no radio except for the damned news which I detest. Nothing to do but read, read, read.

Wednesday 20 November Walked round lunchtime and saw a couple of nasty hits scored over in Somers Town last night. One on a block of flats in Ossulston St another alongside the church in Charlton St, just midway between St Pancras and Euston stations. Had shelter radio on for most of the evening instead of just for the news. Home station transmissions being so bad, had to resort to foreign stations.

Sunday 24 November Early lunch at 12.15, read papers then out for afternoon walk, by roundabout route to St James's Park and back. Sat in the park by the lake for half an hour or so. Lovely day for November, especially this November. Yet I felt sad and depressed. These fits of melancholy beset me every weekend now as I wander around on my mind, but retrospective thoughts of how sublimely happy I was in the spring and summer by contrast with now. It's no good evading the fact – I still can't get E off my mind, not by long chalks [*sic*]. Didn't discover much more raid damage – except in the Adelphi where instead of bombing the hideous new building that has replaced the picturesque side of Adelphi Terrace, the indiscriminating Germans have demolished practically all that was left of the old Adelphi down by York Buildings.

Monday 25 November No raid all night. Only the second time this has happened since the Blitz started.

Thursday 28 November The army service corps are clearing up the ruins of London very rapidly. They'll be out of work again soon if the raiders don't get busier than they have been of late.[75] And still more darts in the evening. I play with an old fellow called Austin who is a slightly more slender version of Mr Pickwick

---

75 See entry for 12 October and note. Some 8,700 Pioneer Corps men had joined the 10,000-strong civilian labour force clearing debris across the region. See also Woolven, 'London's Debris Clearance', p. 64.

Friday 29 November More rationing on the way. Milk supplies to be reduced by a tenth, meat from 2/2 worth a week to 1/10, and supplies of fruit from abroad likely to be cut off all together. Had difficulty in getting filter tips for my 'home made' cigarettes. Tried three tobacconists before I succeeded. So got a good supply of 200 to last me a while.

Sunday 1 December To Regent's Park. Found the greater part of it (the whole extent west of the Broad Walk) fenced off with iron railings which at regular intervals bear the cryptic inscription 'Closed to the public – Danger' – as for any reason, there is no indication what. Possibly it is to be used for the disposal of unexploded bombs.[76] Neither is there much of Primrose Hill left to the public now, what with the trench shelters and the anti-aircraft base, which has extended its areas of ground even further round the slopes. Huge red-brick barracks are now being built to replace the wooden huts put there a year ago. So presumably the war can be guaranteed to last several more years yet if only to justify the erection of these sort of places. Primrose Hill will never be the same place again. Also wandered round Swiss Cottage way. Two or three nasty hits close to the station. The Embassy looks as if it's been knocked about a bit too. Woman bus conductors are becoming as much a part of the London scene as they were in 1917–18. They do however look a degree or two less hideous than their predecessors of a generation ago. I refer mainly to the uniforms!

Saturday 7 December Lunch at home, Mother having a few days leave. Had a fire in the sitting room for first time this winter. Going to the shelter every evening is saving us no end of money on lighting and heating. To Hampstead in afternoon. Glorious day for December. The old houses opposite the Bull and Bush together with the Hare and Hounds alongside all damaged by bombs two months ago now almost demolished by house breaking. I wonder what architectural abominations they'll eventually replace them with. The shelter half empty tonight.

Sunday 8 December Went up to Muswell Hill to lunch with Phil and Kath. At 8.30 the warning went and it soon became evident that the last two nights had been but the lull before the storm. Wave after wave of planes flew over to the accompaniment of a heavy gun barrage. Was in by 7.40, changed and went straight round to the shelter, full house again. They weren't so hectic here the way they were up at Muswell Hill where a good many of them entering London from the north turned back by the barrage and a good steady flow of activity was maintained throughout the night and the all clear didn't go till we

---

76 More probably for the spreading of debris from roads and bombed sites. The land immediately to the south of the Zoo was raised by several feet (the footpath is high above zoo level). The arm of Regent's Canal down to the Cumberland Market was filled in with rubble. The northern section is now the Zoo car park.

left at 7.0 in the morning. Several incendiary bombs were dropped in the near vicinity and the fires quickly got under way.

Monday 9 December According to the Berlin radio, last night's raid was the heaviest London has had since the severe night raids began. 700 tons of high explosives [and] 100,000 incendiary bombs are alleged to have been dropped in the course of it. The whole of London was said to be lit up by huge fires in the dock area early this morning. Would like to have seen it, quite a gala night!

Wednesday 11 December First two quiet nights than a noisy one. Raid started at 6.0 and went on throughout the night with continual gunfire. A lot of ill-natured squabbling about the position of the camp beds. As usually happens when women – specially old women – are in a majority. The adult mentality is sadly lacking in the shelter.

Thursday 12 December Walked to Ryman's in Poland St and back after lunch and got a new book for next year's diary. On getting back found the back part of it somewhat soiled and dented by wetting or something. Just my luck. Saw the shell of Wolff and Hollander's furniture shop on Tottenham Court Rd on the way. Was burnt out on Sunday night. T. C. Rd from the Horse Shoe up to Goodge St has come in for it pretty well all round. Dense fog as we came home at 7.0.

Friday 13 December A haircut lunchtime. A jar of Brylcream formerly cost 1/- now costs 1/2½d, Gibbs dentifrice has advanced from 6d to 7½d and shaving soap from 10d to 1/-. A quiet night with but a brief alert in the early evening and no round of gunfire even during that.

Saturday 14 December Was devilish cold in the cinema. Soon had to don my overcoat I'd doffed on entering and even then my feet remained frozen. In to tea at 4.45 and round to shelter at usual time 6.0. Had an alert about 6.30, nothing more after. Very few there tonight. So uncommonly quiet was it that we were able to hear an excellent Jack Buchanan programme on the radio without distraction or interruption. Extraordinary. Usually the news is the only thing that is listened to in complete silence.

Monday 16 December Sent off 10/- for the Homeopathic Hospital's Annual Christmas Appeal. A quiet night. All-night raids are now the exception rather than the rule. As for daylight raids, we've almost forgotten what they were like.

Tuesday 17 December As in the last war we are now reduced to saccharine to supplement the sugar ration, our small stock of sugar is getting very much diminished. The meat ration, too, is being reduced from 2/2 a week to 1/6. Restaurant and canteen supplies being cut down by a third. Our daily 'cut off the joint' is, alas, very much out these days.

Wednesday 18 December The general notion is that Hitler has something up his sleeve. A lot of discussion in the shelter about the proposed introduction of three tier bunks to hold forty by the ARP authorities. Most of the inmates, having bought folding beds are opposed to the idea and trying to make some sort of protest about it. Not that it is likely to have any effect.

Thursday 19 December The protest re. the bunks in the shelter was forestalled today by the installation of thirteen of them. Much consternation was caused thereby, squabbling broke out as to who was having which bunks and tempers ran high. However things quietened down eventually and they sought solace in deciding to send the protest in spite of all. Actually it hasn't improved the place but made it much more cramped and uncomfortable. And though I gain a bed by it, for before I slept on a mattress on the floor, this advantage is far outweighed by the fact that there's now no room to play darts. And I didn't sleep too well either on the top of our three tier bunks with Mother on the bottom one, the centre tier empty. Had an early evening alarm from about 6.30 till 9.15. Got up and walked up and down Euston Rd as soon as the all clear went. The air in that place gets stifling.

Friday 20 December Paid Casual Labourers and Watchmen at Inverness St depot in afternoon. Left thermos flask behind last night so on getting to the shelter, had to bring it home, make cocoa and fill it and take it back again. Quite like old times tonight. Warning went just before 6.0 p.m. and lasted till about 3.30 a.m. plenty of gunfire. A shelter inspector from HQ came down about 9.0 and informed the carpers that, protest or no protest, the regulations must stand. The bunks were there and must stay put. It was most pleasing to see the discomfiture of the smug little cretins. But we still haven't found a place for our dart board.

Saturday 21 December Only fourteen of us down there despite the frequent gunfire and the raid lasting all night. Home by 7.0 and for the first time in many weeks tumbled into my own bed for a couple of hours.

Sunday 22 December At 5.55 the alarm went and I [to] the shelter, just read my book or tried to anyway. Was so perishing cold down there with no heating and very draughty blowing through that I had to sit in my overcoat. All clear about 5.0 a.m.

Monday 23 December Colder than ever. After collecting rents had to make up Wardens' pay packets for tomorrow instead of Thursday in order to let them have their money for Christmas. Manchester was the main target of last night's raids. London is still being let off lightly for the time being – while the provincial tour is progressing.

Tuesday 24 December A raid-less Christmas Eve. Does this imply a tacit understanding on both sides to hold a truce over Christmas as happened on the Western Front in 1914? The general consensus of opinion is that it doesn't. Mistrust of the 'Jerries' being the dominant feature in the English mind. Yet I wonder. Despite the small attendance – 15 or so – something of what is termed 'Christmas Armistice,' refraining from jumping down each-other's throats in order to do so with more vigour after Christmas and the rest of the year – prevailed in the shelter. Hatchets were buried for once. After lights out some seven or eight lay in the dark listening to the other seven or eight singing carols out in the passage and in the morning small paper stockings, a few sweets and a few nick nacks (mine was a collar stud, Mother's a bath cube) were found pinned to our bunks. Charming! Home at 7.15 and to bed for a couple of hours.

Wednesday 25 December Presents: From Mother a pair of bedroom slippers, three pairs of socks. Two cigars. From others, nil. Given, nil. As is my customary habit on Christmas Day went up to Hampstead in the morning and bestrode the heath. Plenty of people about. Our Christmas dinner consisted of rump steak, chips, beans, mince pie and a glass of port. I could wish for none better. Heard King's broadcast at 3.0. As usual slow, hesitating and unimpressive. Sat by fire reading book and listening to radio for rest of afternoon. Then after tea round to the shelter for the Christmas party. This was held in conjunction with the Quakers (who have a shelter of their own) up in one of the halls. A jumble of concert, games and dancing with nothing but soft drinks and sandwiches and suchlike as refreshments. It was all very tame, so tame that when they went downstairs for the aforesaid refreshments I went over to see old Austin who, wise old man, preferred to sit at home by the fire with a book. Stayed talking for an hour or so and, with the help of a couple of drinks and a few swigs from a bottle of port we surreptitiously smuggled out of the shelter, I managed to get through the evening. But 'twas tough going and I was mightily glad when it was all over at midnight and we went down and turned in. This sort of thing never was my idea of fun. 'I leave that to the children' as the père Austin puts it. There was no raid after all. So they could trust each other. And if for Christmas why not for good? Alas but that's too much wisdom to expect of mankind.

Thursday 26 December A working Boxing Day. At least, so it was supposed to be, and for us it actually was for the Town Hall opened for business as usual. But like the last two Bank Holidays which were likewise cancelled, it was a half and half sort of day. Practically every shop was shut as well as many business houses and for the majority of Londoners it undoubtedly was Boxing Day. No morning papers were published but the evening papers made a somewhat emaciated appearance. Brought some wage sheets home to finish off in the evening. No raid again tonight. The shelter was emptier than ever and those of us who did use it went round to the BMA shelter[77] Boxing Night revels at which Collins, our fellow inmate at the FH, gave us a turn. He topped the bill last night and did it again tonight. An exasperating clown off the stage but most entertaining one on it with a decidedly professional touch. Anyway strolling round there for an hour or so made quite a pleasant break and I enjoyed it more than any part of yesterday evening and much more robust and spontaneous affair. Turned in at 10.30 very tired and slept soundly. Not even the snorers could wake me.

Friday 27 December Office colleague being away for the week, had to do his pay outs today. To ARP HQ in morning to pay office staff. And round to the estates by taxi with Ballard, Housing Superintendent, in afternoon to pay the workmen therein. Another raid at last, the first since Monday night. Alarm sounded 6.35 and lasted till 10.40. Fairly full house again.

Saturday 28 December Lunch at Lyons, home to change then to the Coliseum for the 4.0 performance of *Aladdin*, the West End's one and only pantomime this year – in fact almost the only show of any sort. But of all the awkward times! 12 noon and 4 p.m. And this year when Christmas means so little and evacuation of practically the entire infant population leaves little real demand for pantomime surely the money lavished on this production would have been better employed in providing a good colourful spectacular musical play. It's not even an exceptionally good pantomime. Stalls about two thirds full, circles packed. Out at 7.0 home by bus. In at 7.20 and round at the shelter by 7.40. No warning having gone it was practically empty. Remained quiet all night. Had a gorge of sardines, tomatoes, buttered rolls, crisps and cakes and cocoa, read book for a while and turned in early. Slept eight hours straight off without waking, which I can very rarely do. Dreamed a good deal though.

Sunday 29 December Lunch at 12.30. Chops, chips, beans, mashed turnips, prunes and cream, coffee. Sat by fireside in afternoon. Wrote letter to Norah. Listened to symphony concert including Beethoven's 7th on radio. Then read. A terrific Blitz this evening, presumably a return visit for our heavy raids on the invasion ports last night.[78] Though of

77 British Medical Association House, Tavistock Square.
78 This was the notorious fire bomb raid on the City. The numerous incendiaries dropped overwhelmed the London firefighters at a time when the Thames was at low tide, so pumping river water was difficult. Further, the high explosives dropped with the incendiaries fractured many water mains, drastically reducing the water pressure. The resulting changes in the defences included the formation, in August 1941, of the National Fire Service to replace the individual Fire Brigades, and the introduction of the Fire Guard organisation (requiring 48 hours of duty from eligible persons per 28 days) in place of the voluntary Fire Watcher system previously employed by business premises. In addition, much more 'static water' was made available to firefighters by filling basements of demolished houses and building special tanks: by January 1942, some 88,700 gallons was made available across

1940

comparatively short duration it equalled in intensity anything we've yet had. The alert sounded just after 6.0 and for the first three hours they came in waves every minute or two to the accompaniment of constant gunfire and dropped loads of incendiaries and high explosives. Some tremendous fires were reported over in a south easterly direction which lit up the whole town all night. They were still casting a glow in the sky when we came home in the morning. But after 9.0 it was fairly quiet till the all clear went about midnight.

Monday 30 December Last night's attack was concentrated on the City in an attempt to destroy it by fire. The Guildhall was destroyed together with several Wren churches including St Brides in Fleet St. The Old Bailey was damaged and St Paul's only just escaped, with fires raging all around it. For once the press have been allowed to throw secrecy to the winds and they blazon forth all today in headlines and pictures. I should rank the loss of the Guildhall as the worst calamity that has yet befallen London, which has few buildings more historic. As I expected nothing at all happened tonight. Had supper (cocoa and meat rolls) and took a turn up and down Euston Rd before turning in.

Tuesday 31 December An informal party in the Quakers' shelter to celebrate New Year's Eve. About forty of us altogether. Mostly games, some invariably silly and childish, either embarrassed or bored me. Others uproariously funny, had one doubled up with laughter. It was like one of those old Holborn Rover New Year parties only without Ralph Reader's organising pep and ingenuity. The only breaks in the games were for 'refreshments' (if such they can be called), a lukewarm attempt at dancing and a very tedious mock trial at one time. At midnight we stood in a ring and sang 'Auld Lang Syne' and it was all over. And so to bunk. There was no raid all night. Thus passed out 1940 however I'm so glad to see the last of a year that was an unhappy one for me.

RETROSPECT – 1940

More happened to me in 1940 than in the whole previous ten years put together. And that more consisted largely of two things:

For the first time in my life I fell really and truly in love. It was a 'grand passion' fated, alas, not to survive the year in which it started. It was an emotional upheaval such as I'd never experienced before and from which I have not even yet fully recovered – and may indeed never quite do so.

---

the London Region and forty-one powerful pumps had been installed on twenty-one of the Thames bridges (TNA, HO 186/952 and HO 186/2352). See entry for 5 January 1941 for Heap's tour of the City to see the damage.

Part Two

The story of Eilleen I have recounted at length in my diary and elsewhere.[79] There is no useful purpose to be served in dwelling at length on it again here and reopening old wounds which are still healing. Suffice it to say that I never dreamed I'd ever love anyone as I loved Eilleen. Or that my love would be reciprocated such as it had never been before. It made me sublimely happy and owing to the difficulties and complications involved by the fact that she was married and had children, together with my proneness to frequent fits of jealousy and depression [made me] desperately miserable. I alternated between ecstasy and despair. But attaining the height of the former was worth descending the depths of the latter a hundred times over. It made the spring and summer of 1940 what, I feel, will prove to be the most memorable phase of my life. A beautiful exquisite dream from which the awakening was sudden, abrupt, unexpected, painful and worst of all, utterly incomprehensible. Thus did I love and lose Eilleen. There is no more to say.

The other thing which made 1940 a destiny year for me (thus confounding the science of numerology which would put it at 1935 or 1944) was the fact that after 13½ years at Peter Robinson's, I at last lost my job and, even more remarkable, got another with St Pancras Borough Council. I was out of work for seven weeks (though paid for three of them) and it was quite long enough for me even though it coincided with the holiday period (late July till mid-September) and a fine spell of weather. However, I was really exceptionally lucky to get a job at all in view of my being 30 and so of military age. I owe the fact that I wasn't called up to the fluke of my work being classified as a reserved occupation from 30 – both at PR's and the Town Hall. Even if I had been eligible for service I might possibly have got off on medical grounds. It just wasn't put to the test.

The war dragged on throughout the year, and as I prophesied in my last retrospect, increased in intensity and momentum. It o'ershadowed the whole of the year and, directly or indirectly, had some bearing on everything that happened in it. It was due to the war that I met Eilleen. It was due to the war that we parted – or rather she parted from me. Had it not been for the war I should probably never have got the sack from PR's; had it not been for the war I should certainly have never got a job at the Town Hall. Of all that happened in 1940 it might well have been said 'C'est la guerre.'

Living in London during the latter part of the year with the continual day and night air raids was a grim experience. Yet provided one suffered no personal loss or injury as so many thousands did, one worth living through. Life became suddenly intense and strangely unreal. So much more exciting and yet at the same time so much more monotonous.

---

79 'Elsewhere' is not identified; perhaps it is a reference to her letters that Heap secreted in his diary covers.

1940

An incredible phenomenon. Working by day and sleeping in an air raid shelter by night – from dusk till dawn. It taught us to value even the simplest pleasures of life to which we'd become accustomed and taken for granted. The nocturnal pleasures – theatres, cinemas, pubs, the company of friends, a night's peaceful sleep in a comfortable bed without the threat of death hovering overhead. As always happens it wasn't until we were deprived of these that we fully appreciated them. Only books and an occasional Saturday afternoon at the cinema were left of all the little things that had made life worth living. I naturally missed the theatre most of all though prior to September when the Blitz started in earnest, I had remained an inveterate first nighter throughout the year. And though I must confess that for a time my interest in the theatre took second place to my interest in Eileen, it nevertheless remained my great enthusiasm and I trust ever will be so.

I read a fair number of books, did a few weekends camping with Phil and Kath and one or two walks with Ron and John, I kept up such friendships as I can long claim to and made one or two more. I saved a few more pounds and end the year worth £160 – £20 up on last year (which considering my spell of unemployment and the constantly rising cost of living is not bad going). I drank no more than usual – in fact a good deal less since the change in my life that has been forced on us since September. And there the list of my minor achievements in 1940 ends.

Apart from Eilleen and the change of job – and not forgetting the war! – everything else was of minor consequence. But of what far-reaching consequence to me were those two major happenings.

A bitter sweet year – A momentous year.

1941

This, another momentous year for the now thirty-year-old Anthony Heap, warrants including 51% of the original 43,600 words of the transcript. It opened with a further five months of sleeping in the basement of the Friends House air raid shelter on Euston Road, accompanied by daily touring of as much of London as possible to record the impact of enemy action. With raids becoming less frequent, but delivering heavier bombs, Heap walked his neighbourhood most mornings and evenings and often spent his lunch hour out of the Town Hall visiting bomb incidents to inspect recent damage. Additionally, his work took him around the borough collecting rents and paying ARP workers in their depots and first aid posts. In the early months he felt the need for female company and unsuccessfully proposed by letter to his pen-friend Norah in Manchester; then he met Joan, who had 'distinct possibilities as a prospective mistress' but she 'failed to make the grade'.

In February Heap and his mother moved up a floor to a better situated flat and, within days of the virtual end of the Blitz on 10/11 May, Anthony was recruited into the St Pancras ARP Control Room staff, requiring him to serve one night in four on (sleeping) duty in the Town Hall. A week later, in the course of his wage-paying duties at a first aid post, he met 'that irresistible madcap' Marjorie and they had several outings. She initially rejected his advances but he persevered, and they married on 11 October, honeymooning close to her mother's small house on a Somerset farm. The couple set up home renting a furnished flat in Queen Alexandra Mansions, Judd Street, next to the Town Hall. Country girl Marjorie, six years Heap's junior and employed as a clerical worker, continued to have moods of depression from which he managed to talk her round. Meanwhile they coped with the routine of shelter life, rationing and other shortages, and living on their very limited joint income. In November, they were delighted when Heap's medical examination confirmed that his 1939 abdominal wound rendered him unfit for conscription. Fewer theatrical productions meant that Heap saw more films than West End shows; he read less and had fewer nights out with the lads, as both of 'the Johns' were now in the services. He kept up a regular exchange of letters with John Hobson, who was in the army.

1941

Wednesday 1 January In the shelter tonight two other men and myself agreed to form a fire fighting team to deal with any incendiary bombs which might fall on the roof during a raid. This was a result of the government's present drive to supplement the present ARP and fire-fighting services by voluntary spare time efforts of this nature, the necessity for which was demonstrated by the firing of the City on Sunday night.[1] Three different alerts between 8.0 p.m. and dawn. The snorers were noisier than the guns.

Thursday 2 January The alert sounded at 7.0, went round to the shelter forthwith. The all clear came some five hours later. Had a preliminary demonstration in the use of the stirrup pump – sans water. I am No 3 in the team, my function being to keep the pumps supplied with water. Simplicity itself.

Friday 3 January Several costive attempts at snowing. Brief shelter lecture this evening by district Warden Avery on incendiary bombs, their inner and outer workings and the tackling thereof. He knew his stuff.

Saturday 4 January An invitation round to the Quakers Shelter to hear bearded, benevolent John Fletcher regale us with a lantern lecture on the medical-cum-missionary work of Dr Schweitzer in central Africa. Rather Sunday school-ish but well intentioned. Simple kindly folk. No alert till 1.15 and that lasted till dawn.

Sunday 5 January Spent the morning touring the City and seeing something of the results of last Sunday's raid. It is no exaggeration to say that the bulk of the City is destroyed completely and utterly. Around St Paul's and Cheapside and for a good half mile north of that area, there are very few buildings left intact. Every street has its huge gaping voids, gutted buildings and choked roadways. The odour of charred wood still lingers in the air. Never have I seen such scenes of widespread ruin and desolation. The damage in the West End is negligible by comparison with this – a harrowing sight. Yet in a way I couldn't help thinking that, apart from the tremendous financial loss involved, it's been a blessing in disguise. The City so badly needed re-planning and re-building. (I can only think of it in the past tense now). It was a huge labyrinth of dark twisting turnings. Its buildings were old and antiquated and in a bad state of decay. Its offices were insanitary, badly arranged and ill-ventilated. Taken all in all it was a drab, dismal, unhealthy, soulless place to spend one's working life. I'm glad I never did. Really it was a gigantic museum piece. A mausoleum of all that was hideous and ugly in the commercial sense during the

---

1   Following the damage of the 29 December incendiary raid, the government announced more stringent fire precaution measures, including the compulsory Fire Guard system and the appeal to which Heap responded.

Victorian age, when it grew up and thrived. Its wholesale destruction would have spelt salvation to all those thousands of people condemned to work in it. Yet nothing short of a catastrophe like this could ever have achieved such a desirable object. War has its victories no less renowned than peace. A resounding blow has been struck at gross materialism. Home to lunch at 1.15. Stewed rabbit – and lucky to get that by all accounts. Sat by fire in afternoon. Read papers and made some cigarettes. Had a brief alert about 3.0 – the first daylight one for weeks. An evening one from 7.0 till 11.30.

Wednesday 8 January Lord Baden Powell, the Chief Scout, died today in Kenya, aged 83.[2] He seemed too aged and out of touch with things for the leader of a gigantic youth movement. And even during my connection with the Scouts Association – and that terminated five years ago, it was beginning to suffer badly from lack of leadership. Still, he was a great man and for all that his achievement gave me, I shall ever be grateful. His portrait still looks down on me from my bedroom wall. It's a noble countenance.

Thursday 9 January I see in *The Secretary* that the London headquarters of the CIS in London Wall were completely destroyed in the city fire. Temporary offices have been taken in Gresham St. A great shortage of meat prevails and seems likely to last. Rations being drastically reduced. The price of lunch in the Town Hall canteen has gone up a penny to 1/4d. Blitz back again. An alert with intermittent gunfire, from 7.15 p.m. till 2.0 a.m.

Saturday 11 January Went to see the second edition of Farjeon's *Diversions* at Wyndham's in afternoon.[3] A short but fierce Blitz in the evening from 6.30 till 9.30.[4] Several fires started. All went into the other shelter to hear a lantern lecture on Holland. I've always looked upon Holland as about the dullest and most stolidly uninteresting country on the face of the earth.

Monday 13 January A quiet night, no raids at all, so shelter emptier than usual. Went for walk before turning in. Quite light despite the full moon being obscured by cloud. Walked as far as the south end of Charlotte St and back. Hardly a soul about anywhere, even Tottenham Court Rd was deserted. The buses were empty. Only the familiar sound

---

2   Heap had seen 'the Chief' at the International Camp in Switzerland in 1931, at Albert Hall meetings and at events at the Downe Campsite in Kent.
3   *Diversion* included the talented performer Joyce Grenfell.
4   Heap makes no mention of the Bank Tube Station disaster that evening which killed 111 people when a bomb exploded in the booking hall. It is unusual that he was not aware of and did not observe the massive temporary bridge that was constructed across the complex road junction; however, press reports were generally delayed by the censor for twenty-eight days if specific locations were named.

of the Marquis of Granby broke the ghastly stillness of the night. The rest was silence.

Thursday 16 January No more going down to the canteen for tea in the afternoon, it's now brought round on the trolley instead. Next, round to the BMA shelter concert in the evening, co-shelterer Collins and the two curates from St Pancras Church being the star turns. A lively affair. The jaunt coincided with the night's first alert from 7.10–9.20. The second started at 10.30 and lasted till 1.30.

Friday 17 January Had to pay Drill Hall staff in morning and do the estates around the town in afternoon. We were awoken at 1.40 by the sound of a bomb dropping in the vicinity and though we didn't hear it, the alert sounded a few minutes after and lasted half an hour or so. In the morning we discovered that there had been two local 'incidents' both uncomfortably near Sinclair House. One bomb had dropped at the end of Flaxman Terrace outside the Kentish Arms, just missing the flats. The other on the derelict building at the back of the petrol station in Bidborough St. Though only a few yards from the Town Hall, our windows remained intact this time.

Saturday 18 January The Flaxman Terrace bomb last night destroyed part of the Kentish Arms and rendered several of the council flats sufficiently uninhabitable to necessitate the evacuation of the tenants. Fewer rents for me to collect on Monday. The other one almost completely demolished what was left of the land mine shattered Euston Cinema.[5] It saved the house breakers quite a lot of work. Had an alert from 3.10 till 4.0, proceeded by gunfire. More often than not lately the only bomb planting or gunfire heard takes place before the sirens blare forth. A humorous but hardly commendable reflection on the efficiency of our ARP system.

Sunday 19 January The papers are full of the government's new scheme for compulsory fire-fighting service for all male civilians between 16 and 60.[6] This involves registration with the local authority and 48 hours duty a month, unpaid of course. Surely a more iniquitous system for mounting up the air raid casualties couldn't have been devised.

Monday 20 January Had to do a different rent collection this week. Montague Tibbles House in Prince of Wales Rd. Bigger and more tricky. A bob out on balancing. I prefer Flaxman Terrace any week.

Wednesday 22 January At long last the government have had the gumption to clamp down on the communists and suppress *The Daily Worker*.[7] A letter from Norah [Morris]. Since it was heavily Blitzed a

5   81 Euston Road, now the site of the St Pancras Youth Hostel.
6   The Fire Guard organisation, which had paid officers for coordination in each borough.
7   The ban was lifted in August 1942.

few weeks back, Manchester is, like London, now completely dead after dark.

Thursday 23 January A lucky break, was notified this morning that I am to be given more responsible duties and moved up into the next grade. Fourth raid-less night in succession. About the longest quiet spell we've had so far. Went out for a forty minute walk before turning in.

Friday 24 January Started new weekly job paying Dustmen, Stokers and Stablemen. Managed to get soap and [tooth]paste at the chemist's on the corner but had the utmost difficulty in getting blades. Not even Woolworths had any. Eventually discovered some in an electrical shop in Euston Rd. The chemist told me that his supply is limited to 14/6 worth for three months – the quantity he normally sells in two days! A preposterous position.

Wednesday 29 January Proclamation issued today calling up the 18s and 19s and 37 to 41 age groups. Accompanied by the usual statement that the schedule of reserved occupations is being drastically revised so as to include only key men and those in jobs which cannot be done by women. They've been working on this revised schedule for the last six months. I suppose one day they'll finish publishing vague statements about it in the press and actually issue it. Then there will be some flutterings in the dovecots, including, no doubt, mine. The blighters are sure to catch up with me sooner or later on the reserved occupation dodge. There will then but remain my trump card – the medical one. The first evening alert for ten days sounded at 5.45. Lasted till 10.0 p.m. A very quiet one however. Had a bad fit of depression down in the shelter, culminating in an attack of nerves and a distressing 'scene' with Mother. I therefore stalked out and took a vigorous walk up and down Euston Road. The raw night air cooled my fevered brow, calmed my temper and soothed my nerves. I should have done that to start with.

Friday 31 January A number of bombs dropped between Hampstead Rd and Albany St during one of the two daylight raids. Heard something come whistling down whilst I was in the Barber's under Brighton Hall Hotel waiting for a haircut.[8] It sounded as if it were heading straight down on us and for the moment I was quite scared. Then silence. No explosion or report of any sort. What it was or where it landed I don't know. Big fires started at Bowman's in Camden High St and Maples depository in Pratt St by incendiary bombs in yesterday's raids. Latest news – among today's bulls eyes – National Temperance Hospital and Post Office opposite in Hampstead Rd, Albany St barracks, Middlesex

---

8   In nearby Cartwright Gardens.

1941

Hospital, pub in Farringdon Rd. Many casualties. Talk by Avery on *Gases* in shelter tonight. Gases are 'in the air' these days.[9]

Monday 3 February Decided to transfer to vacant flat up on top floor overlooking Hastings St, No 25. Looked over it at lunchtime, about same size as our present one – three rooms – but with much more light (I'm sick to death of that miserable dark back bedroom of mine) and for a better outlook. On a fine day Highgate Hill is visible from the front rooms. And yet the rent is 6d less than it is for No 19! Some slight damage to a wall and a broken window – the only one in Sinclair House to get the blast from the Bidborough St bomb in need of repairing. When that's done we can move in.

Wednesday 5 February Letter from John [Hobson]. Devotes the whole of it to describing how, on a three day 'invasion repelling' exercise, they had nothing but bread and jam for practically every meal! Replied after tea. Started *Kilvert's Diary* in evening, got it at lunchtime.

Friday 7 February Phoned John Bell, hadn't seen or heard from him since October. Still managing Burton's branch at Southgate and awaiting his call up for the navy (he had his medical eight months ago!). Meanwhile we both look forward to some nocuous reunions during John H's leave four weeks hence.

Sunday 9 February Devoted the whole day to preparations for moving. Didn't go out at all till the evening, didn't even wash or shave. Spent the morning getting up the oilcloth and carpets from under the furniture (the devil's own job), cleaning them and rolling them up. And the afternoon emptying the bookcase and sorting out the hundred odd books therein into two piles, those to be retained and those to be dispensed with. As we have decided to get rid of the rickety old bookcase as well as my bedstead and washstand, the great majority of those musty old tomes fall into the latter category, in fact, sixty five percent. I then set to work on my cupboard in the same manner. As in the case of the books, though to an even greater extent, it was difficult to decide what to keep and what to throw away as 'old junk.' A rather melancholy task really. Practically all the odds and ends – booklets, souvenirs, letters, cuttings, receipts, notices, and the like – which I'd accumulated and stored throughout the years, bring back past memories. Some date back to my childhood days. Being a born collector and hoarder of old junk I'm loath to part with any of it, but space being limited, it must be kept within wieldy proportions and some of it dispensed with occasionally. And moving to me presents the best opportunity to do so. However, the

---

9 The threat of gas attack was a recurrent issue and the Ministry of Home Security periodically reminded people of the potential gas threat, particularly when the invasion threats resurfaced. In 1944 the Prime Minister's daughter Sarah Churchill was filmed on the roof of the Home Office demonstrating fitting a gas mask (Churchill Archive, Churchill College, Cambridge, Hodsoll Papers 6/2).

percentage of 'throw-outs' wasn't so high as in the case of the books – only about twenty-five percent. The new flat should be ready for us by about Wednesday. They have yet to re-paper the walls. The repairs to wall and window have been done. A two hour alert in evening from 7.45 till 9.40. As soon as it was over, went for a good forty minute walk round as far as New Oxford St and back to make up for my lack of fresh air today. Didn't sleep as well as I expected to after it. Had some awful nightmares.

Monday 10 February After tea went to No 25 with a tape measure to finally decide where exactly to place the various pieces of furniture. Then a final check over the discarded books and papers before they're disposed of, just to make sure I'm parting with nothing of real value either monetary or sentimental. Went for another long moonlit walk this evening before turning in. An alert sounded just as I get back to the Friends House at 10.15. All clear at 11.0.

Wednesday 12 February The evening *Star* has reduced the size of its pages and doubled the number. It now resembles the *Standard*, a great improvement. I wonder that all the papers, morning and evening, don't alter their size in corresponding fashion, for the smaller size paper is much easier to handle. I'm a terribly slow reader these days. The trouble is that it is very difficult to get on with a book, what with people continually talking around me and the radio blaring forth all the time. It requires a real mental effort to concentrate on reading, even a few pages.

Thursday 13 February After tea spent an hour transferring the contents of my cupboard and sundry other odds and ends up to the new flat and depositing them in a cupboard up there. Up and down the two flights of stairs with a suitcase full of stuff I went at least a dozen times before I'd finished. The gas men came and took the stove up this morning. But there's still one room to be re-papered before we can move in. Till then we've got to keep going up for every bit of cooking or hot water we want. This moving business is hell.

Friday 14 February Spent another hour after tea taking things up to No 25 and still that damned room isn't re-papered yet. So our moving-in looks like being delayed over the weekend. This is indeed a bloody business. Ron left a message to meet him at Belsize Park Station at 8.0. So after calling at the shelter and leaving our two attaché cases, went up there by tube from Euston. As luck would have it, after being quiet every evening for practically weeks on end, the Blitz must return tonight in full force for the second evening I've spent out of the shelter since we started going down there. The alert sounded about 7.40 while I was in the tube and as we walked round from one pub to another planes flew low overhead incessantly to the accompaniment of gunfire. We stuck this for an hour or more then gave the evening

1941

up as a bad job. Ron, who suffers from claustrophobia to some extent and can't abide shelters decided to walk over the heath till it eased up while I came back on the tube, the platforms and passages packed with shelterers. Got back to the Friends House at 10.0 whereupon it immediately quietened down.

Sunday 16 February So to all intents and purposes we are now in occupation of No 25 and I write this diary there for the first time. The view from my bedroom window, at which I write, takes in quite a wide sweep. It would be even wider if the massive bulk of Clifton House in the centre of the picture didn't block the view northwards across Euston Rd.[10] Through a gap to the right of it can be seen the network of railway lines and gasometers which form the hinterland of St Pancras station with the ruins of the little Euston Cinema and its adjoining buildings in the foreground and the heights of Highgate Hill in the distance (I can't actually see this now as it's only visible on a very clear day which it isn't). Over to the right the pseudo-Gothic outlines of St Pancras station or rather the Midland Hotel, dominates the scene dwarfing the white squat town hall which stands in front of it. A London scene in every detail. The brightness of the rooms is the most striking contrast to No 19. The kitchen, which is the only room at the back and, facing southwards, looks down on the whole length of the courtyard, is probably the lightest of the three for it gets the sun.

Thursday 20 February Finished *Kilvert's Diary* in the evening. Diaries are an all too rare variety of literature. To me they are particularly fascinating. Partly because I keep one myself, partly because 'it' is a form of literary expression which appeals to me strongly. What makes a good diary? The subject matter or the manner in which it is written? It depends to some extent (but not entirely so) on the occupation and social status of the writer, and, to a lesser extent on his interests and hobbies. Most of the great diarists have had the initial advantage of an affluent position, social prestige and an acquaintance with prominent figures of the day. Pepys is of course the classic example. Evelyn was in the same boat, but the two best and foremost modern diarists, Arnold Bennett and James Agate, fall into a similar category even though their sphere of activity is mainly confined to the literary and theatrical worlds. That alone, however is not in itself sufficient. The diarist must infuse his own personality and idiosyncrasies into his journal and comment on the people and events of the day in the light of his own ego.

A diary should undoubtedly be as frank and intimate as possible but a complete lack of self-consciousness is not, I think, so essential

---

10 The block occupying 83–117 Euston Road (south side), between Judd St and Mapledon Place, then included the Euston Tavern, the Euston Cinema and the multi-office Clifton House; the present post-war block includes the Youth Hostel and a Premier Inn over shops and offices.

or desirable as some critics hold. In fact I rather doubt if any diary has ever been written with an entire absence of self-consciousness and less than half an eye to posterity. While the mere fact that it is 'only a diary' is surely no valid excuse for the casual, slipshod untidy expression which is sometimes taken for 'natural' writing. There is no reason why one should not express oneself in the best prose of which one is capable in this medium as in any other. The same applies to letter writing – another neglected art.

The whole point is provided that one's personality and outlook in recording one's life comments intelligently on such things, people and events as come within its scope thereby throw some light on the times in which one lives, then the social standing of the diarist is only of secondary importance.

That is where a diary like Kilvert's scores. He was merely the obscure vicar of a small parish on the Welsh border, who knew no one of much importance and moved only in a very small circle. Yet his personality is clearly defined (and a very gentle, simple and lovable one it is too) and mid-Victorian England is brought so vividly to life throughout this modest record of his daily comings hither and goings hence that it is a sheer joy to read. His description of the countryside and the mountain scenery and their varying colours contain [sic] some of the loveliest prose passages imaginable. If my diary proves to be as well worth reading a century hence, I shall be more than satisfied with my labour of love.

At last theatres are to be allowed to open on Sundays, subject to Parliamentary approval and be put on an equal footing with cinemas in that respect. To think that it takes a war to achieve this amendment of such a stupid anomaly! Ron suddenly migrated back to his home town of Wolverhampton last Saturday. Apparently Friday night's experience was more than enough of Blitz time London for him!

Sunday 23 February To Hampstead in afternoon, a grand day for walking. The huge sand pits over by the Spaniards Rd are being filled in with bricks and debris from bombed houses. They look worse than when they were empty.

Monday 24 February A different rent collection – Somers Town Estate. Not so bad as I expected. Balanced all right, but inadvertently banked the £5 worth of change I set out with, along with the rents. However that can easily be adjusted with the next collection. A painful boil developing on my neck just where my collar fits. A letter from Norah, she passed the exams she took two months ago. She's dead set on being a successful masseuse.

Tuesday 25 February A really exasperating day, one mad rush from start to finish. Had to pay the First Aid Posts in afternoon. Got money to make up the packets in morning, an hour late which gave me no time to check it over. Made up packets as fast as I could and hoped for the best. Fortunately it passed out all right. Then the car arrived late from Malet Place to take me round the hospitals wherever the posts are situated. We got away twenty minutes behind time and failed to make it up. For in spite of rushing round as fast as we could, delays occurred at practically every post even apart from the long winded procedure whereby everyone has to sign for their pay. Finally when I got back at 4.30 I am greeted with the news that someone had phoned up to say that their packet was a £1 short! And on top of this I had to endure the painful discomfort of my boil at its tenderest. I took a very poor view of today, despite its glorious weather. Wrote a letter to Norah after tea, have decided to sound her on the possibility of our getting married in the distant future. I think it's high time we came to some sort of understanding on that question.

Wednesday 26 February The man with the £1 short yesterday came in and saw me this morning. Assuming what he says is true, he seems to be strangely resigned to the loss. Realising that he should have opened the packet and checked it immediately, he was prepared to let the matter drop, unless someone overpaid a quid brought it back which is very unlikely. Tough luck on the bloke but nothing more can be done about it except me giving him a quid from my pocket, which I'm naturally not prepared to do without definite proof that it's my mistake.

Friday 28 February Met John [Hobson] and went over to the Euston Tavern. His regiment moved to the Ipswich district three days ago. It turns out to be even worse than Colchester for they now live in trenches and dug-outs, apparently a perfect replica of France 1916, except for a trifle less mud. He seemed to wear a rather subdued air, such as is commonly discernible in soldiers home on leave for the first time.

Saturday 1 March Further trouble of Tuesday's £1 short incident. Smith, the man in question, apparently goaded into action by his wife and colleagues, wrote to the Borough Treasurer about it. So Taylor called me in, asked to phone Smith to come down and then when he arrived, threshed the matter out in trio. Eventually I agreed to go fifty-fifty and give him 10/- out of my pocket and the dispute was settled with that compromise. Saw Taylor after, told me he was glad I'd settled the matter satisfactorily 'out of court', that he'd heard very good accounts of my work lately and would therefore make it up to me by putting me up into the next grade soon, which means 7/6 a week more. Home to tea then Horse Shoe by 6.0 to meet the Johns. Much to our surprise we found it shut so repaired to the Holborn, JB [John Bell] going home for his last weekend left us fairly early to catch a tram from Victoria. Eventually we landed up at the Green Parrot where we tarried till nigh on midnight. Went home to change before going to the shelter, where I arrived at 12.30 as the third alert of the evening was sounding.

Part Two

Tuesday 4 March The First Aid Posts pay round again. Everything ran smoothly and according to schedule this time even though I got the money a bit late to start with. Staved off an imminent attack of nerves after tea by going out for a good vigorous forty minute walk before proceeding to the shelter.

Wednesday 5 March John's last evening on leave. To Bounds Green to see a couple of his girlfriends. One of them, Joan, has distinct possibilities as a prospective mistress. Not out of the top drawer by any means but lively enough and physically she has her points. The very antithesis of a prude, she might suit me admirably for a spring diversion.

Friday 7 March For two hours in the evening I was the sole occupant of the shelter. The other half dozen, including Mother who had been to an ARP lecture at HQ, didn't begin to arrive till 9.30. What a welcome break it was to read one's book in peace and quiet without any distractions whatever. I'd almost forgotten what it was like.

Saturday 8 March A sudden revival of the Blitz just before 8.0 this evening brought all the old habitués scampering back to the shelter. Flares were dropped and the guns thundered away incessantly till about 11.0.

Sunday 9 March By all accounts considerable damage was done by last night's raid which was the fiercest for many weeks. The most sensational occurrence was a direct hit on the Café de Paris in Coventry St – one of the West End's most fashionable night haunts. It was crowded at the time and dancing in progress. Several were killed, many celebrities being among the casualties.[11] The news must have raced around London like wildfire today for when I passed it this afternoon crowds were standing outside gaping thereat. Though there was nothing to be seen externally. All the damage must have been confined to the interior. A gruesome sight I should imagine.

Monday 10 March Norah in reply to my proposals politely but firmly – and I think very wisely – turned me down. To which I counter reply that, as it can't lead anywhere and we're unlikely to meet again, I see no point in continuing our correspondence indefinitely. 'Twould be too unnatural, I'm not by nature given to so called 'platonic' friendships with women. To me they seem forced and artificial and altogether unsatisfactory relationships. Anyhow, I now know where I stand. That's something. Hardly a shop or building around King's Cross had

---

11   Two 50-kg bombs passed through the Rialto Cinema above the underground club – advertised as the safest restaurant in London. One exploded among the dancers, band and diners, killing four members of staff, including the bandleader, Ken 'Snakehips' Johnson, the manager and the head waiter, as well as thirty diners. Another eighty were taken to hospital.

1941

any glass left intact in their windows today. A bomb fell on the Met. Station platform last night. So it's now closed down, others dropped up Crowndale Rd way.

Thursday 13 March My 31st birthday. Present consisted of three pairs of socks from Mother and half a dozen handkerchiefs from Fred and family at Manor Park. Otherwise I hardly gave it a thought.

Saturday 15 March Two sidelights on the war. On the debit side – the food shortage is becoming so acute that jam and all similar is to be rationed to half pound a month – about a quarter of our normal consumption. Eggs and fish are extremely scarce and meat still rationed to 1s 2d worth a week. On the credit side is the recent pronounced success of our AA fighters against the night bombers. There are several being brought down every night now.[12] Camelot House rent collection in the morning. A comparison of the cash totals with bank paying in slips makes me a quid short. The sheets have yet to be balanced, but unless that reveals an error, I shall have to stand the loss. A disconcerting thought to bring away with me for the week end. There are now ten West End theatres in operation again. Nine have reopened during the last two months.[13] Things are looking up. I arranged to see Joan this evening but called it off at the last moment, I decided after due deliberation that she doesn't quite come up to the standard I've set myself in my choice of women. Perhaps I'm over fastidious and too discriminating in this respect. But there it is, Joan fails to make the grade, so it is best that the affair be stopped at birth rather than let it proceed and peter out in a disappointing conclusion which I feel would be inevitable. For once I follow the dictates of my intuition and better judgement. Then in the evening comes a final note from Norah in reply to my valediction. Very understanding and sympathetic she rounds off the episode with beautiful finesse. So I am left once more with no feminine attachments whatever. The perfect paramour is indeed difficult to find – if such a phenomenon exists.

Tuesday 18 March Aunt Pop's birthday card, letter and a $5 bill, posted on 24 Feb. arrived today by airmail. Replied after tea. Filled two full sized sheets of note paper, both sides in two hours. The alert sounded tonight at 10.30 and jiggered up the radio just as Churchill was about to speak. It was beautifully timed.

Wednesday 19 March The fiercest London Blitz this year with tonight's alert which lasted from 8.15 till 2.0 a.m. Should imagine they did a good deal of damage. Shelter full once more.

---

12 *The Times* on 13 March reported 'Toll of Night Bombers – Four Brought Down'.
13 *The Times* (various dates) reported that re-openings included the Comedy on 24 January and the St Martin's on 15 February, while the Little presented ballet in aid of the Greek Red Cross on 10 March (but see 17 April and note 21 for further damage to the Little).

Part Two

Thursday 20 March On the Wardens' pay round this morning saw the damage caused by a land mine which fell in the centre of a block of buildings near the corner of York Way and Hungerford Rd close to the Brecknock last night. In order to pay some of the stretcher men digging for bodies there, I was able to go right into the thick of it and see the whole works. Not a building in the entire block was left standing intact. It was part of a gigantic pile of debris surrounded by a jagged shell of shattered walls. Every window and shop front for many streets around were blocked out. The total casualties were unknown but likely to prove heavy. These land mines are the very devil. Another dropped on a block of flats just off Cumberland Market. I walked up to see this after tea. The damage wasn't so devastating here though innumerable flats in the many blocks clustered together hereabouts have been made uninhabitable through blast, that is apart from those directly hit. This particular neighbourhood, between the north side of Hampstead Rd and Albany St has been hit as severely as anywhere in London. The proximity of Albany St barracks may have something to do with it. I noticed the pinnacle of the church spire along there had, like many others in London, been removed and that Cumberland Market is now used as a huge sand dump. It looks awful. The alert this evening was as quiet and brief as last night's was noisy and prolonged. It lasted from 8.30 till 10.0. Went out for a short walk after.

Friday 28 March The latest rationing joke – cheese to be 1 oz. a week from beginning of May.

Sunday 30 March A new radio aerial contraption has been erected on Parliament Hill. About 150 ft high it looks like a miniature Eiffel Tower. Out again in afternoon to Windmill St to see the charred remains of the White Hart where a fire broke out last night. Then a stroll around the West End, by bus to Camden Town and a walk through Regent's Park (i.e. such of it one can walk through which isn't much) and around the lower slopes of Primrose Hill, on which I spied the once familiar figure of old Robin Littlewood, erstwhile dramatic critic of the late (but not over-lamented) *Morning Post*.

Wednesday 2 April The Sunday Opening of Theatres Bill was defeated in the Commons last night by 144 votes against 136, a bare majority of eight.[14] But what a triumph for the mealy mouthed puritans, the smug sanctimonious chapel-goers, joy-killing ecclesiasticals – in fact, for the whole miserable brood of pious narrow-minded humbugs who represent the non-conformist conscience which dominates the country to this day. No wonder we are the laughing stock of the world.

---

14 It had been thought desirable by some to also open cinemas on Sundays for the benefit of workers, but the annulment of the Order closing theatres and music halls on Sundays was lost, as was any extension to Sunday cinema opening. Churchill and Attlee both voted against the annulment (*The Times*, 3 April 1941).

1941

Thursday 3 April The theatres plan to hit back by (a) Forming themselves into clubs with a nominal membership fee of 1/- or 2/6 a year which will empower them to open Sundays and furthermore puts them beyond the jurisdiction of the censor (b) boycotting the numerous charity shows, religious or otherwise, to which artists give their services free. Cochran goes even further and advocates a general strike and a closing of all theatres in protest. That's the stuff to give the puritan prigs. Stayed at the office till 6.0 and did an hour's overtime on the wage sheets – much bigger this week due to arrears of war bonus having to be worked out and included therein.

Sunday 6 April Arctic weather, as cold as it has been at any time during the winter. Walked over Hampstead in morning and took a second look round City ruins in afternoon. Looks even worse now they've cleared it up a bit than it did three months ago just after the Great Fire [raid] and though more of it is accessible to pedestrians, many one-time streets are still closed. However one can now get a better idea of the extent of the damage, which proves to be even more colossal than I at first thought. The odour of charred wood lingers in the air even to this day. And it still attracts crowds of sight-seers. I suppose it has the same sort of grim morbid fascination of the Chamber of Horrors – and it's just as tiring to walk round. We have today acquired yet another involuntary and virtually useless ally in Jugo-Slavia. Unlike Rumania and Bulgaria, they have been tactless enough to resist German demands for allegiance – with the result that Germany declared war on them this morning.

Monday 7 April Today's budget proves to be much less drastic than expected. Income tax is raised to 10/- in the £ and the various allowances correspondingly reduced – but the greater part of the increases thereby payable are to be credited to the taxpayers' accounts in the Post Office Savings Bank for post-war use.[15] A surprisingly philanthropic touch this, and apparently this direct taxation is expected to yield sufficient to cover the ever expanding war expenditure without recourse to further indirect taxation, for the expected increased duties on beer, whisky and tobacco have not materialised. To give the devil his due I think that the Chancellor of the Exchequer, Sir Kingsley Wood, had made a good job of the budget which is both sound and fair. And I may say this despite the fact that I have just worked out what I shall be liable to pay under it – to wit, some £23.10.0 for the year or 9/- a week!

Wednesday 9 April The granting of a holiday on Good Friday to all the council servants (as distinct from officers) has necessitated a re-adjustment of our week's work. This means that someone else has to do my wardens pay round this week. We get Easter Monday off

---

15   Post-war credits were forced saving, as advocated by John Maynard Keynes.

and one extra day. My second increase in salary (promised a month ago) has gone through at last and starts this week. Salonika fell this morning to the Germans after a rapid three day advance into Greece from Bulgaria. This virtually means the imminent collapse of Greece and Jugo-Slavia and is a setback of the utmost gravity for us. And what a bitter pill for those wishful thinkers who maintained that the mountainous Balkans couldn't be invaded and overrun as easily as the Low Countries.

Thursday 10 April The revised schedule of reserved occupations is published at last. Mother went down and bought a copy at the Stationery Office this morning. Apparently there was a long queue six deep waiting for copies.

Monday 14 April Bank Holiday and a wretchedly dull and miserable one it was too. Was wondering what the hell to do with myself this morning apart from getting the blues – when a letter from John Hobson arrived and solved the problem – at least for the best part of the morning by giving me a letter to write in reply. I was never more grateful. In the afternoon went with Mother to Greenwich via London Bridge and Bermondsey. Walked through the park (which is something like a larger and more attractive edition of Primrose Hill) and round the Observatory, from which the view must be quite extensive on a clear day. Finally down to the river where we discovered that the historic Ship Hotel, once famed for its whitebait dinners, had been bombed many months ago. Only the bare ruin of it now stands. Back by train to the Embankment through New Cross and Camberwell.

Tuesday 15 April Strolled around the former Italian quarter in Clerkenwell in the course of the evening walk. Dirty, decayed and desolate, the narrow streets of Little Italy now remind me of *The Deserted Village* only with more sinister effect.[16]

Wednesday 16 April A long alert overnight (11.0–4.0). Some occasional gunfire but didn't hear of any bombs being dropped anywhere. The popular dailies are reduced to four pages (one sheet) every day and the Sunday papers eight. *The Telegraph* runs to six but has gone up to 1½d. in consequence. Lunch at the Salvation Army restaurant[17] seems to be a dubious proposition unless one goes early i.e. soon after mid-day when they open. For by the time I got there at 12.45 all the meat dishes had gone off the menu so I had to resort to fish and chips which like eggs and bacon I find unappetising without sauce – and they had no sauce. This, with fig pudding cost 1/2d. but I hope to fare better next time.

---

16   Little Italy, the traditional 'Italian quarter' of London, was the triangular area around Saffron Hill, bounded by Clerkenwell Road, Rosebery Avenue and Farringdon Road. *The Deserted Village* refers to Oliver Goldsmith's 1770 poem about a depopulated rural Irish hamlet.
17   Now the headquarters of the Royal National Institute of Blind People, 105 Judd Street.

1941

Thursday 17 April About the worst Blitz we've yet experienced broke over London.[18] [Alert] Soon after 9 p.m. last night and lasted a good seven hours. It took us right back to last September, though neither then nor since has there been anything to match this raid for non-stop intensity. By 9.30 the shelter was packed and though we turned in as usual about 11.0 the incessant drone of relays of planes flying low overhead (they recurred at least once a minute), the continual gunfire, and the frequent explosion of bombs in the near vicinity made sleep impossible. Finally, when, somewhere around 3 a.m. a bomb hit the other end of Friends House itself, penetrated two floors and shook the building from top to bottom, we all got up and dressed and kept on the q.v. till the all clear sounded at 4.45.[19] I immediately went out to look around and in the course of an hour's walk witnessed the following fires still raging: The whole of Maples main building between Tottenham Court Rd and Gower St (by far the biggest and most destructive fire of the lot) – The Hotel Russell – Herbrand St Schools – The Express Dairy head offices in Tavistock Place – the south wing of University College and a number of houses along Gower St – a factory and a block of flats in Chenies St – the side of the Embassy Cinema in Torrington Place – a block of buildings on the south side of New Oxford St – Fleming's restaurant in Oxford St and a road crater further up – and one or two fires off Charlotte St. So numerous in fact that there couldn't have been sufficient firemen to cope with them for some were burning away unattended. High explosive wreckage I found around the BMA in Woburn Place,[20] in Bloomsbury St, Alfred Place and along Oxford St just beyond Rathbone Place. Dawn had broken by the time I got back to the shelter at 6 a.m. for a final hour's counting of sheep. Counting was all it came to. Further St Pancras bomb damage seen today. Pancras Square, where a land mine demolished the entire block of flats and shattered all the surrounding houses with heavy casualties. (This was one of the worst incidents the borough has had) – the First

18   This, 'the heaviest raid of the war' to date (TNA, HO186/952) and remembered as 'The Wednesday', caused extensive damage, some of which Heap recorded. T. H. O'Brien's official history of *Civil Defence* (London: HMSO, 1955) quotes German records showing that 685 aircraft had dropped 890 tons of high explosive and 4,200 incendiary canisters. Some 1,180 Londoners were killed and 2,230 seriously injured; 2,250 fires were started. Thus it was the heaviest attack on London in terms of weight of bombs dropped, casualties inflicted (the landmine which destroyed the Pancras Square flats, Camden Town, cost 78 lives) and number of fires caused.
19   Heap's record of the raid corresponds closely with the Friends House Fire Watchers Log, which recorded: 'Very noisy – barrage, bombs, flares and fires. About 3.0 am after incendiaries extinguished on roof and in garden, high explosive hit [south-west corner, second-floor] office smashing rooms around and below, breaking windows and doors elsewhere.' Two of the fire watchers were treated at the nearby Elizabeth Garrett Anderson Hospital for injuries from falling debris, which, incidentally, buried their log book. (Library of the Society of Friends, Ref: YM/MFS/PRM/FW/LB1.) 'q.v.': 'quod vide' = 'which see', i.e. waiting for more information.
20   BMA: the headquarters of the British Medical Association, on the north-east corner of Tavistock Square, WC1.

Aid Post building at the back of St Pancras Hospital – two or three more houses down in Oakley Square – some schools at the foot of Haverstock Hill – A landmine between Gray's Inn Rd and King's Cross Rd near King's Cross.

Just back from two hour evening walk round West End, which took the main brunt of last night's attack. It's in a sorry state. Among the buildings completely written off I found the Shaftesbury Theatre and the block of tenements opposite (the worst damage I've seen today), Jack Bloomfield's in Bear St and all surrounding buildings, Stone's Chop House in Panton St, Buzzard's in Oxford St. Slightly damaged were Selfridges and Peter Robinson's and badly wrecked Warings and Littlewoods, Pritchard's and Drage's (this is the fourth time PR's windows and frontage have been blown in). Big slabs of Oxford St were damaged beyond repair on both sides. Fire-fighting on a big scale was still proceeding in the Adelphi where the Little was damaged,[21] Jermyn St and many other places including some of the aforementioned. Any number of thoroughfares blocked with debris and the air was thick with dust and smoke and the smell of smouldering ruins. Such was but a fraction of the total havoc wrought in London during this one night of Blitz which the papers and radio, both here and in Germany, agree to have been the worst we've had so far.

Friday 18 April Saw still more of the devastation in an evening tour of Holborn area. Here the greater part of Bourne Estate and Gray's Inn Rd was laid waste and the ruins still smouldering. Wallis's, the City Temple and St Andrew's behind it were completely burnt out; So were several shops and buildings in Leather Lane, High Holborn, Gray's Inn Rd and Red Lion St. Also Sentinel St on the corner of Southampton Row and Theobalds Rd with all the shops below and several houses in Old Gloucester St behind it. St John's on Red Lion Square now in ruins, apparently hit by an H.E. bomb, all this was apart from the considerable damage done by blast and various minor incidents in the borough. What a raid!

Saturday 19 April The radio said this morning that St Paul's, Chelsea Old Church, Royal Hospital, Guy's Hospital and Christie's were hit on Wednesday night. The City Temple, Selfridges and Maples (but not Wallis's) were also mentioned in despatches. Went round to the Regent in the afternoon.[22]

Sunday 20 April Another heavy raid overnight lasting from 9.15 till 4.45 though not as bad as Wednesday night's.[23] Slept through most of it. [Cousin] Jack over to see us early this morning. They'd just

21 The Little Theatre was badly damaged and was demolished in 1949.
22 The Regent Cinema, 37–43 Euston Road.
23 'The Saturday', London's next major raid by the Luftwaffe, was claimed by Herman Goering to have dropped 1,000 tons of bombs on London to celebrate Hitler's fifty-second

1941

been evacuated to a Rest Centre owing to an unexploded bomb in the vicinity.

Tuesday 22 April Am laying in stocks of razor blades, shaving soap and hair cream, each of which are becoming very scarce. I now have sufficient supplies to see me through the summer months.

Monday 28 April For the first time this year I had an orange today. Some limited supplies are at last starting to trickle through from Spain. I've missed my regular apple or orange a day badly as I'm apt to get very constipated without it.

Tuesday 29 April On the First Aid Post pay round this afternoon the car broke down at Bayham St. Consequently after phoning the depot and waiting in rain for twenty minutes for another to arrive, I had to get a bus to St Margaret's, another to the Archway, climb up and down Highgate Hill to Highgate Hospital then came back by tube. I was pleased!

Wednesday 30 April Home to supper at 8.30 and round to the shelter an hour later. We now eat at home every night before going round and taking thermos (and sandwiches).

Thursday 1 May Travelling by bus these days isn't what it used to be for on most of them the windows have been rendered opaque by green gauze material spread thereon to prevent flying glass and [they] dim the lights at night. I never realised before what an immense pleasure one used to derive (and still can on some) from looking out of bus windows. Just another case of not appreciating anything until deprived of it.

Friday 2 May The Grecian episode has just ended with the final evacuation of our troops.[24]

Sunday 4 May The first day of the new double summer time for the clocks were advanced a further hour overnight in addition to the already existing hour's advance which has been maintained through the winter. So that it doesn't get dark until after 10.0 p.m. and we need only to get to the shelter at night to sleep and not devote half the evening down there.

Thursday 8 May Was invited to take up ARP Control Room duties at the Town Hall. This makes staying on one night and sleeping in the dormitory one night in every four and all day Saturday and Sunday every month. Voluntary part-time work – four meals provided. As it

---

birthday. Although 1,200 were killed and 1,000 'seriously injured', it apparently did not have as much impact on Heap as 'The Wednesday' three days earlier.

24 The evacuation of some 50,732 men (mainly New Zealand and other Empire troops) was completed on 30 April but some 7,000 had to be abandoned and were forced to surrender.

Part Two

wouldn't do me any good if I refused, I decided to accept it. Besides, it might prove of some interest and break the monotony of things a bit. From what I hear of it, provided there is no raid on, most of the time is spent in playing cards, darts, billiards and going to the pub and back. A new office pastime. Betting on the number of planes brought down at night, 3d a guess, winner gets 90% Red Cross 10%. Last night it was 23, for tonight I plumped for 13.

Friday 9 May My lucky number turned up trumps again. After starting at 9 this morning, the figure for last night gradually mounted during the day till the final announced this evening was 13. So I took the pool of 6/6 less 10% is 5/10.

Sunday 11 May Big Blitz overnight, the first of any magnitude for three weeks. Lasted from 11.0 till 5.0.[25] Stayed in bed and tried to sleep but it was impossible for, as if there wasn't enough row outside, everyone must perforce get up, put all the lights on and talk 'umpteen to the dozen', as if that makes things any better. Not to mention the additional din caused by a host of new arrivals who were so numerous that the shelter began to resemble the black hole of Calcutta. However, I did actually manage to get a couple of hours sleep after the 'all clear' had sounded, and how I needed it. Walking home in the morning, I discovered that the two near hits which shook the Friends House during the night were (a) the pub next to De Gaulle's Free French Forces HQ over the road[26] and (b) the corner of Euston Rd and Dukes Rd behind St Pancras Church, including the Swiss Café, the garage next to it and part of Somerset Terrace behind it. A third bomb had made a crater in Euston Rd further along (it had fallen almost exactly the same spot as the land-mine last Sept) broken in the front of Clifton House and the Euston Tavern and smashed all the windows in the Town Hall again. Those of Sinclair House had remained intact fortunately though the shops underneath had got slightly damaged once more. No water supply up on the top floor so we have to go down to the basement to draw it. Walked as far as Shaftesbury Avenue in morning. Various shops burnt out in Tottenham Court Rd, houses demolished in Fitzroy Square and Fitzroy St, a good part of Charlotte St and Old Compton St (Soho's two main streets) completely destroyed by fire, a nasty hit between Dean St and Wardour St (also on Levita House, Somers Town) – a house on Gower St and a building on Malet St down – unexploded bombs

---

25   This five-hour raid by 550 bombers killed 1,418 Londoners. A total of 4,062 high explosive bombs of weights ranging from 1,800 kg to 50 kg, plus 35 parachute mines, 40 oil bombs and many incendiaries, caused much destruction in the City and inner London in particular (TNA, HO186/952, Report No. 15, 16 July 1941). Unbeknown to Londoners at the time, and apart from the early 1944 'Baby Blitz' attacks, this was the last big raid on London by manned aircraft, although Heap records many of the subsequent smaller raids.

26   Probably next to the Hawarden Castle pub at 3 Gower Place on the Gordon Street corner, now the University College London Union.

1941

in Hampstead Rd, Oxford St, Guilford St – St Pancras, King's Cross stations both closed through bomb damage on platforms – street craters in Oxford St, Barnard St and Bedford Sq. Fire damage on corners of Russell Square and Tavistock Square. Such was the extent of the havoc I viewed on this "morning after the night before."

[Tried] the Empire in afternoon but found they couldn't open through the failure of the electricity, so went round and saw some more of last night's damage instead. I thought I'd seen something this morning but it was nothing to what I discovered this afternoon. Along the Strand the corner of Villiers St was down. In Lancaster Place something had crashed through the new Waterloo Bridge approach into the tram subway entrance below. From the bridge, fires could be seen still burning all along the riverside. In Catherine St there was a crater between the Duchess and the Strand. Buildings opposite both sides of Australia House had been hit and St Clement Danes Church burnt out.

But it wasn't until I hit Fleet St that I came across the really big stuff. Huge areas on both sides of it had been burnt right out, not so much in the 'street' itself as behind it. Ludgate Circus was a shambles and New Bridge St a gigantic network of hose pipes leading up from the river at Blackfriars to fight the fires still burning in Ludgate Hill, Old Bailey. Ludgate Hill was, in fact, in ruins and practically nothing was left of St Bride St, Shoe Lane, Charterhouse St and the whole length of Farringdon St, north of Holborn Viaduct and very little of Smithfield and the south end of Farringdon Rd. These are plain unexaggerated facts. This whole area had been virtually laid waste. EC1 and EC4 last night met the same fate as EC2 and EC3 on Dec. 29th last. But it didn't end there. Proceeding up into Holborn, I found that sorely tried borough had taken it on the chin again and this time it was almost a knockout. What little had been left of Gray's Inn Rd from the last show-down was finally disposed of. The north front of Lincoln's Inn too had taken a rap and more of High Holborn, including the Stadium,[27] had been hit. The best part of Red Lion St and Eagle St were burnt out, Bedford Row had taken three direct hits and, as a piece de resistance, the whole of Theobald's Rd (both sides) from Bedford Row right up to Southampton Row, together with the end of Lamb's Conduit St had been brought to the ground. The casualties must have been enormous and though the main brunt of the attack must obviously have been concentrated on this adjacent area close to the City, I should think that the total damage sustained was as great as anything inflicted in any previous raid. And this is the price we have to pay for so called democracy. Is it worth it? I shall leave posterity to judge. The world is too insane today for anyone to hope to make any sense out of it all. Our water in taps again this evening.

27 Stadium Club, 85 High Holborn.

Part Two

Monday 12 May The papers this morning disclose that the House of Commons, Big Ben, Westminster Abbey, Westminster Hall and the British Museum were hit on Saturday night. I went along and had a look at them in the evening. Very little damage visible from the outside. The famous skyline of the Houses of Parliament from the river remains intact and Big Ben, though scarred still keeps time infallibly. But the internal damage must have been great for the Commons debating chamber was completely wrecked, so was the altar of the Abbey and the Deanery. The British Museum damage I should imagine was very slight – nothing whatever visible there. Turned much warmer today. We would be deprived of light and have to work with boarded up windows and depressing electric light by it just when some really fine weather arrives at last.

Tuesday 13 May One of the strangest occurrences of the war has been the landing by parachute in Scotland on Saturday night of Hess, Hitler's deputy who had fled from Germany in a plane which crashed, apparently a rift in the Nazi lute [*sic*].[28] Saw still more of Saturday night's damage in evening. First the land mine wreckage around Percy Circus and Holford Square. Then got a bus from the Angel to Moorgate and walked through the City which had taken another packet i.e. what is left of it. Moorgate, Queen Victoria St, Cheapside and their various tributaries were all badly damaged again. I discovered that the corner of the Old Bailey itself had been hit. Came back through Holborn of which in reality I've now seen enough to last me a very long time.

Wednesday 14 May Mother goes by coach to Canterbury for two days to see her cousins, this being the second of her two days leave. Our cardboard window coverings at the Town Hall are being replaced by fresh ones with substitute glass panels in the middle of them. They do let some light in but not much as they're smaller than the full size windows and not actually transparent. Not really as good as glass window panes, which they apparently won't chance putting in again, but better than nothing.

Thursday 15 May Two more Saturday night hits just revealed. Queen's Hall[29] and St James's Palace.

Tuesday 20 May Went out for the evening with a girl from the Highgate Hospital First Aid Post where we got acquainted in the course of my

---

28 Rudolf Hess (1894–1987), described by Hitler in 1940 as second to Goering in the Nazi leadership, secretly flew himself on 12 May from Augsburg to Scotland, where he parachuted to earth. He claimed he wanted to negotiate peace with the UK but he was imprisoned and tried at the 1945 Nuremberg War Crimes Tribunal. Sentenced to life imprisonment, he died in 1987 in Spandau prison in West Berlin. Heap very clearly wrote 'Nazi lute'; it is possible that he intended the final word of the sentence to be 'elite'.
29 The Queen's Hall had been the venue for the annual Henry Wood Promenade Concerts. The site, next to Broadcasting House, is now occupied by the St George's Hotel.

1941

Tuesday afternoon calls.[30] Took a bus along to the Spaniards and had a couple of drinks and walked back over the heath to Parliament Hill. After seeing her home to Kentish Town I had to walk all the way down to King's Cross, it being nigh on midnight and no buses running. Which served me damned well for being such a 'sucker.' I'd imagined there were possibilities of a lively affair developing with this tall blonde mass of gay femininity. She struck me as being fascinating in many ways and I thought the attraction might be mutual. But my hunch was wrong. I did induce her to come out for the evening and a wildly flirtatious and crazily romantic evening it was too. At the end of it however, she stubbornly refused to see me anymore. The reason was that she is deeply attached to an eccentric and tubercular young Dutchman and not being promiscuous by nature, had no inclination for anyone else. Were I not so well versed in the realistic school of [Somerset] Maugham – not to mention my limited experience of life – this would have flabbergasted and even pained me. As it is, my main reaction is one of cynical wistfulness. Once more I've backed a loser. That's all there is to it. Perhaps 'twould be better if I took to gambling – 'Lucky at cards, unlucky at love' – There may be something in the old adage. The latter half certainly fits me.

Wednesday 21 May Tired after late night and unsatisfactory sleep. Mother having another bad spell of her old internal trouble – yet struggles on somehow. Won't lay up or go into hospital.

Friday 23 May Going by chance into St Pancras station lunchtime, I saw Winston Churchill, accompanied by the top-hatted station master, strolling along one of the platforms towards a waiting crowd and pausing to look at the recent raid damage in the station.

Monday 26 May Apparently the cardboard substitute windows at the Town Hall were only put up as a temporary fixture for today they were removed, real glass put into the lower window frames and cardboard into the upper ones. Much better.

Tuesday 27 May The cigarette shortage gets worse every week. Not a single shop around King's Cross had any today. It only wastes peoples time going in for nothing. And even when there are a few about, it's the devil's own job to get my favourite, Du Mauriers. I'm not much of a smoker it's true – ten to twenty a week is about my limit – but that only makes it all the more annoying when I can't get any at all through the gluttons having cornered the lot.

Thursday 29 May Slept at home in my own bed for the first time since mid-September last. I've got so sick and tired of going down to that wretched shelter night after night that I can't stand it anymore – unless

---

30 This was Marjorie Heatley, Heap's future wife.

of course, we get another series of Blitzes when I suppose I'll have to. For I've taken an intense dislike to the place and the people in it. I sleep badly there and the air is foul. Besides there's no point in going down there every night when we only get a raid every three or four weeks now. There's been nothing whatever for the last nineteen nights. In fact, the time has come to break the habit, and I've broken it.

Saturday 31 May Went down to the shelter for the night because (a) the weather was an improvement on that of recent nights, Saturday is a favourite night for Blitzes and one is just about due now. (b) An occasional night down there is necessary to keep our places reserved.

Sunday 1 June Clothing ration from today 66 coupons each a year. A suit will require 26 coupons, an overcoat 16, shoes 7, a shirt 5 and so on. Socks at 3 coupons a pair strike me as likely to use up more than their fair share of coupons in a year. Hats and a few other items like shoe laces and braces are exempt. No price limit, nothing very drastic – albeit a complete surprise. Last night we went to the shelter. Nothing happened. Tonight we stay at home and get the first night alert London has had for weeks. A comparatively quiet one it's true, with only distant gunfire on the outskirts. But it kept us vacillating between bed and the damp musty basement below from 12.10 till 3.15, and so deprived us of half a night's sleep. So apparently there's nothing else for it but revert to the regular nightly use of the FH shelter and make the best of a bad job. There's nothing more infuriating than being deprived of a night's sleep.

Monday 2 June Whit Monday – no cancellation of it as a public holiday this year, but travelling discouraged. Our latest withdrawal – Crete. Length of run – 12 days! Took a bus ride with Mother to the Elephant and Castle in evening and had a look at the raid damage around there. This region has obviously had more than its fair share of Blitzkrieg. Devastation on the grand scale, comparable to parts of the City and Holborn. Walked back along Waterloo Bridge Rd and through the 'New Cut', both of which were in a similar plight (even the Old Vic was partly damaged) and so over to Westminster to get bus home.

Friday 6 June The war has taken its first toll of our old Robin Hood-cum-company set. Heard from Phil today that Gus went down in a merchantman and drowned.[31] Poor old Gus, he was a most likeable fellow, even if a trifle erratic in some ways, and was very partial to liquor. I don't think he found life any too easy for he was frequently out of work. The loss of a personal acquaintance like this brings the stupidity and futility of war home to one more than anything else.

---

31   Gus, whose wedding Heap attended on 25 November 1939, and Alby Holmes (see 20 August 1945) appear to have been the only members of Heap's circle of friends killed during the war.

1941

Monday 9 June A rumour that it's to be rationed has caused a run on [tinned] soup. Like cigarettes, it's now unobtainable in the shops.

Wednesday 11 June Met John [Hobson] at the Horse Shoe. After a couple of drinks there strolled round to some of our other old haunts, such as were still standing. Called at the Swan Hotel, the Fitzroy and the Marquis and finished up at the inevitable Green Parrot, which, I beheld for the first time in the unbecoming light of day. An air of dejection and melancholy hung over the place. Apart from the proprietor and a Canadian soldier sleeping by the window, we had the place to ourselves for some time. Later one or two more drifted in, but it wasn't a bit like the old days – meaning Spring 1940. Got home about 11.45 having had far too much to drink and then foolishly ate some fish and chips which made me violently sick. Went down and slept in the basement shelter when the sirens went off at 12.15 and stayed there till the all clear sounded at 4.20 whereupon I came up and went to bed.

Sunday 15 June After tea, met John once more and went for a stroll round Hyde Park. Stood and listened to the Coldstream Guards Band progressing from *The Merry Wives of Windsor* overture to *Lilac Time* via *Invitation to the Waltz*. Then strolled through the deserted, melancholy, Blitz-seared streets of Mayfair to Piccadilly, wound up at the Fitzroy.

Monday 16 June Comfortably warm. I couldn't resist the call of Hampstead. Lay basking in the sun on Parliament Hill for an hour before spending a further hour walking round the heath. 'Twas well worth both the effort and the journey. The view over London from Parliament Hill betrays no hint of the effects of the 'Blitzkrieg.' All the old familiar landmarks still stand out, except the Crystal Palace Towers which were recently destroyed by order. They were apparently too good a landmark – for the Luftwaffe.

Friday 20 June Did my first 24 hour spell in 'control' at the Town Hall. Signed on at 9.0 in the morning and was issued with two blankets, a sheet sleeping bag, a pillow case, a tin hat and an armlet. Plus ticket for four meals in the canteen. Spent the evening with Eric Gaylor, office colleague in same shift (No 4). After tea we went over to the Euston Tavern for a drink or two. Back at Town Hall Eric initiated me into the intricacies of billiards, which I'd never played before. Followed by supper, a walk, a final cup of tea and bed at 12.0. Couldn't get to sleep for some time. Must try a different bed next time. As for the control room itself, I spent but five minutes therein looking round, for being the usual quiet night there was naught else to do in there but look around.

Monday 23 June At last England finds an ally really dear to her heart – Soviet Russia! For Germany, anticipating the inevitable stab in the back from Red Russia while engaged on the invasion of England, has forestalled the Bolsheviks by invading her erstwhile ally. Whereupon Churchill, with characteristic smug hypocrisy, promises all aid to the communist scum and slobbers unctuously over our newly acquired comrades. And needless to say the press dutifully follows suit with a 'white wash act'. The truth is that Communist Russia is a far greater menace to civilisation than Nazi Germany has been, or ever could be. In vanquishing Russia and by doing so stemming the poisonous stream of communism at its source, Germany would in fact be rendering mankind an inestimable service.

Thursday 26 June Went along to the FH shelter for first time in ten nights. Must put in an occasional appearance.

Friday 27 June Received an additional 5/- a week bonus, dating back seventeen weeks to the beginning of March, that is apart from the extra 5/- on this week's pay we received and a further £4 for the previous sixteen weeks. A most unexpected but very welcome windfall. I shall put this sum in the bank together with a further £6 I've accumulated in addition to my regular weekly saving of 10/- banked at P.O Savings Bank fortnightly. And still be left with a surplus in hand of £7 odd to meet such expenses as clothes, subscriptions etc.

Saturday 28 June Being on control either Saturday or Sunday during these summer weekends doesn't seem to mean a thing. Everyone goes out for most of the day and only return to the Town Hall for meals and bed. For my part I took the opportunity to see *Rebecca* at the Gaumont, Camden Town.[32] Whiled away the even partly at the Town Hall and partly at home.

Tuesday 1 July In the affairs of the heart I take after the Bourbons. I learn nothing and forget nothing. Otherwise how, after my experience of six weeks back would I have taken that irresistible madcap Marjorie from Highgate Hospital out again this evening? Once more we went up to Hampstead and after a drink or two at the Bull and Bush wandered back over the heath to Parliament Hill, pausing en passant, for a lengthy idyllic sojourn sur l'herbe. And again I had to walk home from Kentish Town after midnight. Things went much better than last time however. I made love to her even more assiduously than before – and with more satisfactory effect. The defence against my amorous advance proved less invulnerable and her whole behaviour seemed to suggest that only a little patience and perseverance on my part are necessary to make a conquest. Just a question of playing one's cards with care and diligence, and not, as I'm apt to do, slamming the whole lot down at once.

---

32 The 1940 Alfred Hitchcock classic thriller, based on the 1938 Daphne Du Maurier story, starred Laurence Olivier and Joan Fontaine.

1941

Wednesday 2 July Though on control, I nevertheless slipped away for the evening to attend the first night of Noel Coward's *Blithe Spirit* at the Piccadilly. What on earth is Coward up to? I doubt if any contemporary English dramatist has a higher reputation as a master of polished, witty, sophisticated comedy. Yet a play less consistent with such a reputation than this farcical nonsense about ghosts would be difficult to imagine.[33] Really it is neither one thing nor t'other. I was still inclined to agree with the solitary voice from the gallery which above all the rapturous applause that greeted Noel's curtain speech, bellowed forth 'Rubbish!'

Friday 3 July Have noticed lately an extraordinary number of girls wearing small ornamental crucifixes hung round their necks. This is, of course, a catholic custom and would seem to indicate that either the young female adolescents of that religion are being specially encouraged to wear this outward emblem of their inner virtue (if any) or their numbers are multiplying in alarming proportions – perhaps both. Went round to the FH shelter for the night – our weekly penance.

Friday 4 July To Hampstead with Marjorie in evening. Walked to the Bull and Bush and back from Parliament Hill and after a drink or two there lay on the heath in ecstatic embrace for over two hours. It had turned midnight by the time we started to walk back in the moonlight up to the Spaniards Road and over to Parliament Hill again. By the time we got there it was too late to get a bus even down to Kentish Town. So had to walk all the way home, leaving M at Bartholomew Rd where, conveniently situated half way between King's Cross and Hampstead, she lives in digs with her cousin. Her Mother lives in Somerset and her father, a dentist, in Australia. Got home at 2.0, had supper and so to bed.

Sunday 6 July My first taste of Sunday control duty. Not so bad as expected. Up at 7.0, over to the Town Hall to sign on. Back to bed till 10.15. Breakfast, papers, shave and wash, short walk, lunch in canteen. Afternoon, deck chair and book on Town Hall roof. Tea at home (the canteen's foul). Evening (6.0 till 9.0) Hyde Park and back, supper, book and bed.

Monday 7 July A most extraordinary evening I've ever experienced. For me it was crucial and 'twas all totally unexpected too. I met Marjorie up at Highgate at 8.0 and as usual, we took a bus over to the Bull and Bush, had a couple of drinks and walked over the heath. So far so good. All was plain sailing. As soon as we were squatted on the grass however things took a less joyous turn. M told me that she wanted to be honest with me and had come to the conclusion that we

---

33 The public did not agree with Heap, as the production, starring Margaret Rutherford and Cecil Parker, created a new long-run record for non-musical British plays of 1,997 performances.

Part Two

weren't altogether suited to each other, didn't think she really loved me – or anyone else, wasn't at all sure what she really did want – and well, we'd better part before it went any further. And so on and so forth. In fact she put one over the Big Renunciation Act. I naturally endeavoured to convince her she was wrong and though feeling bitter disappointment made an outward show of gallant gaiety. In other words I tried to laugh it off. It didn't work. Then as we walked back over the heath to Parliament Hill, I gradually gave way to despair and ceased even to act a part I couldn't really 'feel.' An air of intense melancholy enveloped me and I suppose I must have looked as miserable as sin for M, suddenly relenting, called a halt and suggested we sat down and proceeded to try and comfort me in my sobbing grief. And then came the incredible part of the whole thing. After about ten minutes of sorrowful silence, she suddenly realised she loved me after all, hugged me to her bosom and promised to marry me. Yes, it happened just like that. I'd unconsciously played my emotional card so well that I'd snatched an overwhelming victory from the very jaws of defeat.

To ask M to marry me was, of course, a momentous decision for me to take especially in view of my life-long determination to remain single. But the last year or two has brought home to me the fact that there's no real kick to be got out of being a bachelor indefinitely – only a hell of a lot of loneliness and I've had enough of that to last me a lifetime. So I'm making a bid for a chance of permanent happiness while the going's good. My immediate reaction to becoming thus informally engaged is difficult to describe. I still feel a little dazed by the suddenness of it. But uppermost in my mind is a strange sense of wistful exhilaration of having probably for the first time in my life made a quick decision on a vital issue, backed my own judgement without hesitation and taken a real chance. It's true we've only known each other for a very brief period and it may seem crazy to come to such decision on such short acquaintance. Maybe, but I had a hunch about M right from the start. I knew as soon as I first saw her less than three months ago, that she was just the right type for me, and I fell for her at once. Our recent association, brief though it may have been, has assured me that not only she's the right type but the right girl for me. I'm dead certain that my hunch is no illusion and I'm backing it up for all I'm worth.

The practical problems which will inevitably arise e.g. Mother, finance etc can be left till later. All that matters now is that M and I have decided to make a go of it. I've wooed and won her in a week in spite of old established competition – was ever a courtship more swift or so sure? Naturally I feel somewhat elated at the achievement. I consider Marjorie a prize worth having and by sheer perseverance and tenacity of purpose, I've won it.

My dominant sense of adventure must surely be making itself manifest at last.

Thursday 10 July Called on Marjorie for a fleeting half hour on my way back from Bar. [Bartholomew] Rd depot this morning. This is the last I shall see her for a week as she goes away tomorrow for five days with her mother and aunt in Somerset. Gosh, how I shall miss her! Went for a long stroll after supper. But though quite tired on turning in, slept badly. Just can't get used to that Town Hall dormitory.

Tuesday 15 July Had a charming little letter from Marjorie, sent from Somerset on Sunday. So typical of its writer – fresh, fragrant, affectionate, irrepressibly gay and containing among other things the joyous intimation that our reunion will be a day earlier than expected.

Sunday 20 July To Hampstead in morning. Extensive Home Guard manoeuvres on Parliament Hill. Nearly got run in for not having my identity card with me, for the sentries posted at the approaches to the heath were halting people, especially young men, and demanding their production. Fortunately they let me pass unchallenged and tackled two youths walking just behind me instead. I can never keep to transferring the damned thing from the pocket of one jacket to another. Called for Marjorie after lunch and went to the Zoo.[34] Not a place I'm particularly keen on, but M likes it and, in the circumstances, it made a pleasant afternoon's diversion.

Monday 21 July Had Marjorie for tea with us. She and Mother took to each other at once and the evening passed off as smoothly and amicably as could be. Mother went up to ARP HQ for a couple of hours and left us on our own, returning in time for a drink with us over in the Euston Tavern, after which I saw M home.

Tuesday 22 July Bought an engagement ring at Bravington's for a fiver and presented it to Marjorie as we drove down from the hospital after the pay-out this afternoon. Not, perhaps, an appropriately romantic occasion though I've a weakness for doing things in incongruous settings. M having to go to a lecture this evening and I being on control, I betook myself to the first performance of *Quiet Week End* at Wyndham's. Back by 9.30 in time for supper at the Town Hall.

Friday 25 July After tea with Marjorie, took her up to meet Phil and Kath. On the way home M developed one of her difficult moods. She couldn't understand my friends and had nothing in common with them, was doubtful as to whether we'd really hit it off together and afraid of making me unhappy and All That. Actually this is the third time this week I'd had to cope with these temporary but recurring misgivings.

---

34 London Zoo closed briefly from 3 to 9 September 1939 but otherwise remained open during the war, although the giant pandas and the elephants were sent to Whipsnade. Regent's Park itself remained open, other than areas taken over by the military and the local authorities for public air raid trench shelters. Other areas were used for the disposal of bomb damage debris, which was buried and covered with turf and topsoil.

It took me an hour's hard work to dispel her doubts and for my pains I had to walk home from Kentish Town. Poor Marjorie! Like me she's a bit of a misfit with a touch of masochism in her emotional makeup. She seems to so love making herself unhappy now and again.

Sunday 27 July In the afternoon we took a bus to Hampton Court, wandered around the grounds, had tea and spent the evening sur l'herbe in the adjoining park. Though the morning had been dubious and unpromising it turned out to be a glorious afternoon and evening and we had a truly blissful time. After a drink in the over-crowded and exorbitantly expensive Mitre Hotel (I was charged 2/6 for a Mousec and a draught lager), we got a bus home at 9.30, arriving back at 11.0 most pleasantly tired. I could have done with a good night's sleep but, alas, one was not allowed to slumber undisturbed. For the first time for many weeks the alert sounded at 1.45 a.m. heralding a sharp two hour raid. Few bombs seemed to be dropped (the docks and East End were apparently the main targets) but the gunfire was noisy and prolonged. Went down to the basement and stretched out on a bunk but the place was too full of vociferous old women to enable me to doze off. So I just had to lose two hours of much needed repose.

Tuesday 29 July Reply to John Hobson's letter before going up to meet Marjorie emerging from a lecture at ARP HQ in Camden Town at 8.45. She was evidently experiencing a mild attack of the blues so I took her down to the Fitzroy and, with the aid of a few sherries, managed to effectively dispel them. By the time I saw her home, she was so jubilant as could be. Missed the last bus down to King's Cross but got the tube from Camden Town. Got home as midnight struck.

Thursday 31 July To tea with Marjorie who was again in the throes of one of her difficult depressing moods. These seem to recur regularly every two or three days and come on without warning or any apparent reason whatsoever. She just isn't keen to help herself. I've yet to find a permanent remedy for these strange bouts of unwarranted melancholy, though I can usually manage to dispel them temporarily. Unfortunately I didn't have time to do so this evening, so I had to leave her up at Highgate to attend a lecture at 7.30. Whereupon I came home, had supper and went to bed early, hoping for the best. Thus ends July 1941, the most remarkable, erratic and egotistical month.

Saturday 2 August Went up to Marjorie's at 4.0, had tea and stayed there till 8.0 when we sallied forth to Hampstead Heath and had a couple of drinks at the Bull and Bush and walked back over to Parliament Hill in time to catch the bus home. M was in an exceptionally joyous and loving mood this evening. So was I.

Sunday 3 August Signed on for control at the Town Hall at 9.0. Came back to breakfast, shaved, washed, dressed and went up to call for

1941

Marjorie at 11.15 and take her for a walk over Hampstead. As she was on her own for the weekend I went back and had lunch with her. And a very nice lunch it was too. Thank heavens she can cook. At 4.0 we went up to Hampstead again, had tea at a café on that steep hill going down to Hampstead Tube from the Whitestone Pond and then walked slowly over to Parliament Hill and listened to the band for a while. But as M's bare legs were being bitten by gnats and midges, we didn't hang around too long and went back to Bartholomew Rd shortly after 8.0. Had some supper and stayed on till 10.0 when I reluctantly had to drag myself away, come home and get over to the Town Hall by 10.30 (Blackout time).

Monday 4 August Bank Holiday. Though not a very lively one, a subdued, dejected air hung over London like a pall. To Marjorie's after lunch. Later in the afternoon we went up to Hampstead, where all plebeian London seemed to be gathered in search of a fair.[35] All that was offered was the very archaic affair in the Vale of Health.

Tuesday 5 August The first day for a fortnight during which I haven't seen my beloved. I feel quite lost of an evening without her such an inseparable part of me has she already come to be. Having no letters to write, odd jobs to do or plays or films to see, I just had to resort to that trying task of filling time. The best I could think of in this direction was to walk to the West End and back. It was all very depressing.

Wednesday 6 August Met Marjorie at 5.30 and went for a walk over the heath, had a couple of drinks at the Bull and Bush and got a bus from the Spaniards along to Highgate. Had to cope with another of M's awkward moods. Happily it didn't survive the evening and melted right away at the last moment, otherwise it'd have probably come home with me as well. Still, they're getting much less frequent. This was the first for nearly a week. Mother taking over new job on Friday. Being transferred from the Wardens Post in the crypt to HQ and put in charge of the catering there. Different hours, 10.0 till late evening with afternoon break. Should suit her better.

Sunday 10 August Marjorie's moods wax and wane like the moon – only with greater profundity and frequency. Today I was hard put to keep up with them, so swiftly and surprisingly did they come and go. The first came on whilst we were walking over Hampstead in the morning. We hadn't gone far before she suddenly lapsed into a sullen silence and wanted to go back. So back we went. A couple of drinks in the Abbey Tavern[36] however saved the situation. Marjorie was herself again. After lunch we got a bus to Kew Gardens, had tea and wandered around while two more moods came and went in quick succession. About

35 See note for 23 March 1940 on bank holiday fairs.
36 124 Kentish Town Road, NW5.

Part Two

7.0 it started to rain and set in for another wet evening whereupon we posted back to town and finished the evening in the Fitzroy, four sherries combined with the gaudy gaiety of the place had quite a cheering and exhilarating effect on M. My own dampened spirits rose in unison. Alas it had worn off by the time we got back to Bar. Rd and given place to a final mood of Marjorie's dejection thus making a consistently imperfect end to an imperfect day. The trouble is, I think, that inadequate sleep and rest together with a strained atmosphere at home due to the unsympathetic attitude of her cousin's own engagement is reacting adversely on M's highly strung temperament and making her overwrought. Hence these unfortunate vicissitudes. This continual depressing wet weather doesn't help matters either. It's apt to try even the liveliest spirits. I'm beginning to feel the effect of it myself.

Tuesday 12 August Met Marjorie coming off duty at 8.0 and went down to the Coventry St Corner House Brasserie, where we ate hors d'oeuvres and drank draught Bass. The place was, as usual, packed. We sat on for a couple of hours or so, listening to the music, drinking more beer and chatting gaily on this and that. Until some chaffing remark of mine, possible tactless, but certainly not intended to be taken seriously, rather hurt M, and caused her to lapse into strong silence. However, it soon passed. As soon as we got outside and started walking along to the bus, I quickly convinced her that she's 'Got it all wrong' as they say in the films, and all was well – very much so in fact! Saw her home, then walked home myself and ate a supper of lukewarm bacon and tomatoes which had been left under the grill since 11.0 for me.

Thursday 14 August Tried a different warden's pay round this morning – Division 1, the northernmost part of the borough up Highgate way. Highgate village being the apex of the triangular area it roughly covers. A much nicer run than Division 2 which I've always done before – or either of the other two divisions for that matter – and I got on well with Barnberger, the gigantic District Warden, who ran me round in his car. Finished up at the Stretcher Party Depot at Old William Ellis School, but went along to Meaker's in Kentish Town to buy a fur-lined gabardine raincoat (Sale price 29/9 and 16 coupons) before returning to the Town Hall.

Saturday 16 August To the Horse Shoe to meet John [Hobson] at 7.0. Had a few drinks and talked with a communistically inclined but perfectly charming Canadian soldier at Bodega in Glasshouse St[37] before returning to the Horse Shoe at 8.30 to meet Marjorie and to proceed round to the Fitzroy. From there to the Wheatsheaf and finally to the Green Parrot which, judging by the crowd up there, seems to have gone down somewhat in the social scale lately, from saloon to

---

37 Bodega, 42 Glasshouse Street, W1 – an Italian café/restaurant.

public bar. Hadn't been there long before I began to feel the worse for drink for I'd made the old fatal error of mixing drinks, abandoning beer half way through the evening and going on scotch. With the result that I was sick and, well, not exactly the life and soul of the party. Was glad to get out into the air when we left at 1.0 and walked up to Hampstead Rd and got a cab, drove M home then home myself. To bed about 2.0 after being sick again. Quite a lively spree!

Tuesday 19 August Round to King's Cross Kinema[38] with some of the other control boys in the evening and saw *The Death of Miss Jones*. Accompanying it was the inevitable *Target for Tonight*.[39] Inevitable because it is on this week at every cinema in London and one cannot go to a cinema without seeing it. This is the much publicised full length documentary film depicting a raid on Germany by the RAF of the whole operation from start to finish. For once in a while fact was not as strange as fiction – and definitely not as exciting.

Wednesday 20 August One of Marjorie's difficult evenings. Met her up at the hospital at 8.0 and went down the Fitzroy wherein came the calm before the gathering brain storm. It burst as soon as we got outside and gradually subsided as I stood and gently relaxed with her. Eventually the cloud of depression cleared completely, the sun of M's natural disposition blazed forth and we parted as happily as could be. But it was tough going while it lasted.

Friday 22 August A much bigger pay to do this week. Casual labourers and watchmen. Nigh on a thousand quid altogether. Brought M down to Sinclair House this evening by way of a change. Made some coffee and sat listening to the radio for nearly two hours. Saw her home after.

Sunday 24 August Up to M's again after lunch and met M's brother who, with his very young and shy girlfriend Audrey, arrived soon. Had some tea and sat around talking till about 6.15 when we made tracks for the West End and divided the evening between the Tartan Dive[40] and the Fitzroy. And a right merry evening it was too! I liked Charles immensely. He has all the natural, carefree impetuosity of youth combined with an engaging frankness and charm of manner. In fact he's perfectly cast for the role of M's brother!

Tuesday 26 August Out for the evening with Marjorie, Charles and Audrey. Had tea at the Heather Bell Café. And what a tea! It nearly ruined a good evening. No jam, no cakes and shocking service. Charles and I ordered fish and chips. After about ten minutes we were informed that there was no fish. Would we have egg and chips. We

38 275–277 Pentonville Road, N1.
39 This 45-minute Crown Film Unit film of a Wellington bomber crew's raid is available on youtube.com.
40 The basement bar below the Sussex, 20 Upper St Martin's Lane, WC2.

would. Another ten minutes go by and we're told there were no chips left. As a last resort we consent to egg on toast and eventually get egg and chips. They found some more chips somewhere! Really they could almost have grown them in the time we were kept waiting. We left no tips. Walked up to Covent Garden and had a couple of drinks before going into the Opera House, now given over to nightly dancing. Quite a bright and pleasant affair and not uncomfortably crowded. The services predominated among the male element instead of the usual crowd of Jews they tend to get at these places. Unfortunately they only have a licence for Thursdays and Saturdays so we had to go out for drinks. During our first excursion to the local pub, we got talking with a couple of Canadian soldiers, one old and one young but both equally charming. I took quite a liking to the old boy – who was named Arthur – and by way of being a writer and a philosopher with a wider experience of life. On getting back to the dance the two of us just stood and talked while the others danced. We discussed drama, music, literature, travel, solo whist – all manner of topics. He told me, among other things, that he'd once waited all night to get tickets to see Henry Irving and Ellen Terry in *The Bells* – and I knew at once that we were kindred spirits. One of the most interesting men I've ever met. It grieved me to think that we'd probably never meet again. Our second visit to the local lasted till 11.0, and we returned to find the dance over and everyone emerging. So we reluctantly had to call it a night, break up the merry party and bid farewell to our well met Canadian friends. Walked down to the Strand, saw Charles and Audrey to a bus to Waterloo and got a 77 ourselves to King's Cross. Saw Marjorie to a trolley bus and so home to supper and a very welcome bed.

Wednesday 27 August Had a second rather shorter letter from John Bell. Getting married on Sept. 21 and going to sea immediately after. Being 'on control' in the evening went to the first performance of *Squaring the Circle* at the Vaudeville. Got back to the Town Hall at 8.30 and after supper in the canteen, went indoors for an hour. Finally read my book in the dormitory till I was too tired to read another word. Lovely feeling!

Sunday 31 August Back to Bartholomew Rd we go and up turns Charles half an hour later. Explanations vague. Had tea and sat around talking till 9.30 when I return to the Town Hall for supper and rejoin Charles and Marjorie in the Euston Tavern an hour later. Thence to the Fitzroy till 10.0. Left them in Tottenham Court Rd to proceed to the Corner House for supper, while I wend my solitary way back to the Town Hall for the night. A delightful day in every way.

Monday 1 September Have had a new Yale lock put in the door of our flat as a precaution against further burglaries following the loss of my gold watch chain and gramophone records.[41] To the Horse Shoe at 6.30 to join Marjorie, Charles and Joan.[42] This being Charles' last day of leave, they'd been to a tea dance at the Astoria in the afternoon and obviously hadn't enjoyed overmuch. I sensed a strained atmosphere as soon as I went in. Marjorie was tired and overwrought. Charles, though as gay and natural as ever, seemed to be set on getting tight as quickly and as effectively as possible in the remaining few hours. Joan, playing her self-appointed role of the fly in the ointment was also rapidly getting tipsy and being as infuriatingly stupid and as spiteful as only she can be. Things got no better when we proceeded to the Fitzroy. Charles and Joan got more and more drunk and, worse still, loving, while Marjorie got more and more irritable and upset. I could gladly have strangled that callous little bitch Joan. From the Fitzroy we got a cab to Bartholomew Rd, put Joan to bed, tried to sober Charles up a bit with some supper (actually it made him sick), gathered up his luggage and saw him down to King's Cross and on to the 10.15 train. At the last moment Marjorie broke down and wept bitterly. She was so certain she'd never see him again. I saw her home and did my best to console her. But she was feeling too utterly miserable for sympathy to be of much avail. So I left her to bear her sorrow in solitude and came home. A most deplorable and distressing evening. One that I definitely did not enjoy.

Tuesday 2 September Passing reflections on wartime London at the end of the 2nd year of war: Women (and what women!) working as dust collectors and road sweepers. Matches becoming even more scarce than cigarettes. Bottled beer practically unobtainable, draught beer fouler than ever. Twenty West End theatres open.

Wednesday 3 September Tea at Marjorie's. Both feeing rather tired, we decided to make an early night of it and were home by 10.0. But 'twas a perfect evening for aw' that – Marjorie being now right back to normal and altogether her own sweet self once more.

Thursday 4 September Marjorie to tea with me. Had to put her onto a bus home [as] I went back to the Town Hall for control duty. Did an hour's practice in the control room after supper, then an hour's read in bed. And so to slumber.

Sunday 7 September Met Marjorie coming off duty at the hospital at 12.0, took her for a walk over Hampstead and brought her home for lunch. In the afternoon we went to Hyde Park, strolled through to Kensington Gardens and had tea therein, a dubious delight which involved me waiting forty minutes in the queue at the cafeteria, the

---

41 See entry for 27 November for resolution.
42 Marjorie's cousin and flatmate.

place swarming with Jews. Turned very chilly about 6.0 so we went back to Marjorie's. Left about 10.30. A very nice day indeed.

Monday 8 September Tea at Marjorie's which will be the order of the week since we intend to take full advantage of Joan's very welcome absence. Unfortunately I could only stay a couple of hours afterwards for the evening, for being on Control I had to leave soon after 8.0 and hie me back to the Town Hall by nightfall.

Sunday 14 September Came home to lunch then to the Labour Exchange in St Pancras Way at 3.0 to register for fire watching duty[43] under the new compulsory registration scheme for all men between 18 and 60, 18 to 35 today. Later ages next Saturday and Sunday. After giving my details, got a form on which to apply for exemption on the grounds that I already do 48 hours a month on civil defence duty (on control). We've decided to get married at the Town Hall Registry Office on Oct 11, spend a week in Somerset and get a furnished flat until I'm called up, which surely can't be long delayed now. Marjorie's got to leave Bartholomew [Road] soon anyway, for life with Joan has become intolerable lately. And we feel we'd like to have some experience of married bliss to look back on when I get called up, even if it's only a month or so. So we take the plunge in four weeks' time. Told Mother tonight when I got back. It naturally rather upset her, though she did her best not to show it. After all it is going to be a bad break for her, and I don't feel at all happy myself about leaving her on her own after all these years. But I can't really see what I can do about it at present and in any case it would be just as bad a break when I got called up, married or not.

Tuesday 16 September Gave in the requisite 21 days' notice of 'marriage by certificate' to the Registrar this morning. Incidentally this is the first anniversary of my starting work at the Town Hall. Little did I realise then what 'twould lead to! Walked over the heath again in the evening, had a drink at the Spaniards and left M at the hospital at 8.0, the same as yesterday but, being on control tonight, went back to the Town Hall for supper and came indoors for an hour afterwards. Back at 10.0 to bed and book.

Thursday 18 September My income tax assessment for the year amounts to £22.10.0 payable by weekly deductions of 8/8 from my salary, starting in November – an increase of 5/1 on my present deduction. Assuming, I suppose, that I'm still around in November earning a salary from which it can be deducted.

---

43 The popular name for the compulsory Fire Guard, which required those eligible to serve a minimum of 48 hours on call every 28 days.

1941

Monday 22 September Met Marjorie coming off duty at 8.0. What to do with ourselves on these chilly dark evenings looks like being a bit of a problem for the next fortnight. Tonight we solved it, though somewhat unsatisfactorily – by first going down to M's to leave her case and then wandering along to Camden Town and having a couple of drinks at the Mother Redcap.[44] M still feeling tired and off form, I also that way inclined. So what with one thing and another it wasn't at all a lovely evening. Still, we got through it somehow.

Tuesday 23 September To the hospital again at 8.0 to meet Marjorie emerging into the 'emerging dusk.' Bus to the Bull and Bush, two gin and limes for Marjorie and two Basses for Anthony in the quiet, almost empty lounge. Back over the heath to Parliament Hill Fields. So dark and misty that if I hadn't known my Hampstead as well as I do, we'd have got hopelessly lost. 'Spooky' as M put it. And very enjoyable too in its mildly adventurous way.

Thursday 25 September Up to Highgate to meet Marjorie at 8.0, brought her down to Sinclair House to have some supper and spend the evening with us. Stayed till 11.0 when I went round and saw her onto a bus from King's Cross.

Saturday 27 September Twice over Hampstead. On my own in the afternoon and with Marjorie in the evening after meeting her at the hospital at 8.0. Had a few drinks at the Bull and Bush and came back from the Spaniards. To please M I've promised to (a) discard my dirty and torn old Telemac (b) refrain from wearing my white interlock sports shirt any more (c) get a new pair of flannels to replace the ill-fitting pair I wear at present and (d) use a nail brush. C'est l'amour!

Sunday 28 September Fred and family to tea. They'd obviously come fully expecting to be invited to the wedding so were disappointed when I intimated that we wanted it to be as quiet and informal as possible, with no more present than was absolutely necessary. However they made me a present of some clothing coupons which will come in very useful. I want nothing more. We also had an unexpected visit from my old school friend Ellis, now in the Air Force and training to be a pilot. He came about a letter he's written to his mother concerning the possibility of her leasing her furnished flat in Queen Alexandra Mansions to us (the Housing Society had given us her name and address). Apparently she expects about 35/- a week for it, which is more than we can really afford to pay for rent. However, knowing one as he does, Ellis promised to try and get her to let us have it for less, at any rate for a maximum of 30/- that being the figure we decided was to be our upper limit. So there the matter rested for the time being.

---

44   174 Camden High Street, now 'The World's End'.

Monday 29 September Up to the hospital to meet Marjorie at 8.0. Bus to Bull and Bush, two drinks therein. Walking back over the heath M unexpectedly came over 'temperamental' but the mood had subsided by the time we got to Parliament Hill Fields – on to the bus home. They never last a long time, thank heaven.

Tuesday 30 September Hopped out for few minutes at 10.0 this morning and looked over the Ellis flat in Q.A. [Queen Alexandra] Mansions with Marjorie and Mother. Ellis himself showing us 'the works.' A bit dusty and grim from neglect but could be quite attractive when cleaned up. Provided we can get it at reasonable terms we shall take it.

Thursday 2 October A letter from Mrs Ellis agreeing to let us have the flat for 30/- a week. We decide to take it on these terms and now wait a call from Ellis to tell him so and get him to arrange for his mother to come up as soon as possible to settle final details.

Saturday 4 October The front of the Town Hall has just been bedecked with red flags and banners displaying the hammer and sickle and such like communist emblems in preparation for the so called St Pancras Anglo-Russian Civic Parade through the borough from the Town Hall to Parliament Hill tomorrow – ostensibly in aid of the Russian Red Cross. In actual fact, the whole stunt is organised by the Communist Party and is nothing but a Bolshevik rally, march and demonstration to which the stupid sheep-like council and civil defence services give their support. Such is the appalling state of affairs to which we have sunk in this year of disgrace, 1941.

Monday 6 October Called in at 93 Queen Alexandra Mansions with Marjorie in the early afternoon and saw Mrs Ellis, down from Bletchley for the day. She'd had the flat cleaned and tidied and it now looked much more presentable, a plump, pleasant homely old soul and as voluble as her son. They seemed to be having a competition as to which of the two could talk the most as they showed us the place, what had been done and what still needed doing. Practically everything we need is there except bed linen which we'll have to buy and pillows which I can take from home. An out-of-work radiogram will also require the attention of a wireless engineer and the windows that of a cleaner. Otherwise it's just waiting for us to move into. We're having the keys on Thursday so that we can get our clothes and that in before Saturday. M came down again later in the afternoon – to have tea with us. She'd also been to buy the tea set presented to her by the post earlier in the day – was much enamoured with it. Saw her over to the bus at 7.0 and off to night duty. Couldn't accompany her up to the post. For I was on control duty myself – the last for over a fortnight.

Tuesday 7 October Went along to the West End lunch time and bought two collar attached shirts, one blue and one grey (7/11 and 5 coupons each) and a tie (2/6 and 1 coupon) at the Five Shilling Shirt Co shop in Shaftesbury Avenue. Also a pair of medium grey flannels (27/6 and 8 coupons) at Meakers. Had a haircut after work then up to Marjorie's for tea. Set out for the hospital at 7.30 and groped our way up from Swain's Lane through a dense damp fog.

Wednesday 8 October Ran into another old school acquaintance the other evening in the Town Hall dormitory of all places! I didn't recognise him but he knew me at once and introduced himself as Jacobs, at present acting as Gas Identification Officer for St Pancras.[45] Went to Bravington's and bought a wedding ring after lunch. Marjorie came down to tea with us. Had been buying more presents in the afternoon – a dinner service and a coffee set among other things. Mrs Zelger was to have come to tea also but didn't arrive till 7.0, just in time to present us with a silver bowl and wish us joy before we left for the hospital a few minutes later, calling at Bartholomew Rd en route.

Thursday 9 October A wet, trying day. Called for Marjorie on way back from pay round and helped her bring a suitcase full of stuff to the flat, then went round to Bravington's to change the ring I got yesterday for a more solid one. Did an hour's overtime and went straight from the Town Hall at 6.0 up to Marjorie's and fetched two more cases full of stuff down to No 93. Emptied them, took them back to Bar. Rd and finally saw M up to Highgate. Home at 8.30. Had intended taking some of my own clothes over this evening but got no further than getting them ready and putting some in a suitcase. They'll have to go over tomorrow. Didn't feel like fumbling around in the dark over there tonight for there's no blackout curtain in the bedroom. Another thing to get.

Friday 10 October My last day of bachelorhood, and a very busy one it was too. Took a suitcase full of clothes across to No 93 before work and another after lunch. Then replied to a letter from John Hobson. On knocking off work at 5.10 came in, changed, gulped down a cup of tea, dashed up to M's and brought down another suitcase full of her things, including a pair of sheets and some blackout curtains she'd bought today. Fixed up the blinds, emptied the case, tidied the place up, came over to Sinclair House for a few minutes and up to the hospital via Bar. Rd. Had supper as soon as I got back. Ellis called up about 9.30 and came over to the 'Mansions' with Mother and myself when we took some more clothes, an eiderdown and pillows and bolster. As it was too late for him to get a train, we agreed to let him sleep in the flat for the night and hand us over the keys in the morning.

---

45 Presumably the 'Mr S Jacobs of the Gas Identification Service' from 1937, mentioned in C. A. Newbery, *Wartime St Pancras: A London Borough Defends Itself* (London: Camden History Society, 2006), p. 63.

Part Two

Saturday 11 October A very red letter day in my life, the reddest of all I suppose. For today at noon I was married to Marjorie at the Town Hall. The ceremony, which took place in one of the committee rooms upstairs, was pleasantly informal, very much to the point, and despite the considerable amount of writing by the registrar and his clerk which seemed to be involved, admirably brief. Mother and Joan acted as witnesses and three of M's colleagues from the post were present. And the sun shone for us, so everything was lovely. Went for a drink in the Euston Tavern after Joan left to catch a train. Mother, Marjorie and myself went to the Cumberland Hotel at Marble Arch for lunch. Lobster salad, mushrooms on toast, pastry, lager, coffee. Excellent. Got a bottle of wine to take to Somerset in Soho on way back. Came indoors (i.e. our new flat) for an hour or so. Out again for half an hour's stroll around. Had Mother over to tea. Set out soon after 6.0 for the Strand Palace, where we dined, drank half a bottle of Sauternes and a bottle of claret. The band kept playing show tunes of the 'twenties, a nice nostalgic evening. Left at 10.30, cab home and, as Pepys so slyly says, so to bed. About my own 'first night' I shall say nothing except that it was somewhat restless. We kept getting very thirsty and got very little sleep. And there were no critics present!

Sunday 12 October Down to Somerset for five days. Mother came and saw us off on the 12.30 from Paddington. Had to change at Chippenham – wait an hour for a terribly slow train which stopped twenty minutes at every station. And the fact that we both felt very tired and very hungry didn't make the journey any more enjoyable for us. What a relief it was when we at last crawled into Frome station at 6.0 and were wafted away in a waiting car to Coombe Farm where we're to stay. This is M's cousins' place, about four miles from Bangle Farm where M's Mother lives – there wasn't quite enough room for us to stay there. After some much needed tea we set out for Bangle Farm in the car. There I was introduced to my mother-in-law and innumerable relatives who had all foregathered for a feast in our honour. Simple kindly farming folk. Never was a good dinner more welcome than this sumptuous repast.

Monday 13 October All is peace and tranquillity down here. Except for the drone of the planes flying by overhead, the war and all connected with it can be completely banished from one's conscious thought in this quiet serene unspoilt countryside of rich fertile soil and yonder undulating hills. They have however had a few bombs in the vicinity for it's on the direct route from the South coast to Bristol which the raiders usually take when making for that much-bombed city. In contrast to our hectic activities of the last few days, we spent a lazy easy going sort of day beginning with a late breakfast in bed, which I'd have enjoyed better if we'd had a pot of hot tea with it instead of a lukewarm cup each. Still, we do get plenty of new laid eggs, they being so rare in London now. We were up so late that there wasn't time to do anything but take a short stroll over the fields before lunch – plentiful affair of lamb, potatoes and turnips and baked plums and custard. They certainly know how to feed well. Walked over to see a secluded lake[46] and grotto which M is very fond of in the afternoon. An exquisite and unique spot, well worth seeing. Then to Bangle farm for tea. And again for supper after a walk over to Chantry to get a drink and some cigarettes at the White Horse. Called in on a churchyard en route and saw the graves of M's ancestors. They've been farming round these parts for two centuries or more. Stayed sitting talking round the fire with M's mother and aunt till about 10.0. Half an hour walk back to Coombe Farm, a cup of cocoa and then to bed.

Tuesday 14 October Nunney is a rather picturesque old village very reminiscent of some of the Cotswold towns with its square towered church, a stream running alongside the main street. It also boasts a ruined castle and the uncommon novelty of an inn sign (The George) placed right across the street like a banner.[47] Called in at Coombe to get our coats and a suitcase in which to carry back the wedding presents and then went over to Bangle for the evening. Called round to the nearby Manor Farm to see Uncle Ernie and Aunt Annie before supper. Back to Coombe and at 11.0, very tired, very hot, to bed.

Wednesday 15 October Drove into Frome with cousin Frank in the morning for marketing day. Not a particularly interesting place. It's built on a hillside, has hundreds of shops but very little else. Walked over to Bangle, and there had more tea thrust upon us, closely followed by an early supper, for we had to leave soon after 7.0 to get back to Coombe in time to join a party setting off by car to a Home Guard Dance in a nearby village. A terrible dance, small dingy church hall with a floor as unpolished as the swarm of lads of the village who filled the place. We took one look at it and immediately went round to the nearest pub and drank as much sherry and bass as we could drink before closing time in order to make the thing tolerable. I shudder to think what it would have been like without such stimulant.

Thursday 16 October This soft sleepy Somerset air doesn't suit me at all – any more than it did when I stayed over at Brean two years ago. It's far too enervating, I feel tired and listless all day. Poor M very upset at leaving her mother. However I continued to [urge] her to sleep and all was well.

Saturday 18 October Back to London on the 10.30 from Frome. And a nice wet morning made going back much more welcome than it

---

46 Presumably Chantry Pond.
47 More complete entries on Heap's time in Nunney were supplied to that village's website and are included, with photographs of the farms and pubs mentioned, on the web pages. Many of the locations remain and some are still inhabited by Marjorie's distant relatives. See http://www.visitnunney.com/index.php/wartime-visit-nunney/ (accessed September 2015).

might have been had the weather been better. Got into Paddington at 1.20 having taken half the time it did going down. Cab home, lunch, unpacking, shopping, tea. What with overwork, ill health and the loneliness she must be feeling now, old Mother wasn't looking too good. I don't feel at all easy in my mind about her.

Sunday 19 October Have had a swollen nose for the last few days. Must have got bitten by some insect or other while away. Am trying to get it down with iodine ointment. Marjorie up and away by 7.30 being on duty mornings (8–12) this week. I got up and prepared some breakfast and had just washed up and dressed when someone came to have a look at the radiogram. Said it would need three new valves. That is the cost of financing overhauling etc amounting to about £2.10.0. Will have to let Mrs Ellis know about this before proceeding further.

Monday 20 October Back to work. And not at all sorry about it either. Congratulations and handshakes from all my office colleagues who had heard about my marriage during my absence. Paid the rent of our flat (22/9) into the office for the first time today. Am sending in the balance (9/6) to Mrs Ellis fortnightly.

Thursday 23 October Had a filthy car for the Warden's pay round this morning. Continually filled with smoke escaping from the faulty exhaust through the back of the seat which necessitated having the windows wide open to let it out. I don't know which was the worst ordeal, being well-nigh choked or getting chilled to the bone by the very draught. But I know that if they send that car again next week, I shall refuse to go round in it. Out for the evening with John [Hobson] and his girlfriend Nan.

Monday 27 October M on night duty this week (8.0 p.m. – 8 a.m.). Mother came in about 9.0 and got me some supper. Will go over to her for breakfast. Bed at 12.0.

Friday 31 October Had an unexpected increase in salary of 6/6 a week. Apparently a new scale of pay has been adopted. Also put £1 in the PO Bank. Am going to start putting £1 every fortnight again. To try and recoup the £17 I withdrew a month ago. There's not much of that left now.

Wednesday 5 November Went along to Ryman's in Poland St after lunch in the Town Hall canteen to get another book like this for next year's diary.

Friday 7 November Received a notice to attend for medical examination at Holloway at 12 noon on Tuesday next. So they've caught up with me at last! I was beginning to think they'd lost trace of me, for I registered as long ago as 22 June 1940 and had heard nothing further since. Still,

1941

whatever the result may be, I've at least had a good run for my money! Control night in the Town Hall dormitory.

Tuesday 11 November Up to Holloway at noon for my medical. Was there for two hours being given a twenty minute selective intelligence and observation test prior to the actual medical examination. Surely a case of putting the cart before the horse as if one is medically rejected then the selective test is just a waste of time. Thus it was in my case. But I should worry! For the result was the best I could possibly have hoped for. I was put in Grade III, told I wouldn't be wanted and sent joyously packing out into Seven Sisters Rd! So my two year old operation for perforated appendix saved my bacon after all. That and my doctor's letter about the hernia still present in the wound worked the trick. Peritonitis be praised! The relief is terrific, the dark clouds have lifted and my spirits soar once more. Phoned the glad tidings to M as soon as I got out and then went and had lunch at ARP Headquarters. Got back to the office at 3.30. I sent Mrs Ellis our fortnightly PO straightaway. Took a night off from control to celebrate my reprieve. As soon as M got home we sallied forth in the pouring rain to the Oxford Corner House Brasserie and had soup, hors d'oeuvres, lager and coffee. But we didn't enjoy the evening as much as we expected. Partly, perhaps, because we expected too much of it, but mainly I think because we are too tired and exhausted after the tension of the last day or two to enjoy anything much.

Thursday 13 November The wireless repairers came again this evening and after spending four hours on the radiogram at last got it into perfect working order. The total cost including replacement of valves came to £2.10.0 which, considering the time and trouble they've expended, is very reasonable indeed. Mrs E has agreed to pay half of this so we won't be much out of pocket.

Monday 17 November Went in and saw Taylor this afternoon about filling in the Ministry of Labour questionnaire. Had quite a long chat about my job, marriage and my prospects at the Town Hall. As I've passed the General Schools Exam and passed in addition the ACIS degree, there's a possibility of my being kept on after the war. A chance not to be sneezed at for unemployment will be widespread and there'll be a terrific scramble for jobs.

Saturday 22 November With Marjorie to the Hippodrome in afternoon to see *Get Ahead of This* by James Hadley Chase. M off to 'work' at 7.30. Over to Mother's an hour later for supper. Went round to the Friends House shelter after and brought back case full of diaries left there with bedding some time ago. Bed 11.15.

Tuesday 25 November Mother's 60th birthday. I gave her a pair of gloves as a present and Marjorie, a bottle of Eau de Cologne. We went to the ARP HQ to call for Mother, have a drink or two and a game of darts and bring her home to supper.

Thursday 27 November Mother has unexpectedly come across the jewellery and gramophone records which we believed had been stolen from the flat some months ago.[48] A joyous discovery, especially as the jewellery, comprising gold watch and charm and cuff links, diamond dress stud and a set of dress waistcoat buttons were all mine. Control duty in evening.

Saturday 29 November Mother indoors waiting for us when we got back at 10.20. Had brought us over a letter from Aunt Pop containing the somewhat overdue wedding gift. But it was worth waiting for – $21, which at the present rate of exchange is just over £5.[49] Dear old Aunt Pop! She's about the most generous soul I've ever known.

Sunday 30 November Took M for a walk around Lincoln's Inn Fields, the Law Courts, the Embankment and the Adelphi in the afternoon. Showed what is still left of my old school in Houghton St, The Old Curiosity Shop (which now empty and neglected, fascinated her enormously), the one corner of the Temple still intact after the Blitzkrieg, Cleopatra's needle and Scott's ship *Discovery* lying anchored in the Thames alongside the Embankment. Actually this was a discovery to me as well. I don't know how long it's been there.[50] I may have casually noticed the ship before but, if I had, I didn't know what it was. Rather to my surprise M found this jaunt full of interest and enjoyment. We must try some more. I may possibly get her to love London as much as I do in time. Home to tea at 5.30. Wrote a brief letter to Aunt Pop after, thanking her for the present and telling her about the 'medical' result. Mother came over at 7.0 and stayed to supper. A short read before bed.

Monday 1 December Went up to Holborn after lunch to get my usual 'at a glance' calendar for 1942. Couldn't get one – but at least they didn't insult [me] by meeting my request with the current parrot cry 'There's a war on you know' which is universally adopted as an excuse for unnecessary delay, bad work and gross inefficiency. Tinned foods are rationed from today on the 'points' system. The number of coupons required vary according to the demand for different foods, but may be exchanged at any shop – not, as in the case of the other rationed foods (and very few aren't now) necessarily at the retailer one is registered with. The object of this extension of rationing is ostensibly to stop the

---

48 See entry for 1 September above.
49 The pound was devalued from $4.03 to $2.80 in September 1949.
50 The three-masted sailing barque with auxiliary engines RRS *Discovery* was the ship built specially for Captain R. F. Scott's First Antarctic Expedition (1901–1904). Laid up after further service, from 1936 it was used for Sea Scout training, and then by the Admiralty on the Thames at Westminster, before being transferred to Dundee in 1985.

food racketeering which had been very prevalent lately. 'Ostensibly' is, I think, the operative word.

Wednesday 3 December According to Churchill's statement in the Commons yesterday, conscription for military service is to be extended to cover all men between the ages of 18½ to 51 instead of 21–41 as it stands at present. Women of 20–30 are also to be conscripted for the women's services and not merely directed to them as they have been hitherto. Furthermore block reservation is to be scrapped altogether and replaced by a system of individual deferment according to the importance of the actual work one is engaged on – the screw turns.

Sunday 7 December Took M for another walk 'in search of London', this time round the City i.e. what was the City before most of it was razed to the ground. From Holborn to the Bank and Monument and back via St Paul's and Fleet St. Have got a bit of a pain around my right thigh. May be just wind or I may have turned my muscles somehow. Hope it's nothing more serious.

Monday 8 December Today's papers carried the sensational news of Japan's declaration of war on England and America. The Japs already going great guns in the Pacific and the US Navy losses are heavy.[51] So the Yanks have been forced into fighting the Japs. The war has now spread right around the world.

Wednesday 10 December The Japs have got off the mark with a flying start. They've already sunk two of our biggest battleships, the Prince of Wales and the Repulse off Malaya. M's mother having sent us a couple of pigeons from Somerset, we had pigeon pie for lunch today. A dish I'd never had before or even heard of outside the pages of Dickens. I wasn't o'er enamoured with it.

Friday 12 December America has now declared war on Germany and Italy. And of course, vice versa. Which makes it a real 'all in' world war, the main line up being Germany, Italy and Japan v Britain, America and Russia – with the proviso that Japan and Russia discreetly refrain from declaring war on each other or nullifying their neutrality pact in anyway.[52]

Tuesday 16 December Didn't get such a good night's sleep as I expected – thanks to the constant ringing of a phone bell in a flat upstairs. It never ceased all night.

---

51 The Imperial Japanese Navy had attacked the American fleet at Pearl Harbor that Sunday morning (local time) without a declaration of war. On 8 December the US Congress complied within minutes to President Roosevelt's request that the US declare war on Japan. Germany and Italy declared war on the US three days later.
52 After a brief war in 1939 between the Soviet Union and Japan, in April 1941 the two countries signed a pact to ensure their neutrality in any future war.

Part Two

Friday 19 December Had a haircut after lunch. I scribbled and addressed my Christmas cards in the evening ready to send off tomorrow. Also wrote 'Retrospect 1941.' The former accompanied by a bout of toothache.

Saturday 20 December Up to Highgate to meet Marjorie off duty at 8.0. (shades of my courting days!) and take her to the Load of Hay on Haverstock Hill, which we'd heard was an uncommonly lively pub, replete with music and dancing. Actually it proved to be quite dull and uninteresting. The dancing was conducted in a hall quite apart from the bar and they were charging 1/6 for entry thereto. We took one look at it, saw half a dozen couples mournfully gliding round, went back to the bar, drank up and departed. So much for the Load of Hay. From there we walked up to the more familiar and certainly more comfortable Haverstock Arms where I often used to go with Ron. Had a couple more drinks then came home by tube from Belsize Park.

Sunday 21 December The First Aid Post at Highgate is being closed down in four weeks' time. Which seems to mean that M will have to look for a new job.

Tuesday 23 December On getting home at 9.30 found M had brought a radio set home on trial. A second hand Echo, for which they ask £5.10.0 knocked down from £6.10.0 since M bargained for it. Sounds all right so I suppose we might as well buy it. We've got to get a set of our own sooner or later and the Ellis set appears to be a washout anyway, so why not now?

Wednesday 24 December It's been a hectic three days in the office, trying to get a week's work into half a week. Though the Town Hall opens Boxing Day, which is not officially a bank holiday, practically everyone (including myself) has got the day off, as we've been given an extra day's holiday in addition to Christmas Day. Those of us to whose lot it falls to be in control tomorrow will get a further additional day off later. Met M at 8.30 at the ARP Headquarters, whither we went to join Mother in a drink or two in the canteen. Didn't stay very long however for it wasn't particularly pleasant there tonight.

Thursday 25 December The usual quiet Christmas Day at home. Got up at 9.30, shaved, washed and dressed and went over to the Town Hall to sign on for control before breakfast. Went for an hour's brisk walk over Hampstead in morning. Back at 1.0 in time to hear *Brains Trust* programme on radio.[53] Mother came over to dinner at 2.0 and stayed for the rest of the day. Our dinner consisted of roast chicken

---

53 Heap regularly listened to this radio programme, in which a panel of five intellectuals and experts discussed and answered listeners' questions. The regular contributors were the Hampstead resident and Birkbeck College philosopher Dr C. E. M. Joad, the anecdotist Commander Campbell RN and the scientist Professor Julian Huxley.

1941

(M's Mum had sent us one from Somerset) in lieu of turkey, with sausages, roast potatoes and swedes, followed by home-made Christmas pudding. Washed down with a bottle of port which Mother brought over, accompanied by a bottle of whisky. We did very well as things are at present. Sat and listened to the radio throughout the afternoon and evening. The tone of it wasn't at all good, sounded rather tinny. We'll have to have it seen to already I suppose, after only two days use. We do seem to damnably unlucky as regards radio sets. And to aggravate the matter the programme was pretty poor too. This in turn aggravated the heavy dull oppressive feeling of despondency which invariably besets me at Christmas time. Until 8.0, when we turned off the light and sat silently listening to a Mozart symphony in the firelight glow. Then all was peace, perfect peace. Immensely soothing. And so to supper at 10.30 over to the Town Hall for the night. I'm never really sorry to come to the end of Christmas Day.

Saturday 27 December The usual rent collection at Ferdinand Estate. An hour's brisk walk over Hampstead in the afternoon, terminating at Highgate Hospital First Aid Post, M and her colleagues having asked me up to have tea with them.

Monday 29 December M took the faulty radio set back to the shop today and left it to be brought back and fixed up later in the week. Before doing so, however, she'd tried to put it right herself and fused the electricity supply in the process. With the result that we are without electric light this evening, for despite repeated phone calls to the supply company, an engineer has failed to come along and repair it. Not such a calamity as it might have been however for M starts her week of night duty tonight and I'm on control. For such little time as either of us have had to spend at home, we've managed to make do with two candles.

Tuesday 30 December Was astonished to find the electric light supply back again when I came in early this morning to shave, wash and change. Unknown to me the repairer had called and fixed it yesterday evening while I was over at the Town Hall for the control practice. Town Hall topics: Breakfast getting worse, usual dish is two solitary rashers of fat salt bacon American fashion. Nothing with it, not even a fried bread or potato. There's a movement afoot to form a Home Guard for the staff. Meeting to discuss scheme Friday. Little enthusiasm evidenced thereof so far.

Wednesday 31 December M went to the hairdresser's this morning and had her hair set and dyed dark ginger. She's very smitten with it. So am I. Stayed in till midnight to see the Old Year out (or rather hear it on the radio) and back to bed and 1942.

Part Two
RETROSPECT – *1941*

Things happened to me in 1941. Or, to be precise, one big thing and a few small things. But the big thing was really big. I reached the most important milestone in my life. I met, wooed, won, and married Marjorie.

It all happened in the second half of the year. The first few months of 1941 were just a continuation of the last few months of 1940 – an empty, monotonous, irksome existence, working by day and sleeping in a shelter at night, my only escape being a Saturday afternoon at the theatre or cinema. It was all very melancholy and depressing. I yearned incessantly for company of some sort, something to make life really worth living. Then came the summer, the end of the air raids (the last big Blitzkrieg was on May 10) and the advent of Marjorie. Instantly my life was transformed. For the first time it was full and complete. I experienced an all-absorbing interest and enchantment such as I'd never known before – not to the same extent anyway. And there were no snags in it this time! It was a strange, swift, erratic courtship that terminated on Oct 11 – the day on which I embarked on the biggest gamble of my life and married Marjorie.

After a week's holiday in Somerset, we set up house together (if renting a furnished flat can be so termed) at 93 Queen Alexandra Mansions and commenced what has so far proved to be a happy and well favoured partnership (Incidentally this was my second move this year, for in February Mother and I had moved up from 19 to 25 Sinclair House). All else that happened during the course of the year was of small significance by comparison.

In November, seventeen months after I'd registered for military service. I was at last called up for medical examination, but, being put in Grade 3 on account of my abdominal wound, was not conscripted. I saved quite a bit of money during the first six months, for, despite the high and ever-increasing cost of living, I had so little to spend it on. However, I spent most of it during the following months – courtship and marriage, proving I found, somewhat expensive businesses. But I guess it was worth it. And I still finish the year worth approximately £176, which is £15 more than I started it with.

My interest in the theatre was evidently maintained in spite of the comparative dearth of new productions throughout the year, which led me to resort to the cinema for entertainment to a far greater extent than had been my practice hitherto. For the first time since 1927 I actually saw more films than I did shows and came perilously near to becoming something in the nature of a film fan. My book reading, like my play-going was also well below the average for the last few years. I seemed to find so little time or opportunity for it, especially during the summer. Still, I managed to get through quite a few good books all the same.

1941

I did practically no rambling or anything of that sort and except for the odd week in Somerset, hadn't seen the country from one end of the year to another. My friendship with John Hobson was diligently maintained through the medium of regular letter writing and an occasional week's leave. With the remainder of my erstwhile companions, however I tended to get more out of touch – thanks mainly to the disintegrating process wrought by the war. Though I did continue to correspond frequently with my old PR colleague Cookie. I held my job at the Town Hall, undertook control duty every fourth night, and, with increase in salary amounting to £1.7.0 a week made some little progress. Taken all in all, it was a year I can look back on without regret or recrimination. And how much happier am I at the end of it than I was at the beginning!

1942

Seven months into what was to become the thirty-one-month virtual lull which followed the end of the Blitz in May 1941, and three months into their marriage, both Heap and Marjorie had misgivings and doubts on their decision to marry. Both experienced recurrent periods of depression, Marjorie moving from job to job; unhappy with office work, in August she decided to join the Land Army, but her office would not release her. Occasional air raid warnings reminded them of the Blitz but the 'Baedeker' raids on historic English towns, which opened in April, avoided central London, so Heap, having already retrieved his old diaries from the public air raid shelter, now collected the rest of his bedding. Marjorie's family farm in Somerset provided a summer holiday but generally 1942 was uneventful for the couple. Meanwhile, the war did not go well until November, when church bells were rung to celebrate military success in Egypt. Although Heap kept up his attendance at theatres and cinemas, for this uneventful year of 'doubt and despair' only 27% of his original 42,600 words warrant inclusion.

Thursday 1 January Made a stoic start to the new year by getting up half an hour earlier than usual at 7.0 and following up my shave with a shampoo and bath. Called at King's Cross Post Office on my way back from the morning pay round, withdrew £2 from the savings bank, bought a new wireless licence (10/-) and sent off my annual C.I.S. subscription (31/6), then to Boots to renew library subscription (19/6). Our new radio set arrived back from the dealer in Highgate this afternoon, reception now perfect. Took M to the Town Hall's New Year Party and Dance at the Adolf Tuck Hall in Upper Woburn Place.[1] One of those terribly jolly adolescent affairs consisting of dancing to a very indifferent amateur dance band, interspersed with a few even more indifferent amateur cabaret turns. Nor did the crowd help to improve matters, comprising as it did, the normal wishy-washy gathering of callow youths and nit-witted girls such as one inevitably finds at any third rate dance hall. And to fill my cup of woe to overflowing there was, of course, no bar. [We] Finished up our Christmas bottle of Scotch before starting out, rounding it off with two gins and lime at the Euston

---

1   In Woburn House, on the junction with Endsleigh Street.

Tavern on the way and repairing to the Kentish Arms for two more drinks during the interval. We stuck it till about 10.0 [when they] set up a shrill and insistent clamour for the tango and the conga, whereupon we left.

Friday 2 January The specific gravity of beer is now being further reduced by 5%.[2] Even so, an acute shortage of beer is arising in some districts. Wines and spirits are now very scarce and, unless the import ban on them is lifted, look like becoming unobtainable in a month or two. On control in the evening.

Sunday 4 January With M to St James's Park, along the Embankment to Charing Cross. Noticed that they seem to be making some sort of temporary bridge over the Thames between Westminster Bridge and Hungerford Bridge.[3] For what purpose I know not.

Wednesday 7 January Went pub-crawling with John Hobson. As this was our last session before he goes back on Monday we made quite an evening of it.

Monday 12 January M calls at the New Veterinary College First Aid Post,[4] whither most of the Highgate post are being transferred next week, takes an instant dislike to the sister-in-charge, the people already there and the place itself, sends in her resignation to the Town Hall, goes up to the Labour Exchange and lands a job as a telephone and telegraph tester at the Post Office in Islington, starting next Monday. Good going!

Tuesday 13 January Going up to Highgate Hospital for the last time today on the First Aid Posts pay round aroused in me feelings of sweet melancholy. Yes, I shall always have a warm sentimental affection for Highgate Hospital and its First Aid Post, even though after Saturday next it will, alas, be no more. It has played a very important part in my life and acquired a very soft spot in my heart.

Wednesday 14 January The view from our windows this morning presenting that fascinating spectacle of white snow-covered roofs set against a lugubrious leaden sky. The snow had been falling all night and today it 'lay around about, white and crisp and even' to a depth of two or three inches.

Monday 19 January M went down to Somerset on the 12.30 from Paddington to Frome today, staying with her Mother at Bangle Farm

2   The Brewers' Society announced that, owing to the acute shortage of labour in the malting industry and to conserve available malt, the gravity of beer was to be reduced. The Minister of Food stated that the price of beer would not be reduced (*The Times*, 31 December 1941).
3   Presumably a wartime emergency bridge rather than the temporary bridge in place between 1936 and 1943 during the building of the replacement Waterloo Bridge, which was partially opened on 11 August 1942 and completed in 1945.
4   Royal College Street, NW1.

till Thursday. I certainly don't envy her the trip this weather. It's still bitterly cold and tonight another heavy fall of snow is beginning to lay.

Saturday 24 January M not too enthusiastic about the new job which she started this morning. Reasons: (a) She's not being given nearly enough work to do. Apparently they're waiting for a sufficient number of women to form an instruction [quorum]. (b) Her associates are rather on the common side and therefore she doesn't get on with them too well. (c) There's a possibility of her having to do overtime on Sundays.

Monday 26 January Turned bitterly cold again. One of our greatest problems at the moment is procuring of coal. Like most people nowadays whose business is to sell a somewhat scarce commodity much in demand, the coalmen have become very surly and independent and refuse to carry coal up to such a dizzy height as the third floor. It's all very tiresome and trying.

Tuesday 27 January Managed to get a small bag of coal from the grocers, about enough to last a couple of evenings. More snow this afternoon. M, who comes home from work more depressed each day, has now decided to turn the job in and give notice.

Wednesday 28 January Lost my cigarette case this morning. It dropped out of my trouser pocket while enthroned in the Town Hall lavatory and I forgot to pick it up when I came out. Put up a notice as soon as I discovered the loss but no one brought it back. I bought it for a bob at a Mornington Crescent tobacconists in March 1935 – and I became quite attached to it.

Thursday 29 January Cigarette case regained. Someone turned it in to the caretaker replete with the three Du Mauriers it contained.

Friday 30 January The coal problem solved, Mother managed to get a coalman to deliver two cwt [hundredweight] here yesterday with a guarantee of future deliveries when required. Thank heavens for that.

Saturday 31 January Arrived home lunchtime to find soldiers posted at the entrances to Queen Alexandra Mansions and police searching the courtyard, passages and staircases. They were on the track of a deserter who had been seen to enter the Mansions and then disappear. Whether they eventually found him or not I don't know.

Monday 2 February Wore my old nailed hiking boots today – incongruous though they looked with black coat and striped trousers, the streets were in such a foul mess underfoot. M arrived home highly elated teatime. She'd finished up at the Post Office, been to the Labour Exchange, had an interview and arranged to go along again tomorrow with a view to getting an office job somewhere. So M is herself again. The depression which has hung over her for the last nine days is lifted at last.

1942

Friday 6 February M tired of waiting to hear from the Exchange, phoned them this afternoon, whereupon they sent her along to Ibex House in Minories [EC3] for an interview re: a clerical job in the Tax Collector's office. She got the job, starting Monday – wages 57/6 plus 11/8 overtime for a 51 hour week. I think she's done very well for herself.

Monday 9 February Soup rationed from today. We weighed ourselves on the tube platform scale yesterday afternoon. I was just on 13 stone. M was 11 stone 9 lbs. M started on her new job in the Tax Collector's office this morning. She finds it considerably more congenial than the P.O., more pleasant surroundings, more people to work with. I feel quite relieved that she's taken so warmly to the job for yesterday she was very apprehensive and worried about it. Unduly so really.

Saturday 14 February In the course of my afternoon's walk over the heath I observed a sailor and his lass locked in close embrace on the grass. If this doesn't suggest spring, what does? Mother still very ill ('old bowel problem'). She will insist on going to work however and I fear she'll go on doing so till she drops. Nothing will stop her.

Monday 16 February The fortunes of war continue to go dead against us. Singapore has been surrendered to the Japs, we are on the retreat in Libya once more and three German battleships have escaped from Brest and passed up the Channel, through the straits of Dover and safely back to home waters unscathed in spite of our fierce shelling and aerial attack.[5] So far as we're concerned the war has only brought one damned setback after another.

Friday 20 February Many of London's streets, squares and parks have a strangely bare and unfamiliar appearance these days. For all unnecessary iron railings surrounding little private houses or open spaces have been requisitioned by the government for the manufacture of munitions, and most of them have by now been torn down and taken away. At Camden Town they are even beginning to pull up the old disused tramlines for their steel content.

Sunday 22 February M's 26th birthday. Mother and I presented her with a small wine-coloured handbag which she bought herself in the City on Friday for 17/6. In addition Mother has given her a pair of small pale blue vases for the mantelpiece and a tin of grapefruit – M having been longing for some tinned fruit, now almost as scarce as fresh fruit.

Thursday 5 March Men's fashions look like being set back thirty years or so when the new 'utility suit' is introduced. In order to save cloth,

---

5   The battleships *Scharnhorst* and *Gneisenau* and the heavy cruiser *Prinz Eugen* broke out of Brest harbour under cover of darkness and successfully ran the Royal Navy and RAF blockade through the English Channel to reach German home waters.

the Board of Trade has ruled that this is to be the only type of suit made in future, and according to the specification double-breasted styles, sleeve buttons and trouser turn ups are to be discontinued and both sleeves and trousers are to be cut narrower. The only corresponding regulation in regard to women's dresses is that they are to be made slightly shorter.[6]

Sunday 8 March Up to Holly Lodge estate[7] to have tea with M's old FAP [First Aid Post] colleagues, one of Mrs K's sons, her vivacious French daughter-in-law and a French soldier. A very nice house, beautifully furnished. Had an excellent and plentiful tea, including preserved ginger and Christmas cake, followed by controversial but quite amicable discussion on the war and things in general. A most enjoyable and agreeable evening.

Monday 9 March It's now an offence, punishable by fine or imprisonment, to throw away a bus ticket, a cigarette packet or any sort of paper that can be utilised as salvage. What a sorry pass we've come to!

Tuesday 10 March Neither of us getting enough sleep lately. Though I don't seem to feel it as much as M – for it takes me a quarter of an hour to get her up in the morning.

Friday 13 March My 32nd birthday. A navy blue pullover from Marjorie, three pairs of socks from Mother and two from Fred and family. Had Mother over to supper. Quite a convivial evening.

Monday 16 March A twenty five minute alert this morning – the first daylight one for nine months.

Wednesday 18 March Further war economy cuts. Newspaper supplies by 10%, clothing coupons by 25%. The next allotment of coupons on June 1st will only number 60 instead of 66, and have to last 14 months instead of 12.

Saturday 21 March The first day of London's 'Savings for Warships' week. St Pancras' effort was inaugurated this afternoon with a procession through the borough. Watched it set off from the Town Hall and march past the Mayor. A tawdry shoddy affair. No colour, no music, no showmanship. Wasn't worth walking across the road to see.

Monday 23 March Alterations in the Town Hall Control duties, North Report has been closed and the personnel transferred to the Town

---

6   Hardie Amies, Norman Hartnell and other designers created thirty-four smart Utility Clothing designs and commented on men's styles ('Fashion or Ration: Hartnell, Amies and Dressing for the Blitz', The National Archives podcast, 18 February 2010, available at http://podbay.fm/show/208318433 (accessed 25 April 2017)).

7   The private, gated estate on the southern slopes bordering Hampstead Heath..

Hall, thus making six shifts instead of four.[8] I have been detailed to alternate the function of Plotting Officer with someone else. So that for the time being I shall only have to go on duty every twelfth night. Had a 'practice' at 6.30 this evening and gleaned something of my new job, which consists of sticking small flags on large scale maps of the borough to mark 'incidents' and road blocks as they occur.

Friday 27 March Having got wind that there are likely to be some changes in the office when Taylor becomes Borough Treasurer on May 1st – I went to see him this morning and ask for a better job. After consulting McEwen who is in charge of the general office and due to succeed him as Deputy B T, he decided to put me on some accountancy work as soon as it could be arranged. So! I came out with the gratifying feeling of having accomplished something after all, it only required a little nerve and self-confidence. I don't expect it will mean any great increase in salary but at least I shall have something more interesting to do than the monotonous weekly routine of rent collections, pay and suchlike.

Wednesday 1 April After a rather gloomy heart-to-heart talk about the obscure depressions which, for some reason or other, we both seem to be experiencing this week, we went round to the Friends House this evening. (It seems a very long time ago now since Mother and I used to go along there to sleep night after night for months on end.) Went down to the shelter, collected all the bedding still there comprising two mattresses, two pillows, and two blankets, lugged them up the five flights of stairs to No 25. Mother hadn't got back so we just dumped our awkward burdens in the bedroom and came away. As soon as we got indoors and switched the light on, it fused. So for the rest of the evening we were deprived of that modern amenity and I felt truly Pepysian as I wrote my diary, supped and 'so to bed' by candlelight. What I should feel however, if we had to make do with it for more than one night is another matter.

Thursday 2 April M comes home from work very depressed and worried again. Apparently she's been making one or two mistakes in the office lately and instead of taking them in her stride she gets worked up into a state of nervous tension and that in turn develops into an awful inferiority complex. It's that old psychological disorder of hers, which manifested itself quite frequently during our three months engagement. Since we've been married, however, it's become more subdued and only breaks out at infrequent intervals. It ended with her sitting on my lap and having a hearty sob on my shoulder after which

---

8 The reserve civil defence control room in Pratt Street, Camden Town, was closed to save manpower.

she felt much better. There's nothing like a good cry to relieve one's overwrought mind.

Friday 3 April Good Friday Took a gloomy walk around the West End in the morning and over Hampstead in the afternoon. A couple of fairs in progress on the heath, both well patronised. They were also starting to dig for allotments on Parliament Hill. I suppose they won't be satisfied till the whole of this beauty spot has been desecrated and made as hideous as Primrose Hill is today. Went for a stroll up Tottenham Court Rd afterwards and had a look at the furniture shops. Fantastic prices even for the shoddiest stuff. The average cost of a bedroom, drawing room or dining room suite being 50 to 60 guineas which is at least 10% more than pre-war prices and about 20% more than they're worth. We had thought of getting another flat soon and furnishing it ourselves but it's utterly impossible for anyone of moderate means to afford such prohibitive prices. A hopeless position altogether. Couldn't even get the damned fire to light. Bloody awful day.

Saturday 4 April Double summer time begins tonight when the clocks are put on the extra hour – a month earlier than last year. Though, why, when it was decided to extend the period, they didn't tack on the extra month at the other end, would not continue the light evenings into September, I can't understand. They'll surely be more welcome then.

Monday 6 April Easter Monday Very windy and doubtful, so we once more abandoned our intention of going into the country for the day and reluctantly obeyed the Government's appeal to refrain from travelling by rail at Easter by staying put in London. Walk over Hampstead where the fairs were in full swing, and an afternoon stroll through the equally crowded parks from Horseguards Parade to Marble Arch. An hour over at Mother's listening to her radio (ours hasn't come back from the dealer's yet).

Wednesday 8 April Started work on the accounts, filling in the pencilled figures for the year ending 31 March 1941, initialling off each account after closely studying the details. Rather bewildering and complicated at first sight, especially after having had no real practical experience of book keeping before for my work at PR's could hardly be called that and such knowledge of the subject as I possess was gained in the course of my studies for the CIS exams many years ago. However, I am beginning to find my way about and get a good rough idea of how the accounts were compiled. I felt really exhausted when I came in at 6.0. Brought in some fish and chips for supper.

Sunday 12 April A glorious spring day, the finest this year so far. Took full advantage thereof by getting out into the country and doing fourteen miles of Surrey. Enjoyed every moment of it, despite the mediocre efforts of the railway companies to engender a feeling of guilt on prospective

1942

ramblers by means of the insolent question which confronts one above every booking office window 'Is Your Journey Really Necessary?'[9] However we weren't unduly troubled by any qualms of conscience as we bought our day return tickets to Leatherhead at Waterloo Station – lunch on Box Hill and tea at 'Hog's Back.' Large number of soldiers, mainly Canadian, loafing about the streets with nothing better to do than get thoroughly bored. There were also a good many on and around Box Hill where the surrounding ground has been transformed into a military camp. Home at 9.40 to a supper of roast veal, baked potatoes, turnip tops and plums and custard which Mother had cooked for us. A grand meal to end up a grand day. We came back with our faces sunburnt and our bodies saturated with fresh air and exercise. The most beautiful sight imaginable.

Tuesday 14 April The most drastic measures in today's budget are the increased duties on beer, wines, spirit and tobacco. Beer will cost an extra 2d a pint. Whisky goes up by 4/8 to the fantastic price of 22/2 a bottle, as compared with 12/6 in pre-war days and even that, three quarters was duty. The price of cigarettes is increased from 9d to 1/- for a packet of ten, exactly double the pre-war price. Both the Entertainments Tax and the Purchase Tax on certain luxury articles are also doubled. Income Tax remains unchanged at 10/- in the £. Small consolation alas, for such a heavy toll on our modest little luxuries.

Saturday 18 April Had a letter from John Bell, the first since November. Actually he wrote it on February 24 when his ship was off the west coast of Africa round about the equator, so it's taken nearly two months to get here. A most amusing letter.

Friday 24 April Have reverted to the light lunch such as I used to have when I was at PR's and took sandwiches and fruit every day. Instead of getting a poorly cooked and unsatisfactory meal in the canteen, I now come indoors and have bread and cheese with possibly beetroot or pickles, washed down with a cup of coffee or Ovaltine. I find this quite as satisfactory and – since I invariably have a good breakfast over at Mother's and a plentiful supper at home in the evening – perfectly adequate. If only it were possible to get fruit still 'twould indeed be an ideal lunch, especially for the summer months. However we should be able to get tomatoes and green stuff soon, it's a decided change for the better – and far more economical.

Sunday 26 April After an early lunch we went to Epping Forest. Went by train to Chingford, the only snag was that M began to get very weary after about six miles, which made her a trifle irritable and depressed. But that soon passed and otherwise all was well.

---

9   This 1940 slogan headed the campaign to ease transport overcrowding.

Part Two

Tuesday 28 April In reprisal for some raids we've been carrying out over Germany lately, Bath, Exeter and Norwich have been severely Blitzed during the last two or three nights.[10] Widespread damage and heavy casualties in each case. Things are warming up again.

Wednesday 29 April Attended the presentation of an inscribed silver inkstand by [Alderman] Davies [to] retiring Borough Treasurer in one of the Committee rooms. Embarrassing ceremony but mercifully brief.

Thursday 30 April Met Ron at the Horse Shoe at 8.30 and went for a short pub-crawl. At the Wheatsheaf I accidentally dropped my 'Shockproof' watch going out of the Gents and it bounced down the whole flight of stairs without breaking or even stopping.

Friday 1 May The sale of cigarettes has declined considerably since the increase in prices. A shortage now no longer exists and it is not an unusual sight to see packets of cigarettes stocked on the shelves of tobacconists' shops once more, instead of hidden under the counter.

Thursday 7 May M feeling tired out after a sleepless night, decided to 'lay in' the morning and have one more day off. It being a gloriously warm and sunny afternoon, I advised her to spend it on Hampstead Heath. Which she did and felt infinitely better thereafter. After tea we got a bus up to Regent's Park, had a look at the spring. Visions to store up in one's mind and recall during the next grim winter.

Monday 11 May Churchill, to celebrate the second anniversary of his premiership, makes a speech on radio threatening the Germans with poison gas if they dare to use it against our dearly beloved Bolshevist allies. The man's a perfect genius at meeting trouble halfway, especially when it is in the interests of the communist rats to do so. Now that furniture has risen to three times the pre-war level the government has decided to stop the ramp by making an interim order 'fixing' the maximum prices at the present level and setting up a committee to explore the possibility of producing more reasonably priced 'utility' furniture. How like a democratic government to wait until it is too late to do anything effective before doing anything at all. In any case all furniture made now is of inferior quality for no good class timber is available for its manufacture. Moreover, I can't see any possibility of the situation improving till after the war.

Thursday 14 May Charles and [Marjorie's] mother 'came up from Zummerzet.' Met them arriving at Paddington on the 7.25 and brought them home in a taxi. M thrilled to death, this being the first time she'd been able to get her mother up to London since they came over here ten years ago, and Charles having got much longer than expected –

---

10   In April and May, these 'Baedeker' raids were mounted against historic English towns in reprisal for RAF raids on the historic German towns of Lübeck and Rostock.

1942

27 days. Apparently the [RN battleship] *George V* collided with a destroyer and is laid up in dock for repairs. We'd just finished supper when Mother came in to meet the family for the first time. Stayed talking for about an hour, during which time Charles and I slipped down to the Euston Tavern for a couple of drinks. And how avidly he knocked them back! He puts down a pint in one gulp ere I've hardly supped mine. I certainly can't keep up with him at drinking. Charles and I in the spare room, M and her Mother in ours.

Saturday 16 May To the Fitzroy with M and Charles in the evening. Spent about an hour and a half there – just long enough to get mildly and pleasantly tight. Unfortunately we had to come home at 9.30 to enable me to get some supper before going over to the Town Hall for control duty.

Monday 18 May Went to a dance at Covent Garden Opera House with Marjorie and Charles, while our two mothers went to the cinema together. They've made the place much more elaborate and decorative since we last went nine months ago, and, even for such a slack night as Monday there was quite a large crowd assembled. But on the whole it was a pretty awful crowd, especially the feminine part of it (the male section consisted as usual of soldiers and airmen) and we didn't enjoy ourselves overmuch. The discordant wails and howls radiated by the dance band and the 'crooners' both depressed and irritated me and I felt entirely out of my element amid the hideous contortions of 'jitterbugs' and such like manifestations of the imbecility displayed by modern youth who seem to belong more to the jungle than a civilised order of society. And since even Charles could find nothing to his liking so far as girls were concerned, the evening could only be written off as a dire failure. Cooked some eggs and bacon for supper when we got home. After which Charles decided to bring his up again. A 'no joy' end to the evening.

Thursday 21 May Our radio came back repaired after two months. Went to Covent Garden again with Marjorie and Charles in the evening. Why, God only knows! Neither M nor myself were feeling in the mood for dancing and Charles didn't need us to keep him company for no sooner did we get inside the place than he got hooked up with some awful little tart who clung to him throughout the evening.

Sunday 24 May M and I are beginning to get a bit washed up. In other words we are inclined to chaff under the stress and responsibilities of married life, yearn for our independence again, and get on each other's nerves now and then. If this state of affairs continues indefinitely, it seems that the only satisfactory solution of the problem is to separate. Still, we are able to discuss the matter quite frankly and amicably without any bitterness or bad feeling and that is definitely something to be thankful for. What it all boils down to is that we both realise we possibly made a mistake in getting married and we are not as well suited to each other or married life as we thought we would be. Unfortunately, a few months' actual experience of married life is the only way to find that out – and then it's a hell of a job to get out if you want to. Went up to see Ron; pub-crawls with Ron provide an antidote to the depression from which I'm suffering at the moment.

Monday 25 May Whit Monday Didn't get up till 11.30. At our wits' end to know what to do for the rest of the day. The weather wasn't good enough for Hampstead and all the cinemas were packed, so we just sat around indoors, got more and more bored until about 6.30 when, with Mother, we all went round to the Euston Tavern and got maudlin drunk. Phil and Kath whom I hadn't seen for six months and a few others of the old Robin Hood crowd came in while we were there, and their presence brought on one of M's temperamental moods. Going round to the Plumbers Arms only made matters worse for the crowd in there was even more plebeian and less congenial than that in Euston had been.

Tuesday 26 May Awoke at 5.0. Couldn't get to sleep again so got up and made some tea. M hadn't any sleep at all and though she got up and dressed ready for work she was so overcome by saying goodbye to Charles and her mother that we decided she'd better have another day off, see them off to Somerset in the morning and go to bed in the afternoon. Poor Marjorie, these leave-takings always upset her.

Friday 29 May Spent a good part of the evening arguing with M about money. Or rather she did most of the arguing and I just patiently listened. The point being that she wanted me to buy her a new blouse and skirt. In the end she succeeded in making me see her point of view and so won the day.

Saturday 30 May Went round to the Food Office in the afternoon and got our new ration books. Much to my surprise I was only kept waiting a few moments for there had been long queues for them throughout the last fortnight.

Tuesday 2 June The RAF is now making a habit of carrying out nightly mass raids on Germany, sending a thousand planes at a time to bomb such places as Cologne and the Ruhr region.[11] If they keep this sort of thing up, we're sure to get it in the neck here again soon. Why not let sleeping dogs lie and let the damned Bolsheviks do their own dirty work.

---

11   The first such raid was mounted by RAF Bomber Command on the night of 30/31 May with 1,047 aircraft bombing Cologne. See I. C. B. Dear (ed.), *The Oxford Companion to the Second World War* (Oxford: Oxford University Press, 1995), pp. 1107–1108.

1942

Wednesday 3 June Had our first night alert for seven months early this morning when a few raiders flew over London and dropped a few incendiaries in a park. The siren woke us up at 2.40 and the all clear sent us to sleep again twenty minutes later. Heard neither planes nor gunfire. On control at night.

Thursday 4 June Went to the Holly Lodge Estate in evening to see M's old FAP [First Aid Post] colleagues, Charles also came along and 'among others present' were Mrs K's French daughter-in-law, Suzy, and a pretty and a much too slender friend of hers named Eve. Had tea in Mrs K's garden and sat out there throughout the evening. It was all so green and clean and bright and fresh that we wished more than ever that we could live in such a delectable spot other than in the grimy depressing purlieu of King's Cross.

Sunday 7 June Home to tea before going onto Hyde Park in the evening to listen to the band for a few minutes – Charles was too impatient to get a drink to stay longer – and then walked all the way to the Fitzroy. As usual it was too uncomfortably crowded to stay for more than one drink, so we proceeded via the Horse Shoe to the Tartan Dive where we stayed for the rest of the evening. Really we had quite a convivial time down there, an amusing encounter with a loquacious and high spirited American girl adding considerably to the gaiety of the occasion.

Tuesday 9 June Awoken at 5.0 by the fire brigade from the school buildings opposite carrying out some sort of practice drill in the streets below.[12] Why they chose such an ungodly hour to make such an unearthly row I can't imagine. At lunchtime, who should I find there [at home] but Jill, the American girl whom I met at the Tartan Dive the other evening. Apparently Charles had been there last night on his own, met her again, fallen for her, and invited her along to spend the day with him. She was still there when I came in again at 5.0 and accompanied us when we sallied forth to celebrate Charles' last night of leave. Went first of all to the inevitably over-crowded Fitzroy for one uncomfortable drink and to the Duke of Wellington, where we settled down for the evening.

Wednesday 10 June M has the day off to keep Charles company during his last few hours of leave. Jill also stayed on till the evening. M completely confounded our expectations by not bursting into tears at the parting. In fact, she remained quite calm and collected and cheerful throughout the evening. We afterwards took Jill down to the Tartan Dive – she lives only a few yards from there.

---

12 The Heaps' flat overlooked the Argyle Street School on Tonbridge Street, WC1, which housed Station B1X of the National Fire Service (William Hickin, *Fire Force: A Short Organisational History and Directory of the National Fire Service of 1941 to 1948* (London: WHF Publications, 2013), p. 132).

Wednesday 24 June Managed to negotiate a 6/- increase in pay, which brings me up to £5 a week.

Thursday 25 June After driving us out of that long-contested theatre of war, Libya, with heavy losses, the Germans are now rapidly following up their strategical triumph with an invasion of Egypt and have already advanced fifty miles over the border. It's the old story of superior enemy strength in men, planes and tanks outnumbering and outmanoeuvring our own inadequate and ill-equipped forces. Sending supplies of war material to Russia to bolster up the Bolsheviks seems to be of much greater importance than keeping our own army adequately supplied. In any case the Reds don't seem to be doing so well, even with our aid, for the Germans look like capturing Sebastopol at any time now. They certainly know how to lose wars.

Friday 10 July Met John Hobson outside the Horse Shoe at 7.0 and went on an extensive pub-crawl round the West End. We made at least ten calls and disposed of about fifteen drinks a head including the pint of lager we had with the inevitable hors d'oeuvres at the Corner House after. I'm afraid we got ingloriously drunk for it seemed likely to be the last time I'd see John for a very long time.

Saturday 11 July Woke up with a thick head and a parched throat. A cup of tea and a couple of aspirins, however, disposed of both within half an hour. Journeyed down to Somerset to stay with Marjorie's mother for our fortnight's holiday. I had the morning off and M got away early, so we managed to catch the 1.15 from Paddington. Train packed. Had to stand in the corridor as far as Swindon and then change at Chippenham. Reached Frome soon after 5.0.

[*The weather was poor for their holiday but they managed days out in Bath and Shepton Mallet, the other days resting and visiting local pubs in Nunney and their local, the White Horse. The sole significant 'family' incident was on 23 July.*]

Thursday 23 July I 'put my foot in it' and 'blotted my copybook' with a vengeance last night. While sitting round the fire over a final cup of tea, I tactlessly allowed myself to be drawn into a political argument with M's mother, who has obviously been 'fed' with a lot of communist propaganda by someone or other. As usual, I gave full vent to my anti-communist views with the result that the old girl lost her temper, flared up in fervent defence of the Bolsheviks and hysterically denounced me as a pro-German unpatriotic scoundrel, a traitor and all the rest of it. Followed a distressing scene in which M broke down and wept, her mother cooled down a little and I declared my intention of leaving on the morrow. Later M persuaded me to stay on till Saturday for the sake of appearances and so prevent the gossip and conjecture to which my premature departure would give rise.

Sunday 26 July The last day of our holiday is about as lugubrious an occasion as the last night of a play. One seems to get neither the opportunity nor the inclination to do anything apart from packing and aimlessly hanging about waiting until the time to leave. At 5.30 the car at last arrived to waft us off to Frome station to catch the 6.8 back to London. Much to our surprise we managed to get seats on the train and so had quite a comfortable journey. Arrived Paddington 9.15, forty minutes late and home by 9.40. Avidly devoured the ham and tomatoes Mother had ready for us, unpacked, got ready everything for the morning and were in bed well before midnight.

Monday 27 July Had two short air raid alerts round about 7.0 this morning. No bombs dropped on London. All I did was to take M and Mother over to the Euston Tavern and have a few drinks.

Tuesday 28 July We were awoken at 3.0 a.m. by gunfire and heard a plane flying over a couple of minutes later. When it had gone, the alert sounded and lasted till 4.15. Further bouts of gunfire kept us awake throughout but there didn't seem to be any bombs being dropped anywhere. Spent nearly two hours this evening ploughing through the last fortnight's newspapers.

Saturday 1 August I've just set up a new personal theatre going record. I've frequently done two theatres in one day – sometimes two in one evening – and I've occasionally done three theatres in three days but never before have I done three theatres in two days – in fact, within twenty four hours.

Wednesday 5 August M has been 'lent' to the Euston District Tax Inspector's office for a few weeks during the holiday period. As it is only two or three minutes' walk from Queen Alexandra Mansions, she is now able to leave later in the morning, get back earlier in the evening and come in for lunch at the same time as I do. Rather wishes she could be transferred permanently. The young scallywag who came and took the Ellis radiogram set away to be repaired over six months ago, at last brought it back this evening and fixed it up. It went perfectly by the time he'd finished, and all was forgiven.

Saturday 8 August News from the two Johns arrived almost simultaneously. A brief letter from John H posted as he was about to embark for overseas and with the date deleted by the censor. And an airgraph from John B, still roaming the seas, fed up and far from home.[13] To the New Victoria,[14] an uncommonly good double feature programme. My enjoyment of both films was somewhat marred however by an air raid alert signal which was displayed just after 6.0. As I was supposed to be on control duty at the Town Hall this naturally caused me some concern, especially as no all clear followed during the remaining two hours we were there. For if, by any unfortunate chance, a heavy raid had occurred, my absence would have landed me in the soup. On getting back I went to the Town Hall with some trepidation – only to learn that the alert had lasted but half an hour or so and had been entirely without incident. So it was a case of much alarm about nothing. But why the hell didn't the damned cinema announce the all clear as well as the warning.

Sunday 9 August Went for a walk over Hampstead in the evening and had a drink at The Spaniards. The strains of music followed us all over the heath for there was not only the small brass band playing at Parliament Hill Fields, but also a military string orchestra giving a concert up by Whitestone Pond. Presumably a feature of the extensive outdoor entertainment programme which has been organised by the LCC for the benefit of Londoners spending their holidays at home.

Friday 14 August On control at night. M having at last decided to join the Land Army, gave in her notice at the Tax Office this afternoon and later went along to the Land Army office at Marble Arch to get an enrolment form and arrange for an interview.[15] Not that she wants to leave me, but she just can't take to office work and apart from going into a factory or one of the women's military services, which would be equally repugnant for her, there is no other alternative from compulsory national service but the Land Army. On top of this she hates King's Cross and the Ellis flat even more than I do and longs for the freedom and freshness of the countryside. She will, of course, get placed as near as possible to her mother in Somerset, while I shall have to go back to live with mine. We shall miss each other terribly, for despite all the difficulties and set-backs, financial and otherwise, which have marred our brief married life, and regardless of our difficulties and temperament and taste, we have become most deeply devoted to each other during the last few months. But our better judgement tells us that this break is somehow to be for the best of a bad job and endeavour

---

13 To reduce the physical bulk and weight of mail to and from forces overseas, the original was written on a standard form and then photographed, the film being sent by air. At the destination the film was developed, enlarged and printed, and the letters delivered to the individual addressees.
14 Cinema at the corner of Vauxhall Bridge Road and William Street, SW1.
15 The Women's Land Army was formed in the First World War and again in 1939 to provide civilian women ('Land Girls') – initially volunteers – for farmwork. By July 1943 some 87,000 women were so employed. See Juliet Gardiner, *Wartime: Britain 1939–1945* (London: Headline, 2004), pp. 449–455.

1942

to readjust our lives for the duration as best we can. It won't be easy though.

Wednesday 19 August It looks as though we are likely to attempt a continental invasion shortly now. A large scale combined forces daylight rehearsal raid on the Dieppe area was carried out today, including the landing of tanks. It lasted nine hours, met with strong resistance and involved heavy losses on both sides. The object of the raid has not been made clear though it was repeatedly stressed that it was not an invasion.[16] The communists' continual clamour during the last few months for a 'second front' to relieve the pressure on their precious Russia is apparently about to be gratified at last. The cost doesn't seem to matter.

Monday 24 August I see that the Board of Education has recommended some forty books extolling the glories (!) of Soviet Russia to teachers for use in schools. In other words, the minds of the rising generation are about to be stuffed with the foul doctrines of communism. What an outlook!

Wednesday 26 August The Duke of Kent was killed last night in an air crash in Scotland while proceeding on a flying boat to Iceland. Since the Duke of Windsor went into exile, he has been the most popular member of the royal family apart from the King and he excelled even him in personality, while his wife has always been le dernier cri[17] in regal elegance. A lamentable tragedy.

Troubles in the Borough Treasurer camp. A woman came along from Ferdinand Estate this afternoon and accused me in front of the Treasurer of taking her week's rent of 17/4 on the Saturday before last and not giving a receipt for it on her card – an omission which she alleged she failed to notice until last Saturday when I myself drew her attention to it by asking her if she was paying one week's rent or two. As there was no entry against her number on my collection sheet either and I accounted for all cash received that morning in balancing, I maintained that it could not possibly have been paid in. Neither could there have been any possibility of an error on my part. The woman continued to swear that she'd paid it however, and could bring a witness to vouch for it. So Taylor told her to bring her witness along [and] adopted a solemn suspicious attitude towards me and left it at that. If she persists with the accusation and Taylor continues to doubt my honesty it seems the only way I can possibly clear myself is to

---

16   The first major combined operation of this war involved some 6,000 men (predominately Canadian) in an amphibious landing on an enemy shore. It achieved virtually none of its objectives and some 60% of Allied men were either killed, wounded or captured. Many useful lessons were learned that benefited future operations. See Dear, *Oxford Companion to the Second World War*, pp. 298–299.

17   'The last word'.

Part Two

bring an action for defamation of character against the party concerned. Though I don't exactly relish the experience and trouble and general unpleasantness which a legal action involves.

Thursday 27 August The nineteen months old ban on the *Daily Worker* is at last lifted.[18] Another concession to communist clamour. Saw *Mrs Miniver* at the Regent. Gets nearer to recapturing the Spirit of England in 1940 than anything else I've yet seen.

Friday 28 August Having heard nothing about the rent dispute since Wednesday I went to see Taylor in the hope of coming to some sort of understanding on the matter. He, however, adopted the same attitude as before and maintained that he had to keep an open mind in cases of this kind and, in the absence of conclusive proof one way or the other remain strictly impartial towards both parties. At the same time intimating that though he was willing to overlook this occurrence it would be my last chance and should I be involved in any future disputes over money, then I would forthwith be banished from the sacred precincts of the Town Hall for evermore. At which point I came to the conclusion that, in view of the sympathetic and understanding treatment one receives within those sacred precincts, nothing would suit me better for it would save me the trouble of trying to get released by the Ministry of Labour and finding another job of my own account. I put my case to him from every possible angle but he just wouldn't see it. All I could get out of him was that it was up to me and the tenant to settle things between us and that the best thing I could do was to go and see her personally. So as a last resort I did so – immediately after tea this evening. But though we talked over the problem at considerable length and without any bad feeling I failed to arrive at anything satisfactory. She seemed to be quite genuine in her conviction that she'd paid the rent and I remained equally certain in my own mind that she couldn't have done. What really happened to it remained a baffling mystery and in the end we had to leave it at that. Since neither of us could remedy things in any way we agreed to let the matter drop. But I'd give a lot to have that Saturday morning reinstated. The one thing that was brought home to me in the course of our talk was that I could have saved myself a lot of trouble and unpleasantness by seeing her and talking things over in the first place instead of thoughtlessly and exasperatedly telling her to come to the Town Hall and having it out. In other words it pays to keep things dark and hush them up rather than to come out into the open and thrash them out there. At least such seems to be the case so far as money disputes and Taylor are concerned.

Monday 31 August Went in and saw Taylor about the rent dispute for the third and last time. Gave him a full account of my call on the tenant

18   See entry for 22 January 1941.

and suggested that as I had now satisfied myself that the woman had acted in good faith and couldn't afford to lose the money, I would be prepared to stand the loss myself rather than let her go on thinking that the council had been responsible for losing her week's rent. He said he was glad I'd been to see her and settled the matter between ourselves and agreed that my solution seemed to be the most satisfactory way in which to clear the matter up. Actually I'd willingly have paid the 17/4 out of my own pocket in the first place, had I realised that it was going to involve such a lot of fuss and bother and beastliness. It's certainly taught me a lesson. Saw Dr Cutner in the evening about my right ear which keeps getting chocked up with wax. He always remembers me as the patient who staggered into his surgery one morning with an attack of peritonitis.

Wednesday 2 September The dismally empty shelves and windows of the confectionary shops which has become an all too familiar sight during the last year or so are now choc-a-bloc with sweets and slabs of chocolate – the result of confectionary rationing a month ago. The present ration is a pound a month.

Thursday 3 September Three years old and still this dreary war drags on, seemingly without hope of an ultimate ending for many years to come. In many ways the third year has been the most uneventful of the three. The problem is still very much the same as it was a year ago except that America and Japan have entered the war, though that hasn't affected the course of it to the extent that one might have expected.

Friday 4 September Had a letter from John Hobson. The envelope marked 'received from H.M. Ships' and decorated with stamps of two different censors. Couldn't give me much news on account of censorship difficulties and in any case he was anywhere in the middle of the ocean bound for an unknown destination. Cigarettes are fantastically cheap on board and the beer foul. And that's about all. Poor old John, years it will be 'ere we see him again – if ever. Pub-crawled with Ron in evening. Freemasons Arms, George, Haverstock Arms – Load of Hay [Hampstead].

Sunday 6 September Found Phil waiting for me when I got back at 2.0 from my morning's walk over Hampstead. Apparently he's been finally rejected by the RAF because they can't fix him up in his trade therein and is now waiting to be called up for the army.

Tuesday 8 September Had a fifty minute alert last night 10.45 till 11.35, flares and gunfire but no bombs. We were summoned to the control room as soon as the warning sounded and stayed there until the all clear came through. We've at last managed to get a man along to mend the bathroom sink fittings and pipes which have been collapsing and leaking for two or three months past.

Part Two

Wednesday 9 September M isn't going to the Land Army after all. In fact she couldn't because the Inland Revenue won't release her from her present job. So that's that!

Thursday 10 September The sink repairing has proved to be very unsatisfactory, the crudely cemented fittings have started to come loose again, which means we've got to go and make a further complaint. There's no end to it. It seems impossible to get anything done properly nowadays. Inefficiency and slovenliness are the order of the day.

Monday 14 September I complete my first two years at the Town Hall this week. Which means that I automatically come into the Council's superannuation scheme and will henceforth have 6% of my salary deducted each week as contributions thereto.

Tuesday 22 September M apprehensive at the prospect of the grim winter before us is at present in the throes of a 'preserving' mania. Her total bag to date being seven jars of pickled onions, four of tomatoes and four of fruit. All lined up in our store cupboard along with jars of green tomatoes, preserved ginger and home-made jam. They present a colourful succulent sight. After a lapse of nearly three months, the *Brains Trust* is back on the air again this evening. Without the familiar presence of Professor Joad and Commander Campbell it was hardly its old jocular self.

Friday 25 September Had a wretched evening. After an hour's control practice from 6.0 till 7.0 I came in and was involved in a long depressing argument with M about money. She'd just laid out nearly £5 for a table lamp. If she got an electric fire as well, would I put up five or six quid for a small table? Though I agreed, 'twas very reluctantly. For, however much I try to do so, I just can't reconcile myself to the idea of paying as one has to these days two or three times what these things are actually worth. Which of course set her off on her old moan about my selfishness and our present unsatisfactory way of living. I can't stand much more of it. The worry and strain and expense of married life is becoming well-nigh intolerable. I just don't know what to do for the best. There are no other alternatives.

Monday 28 September For some reason or other the onset of autumn fills my mind with nostalgic memories of early autumn in happier years – 1935 – '36 – '37 – '38. How much more carefree and contented I was then. Such were the thoughts with which I spent an evening of sweet melancholy.

Thursday 1 October We have decided to gradually get together sufficient furniture for a small flat as and buy when opportunities to buy good second hand stuff at reasonable prices arise. It seems futile to wait until after the war before getting a home together as we originally intended. For the war looks like going on many years yet, and even when it does end, it will be several years afterwards before prices get back to anything like the pre-war level. Besides it's absurd to go on paying so much rent for a furnished flat when we could get an unfurnished one so much cheaper. As for the possibility of further air raids well, we'll just have to take a chance on that. So during the next few months we're going to keep a sharp look out for furniture bargains. M made a start today by buying two small tables, one oak one walnut, for £6.0.0 at a second hand dealers in Camden Town. She's tremendously enthusiastic about it all.

Saturday 10 October Celebrated our first wedding anniversary (which actually falls tomorrow) by having our photograph taken together in the afternoon and going to dine and dance at Frascati's.[19] Had hors d'oeuvres, lobster salad and 'prime cardinal' to eat and a bottle of ersatz hock (Australian vintage) to drink, which, even on top of the sherries we had on the way, had no effect on me whatever. Not excessively expensive, the dinner cost the legal maximum of 5/- each, plus a 'house charge' of 2/6 for dancing and 6d for coffee, the wine 14/-. Total 30/-. Danced quite a lot and enjoyed the evening so far as I possibly could, M being more in her element and fonder of dancing than I am, certainly enjoyed it. And that, so far as I was concerned was all that really mattered on this festive occasion.

Monday 12 October The war has so debased and blunted the sensibilities of mankind that England and Germany are now venting their spleen on each other by putting their prisoners in chains. The Germans allege we manacled some of their soldiers during a raid on Sark[20] and in retaliation put into chains the captives they took in the course of our raid on Dieppe. Whereupon we proceed to do likewise to a similar number of German prisoners here. And so it goes on – reprisals and counter-reprisals – viciousness and still more viciousness. 'Man's inhumanity to man' has never sunk to such abysmal depths as it has this year of grace 1942.

Tuesday 13 October M's latest furniture 'discovery' – in a second hand dealer's in Tottenham Court Rd – a mahogany dining room table with six chairs to match – £22.10.0, French polished for £2.10.0 extra. She has quite set her heart on them.

Thursday 22 October Tonight's papers announce that youths of 18 are about to be called up. In other words the government propose to by-pass the third of Shakespeare's seven ages of man. The unwilling schoolboy of today won't have time to pass through the sighing lover

---

19   32 Oxford Street, W1.
20   On the night of 3 October, a twelve-strong Commando Raiding Party landed on Sark (Operation Basalt) and captured four German prisoners, three of whom died when attempting to escape. The fourth was brought to England.

stage before becoming the unwilling soldier of tomorrow. And even then, his prospects of playing the remaining three parts won't be particularly promising.

Wednesday 28 October Our dining room suite arrived this morning, newly French polished. It certainly looks impressive. In fact, I'm beginning to think it's worth the money!

Wednesday 4 November Another hectic lunch hour dashing round West End – vainly trying at various Ryman's shops to get another of these books for next year's diary. They are now unobtainable. If only I'd had the foresight to lay in a stock of them! At the Brewer St branch, the salesman was most amusingly disgusted with the rubbish they'd got to sell and kept picking books at random from the shelves, showing them to me and unfavourably comparing the inferior paper and inadequate thickness with the exorbitant prices charged therefore. That's the sort of shop assistant I like!

Thursday 5 November My search for a suitable book in which to keep next year's diary has already born fruit. I found the very thing at lunchtime today in a stationers on the corner of Fleet St and Chancery Lane – identical in every way with this volume except that the cover is of black American cloth. So I bought a couple and made my way back through the pouring rain, rejoicing.

Saturday 7 November Consternation in the control camp! Unbeknown to me, Bainbridge[21] called a meeting of Shift 4 prior to the practice last night and announced that in future everyone on duty had to stay in the building after blackout unless given special permission to go out, an edict which naturally aroused much resentment among those of us accustomed to going home or elsewhere for the entire evening. Nevertheless I shall continue to slip indoors in the course of my control evenings – if I can get away with it. After all, when I only live across the road and can dash in and get down to the control room as soon as anyone else when an alert sounds, I can't see any possible objection to my going home for two or three hours, except of course the childish dog in the manger attitude which is so oft to enter into this petty sort of business. And as a precautionary measure against that, I suppose it will be advisable to curtail the duration of my absence for a few weeks or at least until the fun dies down and one can gauge how strictly the new ruling is likely to be enforced.

Monday 9 November At long last we are meeting with some success in the theatre of war.[22] Simultaneously with our driving the Germans

21   Cyril Bainbridge, the St Pancras Borough Engineer and Surveyor and ARP Controller.
22   Heap has not previously mentioned the recent successes of the British Eighth Army in holding the advance of the German General Rommel's Afrika Korps and Italian forces just 65 miles west of Alexandria at El Alamein. The Germans were eventually routed at the

1942

out of Egypt back into Libya, the Americans have landed in Algeria and Morocco virtually taken control of French North Africa from the puppet Vichy government. These tidings have naturally given rise to much jubilation but whether this sudden turn of fortune will prove to be just a passing phase remains to be seen.

Thursday 12 November Control Duty. Made my first acquiescence to the new ruling by going back to the Town Hall immediately after tea and staying till 8.0 when I came in for supper finally returning at 9.0. Spent most of the evening laying on my bed in the gloomy dormitory reading. There isn't really much else one can do these days, for I don't play table-tennis or billiards and the 'rest-room' is usually full of chatting females. In fact, I might just as well have been at home all the evening. A gradual return to my former practice is clearly indicated, rule or no rule.

Sunday 15 November In celebration of the British army's success in the Battle of Egypt, church bells throughout the country were rung this morning for the first time since June 1940, when they were banned in order to be used as a warning in the event of invasion. We heard one or two bells chiming as we lay in bed drinking our morning tea but they sounded very dim and distant.

Wednesday 25 November Mother's 61st birthday. Gave her an overall and took her round to the Regent with us in the evening. Earlier in the evening we had an unexpected visit call from Young Bernie[23] who used to stay with us a good deal. I hadn't seen him since he was evacuated to Cornwall over two years ago, and he'd grown so much in the meantime that I failed to recognise him at first. His mother was taking him back to Penzance on the midnight train and he'd insisted on coming to see me before he went. Which made me feel I was rather letting the kid down when I had to explain that we'd arranged to go to the cinema and thus hint that they wouldn't be able to stop more than a few minutes instead of staying in and keeping him with us for the evening. And the shilling I gave him as we parted did little, alas, to salve my conscience. He's a dear little chap and I shall always have a warm affection for him. For though he's already eleven years old and rapidly growing up, to me he will always be the lively loveable little vamp of five or six who helped to provide me with some of my happiest memories.

Sunday 29 November To Hampstead. Noticed further large tracts of Parliament Hill Fields being dug up for allotments. Is there to be no end to this unsightly despoliation of London's loveliest and most extensive

---

Second Battle of El Alamein, 4–11 November, which coincided with Operation Torch, the Allied landing along the western Mediterranean in French Morocco and Algeria which Heap is recording here.
23   Bernie MacLavey – see Appendix A.

open space? Further over were hordes of Home Guards carrying out manoeuvres, replete with tanks. Such melancholy sights hardly add to the enjoyment of one's walk.

Wednesday 2 December The long awaited Beveridge Report on Social Insurance has at last been published.[24] Its main recommendation is a levying of a compulsory contribution of 7/6 a week (6/- for women) to be borne jointly by couples and paid into a central fund administered by a new Ministry of Social Security. Out of this fund would be paid every sort of benefit, sickness, unemployment, old age pensions and family allowances at rates considerably in advance of the present scale, which is grossly inadequate. A splendid scheme if it can be brought into action. The two great obstacles to be overcome are (a) the unemployment problem for the plan's success depends upon the abolition of that modern curse, and (b) the formidable opposition of the big insurance companies to whose interests it runs counter. Even if it does eventually get put into operation, I imagine it will be in a modified form.

Friday 4 December The most scarce commodities at the moment appear to be razor blades and No 8 torch batteries.

Sunday 6 December M discoursing over lunch on the pretensions, false values and the lack of conviction displayed by many films and plays nowadays, put her argument in a nut shell by saying 'I'd rather see 'cat' spelt correctly than 'psychology' spelt incorrectly'. I thought that was rather good. Though I was really supposed to be on control duty today, I nevertheless took a chance on the remote possibility of an alert occurring and went up to Hampstead for my usual Sunday walk over the heath before lunch. Didn't go out again until 9.15, at which hour it behoved me to go round and spend ten of my official twenty four hours in the precincts of the Town Hall.

Wednesday 9 December M given the afternoon off from work to do her Christmas shopping makes an extensive, exhaustive and disappointing tour of the crowded but barren shops and arrives home at 5.0 with a fruit dish and three knives. Went carousing around the West End with Charles to celebrate his last night of leave. After a preliminary drink in the Euston Tavern we entrained to Piccadilly Circus and eventually arrived at Maxim's, a Chinese restaurant in Wardour St, where we ate a

---

24 'Social Insurance and Allied Services', Cmnd 6404, the best-selling White Paper proposing a comprehensive policy of social progress to conquer 'the giants of Want, Disease, Ignorance, Squalor and Idleness'. It proved very popular with the British public but met with a cool response in Whitehall and from the government, which eventually committed itself in principle to Beveridge's proposals (see entry for 26 September 1944). It became the blueprint for the welfare state legislation of 1944 to 1948. For an excellent summary of the report and its reception see Peter Hennessy, *Never Again: Britain 1945–1951* (London: Vintage, 1993), pp. 72–77.

soggy mixture of messes tasting like an indifferent Irish stew sans meat and drank some somewhat livery lager (the bill amounted to £1.3.4 even half of which would have been exorbitant for what we had). Charles and Marjorie also danced occasionally. Not feeling in a festive mood myself, I merely sat and played the role of the cynical misanthrope and though my inconsiderate behaviour wasn't deliberately calculated to ruin M's evening as well as my own, that, alas was its ultimate effect. Fortunately the irrepressible Charles failed to react in the same manner and at 11.15 he left us at Leicester Square to continue his nocturnal carousal elsewhere. Whereupon we silently stole homewards and glumly sought our connubial but temporarily unconvivial couch.

Tuesday 15 December Had an airgraph from John Hobson dated Nov 27 and saying he'd just got my letter of Aug 1st. Replied in like manner. Since this method of transit only seems to take two or three weeks as compared with three or four months for a letter and costs but 3d, I think I might as well continue to use it in future. I find it the deuce of a job to condense myself into about 150 words in a letter.

Saturday 19 December Bought a plain green carpet for £20. Mother discovered it in a second-hand dealer's in Camden Town and, deciding it was a hell of a bargain, put down £5 deposit and dashed home to apprise us. Whereupon we went straight up there and, paid the balance and brought it home in a taxi. Though not exactly inexpensive, it's quite good value as prices go nowadays. As good as new so far as wear is concerned and so big in size that it would easily cover two small rooms if cut up. Incidentally I've not written off my violet ray scalp treatment as a failure. My hair still comes out when I brush it in the mornings and doubtless will continue to do so till my dying day – if I still have any left by then!

Wednesday 23 December I forgot to mention the parcel which arrived from Somerset yesterday afternoon, containing a plump chicken for our Christmas dinner in lieu of turkey, some home-made butter, holly, nuts and ten eggs, half of them broken in transit. Turkeys this year are as scarce and expensive as tickets for the first night of Cochran's first post-war revue will be.

Thursday 24 December Knocked off work at 1.0 and went over to lunch at the Londoners Meal Service place which has just opened in Euston Rd. Though these 'British Restaurants' as they are called, have become a national institution during the last few years this was actually my first visit to one.[25] I had roast pork and two vegetables for 10d and

---

25 Originally 'community feeding centres' and opened across the country, particularly in London, these 'British restaurants' were set up by the Ministry of Food and run by local authorities or voluntary agencies to provide reasonable meals for all at a set price. Heap here used the one in Clifton House, Euston Road (see note to entry for 18 February 1941). For 'British restaurants', the Londoners' Meals Service and civic restaurants, see W. Eric

Christmas pudding and custard for 3d. And even if the portion of pork was infinitesimal and the pudding hardly a 'blow out', it was still quite good value. There are, of course, no waitresses in attendance. The food is obtained at a counter and taken to a table to be eaten, the empty plates being subsequently returned to another counter near the exit – a procedure which neither wastes one's time nor taxes one's patience in the way that the ordinary restaurant does. Nor does it involve the accursed tipping system. Economy combined with self-help is in fact the merit of the British Restaurant. The crowd they attract is on the whole decidedly plebeian in character, but not repugnantly so. I may go there quite frequently throughout the winter for I'm getting tired of lunching so often on bread and cheese, which is hardly a suitable diet for the cold weather anyway. Most of the evening attending a Shift 4 Christmas party at the Town Hall and, of course, being on duty tonight. Started with supper in the canteen at 7.30 after which we proceeded to sing, dance and frolic in a hall upstairs until 1.0 when the party petered out. It wasn't very a well organised affair and things fell flat at times, but with the aid of a few beers, I somehow continued to enter into the spirit of it and extract some measure of enjoyment there from.

Friday 25 December A cold but otherwise unexceptional Christmas Day. Mother came over to spend the rest of the day with us, bringing with her a bottle apiece of port and sherry which added considerably to the gaiety of the occasion. Our Christmas dinner, partaken at 2.45, was really excellent, both the chicken and the plum pudding being perfectly cooked and not too heavy. Neither was the port we washed it down with. Nor even the homemade cake we had for tea. Consequently I felt free from the depressing drowsiness one usually experiences during the latter half of Christmas Day and on the whole quite enjoyed the easy going afternoon and evening we spent sitting around the fire, listening to the radio. I discovered that Christmas can be tolerably pleasant provided a surfeit of over-rich food is avoided and my leanings towards cynicism or misanthropy are held gently in check for the duration of the festivities.

Thursday 31 December Renewed wireless licence and sent off CIS subscription. Sat up till midnight and saw the Old Year out with Mother and the residue of the Christmas wine.

Jackson, *Achievement: A Short History of the London County Council* (London: Longmans, Green and Co., 1965), pp. 40–41.

RETROSPECT – 1942

A year mainly devoted to getting – or rather trying to get – used to married life. I'm not sure even yet, after fourteen months of it, whether I'm really suited to marriage. Sometimes it seemed to work quite well. At others an undercurrent of discontent and doubt comes to the surface and then I'm not so sure. Marjorie, too, has experienced these occasional misgivings as to whether we were wise in getting married in view of our different tastes and temperaments. We discussed the matter frankly – and, for the most part without bad feeling – at various times throughout the year, and yet found no satisfactory solution to the problem. Were we really suited to each other or to married life in general? One day we'd think yes, the next, no. And so we've gone on, alternating between spasms of marital bliss and deep despondency. I suppose that the trouble is that neither of us properly knows our own mind. We're not really sure what we want and the added strain imposed by the war hasn't made things any easier for us financially or otherwise. There are so many different and conflicting angles to the problem. I'd got so set in my ideas and outlook before I married that I couldn't somehow shake them off and readjust myself to the tame process of domesticity. At times we've both thought it would be better if we separated and I went to back to live with Mother. I'd have my independence again, no responsibility and more money to spend. On the other hand I should miss Marjorie considerably if I did so, and have to contend anew with the dreaded horrors of loneliness, to avoid which was the chief reason for my getting married. Whereas remaining together and trying to make a success of our marriage merely presents the reverse side of the picture. One has companionship and, taking a longer view, a certain extra degree of comfort, offset by ties and responsibilities and continued financial worries. I have moreover an innate dread of 'settling down' to home life, and, possibly having children. But which is the greater or lesser of the two sets of evils I can't for the life of me decide.

So there the matter rests at present. We're just jogging along as best we can, living for the day, getting as much fun out of life as the war permits, and endeavouring to get together sufficient furniture to escape from 93 Queen Alexandra Mansions and get a flat of our own. Marrying in wartime can at the best only be an uphill struggle. With our divided minds the hill has been rendered even steeper.

Theatres, cinemas and books continued to form my chief source of recreation. Again the restricted stock of wartime theatrical productions resulted in my going to the cinema as frequently as I did to the theatre – though the latter remained my paramount interest. And once more my book reading wasn't nearly so extensive as it was in years of yore

– partly laziness, partly lack of time and opportunity. To read more is the one and only relaxation I shall attempt to carry out in the New Year.

I made some progress in my work and had my salary increased by 9/6 a week. During the early part of the year, I made desperate attempts to save sufficient money to have £200 by the end of it. But what with income tax and many calls on my slender resources, the odds against me were, alas, too overwhelming and I had to regretfully abandon the attempt in June. Actually my total savings at the end of the year amount to £160 which, owing to a certain outlay on furniture, represents a net decrease of £15 on the balance brought forward from 1941. Whereas if I hadn't got married, I would now be worth at least £250 – probably a good deal more. So I can hardly feel elated about my financial position.

My few remaining friendships were assiduously maintained so far as they possibly could be. Ron after eighteen months absence in the provinces returned to London in the spring and soon after followed my example of getting married. However that hasn't prevented us from seeing quite a lot of each other since. John Hobson unfortunately got sent overseas in July, since when his despatches have become few and far between. John Bell continued to sail round the world and send me a few lines every few months. Phil I saw but twice. Bill Colbourn whom I haven't seen for three years, I've virtually given up as 'lost and gone for ever' – as a friend anyway. Really I need a bigger circle of friends than I possess at present but outside the services, there seems to be little opportunity of acquiring any these days. Especially if one doesn't make friends very easily.

I had my first real summer holiday for three years when in July we went down to Somerset for a fortnight and stayed with Marjorie's mother at Bangle Farm. But for a variety of reasons – chiefly the bad weather – it wasn't a very enjoyable holiday, and though undoubtedly beneficial from the health giving point of view, I can't honestly include that fortnight among my happiest memories of 1942. There were very few of them in any case. It was far too difficult a year, both from a general and a personal aspect, to look back on with pleasure or nostalgia. The war dragged on slowly, sluggishly, and seeming indifferent as to how many long wearisome years it continues to blight and stultify and cramp our lives. It formed the sombre, sinister background to our personal difficulties and problems and from it they derived their tone. Perplexity, doubt, insecurity, worry, strife, stagnation, despair ..... Such were the keynotes of 1942.

1943

Marginally more reconciled to married life, both Anthony and Marjorie Heap nevertheless continued to suffer moods of depression. Marjorie's were somewhat relieved by their moving, in March, to a cheaper flat and buying more second-hand and some new (utility) furniture, and Anthony's by occasionally pub-crawling with his old friend Ron. Heap's medical condition was degraded when he developed an abdominal rupture, the legacy of carrying the couple's chattels up six stories to the new top-floor flat. Luftwaffe 'nuisance raids' continued to disturb their sleep patterns but further military successes in North Africa and then in Italy boosted morale. By the end of the year, Churchill appeared to have at last gained Heap's grudging support.

Heap's roughly weekly theatre-going continued through the year, while his reading and film-going maintained their high wartime level. Very few diary entries are unedited below and only 26% of Heap's original 41,000 words are here reproduced.

Friday 1 January Sent off an airgraph to John Hobson at lunchtime, then went to Boots to change book and pay annual subscription. Instead of renewing my 'Class A' subscription, I changed over to the 'On Demand' one, for though this costs £2.5.0 a year as compared with the 19/6 I've paid hitherto, the satisfaction of being able to obtain any book I wanted as soon as it was published will, I think, justify the extravagance. I'm tired of having to wait several months, sometimes a year or more, for desired books and, as often as not, being unable to get anything on my list at all.

Saturday 2 January Went to Moody's[1] immediately after lunch and bought the wardrobe and dressing table without the washstand for £35, £3 down, balance payable on delivery next Friday. The dressing table has several markings on it, otherwise the suite is in excellent condition. Somewhat old fashioned in design but of first rate quality.

Saturday 9 January The wardrobe and dressing table from Moody's arrived after lunch. On second sight I wasn't so pleased with them, they seem too old fashioned in design and too bulky in dimension, especially the wardrobe. These misgivings, aggravated by the bitterly

---

1   Harry Moody, second-hand furniture dealer, 1a Delancey Street, NW1.

cold weather sent me into a depression which reached its zenith when we went along to try and get into the Paramount[2] and found it packed out.

Thursday 14 January To Caxton Hall whither we were invited by the *Daily Express* 'Centre of Public Opinion' to 'Ask the Experts' questions related to the war – the experts being nine of that paper's featured writers under the benign and beaming chairmanship of Leslie Hore-Belisha MP.[3] The main attraction as far as we were concerned was [theatre critic] James Agate who answered questions on literature and drama in his usual witty and ebullient manner and aroused the vociferous wrath of a noisy Red element present by venturing to suggest that Rome should remain [free] from bombing on account of its beautiful architecture. Needless to say, he stood his ground boldly and triumphantly. It was, on the whole, quite a lively evening, in fact I rather enjoyed it.

Sunday 17 January Latest wartime problem is the manufacture of hair fixture – cream, brilliantine etc – owing to the necessity of conserving their main ingredient, petroleum oil, for war purposes. I now have to go and take myself over to the Town Hall and slumber fitfully through a spell of control duty.

Monday 18 January Thought the latter part of last night's entry was written somewhat prematurely – actually I'd still to have supper before repairing to the Town Hall – it proved to be truer than I imagined. For no sooner had I laid down my pen than the sound of an air raid warning, followed immediately by my taking myself over to the Town Hall and down to the control room a damn site quicker than I expected. Quite like old times in fact. But though the anti-aircraft guns continued to thunder away for some time there was no indication of any bombs being dropped – not in St Pancras anyway, and after half an hour or so the Controller provisionally dismissed us. Whereupon we went into the canteen. A wretched meal. I took the opportunity to dash in and collect all the things I'd left behind in my hasty exit – book, spectacles case, comb, watch, lighter, toothbrush. And so finally back to the Town Hall for the night – after an alert lasting only five minutes came the All Clear. Which meant that I was able to slumber fitfully in my dormitory bed after all – at least until 4.45 when a second alert caused us to be summoned to the control room once more. This raid was merely a repetition of the earlier one – plenty of gunfire but no bombs – and after a cup of tea we were allowed to go back to bed. A few minutes later, at 5.45 the All Clear lulled us off to sleep again and that was the end of the night's alarums and excursions. Today the papers reveal that

2 Cinema on the Grafton Way corner of Tottenham Court Road.
3 War Minister 1937–40 and alleged victim of anti-Semitism. See entry for 6 January 1940.

the raids were intended as reprisals for our raids on Berlin on Saturday night. As much damage and injury seems to have been caused by our own AA shells as the enemy bombs! Is it worth it? Why the hell can't they leave Berlin alone and let sleeping dogs lie, inducing the reprisals on London which inevitably follow all such foolhardy attacks. M heard this afternoon that one of the major catastrophes last night was a direct hit on Jones & Higgins, the drapery store in Peckham Rye at which Cookie recently got a job as Assistant Counting House Manager.

Wednesday 20 January Things are certainly warming up in the inter-capital bombing contest. German raiders came over and carried out the biggest daylight raid on London since the Battle of Britain at lunch time today. According to the evening paper, a 'thickly populated area' was dive-bombed and a railway station machine-gunned – considerable damage being done and several casualties incurred. We heard some spasmodic gunfire issuing from the AA batteries not far away but no bombs, so presumably the suburbs bore the main brunt of the attack again.

Thursday 21 January The official casualty list of yesterday's raid comprises 102 killed and 152 injured within the Metropolitan Police District. Most of the fatal casualties occurred at a school in Catford where they're still digging for the bodies of children buried under the debris.[4] Such is the price that has to be paid for the gratification of the insatiable 'Bomb Berlin' maniacs. They must be well satisfied with themselves! I managed to get through to Cookie on the phone this afternoon. Apparently there's still a part of Jones & Higgins left intact, including the counting house.

Sunday 24 January One sees surprisingly few people over Hampstead Heath on Sunday mornings (or rather early afternoons) lately. Even that erstwhile car-infested and Jew-ridden 'monkey parade', the Spaniards Road. Or is it that I don't embark on my pre-lunch perambulations until the rest of London is carving its Sunday joint?

Wednesday 27 January M goes to the dentist's to have three teeth out with gas. He extracts two, breaks the third, leaves the root in and tells her to come back next Tuesday to have that out. With the result that the lacerated gum bleeds and aches all the evening and instead of having an unpleasant experience over and done with, poor M has to have the wretched business hanging over her head for a further week. What deplorable incompetence! M eventually has to go over to the Elizabeth Garrett Anderson Hospital on Euston Rd to get something to stop the bleeding. Otherwise it would probably have gone on all night.

---

4   This daylight raid killed thirty-eight children and six teachers at lunchtime at Sandhurst Road LCC School.

Friday 29 January M is directed by the local National Service Officer to 'enter the services of the Holborn Borough Council as a part-time warden' and 'for that purpose to present herself at Holborn Town Hall on Monday 8th February.'5 [M] is going to see if she can volunteer to do 'fire watching' at the office instead. The whole thing is a stupid imposition anyway. Whilst with her 51 hours a week job and her housework on top of that, she has quite enough to do already without being compelled to waste time on futile civil defence duties as well.

Saturday 30 January Apparently M can't volunteer for 'fire-watching' at the office as women are not allowed to do it in the City. So she's going to send in a straightforward appeal against the order on the grounds of overdue hardship. What a hope!

Saturday 6 February The extent to which the public have developed queue mania lately is astonishing. As I came back on the bus, there were some two dozen people outside Kentish Town station to buy – newspapers!

Sunday 21 February By way of a change from my customary walk over Hampstead this morning, I turned my steps towards the West End – to be more precise that south segment of it signified postally to be the cipher 'WC2.' Beheld and set forth for the first time the new and recently opened Waterloo Bridge[6] – the replacement of the old bridge by a new one having taken eighteen years to complete. An elegant streamlined structure with a light freshness which the sooty air of London will doubtless soon mellow. Two other equally unfamiliar sights were the temporary bridge spanning the river from the Air Force memorial on the Embankment over to the east side of County Hall and the squat concrete impregnable looking building that has been erected just outside Admiralty House,[7] no idea what use either of them are put to. Incidentally I noticed for the first time how different the trams sounded along the Embankment to what they do anywhere else. A study of the windows of tailors and hosiers shops on the Strand indicated that the cost of male attire is about twice the pre-war sort. The cheapest ready-made utility suit obtainable today cost £4.5.0. the price of a reasonably decent made to measure (but also, alas, utility) suit, is however more in the neighbourhood of ten or eleven guineas even

---

5   Marjorie, a St Pancras resident working in the City of London, was probably called to Holborn Town Hall as that borough, in the same Group 3 of inner London authorities as the City and the East End, needed additional ARP 'volunteers'.

6   Designed by Sir Giles Gilbert Scott, this second Waterloo Bridge was opened on 11 August 1942 and finished in 1945.

7   The Admiralty Citadel, constructed 1940–1941 as a bomb-proof operations centre with 30-foot deep foundations and a 20-foot thick concrete roof was described in his memoirs by Churchill as a 'vast monstrosity which weighs upon Horse Guards Parade'. He never used it and, now covered with Russian vine, it serves as the Admiralty Communications centre HMS *St Vincent*. Its appearance was the subject of a brief adjournment debate in 1955 (HC Deb, 27 October 1955, vol. 545 cc. 526–532).

at the most unfashionable and normally inexpensive tailors. Prices of shirts, pyjamas, underwear etc appear to have likewise soared in about the same proportion. Since Maison Lyons was converted into a club for U.S. forces, the Shaftesbury Avenue corners of the 'centre of the world' have become infected at all hours of the day and night with scores of dissipated looking American soldiers lecherously loafing around in the hope of picking up any stray tarts passing by. Why on earth bring them over here if they can't find anything better for them to do than run to seed like this?[8]

Monday 22 February Marjorie's 27th birthday. My present consisted of half of the cost of a dark green frock which she's managed to get at a pseudo-second hand clothes shop on Edgware Rd without giving up coupons. Mother gave her a pair of green suede bedroom slippers. Celebrated the occasion by having Mother over to supper – tinned turkey and ham, potatoes baked in jackets and blackberry tart and custard, washed down with light ale and coffee. After, I duly proceeded to the Town Hall for control duty.

Saturday 27 February M off to Somerset to see her mother before she leaves Bangle Farm next month and goes to live with her sister nearby (which means of course we won't be able to go down there for our holidays anymore). Returning Monday evening.

Monday 1 March M arrived laden with a large parcel of pots and pans which she's managed to get at the village store. Also brought back nine eggs (the present ration is one a month). Took her over to see 88 Sandwich House as soon as we got home. Much to my surprise she liked it and after debating all the pros and cons over supper and worrying ourselves sick with indecision, we at last decided to take the flat, despite its snags. We'll at least save 11/- a week in rent on what we're paying now and it's doubtful if we'd get offered another flat if we turned this one down. Besides, we can also move again if it proves too uncongenial. So – the die is cast! We move at last!

Tuesday 2 March A new prospect arises. The letting office informs us that someone in Jessel House[9] wants a larger flat and may be induced to take 88 Sandwich House in which case we could have an option on the Jessel House one if we preferred it. We await developments.

Wednesday 3 March The reprisal raid at last! 'Twas heralded by the sirens at 8.20 this evening and lasted an hour and a half. Heavy gunfire

---

8 The huge American Red Cross 'Rainbow Club' opened on 11 November 1942 on the corner of Denman Street and Shaftesbury Avenue and operated 24 hours a day, providing food, welfare facilities and entertainment, often by Hollywood stars and leading bands, for American servicemen, until it closed on 8 January 1946 with a ball attended by Eleanor Roosevelt and Anthony Eden.
9 Jessel House, Judd Street, is a seven-storey block of flats similar to Sandwich, Hastings and Thanet Houses in surrounding streets, all built just before the First World War.

Part Two

throughout. A seemingly insignificant air raid for all 'the sound and fury' of the AA barrage.

Friday 5 March Today's papers reveal that during the raid on Wednesday evening, 178 people were suffocated to death through rushing panic-stricken down a darkened stairway leading down from the street to a tube station (Bethnal Green according to the rumours) and thereby falling on top of one another. I've never heard of anything more utterly fantastic and incomprehensible than this extraordinary catastrophe.[10] A sign of the times – so widespread has Venereal Disease become lately that the Ministry of Health now boldly take advertising space in the press in which to freely discuss its dangers and advise as to prevention and treatment.[11]

Monday 8 March Negotiations for the Jessel House flat having since come to nought, we are given a further last minute alternative to 88 Sandwich House – to wit, 61 Rashleigh House.[12] Top floor, two fair-sized rooms at the front, plus a not so light kitchen-cum-bathroom at the back. Not particularly keen on Rashleigh House (there isn't even a lift there) but as the flat suits our requirements so much better than the other one and the rent only 13/1 a week as compared with 18/11, we decided to take it. 'Twill serve until the end of the war anyway.

Tuesday 9 March Slipped round to the letting office at 10.0 to hand over our contract of tenancy and pay the deposit. Though we won't actually move in until the end of next week, we take possession as from Monday the 15th.

Thursday 11 March First night of *Brighton Rock* at the Garrick – I'm sure Satan's domain couldn't possibly be as sordid as 'Brighton Rock.' The wartime substitute for ices – jellies! The attendants were hawking them round the stalls this evening and doing a roaring trade.

Saturday 13 March My 33rd birthday. Presents – pale blue pyjamas from M, bedroom slippers from Mother. Went up to Camden Town in late afternoon and blued £7 on a roll of linoleum for the new flat, 43 square yards of it and as heavy as hell. Brought it back in a cab and with the aid of the taximan somehow got it to the top floor of Rashleigh House and dumped it in the flat, the occupants being in the process of

---

10   This, the worst civilian incident of the war, occurred at the uncompleted Bethnal Green Tube Station when 173 men, women and children were crushed as they converged down the steps of the single entrance to the underground station being used as a shelter. There was no enemy activity in the immediate area and an inquiry, not published until 1945, found that people descending the steps of the single entrance had panicked when a new anti-aircraft multi-rocket launcher was fired from the adjoining park.

11   *The Times*, 2 March 1943, p. 2, carried the Ministry of Health display advertisement 'Venereal Diseases – Plain Speaking', which gave 'Ten facts about VD' and the signs of both syphilis and gonorrhoea. It advised checking with a clinic as 'it is best to be sure'.

12   Overlooking the corner of Thanet and Leigh Streets.

moving down to a lower flat. The cabby badly bruised his thumb (for which I felt bound to compensate him with a 200% tip on the 1/6 fare) and we both strained our guts to get the damned stuff laid down before the furniture's moved in early next week. As we've just got enough to cover all the floor space, it won't be necessary to use our precious green carpet. Rather than cut it in two we prefer to wait till we get a flat with a room big enough for it. Subsequently decided to double it in half and use it over the lino.

Sunday 14 March Awoke feeling stiff and costive. A vigorous five mile walk over the heath in the glorious spring sunshine effectively disposed of the stiffness but the costiveness returned for the rest of the day. Went over to the new flat after lunch to lay the lino – a job which we expected to complete in about an hour. Actually we were still there at 7.30 when the fast falling shades of night put an end to our labours. Even then we only covered the two front rooms, leaving the kitchen and hallway still to be completed. However we got the bulk of it done and four hours of that sort of thing is quite enough for one day. Felt absolutely whacked by the time we got back to a very tardy tea.

Monday 15 March M has been informed by the local National Service officer that they have decided to withdraw the directive to undertake civil defence duties. In other words, her appeal's succeeded and she's been exempted. A most unexpected stroke of good luck. Spent another strenuous evening over at the new flat putting up black-out blinds and laying down the rest of the lino.

Wednesday 17 March Had our furniture moved over to Rashleigh House during the afternoon (Mother attended to the job for us) and followed up ourselves in the evening with suitcases full of clothes, etc which we put away in the wardrobe and cupboards. There's very little of our stuff left in the Ellis flat now, though we'll have to stay on until Friday night to get the place cleared up and straightened out before we finally leave.

Friday 19 March A final hectic evening of cleaning up and transferring the remainder of our belongings, we locked the door of 93 Queen Alexandra Mansions behind us for the last time and after three treks up to Mother's flat to collect a kitchen table and two chairs she doesn't want, we at last settled in 61 Rashleigh House, where all we now have to do is to sort things out and tidy up. Had some supper and went to bed at 11.30. What a week!

Saturday 20 March Our first night in our new abode was a far from comfortable one. What with some troublesome woman in the flat below first setting our already frayed nerves on edge by shouting up in protest at our making so much noise at such a late hour (actually we were both creeping around in bedroom slippers and couldn't possibly have been quieter) and then the bed being so hard and uncomfortable in comparison with the one we've been used to, one got practically no sleep at all. Consequently we feel even more exhausted today than we have done all the week. However, we've at last got the noise question settled, for I went down and had a few words with the woman below on getting home at 1.0. Whereupon she instantly climbed down and apologised. I don't think I'll have any more trouble from that source, I hope not anyway. Otherwise, things are going to be very impolite around these parts. An hour's rest on bed before tea and then to revival of Shaw's *Heartbreak House* at the Cambridge.

Wednesday 24 March Registered our change of address at the Town Hall and had identity cards and ration books altered accordingly. Also filled in and sent off a form applying for permit to buy a couple of the new 'utility' easy chairs, which is all we now need to complete our furnishing for the time being anyway. In the distant future we hope to add a writing desk, book case, and sideboard to our modest possessions.

Saturday 27 March Two theatres in one day. And what a contrast! Firstly to the matinee of *It's Foolish But It's Fun* at the Coliseum. Home to tea and then with M to the Westminster for the revival of *Hedda Gabler*, which is as far removed from foolishness and 'fun' as any play could be.

Thursday 1 April After supper went round to the Section House in Judd St and got a policeman to come up and see a glaring light which we've noticed several times shining from one of the back windows of the Brighton Hall Hotel over in Cartwright Gardens. He went straight round and within a few minutes 'twas duly blacked out. A fair cop.

Monday 12 April Budget Day. Income Tax remains at 10/- in the £. The main brunt of increased taxation falling, as usual on the indirect sources of revenue – tobacco, beer, wines, spirits, entertainment and luxury articles. Cigarettes will cost an extra 2d on a packet of ten, i.e. 1/2d. Beer going up by 1d a pint, spirits by 2/4 a bottle. Entertainment tax increase not given in detail though it's expected that theatres will get off more lightly than the cinemas – the war is now costing over fifteen million a day.

Wednesday 14 April Razor blades are so extremely difficult to obtain now that I've had to resort to using old discarded blades again – a different one each morning. Which makes shaving more of an ordeal than ever. But I suppose it's better than a beard.

Monday 19 April The sound of sirens is becoming almost as familiar a feature of London life again as it was in the winter of 1940–41. Had another alert at 1.0 a.m. this morning, presaging the usual negligible one plane raid and duly petering out after rounds of gunfire. While yesterday we had two brief alerts which were both admitted to be false alarms due to a couple of British planes being mistaken for German ones. Apparently we can't tell the difference even yet!

Friday 23 April Easter has fallen so late this year that today, Good Friday, clashed with St George's Day. What more directly concerned me was the fact that it also clashed with control duty, which meant that I had to go to the office as usual and have another day off later instead. Just as well really for 'twas a wet and dismal day. Town Hall at 6.15 after a two hours 'exercise.' Home again to supper afterwards and finally back to the Town Hall for the night.

Tuesday 27 April Charles goes back to sea. We go back to work. M also goes to the Labour Exchange to lodge another paean against a further order she's recently received directing her to become a part-time member of the NFS [National Fire Service]. Result pending.

Friday 30 April Went along to see Dr Cutner in the evening about a swelling on my groin that has been causing me some anxiety during the last month or so. As I suspected it proved to be a rupture, doubtless due to overstraining my abdomen in the course of moving stuff into our new flat last month. So I've now got to attend the Homeopathic Hospital for a course of some new abdominal massage treatment they're trying out there and then if that isn't successful, undergo an operation. Damned nuisance, [but] I hope for the best, which, after my peritonitis experience, is so very difficult. Came home, flopped dejectedly into one of the two new utility armchairs we've just acquired (72/- each!) and made a determined effort to take my mind off medical matters by reading.

Tuesday 4 May My initial visit to the Homeopathic this morning proved to be somewhat disappointing. I went along blithely expecting to be attended to at once, whereas what actually happened was that I not only had to wait nearly two hours with several dozen other out-patients, but even when I did succeed in getting into the massage room and see Dr Cutner, he was unable to start my treatment straight away for it seemed that he and his assistant were rushed off their feet with the morning's phenomenally large influx of patients. So the best I could do was to arrange to go again at 5.0 tomorrow and hie me back to the Town Hall where I belatedly arrived at 11.20. What a waste of time!

Saturday 8 May The sirens just forestalled our alarm clock this morning by waking us up about a couple of minutes before our accustomed time 7.15. Lasted about an hour, the longest daylight raid since Feb '41.

Monday 17 May Kept awake half the night by a succession of three alerts between midnight and 4.0 a.m., but the only bomb we heard preceded the first alarm. To the hospital for massage in evening. Was also shown some exercises to carry on with at home. I must confess that my abdomen seems to be getting stronger. Night at the Town Hall on control duty.

Tuesday 18 May Had to get up twice during the night and sit out a couple of alerts in the control room. The last all clear didn't sound until just after 8.0. I only had about four hours sleep for the second night in succession. If they keep this sort of thing up, they'll soon get us down.

Wednesday 19 May Alas my hope of making up for lost sleep! For the third night running the sirens were set wailing and the guns thundering throughout the small hours by a handful of 'nuisance' raiders. The first alert came, as usual, round about midnight and was of very short duration – a second one following at 2.30 and lasting an hour or more. As happened on Sunday night there was apparently a loud bomb explosion before the first alert, though I didn't hear it myself. Not that I wanted to, I was kept awake quite long enough as it was. Met Ron at the Chandos[13] at 7.0. Had our second drink at the Duke of Wellington and the third, fourth and fifth at the newly reopened Bricklayers Arms (or Burglars' Rest as we used to call it) then up to Haverstock Hill and had as many more at the Load of Hay and finished up at The George, the excessive intake of beer enabled me to enjoy a good night's sleep, despite the inevitable brace of alerts, it wasn't entirely wasted. Exceptionally heavy gunfire did wake me up round about 3.0 but I was asleep again within a few minutes. There's no sedative in the world to compare with a few pints of beer. I wonder that the brewers never stress this property in their advertising. Perhaps they will if these nuisance raids continue indefinitely.

Sunday 23 May The first raid-less night for a week. Found Mother very downcast when I went up to see her this morning, and with good reason. Has lost her wallet containing £8 in notes, 35/- in insurance stamps, coupon cards etc in Camden High St yesterday morning. The chance of recovering it is, I fear, very slender.

Tuesday 1 June A short but very noisy raid at 3.0 a.m. this morning. Had the day in lieu of the day I should have had off at Easter. Spent the entire morning at the hospital waiting to see Dr Cutner. He seemed to be quite satisfied with the progress I'd made so far and intimated that, provided I continue to carry out my abdominal exercises regularly at home and keep my stomach drawn in as much as possible at all times, I should have nothing much to worry about, it will at least enable me to get along comfortably until an operation is convenient – and that won't be until the end of the war if I can help it!

Thursday 10 June It is now over a year since tailors were forbidden to make suits with trouser turn-ups and double breasted jackets. And

---

13   29 St Martin's Lane, WC2.

yet a man wearing an 'austerity' suit today would still be regarded as an oddity. One never sees trousers without turn-ups and there are just as many double breasted jackets to be discerned as there ever were. In other words, it would appear that, so far as the Board of Trade's restrictions are concerned, evasion is nine tenths of the law!

Saturday 12 June Had a letter from Aunt Pop enclosing a second birthday card and a five dollar bill to replace [those] that presumably found their way to the bottom of the Atlantic in March. She won't let the war defeat her good intentions. That's the spirit.

Friday 18 June How deceptive are the distances of fires at night. Having heard a bomb descend disconcertingly close to us just after the alert had sounded at 1.0 a.m. this morning, we got up and went to the window and found that a big fire had been started just behind Clare Court (so we thought at the time) – a mere hundred yards or so from out flat. Actually it was Mount Pleasant the big Post Office depot on the corner of King's Cross Rd and Roseberry Avenue – a good half mile away, that was ablaze.[14] And how it blazed! Not until well after daybreak were they able to get it under control. The sight of the brilliant glow over the house tops with clouds of dense white smoke ascending above the sky line vividly recalled the hectic nights of the Blitz. It's well over two years since we saw anything like this. I did, however, trudge round to King's Cross and buy a new pair of black shoes (24/9 and 7 coupons). There is every indication that only wooden soled shoes will be on sale soon, I thought it advisable to lay in an extra pair of leather shoes while they're still available. M did likewise with her last five coupons. There's quite a rush on the shoe shops this week – thanks to the recent radio appeal to the public not to buy unnecessarily at present! If we'd left it another week I doubt if we'd have got any.

Saturday 19 June The Derby run at Newmarket and won by Straight Park (15–1). Went along to see what's left of Mount Pleasant after lunch. The old building completely destroyed, but the new one at the southern wing, didn't seem to be damaged at all. Plenty of sightseers there. Came home and devoted the remainder of the afternoon to cleaning windows. Merely to please Mother we went to the Conservative Association Dance in aid of The Prisoners of War Fund at the Royal Hotel. Dreadfully overcrowded and rough. Even half a dozen drinks at a nearby pub couldn't endear me to it. In fact I had such a wretched

---

14. Dropped by a single aircraft under a full moon, the bomb exploded in the basement of the huge sorting office. Although the National Fire Service was on the scene within four minutes and eighteen pumps were used, the intense fire destroyed some 75,000 parcels (W. G. Ramsey, *The Blitz: Then and Now* (London: Battle of Britain Prints International, 1987–1990), vol. 3, pp. 282–283).

evening that I made up my mind never to go to a dance again if I can possibly help it. There is really nothing I enjoy less.

Sunday 20 June Another very noisy nuisance raid during the night. Didn't keep us awake for long though. Glorious day. The first really fine one for a long time. Got lunch over early and set off for Kew Gardens immediately after. Had tea there and in the evening strolled along the river towpath down past the Observatory –a delightful walk I'd never done before. Took the ferry over to Isleworth and back to see the old church – or rather charred one which is all that remains of it since the Blitz – then proceeded along to Richmond and caught the train back to Camden Town. An exceedingly pleasant trip. I doubt if we'd have had a more enjoyable day even if we had have gone down to Leatherhead.

Tuesday 22 June Latest despatch from John Hobson dated May 27 reveals that after one hectic day's leave in Tunis, he has now returned to the desert and peacetime soldiering again. Thanks to two prolonged alerts and M having to get up in dark to report for fire guard duty round at the Tonbridge Club,[15] we only got about three hours sleep last night. Consequently felt more than somewhat weary today and being on control duty myself tonight I couldn't even go to bed early and make good some of the lost sleep.

Tuesday 29 June Walked round to Museum St at lunchtime and bought the reproduction of Degas' *La Repetition* we had so often admired in the shop window when passing that way on Sunday evening. Only 15/9. Left it to be framed, which takes three weeks and cost more than the actual picture! Evening at home, washing and book and radio.

Friday 2 July An airgraph from John Hobson. The only news that he has to send is that the brothels are closed for repairs – and presumably the staff's annual holiday! Not that it worries him much. The sight of one or two hundred of his comrades in arms queued up outside damps any ardour he might feel!

Tuesday 6 July Took morning off in lieu of the Saturday morning I should have had at Whitsun and went along to the Homeopathic for periodic examination by Dr Cutner. Had to wait nearly four hours before I actually saw him. I came away almost feeling that it was worth it. Have now only got to attend once a fortnight for massage.

Wednesday 7 July Second anniversary of our engagement. Intended to celebrate it as we did last year – by making a sentimental journey up to Hampstead and reclining under the same tree that beheld our betrothal on that night back in '41, but unfortunately that sort of project calls for

---

15 Behind Queen Alexandra Mansions on Tonbridge Street.

a fine warm evening, whereas tonight was cool and showery. So we reluctantly abandoned the plan and stayed in.

Friday 9 July Thank heaven we decided to go easy for a fortnight later this year for the prevailing weather is exactly the same as it was when we went away this time last year – cold, wet and despondent. What is even more fortunate though is that M's mother's staying on at Bangle Farm for the summer so we have again got somewhere to go for our vacation. Somewhere that is not unduly expensive or involving a lot of worry and inconvenience. And there is preciously little holiday accommodation nowadays.

Saturday 10 July The war extended on yet another new phase today with the invasion of Sicily by Allied forces. Though this hazardous but obvious move has been expected ever since the African campaign finished two months ago, its actual occurrence nevertheless makes exciting news. On control at night.

Wednesday 14 July Another first-night-less week. Wherefore to break the monotony of staying in every evening we hied us to the Leicester Square Odeon to see *The Life and Death of Colonel Blimp*. Costing a quarter of a million to produce and running nearly three hours, this is understandably the most ambitious British film ever made. Yet its precise purpose isn't at all clear for its central character bears scarcely any resemblance to the Colonel Blimp of the cartoons.[16] He doesn't even bear the same name, so why retain such a misleading title? Magnificent entertainment – sound, solid and satisfying.

Thursday 15 July I see in the papers that three million pounds worth of clothing is being sent to Russia. In heavens name why, when we obviously need it so badly ourselves. Or doesn't our own shortage of clothing matter as long as the bloody Bolsheviks are well clad? Apparently not.

Saturday 17 July Spent the evening carousing around Charlotte St. with Ron. Ran into a crowd of the old Malaya Club habitués in the Fitzroy and went with them to the Bricklayers Arms, the Marquis of Granby and the Duke of York's[17] (all packed to the doors), finally finishing up at the United Nations Restaurant in High St just off St Giles Circus which was the only place that seemed to be open after 11.0. Fish and chips and coffee 3/3 a head. Home at 12.45. Quite an amusing evening one way and another.

---

16   Based on the cartoonist David Low's moustachioed military character and starring Roger Livesey, Deborah Kerr and Anton Walbrook, this famous Powell and Pressburger film was a pro-British satire on perceived government, establishment and military matters.

17   47 Rathbone Street, W1.

Part Two

Saturday 24 July Down to Somerset for our fortnight's holiday. No last minute improvement in the weather alas, London presenting as grey and gloomy an aspect for our departure this morning as it has done for the last three weeks. Left home at 11.30 and got cab to Paddington. Station swarming with hordes of holiday makers. Biggest such since the beginning of the war according to the papers. The 12.30 train, on which we travelled down was crowded to capacity long before it was due to start. I stood in the congested corridor all the way. Disappointed to see the reversion to grey mistiness as we approached Frome. Train on time at 3.15 and car waiting at station to take us out to Bangle Farm according to plan. Tea waiting for us as we arrived. Afterwards unpacked, strolled round the farm and then took M's mother up to Chantry for a couple of drinks at the White Horse before supper. Turned out to be quite a fine evening. Though I've only been down here for a few hours, I feel better for the change of air already.

[*A quiet fortnight's holiday without significant incident followed.*]

Monday 26 July Sensational news from Italy overnight. Mussolini has resigned and Marshal Bodaglio taken his place and proclaimed martial law throughout the country. The reason for this extraordinary step hasn't been made manifest yet, but there seems to be a clear indication that a crisis of some sort has been precipitated by the successful Allied invasion of Sicily and our intensive air offensive. It's exasperating not being able to get newspapers down here, except by borrowing someone else's or going down to the village early in the morning on the off chance of getting a spare copy – especially when such exciting events are taking place. Fortunately we get the news on the radio – so we're not entirely cut off from civilisation – such as it is.

Tuesday 3 August A poor night's sleep owing to M hearing, or imagining she could hear, a mouse. Her terror of rats and mice almost amounts to a phobia.

Monday 9 August An infuriatingly fine day for our return to town. Got up at 7.15 and had had our breakfast and were ready to leave by 9.0 thus leaving a long mournful hour in which to hang about waiting for the car to arrive and take us to Frome in time to catch the 10.30 train. Platform packed with returning holiday makers. Likewise train which arrived 25 minutes late. But by some miracle we managed not only to get on it but easily secure a couple of corner seats in a compartment. Even so I didn't feel too comfortable during the three hour journey. Too hot and hungry. Arrived Paddington 1.55, 40 minutes late. Queued up for half an hour for a taxi and thus got home about 2.10. No food in flat so went round to King's Cross and got a haircut and shampoo while M bought rations etc and got a meal ready. Having at last satisfied our hunger, we went to the shop in Museum St where we bought our Degas picture and had a look through the remainder of their stock of French Impressionist reproductions. Bought one of Monet's *Summer* and two smaller ones of Renoir's *La Loge* and Manet's *Les Servants de Bocks*. Paid £1 deposit and left them to be framed. Had an equally energetic evening, unpacking, putting the furniture back into our now redecorated sitting room and generally getting the flat back into ship shape order again. Mother came in had dinner with us and afterwards went out with M for a couple of drinks while I did some washing and read a few of the newspapers Mother has been collecting for me. Finally a bath and to bed exhausted at 11.30. Hell of a day.

Tuesday 10 August Back to the office, half yearly estimates, and the joyous tiding that my salary has been increased by 7/- a week as from June 21.

Wednesday 11 August Received an amusing letter from John Hobson, mainly about a four days leave in Tripoli and the prices charged in North African brothels. I was particularly tickled by his suggestion that it is placed on record at their 'local' that one woman took 128 men between 12.0 and 6.0 p.m. To which he characteristically adds 'I should have hated to have been the last man in.' Has only taken eight days to get here – astonishingly swift.

Sunday 15 August News items (a) After a further heavy bombing attack the other morning Rome has at last been declared an 'open city.' (b) Fewer coupons required for men's woollen socks, women's seamless stockings and certain lower grade 'utility garments.' More for leather and shoes. Sat on Parliament Hill for an hour. Evening at home reading prior to proceeding to the Town Hall for the night.

Tuesday 17 August Axis powers evacuate Sicily. The whole island now in our hands, five and a half weeks after the first landings. What a lot of geography we're learning in following the course of the war. If, prior to the invasion of Sicily, I'd been asked in what countries the towns of Palermo, Messina, Syracuse and Catania were situated, I could only have hazarded the vague guess that the first two were in Italy, the third in Germany and the last somewhere in the Balkans! I should have been equally hazy about many of the places in North Africa that have since become bywords. In fact, I should imagine that people have gleaned more of the subject from newspaper sketches and diagrams and special wall maps of the world during the last few years than they ever learnt at school.

Monday 23 August Have had a fawn wool-lined raincoat that's seen me through the last two winters dyed navy blue – a great improvement. The thing always looked filthy as it was. Felt very strained around my rupture after doing an hour's washing this evening – seems as if I'll have to give up helping M with the housework for a while.

Friday 27 August Seen in Euston Rd yesterday afternoon – an American soldier and a tart, both so drunk that neither could stand or walk without support of the other, lurching about in the middle of the road trying to get a taxi. Their condition being so obvious, no taxi driver would, of course, stop for them. Apparently they'd just been in the Town Hall and tried to get married on the spur of the moment! Eventually they realised the futility of signalling unsympathetic taxpayers and stumbled up to seek the comparative seclusion and sanctuary of St Pancras Station. On control duty at night.

Monday 30 August Mother being unable to get our rations for us today as she usually does, had to dash round and get them myself before going along to Somers Town in the morning.

Tuesday 31 August Though I haven't been 'discharged', I've decided to discontinue my hospital massage and exercises having failed to remedy my rupture, it seems to be the best thing I can do is to get fitted up with a truss and carry on with that till the war's over. Then have the damned thing put right with an operation.

Thursday 2 September Went along to Mount Pleasant in the lunch hour to collect a parcel which, unbeknown to us, M's mother had sent off to us a week ago but the postman hadn't been able to deliver. They must have been glad to get rid of it, for it smelt absolutely foul. Made me feel quite embarrassed on the bus coming back even though I was the only passenger. Turned out to be a container of sour cream cheese and some eggs that had all got broken in transit and consequently gone bad. No wonder it stank!

Friday 3 September The invasion of Italy this morning made the fourth anniversary of the outbreak of war, quite a dramatic occasion. The war has only just over three more months to run in order to exceed the length of the last one. Conjecture is rife at the moment as to how much longer it actually will last. Wishful thinking optimists once more reiterate their annual prophesy that 'it will all be over by Christmas' as if there were something inevitably conclusive about that dreary festival. The more rational consensus of opinion however, gives it about another three years – one to dispose of Germany and a further two to polish off Japan. My own incorrigibly pessimistic view is that assuming we win the war at all (which still doesn't strike me as being by any means a forgone conclusion) it will take twice that time to achieve victory. In any case, no country 'wins' a modern war except in a purely nominal sense. However and whenever it finishes, we shall all be losers in the long run, and the only real victory will be that achieved by the forces of death, destruction and anarchy.

1943

Had M's friend Mrs Morley to spend the evening with us. Afraid I've no aptitude whatever for entertaining guests.

Tuesday 7 September Awakened in the middle of the night by a brief alert. The first time this has happened for quite a while. Though considering the heavy raids we've recently been inflicting on Berlin and other places, it's a wonder we haven't had a good Blitz before now. Night after night, huge forces of bombers bound for Germany and North Italy incessantly soar their way over London for an hour or two after sunset. Strangely enough most people seem to get quite thrilled by the sight and sound of these sinister carriers of death. I suppose they derive some sort of morbid satisfaction from the knowledge that our airmen are on their way to destroy the lives and property of innocent defenceless German and Italian civilians. Some even stand out in the street cheering. Personally I find it all very irritating and depressing. The whole thing's so damned silly and futile. Went along to Museum St at 5.0 and collected our three new pictures – framed at last. Hung them in appropriate positions on our sitting room walls in the evening. They make a tremendous difference to a room, give it warmth, colour, personality too.

Wednesday 8 September Heard on the radio at 6.0 that Italy had unconditionally surrendered and been granted an armistice – hostilities ceasing at 5.30 this afternoon. This is certainly the best news we've had since the war began. Even I feel quite bucked about it.[18]

Sunday 12 September Despite Italy's capitulation, that ill-fated country seems destined to remaining a major theatre of war for some time yet. The Germans have occupied Rome and many other towns in the north. The British and American forces continue to advance along the coast up towards Naples from the south. A violent clash somewhere in the heart of Italy is therefore bound to take place in the near future. What a bitter reward for plumping for peace!

Tuesday 14 September At last the Mussolini mystery seems to have been cleared up. After seven weeks of wild rumours and conjecture as to what had become of him since he 'resigned', it now transpires that he was kept in captivity by the Badoglio government, from whom he has recently been rescued by the Germans and placed in control of a new fascist government of German-occupied Italy. Which only goes to show you can't keep a bad man down! At the moment the tide seems

---

18 Mussolini had been arrested by order of King Victor Emmanuel and the Italian High Command and was transported to mountain hideaways. The general staff then secretly negotiated with Allied commanders and signed a 'short' armistice on 3 September which was announced on 8 September, the day before the allies landed at Salerno. The Italian army was disbanded and 650,000 soldiers were deported to Germany. The reinforced German forces subsequently fought hard against the Allies, who slowly and expensively advanced northwards.

Part Two

to have turned against us in Italy. A big battle is now raging south of Naples and by all accounts the Germans are gaining considerable ground. This is one of those entirely blank weeks as far as entertainment is concerned. No new plays. No films worth seeing. Nothing to do in fact but stay home and read every evening. Not that I'd have wished to do otherwise this evening since, for once in a while there was actually something worth listening to – a good symphony concert followed by the first of the new season's *Brains Trust* sessions.

Monday 20 September Apparently M won't have to do fire guard duty much longer for a new ruling is supposed to come into force today whereby women who work more than forty hours a week and have one other person to look after at home are exempt. And rightly so!

Wednesday 22 September The library is beginning to let me down again. Nothing on my list forthcoming either last week or this. It's true I have only four books listed at the moment, but they surely ought to be able to get me at least one each week.

Friday 24 September The foremost topic of the day is the new 'pay as you earn' system of income tax payment which is due to come into force next April. Under this scheme, all weekly wage earners are to have their income tax deductions based, according to a sliding scale, on the current week's income, instead of the previous year's as at present. This will mean a remission of a few months' tax that will still be due from such tax payers at that date and a consequent loss to the Exchequer of some 250 million, but the simplification of the whole system of tax collection that will result from the change-over should make it well worth while in the long run – especially as it means the elimination of evasions and bad debts. At the same time, it does seem rather unfair to those taxpayers whose salary happens to be computed at a yearly instead of a weekly rate. Still, it's definitely a step in the right direction.

Tuesday 28 September Apparently I was wrong about M getting exemption from fire guard duty. The new ruling only applies to women who do fire-watching on business premises. My mistake!

Wednesday 29 September One of those thoroughly uneventful days which defy even the most diligent diarist to discover anything worth recording. I shall therefore merely set down the uninteresting fact that, after a tediously slack day at the office, I spent yet another evening sitting by the fire reading – and leave it at that.

Sunday 3 October Off with M to explore Chelsea. Got a bus to Sloan Square and walked from there down to the river along the Chelsea Embankment as far as Cheyne Walk and back along King's Road. Quite a pleasant and interesting stroll, despite the fact that except for a brace of beards and a pair of corduroy trousers we saw nothing to suggest the

1943

bygone bohemianism with which this quarter is traditionally associated. But then I suppose there are about as many artists left in Chelsea today as there were Chinamen in Limehouse. The most peculiar thing we did see was an old wardrobe standing outside a second hand furniture and old junk shop in King's Road, presumably because there wasn't enough room for it inside. In the window was a huge tapestry work and picture of Charles I taking leave of his children. While further along in a shop specialising in religious images was another likeness of 'the Martyr King', this time in china and enjoying the exclusive company of saints and Virgin Mary. Was this just coincidence, I wonder or the modest manifestation of the doubtless determination of King's Rd to live up to its name?

Thursday 7 October Another alert in evening. A real raid this time replete with full gunfire. Lasted over two hours, and what with the heavy AA barrage that greeted the two waves of raiders and the roar of the planes on their way to France in between, we had quite a hectic evening of aerial activity aloft. Still they at least had the consideration to get it all over and done with by bedtime.

Friday 8 October The *Daily Express* this morning described last night's raid as the heaviest since the last Blitz on London on May 10, 1941. It hardly seemed as bad as all that to me. We didn't even hear a bomb drop, though there were a few scattered around London – presumably in the suburbs. But then the *Daily Express* reckoned without the German Radio, which has been propagating news of the raid in very much the same terms. Wherefore the *Evening Standard* must needs refute Goebbels' 'absurd' claim, even though it means openly contradicting its big brother. Thus according to this infallible fount of truth, 'there were only fifteen raiders over London, none of which stayed for more than a few seconds.' And 'Already this year there have been three heavier raids than last night.' Well, well, well. A damned nuisance all the same for I had to leave my supper and dash over to the Town Hall as soon as the sirens sounded at 8.20.

Saturday 9 October Celebrated our second wedding anniversary by going to dine and dance at Oddenino's.[19] Had a drink (gin and orange cordial) with Mother at the Kentish Arms before setting out and another en route at the St James' Tavern,[20] where they only had beer. Even then we arrived at Oddenino's too soon for dinner in the restaurant and so had to have a third drink in one of the many bars – all full of American soldiers and the cheap little tarts that invariably accompany them, giving the place the appearance of a glorified pub. Here there was nothing but whisky to be had. With lemonade and ice in it made a

---

19   54–62 Regent Street.
20   45 Great Windmill Street, W1.

very pleasant drink but didn't mix very well with the gin and beer and in any case wasn't worth 2/5 a glass. Neither was the meagre dinner we proceeded to worth anything like 11/- a head (5/- maximum charge, plus 3/6 'house charge', plus 2/6 'entertainment charge.' What a racket!) All we were given for this was a plate of pea soup, half a lobster unappetisingly showered with lettuce, boiled potatoes, a diminutive piece of trifle, and a third rate dance band. A 12/6 flagon of very poor quality rough red wine and a tip of 4/- brought the bill up to £1.18.6. Total cost of the evening £2.10.0. Utter waste of money. M had to rush out and be sick half way through wretched meal and neither of us enjoyed ourselves in the slightest degree. Apart from the rotten dinner, we didn't like the spurious, streamlined style and the cold, hard, money grabbing atmosphere of the place. It was all horribly shorn, synthetic and artificial, so abysmally lacking in warmth, comfort and genuine unforced gaiety. After taking one or two turns round the cramped little dance floor we decided we'd had more than enough and, the sadder and wiser for the experience, proceeded at 10.30 to wistfully wend our weary way home. Oddenino's will ne'er see us again.

Monday 18 October The sirens again disturbed our slumbers at 2.30 this morning, though 'twas no false alarm this time as well we know when a bomb dropped over in Birkenhead St, only about 300 yards from us. From our front windows, we could see, in the moonlight, a huge black cloud of dust rising up from the spot where the bomb had fallen. We didn't feel like staying up on the top floor after such a close shave, and so hastily dressed and descended to the basement. But apart from a few more rounds of gunfire, nothing further happened and within fifteen minutes or so we were up in our flat again waiting for the all clear, which duly followed a few minutes later. Took M round to see the damage this evening. Hundreds of sightseers there. Several houses down on both sides of Birkenhead St. Rescue squads still trying to recover bodies. Considerable number of casualties by all accounts.[21] I suppose King's Cross station was actually the target – and they weren't far out. Neither were we! Tonight's 'tip and run' raid came shortly before 11.0, the alert being quickly followed by the sound of low flying planes and gunfire. Went down to the basement again and got invited into the old caretaker's flat, wherein we sat chatting by the fire in a candlelit bedroom till the all clear sounded half an hour later.

Thursday 21 October M comes home with the news that she's to be transferred to Somerset House for two months beginning next Monday. Some special work in connection with the new 'pay as you earn' tax

---

21 In this 'tip and run' nuisance raid, the first major local incident since the Blitz, a bomb hit the end of a public surface shelter, killing eleven and seriously injuring twenty-one. As well as the houses destroyed, seventeen more had to be demolished and fourteen were rendered uninhabitable.

deduction scheme. Hours 9.0 till 5.0, 1½ hours less than she is doing now.

Monday 25 October M's first day at Somerset House. Gets home at 5.20 instead of 6.0 so we have tea half an hour earlier and a correspondingly longer evening thereafter. Sirens at 7.30, the rest was silence and no guns! All clear at 8.0 just in time for the weekly *Monday Night at Eight* [variety] programme on radio.

Tuesday 26 October Off to work in a foul temper after discovering that the new pair of long pants I'd just put on were too small for me and, of course, would get smaller still every time they were washed. Will I ever get clothes to fit me properly?

Sunday 31 October Damp and misty. Took M for a walk around the grimy locality of Pentonville Rd in afternoon. Very depressing.

Monday 8 November Direct hits on furniture [shop], pub, milk bar and dance hall in Putney High St last night. Hundreds of casualties, mostly in dance hall that was crowded.[22]

Tuesday 23 November Terrific uproar going on over the recent conditional release from Holloway Prison of Sir Oswald Mosley, who is suffering from acute phlebitis and would have been in danger of losing his life if he had been kept there. What with the yelping of the communist curs, the barking of the trade union tikes and the carping clamour of the Parliamentary pack, the Home Secretary seems to have aroused the ire of the entire left wing, through being sufficiently just and humane to act on the recommendations of the doctors attending Mosley. He's standing his ground with admirable firmness though. His lengthy explanation to the Commons today, given while a raucous rabble demonstrated outside, was a masterly piece of self-justification. I've never admired Morrison so much hitherto, but I certainly take my hat off to him now – or at least I would if I wore one![23]

Wednesday 1 December An amendment to the King's Speech 'regretting the release of Sir Oswald Mosley' was soundly defeated in the Commons today by 327 to 62, which not only vindicates Morrison's actions but puts the communist clamour into its right perspective. Though whether, after this full dress parliamentary debate, the shouting and the tumult will at last be allowed to die down remains to be seen.

Monday 6 December The influenza death role is now rising so rapidly that the Ministry of Health has at last been forced to officially admit that there is an epidemic prevailing – in fact 'the worst since 1937.'

---

22   Some 81 people were killed and 248 injured when a bomb hit 33–35 Putney Bridge Road, mostly young people in the first-floor Cinderella Dance Hall.
23   Herbert Morrison, Leader (Labour) of the LCC 1934–40, then Home Secretary and Minister of Home Security 1940–45.

Part Two

Oddly enough, I can't remember one in '37 at all – and my memory is pretty good on dates.

Thursday 9 December The razor blade scarcity hasn't been so acute lately. I've usually been able to get two or three Gillettes each week during the last few months – and thus accumulate quite a good reserve stock. At the moment I have exactly sixty new blades, enough to last me for well over a year. No. 8 torch batteries, however, are still very difficult to obtain, so is saccharin.

Tuesday 14 December The auditors having temporarily appropriated all my ledgers etc and thus left me with no work to do, I finished off my retrospect of 1943.

Thursday 16 December The news that Churchill is down with pneumonia in Cairo has set everyone surmising who will succeed him if his illness proves fatal – only to realise what a poor field of runners-up there is to choose from.[24] Not one of them has sufficient strength of character or personality – let alone the necessary flair for leadership – to fit them for such a position.

Wednesday 22 December Parcel containing a plump chicken for our Christmas dinner, half a dozen new laid eggs, some homemade butter and a few pieces of holly, arrives from Somerset. Also to hand – first batch of Christmas cards including an illustrated airgraph from John Hobson.

Thursday 23 December From this morning's *Daily Express* – 'The BBC has banned the revival of certain musical comedies because the lyrics were written by P. G. Wodehouse who broadcast from Berlin in 1941.' How despicably petty! How utterly childish! The next column however contains the less nauseating news that the Trades Union and Socialist Party leaders have decided to drop their campaign for the re-imprisonment of Sir Oswald Mosley. That is nice of them.

Saturday 25 December It would of course be my damned luck to be on control duty today of all days. And not only that to have to go to the Town Hall thrice – at 11 a.m. to sign on – at 3.45 p.m. to hang about in and around the control room for an hour waiting to be inspected and addressed by the ARP [Senior] Regional Commissioner Sir Ernest Gowers, who apparently has nothing better to do with his Christmas Day than trail round St Pancras ARP centres accompanied by his wife, and finally at 7.0 p.m. for the Shift 4 Christmas Dinner and party.

24 News of the Prime Minister's illness and the fact that he was remaining in Cairo was announced in Parliament on 16 December by Mr Attlee, his deputy (*The Times*, 17 December). The press reported almost daily on Churchill's 'steady progress at the end of a strenuous year'. Mrs Churchill joined him, taking her paint box, and, on 16 January 1944, *The Times* reported that he was in Morocco for talks with the Allied Generals Eisenhower and De Gaulle.

1943

What little was left of the day, I spent at home with M and Mother, sitting by the fire and listening to the radio and partaking of Christmas Dinner (roast chicken, Xmas pudding, port etc). By comparison, the cold unappetising meal we had in the Town Hall canteen in the evening – even though it did boast a morsel of turkey – only an apology for a dinner, Christmas or otherwise. The party that followed it was pretty putrid, despite the unlimited quantity of beer available, I failed to get either very merry or enjoy myself much. The fun and games dragged on till about 3 a.m. but I didn't stay till the end. I'd had quite enough of it by 1.30, at which time I stealthily stole off to bed.

Wednesday 29 December The Allied invasion of Western Europe (the so called second front) that our bellicose non-combatant communists have been so assiduously clamouring for the last two years at last scheduled to take place, within the next three months. Estimated initial casualties half a million. Something to look forward to! Especially for those taking part in it.

Friday 31 December Renewed CIS and Library subscriptions and Wireless Licence. Have had to revert to a Class A library subscription as the 'On Demand' service has been suspended for the duration. Not that it matters much. I've had almost as much difficulty in getting the books I want on my OD subscription during the last year as I formerly did on the 'A' one. Being on control duty at midnight I had, perforce, to see the Old Year out and the new one in at the Town Hall participating in the Shift 4 New Year's Eve party which was even more flat and boring than the Christmas one, but fortunately of much shorter duration. Bed at 12.30.

RETROSPECT – 1943

On the whole a much happier year than its predecessor – most of the doubts and uncertainties that plagued me in 1942 being either solved or liquidated in 1943. For one thing, I at last managed to reconcile myself to the idea of being married, and to adjust my outlook accordingly. Not that I found it an entirely satisfactory state with no shortcomings whatsoever, no one of my temperament could possibly do that. Neither did the year pass without some occasional tiffs between us or vain nostalgic longings on my part to go back to my bachelor days and relive the past. I don't suppose I ever will be entirely free from such futile yearnings. But we did at least come to understand each other so much better than we had done hitherto – which in turn, meant mutual consideration and toleration and greater harmony in our married life. I further realised how infinitely happier and more contented I was than I would have been had I remained single and how very fortunate I'd been in my choice of a wife. Our marriage did, in fact, show definite signs of proving itself to be a success. I only hope it will continue to prove sufficiently successful to surmount the various difficulties, financial and otherwise, that seem likely to loom up in the near future – especially that harassing head ache the 'to have or not to have' children problem.

What probably helped more than anything else to put our relationship on a firmer and sounder basis was the fact that at last we were able to get a home of our own. Having bought the remainder of the necessary furniture early in the year, we moved from 93 Queen Alexandra Mansions to 61 Rashleigh House and thereupon embarked on the second phase of our married life – a less difficult and trying phase than the first, free from the irksome responsibilities involved in living in someone else's furnished flat, and enhanced by the pleasure of having one's things about one and the satisfaction of being able to save money again as a result of the considerable reduction in rent effected by the move. If all goes well, the total cost of our furniture will thereby be recouped within two or three years. After that we hope to find another flat in a less slummy and grimy neighbourhood. But until then, Rashleigh House provides us with a conveniently situated (and certainly conveniently priced) temporary domicile.

In the course of moving, I overstrained myself and acquired a rupture, which reduced myself to a rather low level throughout the greater part of the year. A course of abdominal massage at the Homeopathic Hospital failed to put it right but, with the aid of some home exercise, I have been able to keep it in check to a certain degree and so postpone the operation I must eventually undergo. The one consolation about the handicap is that it will keep me in a low grade if I should happen to be called up for medical examination again. It is undoubtedly a useful sort of thing for a bloke of my age to have these days!

My total savings at the end of the year amount to £155, exclusive of Income Tax Post War Credits to the value of £21, a credit balance of £22 in the Borough Council Superannuation Fund (which of course only becomes returnable if and when I leave) and a reserve of £10 cash in hand for imminent expenditure on clothes. Taking into consideration that fact that I bought over £100 worth of furniture during the six months prior to April, that it, I think, a very satisfactory figure. I had two salary increases amounting to 15/6 a week – and a corresponding income tax increase of 8/6 a week. Rises, alas, aren't what they were!

While the extent of my theatre going has, in accordance with the increased volume of theatrical activity, being greater than last year's, that of my film going has been proportionately smaller. Thus, whereas I went to the theatre 54 times in 1943 as compared with 40 in 1942, my visits to the cinema dropped from 38 to 23. The reasons for this were twofold (a) there weren't so many good or even moderately good films to be seen (b) I reverted to my pre-war practice of only going to the cinema to see films of outstanding merit, and not simply going for the sake of something to do, or as an alternative to the theatre. On the other hand, I read more than twice as many books this year – 58 as against 1942's 25 – and so kept my one and only New Year's Resolution. All these figures, in fact, indicate a gratifying return to pre-war normality.[25]

For the first time in the course of my long friendship with Ron, a potential rift in the bond became apparent. The trouble is that Ron allowed himself to be influenced more and more by his stupidly selfish and possessive wife, who did everything in her power to prevent us seeing each other – usually by inducing Ron to call off our arranged meetings at the last moment. This sort of nonsense happened several times and I got heartily sick of it. If persisted in, it can only mean a parting of the ways. For much as I should regret losing so old and likeable companion there is a limit even to my patience and that limit has almost been reached.

My friendship with John Hobson, however, has continued to flourish unabated through the medium of regular and frequent exchange of correspondence to and from North Africa and Italy. He's about the only reliable friend I seem to have left now. In the absence of any news from John Bell, we have been reluctantly forced to come to the conclusion that he must have been killed. As for Phil Smart, well, our erstwhile friendship just seems to have died a natural death through lack of nutrition.

Despite some bad weather in the second week our fortnight's holiday in Somerset proved to be more pleasant and enjoyable than it was last year. Likewise the three or four Sunday rambles in the country in the early part of the summer. The first of these, a mid-May tramp in Surrey will always remain one of my most treasured memories. Never have I seen a more completely perfect picture of spring than I saw that day.

The war, with all its attendant worries and difficulties, continued to overshadow and regulate our life in one way or another. Though the hopeful turn it took did help to make life a shade brighter and more endurable than it had been through the bleak hopelessness and stagnation of the previous years. 1943 can therefore be set down as a year of progress. We gradually emerged from the darkness into the light and began to get somewhere to achieve something. If only for that reason, it is a year to look back on, if not exactly with joy, at least without regret.

---

25 None of these figures – presumably taken from the missing annual loose sheets – correspond exactly with the totals given for theatre and cinema visits and books read in Appendix B – the latter being calculated from Heap's mentioning them in the diary.

1944

With the expectation of a 'second front' promising an exciting year, from late January to April London suffered another manned bomber campaign – the 'Baby Blitz' – but most of the high explosive bombs avoided St Pancras, although the borough received its share of incendiary bombs. Then in mid-June, a week after the allied invasion of the continent began, the predicted German V–1 flying bomb offensive opened and was followed in September by the V–2 long-range rocket offensive. The Heaps understandably reverted to sleeping in public air raid shelters, from where, following the 'all clear', Heap again routinely walked his wider neighbourhood, recording the physical damage being suffered by his beloved London.

Now more settled into married life, the Heaps decided in June to wait for better times before starting a family. Meanwhile Anthony maintained his regular wartime rate of theatre 'first nighting', cinema-going, reading and enjoying the occasional pub crawl with his old friend Ron. He continued to do his regular duties in the ARP Control Room and experienced the wider war vicariously through 'the two Johns': John Bell, now a Lieutenant in the Royal Navy, and John Hobson, a private soldier. Both met Heap for drinks in February, Bell between ships and Hobson on leave between the Italian campaign and training for the Normandy landings. The significance of the momentous events of 1944 is reflected in reproducing some 38% of the 40,200 words of Heap's original volume.

Saturday 1 January My one and only New Year resolution is to get fitted with a rupture appliance. Just as one keeps putting off the necessity of a visit to the dentist for as long as possible, so have I being merely endeavouring to keep my hernia in check without any sort of support in order to avoid consulting whoever in this case corresponds to the dreaded dentist. With the result that the damned thing is now getting me down. Still, my own modest resolutions hardly compare with M's which is nothing less than to give up smoking. Considering she's accustomed to about fifteen cigarettes a day, it will be a tremendous triumph of willpower if she sticks to it. But I doubt if she will, I might not even stick to mine.

Monday 3 January No sooner got into bed last night, than the sirens promptly got us out again and sent M forth on fire guard duty and me into the sitting room with my book, thus to remain until the 'all clear' allowed us to resume our repose some thirty five minutes later. Received John Hobson's monthly digest from the Italian front. Has apparently had a good deal of active service. Also had four days leave in Naples of which fair city he gave a somewhat unappreciative description.

Tuesday 4 January Kept my New Year's resolution by going along to Chancery Lane at lunch time today and getting [fitted] with a Brooks rupture appliance.[1] They appeared to be doing a roaring trade and their service was so brisk and efficient that, despite the waiting room being cluttered up with some seven or eight fellow sufferers when I arrived, I had been measured, fitted, relieved of £2.0.6 and was out again within forty-five minutes. I guess it's going to take some getting used to though doubtless feel more comfortable after the first few days. Anyway, I'm glad I made the effort and got the damned contraption.

Wednesday 5 January Sirens and gunfire in the middle of the night, duration about 35 minutes. Appropriate loss of sleep for 1½ hours. Took the trousers and waistcoat of my most presentable suit round to the local repairs and alterations tailor to have them both let out three inches round the waist and chest respectively.

Thursday 6 January For the first time since they were so summarily ejected by the Germans in June, the Russians have at last begun to penetrate into Poland again. The natural antagonism of all types of the Poles to the Russians who clearly intend to try and retain the half of Poland they acquired at the outset of the war by stabbing that unfortunate country in the back (they call it 'liberating the Polish workers') should give rise to some interesting complications. The Anglo-American attitude to the dispute is still somewhat obscure, but the issue is clear cut. Either we continue to stand by the pact with the Poles that first brought us into the war and support their claim for the restoration of the 1939 frontier, or we betray them in order to appease the Russian Bear, and so help bring about the Bolshevik domination of Europe. And beguiled as this easily-hoodwinked country is by the belated victories of the Red Army and the everlasting spite of government propaganda poured forth by the press into overlooking Soviet Russia's bleak record of bloodshed, tyranny and aggression, it seems much more likely we shall adopt the latter course than the former.

Friday 7 January The Board of Trade 'lets on' that we're to be vouchsafed twenty four clothing coupons over the next six months.

Saturday 8 January Eager to get some fresh air and exercise now that my rupture appliance enables me to do so without feeling strained and fatigued. I went for a vigorous walk over the heath in the afternoon –

---

1 R. Brooks Appliance Co., 80 Chancery Lane.

Part Two

and felt duly invigorated thereby. The 'Brook' is still far from being sufficiently comfortable for me to be unconscious of it (except when sitting). But I'm gradually getting inured.

Wednesday 12 January Latest move in the Russo-Polish showdown is Russia's 'offer' to give the Poles East Prussia and Silesia (neither, of course, being theirs to give) in exchange for the Eastern half of Poland they covet. The whole thing is, in fact, as foul and filthy a frame up as any that have hitherto been devised by the scheming scum that make the name of 'Soviet Russia' stink.

Saturday 15 January Brace of bombs dropped by lone raider on a crowded cinema and adjacent department store in Croydon yesterday. No alert, no gunfire, but plenty of casualties![2]

Sunday 16 January My pre-lunch perambulations were confined to a brisk walk as far as Piccadilly Circus whence I returned by bus. The West End streets used to be practically deserted on Sunday mornings, now they're so crowded with American soldiers – and of course the cheap little pick-ups that are usually to be found in their employ – that the ordinary Londoner venturing therein is made to feel almost like a foreigner in a strange land.

Tuesday 18 January Except as far she persuaded me to give her one cigarette every evening as a special treat, M has kept to her New Year resolution to give up smoking and thereby saved about 13/- a week. A propos saving money we are now putting £1 a week into a special 'furniture fund.' It makes me quite depressed when I think of the amount of stuff we've still got to get before we'll have an acceptable home.

Thursday 20 January A night out with Ron. Our first get-together for eight weeks. Met in the George at 8.15, proceeded to the Tunnel Club[3] an hour then we tarried, playing darts and quaffing Worthingtons until they closed at 11.15. In all I spent 7/3, drank eight beers and smoked ten cigarettes. The depths of dissipation!

Saturday 22 January Another lively raid early in the morning. Got up and dressed as soon as the siren sounded at 4.30 and went downstairs

---

2   On the evening of Friday 14 January, the 3,275-seat Davis Cinema at 73 High Street, Croydon (the second-largest cinema in Britain) was hit by one of two bombs from a lone raider. It did not explode when it fell through the roof and landed in the front stalls, but it killed 7 of the 1,500 audience present and injured 31 others. The second bomb exploded in Allders store in North End and blew out many shop windows (W. C. Berwick Sayers, *Croydon and the Second World War* (Croydon: Croydon Corporation, 1949), pp. 88–89).

3   Presumably close to the air vents of the railway tunnel under Haverstock Hill, down from the George or close to Hampstead Town Hall and Belsize Park Deep Shelter under the tube station.

immediately the gunfire started about fifteen minutes later.[4] The barrage was even fiercer than it had been during the earlier alert. There also seemed to be more planes taking part in the second attack. But fortunately it didn't last any longer. After half an hour or so the tumult died down once more and we came up waiting for the all clear which, at last, issued forth at 6.0. And so back to bed for the briefest of sleeps 'ere rising at 7.15.

Tuesday 25 January Great news! The unpopular austerity restrictions on men's clothes, in force since May '42, have been lifted. So that, from February 1, one may have a suit made with trouser turn-ups, a double breasted jacket and full complement of pockets, pleats and buttons. My heart leapt up when I beheld these tidings in the newspapers. In fact I could hardly have been more overjoyed if peace had broken out. I've been in desperate need of a new suit and a sports jacket for some time, but loath to waste my precious coupons – and money – on hideously looking 'austerity' garments, have been putting off going to a tailor's for as long as I could in the hope that some miracle might happen and my patience rewarded at long last and able to gaily sally forth and order some new clothes. Went down to the Strand at lunchtime in search of a suitable book in which to keep next year's diary. Dared not leave it till the end of the year in case the paper restrictions get worse 'ere then and I should find it impossible to get anything like what I require. I couldn't get exactly what I wanted today as they apparently don't make books like this, an inch thick, any longer but I managed to get the next best thing, a couple of uniform volumes exactly half that thickness. The story of my life for 1945. 'C'est la guerre!'

Saturday 29 January M bought herself a hat. Stayed in evening, for the seventh Saturday running. Had a nice hectic hour's raid 8.15 to 9.15 – presumably a reprisal for our heavy raids on Berlin the last two nights. What with the avalanche of bright flares descending from the skies and the cascade of anti-aircraft shells ascending aloft, we were given quite a lively and colourful fireworks display – a little too many though for my liking.

Friday 4 February Like a veritable bolt from the blue, John Bell, gold braided and bearded, blithely [came] into the Town Hall today, thus proving himself not to be dead or missing as I had surmised from the lack of news from him, but to my great joy and surprise very much alive and kicking. Needless to say we at once repaired to the Euston Tavern and, over three or four beers, exchanged our life stories for the last two years, most of which he spent sailing round the Indian Ocean.

---

4   This was the first raid of the 'Baby Blitz' offensive by manned aircraft, which continued through to April. Heap mentions the raids which affected St Pancras (19 February, 15 and 22 March), but most were directed at riverside and West London boroughs.

Now a fully-fledged lieutenant, he was just passing through London on his way north to join his new ship.

Sunday 6 February Sirens at 6.0 followed by two or three short bursts of gunfire. Which meant that we had to get up, dress, go round to the control room and hang about there until the all clear went half an hour later, and allowed us to go back to bed for another couple of hours. All very exasperating.

Tuesday 8 February I can keep next year's diary in one volume after all. M found just the sort of book I use on Aldgate Station today. Three quarters as thick as this one yet only ten pages less, 3/- each. Inferior paper of course. Must get another one for luck as well. I wish now I hadn't been so quick in buying other books a fortnight ago, though I'll doubtless find a use for them some day.

Saturday 12 February I'm certainly getting some surprises these days. First John Bell, whom I imagined lying in a 'watery grave', appears on the scene. Now John Hobson whom I mentally thought to be still in Italy does ditto. When he phoned me up this morning and told me he'd come home on a fortnight's leave I was, like [comedian] George Robey, more than surprised, I was absolutely amazed. Not quite so dumbfounded, however, to be incapable of making a date for this evening and at 6.0 he duly came up to call for me. Apparently his regiment has come back to be equipped and trained in the use of new guns prior to taking part in the invasion of Western Europe. Gave him some tea and a tankard of beer, then off to the Horse Shoe to meet Ron. One drink there, one at the Bricklayers Arms and one at the Fitzroy – and so up to Belsize Park in order that Ron could rush home and hold Iris's hand if the sirens went. After three potent Younger's No 1 Ales at The George we proceeded to the Tunnel Club and stayed there for the rest of the evening. I drank too much and upset my stomach. By the time I got home I felt wretchedly sick and went supper-less to bed. Hardly the jubilant night out John's homecoming called for.

Saturday 19 February Reprisals for Tuesday night's 'greatest ever' raid on Berlin were duly administered between 12.45 and 1.30 a.m. this morning when some sixty planes scattered incendiaries on a grand scale. Still, I suppose we ought to be thankful we didn't get hit for there were quite a number of bombs dropped half a mile or so to the north. From the roof afterwards we could see the glow of fires blazing away in several directions. This morning I heard that among the direct hits had been West Hampstead station, part of William Ellis School at Parliament Hill Fields, a pub at Gospel Oak and a factory at Chalk Farm. I also discovered that Camden Town was so full of delayed action bombs that no buses were running that way from King's Cross so I had to get up to Ferdinand Place Estate as best I could by tube. Yes, it was certainly the heaviest raid we've had for a very long time.

1944

Pub-crawled around West End with John in evening. Soberly supped on fish and chips and coffee at the United Nations Restaurant. Home at 10.40. A dreary and disappointing evening.

Sunday 20 February The most conspicuous feature of the West End streets these days, and perhaps even more so, these nights, is the new uniform of the American Military Police.[5] Their glaring white helmets, belts, gloves and spats continually attract the passer by and can even be seen in the black-out quite a good distance away. A pair of these tough looking stalwarts are now posted at regular intervals all the way along the main thoroughfares. About time too, the Yanks have been allowed to run wild around the West End long enough.

Monday 21 February Another big incendiary raid last night between 10.0 and 10.30. Extensive ring of fires started around central London. Beheld these big blazes from the roof afterwards – one in Holborn (Hatton Garden), another up at Islington (Chapel Market), the other just beyond Kentish Town (Highgate Rd). And the glow of several more conflagrations lighting up the town over to the west. Quite a fascinating spectacle really. Only 'twas much too cold to stay up there and watch it for more than two or three minutes.

Tuesday 22 February Casualty figures for Saturday morning's raid – 215 killed, 619 injured. Quite an appreciable 'bang' for the 'Boche.' Had our flat broken into and burgled during the afternoon. In the bedroom the wardrobe, the cupboard and every drawer in the dressing table had been ransacked and the contents strewn all over the bed and floor while in the kitchen the fire poker was laying on the table. It looked as if the thief had been searching for money yet the bank book cover in which I'd been keeping some £20 in notes and various other odds and ends such as PO Savings Bank book, clothing coupon books, savings certificates and Income Tax Post War Credits was lying on the floor and my clothes all intact! Must have overlooked it in his haste to rifle the wardrobe – a most clumsy burglar to be sure. Pity he didn't overlook my best suit as well, for that, one of M's dresses, my third best pair of pyjamas, the oldest and least valuable of our three suitcases and a bar of chocolate comprised his total [haul].

Wednesday 23 February Arranged to have a Mortise lock put on door at the exorbitant cost of 30/- . Got application form for extra clothing coupons from Town Clerk's department ready for endorsement by the police. The detective was to have called today at 5.0 to collect detailed list of missing articles but didn't. So suppose I'll have to take

---

5   With huge numbers of US forces assembling in the UK preparing to invade the European continent, central London was the focus for thousands of US servicemen enjoying the (liquid and female) entertainments they found and attracted. The US authorities, like the British wherever large numbers of their troops were 'ashore', deployed a substantial visible military police presence to deal effectively with potential troubles.

them both along to the Gray's Inn Rd station tomorrow. More casualty figures – Sunday night – 217 killed, 479 injured.

Thursday 24 February Went up to the Gray's Inn Rd Police station at lunchtime and handed in list of stolen articles. The coupon application didn't have to be endorsed after all, so sent it off with a brief covering note referring them to the Police if they wanted verification. Saw John in evening, his last night of leave. Called at the flat first and tried on the suit he's letting me have; offered John £3 for it but he wouldn't take a penny.

Saturday 26 February Went along to the West End to see the raid damage that had occurred there during the last few nights. The Wardour St end of Old Compton St was in rather a nasty mess. So was King St where the St James's Theatre had been damaged and only just missed being flattened right out. The western end of Pall Mall also looked somewhat battered, and the northern side of Whitehall, just behind Downing St, had evidently 'caught a packet' as well. And that seemed to be the lot. Didn't really amount to much by comparison with the damage inflicted during the 1940–41 raids, but quite enough to give one an unpleasant reminder of those dark days all the same.

Tuesday 7 March After tea then set out for Paddington to meet M returning from Somerset. Train in at 8.55 only ten minutes late. M comes along laden with plants and escorted by a compartment full of American soldiers and airmen with whom she had been talking, smoking and chewing gum throughout the three hour journey. Amusing and entertaining bunch of blokes by all accounts. And so home by tube and supper and slumber.

Wednesday 8 March Am having John's suit altered by the little tailor round the corner. Was delighted to learn that he could 'let out' the jacket for me as well as the waistcoat and trousers. And of course shorten the sleeves. Will probably cost about 15/- altogether but 'twill be well worth it. Ready next week.

Monday 13 March 34th birthday. Getting on! Presents: cigarettes and a tie from M, pyjamas from Mother, handkerchiefs from Fred and Minnie, Aunt Pop's dollars presumably still on the way. Had Mother round for the evening and celebrated the occasion with a supper of roast lamb, Christmas pudding and beer, which we had to have in the kitchen as owing to the chimney being choked up with soot and urgently being in need of sweeping, we can't light a fire in the sitting room without getting the place filled with smoke.

Wednesday 15 March Big scale incendiary raid last night. One of the heaviest since the Blitz in every respect: number of planes over, quantity of bombs dropped, volume of gunfire. Extensive fires were started all over London. Went round and saw some of our local ones as soon as the raid ceased about 11.30. Biggest blaze was only some 200 yds. away at Handel St Drill Hall, where soldiers were salvaging huge rolls of corrugated cardboard, bundles of newspapers and books and flinging them all out on the roadway. Apparently the place was being used for the distribution of parcels and papers to the forces. Another fire was raging round at the corner of Coram St and Herbrand St and a third just behind Kenton St. Crowds of sightseers everywhere but no sign of the fire brigade. Though these were the only three fires initially located, the glow of several more could be seen within a mile radius from the roof of Rashleigh House. Rumour specified some of them as being (a) St Pancras Goods Station (b) a block of flats by Cumberland Market (c) the Children's Hospital in Gt Ormond St and (d) 'Frames Tours' in Southampton Row. In the meantime M had been on Fire Guard duty over at Jessel House and helped to put out an incendiary bomb that had fallen in the courtyard. So altogether we had quite a lively and exciting time despite, or should I say thanks to, the disconcerting proximity of some of the conflagrations.

Friday 17 March Got John's suit back from the 'repairs-alterations' tailor. He's made a splendid job of it. Now fits me almost as well as if it had been made for me. Also journeyed to the District Post Office during my lunch hour to collect a registered letter containing a permit to buy curtain material which we applied for a fortnight ago. Without this, one has to give up clothing coupons for the damned stuff.

Sunday 19 March My 'Gillette' safety razor gave out just as I was about to shave this morning. Fortunately I had an old spare one that was given away free with a box of half a dozen collars I bought in '27 or thereabouts. Good job I got those collars otherwise I'd have to go without a shave today, and might even have been compelled to grow a beard for I believe it's practically impossible to obtain safety razors these days. I'm sure I could never contemplate a cut throat successfully – not for shaving anyway!

Wednesday 22 March Heavy raid at 1.0 a.m. this morning after a week's lull. Big fire started up in Islington and a big HE bomb dropped just behind the *Daily Sketch* building on Gray's Inn Rd. Heard this whistle through the air while we were sheltering down in the passage and we imagined that it was heading straight for us. Went along there at lunchtime and saw the damage which was considerable. Not much of Mount Pleasant left intact anyway. Also called at the Customs Office in Southampton Row to find out what was happening about the clothing coupons. Was told that 41 coupons (the full number applied for) had been sent to me three weeks ago and returned undelivered. Why the registered letter wasn't returned to the West Central District Office and [I didn't get] the usual printed notice asking me to call for it there, I don't know. And I was much too elated at getting the coupons at all to bother about finding out. Have got to go along and collect them tomorrow.

Thursday 23 March Called at the Customs and Excise offices again at lunchtime and duly collected the coveted coupons.

Saturday 25 March Clicked [happened to be my lot] for the longest raid we've had for a year on control duty last night – 11.20 till 1.0. Only two minor AA shell incidents in the borough but plenty of damage [near] here by all accounts. Back to King's Cross via Fleet St where one or two buildings, including St Dunstan's Church,[6] had been hit by incendiary bombs last night. Had a haircut, dashed home for a hasty tea then off with M to approve and buy for £13 a dark oak bureau she's just discovered in a second hand shop in Chalk Farm Rd.

Monday 27 March The bureau duly arrived at 5.15 this afternoon. Tones perfectly well with the rest of the furniture – and what a joy it is to be able to sit down at a desk with diary, pen, ink, blotter, paper, eraser, with everything else one could possibly want immediately at hand instead of having to lug the whole lot out of a cupboard onto a table and put it all back afterwards.

Monday 10 April Easter Monday. Ergo another dismal day of aimlessly wandering around, wondering what to do with myself. What I actually did was to get up at 10.0, shaved, dressed and had an hour's read, strolled around the Squares, take a bus up to Hampstead, wander round the crowded fairs, get one of the heels wrenched off the old pair of shoes I was wearing, walk down to Hampstead tube, find a queue about half a mile long outside it – walk on to Belsize Park station – hobble on to the shorter queue there minus heel, which, much to my mortification and embarrassment detached itself half way down Rosslyn Hill, reach booking office after twenty minutes so arrive home by tube for tea for a further fireside evening with book and radio.

Thursday 13 April Sirens sounded just after we'd gone to bed last night. Got up, dressed and went down stairs as soon as the guns started barking, but the raid didn't come to anything. All over bar the invariably dilatory All Clear within five minutes.

Friday 14 April Further alarums and excursions without at 1.45 a.m. this morning, on the same minor scale as last night's. Got up and dressed but didn't go downstairs. Simply sat and sucked an orange. All clear at 2.0 just as we were getting back into bed again. I've just noticed that on Jan 18 I recorded the fact that M kept to her New Year resolution to give up smoking. Alas it wasn't kept for very long, she gradually slid back into her old habit and now smokes just as much as she ever did. So much for womanly will-power.

6   St Dunstan in the West, 186a Fleet Street, EC4.

1944

Wednesday 19 April Noisy, fair sized raid from 1.30 till 2.0 this morning. For some reason or other the Luftwaffe now seem to make a point of paying us most of their more informal visits on Tuesday nights. A hospital in north London – the North Middlesex at Edmonton according to rumour – got a nasty direct hit.[7] Where else they left 'cards' I know not. Nowhere in central London, anyway.

Saturday 22 April Both the driver and the conductor of the bus in which we went to the theatre last night were soldiers. The reason being that since over two thousand busmen had come out on strike through some trivial objection to the new service schedules, the Army Service Corps had been roped in to run the more essential services – gratis to the public.[8] But today, alas, all the strikers returned to work, so we shall no longer have the benefit of these fare free rides.

Sunday 23 April There are very few soldiers, American or otherwise, to be seen about on the streets now. Which naturally leads me to surmise that they are being massed on the coast in readiness for the invasion. Yes, it looks as if that long-threatened event is really about to materialise at last. Anyway if it doesn't take place within the next week or two I doubt if it ever will.

Sunday 30 April Down to Leatherhead on the 10.47 from Waterloo for a ten mile tramp – our first this year. We couldn't have chosen a finer day for it. Absolutely perfect weather for walking – and for seeing the gloriously green countryside to the best advantage. Though it has yet to attain its full spring splendour. Home at 8.30, tired as dustmen and brown as berries.

Thursday 4 May First night of *How Are They At Home* at the Apollo, just another piece of Priestley's pink propaganda.[9] Here is no obvious piece of left-wing tub thumping in the guise of a modern parable, but a smooth faux comedy gaily reflecting the lighter and more hilarious aspects of the social changes brought about by the war. Huge crowd of 'rubber-necks' outside the theatre afterwards. Presumably waiting to see cabinet ministers Bevin, Greenwood and Alexander and more especially Air Chief Marshal Tedder emerge. Quite an 'event' forsooth.

Friday 5 May Received letter containing birthday card but, alas, no dollars, from Aunt Pop, postmarked March 9. Has therefore taken exactly eight weeks to get here. What happened to the present, though,

---

7   Eleven people were killed at the North Middlesex Hospital.
8   'Many passengers offered the soldier conductors their fares, but the traffic authority's main concern was to provide transport' (*The Times*, 22 April).
9   Having in his youth contributed a weekly column to his local Bradford Labour Party paper, from June to October 1940, J. B. Priestley gave regular Sunday BBC *Postscript* talks, which many, including the MP Brendon Bracken, demanded should be stopped. The BBC dropped him, possibly on Churchill's orders ('John Boynton Priestley (1894–1984)', *ODNB*, http://dx.doi.org/10.1093/ref:odnb/31565).

Part Two

God only knows. She doesn't even mention it in this letter. Presumably there's still a money order floating around somewhere or other. Unless, of course, she's just dreamed she's sent it, which is more than somewhat unlikely. Being on duty in evening, had to attend a 'refresher' lecture on Control room procedure by Staff Officer Newbery at 6.0.[10] Very brief and to the point and sensibly supplemented by printed précis, copies of which were duly handed round at the end of the talk. Home for rest of evening, returning to Town Hall for night at 10.0.

Sunday 7 May Scaled the heights of Muswell Hill after lunch to inspect a three-piece sitting room suite 'bargain' which M had noticed advertised in *Daltons Weekly*. But, of course, it had already been sold – and in any case, wasn't quite the type of thing we wanted. However, the dealer was expecting another in towards the end of the week so we said we'd call again on Friday and see that. Went for a walk round Alexandra Palace before coming back. Up to Hampstead in evening for a stroll over the heath and a drink at the Vale of Health. Home by tube.

Friday 19 May Am at present in the throes of one of those occasional fits of nostalgia, yearning for the past, that I'm so sadly prone to. It started on Wednesday with my recalling the famous May frost of 1935, which set me thinking about that year in particular and my old carefree bachelor life in general. With the result that these melancholy musings have continued to burden my mind throughout the last three days. I suppose, like all such spells of mental self-torture, it will soon be dispelled by its own futility, but it's damned depressing while it lasts.

Tuesday 23 May No sooner do we arrange to have our holiday in separate weeks this year – and thus commit ourselves to two journeys to Somerset instead of one – than the railway companies suddenly decide to make travelling even more difficult and trying than it has been by taking off long distance trains ad lib and without notice.[11]

Sunday 28 May Weather well up to expectations. Gloriously hot and sunny. So at last we were able to embark on our thrice-postponed second Surrey ramble. Caught the usual 10.47 train from Waterloo to Leatherhead, completing a good round dozen miles. Had a couple of drinks at the Railway Hotel sharing a table with a young couple who were both dumb (and doubtless deaf as well) and kept up a continual conversation by means of hand and finger gesticulation. Yet they didn't appear to be at all self-conscious. We ourselves felt more embarrassed

---

10 C. Allen Newbery, ex-councillor and former ARP officer; his memoir, *Wartime St Pancras*, was published in 2006.

11 As the final preparations for the Allied invasion of the continent progressed by moving even more troops and supplies to the south coast, many trains were cancelled at short notice. Security required other reasons to be published following the Railway Executive's public appeal to travel less, such as increased traffic to Newmarket races, and there was a 'Railway's plan for Minimum Inconvenience' (*The Times*, 23 May).

than they showed any trace of being. Oddly enough, we'd seen other wayfarers similarly afflicted setting out from the station in the morning. [Caught] the 8.26 train, fairly full but not uncomfortably so. Home at 9.40 whacked to the world. A grand day from beginning to end. Couldn't possibly have enjoyed ourselves more.

Monday 5 June Rome is saved! When I picked up the morning paper and read that Hitler had ordered the withdrawal of the German forces to the northwest of the city in order to prevent its destruction, I could scarcely believe my eyes. But there it was – the miracle had happened. In sacrificing an important strategic position to preserve the cultural splendour of Rome, the bogeyman of Europe thus earns the gratitude of the whole civilised world. Not that he will be given any credit for it. The narrow vicious hatred that propaganda induces into the hearts and minds of warring nations – especially the civilian population – allows, alas, of no such graciousness.

Tuesday 6 June After being kept awake half the night by the continual drone of planes flying over, I wasn't altogether surprised when the vague rumours that the invasion of France had started began floating around the office this morning. But even they didn't detract from the thrill of hearing the official announcement on the radio at lunchtime and reading in the afternoon papers that an armada of 4,000 ships and several smaller craft, backed by 11,000 planes had begun landing Allied troops on the coast of Normandy near the mouth of the Seine at 6.0 this morning.[12] So it's really happened at last! From now on, the war news should be really interesting.

Wednesday 7 June Apparently the invasion was due to begin on Monday morning but had to be postponed for 24 hours on account of bad weather conditions. Latest reports several penetrations ten miles inland and fierce fighting in the region of Caen. In glancing at the newspaper maps I notice that the main landings have been made only a few miles from Harfleur where Henry V launched his invasion of France in 1415. To what extent, I wonder, will history repeat itself in this instance. Incidentally a film version of Shakespeare's *Henry V* with Laurence Olivier as the King is about to be presented in the West End.[13] What perfect timing! 'Twill be the most topical entertainment in town.

Saturday 10 June No sign yet of the renewed air activity that was expected over here as soon as the invasion started. In the absence of the real thing however, the St Pancras Civil Defence must perforce proceed

---

12 This was indeed the long-awaited Allied invasion of north-west Europe, 'Operation Overlord'; see I. C. B. Dear (ed.), *The Oxford Companion to the Second World War* (Oxford: Oxford University Press, 1995), pp. 848–853.
13 Heap saw the film on 2 December 1944 and thought it 'a picture that does credit to Shakespeare and the British film industry alike. I shall never forget it as long as I live.'

Part Two

to play at air raids and have 'exercises' every night for a fortnight![14] Which meant that ere finally returning to the Town Hall at 10.0 for control duty, I had first of all to go back at 6.0 and sit in the control room for over an hour waiting to take down make-believe messages.

Tuesday 13 June For the first time for nearly two months, the 'still of the night' has just been broken by the wail of the sirens. To be precise, by a brace of brief alerts that came in close succession as the dawn broke through between 4.0 and 5.0 a.m. this morning. An enemy plane crashed at Bow during the second one and put one of the LNER lines out of action.[15] Otherwise neither were of much consequence except in so far as they jointly served to rob me of an hour's sleep.

Friday 16 June At last the Luftwaffe has now turned to play its trump card – the long-awaited bogey, the radio controlled or rocket propelled pilot-less plane. No soon had the sirens sounded just before midnight last night to herald an all-night alert for its last debut, than the first one came down in flames and crashed in Kentish Town – and caused considerable damage by all accounts. One or two of these gliding over at frequent intervals can easily prolong an alert indefinitely and by drawing heavy gunfire every time make sleep practically impossible. Such was our experience last night. As fast as we fell off to sleep the guns would wake us up again. Occasionally we could hear the sounds of distant explosions as well, for several came down, and once, on getting up and looking out of the window, we beheld a deep red glow on the eastern horizon. M was supposed to be on fire guard duty but none of the other members of the party turned out, she gave it up after an hour or so and came back to bed. We did manage to get a certain amount of sleep during the night but not very much. The all clear eventually came at 9.25 a.m. only to be followed by another alert ten minutes later – and two more in the early afternoon. Fortunately the evening was completely quiet, so, despite being on control duty, I was still able to spend the first part of the evening at home – as usual.

Saturday 17 June Another disturbing night though not nearly so bad as the previous one. We did get a couple of fairly long alerts extending from about 1.0 till 6.0. And we did have to get up and go round to the control room as soon as the first one began. But as nothing of any

14   Since late 1943 the government had been aware that the Germans were developing totally new weapons, and their launch sites in France were first monitored and then attacked as the invasion was mounted. ARP authorities were told to prepare their forces for a new offensive on the UK.
15   This, the first of 2,247 V–1 unmanned 'flying bombs' to hit the London region, struck a bridge in Bethnal Green and killed six people. Having seen the flaming exhaust of its pulse jet motor, observers assumed it to be a crashing aircraft. The offensive proper opened on 16 June, the day that Morrison told the Commons of 'the use of pilotless aircraft against this country' (HC Deb, vol. 400, cc. 2301–2303). For the V-weapons, see Dear, *Oxford Companion to the Second World War*, pp. 1249–1253.

consequences transpired, we were dismissed after an hour or so and allowed to return to our beds whereon we slumbered on until 8.0 a.m. Derby won today by Ocean Swell (28-1) which M had in the office sweep. Got a haircut in afternoon then off to the Saville to see *The Gypsy Princess* revival.

Sunday 18 June My surmise was wrong. There weren't six alerts. There was only one – an all-night affair lasting from 11.25 until 5.30, what with the pilot-less planes gliding over in dribs and drabs, and the loud intermittent bursts of gunfire greeting them, it was rather like Thursday night all over again. And we got just about as much sleep as we did then. Three more alerts during the morning, the third one beginning at 11.40 and lasting right up till 7.45 in the evening. The obvious sensible thing to do today was to spend as much as possible of it in bed and make up for the lost sleep of the last three nights, which I imagine 80% of Londoners did do. So might we if it hadn't been such a damned fine day. For we've had so precious few since the advent of Spring that we just couldn't waste it when we did have one. So after lunch we made our way to Kew Gardens and proceeded to have tea at the open air cafeteria. And a foul tea it was, too weak, colourless, tasteless synthetic cake, stale buns and rancid butter. Threw most of it to the sparrows. Glad we went anyway.

Monday 19 June Heard that among the many direct hits caused by yesterday's consignment of pilot-less planes were the West London Hospital at Regent's Park,[16] the Guards Chapel at Chelsea Barracks (during morning service)[17] and Hungerford Bridge. Two alerts this morning, a plane crashing just behind Tottenham Court police station during the second one.[18] Went along and saw the wreckage after lunch. Scarcely a pane of glass left intact along Tottenham Court Rd, Charlotte St and the other surrounding streets and practically nothing left of that end of Whitfield St and we resented being kept on the move along Tottenham Court Rd by American military police. Methinks they'd be better employed doing what they're supposed to do, keeping their own compatriots in order. Later learned that another had crashed on Clements's [*sic*] Inn alongside the Law Courts earlier in the morning. Went down and had a look at that after tea. Quite a nasty mess but not as bad as the other. Finally M comes home with the news that a couple of the pests had crashed within a stone's throw of Ibex House, one yesterday, one this afternoon while she was there.[19] We've had four

16 A hospital 'for Nervous Diseases', just inside the Park near Gloucester Gate.
17 In fact the missile (possibly the 500th launched) hit the chapel at the east end of Wellington Barracks at 11.20, killing sixty-three service personnel and fifty-eight civilians. Sixty-eight people were seriously injured.
18 The impact point was behind the Tottenham Court Road Police station, on houses in Colville Place, now a small garden site with public seating.
19 Her workplace in the Minories, EC3.

more alerts since 5.0 and it's now only 9.30. If this isn't Sept. 1940 all over again then it's a damned good imitation. 10.30 p.m. – just had a fifth evening alert, and a pretty near miss by the sound of it. Dropped over towards Holborn as far as I can make out.

Wednesday 21 June Tired and depressed after a disquieting night. How to get sufficient sleep is becoming as great a problem as it was in the early days of the 1940 Blitz. It's not the guns that keep one awake now for they've suddenly ceased to function lately (why, I don't know)[20] – but the mental uneasiness of lying in bed listening to the robot planes gradually coming nearer and nearer, until the drone abruptly ceases and the inevitable explosion follows a few seconds later. Only then can one be sure that the infernal thing hasn't, and isn't going to, come to a stop immediately over one's roof. And living on a top floor doesn't help make one's mind any easier, either. If this is going on night after night indefinitely (and it certainly looks as if it is) we shall all be nervous wrecks before long.

Casualties inflicted by the pilot-less planes on London during the first three days of the new phase i.e. up till 6.0 p.m. Sunday, amounted to 468 killed and 1961 injured. Was dismayed to read in the papers that "unless the new Air Raid Precautions are changed, no more Albert Hall Promenade Concerts will be broadcast this season. Other outside broadcasts will be cancelled." Reason: Outside broadcasts are liable to pick up alerts and giving the information to the Germans that specific salvos of pilot-less planes have reached the London area. Was even more dismayed to hear at the Town Hall this morning that all holidays had been cancelled until further notice. The cases of those who, like myself, are due to start their vacation this coming Saturday and had arranged to go away are, however, being given further consideration. So I suppose there's still hope.

Thursday 22 June Through sheer exhaustion, managed to get a few hours' sleep last night despite four alerts. Am to have next week off and Saturday morning as well. My 'special circumstances' win the day. On control duty tonight. Meeting in control room at 6.0 to split the shift up into six sub-shifts, each to man the control room for one hour between raiding and 6.0 a.m. – whenever there is an all-night alert, but no incidents in the borough – while the next sleeps. Not a bad idea. Had an alert immediately after. Stayed on till the all clear at 7.30. Then home to supper, back at 9.0. The night Blitz didn't start till nigh on 2.0, an hour after my watch. Plenty of stuff dropped but nothing in the borough so didn't have to get up all night.

---

20 The guns had been redeployed to form an effective defensive barrage along the south-east coast.

1944

Friday 23 June A busy day bustling around see to all the odds and ends one has to do 'ere one gets even a week's holiday e.g. pay my rent, settling up with the milkman and changing library book, and of course tackling the inevitably exasperating problem of how to get a quart into a pint pot – in other words, packing. Nevertheless I still found time to inspect the damage wrought by a flying bomb (the latest) that landed in Shelton St (a narrow turning off Drury Lane opposite the Winter Garden) at 7.0 yesterday evening. The [Drury Lane] Theatre just missed it by about twenty yards, and Oldham's Press also escaped with nothing more severe than a kick in its fat behind! A very nasty mess all the same. Much less devastating in effect was the one that dropped dead in the middle of Russell Square at 2.0 a.m. Needless to say there won't be a pane of glass left in the square otherwise the damage is negligible. Saw some women and children queuing up outside Russell Square station at 1.30 p.m! in order to spend the night down the tube. This is definitely Sept. '40 all over again. Latest casualty figures – Sunday evening to Wednesday evening – 423 killed, 703 injured. Waterloo and Victoria copped it this evening. I wonder just how much of London will be left by the time we get back.

Saturday 24 June Woken at 6.30 a.m. by a flying bomb that was doubtless labelled 'King's Cross Station' but actually landed about 200 yards short and landed on a block of flats at the bottom of Pentonville Rd.[21] A rousing send-off for our holiday! Our good luck held to the extent of securing a couple of window seats on the hot, stuffy, crowded 1.15 down from Paddington. Unfortunately this was a Bristol train which meant changing at Chippenham on to a crawler that stopped about fifteen minutes at every station big or small and finally got us into Frome at 5.50 – an hour and a quarter late. However there was still a car outside to waft us to Bangle Farm. That was something. Did nothing much in the evening except wander around the meadows, breath the soft, fresh, balmy air and relish the thought of being able to look forward to a week of peace and quiet and undisturbed sleep away from the incessant wailing of sirens, droning of aircraft and crashing of bombs, in fact from the whole infernal nerve racking racket. Here is the complete antidote to London at the moment – and never was such an antidote more acceptable.

Tuesday 27 June Exactly three weeks after the beginning of the invasion comes news of our first major victory – to wit the capture of Cherbourg, which not only completes our conquest of the entire

---

21 All London-bound V–1s were aimed at Tower Bridge, but small range and bearing errors distributed them widely across the London region, although centred around Dulwich, some 4 miles south of the bridge. Their accuracy was a tribute to German engineering: one, on 12 July (see entry below), went into the river having passed between the towers of the bridge.

peninsula but gives us a port of the first order. At this rate we shall get the whole of France back within three or four years!

Sunday 2 July Rains harder than ever for our last day in Somerset. Catch the 6.8, actually the 6.48 by the time it came. And so back to London, flying bombs and sleepless nights. Yet I can't say I'm sorry to get back for it's been a thorough wash out of a holiday. Into Paddington 9.15 and home by tube to find Mother waiting for us with a hot supper ready – and very welcome it was too.

Monday 3 July Had the flying bombs over in force to welcome us back during the early hours. Worst night since we went away. Lay on the bed in our clothes with just an eiderdown over us, ready to jump up and make a hasty exit whenever a bomb loomed over, which happened every few minutes. Consequently, didn't get a wink of sleep until about 6.0 when I dreamed that the window had been blown in by blast! Small wonder, therefore, that I returned to the office feeling dead tired and more in need of a holiday than just back from one. Still, 'twas an ideal day for going back to work, the rain teeming down from a leaden sky even more viscously than it did in Somerset. Wonderfully wet! Three or four alerts during morning, the last one extending from 11.50 until 6.30 p.m. and yet three more 'ere midnight. Scan through last week's newspapers till 10.30 then we sallied forth with cushions and blankets to spend the night in the shelter under Sinclair House. But the place was so revoltingly filthy and the air so foul and stuffy that we promptly abandoned the idea and after trying unsuccessfully to get into the more tolerable Salvation Army building shelter across the way, came home again. Better to risk being killed quickly by a bomb than slowly ruined in health by the disease-laden atmosphere of that vile dungeon.

Tuesday 4 July A quick run round the West End by bus at lunchtime to inspect last week's bomb damage at: (a) the junction of Kingsway and Aldwych.[22] (b) the hinterland of the Regent Palace Hotel and (c) the corner of Tottenham Court Rd and Howland St. Nothing much to be seen at either of the first two apart from minor blast damage to the East Wing of Bush House and the buildings opposite which being of strong modern construction, stood up to it pretty well. Aldwych and Piccadilly Theatres both put out of action but only temporarily so. On the other hand, the older property of the Tottenham Court Rd area presented a much more ruined aspect. As happened in the nearby [19 June] Whitfield St 'incident' several houses and shops were

---

22 As people were returning to work from their lunchbreak on 30 June, this V–1 had landed 40 feet in front of the then Adastral House on the eastern corner of Kingsway, killing forty-eight people. The injured were taken into Australia House.

entirely demolished here.[23] Obviously nothing less than concrete will withstand the powerful impact of these things. Nine alerts today with brief intervals of fifteen or twenty minutes between each. On control duty at night. Came home from 5.0 till 6.0 for tea, and again from 7.30 till 9.0 for supper and *Brains Trust*. Rest of evening at Town Hall reading – apart from a stroll up towards Islington to discover the resting place of a bomb we'd heard whiz down and drop fairly close in the early evening. Located it right in the heart of the slum area between Caledonian Rd and Barnsbury – not far from the spot where, on the Saturday morning, we went away. Extraordinary how many bombs are falling within about two hundred yards of previous ones. Or is it so extraordinary? Knowing the German genius for thoroughness and precision, I should be more inclined to consider it part of an ingenious and carefully devised system. Another fairly quiet night. Bed at 11.0 and up at 2.0 for control room watch. Back to bed again from 3.0 till 7.15. About four hours sleep in all.

Wednesday 5 July Bomb on Hampstead Heath fairground alongside the ponds at 5.15 this morning. Just missed the A.A. gun site by a few yards. And another early in the afternoon at the corner of Ossulston St and Phoenix Rd in the heart of Somers Town.[24] Gave us quite a shaking in the Town Hall, though windows stayed intact. About the closest shave we've yet had in the flying bomb Blitz. Another close shave while we were having supper. Hearing a bomb, we dashed up on to the roof and saw it come down and explode behind. On going round to find the actual [spot] it appeared to be the Royal Free Hospital in Gray's Inn Rd – a direct hit! After [that] we decided to have another shot at finding a shelter. Had heard that there was still room in the one under Noile & Wortley's in Bidborough St[25] so went along to investigate. Finding it reasonably clean, airy, quiet and reasonably well conducted, we straightaway got ourselves booked in, fixed up with a couple of bunks, dashed home for pillows and blankets and settled down there for the night. Didn't sleep much though I suppose one could hardly expect to do so first night. The comparatively hard bed and the convivial surrounds have to be got used to. But at least one can feel fairly safe in such a place. On the top floor of Rashleigh House one has no chance of enjoying either sleep or peace of mind.

Thursday 6 July Doubtless the change of weather accounted for there not being so many bombs over today apart from a handful early in the morning, one of which landed in Hawley Rd [NW1] and damaged the Metropolitan Railway line. This was Camden Town's second bomb

23 The damage and fatalities caused by these incidents, and those in Camden Town in early July, are detailed in C. Allen Newbery, *Wartime St Pancras: A London Borough Defends Itself* (London: Camden History Society, 2006), pp. 35–37.
24 On the St Pancras Coal Yard.
25 A liquorice merchant's premises, 400 yards from Rashleigh House.

within the week. The other fell on Rochester Place just off Camden Rd on Sunday morning. Churchill states in the Commons that up till 6 a.m. today 2,754 flying bombs had been launched against London at the rate of 100 to 150 a day. Fatal casualties 2,752 (about but not exactly one per bomb). Injured approx 8,000. Walked round Camden Town seeing what little there was to see of the two lots of damage in evening winding up our stroll with a drink at the Mother Redcap, round to the shelter at 10.30.

Friday 7 July Everyone in the shelter seems to go to bed at 11.0 and get up at 6.0. Why they have to get up at such an unearthly hour I can't imagine. But since they do, and there's no hope of getting any more sleep once the lights are switched on and the hustle and bustle begins, we have no option but to fall in line. Busloads of children pouring into St Pancras [station] every morning. Several thousands of them have been evacuated since Monday.

Saturday 8 July How deceptive is the sound of these flying bombs as they near their destination. Heard one ominously roaring towards us last night while we were having supper and feeling certain that it was going to land on Rashleigh House or within a few hundred yards of it, bolted downstairs and crouched down at the end of a landing. Actually it came down the other side of Hampstead Lane, near The Spaniards, a good five miles away. Heard several others drop soon after and a few more round about 12.30. One is said to have fallen on the Embankment near Charing Cross. Where the rest fell, I know not.

Monday 10 July Only twelve West End theatres remain open. Thirteen closed down on Saturday night. The Albert Hall Promenade Concerts have also been suspended though they are continuing to be broadcast from a B.B.C. studio, which is something to be thankful for.

Tuesday 11 July Present clothing ration of four coupons per month to be maintained for a further five months. Bacon ration to be increased from four to six ounces a week for eight weeks. Another bomb land[ed] by Camden Town railway station this afternoon. Landed at the south end of St Pancras Way on a small factory next to the Labour Exchange only a stone's throw from Rochester Place where a previous bomb dropped. What with these and the other pair at Torbay and Hawley Rd, Camden Town doesn't seem to be a very healthy spot these days. This was the nearest we've had since when one fell in the Broad Walk in Regent's Park. That's the place for 'em.[26]

Wednesday 12 July Another quiet night. Plenty of stuff over today however. Heard several bombs drop during the afternoon and evening. One of the afternoon's crop came down near Holloway prison, just off

---

26   A dozen V–1s hit Regent's Park in 1944–1945.

1944

the top of Camden Rd. Two others at Moorgate (according to M who seems to be in the thick of it every day at Minories) and another on a barge alongside the Tower. Have just seen a couple of this evening's consignment fall over to the east, somewhere around City Rd as far as I can judge, or possibly beyond. One always imagine these things fall much nearer than they really do.

Thursday 13 July Why the series of nocturnal lulls? Can it be that our own planes are better able to locate the flying bomb installations when they're used at night? I wonder. Official Town Hall embargo on holidays lifted for the moment.

Friday 14 July News item: more Londoners have been evacuated during the last four weeks than in the whole of the 1940/41 Blitz. A mysterious bang in the middle of the evening which turned out to be a gun shooting at a doodle bug in the middle of Regent's Park.

Sunday 16 July Nocturnal raids resumed again. Surprised to hear this morning that another bomb had dropped on Regent's [Park] round about 5.0 and woken everyone up, for it didn't wake me. Didn't even hear the alert sound just after midnight, so soundly do I sleep in the shelter. Would be my misfortune to be on duty today – one of the very few fine Sundays we've had this summer. Still, it could have been worse. At an 11.0 meeting in the control room it was decided that as at least half a dozen members of the shift intended staying in the building throughout the day in any case the rest of us need not do so. And so it came to pass that I was able to spend the best part of this sunny day at home, and even ventured as far as Hyde Park for an afternoon stroll.

Monday 17 July A quiet night until 4.35, when the sirens sounded and a bomb came down over in Copenhagen St a few minutes later. Walked up that way after lunch and saw the damage. What with this bomb and another that fell in the very same spot three weeks ago, the area surrounding Copenhagen St between York Way and Caledonian Rd has been virtually reduced to ruins. And yet – apart from the loss of life and the personal property involved – I couldn't help reflecting as I wandered around those mean, ugly, dirty, desolate little streets, what a benefit the Germans are bestowing upon us in ridding London of such squalid slums. They all ought to have been demolished and replaced by buildings fit for human habitation long ago. In so far as Germany is thus partly doing for us what we should have done with the money and effort we've been wasting on fighting Germany, the situation is not without a certain touch of irony. Also journeyed to the West End to view the wreckage wrought by a bomb that fell on Conduit St yesterday morning and found Regent St one shattering mass of broken glass. But how much more gratifying the journey would have been if I found that, instead of knocking down a building in Conduit St, the bomb dropped just a couple of hundred yards to the NE and knocked down one in Oxford Circus![27]

Tuesday 18 July Kept awake half the night by the loud incessant snoring of the other shelterers, most of whom are old people who seem to make a point of sleeping on their backs. Solos, duets, trios, quartets, full orchestrations – every possible combination and variety of snores – we had to be awake and endure them all. Not even the flying bombs spoil one's slumbers to the extent that this infernal row does. Must seriously consider staying at home again if we lose much more sleep through it. Wouldn't mind so much if snoring was unavoidable, but it isn't. It's just a downright selfish lack of consideration for other people.

Wednesday 19 July Apparently bombs were heard dropping all night up in North London where most of the 'boys' live. Didn't hear anything here apart from one bomb that fell shortly after the alert. So that if there were any further alarms and excursions without, I must have slept through them. 'Smiles' Smith, the doyen of the office had one of the narrowest escapes I've heard of on his way up this morning. He'd just come out of Cannon St station and was walking through St Swithin's Lane to the Bank when a bomb fell right outside the station. The blast blew him into the ruined shell and sent him sprawling on the ground therein. Luckily, apart from being shaken and bruised, he was unhurt. Whereas if he'd emerged from the station a few seconds later, or the bomb had dropped a few seconds earlier, he almost certainly would have been a dead'un.

Thursday 20 July Our patience, like Hitler's, is exhausted. After being kept awake again by snorers for the best part of the night, we definitely decided this morning to forsake the shelter and try sleeping at home again. Had printed War Office postcard from John Hobson advising me of his new address – British Western Expeditionary Forces. In other words Normandy, France.

Friday 21 July Considering it was our first night at home for over a fortnight, that it was far from being a quiet one, and that in order to protect ourselves as much as possible from blast, we lay half-dressed not on the bed but on the floor alongside it, we didn't sleep at all badly last night. Everyone was excited this morning over the unsuccessful attempt on Hitler's life that a few discontented German generals are alleged to have made.[28]

Sunday 23 July Went for a walk through Regent's Park and around Primrose Hill after lunch. Despite the three or four bombs that are supposed to have dropped in it, the former looks much less of a

27 i.e. Peter Robinson's, Heap's former workplace.
28 In the '20 July Plot', Lt-Col. Claus von Stauffenberg placed a bomb in an attaché case close to Hitler in his field headquarters. It injured Hitler, but did not kill him.

shambles than it did when I last saw it, though the best part of it is still closed to the public. As for Primrose Hill, what with the anti-aircraft base and the extensive area taken up by allotments, there's scarcely any part of that erstwhile delightful place left to walk over at all. Up to Highgate with M in afternoon for a stroll around the 'village' and Waterlow Park in which we hadn't set foot since our courting days three years ago when M was still at Highgate Hospital FAP [First Aid Post]. A bomb had come down just at the top end of the park on Thursday morning and damaged some houses in Bishops Gardens. Nothing spectacular however.

Monday 24 July Ventured to sleep on the bed again last night, trusting to black-out blinds, curtains, spare blankets and providence to protect us from blasted windows. Woken at 4.45 by the roar of a flying bomb so low overhead that we thought our last minute had come. But it roared on for two or three more miles and eventually came to earth in Kilburn. Had to cover the Brookfield Estate rent collection in morning. Went there via Dartmouth Park Hill where a bomb crashed early yesterday afternoon amid the houses facing the reservoir. Had completely demolished several of them (including one to which we went after a furnished flat when we were about to get married) and caused considerable blast damage all-round the neighbourhood. We'd no idea this had happened here only a couple of hours previously when went up that way yesterday.

Wednesday 26 July Yesterday's 17½ hour's lull was definitely the longest since the flying bomb Blitz began. It ended at 11.30 when the sirens announced the regular night alert lasting up till 6 a.m. It seems as if these nocturnal alerts continue merely as a matter of routine regardless whether any bombs get through or not. We haven't heard many about during the last few nights anyway. Or perhaps we've been singularly fortunate in central London.

Thursday 27 July Went to Stanhope St after to see the damage done by a bomb that fell there at 2.15 this morning. Had knocked two or three empty houses on the next site, just to the north side of Varndell St and blasted the block of flats overlooking Augustus St at the back. Sorry to see that Rex Whistler has been killed in Normandy.[29] He was about the most brilliant of the set designers of the London stage.

Monday 31 July Tired and inert through being kept awake for a good part of the night by flying bombs. About the worst night we've had for two or three weeks. Certainly the busiest since we've been back at home again.

---

29   Rex Whistler (1905–1944), artist and Guards Armoured Division officer.

Wednesday 2 August Instead of issuing forth as it usually does round about midnight, the night alert didn't start until 3.45 this morning. Heard three or four bombs drop a few minutes after, one of them landing amid the allotments on the southern slope of Parliament Hill. There wasn't much chance of getting any more sleep 'ere rising at 7.15. Nevertheless we did manage to snatch an hour or so. Latest flying bomb scores up to 'close of play' this morning:

Bombs launched	5,340
People killed	4,735
seriously injured	14,000 (approx)
evacuated from London	1,000,000
Houses and buildings demolished	17,000
" " damaged	800,000

These figures covering the first seven weeks of the bombardment of London were announced by Churchill in the Commons this afternoon, after which our gallant rulers, doubtless in need of a change of air, proceeded to set the country a shining example by adjourning for seven weeks holiday.

Thursday 3 August Had one of the heaviest flying bomb attacks yet launched against London during the night and early morning. Waves of bombs over every half hour or so. The nearest to us fell at the junction of Crowndale Rd and Charrington St round about 4.0. Walked round there and saw the devastation at lunchtime, and there was plenty of it to see too. Double Summer Time which was due to finish on August 13 has now been extended, despite agricultural opposition, to September 17, and rightly so. It should have carried on until mid-September [as] in the three previous years of DST instead of ending so absurdly early as the second Saturday in August.

Friday 4 August M comes home with the tidings that her office colleague, cum theatre-going companion, Mrs Colman had offered us the use of her house at Hayes, Kent while she is away over the weekend. The only snag about Hayes is that being due SE of London and only just outside the metropolis it is really, so far as the flying bombs are concerned, an even more vulnerable area than St Pancras. For apart from those that fall short of their target, quite a good number are shot down thereabouts before they reach it. Still, at least we shall be able to enjoy a welcome change of scenery and surroundings for a couple of days and can always bolt into the surface shelter in the garden if things get too hot for us!

Saturday 5 August Down to Hayes on the 5.7 from Charing Cross laden with joint, loaves, vegetables, fruit and all the rest of the seemingly enormous quantity of food one needs to take with one nowadays in order to spend even a couple of days away from home. Had to walk at least a half mile from Hayes station and we reached our ultimate destination – 79 Baston Rd, which proved to be the upper part of an ultra-modern semi-detached red-brick maisonette. All very light and airy and nicely situated in a pleasantly green and leafy surrounding on the verge of the open country.

Sunday 6 August Up late, after being awakened several times during the night by flying bombs passing over en route to London. A good many more over during today, one lot at lunchtime and another at tea time. Mother arrived just before mid-day to spend the rest of the weekend with us Chez Colman.

Monday 7 August Bank Holiday. Went for a walk, taking in Keston to (a) have a look at the intensive damage done by a bomb which came down right in the centre of the village a week or two ago (b) get some aspirins for M's headache and, of course, something to wash them down with. Couldn't get any mineral waters or even tea. Only coffee, and foul stuff at that. Still, it served its purpose. Back to tea and to pack and tidy up the flat in time to catch the 7.12 to London Bridge.

Friday 11 August Two bombardments yesterday evening, another this morning at 7.30 when the Gaumont Cinema at Holloway got a direct hit and yet another in the afternoon when St John's Wood 'caught a packet.' Heard the new local immediate danger warning during a couple of these alerts – three two-second blasts on a klaxon with a continuous six second blast to indicate danger passed.[30] The one we hear is rumoured to be on the top of the six storey sky-scraping building of London University (now occupied by the Ministry of Information) on the west side of Russell Square. From that distance it sounds just like a motor hooter down in the street.

Sunday 13 August Walked up through Epping Forest to High Beach expecting to get tea at the King's Oak but found it shut when we got there. Fortunately The Turnpike Home a hundred yards or so down the hill proved to be more accommodating. In fact the tea we got there for 1/6 was an exceptionally good one by war-time standards, reasonably strong tea, plenty of bread and butter and a big jar full-up of marmalade and a selection of eatable cakes.

Monday 14 August Awakened thrice during the night. Firstly at 4.30 by the buzz and explosion of three or four bombs (one of them coming down in the playground alongside the railway at the foot of Parliament Hill), secondly by the usual 6.0 all clear that always ends

---

30 Formerly, workers went to their shelters and work stopped as soon as the sirens sounded. To save wasted time if the V–1s were not threatening particular areas, it was decided to post 'spotters' high on the roofs of buildings to sound an 'immediate warning' if a missile appeared to threaten their works, whereupon the workers would rapidly take cover in nearby shelters.

the inevitable seven hour night alert. Thirdly by the customary brief follow up alert at 7.0 and the deafening descent of a bomb on a coal dump in a goods yard at the back of St Pancras station. Yes, some of them are getting disconcertingly close again. The one that landed between Chancery Lane and Fetter Lane yesterday morning was less than a mile from here too; yet on the whole the Blitz has slackened off considerably within the last week or two. Thanks to the fine spell of summer weather we have been getting lately, alerts during the day have become the exception rather than the rule, and even the nights aren't so bad as they were a few weeks back. It is exactly five years to the day that I lay hovering between life and death in the Homeopathic Hospital after being operated on for peritonitis. I wonder where I, or what might have been left of me, would have been now had not that catastrophe subsequently saved me from the even worse catastrophe of conscription.

Saturday 19 August Got to Paddington at 11.0 and found a queue of some three thousand people lined up along the whole length of Eastbourne Terrace (both sides) waiting to move into the station. By the time M arrived at 11.30 however it had practically disappeared and we got onto the platform quite quickly and scrambled to find a couple of window seats. Finally arrived at Bangle Farm at 6.30 and unpacked. Have just become aware of a certain stiffness in the muscles of my right arm due no doubt to (a) stumbling over a suitcase that some bloody fool had left in my way on the platform at Paddington and breaking the fall by throwing out my arms and landing on my hands (b) the suitcase handle breaking off as we alighted from the train at Chippenham which necessitated my carrying the damned thing under my arm for the rest of the journey. No wonder it feels strained.

[*A week's holiday in Somerset.*]

Sunday 27 August A really perfect day at last – making the most of our last few hours in Somerset 'ere the car came at 5.45 to convey us to the station. Caught the 6.8 with ease and secured a couple of excellent seats and duly arrived at Paddington at 8.50. Then home by the overcrowded tube to a supper of rabbit stew that Mother had prepared against our return.

Monday 28 August Didn't seem to have missed much in the way of bombardments while we were away, the only architectural casualties during the week being Staples Inn and Falk Slade Piano's factory in Farringdon Rd. A brief alert yesterday morning brought 48 hour lull to an end but apart from this there was nothing between Friday morning and this afternoon when a brace of alerts broke up a 30 hour silence.

1944

Evening at home washing soiled linen, and cooking supper while M goes to the dentist.

Tuesday 5 September It's been revealed today that the total number of flying bombs launched during the eleven weeks ending last Thursday was 8,070, 2,300 of them reaching London.[31]

Wednesday 6 September Monday's reports concerning the Channel ports turned out to be somewhat premature, to say the least of it. Far from being captured, the battle for these vital supply bases is only just beginning. And judging by the large forces of enemy troops defending them, it's going to be no walk over either.

Thursday 7 September A partial lifting of the blackout is to come into force as soon as Double Summer Time finishes at the end of next week. Street lighting will be considerably brighter and windows need only to be 'dimmed out' by normal curtains instead of black out material except in the event of an alert when the latter must be resumed. But the powers that be don't expect many more raids or the present restrictions wouldn't be relaxed. Or would they?

[*On 7 September the responsible minister, Duncan Sandys, confidently told a press conference in Senate House, Malet Street, that 'Except for the possibility of a few shots, the Battle of London is over. ... I am a little chary of talking about the V–2.' The first of these ballistic missile rockets hit Staveley Road, Chiswick the following evening.*]

Friday 8 September Control duty. Wonder how much longer I'll have to do this. Not more than another month or two I don't suppose, for voluntary part-time service in both the Home Guard and Civil Defence seems likely to be almost completely dispensed with in the near future. In a way I should be sorry to give it up. Having to sleep in the Town Hall every sixth night is a bit of a nuisance sometimes but the 4/6 or 6/- 'subsistence allowance' I get for doing so comes in very useful as extra pocket money and I shall surely miss it when it ceases.

Monday 11 September Much mystified over the weekend as to the purpose of certain projections that were being fixed up all around the Town Hall on a level with the first floor. Heard today that they were for floodlighting the building. What sublime optimism!

Tuesday 12 September Awakened at 6.20 by an explosion at Kew, another even more distant following just before 9.0. What with these two occurrences and that other mysterious affair at Chiswick on Friday evening which was heard all over London but hushed up by the press and radio it looks very much as if V2, the new German bigger, better

---

31   'London' was defined as the 720 square miles of the Metropolitan Police District.

variety of flying bomb has arrived on the scene.[32] By all accounts this latest secret weapon can be fired at very much longer ranger than its predecessor VI, is considerably more devastating in effect and since it descends from a height of sixty or seventy miles, no warning can be given of its approach. On the other hand the disturbance might, by some strange coincidence have been due to either factory explosions or delayed action bombs going off. Though in that case why doesn't the government say so instead of pretending nothing has happened at all? In the meantime, the wildest rumours as to the nature and whereabouts of these incidents fly around the town – the evacuees continue to return to London in thousands and the Americans make their first thrust across the German frontier.

Wednesday 13 September Number of alerts sounded during the eleven weeks flying bomb Blitz amounted to just over four hundred – this brings London's total score since the beginning of the war to 1,143. Arranged for a parcel of 200 cigarettes to be sent to John [Hobson]. Being duty free for the forces overseas they cost but 5/6 – less than a quarter of the ordinary retail price.

Thursday 14 September A few more mysterious explosions early this morning including one at Walthamstow and another at Eltham. And still we are kept in the dark as to what exactly is happening. What's more the Lights o'London aren't going up on Sunday after all. As one expected 'technical difficulties' have arisen to prevent our benefiting by a relaxation in the blackout regulations for some time yet. I had a hunch it would be too good to be true.

Sunday 17 September Up to Hampstead after lunch and did the same four mile walk we did last Sunday only the other way round. Dim Out begins.[33] It wasn't very impressive, the streets were no lighter and the vast majority of windows were still blacked out. Perhaps because, like us, most people deemed their ordinary curtains inadequate. And even the fear that we're merely 'dimmed out' soon had to be 'blacked out' again. For I'd no sooner got to Euston Rd than the sirens went and a flying bomb came whizzing over. Dropped about a mile away on a north-westerly direction – the all clear following immediately afterwards. So much for the first night of 'dimming out' – an utter farce if there ever was one – the Germans saw to that.

Monday 18 September Heard this morning that last night's flying bomb came down in Regent's Park which was just about where I thought it

---

32 Heap was correct in assuming that these explosions were caused by V–2 long-range rockets; officially, they were described as 'gas explosions'. Rockets were not confirmed until 10 November, when Churchill informed the Commons of their use, two days after a German statement: see entry for 11 November below.
33 Relaxation of blackout regulations.

had landed. All the theatres that remained closed throughout the flying bomb Blitz are re-opening in rapid succession.

Tuesday 19 September More flying bombs over at 4.15 this morning. Heard at least five drop in the twenty five minutes alert. Quite like the old times again! Meanwhile the mystery explosions continue to recur daily.

Wednesday 20 September Sleep broken again by another alert in the middle of the night. Lasted nearly an hour this time, but only heard two bombs drop. Apparently these latest batches of flying bombs are launched by 'pick-a-back' planes from over the North Sea.[34] So that by sending across a handful every night, they can, of course, continue to disrupt our slumbers indefinitely.

Friday 22 September The government gives premature birth to its demobilisation plans in the form of a 'White Paper' published today. The main point being that the order of discharge from the services will depend largely on two factors – age and length of service. All very enlightening no doubt, but how stupid to talk about demobilisation now when our forces in Holland are at last coming up against stiff opposition.[35] The real fighting is only just beginning, not ending.

Tuesday 26 September The best part of today's papers are given over to explaining not the serious set-backs our forces are suffering in Holland but the government's plans for carrying out its slightly modified version of the Beveridge Social Insurance scheme – in the sweet by and by. I thought this quite a good idea when it was first mooted nearly two years ago. Since then, however, I've come to realise what it really signifies – an essential part of that hideous conception we are to have foisted upon us after the war; to wit the 'Brave New World' in which bureaucratic state control is apparently to be expanded to the maximum and industrial enterprise and initiative is to be reduced to a minimum. In short the thin end of the communist wedge. The fact that the country will be left bankrupt by the war and quite unable to afford any such scheme is, of course, conveniently overlooked. As is the much more urgent need to put the export industries on their feet again, regain our world market and thus obviate unemployment, which is after all the main cause of poverty and insecurity. But to get at the root of the trouble

---

34 The Allies' advance on the continent had overrun the launching sites in northern France, so Heinkel-111 aircraft were modified to launch V-1s from over the North Sea. Over 1,100 V-1s were air-launched.

35 In an attempt to outflank German defences and establish a bridgehead across the River Rhine – and thus speed the end of the war by capturing the Ruhr – on 17 September the Allies had launched Operation Market Garden, a massive airborne assault to capture eight bridges across rivers and canals to speed their advance into Germany. But the German forces, recently exercised in repelling an airborne landing, reacted quickly and in force, with the result that the vital bridge at Nijmegen was not captured and the Germans took 6,000 allied prisoners. See Dear, *Oxford Companion to the Second World War*, pp. 718–719.

and solve the real problem is obviously the last thing the government wants to do. As long as the left wing is appeased nothing else seems to matter. Heard the first of the new season's series of *Brains Trust* 'ere repairing to the Town Hall for control duty. First rate fun!

Thursday 12 October Took M to the New once more to see the third of the three plays in the Old Vic's present repertory – *Peer Gynt*. Met Ralph Reader going in and had a chat with him in the interval, mainly of course about old times and the old Holborn Rovers he'd bumped into all over the world since the war began.[36] Quite a nostalgic encounter, one way and another.

Wednesday 18 October Got a letter from John Hobson now in Holland – mainly on the inferiority of Belgian and Dutch beers.

Thursday 19 October For the first time since the war began, the weather has become news again. Not exactly red hot news, but the papers can now at least say what it was like the day before yesterday instead of having to wait ten days before mentioning it. Took M up to the Plaza, Camden Town. Was surprised to see so many people trooping out when an alert was sounded at 8.25. Mostly women, of course, but in a West End theatre or cinema no one would have stirred.

Monday 30 October Bought a copy of *Everybody's*, a popular weekly magazine I recently 'discovered' in the dentist's waiting room, and spent the best part of the evening reading it.[37] Contains a dozen lengthy, informative, well written and choicely illustrated articles. Must get it every week.

Wednesday 1 November On duty at night, have been given a new job in Control Room. Instead of being 'Service Telephonist' I am now 'Resources Officer', the sole function of whom is to indicate by means of tabs affixed to hooks on a big wall chart, the number of rescue cars and ambulances in or out of the various depots during a raid. Don't suppose I shall have any nervous breakdowns over that!

Saturday 4 November A wave of sexual mania comparable to that which beset Berlin in the 'twenties is now sweeping over London and making itself manifest everywhere. Particularly in the West End at night where, discreetly ignored by the police, prostitutes post themselves every two or three yards along the main thoroughfares. Some, of course, are genuine professionals, but the vast majority are obviously amateurs – girls in their 'teens for whom the thousands of overpaid and over-sexed American soldiers roaming around are easy prey. To see vice flouted so

---

36 The founder of the Scout *Gang Shows*, Reader had been a leading member of Holborn Rovers with Heap. See note to entry for 14 January 1931.
37 A new weekly rival of *Picture Post*.

openly and crudely and on such an alarming scale as it is in the streets of London is enough to nauseate even the most broadminded observer.

Monday 6 November Heard that the last and loudest of the three rocket bombs we heard fall yesterday landed hard by the Archway junction at Highgate. The nearest we've had yet – sounded like it too!

Tuesday 7 November Put in three hours overtime on Bomb Damage Repairs Accounts which accumulated to such an unwieldy extent as a result of the flying bomb Blitz that the Cost Office finally had to send out an SOS for volunteers to stay late this week and help in clearing up the arrears of work involved. With overtime paid for at the rate of 4/9 an hour.

Friday 10 November St Pancras leads the way in starting the new system of brighter street lighting which the Home Secretary has at last authorised London boroughs to go ahead with. Although I didn't notice it when I left the Town Hall at 8.0, Euston Rd was already lit up last night. The rest of the borough is to be likewise illuminated over the next week or two.

Saturday 11 November Following Churchill's statement in the House yesterday, this morning's papers carry the full story of the V2.[38] Apparently these rocket bombs have a range of about 200–250 miles, ascend some 70 miles into the stratosphere and descend at a rate of 2,000 miles an hour. The blast effect isn't as great as the flying bomb but they penetrate further and have a higher explosive effect. In fact they promise to provide us with quite a lively winter.

Monday 13 November Heard two rocket explosions overnight, one fairly near, the other more distant. The former alleged to be in the vicinity of Victoria. Bought a second-hand fender in Judd St for 10/-. Also paid the same amount for an unworn shirt and two collars left by the deceased uncle of one of M's office colleagues. Actually it's half an inch too small for me round the collar but, whereas that can be remedied by letting out, one doesn't get a chance to buy brand new clothes without giving up coupons very often.

Wednesday 15 November Two further nocturnal alerts at 12.15 and 6.0 a.m. Heard a flying bomb drop fairly near during both of these. One landed in Kentish Town, the first incident in the borough since the end of the Blitz in August. Where the other fell I couldn't discover. What with the rupture and the rib trouble and now this [blocked ear] I'm beginning to feel like a real old crock!

---

38 The government had not confirmed the use of long-range rockets until after the Germans themselves announced the start of their V–2 offensive on 8 November (Basil Collier, *The Defence of the United Kingdom* (London: HMSO, 1957), p. 413).

Part Two

Friday 17 November Woken up twice early this morning by rocket explosions. Presumably to console us for the fact that the war in Europe has virtually come to a standstill for the winter, the government simultaneously issues another premature White Paper vaguely outlining demobilisation plans and lifts the ban on the manufacture on ice cream! Surprised to get another letter from John [Hobson], only nine days after the last one. For the first time in the course of our four year exchange of correspondence, he'd replied by return of post. I managed to fill my usual four pages somehow or other. Knocked off an hour earlier tonight and came home at 7.0. For the 13 hours overtime I put in for the week ending Tuesday, I earned £3.2.0 which amount exactly equals my income tax deductions for the week! Thus as well as allowing for this as well as superannuation and national Insurance, all I actually get out of the £9.6.0 I grossed this week is £5.14.9. what a vamp!

Wednesday 22 November Nearly all the main streets in central London, including the West End, are now illuminated at night by artificial 'moon lighting.' At least eleven however of London's twenty nine boroughs, intend to stick to their old excuse for doing nothing – 'technical difficulties' – and remain in darkness to the bitter end.

Friday 24 November Learned that last night's rocket bomb landed on a chemical factory in City Rd. Not a bad guess on my part. Another rocket explosion around about the same time as last night's. About the same distance away too, I should imagine.

Saturday 25 November Flying Bomb in King Henry's Rd, just behind Primrose Hill during 5.0 a.m. alert. Followed six hours later by a rocket destined for Warwick Court, Holborn[39] – the nearest we've yet had. Went along there to see the damage after lunch. Not so extensive as I expected possibly because that particular area of Gray's Inn Rd and High Holborn had been pretty well devastated during the 1940–41 raids. Still. It was bad enough, and the number of casualties must have been considerable.

Tuesday 28 November The most interesting item in today's papers concerns the committal for trial at the Old Bailey of an American soldier and a striptease dancer for the murder and robbery of a taxi driver.[40] Before the war I never bothered to read detailed reports of murder cases but nowadays when the papers are filled with nothing but news of mass murder, which is all the war really amounts to, I

---

39   Warwick Court is the passage leading north from High Holborn to Jockey's Fields. Heap did not mention the V-2 which hit New Cross Woolworths at lunchtime, killing 168 people.
40   In the case known as the 'cleft chin' murder, a twenty-two-year-old American paratrooper, Karl Hulten, and his eighteen-year-old nightclub dancer friend Elizabeth Jones were accused of shooting and robbing a cleft-chinned taxi driver, George Heath. Both were found guilty at the Old Bailey in January 1945 and Hulten was executed on 8 March.

1944

find it quite a pleasant change to read of an individual case. It brings a welcome touch of colour and variety.

Friday 1 December The first pennies to be minted since 1940 are gradually beginning to come into circulation. But they are not as bright as pennies usually are.

Monday 4 December The street fighting between loyalists and communists now taking place in Athens, Rome and Brussels, gives a clear indication of the way things are going in all the countries the Allies have 'liberated.' No sooner are the Germans out of the way than the communist rats, taking advantage of the ensuing chaos and confusion seek to discredit and overthrow the restored legally constituted governments and by force of arms acquired as members of the erstwhile underground resistance movements set up Red Dictatorships. Which, like the Bolshevik tyranny in Russia, would be looked upon by the poor dupes in this country – who have been fed on nothing but communist propaganda for the past 3½ years – as 'democratic utopias.' While anyone who dared to utter a word against them would of course be automatically labelled 'reactionary' or 'fascist' – just as anyone who ventures to express anything but abject adulation of the barbarous brutes who to our everlasting disgrace we make our allies today. It makes my right-wing blood boil to think on it!

Tuesday 5 December Good to glean that British forces on the western front are to start coming home for a week's leave in the new year – which means that, with my luck I shall be seeing John again within two or three months. M gets three pairs of white linen American made pants from someone or other in her office. 5/- a pair – no coupons. A bit on the big side but that can easily be remedied.

Thursday 7 December Terrific rocket explosion just after we'd gone to bed last night. Sounded as near as the Holborn one did twelve days ago. Actually the thing landed on a pub in Duke St down by the side of Selfridges whither I went to quiz the damage at lunchtime. Couldn't see much of it from Oxford St, but what little I could see looked a hell of a mess.[41] Quite a few casualties too by all accounts. Had a post-overtime drink with two of the Town Hall boys at The Skinners Arms[42] before arriving home to supper. Were just discussing last night's rocket calamity when damned if another distant explosion didn't rend the air. Talk of the devil!

Monday 18 December Two alerts early this morning, got up for the first one and stayed in bed throughout the second. Heard no bombs

---

41   This V–2 hit the Red Lion (now the Henry Holland) at 39 Duke Street, opposite the Selfridges Annex and housing the US Base Transportation Office. Although behind a 12-foot-high blast wall, seven US servicemen and twelve civilians died.
42   114 Judd Street.

Part Two

during either. Had a letter from John, mainly an account of forty eight hour's leave in Brussels which, needless to say, he enjoyed very much. Replied forthwith. M home at 4.50 all week, I therefore came in for tea before starting on overtime work.

Tuesday 19 December The big German breakthrough into Belgium and Luxembourg now taking place provides yet another clear indication that the war is not likely to end for a long time yet.[43] And, incidentally proves how preposterously absurd were the prophesies of the 'Over by October and Lights Up for Christmas' optimists whose smug complacent voices were raised so loud in the land three or four months ago. The invasion of France had been started far too late in the summer to allow for any hope of the Germans being defeated before the winter sets in. Yet even now there are some fatuous fools who go around bleating out their half-witted theories that the latest setback is really to our advantage. How pitifully puerile is the mentality that war, with all its artificial hate propaganda, engenders among the ill-educated masses the notions involved therein.

Thursday 21 December Recently discovered to my utter astonishment that I've been spelling the word 'pantomime' wrong all my life. I always imagined it ended in 'ine.' M happened to point out my error. We live and learn. Received our annual Christmas parcel from Somerset the day before yesterday. Contents – chicken, eggs, apples, nuts, holly. Still working till 8.0 every night, and by the look of things likely to continue doing so for some time yet.

Saturday 23 December Much perturbed by the government's plan to call up a quarter of million men within the next month. This week's German advance into Belgium seems to have sent the powers that be into quite a panic. Less disturbing is the news that Charles is due home within the next month to take a three month training course at Portsmouth. It's going to be a bit awkward fixing him up with accommodation when he arrives but 'twill at least make a break in the monotony of our dull lives.

Monday 25 December As usually falls to the lot of our shift at Christmastide, we were on duty today, which meant my having to go over to the Town Hall to sign on and in the evening again to participate in the party. The interim I naturally spent at home with M and Mother following in the wake of an ironing board for M and a pipe for me. Came up at 1.30 laden with port and vermouth to supplement our half bottle of gin and half a dozen bottles of beer. We then partook of roast chicken and Christmas pudding, duly stuffed ourselves to saturation

---

43 This German Ardennes offensive – 'The Battle of the Bulge' – delayed the Allied advance towards Germany and, in freezing winter conditions, cost the American army some 19,000 men killed.

point. Followed on by jollification and tea and Christmas cake. And so the Town Hall to sup in the canteen and frivolities in the 'small hall' – Actually it was all a complete and utter wash out. Things at last fizzled out around 2.0 a.m. and this enabled us to bedwards plod our weary way.

Saturday 30 December In accordance with the government's order, all men over 60 and women under 45 to give up ARP work by the end of the year, Mother leaves the HQ canteen tonight after 5 years and four months in the Wardens' Service. As however shelter marshals don't apparently come under the edict, she's to become one such at Russell Square Underground Station as from tomorrow night as well as do part-time office work in the afternoons for the Amalgamated Approved Society. She seems to think this shelter racket quite a cushy job, merely involves having to sleep down the tube at night but it sounds bloody awful to me. It's a pity she has to go to work at all, considering her age and bad health. If I'd still been single and living with her, she wouldn't have had to, poor old girl. All the same I'm sure she could find a much more convivial job than that, especially nowadays.

Sunday 31 December Being on duty, went over to the Town Hall at 10.15 expecting to find a New Year's Eve party in progress. As, however, there was no sign of one, I came home again at 11.0 and, after seeing the New Year in over a glass of port with M, returned to the Town Hall at 12.10. I've never yet seen the Old Year out in bed and I was damned if I would this time, duty or no duty. Not that sitting listening to the special New Year's Eve radio made a very festive ending to the year, but it was at least an ending.

RETROSPECT – 1944

Although 1944 was in many ways the most fateful year of the war, from the strictly personal standpoint it was almost entirely lacking in incident and importance. Nothing whatever happened to my way of living or altered the course of my life. For London in general, it was exciting enough. The last big incendiary raids came and went. So did the long series of flying bomb attacks that the invasion of France brought in its wake – these to be followed in due course by the rocket bombardments. But regardless of these distractions we just went on quietly living our humdrum existence in our little top floor flat and going [about] our business with no more concern than was common to millions of other Londoners who came through these grim ordeals unscathed and materially unaffected.

Despite the fact that Marjorie and myself got on together as well as ever, I continued to be depressed by occasional bouts of vain nostalgia longing for my bachelor days, to console myself with the thought that,

Part Two

in the present circumstances, I was much happier married than I would have been single, and then to be even more depressed by the financial worries that marriage entails and must surely become more and more harassing as the years go by. But for the most part, I continued to forget the vexatious post-war problems that loom so ominously near, and keep my mind reasonably balanced by living for the day and pursuing my old preoccupations – theatre, films and books with undiminished enthusiasm. I went to the theatre 52 times all told, which, taking into consideration the fact that there were practically no theatres to go to throughout the eleven weeks of the flying bomb Blitz wasn't bad going. I also managed to see some 26 films as compared with 23 in 1943. My reading however only accounted for 48 books – a drop of ten on the preceding year. Still, they were all pretty good averages.[44]

My physical condition, though satisfactory enough to make me realise how lucky I was not to be in the forces, still left much to be desired. My rupture got neither better nor, thanks to the Brook's appliance I acquired in January, worse. Thus accoutred, I got more or less comfortably through the year, looking forward to being operated upon and regaining my physical fitness after the war and in the meantime, getting fatter and fatter and flabbier and flabbier for lack of exercise. Perhaps even more trying than my physical infirmity, however, was a lack of male companionship, which I felt more acutely than I ever did before. For having no boon friends to go out with occasionally can be almost as bad as having no loving wife to go out with frequently. Ron, on whom I had mainly relied for such company for the previous two years, left me in the lurch by migrating to Wolverhampton in March, since when I've neither heard nor seen anything of him – and, I don't suppose am ever likely to again, the precious Iris will see to that. And except for three weeks leave between being shipped home from Italy and sent over to France, John Hobson was likewise unavailable. We kept up our regular correspondence, of course, but an exchange of letters every three weeks or so is a poor substitute for mutual pub-crawls. John Bell made a brief appearance to prove that he was still alive – then disappeared into the blue again. Such was the sorry record of my friendships for 1944. The real trouble, of course, is that I still have neither enough friends nor the opportunity to acquire more.

Financially, the year hasn't been so unsatisfactory – my total assets at the end of it being – Balance in Savings Bank plus Savings Certificates, £200. Cash in hand £15. Superannuation contributions £41, Income Tax Post War Credits £12. Altogether much more than I've ever been worth before. I also had a further salary increase. Chief items of expenditure were the purchase of a second hand bureau for £13 and an outlay of £12 or so on replenishing our scanty wardrobe.

---

44 As in 1943, Heap's figures differ from those in Appendix B, which are drawn from his diary entries.

1944

The best part of our holidays in Somerset was marred by the bad weather that prevailed throughout the summer and also prevented our going on Sunday rambles in the country more than thrice. Taken by and large, it was about the most depressing summer I've ever known – nothing but dull skies, drenching rain and flying bombs.

No, it certainly wasn't a very cheerful year, even though the war did begin to show some sign of eventually coming to an end. Yet, apart from the minor mishaps of having my best suit burgled, I've got no cause to look back on it with any misgivings. I came through it alive and without injury, personal or otherwise. What's more I was sufficiently fortunate to remain even at this advanced stage of the war, in civilian life and with a cushy congenial job, to boot. And that, I guess, was about as much as anyone of my age could possibly have hoped for in such a year as 1944 has proved to be.

1 JANUARY–31 AUGUST 1945

Even the cautious Heap thought that the end of the war was in sight as 1945 opened, although victory was by no means certain and the German V–1 and V–2 missiles daily continued hitting London, with St Pancras suffering more impacts until the advancing Allied armies captured the launch sites in late March. When Victory in Europe finally came in May, the relieved Heap and Marjorie joined in London's celebrations by hearing Churchill broadcast in Parliament Square; they then joined the crowd outside Buckingham Palace to see the royal family wave from the balcony. Three months later, so eager were the couple not to miss London's Victory over Japan celebrations that, on their August holiday week in Somerset, they immediately returned to London by train and again spent the day in the Parks, the West End and outside Buckingham Palace before returning to Somerset the next day.

Heap had mixed emotions when peace came. He was, of course, grateful and 'relieved at having come through these five long years of futile slaughter and destruction without injury or damage to oneself and the people and things one holds dear and having no longer to dread the possibility of being conscripted or being blown to bits or maimed for life by a bomb.' To this he predictably added that he was now also rid of the threat of 'getting one's precious diaries or other personal possessions wantonly destroyed'. However, the end of the war brought not a relief from wartime rationing and shortages but further shortages in food, beer and housing, so that, without a real chance of improving their housing situation, the Heaps had 'to eke out a bare and frugal existence as best they could'. Meanwhile Heap's hopes for the future were further dashed in July by 'a Labour government coming into power and communism spreading like wildfire all over the world, [so] things could only go from bad to worse'. Heap had administrative duties at the polling station during the General Election and, three weeks later, at the count in the Town Hall.

As his 'escape from the reality of the Brave New World', Heap maintained his impressive rate of attending first nights and films in 1945. For this final eight months of the war, the original transcript has been severely edited, so that only some 44% of his original 28,000 words appear below. Heap's longest ever single-day entries describe his participation in London's two victory celebrations and the floodlighting of buildings now further illuminated by the 'scintillating [anti-aircraft] searchlights'.

1945

Monday 1 January After unsuccessfully trying to think of a New Year Resolution I could make, I've decided to leave such good intentions to less perfect mortals than myself! Wonder whether this year will see the end of the war in Europe? With the British and American forces still trying to stem the German advance into Belgium, the Russians no nearer to Berlin than Budapest, and the Greek communists continuing to hold out against us in Athens, it seems very doubtful at the moment. On the whole I should say the odds are about two to one against. Got so little sleep last night that I could hardly keep my eyes open this afternoon. In fact, I felt so exhausted by the time I got home from the Town Hall at 8.0 that it was as much as I could do to eat my mutton hash and treacle pudding 'ere flopping into an early bed.

Tuesday 2 January For the first time since the war began, there is a shortage of potatoes. This used to happen quite often in the last war, though for a different reason. Then it was caused by distribution muddles, now it is simply due to the past week's exceptionally severe frosts, which have prevented digging. However we're still receiving our nightly ration of rocket bombs alright! Terrific explosion out Hammersmith way last night and up at Finsbury Park the night before.

Wednesday 3 January Duly delighted to learn that bread is to regain some of its former whiteness. What with this, and the reappearance of ice cream, we seem to be getting right back to – well 1941, anyway. Though I'd be willing to swop all the white bread and ice cream I'm likely to come by in the coming year for a bottle of Heinz Tomato Ketchup, which, so far as the pleasures of the palate are concerned, is the thing I've missed most of all during the war. It makes a world of difference to many a dull dish – especially bacon and eggs. This morning's rocket recipients Chelsea and Enfield.

Thursday 4 January Rocket bomb deposited at Cranleigh Gardens, Muswell Hill just before 12.0 last night. Snapped my Yale key in two when closing the door to the flat this morning, the handle remaining between my fingers, the stem staying in the lock. I never dreamed I possessed such extraordinary strength – anymore than I did when I broke the pump handle in two down in Somerset. Fortunately the door wasn't shut when it happened, so I was able to put the Yale catch up and use the Mortis lock only. Otherwise I couldn't have got in again. Took an evening off from overtime to attend the year's first 'first night.'

Friday 5 January Yesterday was the worst day for rockets we've had since they first started coming over four months ago. I didn't hear them all myself but apparently there were well over a dozen dropped in different parts of London during the afternoon and evening. Have no idea where the majority of them fell.

Monday 8 January Now that the rocket attacks are being intensified, we might get them over during the day again as well as after dark. Heard several drop yesterday, and many more today – some quite near. We certainly live in stirring times A bit too damned stirring for my liking!

Monday 15 January The V2s are at last beginning to bring about a slump in the entertainment world. Not exactly a sensational slump such as occurred in the V1 Blitz last summer, but sufficiently to ensure a considerable falling off in attendances at all theatres and cinemas apart from those showing cast-iron successes – the weather has had something to do with it too.

Tuesday 16 January Ever since Christmas I've tried to spend an hour after supper every night smoking the pipe Mother gave me, and still I can't get used to it. No matter how well I pack it or how vigorously I puff away at it, the damned thing keeps going out every two or three minutes. Consequently I have to relight one pipe full of tobacco about a dozen times before I'm through with it. This is my third attempt to try to take to a pipe, and so far it doesn't look like being any more successful than the other two. As, however, I intend to give this one a really good chance. I shall continue to persevere with it for at least another two or three weeks. It hasn't made me sick yet.

Friday 19 January There is, I suppose, such an acute shortage of coal in London and in getting what little there is delivered that some desperate souls are even taking taxis to the depots for a bag full. I can't say we have any trouble getting all we need. Maybe it's because we only light a fire in the evenings and therefore require but a modest half hundredweight a week. Yet because we live so near the King's Cross depots [we] thereby get a better service than most districts. Or, most likely reason of all, because we give the coalman a pretty good tip and I carry half of it up for him. But whatever the why and wherefore, we certainly get it. In any case I doubt if we'll ever be reduced to the present dire straits of the Parisians, who, if we are to believe our newspapers, are having to use their furniture for fuel!

Wednesday 24 January Had an hour's exercise in 'long range rocket procedure' on control duty this evening. If, instead of being an utter waste of time, these practices were really necessary, I should say it was a bit late in the day to put us wise on the rockets (which so far as the civil defence services are concerned appear to be dealt with in precisely the same way as ordinary high explosives). For we have been bombarded by V2s for 4½ months now – though luckily none have fallen in the borough yet.

Friday 26 January Still in the grip of the most severe and prolonged spell of cold weather we've had for several years.

1945

Monday 29 January The fuel situation continues to go from bad to worse. Still unable to get deliveries, distracted housewives daily besiege the newly-opened coal dumps in their thousands to buy 14 lb for 6d. In addition to which gas and electricity supplies are liable to be suddenly cut off without notice. What will they think of next for making life even more difficult than it is already.

Wednesday 31 January Telegram from Charles – 'HOME AT LAST. GOING SOMERSET WRITING.'

Sunday 4 February At last! A telegram from Charles 'ARRIVING 3.20 MONDAY.' So now we know! Washed underwear and pyjamas in morning. Walked over Hampstead Heath in afternoon. Wrote to John Hobson in evening. Day of rest indeed!

Monday 5 February Being on duty in the evening had to waste an hour footling about in the Control Room on a silly 'Exercise', time which would otherwise have been put to the much more profitable task of working overtime and thus four or five bob (in reality 2/9 after the Inland Revenue robbers have taken their toll!). Home at 8.0 to find Charles duly installed as our guest for the next fortnight or so. Actually he's got another three weeks leave before returning to Portsmouth for his six month course, but he will probably be going down to Somerset with M for the next few days of it. And so, after supper and a few drinks in the Norfolk Arms[1] and the Euston Tavern, back to the Town Hall for the night.

Tuesday 6 February An evening of pub-crawling with M and Charles. First to the Fitzroy where we tarried for an hour or more and bumped into Ralph Reader for the second time within four months. Then to the Sussex where we found the famous Tartan Dive shut and the ordinary ground floor bar as dead as Queen Anne. From there to the Duke of Wellington, which like all the others around Shaftesbury Avenue and Piccadilly Circus [was] closed, even though it was only 10.30 or thereabouts. So there was nothing for it but to come home, and after glumly munching bread and cheese and sipping tea, subsequently went to our respective couches. What is the West End coming to?

Friday 9 February The first rocket to land in the borough fell soon after 4.0 this afternoon alongside the Scottish Church around on Tavistock Place barely two hundred yards from Rashleigh House.[2] Windows were shattered all around – along Leigh St, up Marchmont St, down Judd St as far as the Town Hall, but luckily ours were spared. Even the mirror which had fallen from the sitting room wall onto the floor wasn't cracked. Unfortunately I wasn't in the Town Hall but up at

1 29 Leigh Street, WC1, 60 yards from the Heaps' flat.
2 At 16.08 a V-2 hit the Presbyterian church on the south-west corner of Regents Square, where a conference was being held.

Camden Town when it happened and so missed the exciting experience of being about as near to a rocket explosion as one could be without getting hurt. I would!

Saturday 10 February Heard that there were at least forty fatal casualties incurred in our local incident yesterday. After clearing debris all night the rescue workers had unearthed twenty bodies by this morning – and have continued digging for the remainder throughout the day. They're still at it tonight.

Tuesday 13 February So Churchill and Roosevelt have at last been persuaded by Stalin to agree to the callous carving up of Poland. Russia to retain the eastern half which her barbarous hordes overran and ravaged in Sept '39. Poland to be fobbed off with a bit of Germany as compensation. Thus are the first seeds of World War No 3 well and truly planted. With the Red Army only about 50 miles or so from Berlin, all this is, of course, acclaimed as a most fair and reasonable settlement of the Polish Problem by our servile pro-Soviet press – the same press that continually denounces the handing over of the Sudetenland to Germany at the Munich Conference as a betrayal of Czechoslovakia. There is no suggestion now of Poland being betrayed, Oh dear no! Our 'brave ally' Russia, the unassailable holy of holies, can do no wrong. How, then, could their demands and annexations and incessant bullying of the wicked little countries surrounding them be other than just? What, after all, does it matter if all Europe is allowed to fall under communist tyranny so long as Saint Stalin and his red disciples are satisfied? And so the dirty degrading business of appeasing the Bolshevist Beast goes serenely on.

Wednesday 14 February The Tavistock Place incident last Tuesday has been much in the news this week on account of the fact that among the fatal casualties were several who were apparently attending a conference in the hall adjoining the church round there. The entire office staff were also killed.

Thursday 22 February M's 29th birthday – wherefore I present her with a longed for electric iron, tactfully she had it in advance – about 12 days ago. To first night of *Madame Louise*.[3]

Tuesday 27 February Our overtime work having at last been completed, I now come home at 5.0 again instead of 8.0. I can't say I'm particularly pleased about it for I rather enjoyed staying on at the office for two or three hours on three or four nights each week, and I certainly enjoyed the extra money put into my pay packet every Friday. Altogether I've worked 178 hours overtime during the last 16 weeks and thereby earned £43.11.9 – actually about £24 after deduction of Income Tax.

---

3 A farce at the Garrick, starring Robertson Hare.

1945

Saturday 3 March Flying bombs again – a short alert at 3 a.m. the first for two months, couple more this afternoon. Just like old times!

Sunday 4 March Two more alerts. According to the 1.0 news, piloted planes came over during the night for the first time since last June.[4] Very much like old times! Took M for a walk around Belsize Park – primarily to peer at 'Flat to Let' advertisements outside newsagents' shops in the vain hope of finding one suitable to our modest requirements. But of course there was nothing for us whatever. Having endured the discomforts and dreary surroundings of Rashleigh House for two years now M is intent on getting another flat this spring. Though when we're going to obtain one at a reasonable rent and within a reasonable distance from the Town Hall while the present acute housing shortage prevails, heavens only knows!

Thursday 8 March Rocket explosion at corner of Charterhouse St and Farringdon Rd this morning.[5] First night of 'Gay Rosalinda' at the Palace. A timely, and indeed triumphant revival.

Monday 12 March Several V2s over during the night after a short weekend lull. I suppose that one of these days our armies will make some attempt to advance northwards into the Netherlands as well as westwards [*sic*] into Germany. Then we might get some peace from these damned things. But we're certainly not likely to while the Germans continue to hold the best part of Holland.

Tuesday 13 March Today I attain the ripe age of 35, exactly half way through the 'three score and ten' that is generally considered to be man's span of existence.

Thursday 15 March The cheese ration is again to be reduced from 3 to 2 oz. a week. A reduction in the present meagre sweet ration of 1/2 worth a week (approximately one pound) is also threatened, while clothes are expected to be shortly unobtainable by the end of the year. In fact about the only thing we don't seem shortly to be short of is V2s! A pleasant outlook forsooth.

Saturday 17 March Awoken by a terrific rocket explosion at 5.20 this morning. Turned out to be in the vicinity of Finchley Rd Station which is, I guess, a good three [miles] from here.

Sunday 18 March Another shattering explosion at 9.30 this morning. Saw a cloud of dust rising a mile or so over to the west in the direct line of Marylebone immediately after, but I had no idea exactly where the V2 had landed until, going up to Hampstead on the bus after lunch, I heard that it was Marble Arch. Whereupon I promptly changed course

---

[4] 'Six piloted aircraft were shot down having crossed the coast over East Anglia yesterday' (*The Times*, 5 March)

[5] See entry for 27 April below – this was the costly Smithfield Market incident.

and journeyed thither instead. The thing had fallen right bang in the middle of the open space where the orators usually hold forth. Had it happened two or three hours later with the meeting in full swing, there would have been hundreds of casualties, especially on such a glorious day. But I don't suppose there were many people about at that time of the morning. A few trees had been blown up and the big buildings facing the Marble Arch such as the Cumberland Hotel and the Regal Cinema had all their windows blown in. Otherwise there wasn't much material damage apparent.

Tuesday 20 March I have now been staying at 61 Rashleigh House for exactly two years. And for all the chance we stand of getting another flat, look like being stuck here for another two years. Managed, with some difficulty, to get hold of *The Hampstead and Highgate Express* for the last two weeks only to find that under 'Unfurnished Flats to Let' the same six advertisements each week. Four of them offered houses for sale, one a single roomed 'flatlet' for one person and the other one an actual flat – at £4 a week! Sorry to read of the death of Lord Alfred Douglas in the evening papers, for England thereby loses not only a fine poet but a High Tory who possessed both the courage to voice incomprehensively right wing views with complete candour and the ability to get them published.[6] Such brave and noble spirits are rare today. That his life should have been so darkly overshadowed by the Wilde scandal was nothing less than a tragedy.

Wednesday 21 March The second V2 to fall within the borough landed on Primrose Hill at 11.30 this morning.[7] Only four minor casualties.

Friday 23 March Compulsory fire-guard duty, first introduced in the autumn of '41, officially ends tomorrow. About time too! Not that it affected me, being on the voluntary control room staff at the Town Hall, I was automatically exempted therefrom. I must say I have been fairly lucky in this war, one way and another.

Monday 26 March No sooner had I arrived at the Town Hall last night than a V2 landed on Whitefield's Tabernacle in Tottenham Court Road[8] and this provided Shift 4 with its first 'incident' since I joined it in June '41, which meant sitting in the control room for 2½ hours listening to the continual ringing of 'phone bells and watching everyone excitedly darting about like cats on hot bricks. According to reports received there were about a hundred casualties – ten per cent of them fatal. And when everything that could be done for them was done we at last got to bed at 1.0. Only to be awakened throughout the night by further V2

6   Lord Alfred 'Bosie 'Douglas (1870–1945), author, and friend of Oscar Wilde.
7   It landed by the path between the West Gate and the reservoir, creating a deep crater and destroying the tea rooms and the men's toilet.
8   No. 79a, opposite Heal & Co. and backing onto Whitfield Street. Rebuilt as the American International Church.

1945

explosions (fortunately no more occurred in the borough) and a short alert. Still, I suppose we can't complain at having to earn our over-generous 'subsistence allowance' once in a while. Saw the damage today. Nothing of the church left but a few ugly red brick rows and a huge pile of rubble. And of course there was considerable blast damage all round, especially along Tottenham Court Rd. It would hardly have been maintained, however, that the Tabernacle or the buildings around it were actually of any architectural artistry. From that angle at least, their demolition is no great loss.

Tuesday 27 March What with two alerts and about ten V2 explosions, last night was about the worst night we've had for some time. Not that I lost much sleep on that account, I was too damned tired to care.[9] Lloyd George died yesterday evening at the grand old age of 82. To the credit of the popular press it should I think be recorded that despite the scanty space at their disposal and the exciting news of big advances across the Rhine, all the papers 'did him proud.'

Tuesday 3 April With the Germans retreating out of Holland and the British and Canadian forces advancing northwards from the Rhineland towards the Zuider Zee, it looks as if the V2 menace has come to an end at last. No rockets have reached London for over a week now. Nor any other parts of the country for five days. Which is, of course, a great relief. But I doubt if we've had the last raid yet. Not until the war is formally finished will we be entirely free from the threat of the flying bomb on piloted plane attacks – and it's obvious that Germany intends to fight to the last gasp.

Wednesday 4 April One of the things I most look forward to after the war is the prospect of seeing fewer and fewer – and eventually I hope no more – seedy, sex-crazed American soldiers sloppily slouching along the streets clutching, as often as not, the arms or crimson-nailed claws of the common little sluts, for whom 'Yankin' has become a full time occupation.

Sunday 8 April A wretched day. Felt like a wet blanket and behaved like one. No initiative whatever. Just couldn't bring myself to be sociable. A long afternoon walk over Hampstead Heath failing to dispel my depression, the evening, which for some unaccountable reason we elected to spend sitting about at home with nothing to do but listen to dreary radio programmes was automatically doomed to deadly gloom. I became more and more self-consciously bored, M and Charles more and more embarrassed. Until at 9.0 poor Charles, unable to endure it any longer, went out in search of a drink leaving M and myself to

---

9 The final V–1 and V–2 weapons fell on London this day; the last V–2 on inner London hit Hughes Mansions, Vallance Road, Stepney, at 7.20, killing over 130 people.

engage in an inevitable scene. After patiently allowing M to give full vent to a vituperative flow of bitter reproaches I managed to pacify her after managing to put up a pretence of still being on speaking terms when Charles returned. We saw him off an hour later.

Monday 9 April The storm blows over and the domestic peace prevails once more in Rashleigh House. M takes a day's leave to regain her poise and composure. I am only too glad to get back to work and have something to do. The whole trouble is that I find it virtually impossible to feel happy and contented unless my mind or body is occupied with some form of a mental or physical exertion. In other words, I just can't relax – at least not while I'm sober, which is naturally my normal state. For once in a while do I get other than inclination or the opportunity to get merrily and convivially drunk. If therefore, I have to be idle for one reason or other, it's always best for everybody concerned that I should be alone. Polite small talk never was and never will be one of my accomplishments.

Friday 13 April Even the rapid progress of the war and the prospects of an early end to it take second place in today's papers to the dramatic news of President Roosevelt's sudden death from cerebral haemorrhage, at the age of 63. He was, of course, worn out by the stress and strain of successfully steering America through the war. Of more personal concern to one is the news that no more men over 31 are to be called up after the end of the month. Which means that at long last I shall be finally free from the fear of conscription – thank God!

Tuesday 17 April Furious at being kept awake during the night by incessant roar of low flying planes. In fact I found it so intolerable lying in bed unable to sleep that at last I got up and went along to the sitting room and read my book until the din quietened down a bit. Eventually I did manage to get two or three hours sleep before being prematurely woken out of it by the same planes returning. And today I read this: 'The biggest RAF bombing armada ever to be sent over London roared over hour after hour during the night on its way to bomb targets on the German/Czech border. And Londoners who lost sleep must make the best of it. For there are likely to be more and more sleepless nights until Germany is finally beaten. London is now on the air bombing "bus route." The capital lies in a direct line to many of our targets in Germany and the German Atlantic strongholds. It has long been on the route to targets but until now it has been by-passed because:

(1) the balloon barrage made it a highly dangerous spot for our aircraft.
(2) while there was still a prospect of piloted-plane raids in the capital, the risk of our own bombers getting mixed up with them or of the defences being paralysed could not be taken.'

Must make the best of it indeed! Is the continual loss of sleep by seven or eight million Londoners and its mental detrimental effect on the health of the population of so little account that London couldn't continue to be bypassed. Haven't we been kept awake at night often enough in the last few years by enemy planes without our own planes inflicting the same ordeal on us! What in heaven's name has London done to deserve such scurvy treatment? Had John up to see us in the evening. After accounting for eight pints in the course of the evening, had just about reached saturation point by closing time. Another half pint and I'd surely have spewed the lot up. As it was I simply staggered home and flopped into bed like an overblown balloon.

Saturday 21 April Another cigarette shortage – almost comparable with the famous fag famine of '41 – has declared itself. Looks as if the wholesalers are holding back stocks in expectation of a rise in prices after Budget Day next week. Heat wave ends, just in time for weekend.

Tuesday 24 April Budget Day. Like its predecessor, Sir John Anderson's second budget is more or less a case of 'no change.' That is to say Income Tax remains at 10/- in the £, cigarettes at 2/4 for 20, beer 1/3 a pint and whisky (when you can get it) at 25/9 a bottle. Only whereas a year ago everyone expected increases in taxation, it seemed to be generally assumed that there wouldn't be any alterations this time. Why, therefore the racketeers, responsible for the cigarette shortage should have gambled so heavily on an increase in tobacco duty, passeth all understanding. Anyway now that they know the worst, the tobacconists shops will, perhaps, have something to sell again.

Friday 27 April At last the papers are permitted to print the 'full story' of V2. Of how, between Sept 8 and March 27, 1,050 rockets were launched against London, killing 2,754 and seriously injuring 6,523. The rest of the story including details of the three worst incidents at New Cross, Stepney and Smithfield market[10] and of all the other newsworthy incidents that occurred during those seven months of terror is, as far as Londoners are concerned, only too familiar.

Monday 30 April Revolted to read of the cold-blooded murder of Mussolini by Italian 'partisans' and the dumping of his body along with his mistress and a member of his followers in the Piazza Loreto, Milan where '25,000 hysterical people fought like animals for a chance to kick or spit upon him.' A typical manifestation of the foul bestial mentality of the communist mob. Other sensational news items, following on the splitting of Germany into two by the recent link up of Russia and American forces, relate to the capture of Munich, the imminent fall of Berlin, rumours of Hitler's death and reports of peace negotiations

---

10   The Smithfield V–2 killed 110 people; when Heap recorded it on 8 March (see above), he did not identify the exact location.

based on Germany's unconditional surrender between Himmler and the Allies. Well we'll soon know – or will we?

Wednesday 2 May Peace prospects not so good. German radio announces death of Hitler while directing defence of Berlin and the appointment of Admiral Doenitz as his successor. And the admiral defiantly declares 'We fight on' but where is Himmler? Where is Goebbels? What has become of Goering? Where is Ribbentrop? How is the last act of that lurid melodrama 'The Third Reich' working out? History can be relied upon to realise that. Abandonment of Civil Defence begins today – part-time volunteers are 'standing down' at once and, of course, means no more control duty. And therefore no more weekly subsistence allowance to supplement my pocket money. Ah well, it's been a good game while it lasted – even if it was a damned nuisance when control nights clashed with first nights. The siren system of air raid warnings and all clears also officially came to an end today – total number of alerts sounded in London during the war 1,224. And evacuees were given official permission to return to London. All of which seems to indicate that the government must be mighty sure we're not going to have any more air attacks. Rather hope they're right!

Thursday 3 May The entire German army in Northern Italy and Western Austria numbering nearly a million unconditionally surrenders and Berlin finally falls to the Bolsheviks – Hamburg captured by the British forces – Hitler and Goebbels now alleged to have committed suicide a week ago. With sensational news items such as these jostling each other on the front pages of today's papers the war swiftly sweeps on to its grand finale. Spent a solitary and sweetly melancholy evening sweeping into and reading pre-war diaries.

Friday 4 May Surely the end can't be delayed much longer for all that now remains in German occupation is Norway and Denmark, a chunk of Czechoslovakia, a fragment of Austria, a morsel of Jugo-Slavia, and a small scrap of Germany. When it comes to taking a long time a dying however Germany makes Charles II's end seem swift by comparison. Waiting for VE [Victory in Europe] Day to arrive is becoming almost as exasperatingly monotonous as waiting for D-Day was this time last year.

Saturday 5 May All German forces remaining in Denmark, Holland, and North West Germany surrendered at 6.0 thus bringing another million in the bag! Charles up again on weekend leave solved the problem of what to do on a depressingly damp evening by [us] all going to the Tivoli.

Monday 7 May Even the weather seems to have bucked up at the now very imminent prospect of peace. For after a fortnight of intense cold and grey skies, the temperature shot up into the seventies and the sun shone forth in all its golden glory. A propitious omen, forsooth! A hushed and tense hour of expectancy hung over London tonight. Flags fly everywhere, floodlighting installations are in position ready for use. The flood-gates of jubilation and rejoicing are all about to burst wide open. In plain English, the moment is on hand. Yes, the long-awaited news of Germany's unconditional surrender, tomorrow will be VE Day and, together with the day following, a public holiday. Churchill broadcasts at 3 p.m., the King at 8.0 p.m. Strikes me as being rather a mistake to announce all these plans tonight instead of waiting till the morning news and give the PM [the opportunity] to announce the end of the war in Europe. Robs the occasion of the spontaneous sense of drama it should possess. Historic events like this don't lend themselves to such cut and dried formalities. But how English to try and make them do so!

Tuesday 8 May Not realising that the victory celebrations would unofficially begin late last night, went to bed as usual at 11.0 – only to be kept awake for two or three hours by the incessant moan of fog horns from ships on the river and distant sounds of revelry by night. Bonfires blazed out all over London, the West End crowds sang and danced and cheered and went generally mad and Mafeking was the order of the night, until about 1.30 when a terrific thunder and lightning storm brought the hectic proceedings to a close. Odd that we should have had thunderstorms on the night before the war started and on the night that it ended. If I'd known all this was going to happen, I'd have gone along to the West End and seen it instead of just reading about what I'd missed in the morning papers. But I never dreamed that the staid and solemn citizens of London would start painting the town red so soon. And so, after the preliminary nocturnal junketing, the Great Day dawns and this battered old town tastes the joys of peace once more. Of course it's not really the end of the war as Japan has still to be beaten yet. Still to all intents and purposes this is the day we've been patiently looking forward to for five years, eight months and five days.

Yet overjoyed as one must feel, one can't help looking back on the war with a feeling of nostalgia or looking forward to the peace with some degree of apprehension. After all, it's only natural that one should experience a tinge of melancholy when any phase of one's life, however difficult and unhappy it may have been, comes to an end. And war becomes much more of a part of one's existence than peace ever does. On the other hand, the restoration of peace doesn't seem likely to bring prosperity and plenitude in its train for some considerable time. Fresh worries and anxieties are looming large [and] will supplant those that once beset us in wartime. I'm certainly not looking forward to the communistic Brave New World that the left wing is so determined to foist upon us and probably will in some degree or other. Give me back the Bad Old World any day.

Part Two

However such doubts and misgivings are scarcely worthy of so joyous a day as this. For above all else one can only feel immensely relieved and intensely glad. Relieved at having come through these five long years of futile slaughter and destruction without injury or damage to oneself and the people and things one holds dear – at having to no longer dread the possibility of being conscripted or being blown to bits or maimed for life by a bomb or of getting one's precious diaries or other personal possessions wantonly destroyed. Glad that there is now nothing to deter one from going into hospital and having a rupture put right and thus regaining one's physical fitness – that the innumerable shortages and inconveniences and petty annoyances we've had to endure all this time will gradually be remedied so that one will in time be able to buy as many decent clothes and as much good food and drink as one needs at reasonable prices that one can afford to pay out of an income that isn't so depleted by heavy taxation that all the irksome rules and regulations we also had to suffer throughout the war will likewise be relaxed. Yes, we've certainly a lot to be thankful for on the jubilant day and despite the wistful reflections and apprehensive fears that beset my mind, no one is more conscious of that fact than I am – or with better reason.

Spent most of the day roaming around the West End seeing the sights with M. Started out at 10.30, got a bus to Charing Cross and walked down Whitehall to Westminster thence through the Parks up to Piccadilly. Had some lunch at the Kardomah Café[11] followed by ice cream at a Milk Bar in Leicester Square. Huge, gaily dressed crowds which gradually got bigger as the day wore on thronged the main thoroughfares and gathered en masse at places like Trafalgar Square, Whitehall, Piccadilly Circus and the front of Buckingham Palace – many of the more youthful and boisterous element wearing paper hats and waving flags, streamers and rattles. Just like Hampstead Heath on a Bank Holiday. The Parks were likewise crowded, especially St James's Park whither we returned to sit and bask in the sun for an hour or so before going round to [join] the thousands waiting in Parliament Square to hear the broadcast of Churchill's speech officially announcing the end of the war with Germany at 3.0. As soon as it was over, wound our way out of the crush on to the Embankment and along to Charing Cross to get the tube back home and have a much needed wash and cool off (for it was a sweltering hot day) followed by tea and a couple of hours rest, and an early supper.

Off to the West End again at 7.30, Piccadilly station being shut, had to get out at Leicester Square, by now the crowds had got so dense and unwieldy that all road traffic had stopped. People were beginning to loosen up more and let themselves go – despite the fact that the pubs, though allowed to keep open till midnight, were nearly all closed. The

---

11   The branch at 186 Piccadilly, which sometimes provided a string quartet entertainment.

cinemas, unlike the theatres were also shut. Made our way down to Buckingham Palace where we heard the King's broadcast speech at 9.0 and subsequently saw the Royal Family come onto the balcony to acknowledge the cheers of the multitude that had gathered outside and wouldn't budge until they had seen their sovereign liege in the flesh.

By the time we'd fought our way out into the Mall (the only thoroughfare in the West End to have its street lights lit tonight) it was dark enough to set about seeing the floodlighting. Westminster, with the Middlesex Guildhall, the Houses of Parliament and the County Hall making a most lustrous trio of gigantic stage sets, Horse Guards Parade – Trafalgar Square with a spotlight on Nelson – Pall Mall with naphthalene flares flaming outside, we saw it all. We even saw the Prime Minister when, just as we were crossing the top of Whitehall, he suddenly appeared on the balcony of the Ministry of Health and, after acknowledging the acclamation of the huge crowd that – like us – rushed towards the building, made a short impromptu speech. It was a great moment – even more thrilling than the scene at Buckingham Palace an hour earlier – and provided a fitting climax to a magic and memorable evening. In many ways it was reminiscent of the Jubilee and Coronation celebrations – both held in the same month exactly ten and eight years ago respectively, though, even then, the town didn't go so wild with joy as it did tonight. Fireworks exploded, searchlights scintillated and everyone sang and danced and skylarked to their hearts content. One small incident we witnessed in St James's St – a dozen or so young revellers dancing 'ring a ring a roses' round Philip Page, the gouty and arthritic critic of the *Daily Mail*, as he slowly hobbled across the road was typical of the hundreds of similar high spirited gaiety that we saw tonight, a night that, I suppose, can only be compared with that of Nov 11, 1918, and I doubt if even that Armistice Night was celebrated on such a scale as this one.

No one seemed to bother much about getting home, for though the last trams to the suburbs had left the West End at the ridiculous early hour of 11.15 or thereabouts, there were still as many sightseers about when we started to walk home just before midnight as there were when we arrived on the scene in the early evening. While outside Leicester Square Station there was a queue extending all the way up to Cambridge Circus waiting for the first trams in the morning! A sight which made us truly thankful that we were able to walk home, footsore and weary, though we were trudging through Bloomsbury, dark and drear by comparison with the brightly illuminated West End. Finally dropped into bed at 1.0, completely tired, ... it had been a grand day ... We were in fact VE Day'd.

Wednesday 9 May VE Day+1 as the newspapers describe it, and another public holiday. No evening papers tonight, no morning papers tomorrow. Naturally didn't get up so early today but went out to lunch again at the same place as yesterday. Even adhered to the same programme to the extent of getting in St James's Park for an hour or so in the early afternoon and after catching another glimpse of the Royal Family as they set out from the Palace on a tour of the East End, coming home about 3.30. Incidentally a military band was playing in the grounds of Buckingham Palace today and thus doing something to remedy the one great deficiency in yesterday's proceedings – lack of music. Once more into the West End in the evening, more or less a repetition of last night. The same good humour of crowds, the same high spirited skylarking. The same awe-inspiring floodlighting. Wasn't perhaps so overwhelming an occasion but was near enough to being so as made no difference. After waiting in the rain for an hour outside the Palace in the hope of seeing the King and Queen appear on the balcony, strolled through the Mall to Trafalgar Square, circled round via Piccadilly Circus and Leicester Square, and finally wandered down the Strand for a last enchanting eye-full of the floodlit splendour of St Paul's Cathedral, Houses of Parliament and Waterloo Bridge. Then back on what must have been the last 68 bus to Euston Rd which was completely illuminated from end to end with its full pale blue peacetime lighting.[12] And so we came to the end of two perfect days. They couldn't have furnished a happier set of memories to look back on in my old age.

Thursday 10 May Back to work, weary but well content. The transition from total war to partial peace begins in grand style with the scrapping of no less than 84 of the emergency wartime regulations restricting civil liberties, including the iniquitous [Defence Regulation] '18B' that authorised the arrest and imprisonment of suspected persons without trial. A further 25 have been 'modified.' I never realised there were so many! And how pleasant it is to see weather reports and forecasts in the newspapers again. I've missed them.

Saturday 12 May Had our Sunday joint for dinner in evening. Afterwards sallying forth for a stroll through the City – primarily to see the Tower of London floodlit. Also saw, for the first time, Ibex House, where M has been working these last three years as well as the illuminated facades of the Royal Exchange and the Mansion House. Finally to St Paul's for a second and closer view of floodlit dome – and the tube home. Unfortunately had to change at Holborn where the platforms and trains on the Piccadilly Line were so hopelessly overcrowded that there was nothing else for it but to get out and walk, which wasn't so good. For what with M's feet aching and me perspiring profusely from head to foot, we were both in a pretty vile temper by the time we got home.

---

12   Floodlighting of government buildings ceased on 14 May and the Ministry of Fuel and Power decided that the need for continued fuel economy meant that all outdoor decorative and display lighting should cease on 25 May (*The Times*, 26 May).

1945

Luckily M had the good sense to go straight to bed without saying a word and leave me to cool off in silent solitude while I wrote up this page of diary. A case of least said, soonest mended.

Sunday 13 May Down to Surrey for the day. Decided to start our tramp from Box Hill for a change, to which end we caught the train we usually get to Leatherhead – the 10.47 from Waterloo. Might as well have stayed in town and seen the Royal procession to St Paul's for all the pleasure we derived from that uncomfortably wind swept walk, however we did hear Churchill's full-dress broadcast at 9.0. So the day wasn't really wasted. Or was it?

[*Heap attended first nights on the consecutive evenings of 15, 16 and 17 May.*]

Tuesday 22 May The food shortages we've had to endure throughout the last few years show no sign of being alleviated with the restoration of peace on the continent. On the contrary we are now about to have even further cuts made in our meagre ration of meats, fats etc in order to help feed starving Europe. Thus the bacon and lard rations of 4 and 2 ozs respectively are to be reduced to 3 oz and 1 oz and the monthly soup ration cut by one eighth. But who is going to feed starving England when we've carried out this altruistic task? One certainly has to pay dearly for the privilege of winning a war these days! Meanwhile another acute [shortage] of beer. As for clothes, there doesn't seem to be any hope of an adequate supply being forthcoming for several years.

Wednesday 23 May The five year old National Coalition Government came to an end today with the resignation of Churchill – which means the dissolution of Parliament three weeks hence. A newly appointed 'caretaker' government will, however, carry on till the general election is held on July 5. This is unusually the first election we've had since Nov '35 and with its approach the party strife that has merely smouldered throughout the war years, flares up anew. 'Twill be interesting to see whether Churchill's personal popularity is still strong enough to counter the swing to the left that has been going on for some time past and return the Tories to power, or not. It looks like being a very close contest anyway. Mother also officially 'resigned' today – from the Wardens Service. Continues to work afternoons only at offices of National Amalgamated Approved Society for the time being.

Saturday 26 May M goes off to Somerset for three days. Up to Mother's for supper after, then home to read till bed time. Incidentally a vacuum cleaner we ordered from Barker's a week ago and paid £6.7.8 for was duly delivered today. Queer looking contraption. Have no idea how it fits together or works. What's more I don't propose to try and work the thing. Will leave it for M to play with, it's her toy.

Wednesday 30 May Glad to see that the more forthright and outspoken American newspapers are openly attacking Russia's overwhelming and aggressive foreign policy – even to the extent of advocating war against the Bolsheviks to prevent them gaining the complete domination of Europe that they're obviously set on. It's just as well that some reflection of the free presses of the Western democracies has the courage and the sense to make a stand against Red tyranny instead of abjectly crawling to Stalin and his thugs as the governments of both Britain and America are so pathetically prone to do. For, so far as the British press is concerned, only one prominent journalist has the temerity to tell the truth about Russia and that is the intrepid Douglas Reed of the *Sunday Graphic*, whose lone but stimulating voice cries in the Fleet St wilderness weekly against the evils and the growing menace of communism. But what is one such brave spirit against so many mouthpieces of the communist movement from whose small but vociferous ranks most of the staff of the timid Tory papers seem to be recruited!

Thursday 31 May Apparently the French feel they haven't had their fair share of war yet, for they've now started up one of their own in Syria and Lebanon – to which ancient lands they'd promised independence from the mandatory control that had formerly been exercised over them, but finding parting such a sweet sorrow, failed to carry out their good intentions, or themselves, quickly enough. So the native hosts attempt to speed the parting guests, who thereupon proceed to land more troops to uphold the 'honour' of France. Tempers and – c'est la guerre! Just like that!

Friday 1 June Sidelight on Syria. Britain intervenes – France climbs down – the fighting ceases. The war is over! Prospects of our getting another flat are gradually becoming more and more remote now that the evacuees are flocking back to town in their thousands and so putting a terrific premium on the scanty accommodation still available – as well as helping to make the shortage of cigarettes, beer etc in London worse than it is anywhere else. There is a very vague possibility of our obtaining a flat in a house in Oakley Square if ever its owner and sole occupier (Mrs Cuddiford of the Conservative Association) can make up her mind whether to stay on there or sell the place. But we're not banking on it. Meanwhile Rashleigh House and its environs get glummer every day.

Tuesday 5 June The Chancellor of the Exchequer informs us that, taking the 1914 value as equal to 20/- the domestic purchasing power of the £ sterling fell, between 1938 and 1944, from 12/10 to 8/4. The pre-war £ is therefore now worth 13/- if that! If I were a socialist I suppose I should also class Attlee's Election Address as such, but being a diehard Tory, I can of course dismiss it as a piece of Bolshie propaganda!

1945

Friday 8 June In view of the fact that M will be 30 next year, we'll have to make up our minds soon whether we're going to have any children or not. M naturally wants to have at least one. I, on the other hand, have serious doubts as to whether (a) it would be worth all the worry and responsibilities entailed (b) we could really afford it, especially in these difficult times. We would, for instance, need a larger flat and the extra cost of food, clothing, schooling etc. would be a considerable and increasingly heavy strain on my scanty resources. Children are liable to be an expensive luxury, particularly if one possesses other interests outside the home and unless one has plenty of money to devote to their upbringing, I think, apt to be more of a liability than an asset. At the same time I realise that M's future existence is likely to be pretty empty and barren without any children and it would be a shame, be selfish of me, to deny her the chance to fulfil woman's main function in life. It is indeed a hell of a problem. Though not fortunately of so urgent a nature that it can't wait for a few months more for a final decision.

Monday 11 June M's Derby Sweepstake winnings turn out to be not £57 as she'd expected – but only £3.10.0. A slight difference! How many [*sic*] longer is this pampering of servicemen and women at the expense of the sorely tried civilian population going on? With all due respect to the part played by the forces in winning the war, there's no getting away from the fact that the civilians – especially the Londoners – have had to endure much greater privations and hardships in the way of food and clothing shortages as well as be continually subjected to the various forms of air attack. And now in addition to the payment of huge cash gratuity and the issue of complete civilian clothing outfit on demobilisation, the forces are to be given, not only an ordinary civilian clothing book containing coupons for the rest of the current rationing period but a further 90 coupons (as many as we get in two years) on top of that. Meanwhile, we poor un-favoured civilians go about in rags and tatters, wondering where our next [are] coming from! But joking apart, there's nothing fair or equitable about this. It's a downright disgrace.

Friday 15 June Invited to take part in the polling on July 5 and also in the vote counting at the Town Hall, which, in order to allow sufficient time for services votes to come in from overseas, doesn't take place till three weeks later. So I get my chance to get some easy money after all.

Saturday 16 June Round to King's Cross after lunch to collect new ration books and a haircut.

Sunday 17 June Little did I dream as I made my way up to Mother's this morning that I was about to see Ron again for the first time since he migrated to Wolverhampton fifteen months ago. But there he was, newly returned to town on his own and seeking me out at the only address he could remember. Straightaway took him over to the Euston Tavern for a couple of drinks and then, still somewhat stupefied with surprise, brought him back to lunch with us. Pleased though I am to have Ron back in London, I do hope our occasional evenings out together are going to be a bit more convivial than this. If only John could get his discharge soon and join us in those beery perambulations, there's nothing like a threesome or better still a foursome, when it comes to a pub-crawl!

Saturday 23 June And so to Somerset on the newly restored 12.30 from Paddington. It's a boon to be able to travel by the fast direct train again, instead of having to go by that long roundabout route on the 1.15. A bit of a crush at Paddington but not nearly so bad as it was last year. Managed to get seats for the best part of the way and so had a comparatively comfortable journey down. On detraining at Frome, duly found the taxi waiting to waft us out to our rustic retreat, where we arrived in good time round about 3.45 and proceeded to make the best of a good tea.

[*A week's holiday in Somerset.*]

Sunday 1 July Returned to London on the 6.5, and never was I more glad to get back. It's been a most disappointing week. Only two really fine days, the rest varying between wet and unsettled. Not quite as bad as last year but a very 'poor show' nevertheless. Maybe if we go again at same time next year, it will be a case of third time lucky. But I doubt if we shall.

Monday 2 July Back to work just in time to receive appointment to act as poll clerk on Thursday from 7.0 a.m. till 9.0 p.m. at a meeting held in the Assembly Hall during the afternoon. Some three hundred or so present. All men – which apparently accounted for M's offer to serve being rejected. After about twenty minutes explanatory talk by the Town Clerk, we all filed up in order of Polling station number (mine being 66 situated, as luck would have it, in Thanet St School right next to Rashleigh House!), handed over our statutory declaration of secrecy, and received official appointment form. And home to tea, half an hour late. M went to the dentist's. Came home at 9.30 highly elated at having seen and heard her hero, Mr Churchill, speaking at Mornington Crescent, on the way back. How that man thrills her!

Thursday 5 July Election Day Up at 5.0 and at the Town Hall at 6.30 to help carry the ballot boxes round to our polling station at Sandwich St School and got everything ready in time to open at 7.0. Three of us in a room on our own with an election register of 870 voters and a services register of 90 to handle. My particular job for the best part of the day being to enter the electors' numbers, read out to me from the register, on the counterfoils of the ballot papers, tear the papers off and hand them to the presiding officer who, in return, stamps them and hands them to the voters. Simplicity itself! Only had a slow steady stream of voters averaging 30 to 40 an hour to cope with throughout the morning and afternoon. But in the evening the average rose to about 70 an hour and, by the time we closed at 9.0, 587 civilian and 92 service voters (the latter mainly by proxy) had been recorded, roughly two thirds of the register. Incidentally I'd recorded my one Tory vote at another station in another part of the building. After clearing everything up and taking the ballot boxes etc over to the Town Hall with police escort, finally got home for supper at 9.40. It had been a long day's work, 15 hours altogether, including three short breaks for refreshment. Yet the time passed quickly enough. Wasn't exactly an exciting sort of job, but it was certainly an interesting experience and at least a welcome break from the daily routine. And now we've got to wait nearly three weeks for the count to reveal the result of it all. How too, too tantalising!

Sunday 8 July Sweated out to Kew Gardens in afternoon. Wasn't worth it. A dreary and extremely uncomfortable train journey in a stuffy stifling hot compartment crammed with wan women and bawling brats, followed by a tedious trek through the Gardens to the Tea Pavilion. Half an hour's queuing for an indifferent tea. More wandering round the Gardens trying to find some quiet peaceful spot in which to lay and relax. But nowhere could one get away from people – young people, old people, gay people, grim people, American and Canadian soldiers with their doxies, harassed husbands with their wives and families, lovers locked in ecstatic embrace, kids yelling their heads off. Especially the latter. All the children in London seemed to have been brought to Kew today. Crowds, crowds everywhere. Came home on an early train in the hope of avoiding the rush. Though of course we didn't and consequently had to stand most of the way. Just another waste of time and energy.

Thursday 19 July Latest of the ever increasing number of commodities to disappear from the shops is coffee – plentiful enough up till a month or so ago, but now completely impossible to obtain anywhere. Causes of shortage are generally believed to be:

a. The large quantities being smuggled over to Europe for sale at fabulous prices on the continental black market.
b. The considerable hoarding that took place earlier in the year at the reported rumour that coffee was to be rationed.
c. The big demand for the stuff by American and Canadian forces over here.

Whereof it looks as if we'll have to get used to going without our customary afternoon cup for a while.

Monday 23 July Received appointment as Counting Assistant on Wednesday and Thursday, Fee 30/-. Letter from John Hobson. Little to say for himself except how pleased he is to be able to go into beer houses now that the ban on fraternisation had been relaxed, which apparently has also had the odd effect of rendering the frauleins both less desirable and more frigid than hitherto. A case of stolen fruit tasting sweeter.

Wednesday 25 July Round to the [Town Hall] Assembly Hall at 9.0 a.m. for preliminary checking of the service votes in preparation for tomorrow's count. Tables arranged lengthways round three sides of the hall. One set, seating about sixteen of us for each of the three divisions of St Pancras (I was on North). A corresponding number of candidates' agents and scrutinizers sitting on the other side of tables facing us. First of all, had to go down to the basement, get the hundred or so ballot boxes out of the safe and send them up on the canteen lift. Then, on coming back, started to open envelopes containing service postal votes, sort out declarations of Identity and Ballot Papers, compare numbers etc. After that, proceeded to open the ballot boxes, and count the total number of ordinary (white) and proxy (green) ballot papers in each – the latter being subsequently being checked with services list to ensure no duplication with postal votes and afterwards put back with rest of ballot papers for formal sorting and counting. On the morrow, working in pairs we thus disposed of five boxes (with an average of six hundred votes to a box) each, eventually completing the job at 1.45. Until the ballot papers are actually sorted according to the votes cast for the various candidates, it's difficult to tell exactly what the results will be. But from what I saw of them this morning I should be very surprised if the Reds don't romp home in St Pancras. If they fail to, it won't be for any lack of support from the forces who have obviously been badly bitten by the bolshevist bug. At least about 95 per cent of them.

Thursday 26 July And so the fateful day dawned and once more we went our apprehensive way to the Assembly Hall for the final count. Firstly the sorting of the ballot papers into separate piles according to candidates voted for. Secondly the counting and fastening of each pile into bundles of fifty and cross checking thereof. Lastly the checking of the total number of bundles for each candidate and the compilation by the chief counters of the final figures. All of which takes but two hours. At 11.15 the candidates join the Town Clerk on the stage and hear him announce the results. Huge Labour majorities in each division.[13]

---

13   Reflecting the national swing to the left, Labour candidates beat their Unionist (Conservative) opponents in all three St Pancras constituencies. In St Pancras (North), G. House won a majority of 7,630 over the sitting Unionist, Wing Cdr Grant-Ferris; in St Pancras (South-East), Dr S. W. Jeger defeated the sitting Sir Alfred Beit with a 4,710 majority; in St Pancras (South-West), H. Davies won a 3,671 majority over the Unionist Air Commodore L. F. Heald. At the previous (November 1935) election, Unionist candidates held the three seats with majorities of 10,233, 9,380 and 11,223 respectively. In 1945, Unionist candidates just held the two neighbouring constituencies of Hampstead and Holborn, with small majorities of 1,358 and 925 respectively.

1945

Looking like the rest of the candidates – either elated or deflated – the two polling the largest and smallest number of votes make brief speeches then all shake hands and though the curtain come down on this traditional finale, one feels that it ought to, for the drama is over. As the other results begin to come out, it became apparent from the large number of Labour gains that dozens of constituencies had gone the same way as St Pancras – the way to Red ruin. By 2.0 p.m., with two thirds of the results known, it was clear that Labour had swept the country and all was lost. Thereafter it was only a question of how big a majority the new Socialist government would have – the 6.0 radio news ultimately confirming our worst fears by revealing that it was about 150. This evening Churchill handed in his resignation to the King who thereupon sent for Attlee and asked him to form a new government. Needless to say he didn't need asking twice! At 9.0 p.m. with 15 results still to be declared, the state of the parties – Labour 389, Conservatives 197, Liberal Nationals 14, Liberals 10, Others 15.[14]

So now we know the worst, and what an appalling worst it is too. A great triumph for the Reds of course but a terrible calamity for the country. Why, it even made the heavens weep for no sooner had the issue been decided than the heat wave we've had throughout the past week promptly gave way to a heavy fall of cooling rain. I didn't wonder at it. I felt to be weeping myself. To think that England should sink to this!

Friday 27 July As usually happens in General Elections, the number of seats gained by each party is quite out of proportion to the aggregate votes. Thus with approximately 12 million votes for Labour, 9 million for the Conservatives and 2¼ million for the Liberals, the three parties should be represented not by 390, 195 and 10 members respectively, but by approx 310, 290 and 55 with Labour governing by a small clear majority of 25 or so. The only remedy for this anomaly is, I suppose, proportional representation. Unfortunately that is generally considered to be so unsatisfactory a proposition as to be practically impracticable. First inevitable effects of the unexpectedly violent swing to the left have been to create an unfavourable impression in America and cause a slump in the London Stock Exchange. What with the wholesale nationalisation of industry that the new government threatens to carry out, together with the indefinite continuance of wartime controls, the incessant fostering of class hatred, the stamping out of individual enterprise and initiative, the subjugation of everything and everybody to a totalitarian system of state control manipulated by a gigantic army of smug little bureaucrats and a foreign policy dedicated to helping Russia spread communism throughout the world, the next five years

---

14 The final distribution of seats was: Labour 393, Conservative 213, Liberal 12, Communist 2, Common Wealth 1, Others 19.

under Socialist rule look like being even more bleak and grim than the last five years under the stress and strain of war have been. What an abominable age to live in!

Sunday 29 July Even the most wildly imaginative of Hollywood scenario writers never descended to anything quite so melodramatic as the tragedy that occurred in New York yesterday morning when a low-flying bomber crashed into the 98th floor of its tallest skyscraper, the 102 storied, 1,248 feet high Empire State Building, and set ten floors on fire and killed 13 people and injured Lord knows how many more.[15] Something like a sensation!

Tuesday 31 July Riding on buses these days is more enjoyable than it has been at any time during the last five years. For now that all the anti-blast gauze netting has been removed, one can at last see through the windows again. Our latest acquisition – a second hand mahogany dinner wagon, purchased by M from a shop in the city for £5. Surely the sort of thing I'd never have thought of buying myself although I can appreciate its usefulness from the feminine point of view although I must admit it's good value, especially at today's prices.

Friday 3 August Nice to know that about a third of the American forces over here have been transported back to the States or to the Far East during the last three months. Another third will have disappeared by the end of the year, and the rest by next May. Then perhaps London will be itself again.

Monday 6 August Had the rare experience of seeing the dawn break over London between 4.30 and 5.0 this morning whilst watching the police searching the roofs, interiors and backyards of the derelict houses over in Judd St that our windows look out on. Apparently they were after some soldier – a burglar, but though he was spotted by several onlookers in different parts of the block, they never caught him. At least they didn't during the hour and a half we spent watching the chase.

Tuesday 7 August Much ado in the press today about the new 'secret weapon' we're using against the Japs – to wit, the atomic bomb which is alleged to have a destructive power equal to twenty thousand tons of the ordinary high explosive (the equivalent of what would be dropped in five 1,000 plane raids).[16] It is a pity that our scientists can't be as adept

---

15 In low visibility at 09.49 on 28 July, a US Army B–25 Mitchell bomber descending to land at Newark Airport hit the north side of the tower between the 78th and 80th floors, killing its three crew and eleven workers in the building. The fire was extinguished and the building was back in operation two days later.
16 The first atomic bomb was dropped on Hiroshima on 6 August. Three days later a second atomic bomb was dropped on Nagasaki. See I. C. B. Dear (ed.), *The Oxford Companion to the Second World War* (Oxford: Oxford University Press, 1995), pp. 530–531, 773.

at making discoveries that could be put to constructive use by mankind as they are at inventing these diabolical weapons for its destruction.

Thursday 9 August At long last, Russia fulfils her obligation to her Allies by declaring war on Japan. Trust the Bolshevik vulture to be in at the kill for a share of the spoils.

Friday 10 August Japan intimates willingness to accept Allies surrender terms provided 'the Emperor's prerogatives as ruler are not prejudiced'. Whether this condition will be accepted by the Allies remains to be seen. But it certainly looks as if the war is as good as finished. I first heard the glad tidings at the booking office at Paddington, whither I went at lunch time to get our tickets to Somerset. By the time I got back to King's Cross the news was in the papers and all over the town. If it does mean the end of hostilities and, though everyone takes it as a foregone conclusion, it's still a big 'if', then the Far Eastern War will have come to an end much more suddenly than the European War did three months ago. No one expected it quite so soon. Apparently the double blow of the Russian invasion of Manchuria and the dropping of atomic bombs on two of their ports has proved too much for the Japs. Well there it is, we just didn't know where we stand at the moment. The chances are ten to one on peace. I am very loath to leave London and thereby risk missing the Victory celebrations. In fact it's a damned nuisance this happening just now when everything arranged so well for our holiday, even the weather, after behaving badly all the week, proved to be good for the next few days. But in the absence of anything definite to work on, there is really nothing else for it but to go ahead with our plans as if nothing had happened and hope for the best. My heart, however, will stay behind in London.

Saturday 11 August After crawling and squeezing our way through the Paddington queues and crushes, just managed to catch the 12.30 with five minutes to spare – miracle of miracles – secured two seats thereon. Arrived at Frome 3.30. No taxi waiting for us. Phoned garage. No reply. Phoned up more garages with same result. At the fourth attempt however we struck lucky and at long last our saviour came along to the station and drove us to our destination. For which service he charged us double the normal fare – to wit 10/-. Still, in the circumstances we were thankful enough to get a taxi even at that price. Spent the evening sitting out in the orchard reading and wandering round the neighbourhood with Charles and M who [i.e. Charles] is also down here for four days leave. And surprisingly enough on the wagon. According to the 6.0 radio news, the Allies have replied to the Japs' offer of conditional surrender with a series of proposals for them to accept or reject. Wonder how long this game will be kept up.

Wednesday 15 August The Japs having at last made up their minds to accept our surrender terms, the war is now finally over and, for the first time for a decade or more peace prevails throughout the world. It scarcely seems possible! Apparently the news was broadcast by Attlee at midnight – about an hour after we'd gone to bed. Consequently we didn't know anything about it till early this morning. As soon as we heard, however, that today and tomorrow were to be the long-awaited 'VJ' Days (Public holidays celebrating Victory over Japan) we immediately decided to dash up to London for the celebrations [and] arrange to have next Monday and Tuesday off in lieu of the two VJ Days and return to Somerset for a further five days holiday on the morrow. A crazy whim and an expensive one to boot, but I couldn't stay away from London – least of all on a remote farm 111 miles from it on this day of days.

Caught the 7.20 train to London. Arrived at Paddington at 11.15 and after hurrying home for some lunch, got out on a preliminary tour of the West End. Not quite so thrilling as we expected. The expected crowds gathered en mass in Trafalgar Square, Piccadilly Circus and Buckingham Palace listening to the tinned music emanating from loudspeakers. But otherwise the rejoicing seemed rather subdued. Just thousands of weary looking people wandering round the streets or sprawling on the grass in the parks. Began to wonder whether it was worth it – especially as we seemed to have missed all the pageantry through not being around in the morning when the King and Queen had driven to Westminster for the State Opening of Parliament (what a dash!). Still, it was at least reasonably fine in the afternoon – and even better in the evening, whereas in the morning it had been pouring with rain. So, on that dubiously consoling thought, we came home to have some tea and rest our weary limbs 'ere embarking on the evening excursion.

Had to walk there and back this time, but as it turned out to be so much more lively and jubilant a jaunt than the afternoon one, we didn't mind that so much. We waited among the multitude outside Buckingham Palace to hear the King's Broadcast Speech and see the Royal Family appear on the balcony afterwards. We stood among the crowd in Whitehall and saw Attlee, Morrison and Bevin on the balcony of the Ministry of Health building, though we couldn't hear what the former was saying as his speech was continually drowned by shouts of 'We want Churchill' (whom we had both seen and heard from the same balcony on that other memorable night three months ago). We saw the floodlighting, we saw the fireworks, we saw the town literally and figuratively lit up – despite the deplorable dearth of drink – as it's rarely been lit up before. In fact we saw just about everything there was to be seen in the West End. And it was all well worth seeing – even 'coming up from Somerset.' So far as revelling by night was concerned, VE day had nothing on VJ day. It was London with the lid off! To bed at 1.15 'whacked to the wide.'[17]

Thursday 16 August Disconcerted to discover that a rash has broken out all over my legs and stomach. Have no idea what these large pink spots signify, but in the hope that it's nothing more serious than heat rash, am treating it with calamine lotion. Felt highly embarrassed when we ran into Phil Smart this morning on our way to Paddington. For, clad as I was in my oldest and shabbiest sports coat and flannels and dirty frayed sports shirt, I was looking anything but smart! And how could I explain that I'd set out from Somerset in a heavy downpour with these unsightly rags hidden under a presentable mackintosh that I expected I'd have to wear till I got back! Fortunately though we didn't have much time to spare, so after a quick drink in the Dolphin, we were able to dash off to catch the 12.30, which was quite a relief. I was however very sorry to hear from Phil that Alby Holmes, one of our erstwhile mutual friends, had been killed in Germany a week before VE Day. He was a decent, easy going good hearted fellow and I shall always remember how, at his wedding party in Nov '39, I came to enjoy my one and only experience of being blind drunk – in other words, flat out. Fortunately he little realised what a dirty trick fate was to play on him five and half years later. Arrived at Frome a quarter of an hour behind time. Just as well really as we still had to wait three quarters of an hour for the 4.15 flyer to Nunney and there's no deadlier way of filling time than wandering as we did – especially on early closing day. Never was I more thankful to behold Bangle Farm that I was at 4.50 today.

[*A further five nights in Somerset.*]

Tuesday 21 August Up betimes and off to Frome by taxi to catch the 10.30 back to London. Much to our surprise we managed to get another taxi home from Paddington.

Wednesday 22 August Back to work in the morning and back to the West End in the evening for the first night of Noel Coward's *Sigh No More* at the Piccadilly.

Saturday 25 August Charles and his beloved Lois duly arrive at 3.45 to spend the weekend with us. The latter who for some obscure reason prefers to be known as Audrey, turns out to be a plump little blonde, vivacious, talkative, sociable, and though far from being a beauty, reasonably good looking. Certainly easy to get on with and, I should imagine, to get off with!

---

17   Although some public buildings were illuminated, *The Times* (16 August) reported 'a sad lack of some official mark of a notable day' to supplement London's 'street revelry, flags, church bells, whistles, hooters, fireworks, music and singing'.

Part Two

Friday 31 August What with our meagre rations being continually reduced, beer and cigarettes being increasingly difficult to come by, food and fuel supplies getting smaller – and now a 25% cut in clothing coupons and an acute shortage of soup, it's difficult to see what material advantage peace has brought us. Needless to say no government spokesman attempts to give any explanation for this dire and distressing state of affairs!

RETROSPECT – 1945[18]

1945 was rather a paradox, and not a particularly amusing one at that for though it saw the end of the war against Germany and Japan and was, therefore, a year of jubilation and rejoicing, it was also, in so far as the aftermath of the war proved to be a bitter disillusionment, a year of depression and despondency. Thus no sooner did we awake from the six years nightmare of war and feel free to enjoy life once more, than the means to do so immediately became even scantier than they had been during the war. Housing, food, clothing, fuel, beer, tobacco – the ordinary comforts of life we'd taken for granted before the war and naturally expected to become more plentiful again when it ended, became instead more and more scarce and difficult to come by.

And so we proceeded to eke out a bare and frugal existence as best we could. It wouldn't have been so bad if we'd at least had some hope for the future. But there was none. With a Labour government coming into power and communism spreading like wildfire all over the world, things could only go from bad to worse. In the meantime prices and taxes stayed up, while incomes stayed down. Even the weather had to be about as miserable and wretched as it possibly could be and, as usual, to do its damnedest to spoil our two weeks holiday in Somerset.

Without getting any further increase in salary, I continued to hold my job at the Town Hall, and, in view of the imminent discharge of the pre-war staff from the forces, to wonder how much longer I would do so. Which, together with the prospect of M giving up her job in the near future and our inability to obtain a better flat in more congenial surroundings, all helped to make the outlook grimmer still.

I did, however, get through the year without breaking into my little bit of capital. In fact, despite the expenditure of some £13 on clothes and a further £15 on household requisites such as an electric iron, vacuum cleaner, dinner wagon and knives, I actually contrived to increase it by a few pounds and thus end the year with a total of £210 invested in Savings Certificates and Savings Bank, £125 cash in hand, £61 in the Superannuation Fund and £55 worth of Income Tax Post-War Credits.

18 Covering the whole of 1945.

1945

First nights, films and books remain my chief means of escape from the bleak reality of the Brave New World. In all I did 48 theatres, saw 50 films and read 35 books – about the same number of theatre, twice as many films and three quarters as many books as last year. Not bad averages on the whole. Though I must confess that I spent more money on theatres than I have ever done before. Not from choice but from necessity. For, like everything else, the prices of theatre seats went up by leaps and bounds.

I didn't suffer from such a lamentable lack of male company as I did during the previous year. For in the summer Ron returned to London once more and settled down in Thornton Heath in close proximity to my old boon companion, Bill Coulbourne, with whom I thereby came in contact again, after a lapse of nearly six years in our long association. Thus it came to pass that I saw almost as much of those two unreliable rogues, Bill and Ron during the last quarter of this year than I did of that most constant and staunch of friends, John Hobson, throughout the whole of 1945, which, apart from two short leaves, he spent entirely in Holland and Germany. John Bell we neither saw nor heard from – until Christmas when after nearly two years silence, news of his imminent homecoming and demobilisation blew in from Bombay.

My health gave me no undue cause for concern or anxiety. For the second year running I cheerfully endured the discomfort of wearing a Brook's rupture appliance, until with the war over and a rupture therefore no longer a useful thing to possess, I duly went into the Homeopathic Hospital in December and had an operation for its repair – from which I am still recovering. In two or three weeks' time, however, I should, all being well, be really fit again for the first time since '39.

So at least I've got something to look forward to in 1946. Alas, there isn't much else. I ought, I suppose, to still feel thankful I'm alive and have come through the war without injury or mishap or being forced into the forces. But I can't go on feeling thankful for ever – not in that negative sense anyway – and when peace proves to be so much more irksome and much less exciting than war – one has precious little reason to do so.

On that appropriately dismal note then, I hasten to bring this solemn summing up of this depressing year to a close. Depressing is scarcely the sort of epithet one would expect to apply to the last year of war and the first year of peace. Nevertheless there's no other that suits 1945 half so well – unless it is disappointing. I can remember few years I've been happier to see the end of.

EPILOGUE

This volume closes at the end of the final month of the war but Anthony Heap continued writing his daily diary entries for a further forty years – until some thirty-six hours before his death, at the age of seventy-five, in October 1985. Unfortunately, post-war life brought little improvement in the Heap family's wellbeing or their enjoyment of peace. Following their decision to delay starting a family until the international situation improved, Marjorie had their only child, Anthony Charles, at a private maternity home in Hampstead in 1949, just as the Cold War was developing. Heap continued working in the Borough Treasurer's Department of St Pancras (from 1974 Camden) Council, becoming 'established' (i.e. pensionable) in 1947. But with Marjorie unable to hold down even a part-time clerical job, he recorded in 1950 that they were 'perpetually hard up'. By working overtime and economising whenever possible, he was able to send young Anthony Charles to a private nursery and then to a Montessori school, before the boy passed the 11-plus examination and moved up to St Marylebone Grammar School.

In 1957, the family moved across the top floor of Rashleigh House to a three-roomed flat where the then eight-year-old Anthony Charles occupied his own bedroom, remaining there when he started his own clerical career and later joined the civil service. Unable to afford or find a better or larger flat, Heap and Marjorie continued living on the sixth floor of Rashleigh House, without a lift, until 1971, when the then twenty-two-year-old Anthony Charles moved out and Heap bought a smaller flat back in Queen Alexandra Mansions. He retired from the Council in 1975 to work part-time for three (and then two) days a week book-keeping for a local businessman friend. He spent his non-working winter days reading theatre-related articles at the Colindale Newspaper Library or occasionally attending the public gallery at the Old Bailey. In the summer months, he took long bus rides around and out of London and occasional longer day trips to the seaside.

Overall Heap's was not a happy or cosy life as it became dominated by the understandable 'stress and strain' of Marjorie's deteriorating mental condition and his responsibilities as a virtual single parent. Having shown signs of depression and suffering 'moods' before their marriage, Marjorie could not settle in jobs and, by 1953, she was 'hearing voices' and becoming violent. When she threw pots and pans into the street six floors below, the police were called and she voluntarily entered a mental hospital. Later, having insisted on returning home, she soon had to be returned compulsorily to hospital. This cycle of alternating periods in hospital and home continued. For Heap, 1956 opened with her 'sudden new manifestation of persecution by television mania symptoms only two months after her discharge'.[1] He nevertheless bought a television set at Christmas 1956 and this provided another medium whose artistic productions he could criticise at length in his diary entries.

Marjorie continued to decline and in 1958 Heap recorded:

> Without a doubt, the unhappiest and most calamitous year of my life so far. I shall remember it mainly for three misfortunes. First, and most distressing of all, the death of my beloved mother. Then the fire that [young] Anthony accidentally started in the kitchen one afternoon, and finally two months later, the sudden disappearance of Marjorie from home, which would appear to be a case of desertion. Though whether this was a misfortune or a piece of good fortune for me is a point on which I'm still not quite clear in my mind. Coming as it did after five years of desperately unhappy home life, with Marjorie continually in and out of hospital with her mental illness, the break was, and still seems, something of a relief. Nevertheless I still have lingering doubts as to whether I'll be happier in the long run or not.[2]

In April 1959, Heap found:

> a letter from Marjorie on my desk at the office this morning – the first I've had from her since she disappeared nine months ago. Written from Horton Hospital, Epsom,[3] she says she 'left the flat because of the voices and found my way here.' She had written to the Town Hall because she couldn't remember the Rashleigh House address and would I go down and see her on Sunday?
>
> Found her looking fairly ghastly – straight short hair, no front teeth (she's lost her denture long since), no make-up and much thinner, as well she might be considering what she's been through. It seems that for four or five months after she left home she led a tramp-like existence, begging for coppers, living on tea and buns, sleeping on Embankment or park benches in the afternoon and roaming around at night, until one evening early in December she'd struck a railway official who'd accused her of begging in

---

[1] This is Heap's description of her apparent psychosis (Retrospect for 1956).
[2] Retrospect for 1958.
[3] Opened in 1902, Horton Hospital was the second of the London County asylums in the Epsom cluster built by the LCC on 88 acres at Long Grove Road, Epsom. In 1956 it had 1,554 patients. See 'Lost Hospitals of London', http://ezitis.myzen.co.uk/horton.html (last accessed 9 May 2017).

Epilogue

Charing Cross Station buffet. Charged with assault and sent to Broadmoor where she'd promptly gone into the hospital, stayed there over Christmas, been certified and sent down to Horton – all the while calling herself Mrs Heatley [her maiden name].[4]

In that year's 'Retrospect' he recorded:

> Marjorie came back into our lives after nine months absence, half the time wandering round London like a tramp, the rest in an Epsom mental hospital whence somewhat to our regret she was transferred to Friern in July, there to remain for the rest of the year. I've abandoned all hope that I will ever resume a normal married life with her again. It's a depressing thought that I shall probably have to spend every Sunday afternoon for the rest of my life – or as long as poor Marjorie lives – visiting her in grim mental hospitals. Yet I dread the possibility of her being discharged from hospital and coming home even more. So I continue to bring Anthony up on my own which, though hard going at times, is a true labour of love. I wouldn't be without him for the world and only regret is that he's growing up so quickly. I shall be a lonely soul indeed when I no longer have the cheerful company of a young son to console me for my marital misfortunes.

Marjorie was transferred to the dismal but more local Friern Barnet mental hospital, where she remained for eight years, Heap making dreary Sunday afternoon visits and caring for their son. Each year he took the boy on summer holiday coach trips around the British Isles and on occasional day trips to seaside resorts. After some years, Marjorie was allowed to make home visits and was eventually 'returned to the community' to spend hours each day in a variety of day care centres. Their family life was never recaptured and Heap lived a bachelor existence. Only once did he mention a relationship with another woman, when, in 1971:

> on a six day coach tour of Ireland I got to know and became attached to a certain likewise not too happily married, theatre loving lady and so, for a month or two after, [I] found life even more frustrating and melancholy than usual.[5]

He terminated the relationship but kept that unnamed lady's final letter to him tucked inside the covers of that year's diary.

The later diaries show that Heap retained his right-wing political views, although these wavered when the Conservative Rent Act decontrolled rents so that his payments more than doubled in 1957. He tried to attend a weekly beer drinking session with friends but,

---

4 Entry for 14 April 1959.
5 Retrospect for 1971.

Epilogue

from 1964, he suffered with arthritis – 'the curse of my old age' – and eventually with tinnitus. Nevertheless he got out of the flat as much as possible, greeting the result of the May 1979 General Election by recording:

> Attended the Thorpe trial at the Old Bailey No. 1 Court.[6] The outcome of the General Election is a Tory overall majority of 43. The state of the parties is: Conservative 339, Labour 268, Liberal 11, Ulster Unionist 9, Scottish and Welsh Nationalists 4 (two each) and Others 3.[7] Margaret Thatcher therefore becomes Britain's first woman Prime Minister. To my mind, it's not a job for a woman, but if there has to be one, then it's as well she should be as good looking and right wing as the radical and glamorous Maggie – as the popular press familiarly calls her.[8]

With all his domestic worries, Heap found some relief in keeping up his regular theatre first-nighting at roughly his high pre-war level until the 1970s, when his visits fell to about fifty a year. He maintained his frequent cinema visits and, in 1968, he took up opera-going. His amateur theatrical criticism peaked in 1970, when, having attended the preview of the semi-pornographic *Oh! Calcutta!* at the Round House, Chalk Farm Road, NW1, his comments of disgust on leaving the theatre were recorded and broadcast next morning in the BBC Radio *Today* programme. He subsequently complained to the police and his letter was one of the four passed to the Director of Public Prosecutions, who eventually 'considered that there was very little chance of a successful prosecution for obscenity'. This was accepted by the Attorney General so no action resulted.[9]

By 1981 Heap's first-nighting had declined to some thirty visits in the year, and on 30 December 1982 he recorded that 'My theatre and film going continues to dwindle. The theatre, alas, is not what it used to be. And neither, I suppose, am I.' On 29 October 1985, two days before he died of acute cardiac failure in University College Hospital, he ended his final diary entry with his criticism of that evening's production of *Camille*:

---

6   Jeremy Thorpe MP (1929–2014) was leader of the Liberal Party from 1967 until 1976, when he resigned as strengthening rumours of a homosexual relationship brought embarrassment to the Party. In 1975 he was charged (with others) with a related conspiracy to murder, but all the defendants were acquitted after a six-week trial.
7   The final result was: Conservative 339, Labour 269, Liberal 11, Scottish and Welsh Nationalists 4 (2 each) and Others 12.
8   Entry for 4 May 1979.
9   See Robin Woolven, '"A Tendency to Deprave or Corrupt in Chalk Farm?" A Camden Resident and *Oh! Calcutta!* at the Round House, July 1970', *Camden History Review*, No. 38 (2014), pp. 21–26.

Epilogue

Pam Gem's new version, much praised (God knows why!) when presented by the Royal Shakespeare Company of *The Lady of the Camellias*. Definitely not for the sentimental, old fashioned likes of me.

Marjorie Heap lived on for another ten years and died in a Camden council old people's home in Gospel Oak in 1995. Their son, Anthony Charles, who for some reason, had changed his surname to O'Connell by the time he registered his father's death, duly executed Anthony Heap's will and donated all fifty-six diary volumes to the British Records Association to be archived for posterity.

APPENDIX A: PRINCIPAL PERSONS MENTIONED IN THE DIARY

Beatrice (Trixie): Surname unknown, but possibly Cole. Heap's girlfriend 1932–1933.

Bell, John: One of Heap's three lifelong friends and regular drinking companions. Served in the Royal Navy during the war.

Bill: *See* **Colbourne, Bill or Redfern, Bill.**

Chamberlain, 'Tiny': Senior member of the Holborn Rovers.

Cherub: Real name unknown. Senior member of the Holborn Rovers.

Colbourne, Bill: One of Heap's three lifelong friends and drinking companions. Married to Margaret (Peggy).

de Hegedus, Adam (1906–1958): Hungarian intellectual, author and member of the Holborn Rovers. Became a British citizen in 1935.

Ellaine: Surname unknown, possibly Gaston. From Welwyn Garden City. Employee of Peter Robinson's Department Store on Oxford Circus until 1940. Despite being a married woman with two children, had an affair with Heap for some months in 1940, before returning to her husband.

Gus (surname unknown): Heap's friend. Became a merchant seaman and was lost at sea in 1941.

Heap, Anthony (1910–1985): *See* Introduction for his biography.

Heap, Anthony Charles (b. 1949): Only child of Anthony and Marjorie Heap.

Heap, Fred (1878–1933): Heap's father. Dentist who lived and practised in rooms at 139 Gray's Inn Road from at least 1922. Took his own life in March 1933, owing to severe financial problems.

Heap, Emily (1881–1958): Real name **Emily Louisa Shepherd** (she and Fred Heap never married). Heap's mother. Worked as Fred Heap's dental nurse and kept house for the family.

Heap, Marjorie, née Heatley (1916–1995): Heap's wife. Daughter of an Australian dentist and a mother who lived on a farm in Somerset. Worked in the Highgate First Aid Post, where she met Heap in the summer of 1941. Generally referred to as 'M' in the diary.

Heatley, Charles: Marjorie Heap's younger brother. Served in the Royal Navy 1942–1948 and was later commissioned. Married Audrey in 1945.

Hobson, John: One of 'the two Johns' in the diary and one of Heap's three lifelong friends and regular drinking companions. Post Office telecommunications

Appendix A

engineer. Spent four years in the Army during the war as a sapper, serving in North Africa, Italy and north-west Europe.

Holmes, Alby: Camping friend of Heap's and one of the 'Robin Hood' crowd. Died June 1945, while serving in the Army in Europe.

Kaye, Bunny: Senior member of the Holborn Rovers.

MacLavey/McLavey family: Residents of the basement flat at 20 Harrington Square when Heap and his mother lived in the top-floor flat (1934–1937).

MacLavey, Bernie (b. 1931): One of the MacLavey family. Looked after from 1936 by Heap's mother.

Morris, Norah: Civil servant whom Heap met in 1933. Rejected Heap's offer of marriage in 1940.

Nigger (c.1927–1938): Heap family's much-loved black dog. Daily walked by Heap around the streets and on Hampstead Heath and Primrose Hill.

Reader, Ralph CBE (1903–1982): Choreographer and theatrical producer. Started the Boy Scouts' annual *Gang Show* in 1932. Member of the Holborn Rovers and a long-term friend of Heap's.

Redfern (Ewart) 'Bill': One of Heap's occasional drinking friends. Associate of the Royal Institute of British Architects.

Reynolds, 'Joshua': Member of the Holborn Rovers.

Ron: Surname unknown. Somewhat unreliable drinking friend of Heap's. Appeared irregularly in London when between jobs and houses in Wales and the home counties.

Shelmerdine: Surname unknown. Heap's girlfriend 1931.

Shepherd, Emily: *See* Heap, Emily.

Shepherd, Fred: Heap's mother's brother; husband of Aunt Minnie and father of Mary and Jack. Lived in Walthamstow and then Forest Gate.

Shepherd, Pop (d. 1959): Heap's mother's elder sister. Moved to America 1931.

Smart, Phil and Kath: Married couple living in Muswell Hill. Heap frequently spent camping weekends with them at a farm in south-east Hertfordshire.

Sperni, John, Senior (1887–1966): Originally **Giovanni Celeste Geraldermo Sperni**. Leading member of the Italian community in Clerkenwell. Mayor of St Pancras 1937–1938. Had two families in London and owned several substantial properties in Bloomsbury.

Sperni, John, Junior (c.1910–1993): Known as 'Little Johnny'. School friend of Heap's. Left London for Rome in 1940, later broadcasting on Rome Radio. Known as 'The Italian Haw Haw'.

Sprackton, Lilian: Heap's girlfriend 1933–1934.

Zelger, Mrs: Friend of Heap's mother. Lived in rooms above those rented by the Heap family at 139 Gray's Inn Road.

APPENDIX B: ANTHONY HEAP'S ANNUAL CULTURE CAPTURE JANUARY 1930–AUGUST 1945

To publish Anthony Heap's diaries without making proper mention of his primary hobbies of theatre 'first nighting', cinema-going and reading would do him an injustice. His long theatrical, film and book criticisms have been omitted from this volume but these annual tables illustrate the range and depth of his interests. They do not include the talks Heap attended or the radio programmes – including Promenade concerts, other music, plays and talks – he listened to. Each listing gives the date, the title, the theatre or cinema (or the author of the book) and any particular comments that Heap made.

The tables have been drawn up from his diary entries, which do not always agree with the totals that Heap sometimes claimed in his annual 'Retrospects'. Another source of discrepancy is that the number of films seen is not necessarily the numbers here tabulated, as most cinemas presented a 'second feature' with their main attraction and the tables generally record only the latter. Theatre, film and social historians seeking more detail can read his theatre, film and literary criticisms in the original volumes of the diary in the London Metropolitan Archives.

Appendix B

Culture Capture 1930 – from Heap's Pocket Diary (not included in this volume)

		Theatre Visits		*Cinema Visits*
January	4	*Pygmalion*/Court	3	*This and That*/Regent
	8	*Man and Superman*/Court		
	11	*French Leave*/Vaudeville	12	[film not identified]/Regent
	17	*The Doctor's Dilemma*/Court		
	18	*The Last Enemy*/Fortune		
	20	*The Philanderer*/Court		
	22	*Darling I Love You*/Fortune		
	23	*The Way Out*/Comedy	28	*Paris*/New Gallery – Jack Buchanan talkie
February	18	*A Night Like This*/Aldwych – farce		
	22	*Silver Wings*/Dominion – rotten show		
	25	*Paris*/Garrick	27	*The Last of Mrs Cheney*/Regent
March	1	*Here Comes the Bride*/Piccadilly		
	8	*The Lady of the Camellias*/Garrick		
	13	*Honours Easy*/St Martin's		
	15	*Appearances*/Royalty		
	22	*A Warm Corner*/Prince's		
	29	*The Three Musketeers*/Drury Lane		

Culture Capture

		Theatre Visits		*Cinema Visits*
April	5	On the Foot/Wyndham's		
	17	Cochran's 1930 Revue/Wyndham's		
	19	Suspense/Duke of York's		
	21	Silver Wings/Globe	26	*The Green Goddess*/Marble Arch Pavilion – equipment broke
			29	*The Green Goddess*/Marble Arch Pavilion – readmission
May	3	Heads Up/Prince Edward		
	20	The Beggar's Opera/Lyric, Hammersmith		
	22	Trelawney of the Wells/Cripplegate Theatre		
June		Continental camping holiday 2–18 June]		
	28	The Way to Treat a Woman/ Duke of York's		
July	18	The Silent Witness/Comedy		
	19	Sons O'Guns/Hippodrome		
	20	Here Comes the Bride/Lyceum		
August	13	The Gondoliers/Kings, Hammersmith	6	*Raffles*/Tivoli
September	27	The Barretts of Wimpole Street/Queen's		
October	4	The Breadwinner/Vaudeville		
	7	Dear Brutus/Cripplegate Theatre	11	*Eldorado*/Daly's – good show
	18	It's a Boy/Strand		
	25	Leave it to Psmith/Shaftesbury		

Appendix B

		Theatre Visits		*Cinema Visits*	
November	8	The Grain of Mustard/Ambassador's		Sleeping Partners/Bloomsbury	1
	22	Little Tommy Tucker/Daly's		Disraeli/Madame Tussaud's Kinema	15
	29	Oh Daddy/Prince's – good show, full house		Bolachova(?)/King's Cross Kinema	30
December	4	It's a Boy/Strand [2nd visit]			
	6	A Murder Has Been Arranged/St James's – clever play		[film not identified]/King's Cross Kinema	7
	13	Wonder Bar/Savoy – good show		[films not identified]/Tussaud's Kinema – rotten films	14
	16	[Variety show]/Palladium – with ten office chaps			
	20	Ever Green/Adelphi (new) – 5/9 seat!			
	23	Smoky Cell/Wyndham's			
	26	Robinson Crusoe/Lyceum – good panto, balcony seat			
Totals		**44**		12	

Recorded Culture Capture 1931

		Theatre Visits		Cinema Visits	Books Read
January	3	*The Private Secretary*/Apollo – 80s' farce	4	*Song O'My Heart*/Trocadero Elephant & Castle	*Man of Property*/ Galsworthy
	10	*Folly to Be Wise*/Piccadilly – Cicily Courtneidge			
	17	*Song of the Drum*/Drury Lane – Ralph Reader			
	24	*The Improper Duchess*/Globe – comedy			
	31	*The Blue Rose*/Gaiety – musical comedy			
February	7	*Tantivy Towers*/Lyric, Hammersmith	1	*The Bad One*/Trocadero E&C – not bad tripe!	
	14	*The Silver Box*/Fortune (People's) – Galsworthy	8	*The High Road*/Trocadero E&C – Lonsdale play	
			21	[film not identified]/Tatler Cinema Charing X Rd – first visit	
March	7	*The Circle*/Vaudeville – good typical Maugham	1	*Monte Carlo*/Carlton – excellent Buchanan film	
	13	*Stand Up and Sing*/Hippodrome – new Buchanan musical			
	21	*Cochran's 1931 Revue*/Pavilion – very good			
	28	*Chauve-Souris*/Cambridge			

517

Appendix B

		Theatre Visits	**Cinema Visits**	**Books Read**
April	3	Paris Revue/Casino de Paris – spectacular!		
	4	Revue/Folies Bergère, Paris		
	5	Faust/Paris Opera – great show, house packed		
	8	The Perfect Command/Players		
	11	White Horse Inn/Coliseum – a magnificent spectacle		
	18		The Devil To Pay/New Victoria	
	25	Bitter Sweet/Lyceum – not so good as before		
May	2	London Wall/Duke of York's – entertaining		
	8		Le Million/Phoenix – very good	
	9	Land of Smiles/Drury Lane – Richard Tauber		
	10		The Front Page/Tivoli	
	10	The Good Companions/His Majesty's – Priestley		
	23	Autumn Crocus/Lyric – dragged a little		
	23		The Big Pond/Euston Cinema – very good	
June	13	The Millionaire Kid/Gaiety – good dancing tuneful music		
	15	The Shops/Fortune – a fine St John Ervine play		
	17		A Yankee at King Arthur's Court/Regal	
	18	Lean Harvest/St Martin's – brilliant and well-acted		
	20		The Millionaire/New Victoria – George Arliss	
	23	After All/Criterion – not greatly to my liking		

518

Culture Capture

	Theatre Visits		Cinema Visits		Books Read
June	26	Turkey Time/Aldwych – the latest farce			
	30	Late Night Final/Phoenix – with revolving stage			30 The White Monkey/Galsworthy
July			7	Passion House/Bloomsbury – awful tripe	
	10	Nina Rosa/Lyceum	15	Lin Takes a Holiday/Stoll – good	16 To Let/Galsworthy
	25	Old Man/Lyceum – Edgar Wallace, satisfactory	18	Dirigible/Tivoli – very good film	
			26	Grumpy/?	
			27	These Charming People/Plaza	21 London Venture/Michael Arlen
August		[Holiday in Switzerland 28 July–9 August]			
	10	The Hour Glass/Victoria Palace	13	On Approval/Regent	
	14	The Midshipmist/Shaftesbury – musical comedy	15	Jenny Lind/Trocadero	
	18	Waltzes from Vienna/? – colour, charm and melody	16	My Wife's Family/Dominion – good for a Sunday show	
	20	The Case of a Frightened Lady/Wyndham's – Wallace's best form	25	Inspiration/The Cinema House – Garbo	

Appendix B

	Theatre Visits		Cinema Visits		Books Read
	28	Take a Chance/Whitehall – an amusing trifle			16 Swan Song/Galsworthy
September	1	Those Naughty Nineties/Criterion – mildly amusing			
	3	The Counsel's Opinion/Strand – smart and clever	5	The Secret Sax/Empire – American gangsters	
	8	Grand Hotel/Adelphi – novel with revolving stage			14 Peacock's English Essays
	26	The Old Bachelor/Lyric, Hammersmith – Congreve			
	30	Victoria and Her Hussar/Palace			
October	2	Elizabeth of England/Cambridge – fine historical play	3	Reaching the Moon/Regal – disappointing	
	10	The Queen's Husband/Ambassador's – comedy	4	Hell's Angels/King's Cross Kinema – a fine film, an epic of the air	
	14	For the Love of Mike/Saville – mild farce	18	My Post/Trocadero – awful tripe!	16 Piracy/Michael Arlen
	17	Cavalcade/Drury Lane – Coward's new spectacular			
	21	Suspense/Lyceum			

520

Culture Capture

	Theatre Visits		Cinema Visits		Books Read
	22	*Taming of the Shrew*/Sadler's Wells – now a smart and modern theatre	24	*Trader Horn*/Stoll	
November	7	*Lady in Waiting*/St Martin's – amusing enough			10 *Cakes and Ale*/Maugham
	18	*A Midsummer Night's Dream*/Sadler's Wells	25	*The Smiling Lieutenant*/Stoll – M. Chevalier	23 *Lily Christine*/Michael Arden
	28	*And So to Bed*/Globe – very clever play			24 *On Forsyte 'Change*/Galsworthy
					26 *The Magician*/Maugham
December	21	*The Nelson Touch*/St Martin's – political satire	3	*Man of Mayfair*/Carlton – a very good Jack Buchanan film	7 *Ashenden*/Somerset Maugham
			17	*Congress Dancers*/Tivoli – satirical and ingenious	18 *Men Dislike Women*/Michael Arlen
			31	*Daddy Long Legs*/Stoll	25 *Five Tales*/John Galsworthy
					28 *Twelve Tales*/Gilbert Frankau
					30 *Dance Little Gentlemen*/Gilbert Frankau
Totals	**49**		**29**		**16**

Appendix B

Recorded Culture Capture 1932

		Theatre Visits		Cinema Visits		Books Read
January	6	The Gay Adventure/Whitehall – smart comedy	2	Sunshine Susie/Capitol – the best English talkie yet	2	Dance, Little Gentleman/Gilbert Frankau
	13	Bow Bells/Hippodrome – many new mechanical devices, dances by Ralph Reader	21	The Blue Danube/Tivoli	2	Angel Pavement/J. B. Priestley
			30	The Cheat and Playing the Game/Carlton – Tallulah Bankhead	15	Martin Make-Believe/Gilbert Frankau
					20	Gerald Cranston's Lady/Gilbert Frankau
February	11	Julius Caesar/His Majesty's (7th time)			12	Masterson/Frankau
	13	It's A Girl/Strand – successful farce				
	16	Julius Caesar/Sadler's Wells (6th time of seeing)	20	Broadminded/Bloomsbury Cinema		
	18	The Green Pack/Wyndham's – Edgar Wallace	24	Merely Mary Ann/Stoll	25	Reflections of a Financier/Otto Kahn
March	1	Helen/Adelphi – Cochran's latest splendid achievement				
	9	Fruit/Sadler's Wells – perfect singing				

Culture Capture

	Theatre Visits		Cinema Visits		Books Read
	12	Cat and the Fiddle/Palace	19	A Nous Liberté/Rialto – a most entertaining film	3	The Contemporary Theatre/Agate
	23	While Parents Sleep/Royalty – an amusing comedy			8	Who's Who/Hannen Swaffer
	26	A Mixed Grill/Theatre Royal, Guildford – pitifully bad variety show				
	31	I Lived With You/Prince of Wales – Ivor Novello				
April	5	Precious Bane/St Martin's – a play for serious playgoers	3	Goodnight Vienna/Capitol – Jack Buchanan	2	The Romance of Great Businesses/?
	12	Can the Leopard?/Haymarket – as silly as I've seen				
	16	The Miracle/Lyceum – spectacular	17	The Silent Voice/Pavilion – George Arliss		
	19	Vile Bodies/Vaudeville – Evelyn Waugh adaption			21	Candida/G. B. Shaw
	23	Napoleon/New – historical play	30	Lily Christine/Plaza – from Michael Arlen's novel		
May	2	Musical Chorus/Criterion – dreary and repulsive			2	Man and Superman/G. B. Shaw
	7	Heartbreak House/Queen's – quite amusing				
	11	Pleasure Cruise/Apollo – farcical comedy				

Appendix B

	Theatre Visits		Cinema Visits		Books Read
	20	Jack Pot/Prince of Wales – new revue		23	Dramatic Opinions and Essays Vol 1/Shaw
	28	Parity/Strand – Ivor Novello's new satirical play			
June	4	Dangerous Corner/Lyric – J. B. Priestley's new play		2	Dramatic Opinions and Essays Vol 2/Shaw
	9	The Vinegar Tree/St James's – Marie Tempest			
	11	Out of the Bottle/Hippodrome – an adult pantomime			
	22	Tell Her the Truth/Saville – new Bobby Howes show			
	28	Hocus Pocus/Garrick – most delightful comedy			
	29	Fanfare/Prince Edward – new revue			
July	5	Evensong/Queen's – a bitter satire			
	8	Love's Labour Lost/Westminster – enjoyed it		11	Not That It Matters/A. A. Milne
	13	The Savoy Follies/Savoy – good enough for seaside!	16	One Hour With You/Carlton – Chevalier	15	Review of Revues/C. B. Cochran
	20	Escape/Garrick – Galsworthy revival	17	The Struggle and C.O.D./Dominion – puerile!		

524

Culture Capture

	Theatre Visits		Cinema Visits		Books Read
	26	*Prince of Wales Revue* – new craze of non-stop revue	23	*The Wet Parade*/Empire – an epic film	27	*Apes and Angels*/Priestley essays
	27	*Twelfth Night*/New – novelty production in black and white	24	*Strictly Dishonourable* and *X Marks the Spot*/Bloomsbury – both dud films!	5	*The Man with Four Mirrors*/Knoblock
August	3	*Non-Stop Revue*/Leicester Square Theatre				
	9	*Orders Are Orders*/Shaftesbury – military farce				
	15	*Promenade Concert*/Queen's Hall – Wagner night				
	16	*Behold, We Live!*/St James's – Gerald Du Maurier and Gertrude Lawrence starring				
	17	*Non-Stop Revue*/Leicester Square Theatre – many of the same items as on 3rd August				
	22	*The Entertainers*/Oval (open air) – too cold to stay!				
	26	*Firebrand*/Playhouse – Gladys Cooper play				
	31	*Night of the Garden*/Strand – uproarious farce				

Appendix B

		Theatre Visits		***Cinema Visits***		***Books Read***
September	1	*Rhyme and Rhythm*/Winter Garden – new revue				
	3	*Over the Page*/Alhambra – exceedingly good				
	5	*Fifty Fifty*/Aldwych – farce				
	10	*The Way to the Stars*/Wyndham's – patchy play				
	11	*What Price Hollywood?*/New Gallery – satire			14	*Crazy Parliaments*/Beverley Nichols
	15	*Too Good to be True*/New – Shaw's new play				
	20	*Will You Love Me Always?*/Globe – Yvonne Arnaud			21	*Are They the Same at Home?*/Beverley Nichols
	21	*Caesar and Cleopatra*/Old Vic – Shaw play			23	*A Modern Vanity Fair*/Stephan Graham
	24	*Words and Music*/Adelphi – Noel Coward			27	*Everybody's Business*/Withers
October	1	*The Merry Widow*/Hippodrome – revival	1	*Marta Hari*/Euston Cinema – Greta Garbo	3	*Company Accounts* (text book)
	7	*Strange Orchestra*/St Martin's – clever	2	*Grand Hotel*/Palace – talkie version		
	8	*Justice*/Garrick – Galsworthy – rather disappointing			10	*The Quicksands of the City* (text book)

526

		Theatre Visits		Cinema Visits		Books Read
	11	*Children in Uniform*/Duchess – an all women play			14	*Portrait in a Mirror*/Charles Morgan
	13	*Il Trovatore*/Sadler's Wells – 5th time of seeing			17	*Orange Street*/S. P. B. Mais
	15	*We Are Angels*/Lyceum – not impressed	16	*Indiscrete* and *The Range Feud*/Bloomsbury Cinema		
	18	*Service*/Wyndham's – Dodie Smith's new success			28	*Nor Many Waters*/Alec Waugh
	22	*Roadhouse*/Whitehall – Walter Hackett comedy				
	29	*Never Come Back*/Phoenix – Lonsdale's new play	30	*New Morals for Old* and *After Hours*/Majestic, T C Rd		
November	5	*For Services Rendered*/Globe Maugham's fine new play			4	*Patchwork*/Beverley Nichols
	12	*Springtime for Henry*/Apollo – American farce			16	*Those Barren Leaves*/Aldous Huxley
	18	*Wild Violets*/Drury Lane – charming				
	19	*Tonight or Never*/Duke of York's	20	*Rome Express*/Tivoli		
	26	*Potash and Perlmutter*/Gaiety – Yiddish silent comedy	22	*Say It with Music*/Dominion		
	29	*A Kiss in Spring*/Alhambra – a massive failure			28	*Pending Heaven*/William Gerardi

Appendix B

		Theatre Visits		**Cinema Visits**		**Books Read**
December	3	*Another Language*/Lyric – an American success				
	6	*School for Husbands*/Court – theatre reopened				
	10	*The Cathedral*/New – Hugh Walpole				
	15	*Business with America*/Haymarket – Viennese com.			18	*Flowering Wilderness*/ Galsworthy
	21	*The Streets of London*/Ambassador's				
	22	*Ballyhoo*/Comedy – terrible blasé				
	26	*The Sleeping Beauty*/Lyceum				
	28	*Dick Wittington*/Hippodrome – beautiful production	31	*Trouble in Paradise*/Carlton – new Lubitsch masterpiece	29	*Star Spangled Manner*/ Beverley Nichols
Totals		**74**		**20**		**31**

528

Culture Capture

Recorded Culture Capture 1933

		Theatre Visits		Cinema Visits		Books Read
January	7	*Dinner at Eight*/Palace – Cochran's new production			3	*Twenty Five*/Beverley Nichols
	11	*Fresh Fields*/Criterion – Ivor Novello's new play			10	*Women and Children*/Beverley Nichols
	16	*Double Harness*/Haymarket – comedy and drama			17	*First Night*/Lorna Kea
	21	*Flies in the Sun*/Playhouse – Novello's new play	22	*A Successful Calamity*/Globe – George Arliss – good	25	*For Adults Only*/Beverley Nichols – a dialogue
	27	*Mother of Pearl*/Gaiety – Cochran's new witty show	29	*Yes, Mr Brown*/Tivoli – Jack Buchanan – an excellent film	26	*The Fountain*/Charles Morgan
	30	*A Bit of a Test*/Aldwych – Ben Travers farce				
February	2	*The Green Bay Tree*/St Martin's – by Mordant Sharp			3	*Meet These People*/Reginald Arkell – satirical poems
	4	*Richard of Bordeaux*/New – historical drama			6	*Blessed are the Rich*/James Agate
	7	*Half a Million*/Vaudeville – a stupid and dreary farce				

529

Appendix B

		Theatre Visits		Cinema Visits		Books Read
	8	Ten Minute Alibi/Haymarket – by Anthony Armstrong				
	9	Don Giovanni/Sadler's Wells – enjoyed every minute!	16	The Sign of the Cross/Carlton – magnificent film	15	Bizz Busy/James Agate
	18	Holmes of Baker Street/Lyric – clever idea of a play	19	14 Juillet/Academy Oxford St (in French)	17	I Had Almost Forgotten/C B Cochran – memoirs
	23	Mary Stuart and Shaw's The Admirable Bashkerville/Sadler's Wells	24	For the Love of Mike and Tiger Shark/Alhambra (Talkies)	23	Playgoing/James Agate
	25	It's You I Want/Daly's – by Seymour Hicks			24	Imperial Palace/Arnold Bennett
March	1	Once in a Lifetime/Queen's – a satire on Hollywood				
	4	The One Girl/Hippodrome	14	Cavalcade/Tivoli (seats booked on 1st March)		
		[Heap's father took his own life on 6/7 March]				
	18	Jolly Roger/Savoy – George Robey				
	25	This Inconsistency/Wyndham's – a disappointment				
	29	The Wanted Adventure/Saville – from Walter Hackett			30	The Magic Mountain/Beverley Nichols

Culture Capture

		Theatre Visits	Cinema Visits		Books Read
				31	*Nymph Errant*/James Lewes – frivolous and amusing
April	8	*The Rats of Norway*/Playhouse – a great play			
	13	*The Lake*/Westminster – a woman's play		21	*Good Time*/J. W. Drawbell
	23	*The Soldiers and the Gentlewoman*/Vaudeville – grim Welsh life		26	*Bernard Shaw*/Frank Harris
	27	*How Do You Do?*/Comedy – Charlot's new revue			
May	9	*The Brontes*/Royalty – five-act dramatic biography		12	*My Northcliffe Diary*/Tom Clarke
	17	*The Late Christopher Bean*/St Martin's – Emlyn Williams; at least 20 curtains!		18	*All in a Lifetime*/R. D. Blumenfield
	23	*Music in the Air*/His Majesty's – with the new Cochran craze of the songs arising out of the plot			
	27	*Diplomacy*/Prince's – good value for money			
	30	*Gallows Glorious*/Shaftesbury – of limited appeal		30	*Just the Other Day*/John Collier and Ian Lang – England since the War
June	1	*Strife*/Little Theatre at the Adelphi – Galsworthy play			

Appendix B

	Theatre Visits		Cinema Visits		Books Read
	9	Clear All Lines/Garrick – farcical comedy			
	10	Wild Justice/Vaudeville			
	15	Proscenium/Globe – New Ivor Novello play – sentimental		15	With Northcliffe in Fleet Street/Sir J. Hommerton
	21	Eight Bells/Duchess – a stirring drama of the sea			
	24	Sally/Strand – stale, trite and obvious		27	The Contemporary Theatre, 1926/James Agate
	29	Give Me a Ring/Hippodrome – musical comedy		29	The English Dramatic Critics 1660–1932
July	1	Wild Decembers/Apollo – a somber, spiritless piece			
	13	After Dark/Vaudeville – a competent new revue	16	A Man Must Fight/Dominion – a stirring film	14	The Gang Comes Back/Reader
	18	Other People's Lives/Wyndham's – A. A. Milne's new play	29	Waltz Time/Dominion	26	My Theatre Talks/James Agate
August	5	A Midsummer Night's Dream/Regent's Park Open Air Theatre – beautiful production			1	Balzac the Man/Francis Gribble
	22	Is Life Worth Living?/Ambassador's – mildly amusing		[On holiday in Cornwall 26 Aug–2 Sept]	3	Failures/Beverley Nichols – 3 plays
	25	The Ace/Lyric – good, the Journey's End of the air			11	The Amazing Mr Coward/Patrick Brybrooke

Culture Capture

		Theatre Visits		Cinema Visits		Books Read
					18	*Dramatic Values*/C. S. Montague (critic)
					21	*Little Man, What Now?* – from the German
			28	*Lord Caruthers's Ladies*/The Kinema, Bude	24	*Gentleman By Birth*/Miles Mander
					15	*London Scene*/H. J. Massingham
					29	*I Take This City*/Glyn Roberts
September	2	*The Wandering Jew*/Prince's – renewal, a ponderous play				
	12	*Ball at the Savoy*/Drury Lane – a decided success				
	16	*Nice Goings On*/Strand – new musical comedy				
	21	*Sheppy*/Wyndham's – brilliant work of Maugham				
	23	*A Sleeping Clergyman*/Piccadilly – by James Bridie				
	30	*Before Sunset*/Shaftesbury – anti-Hitler uproar against Krauss				
October	5	*Women Kind*/Phoenix	3	*That' A Good Girl*/Leicester Square Theatre – Jack Buchanan's talkie version		
	7	*Nymph Errant*/Adelphi – Cochran's production				

533

Appendix B

	Theatre Visits	*Cinema Visits*		*Books Read*
11	*The Cherry Orchard*/Old Vic – a theatrical event			
14	*Ballerina*/Gaiety – from Lady Eleanor Smith's novel			
19	*This Late Idolatry*/Lyric – new play about Shakespeare			
22	*Maternité*/Daly's – previously banned			
November 3	*Gay Divorce*/Palace – a Fred Astaire triumph		5	*All Men are Enemies*/Aldington
8	*As You Like It*/Phoenix – an abridged up-to-date version		6	*Over the River*/Galsworthy
10	*Afterwards*/Whitehall – Walter Hackett's comedy/drama			
15	*A Rose Without a Thorn*/Duke of York's – a worthy effort			
21	*Hay Fever*/Shaftesbury – Cochran revue of Coward's 1925 show			
23	*Please!*/Savoy – Charlot's new revue		23	*Society Racket*/Patrick Balfour

	Theatre Visits	Cinema Visits	Books Read
29	*That's a Pretty Thing*/Daly's – new musical farce		
December 2	*Laburnum Grove*/Duchess – J. B. Priestley's new comedy	4	*The Press in My Time*/R. D. Blumenfield
7	*The Wind and the Rain*/St Martin's – a success		
12	*Escape Me Never*/Apollo – with Elizabeth Bergner		
13	*Measure for Measure*/Old Vic – Charles Laughton and Flora Robson	15	*Writers and Artists Year Book* and *Face the Stars*/Geoffrey Moss
20	*On with the Show*/Cambridge – a terrible show!		
23	*The Old Folks at Home*/Queen's – clever and cynical		
27	*Beau Brummell*/Saville – new musical play		
30	*Whistling in the Dark*/Comedy – good American crook play		
Totals	**68**	**10**	**36**

Appendix B

Recorded Culture Capture 1934

		Theatre Visits	*Cinema Visits*		*Books Read*
January					
	6	*Reunion in Vienna*/Lyric – Robert Sherwood play		4	*Old Flames*/Owen
	8	*The Tempest*/Sadler's Wells – Charles Laughton		5	*Wonder Hero*/Priestley
				19	*The London Roundabout*/ Jane Carr Gordon
				22	*Plays Pleasant and Unpleasant* Vol 1/Shaw
	27	*Henry V*/Alhambra		24	*The Journals of Arnold Bennett* Vol 3 ('21–'28)
February	1	*First Episode*/Comedy		2	*Miracle in Sinai*/Sitwell
	3	*Mr Whittington*/Hippodrome – Jack Buchanan			
	5	*The Importance of Being Earnest*/Old Vic – brilliant!		5	*Nazi Germany Explained*/ Vernon Bartlett
	8	*Within the Gate*/Royalty – Sean O'Casey		9	*He Laughed in Fleet Street*/ Bernard Falk
	15	*Spring 1600*/Shaftesbury – Emlyn Williams			
	17	*Conversation Piece*/His Majesty's – Noel Coward's new play		13	*Selected English Essays*
	21	*Yours Sincerely*/Daly's			

536

Culture Capture

		Theatre Visits		Cinema Visits		Books Read
					27	*The Literature of My Time*/?
	22	*Julius Caesar*/Alhambra				
	28	*Here's How*/Saville – damned fine new musical!				
March	3	*The Country Wife*/Ambassador's – comedy			3	*Frank Harris*/Hugh Kingsmill
	6	*Love for Love*/Sadler's Wells – by William Congreve				
	10	*Magnolia Street*/Adelphi			12	*Characters and Commentaries*/Strachey
	15	*Private Rooms*/Westminster – leftish but charming			13	*Mr Britling*/H. G. Wells
	17	*The Golden Toy*/Coliseum – giant revolving production			15	*People Worth Talking About*/?
	21	*Without Witness*/Duke of York's – Anthony Armstrong				
	23	*The Merchant of Venice*/Alhambra	25	*Morning Story*/Stoll – Katharine Hepburn	28	*Hyde Park Orator*/Bonar Thompson
	29	*Clive of India*/Wyndham's – good in parts			29	*Thank You, Jeeves*/P. G. Wodehouse

537

Appendix B

		Theatre Visits		Cinema Visits		Books Read
April	5	*Macbeth*/Old Vic			9	*Away My Youth?*
	7	*Sporting Love*/Gaiety – musical horse play			10	*I Commit to the Flames*/Ivor Brown
	11	*Three Sisters*/Drury Lane				
	14	*Councillor at Law*/Piccadilly – Elmer Rice play	17	*I'm No Angel*/Carlton – Mae West film	13	*Valentine's Days*/Lord Castleroose
					20	*Under Proof*/Joanna Canman
	25	*Why Not Tonight*/Palace – revue			27	*Magnus Merriman*/Eric Linklater
May			3	*Catherine the Great?*Dominion – outstanding film		
	10	*The Voisey Inheritance*/Sadler's Wells – Granville Barker				
	12	*She Loves Me Not*/Adelphi – new American play			23	*Holy Deadlock*/A. P. Herbert
	24	*Touch Wood*/Haymarket – by Dodie Smith				
June	2	*Happy Week End*/Duke of York's – musical farce				
	9	*Vintage Wine*/Daly's – not farcical enough			13	*BUF: Oswald Mosely and British Fascism*/James Drennan

Culture Capture

	Theatre Visits		Cinema Visits		Books Read
	14 Libel/Playhouse – a success			20	Rude Society/H. P. McGraw
	21 Living Dangerously/Strand – rattling good drama			22	Crowded Nights and Days/Alan Croxton
				27	Hog's Harvest/J. B. Morton (beachcomber)
	28 Queen of Scots/New – acting above reproach			28	Arnold Bennett's Diaries Vol 2
July	19 The Mudlarks/Wyndham's			5	Swinging Apple/Conway Chappell
				11	English Journey/Priestley
		27	The House of Rothschild/Tivoli – very good	20	Hell, Said the Duchess/Michael Arlen
				25	The World Went Mad/John Brophy
	28 That Certain Something/Aldwych – frightful trash	28	All Men Are Enemies/Camden Hippodrome	27	Weep for Lycidas/Michael Harrison
August	9 She Shall Have Music/Saville – new musical comedy	3	Mayfair Girl/Stratford Kinema – murder story British		
	14 The Private Road/Comedy – by John Carlton	6	Love, Life and Laughter/Stratford Kinema – Gracie Fields	16	The Passing Chapter/Shane Leake
	22 Family Affairs/Ambassador's – comedy				

Appendix B

	Theatre Visits		Cinema Visits		Books Read
23	West End Scandals/Garrick – non-stop revue				
25	Blackbirds of 1934/Coliseum – Harlem rhapsody	29	Queen Christina/Granada, Dover		
		31	Coming Out Party/Plaza, Dover		
September 6	Merrie England/Prince's – operetta revival			3	Liza of Lambeth/Maugham
8	The Shining Hour/St James's – by Keith Winter; good			5	To My Son in Confidence/Miles Mander
12	A Man's House/New – by John Drinkwater				
15	East Eden/Duchess – Priestley's new play			18	The Moon and Sixpence/Maugham – superb style
22	Moonlight is Silver/Queen's – by Clemence Dane			19	Ah, King/Maugham short stories
24	Young England/Victoria Palace – lacks sophistication			21	Defy the Foul Friend/John Collier
29	Murder in Mayfair/Globe – Ivor Novello's new play				
October 4	Yes, Madam?/Hippodrome – musical comedy			3	Of Human Bondage/Maugham
6	Streamline/Palace – Cochran's 21st revue; quite a brilliant show				

Culture Capture

	Theatre Visits		Cinema Visits		Books Read
11	Lucky Break/Strand – Leslie Henson's musical farce				
13	Hi Diddle Diddle/Comedy – Charlot's new revue	16	Murder of the Vanities/Camden Hippodrome		
18	Richard II/Old Vic			18	Master Sanguine/Ivor Brown
23	Theatre Royal/Lyric – Noel Coward in a box			22	Memoirs of a Bookman/James Milne
27	Lover's Leap/Vaudeville – light domestic comedy			31	With the Dictators in Fleet Street/R. Stannard
				31	The Street of Adventure/Philip Gibbs
November 3	Sweet Aloes/Wyndham's – Dianna Wynyard stars			5	Author Hunting/Grant Richard
9	Hyde Park Corner/Apollo – new Walter Hackett play	24	Jew Luss/Dominion – outstanding British film	6	First Nights/James Agate
				14	Old Wives Tale/Arnold Bennett

Appendix B

	Theatre Visits	Cinema Visits	Books Read	
			15	*First Person Singular*/Maugham
			20	*The Narrow Corner*/Maugham – Eastern yarns
			22	*London in My Time*/Thomas Burke
			30	*Quick Curtain*/Alan Melville
December	1 *The Moon in the Yellow River*/Haymarket – Irish comedy	5 *Nell Gwynne*/Stoll – a delicious film	7	*An Experiment in Autobiography* Vol 2/H. G. Wells
	15 *Half a Crown*/Aldwych – in a depressing sort of theatre		11	*The Story of 25 Years*/Pearson's Jubilee Book
			14	*In Extremis*/Cyril Butcher
			19	*If I Were Dictator*/St John Ervine
	22 *Blackbirds of 1935*/Coliseum – packed festive audience		20	*While Rome Burns*/Alexander Woolcott
	31 *Cinderella*/Drury Lane – Julian Wylie's last production		31	*C. E. Montague: A Memoir*/Oliver Elton
Totals	60	12	56	

Recorded Culture Capture 1935

		Theatre Visits		Cinema Visits		Books Read
January	5	Jill, Darling/Saville – musical comedy	3	The Count of Monte Christo/Dominion	2	The Nights of London/H. V. Morton
					6	The Green Hat/Michael Arlen
					8	Play Parade/Noel Coward plays
	17	The Dominant Sex/Shaftesbury – new comedy	21	Brewster's Millions/Prince Edward – Jack Buchanan	11	Twenty Nine Years Hard Labour/F. E. Bailey autobiog.
			25	Kid Millions/Prince Edward – Eddie Cantor	21	The Days of War/Yates Brown
					22	Wine, Women and Waiters/Gilbert Maugham
	27	Stop Press/Adelphi – new revue			30	From Bed to Worse/Robert Benchley
February	2	Love on the Dole/Garrick – a fine achievement	13	The Iron Duke/Dominion	1	Celebrities Are Simple Souls/Alfred Sutro

Appendix B

		Theatre Visits		*Cinema Visits*		*Books Read*
	20	*The Man from Yesterday*/St Martin's – drama			8	*Café Royal Days*/Capt. D. Nichols Pigalle
	23	*Youth at the Helm*/Globe – Viennese comedy			18	*Vanity Fair*/W. M. Thackeray
March	2	*Henry IV Part 1*/Haymarket – with George Robey	7	*Private Life of Don Juan*/Forum Kentish Town		
	13	*Mrs Nobby Clark*/Comedy – Marie Ney	9	*The Scarlet Pimpernel*/Dominion – a splendid film	10	*The Ordeal of Richard Feverel*/George Meredith
	16	*The Greeks Had a Word For It*/Cambridge			12	*Monologue*/Lewell Stokes
	23	*Cornelius*/Duchess – new Priestley play	26	*The Man from the Folies Bergère*/Pavilion	20	*Hazlet's Dramatic Essays*
					29	*Three Englishmen*/Gilbert Frankau
April	6	*Strange Things Happen*/St James's	4	*Saunders of the River*/Prince Edward	1	*Ego*/James Agate autobiography
	11	*Viceroy Sarah*/Whitehall – Sarah Marlborough				
	13	*Charlot's Charabanc*/New – revue				
	16	*Bernet's Folly*/Haymarket – West Country comedy				
	17	*Frolic World*/Royalty				
	18	*The Old Ladies*/New – a truly remarkable play				

Culture Capture

	Theatre Visits		Cinema Visits		Books Read
25	*Tovarich*/Lyric – French comedy				
27	*Let's Go Fay*/Shaftesbury – new revue				
May					
4	*Dancing City*/Coliseum – Charlot's production	8	*Royal Cavalcade*/Bedford Kinema	10	*That Which Hath Wings*/Richard Dehan
11	*The Flying Trapeze*/Alhambra – Jack Buchanan				
14	*Shall We Reverse?*/Comedy – gay and witty				
18	*Glamorous Night*/Drury Lane – sumptuous show				
22	*Lady Precious Stream*/Little – traditional Chinese			23	*Gallery Unreserved*/Galleryites
26	*Jack O' Diamonds*/Cambridge			28	*Brighton*/Osbert Sitwell & Margaret Barton
29	*All Rights Reserved*/Criterion – by N. C. Hunter				
June					
4	*The Mark of Virtue*/St James's – Vivien Leigh				
8	*Night Must Fall*/Duchess – Emlyn Williams	10	*The Lives of a Bengal Lancer*/Bedford – magnificent	11	*George IV*/Shane Leslie
13	*Accidently Yours*/Shaftesbury – a dreary farce			13	*Possession*/R. D. B. Bloomfield
22	*Harvey House*/His Majesty's	27	*Four Hours to Kill*/Plaza – sheer trash	14	*Strange Street*/Beverley Nichols

545

Appendix B

		Theatre Visits		*Cinema Visits*		*Books Read*
July	29	Love Lights/Hippodrome – new musical comedy			21	Author – Biography/Cecil Hunt
	13	The Two Mrs Carrolls/St Martin's – only 50 mins			3	The Heart of England/Ivor Brown
	18	Grief Goes Over/Phoenix			5	The Price of Pleasure/Charles Graves
	20	The Desirable Residence/Criterion – A. Rawlinson	22	Ruggles of Red Gap/Camden Hippodrome	12	Queer People/Harold Durden
	24	Close Quarters/Haymarket – only two characters	25	Becky Sharp/New Gallery – in Technicolor; colour crude and artless. What, in short, is all the fuss about?	17	Before I Forget/Bertie Hollender
	27	Someone at the Door/Comedy – thriller			24	The Georgian Literary Scene – Frank Swinnerton
	30	Ghosts/Duke of York's – not impressed!				
	31	The Unguarded Hour/Daly's – neat, crisp				
August	14	Tulip Time/Alhambra – shortened for twice nightly		[Bank Holiday weekend 3–5 August with Bill in Ilford; then walking in the Chilterns 18 – 22 August; with his mother at Margate 24–31 August]	14	Sinister Street/J. B. Priestley's 1,000-page novel
	23	Full House/Haymarket –Novello's new comedy	25	David Copperfield/Dreamland, Margate		
	26	The Jester Entertainers/end of Margate Pier	27	Roberta/Astoria, Cliftonville		

Culture Capture

	Theatre Visits	Cinema Visits		Books Read
September				
28	*On With the Show*/Clifton Concert Hall			
5	*Round About Regent Street*/Palladium – variety			
7	*Accent on Youth*/Globe – an American play		12	*My Seven Selves*/Hamilton Fyfe – autobiography
14	*Stop – Go*/Vaudeville – sophisticated revue		17	*Paths of Glory*/Daily Express serial version
19	*Nina*/Criterion – a delicious diversion			
23	*Peer Gynt*/Old Vic – it will last me quite a time		23	*The Wayward Man*/St John Ervine
28	*Voilà les Dames*/Prince of Wales'			
October				
3	*The Soldiers Fortune*/Ambassador's – Thomas Otway		3	*Arnold Bennett*/Dorothy Bennett
5	*Please Teacher*/Hippodrome – disappointing		11	*Front Everywhere*/J. M. N. Jeffries
12	*The Black Eye*/Shaftesbury – James Bridie			
16	*Espionage*/Apollo – W. Hackett comedy thriller			
19	*Romeo and Juliet*/New – Olivier as Romeo in John Gielgud production		24	*Don Fernando*/Somerset Maugham
31	*Call it a Day*/Globe – Dodie Smith's fragrant new comedy		31	*George the Fourth*/Roger Fulford

547

Appendix B

		Theatre Visits		**Cinema Visits**		**Books Read**
November	2	Seeing Stars/Gaiety – new musical comedy	1	Wings of Song/Dominion – Grace Moore	1	*The Pretty Lady*/Arnold Bennett
	7	Short Story/Queen's – by Robert Morley				
	15	The Three Sisters/Old Vic – worth seeing				
	16	Twenty to One/Coliseum – a vile show	14	Peg of Old Drury/Dominion – a lovely film	15	*Round About England*/S. P. B. Mais
	20	Tread Softly/Daly's – new delectable comedy!	25	Come Out of the Party/Prince Edward – Jack Buchanan	20	*Shakespeare as a Dramatist*/Sir John Squire
	27	Our Own Lives/Ambassador's			28	*Sir George Alexander and the St James's Theatre*/A. E. W. Mason
	28	Romeo and Juliet/New – John Gielgud as Romeo				
	30	[unnamed variety show]/Hammersmith Palace – included Ron's friend Enrico de Sula (hopeless)				
December	7	A Royal Exchange/His Majesty's – Ramon Navarro			6	*The Three Friends*/Norman Collins – a best seller
	11	Distinguished Gathering/St Martin's – murder considered a fine art				
	14	The Sleeping Beauty/Vaudeville – highly polished			16	*The Ghost Walks on Fridays*/Sydney Bhai

548

Culture Capture

	Theatre Visits		*Cinema Visits*		*Books Read*
19	*Mary Tudor*/Playhouse – an interesting play				
24	*Jack and the Beanstalk*/Drury Lane – produced by Ralph Reader				
28	*This'll Make You Whistle*/Streatham Hill Theatre – Jack Buchanan's new pre-provincial tour			31	*Pilgrim's Cottage*/Cecil Roberts
Totals	**67**		**18**		**42**

Appendix B

Recorded Culture Capture 1936

		Theatre Visits		Cinema Visits		Books Read
January	11	*Tonight at 8.30*/Phoenix – three Noel Coward short plays	8	*The Crusader*/Dominion Cecil B. de Mille epic	3	*Gone Rustic*/Cecil Roberts
	15	*Tonight at 8.30*/Phoenix – another three Noel Coward short plays			7	*Blessington-D'Orsay*/Michael Sadlier
	16	*Richard III*/Old Vic – a dismal house	23	*Top Hat*/Dominion – Irving Berlin success	10	*The Way of a Transgressor*/Negley Farson
					31	*The Truth About a Journalist?*
February	6	*St Helena*/Old Vic – by R. C. Sherriff				
	8	*Follow the Sun*/Adelphi – lavish Cochran revue				
	13	*Storm in a Teacup*/Royalty – James Bridie			13	*Byron*/Peter Quenelle
	15	*The Limping Man*/Saville – not good enough			14	*Three Englishmen*/Gilbert Frankau
	20	*Three Men on a Horse*/Wyndham's – US farce	22	*When Knights Were Bold*/Pavilion – Jack Buchanan film		
	27	*Pride and Prejudice*/St James's – adaption			26	*Wild Ass Skin*/Balzac
	29	*Promise*/Shaftesbury – by Henry Bernstein				

550

Culture Capture

		Theatre Visits		Cinema Visits		Books Read
March	4	Red Night/Queen's – by J. L. Hudson with Robert Donat	11	Broadway Melody of 1936/Dominion – spectacular	2	The Strange Life of Walter Clarkson/H. J. Greenwall
	12	All Alright at Oxford Circus/Palladium – not impressed			13	Arnold Bennett's Letters to His Nephew
	14	The Town Talks/Vaudeville – a perfect revue				
	18	No Exit/St Martin's – dull and feeble				
	20	The Show that Jack Built/Alhambra – awful!				
	21	At the Silver Swan/Palace				
	26	Dusty Ermine/Comedy – worth seeing			27	Paris Calling/Henry Greenwall
	28	Wisdom Tooth/Savoy – by Noel Streatfeild				
	31	Love from a Stranger/New – first rate thriller				
April	1	Spread It Abroad/New – a smart intimate show			3	News Hunter/William Holly
	8	The Happy Hypocrite/His Majesty's – a Max Beerbohm story				
	16	After October/Criterion – superlatively good play				

Appendix B

		Theatre Visits	*Cinema Visits*	*Books Read*
	18	*The Frog*/Prince's – by Ian Hay, Edgar Wallace		22 *From Phelps to Gielgud*/Sir George Arthur
	25	*The Shadow*/Playhouse – an original drama	30 *Two's Company*/Piccadilly – an amusing enough British film	
May	9	*Bees on the Boat Deck*/Lyric – Priestley's curious new play		1 *Gone Afield*/Cecil Roberts
	12	*Bitter Harvest*/St Martin's – doubtful about its success		8 *My Own Trumpet*/Dion Clayton Calthorpe
	14	*Ah, Wilderness*/Westminster – not my sort of play		15 *Cosmopolitans*/Somerset Maugham
	20	*The Seagull*/New – John Gielgud		22 *Let's Pretend*/Cedric Hardwicke memoirs
	27	*Boy Meets Girl*/Shaftesbury – American farce		
	28	*Men Aren't Beasts*/Strand – rollicking farce	29 *One Racing Afternoon*/Piccadilly – average film	
June	6	*The Fugitives*/Apollo – by Walter Hackett; boring!		2 *At Half Past Eight*/James Agate – 1921/22
	13	*Green Waters*/Vaudeville – intense but contrary		4 *The Contemporary Theatre*/Agate – 1924
				8 *Alarums and Excursions*/Agate – 1922

Culture Capture

		Theatre Visits		Cinema Visits		Books Read
			11			*Contemporary Theatre 1925*/Agate
			16			*On English Screen*/Agate – 1924
			17			*Agate's Folly* – essays
			19			*Responsibility*/Agate – novel of 1918
			24			*Fantasies and Imperatives*/Agate
			25			*White Horse, Red Lion*/Agate – essays of 1923
			29			*The Common Touch*/Agate – essays of 1925
	25	*Heroes Don't Care*/St Martin's				
	27	*Winter Sunshine*/Royalty – an unpretentious comedy				
July	4	*Mrs Smith*/Duke of York's – two hours including interval	2			*Their Hour Upon the Stage*/Agate – 1927–30
	9	*Blackbirds of 1936*/Gaiety – tremendous Cochran vitality	7			*Regency*/D. L. Murray
	11	*No, No Nanette*/Hippodrome – excellent	17			*The Rocket*/Jeffrey Marston
	18	*Whitehouse*/Playhouse – Mazo La Roche	29			*Labby*/Hesketh Pearson [Henry Labouchère biography]
August	18	*Spring Tide*/Duchess – new comedy		[Walking holiday in Cotswolds, Gloucester and the Welsh Borders, 8–17 August]	6	*Anonymous (1831–1935)* – critical opinions

Appendix B

	Theatre Visits		*Cinema Visits*		*Books Read*
20	The Amazing Dr Clitterhouse/Haymarket	19	Panic in the Air/Britannia Camden Town	26	All Star Cast/Ngami Ryde Smith – stupid book
27	The Two Bouquets/Ambassador's – musical comedy	20	Modern Times/Dominion – new Charlie Chaplin		
		29	Rhodes of Africa/Astoria – a very fine film		
September 2	Swing Bling/Gaiety – new musical comedy; puerile	5	Mutiny on the Bounty/Dominion – magnificent	1	Randlords/Paul Emden
3	O-Kay for Sound/Palladium – a glittering revue	7	Limelight/Camden Hippodrome	8	More Ego/James Agate
9	Laughter in Court/Shaftesbury – by Hugh Mills				
11	Careless Rapture/Drury Lane – a terrific occasion	12	The Great Ziegfeld/His Majesty's	11	Round the World for News/Harry Greenwall
15	This'll Make You Whistle/Palace – Jack Buchanan				
17	Certainly Sir/Hippodrome	19	Things to Come/Britannia – H. G. Wells' most colossal and sensational film	18	There's a Porpoise Close Behind Us/Noel Langley
24	Mademoiselle/Wyndham's – adapted from the French			25	The Card/Bennett
30	Let's Raise the Curtain/Victoria Palace – a new 'all in one show'			28	Tono Bungay/H. G. Wells

554

Culture Capture

		Theatre Visits		Cinema Visits		Books Read
October	1	Transatlantic Rhythm/Adelphi – consistent revue				
	2	The Night of January 16/Phoenix – US court room drama				
	5	The Provoked Wife/Embassy Swiss Cottage – good				
	8	Going Places/Savoy – stereotyped musical comedy			8	Figure of Eight/Compton Mackenzie's latest novel
	10	Charles the King/Lyric – a truly great play	17	Mr Deeds Goes to Town/Bedford – the best film of the year	13	Limehouse Nights/Thomas Burke
	21	A Month in the Country/Westminster – Turgenev			15	Sixty Years Ago/Sir Max Pemberton memoirs
	22	Jane Eyre/Queen's – at Malvern last year	27	The Gay Desperado/Piccadilly – put me in a bad temper	19	Nights in Town: A London Autobiography/Burke
	28	Till the Cows Come Home/St Martin's – dullish house			26	Sparkenbroke/Charles Morgan
	31	Marigold/Royalty – deserves to succeed			30	Hay Walk in the City/Priestley
November	4	Parnell/New – by Elaine Schaffer	5	Under Two Flags/Camden Hippodrome	2	All About Life/Basil Watson
	12	French Without Tears/Criterion – Terrence Rattigan				
	14	The Wild Duck/Westminster – surprised delight!			15	Ego 2/James Agate – diary

Appendix B

		Theatre Visits		*Cinema Visits*		*Books Read*
	21	*Housemaster*/Comedy – new Ian Hay comedy	25	*The King Steps Out*/Bedford – Grace Moore		
	28	*Young Madam Conti*/adapted by Herbert Griffiths				
December	1	*Waste*/Westminster – Granville Barker; magnificent				
	8	*The Witch of Edmonton*/Old Vic – 1821 thriller	9	*Talk of the Devil*/Hippodrome	11	*Cockalorum*/Hannah Maclaren
	12	*Laughter over London*/Victoria Palace			17	*Jill Somerset*/Alec Waugh
	18	*The Boy David*/His Majesty's – by Sir James Barrie				
	23	*Mother Goose*/Hippodrome			23	*Trinity Town*/Norman Collins
	26	*Cinderella*/Coliseum				
	30	*Balalaika*/Adelphi – by Eric Maschwitz				
Totals	**70**		**19**		**49**	

556

Culture Capture

Recorded Culture Capture 1937

		Theatre Visits		Cinema Visits		Books Read
January	7	Bertram Mills' Circus/Olympia	2	Saving Time/Bedford – Astaire & Rogers		
	9	Hearts Content/Shaftesbury – W. Chetham Strode			11	Leaves of My Unwritten Diary/H. Preston – memoirs
	12	Puss in Boots/Lyceum panto			13	Myself, My Two Countries/Marcel Barleston
	14	Busman's Holiday/Comedy – D. L. Sayers drama	16	Anthony Adverse/Camden Hippodrome – a fine film	19	Have You Anything to Declare?/Maurice Baring
	19	The Astonished Ostrich/Duke of York's			21	Our Two Englands/John Hudson
	28	Behind Your Back/Strand – comedy	29	Dark Journey/Piccadilly – Alex. Korda	25	Air For England – feeble!
					25	The East Wind of Love/Compton Mackenzie – new novel
February	2	Home and Beauty/Adelphi – Cochran Coronation revue			3	Ideas and People/Clifford Bax
	5	On Your Toes/Palace – American musical				
	6	Shaw's Candide/Globe – finest production of the season	8	Elephant Boy/Piccadilly	8	My Melodramatic Memories/H. Fink – published today

Appendix B

		Theatre Visits		**Cinema Visits**		**Books Read**
	13	Uncle Vanya/Westminster – Chekov	11	Moonlight Sonata/Piccadilly – Paderewski and Marie Tempest		
	18	Big Business/Hippodrome – Jack Walker musical			18	The Rest of Me/Basil Maine – autobiography
	20	Wise Tomorrow/Lyric – by Stephen Powys	20	Cavalcade of the Movies/Tatler – films of the 1890s	22	Inside Europe/John Gunther
	24	Retreat from Tolly/Queen's – an uneven play				
	27	George and Margaret/Wyndham's				
March	3	The Road to Rome/Embassy – Robert Sherwood play	6	Ziegfeld Follies/Bedford	5	Autobiography/G. K. Chesterton
	6	Night Alone/Daly's	8	Dreaming Life/Pavilion – beyond my comprehension		
	10	Heartbreak House/Westminster – Shaw revival			11	Shaw, Harris and Wilde/?
	20	Suspect/St Martin's thriller	25	Murder in the City/?		
	23	The Taming of the Shrew/New	30	History is Made at Night/Phoenix – a poor film		
	31	Swing Is in the Air/Palladium's new show				
April	3	Mile Away Murder/Duchess – A. Armstrong detective story	8	Theodora Goes Wild/Bedford – comedy	7	Summerson biography (?)
	7	Anna Christina/Westminster	14	Beloved Evening/Bedford – Irish rebellion 1921	9	England Speaks/Philip Gibbs

Culture Capture

		Theatre Visits		Cinema Visits		Books Read
	10	*London After Dark*/Apollo – by W Hackett	17	*Gang Show Film*/Lyceum – not general release		
	22	*And On We Go*/Savoy – quite good	20	*This'll Make You Whistle*/Regal		
	23	*Black Limelight*/St James's – by Gordon Sherry			28	*The Honeysuckle and the Bee*/Sir John Squire – memoirs
	29	*Bats in the Belfry*/Ambassador's – comedy			29	*The Flying Wasp*/Sean Casey – essays
May	1	*The Grand Duchess*/Daly's – Offenbach operetta			5	*Theatre*/Maugham novel
	8	*Sarah Simple*/Garrick – A. A. Milne comedy	15	GB Movietone News Theatre – three *Coronation* newsreel films	10	*Penny Foolish*/Osbert Sitwell
	20	*The Constant Wife*/Globe – Maugham revival			20	*Felicity Greene*/John Brophy novel
	22	*Paganini*/Lyceum – Lehar operetta			27	*A. J. Grein* – biography
	29	*He Was Born Gay*/Queen's – Emlyn Williams				
June	8	*Murder in the Cathedral*/Old Vic – Eliot drama			2	*About Nothing Whatsoever*/'Almost Anyone'
	12	*To Have and to Hold*/Haymarket 'a good play'	12	*Men Are Not Gods*/Trocadero, Elephant & Castle	7	*Musical Memories*/Herman Darewski

Appendix B

		Theatre Visits		*Cinema Visits*		*Books Read*
	15	Judgement Day/Strand – Elmer Rice			10	Midnight in the Desert – new Priestley novel
	19	The Great Romancer/New – by J. E. Goodman; the finest acting to be seen			22	Horatio Bottomley – biography
	23	Satyr/Shaftesbury – disappointing play			23	Aspects of Wilde/Vincent O'Sullivan
	24	Victoria Regina/Lyric				
	29	Floodlight/Saville – Beverley Nichols revue				
July	1	Yes My Darling Daughter/St James's – adapted from American of Mark Reed			8	Rachael the Immortal/Bernard Falk
	10	They Came by Night/Globe – Barrie Lyndon			9	The Naked Lady/Bernard Falk – bio of Adah Isaac Mencken [US actress/painter]
	13	A Spot of Bother/Strand – by Vernon Sylviane			14	Harry Richmond/Meredith
	28	Juno and the Paycock/Golders Green – the Hippodrome revival			28	Thiers biography – a beautiful book
August	5	The Crusher/Prince's – adventure play by Ian Hay	11	Shall We Dance?/Dominion – Astaire & Rogers	3	New Arabian Nights/R. L. Stevenson
	27	After the Thin Man/Palace, Blackpool	14	Cartoons/Tatler – [with young Bernie]	10	Under the Greenwood Tree/Hardy classic

Culture Capture

	Theatre Visits		Cinema Visits		Books Read
30	*Gertie Maudie*/St Martin's by John van Druten		*[On holiday in Northern England, 14–28 August]*	20	*The Cathedral*/Walpole – loan by Youth Hostel Warden
September					
1	*Old Music*/St James's – Keith Waters' new play				
2	*Crest of a Wave*/Drury Lane – Novello's new play				
4	*Time and the Conways*/Duchess – new Priestley play				
7	*London Rhapsody*/Palladium – new show				
8	*Bonnet over the Windmill*/New – Dodie Smith's predestined success			9	*The Citadel*/A. J. Cronin
11	*Wanted for Murder*/Lyceum – rattling good drama				
14	*Busy Days*/Shaftesbury – Stanley Lupino play			15	*Martin Chuzzlewit*/Dickens classic
16	*Going Greek*/Gaiety – Leslie Henson comedy		*Lloyds of London*/King's Cross Cinema	18	
22	*I Have Been Here Before*/Royalty – new Priestley play; 'absolutely above criticism'				
23	*Take It Easy*/Palace – deplorable				

561

Appendix B

		Theatre Visits		**Cinema Visits**		**Books Read**
	25	*Pygmalion*/Old Vic – 1st of their new season			28	*Historical Nights' Entertainment*/Raphael Sabatini
	29	*The Last Straw*/Comedy – thriller, exciting stuff!			30	*Pepys Diary*
October	14	*Hide and Seek*/Hippodrome – musical comedy	2	*Fire Over England*/Odeon, Haverstock Hill	1	*Carnival at Blackport*/J. L. Hudson
	16	*Take it Easy*/Palace – then, later that evening,	6	*For You Alone*/King's Cross Cinema – Grace Moore film	5	*A Pink'un Remembers*/J. B. Booth
	16	*Blondie White*/Globe – Bernard Merrivale	19	*Lost Horizon*/King's Cross Cinema	11	*The Crooked Carrot*/Michael Arlen – novel
	22	*Autumn*/St Martin's – from the Russian			14	*The South Wind of Love*/Compton Mackenzie – novel
	23	*The Laughing Cavalier*/Adelphi – musical romance				
	27	*Chu the Sinner*/Embassy, Swiss Cottage – dull				
	30	*Yes and No*/Ambassador's – not my cup of tea				
November	3	*Good Bye to Yesterday*/Phoenix – Gladys Cooper				

Culture Capture

	Theatre Visits		Cinema Visits		Books Read
4	It's in the Bag/Saville – musical	13	Farewell Again/King's Cross Cinema – good British film	10	My Father's Son/Giles Playfair
16	The Silent Knight/St James's – romantic comedy	18	Wake Up and Live/King's Cross Cinema – Walter Winchell	17	Their Moods and Mine/Reginald Pound – very good book
20	Mourning Becomes Electra/Westminster – Eugene O'Neill			18	Three Comrades/Remarques
24	People at Sea/Apollo – new Priestley play				
25	Robert's Wife/Globe – new St John Ervine play			26	Present Indicative/Noel Coward – autobiography
27	School for Scandal/Queen's – Gielgud revival				
30	Thank You Mr Pepys/Shaftesbury				
December 4	The Phantom Light/Haymarket – comedy thriller				
8	Oh You Letty/Palace – good average mus. com.			10	In Parenthesis/David Jones
11	Think of a Number/Comedy – a tame farce			11	Edwardian and New Georgian/Edgar Jepson
15	Room Service/Strand – riotous enough farce			17	When All's Said and Done/Herbert Swears

Appendix B

	Theatre Visits		*Cinema Visits*		*Books Read*
18	*Me and My Girl*/Victoria Palace – musical comedy; then to				
18	*I Killed the Count*/Whitehall – ingenious thriller				
21	*Choose Your Time*/Piccadilly – Frith Shepherd has backed the wrong horse				
22	*You Can't Take It With You*/St James's – good farce			23	*Coming Sir*/Dave Marlowe
24	*Cinderella*/Prince's – practically the same as Cochran's panto last year			28	*The Big Fellow* – biography of Michael Collins
27	*Beauty and the Beast*/Lyceum panto – exceeded expectations				
28	*Aladdin*/Adelphi – Tom Arnold's panto	29	*Victoria the Great*/Euston Cinema – a notable film	31	*Hollywood by Starlight*/R. J. Minney
Totals	83		25		50

564

Recorded Culture Capture 1938

Culture Capture

		Theatre Visits		Cinema Visits		Books Read
January	6	This Money Business/Ambassador's – Cyril Campion	8	The Good Earth/Regent	3	Hungarian Background/Adam de Hegedes
	19	The Melody That Got Lost/Phoenix – from the Danish	22	A Star is Born/King's Cross Cinema	6	Five Years Dead/B. Falk
	25	Volpone/Westminster – Ben Johnson			10	The Dark Invader/Capt van Rintelin
	27	The Innocent Party/St James's – comedy			20	I Know These Dictators/Ward Price
	29	Three Sisters/Queen's – Chekhov			24	Birkenhead: The Last Phase – by his son
February	2	Herbert Farjeon Revue/Little			2	All The Days of My Life/S. P. B. Mais – autobiography
	12	The Island/Comedy – by Martin Hodge				
	16	Mary Goes to Sea/Haymarket				
	22	Dodsworth/Palace			22	Blasting and Bombardiering/W. L. Lewis
	25	Taffy/Grafton by Caradoc Evans			23	There I Lie/Thompson – journalist's memoirs

Appendix B

		Theatre Visits		Cinema Visits		Books Read
March	26	*Black Swans*/Apollo – promising play				
	9	*Surprise Item*/Ambassador's – comedy	5	*The Life of Emile Zola* and *Jack Buchanan's The Sky's the Limit*/Odeon, Swiss Cottage	4	*Press Gang*/Russell – journalistic parodies
	10	*Death on the Table*/Strand – comedy thriller	14	*Prisoner of Zenda*/Regent – exciting old story	5	*Masquerade*/Hutchinson
	12	*Plan for a Hostess*/St Martin's – comedy	16	*A Hundred Men and a Girl*/King's Cross Cinema	7	*England's Character*/Mais
	15	*King of Nowhere*/Old Vic – James Bridie	23	*Stage Door*/Regent – tragic comedy	17	*The Summing Up*/Maugham
	24	*Idiot's Delight*/Apollo – by Robert Sherwood				
	26	*Toss of a Coin*/Vaudeville – Hackett comedy			30	*This is My Life*/Bartlett
April	9	*Poison Pen*/Shaftesbury – powerful play			8	*Ego*/James Agate – collected criticisms
	13	*Wild Oats*/Princes – 'sing and laugh show'	16	*Smash and Grab*/King's Cross Cinema – Jack Buchanan		
	20	*Elizabeth, la Femme sans Homme*/Haymarket – puerile and stupid	16	*Marie Walewska*/Regent – fine Napoleonic tale	19	*Across the Frontiers*/Gibbs
	27	*Banana Ridge*/Strand – farce				

Culture Capture

		Theatre Visits		Cinema Visits		Books Read
May	7	Palmer's Follies of 1938/Saville	9	I'll Take Romance/Regent	4	Small Talk/Harold Nicholson essays
	12	The Engadine Express/Coliseum – ice show				
	14	People of Our Class/New – St John Ervine; sheer intellectual delight!				
	18	Amphitron 38/Lyric – from the French				
	21	Happy Returns/Adelphi – Cochran revue	21	Inside Nazi Germany (March of Time)/Tatler – 'an atrociously biased film!'	30	Paint and Prejudice/C. W. R. Nevinson
	28	Glorious Morning/Duchess – grim drama	29	Town and Gown/News Theatre – Oxbridge	31	Paris/Jules Bertant
June	2	Spring Morning/Ambassador's – light comedy			9	Without Apology/Lord Alfred Douglas
	9	The Lion Never Sleeps/Drury Lane – melodrama with music				
	11	Lot's Wife/Whitehall – comedy				
	21	Golden Boy/St James's – youthful violinist	25	Break the News/Paramount – Buchanan and Chevalier	28	News of England/Beverley Nichols – in pacifist form
					29	Weekends in England/Mais – travel
July	2	J'Accuse/St Pancras People's Theatre – Agate's Dreyfus play			7	Overture and Beginners/Ronald Adam

567

Appendix B

		Theatre Visits		*Cinema Visits*		*Books Read*
	6	*Maritza*/Palace – Hungarian musical comedy			14	*Tom Jones*/Fielding – classic
	23	*Lysistrata*/Regent's Park Open Air Theatre – anti-war satire			25	*On Foot in North Wales*/Monkhouse – walking guide
	27	*The Joyful Delaneys*/new Hugh Walpole novel				
August	18	*She Was Too Young*/Wyndham's		[Walking holiday in Snowdonia, 30 July–8 August; days out till 14 Aug; holiday camp in Kent, 20–27 August]	17	*Night Lights*/Seymour Hicks
					30	*Northern Lights* – theatrical reflections
	31	*Running Riot*/Gaiety – musical			30	*Confessions of an Inn Keeper*/Fothergill
September	1	*The Flashing Stream*/Lyric – Charles Morgan play; brilliant!	3	*The Vassal of Wrath*/Regent – from a Maugham story		
	15	*Paprika*/His Majesty's – poor reception	7	*A Yank at Oxford*/Regent – Robert Taylor	7	*Germany Speaks* – by 21 leaders of Party and State
	16	*Henry V*/Drury Lane – Novello revival				
	17	*Dear Octopus*/Queen's – Dodie Smith	21	*Snow White and the Seven Dwarfs*/King's Cross Cinema – 1st full-length Disney film	22	*It's Draughty in Front*/Cabbie's tales

568

Culture Capture

	Theatre Visits		Cinema Visits		Books Read
				22	*Those Were the Days*/Sitwell
23	*Goodbye Mr Chips*/Shaftesbury – James Hilton play				
24	*The Corn is Green*/Duchess – Emlyn Williams; semi-autobiographic				
October				7	*World of Action*/Valentine Williams – autobiography
6	*An Elephant in Arcady*/Kingsway – Farjeon musical frolic				
7	*The White Guard*/Phoenix – from the Russian			14	*In My Time*/Huddleston – journalistic reminiscences
8	*Bobby Get Your Gun*/Adelphi – musical comedy				
12	*When We Are Married*/St Martin's – Priestley farcical comedy				
15	*Quiet Wedding*/Wyndham's – domestic comedy				
22	*Room for Two*/Comedy – salacious bedroom farce	2	*Flashbacks*/Palace – movies 1838–1938	28	*Oscar Wilde*/Frank Harris
November					
5	*The Shoemaker's Holiday*/Playhouse – Elizabethan comedy				
12	*They Fly By Twilight*/Aldwych				
18	*Gentleman Unknown*/St James's				
19	*Traitors Gate*/Duke of York's				

Appendix B

	Theatre Visits		*Cinema Visits*		*Books Read*
	24	Under Your Hat/Palace			28	Ego 3/Agate
	30	The Story of an African Farm/New			
December	21	Number Six/Aldwych			
	24	Babes in the Wood/Drury Lane			
	26	The Queen of Hearts/Lyceum			
	28	Marco Millions/Westminster	9	Pygmalion/Paramount	9	It Might Have Been You/Knox
					21	Turner the Painter/Falk
					23	Autobiography of a Cad/Mandervewell
	29	Sixty Glorious Years/Odeon, Swiss Cottage			30	Behind the Censorships/Young
Totals	**60**		**17**		**38**	

Recorded Culture Capture 1939

Culture Capture

		Theatre Visits		Cinema Visits		Books Read
January	14	Sleeping Beauty (amateur)/King George's Hall	7	The Adventures of Robin Hood/Regent	4	Bad Manners – Agate's reprinted articles
	19	They Walk Alone/Shaftesbury – a really scary nightmare play	11	Marie Antoinette/Dominion	6	England Their England/A. G. MacDonnell
	21	Magyar Melody/His Majesty's – from the Hungarian			18	Dawn Express/M. Harrison
	25	Design for Living/Haymarket – by Noel Coward			19	Sporting Times/J. B. Booth
	26	Tony Draws a Horse/Criterion – a tame and trivial comedy			27	Memoirs/Lady Londonderry
	28	Museum Piece/Cameo – pre-war films			30	The Flying Dutchman/Michael Arlen novel
February	2	Gas Light/Apollo – by Patrick Hamilton	1	St Martin's Lane/Regent – Charles Laughton	9	London Guyed – 'a diverting symposium of a dozen diaries'
	4	Nora/Duke of York's – Ibsen revived			15	Lords and Masters/A. G. Mandrell novel
	7	Roland House Panto (amateur)				
	9	Little Ladyships/Strand – Ian Hay adaption from Hungarian	11	If I Were King/Regent – romantic comedy		
	22	Johnson Over Jordan/New – J. B. Priestley	18	Carefree/KC Cinema – Astaire & Rogers	22	Cesar Ritz – biography

Appendix B

		Theatre Visits		*Cinema Visits*		*Books Read*
March	25	*Enemy of the People*/Old Vic – Ibsen				
	1	*The Jealous God*/Lyric – dull and tedious	6	*The Citadel*/Regent	7	*The Ridiculous Hat*/Brophy
	4	*The Mother*/Garrick – by Capek			7	*The Nettle Danger?*/P. Gibbs novel
	8	*Black & Blue*/Hippodrome – intimate revue				
	11	*The Gal's Revue*/Avenue Pavilion			24	*The Beauty of Britain*/S. P. B. Mais – travel anthology
	18	*Sugar Plum*/Criterion – comedy				
	23	*The Dancing Years*/Drury Lane – Ivor Novello	26	*The Cheat* and *Old Bob*/Camden Hippodrome	31	*Revue*/Beverley Nichols novel
	29	*Heaven and Charing Cross*/St Martin's – Mary Clare				
April	1	*The Doctor's Dilemma*/Whitehall – Shaw revival	12	*The Great Waltz*/Euston Cinema – Strauss bio	13	*Charles Laughton and Myself* (?)
	20	*The Women*/Lyric – audacious comedy	15	*Dawn Patrol*/Regent	19	*Love in Our Time*/Norman Collins novel
	22	*The Little Revue*/Little – new Herbert Farjeon show			25	*Goodbye to Berlin*/Isherwood novel
May	6	*The Intruder*/Wyndham's – 'boring play'		[In hospital 30 April–4 May]	2	*Halfway*/Cecil Roberts – autobiography
	11	*Bridge Head*/Westminster – Irish land problem			6	*Christmas Holiday*/Somerset Maugham

Culture Capture

		Theatre Visits	Cinema Visits		Books Read
	13	Inquest/Duke of York's – thriller			
	18	Call It a Day/Fortune – Woolworth Amateurs			
	24	Of Mice and Men/Apollo – 'new American play'		26	Arnold Bennett, A Study/George Lefourcade
	27	Behold the Bride/Shaftesbury – from the French			
June	1	Rhondda Roundabout/Globe – Welsh play		9	Southshire Pilgrimage/Ronald Wild – a tour from Kent to Cornwall
	14	Grouse in June/Criterion – comedy		18	I Took Off My Tie/H. Massingham – East End life
	26	Till Further Orders/City L:It – Peel Players; amateur		21	Cab, Sir?/H. Hodge – cabbie's memoirs
				30	New York/Cecil Beaton
July	6	Alien Corn/Wyndham's – by Sidney Howard (US)	[Walking tour in Derbyshire, 22–30 July]	7	Wolf Among Wolves/Fallada novel
	11	The Gentle People/Strand – American play			
	13	Only Yesterday/Playhouse – strangely enjoyable war play			
	20	The Devil Must Pay/His Majesty's – Faust legend			

573

Appendix B

		Theatre Visits		*Cinema Visits*		*Books Read*
August	8	Summer Revellers/Grove Park Pavilion, Weston Super Mare		[Holiday camp in Somerset, 6–12 August;		*Early Pages*/John Gielgud – autobiography
		[In hospital 14 August–3 September]				*Pickwick Papers*/Dickens
						The King Was in His Counting House/Branch Cabell – American
						Carnival/Compton Mackenzie
September		[All theatres closed 3–14 September]			5–23	*Nicholas Nickleby*/Dickens
	21	The Importance of Being Earnest/Golders Green Hippodrome – Gielgud	23	The Family Next Door + newsreels + Do It Now – ARP film		
	30		30	The Gang's All Here/Regent – Jack Buchanan		
		(During his final fortnight in hospital)				
October	10	Music at Night/Westminster – new Priestley play	7	Gunga Din/King's Cross Cinema	3	*Turn Left For England*/Reginald Pound
	11	The Little Dog Laughed/Palladium	14	Dark Victory/Regent – medical drama	5	*One Pair of Hands*/Monica Dickens
			18	Jamaica Inn/Regent	12	*Listen to the Country*/Mais
	25	Gate Review/Ambassador's – intimate revue	21	The Story of Vernon and Irene Castle/Regent – Astaire and Rogers	18	*Rain Upon Godshill*/new Priestley novel

574

Culture Capture

	Theatre Visits		Cinema Visits		Books Read
27	*The Playboy of the Western World*/Duchess – crude rustic comedy			26	*Gangway Down*/Dave Marlowe
November 2	*Can You Hear Me Mother*/Coliseum – variety show	1	*French for Love*/Criterion – a diverting trifle	2	*Jonathan North* – new Hudson novel
4	*Runaway Love*/Saville – comedy				
7	*His Majesty's Guest*/Shaftesbury – tedious	11	*Goodbye Mr Chips*/King's Cross Cinema		
14	*Black Velvet*/Hippodrome – intimate revue				
15	*Saloon Bar*/Wyndham's – with Gordon Harper				
17	*Married for Money*/Aldwych – a weak little farce	18	*Wuthering Heights*/King's Cross Cinema	19	*Daily Mail Year Book for 1940*
30	*Eve on Parade*/Garrick – Harry Roy and band	21	*Nurse Cavell*/Bedford	29	*London During the Great War*/M. Macdonough
		23	*Only Angels Have Wings*/Regent		
December 2	*Giving the Bride Away*/St Martin's – uproarious farce				
5	*Punch Without Judy*/New – a spineless little play			6	*European Jungle*/Maj Francis Yates-Brown – right wing survey

Appendix B

	Theatre Visits		*Cinema Visits*		*Books Read*
6	*Who's Taking Liberty*/Whitehall – intimate pantomime				
9	*Great Expectations*/Rudolph Steiner Hall – by Actors' Company				
20	*All Clear*/Queen's – captivating revue			20	*Round the Room*/Edward Knoblock
22	*It Had to Be You*/Apollo – rubbish!				
26	*Cinderella*/Coliseum the only panto this year!				
28	*Spotted Dick*/Strand – Robertson Hare comedy				
Totals	**56**		**20**		**39**

576

Recorded Culture Capture 1940

		Theatre Visits		Cinema Visits		Books Read
January	2	*The Golden Cuckoo*/Duchess – by Denis Johnson			4	*I Haven't Unpacked*/William Holt – autobiography
	10	*Bone Idle*/Comedy – a foolish farce			10	*Not Guilty M'Lord*/Seymour Hicks
	11	*This Side Up*/His Majesty's – ingenious revue				
	12	*As You Are*/Aldwych – domestic comedy				
	16	*Follow My Leader*/Apollo – Terrence Rattigan	17	*Up Pops the Past*/Comic cinema	18	*Let the People Sing*/Priestley's new novel
	23	*Believe It or Not*/New – by Alex Cappel	20	*Juarez*/Regent – Mexican revolutionary		
	24	*Desire Under the Elms*/Westminster by Eugene O'Neil	27	*Batchelor Mother*/Stoll – delightful; frolic	30	*To Step Aside*/Noel Coward – short stories
February	9	*Lights Up*/Savoy – Cochran revue – 'the tops'			8	*Living in Bloomsbury*/Thomas Burke
	14	*Then Venetian*/St Martin's – 16th century Italy				
	16	*Fig Leaves*/Adelphi – terrible piece of work!				

Appendix B

		Theatre Visits		Cinema Visits		Books Read
	22	*The Light of Heart*/Apollo – Unimpressive Emlyn Williams	28	*The Stars Look Down*/Euston Cinema	23	*Life, Laughter and Brass Hats*/J. B. Booth – pinkish reminiscences
March	5	*Beggar's Opera*/Haymarket – revival			7	*A Man of Forty*/Gerald Bullet
	7	*Cousin Muriel*/Globe – by Clemence Dane; still born				
	12	*Moonshine*/Vaudeville – Arkell pocket revue				
	16	*Beyond Compere*/Duchess – tame Frankau revue				
	16	*Nap Hand*/Aldwych –tiresome witless farce				
	20	*Silver Patrol*/New – romantic musical comedy				
	21	*The White Horse Inn*/Coliseum – excellent revival	23	*Hollywood Cavalcade*/Stoll – weak film story		
April	2	*Good Men Sleep at Home*/ Shaftesbury Walter Ellis farce			5	*Konigsmark*/A. E. W. Mason
	3	*Jeannie*/Wyndham's – inspirational sentimental play				
	4	*The House on the Square*/St Martin's – liked it!				

578

Culture Capture

		Theatre Visits		Cinema Visits		Books Read
	10	Ladies in Action/Lyric – a worthless trifle				Friends in Aspic/Ian Coster
	11	New Faces/Comedy – Eric Maschwitz	13	Ninotchka/Forum, Kentish Town	12	The Day Before/H. M. Tanburn
	15	King Lear/Old Vic – Gielgud	20	Gone With the Wind/Empire – made me weary	23	
	16	Abraham Lincoln/Westminster by Drinkwater	24	The Hunchback of Notre Dame/King's Cross Cinema		
	17	Up and Doing/Saville – smart and entertaining	25	Gulliver's Travels/Regent – full length film		
May	2	Peril at End House/Vaudeville – tedious detective play			2	When Freedom Shrieked/Rothey Reynolds May
	9	In Good King Charles' Days/New – new Shaw play			3	Self Portrait/Gilbert Frankau
	10	By Pigeon Post/Garrick – spy story, revival				
	14	Present Arms/Prince of Wales – not impressed	15	The Middle Watch/Regent – naval farce		
	26	The Peaceful Inn/Duke of York's	18	The Roaring Twenties/Dominion – grand film, I saw it twice!		
	29	The Tempest/Old Vic				
	30	Ghosts/Duchess – Ibsen put on by Cochran				

Appendix B

		Theatre Visits		*Cinema Visits*		*Books Read*
June	5	Come Out of Your Shell/Criterion – revue	6	We Are Not Alone/Stoll – 'worth sitting through three naively pretentious propaganda films'	3	Can I Help You Sir?/Ethyle Campbell
					12	Master of None/Roland Pertwee – autobiography
					23	Angels in Ealing/Eileen Winnercroft
					30	The Windsor Tapestry/Compton Mackenzie
July	18	Women Aren't Angels/Strand – Robertson Hare farce				
	24	The Devil's Disciple/Piccadilly – Shaw revival				
	25	High Temperature/Duke of York's – puerile bedroom farce			30	Water Music/?
	31	Cottage to Let/Wyndham's – spy play			30	The Reign of Beau Brummell/ Willard Connelly
August	1	Margin for Error/Apollo – anti-Nazi propaganda	6	Thunder Rock/Globe		
			7	I Take This Woman/Stoll – unconvincing drama		

580

Culture Capture

	Theatre Visits		Cinema Visits		Books Read
14	The Body Was Well Nourished/Lyric – mild, ineffectual comedy	12	'A couple of sordid films'/King's Cross Cinema – 'effective escape'	20	I Lost My English Accent/G. V. R. Thompson – New York journalist
22	Dance to Brook/Aldwych	15	Broadway Melody of 1940/ Dominion – Astaire and Eleanor Powell		
		24	The Grapes of Wrath/Odeon, Upper Street, Islington		
September					
		5	Gaslight/Angel Cinema	6	Iron Gustav – a story of a Berlin family
				7	The West Wind of Love/ Compton Mackenzie – vivid tale
				13	Fanny By Gaslight/Michael Sadler
				23	Pound Notes/Reginald Pound
				27	Ego 4/Agate – criticisms
				21	Fifty Years A Showman/?
October					
		19	Bulldog Sees It Through/Picture Playhouse – spies and sabotage stuff	22	Scoop/Evelyn Waugh – one of the bright young men
				29	The Mixture As Before

Appendix B

	Theatre Visits		Cinema Visits		Books Read
November	2	*Diversions*/Wyndham's – devised by Herbert Farjeon; my first time in a theatre for two months	23	*Foreign Correspondent*/King's Cross Cinema – Hitchcock	30 *West to North*/Compton Mackenzie – 4th volume of *West Winds of Love* saga
					14 *London Doctor*/Edward Fuber
					18 *Written With Lipstick*/Maurice Dekobra – French author
December			14	*Waterloo Bridge*/Regent – from Sherwood play	13 *The Voyage*/Charles Morgan
			21	*The Great Dictator*/Gaumont – Chaplin film	14 *Oscar Wilde – A Summing Up*/Lord Alfred Douglas
	28	*Aladdin*/Coliseum – the one and only West End pantomime			18 *Mr Wu Looks Back*/Lang – memoirs
					28 *Unfinished Victory*/Arthur Bryant
Totals	**43**		**22**		**34**

Recorded Culture Capture 1941

		Theatre Visits		Cinema Visits		Books Read
January	11	Farjeon's Diversions/Wyndham's – revue	4	Lucky Partners/King's Cross Cinema – Ronald Coleman and Ginger Rogers		
					21	The Long Weekend/?
					26	Dramatic Criticism/?
					27	This For Remembrance/Julia Neilson
February	1	Dear Brutus/Globe – John Gielgud	8	You Will Remember/Paramount – Myrna Loy		
					5	Kilvert's Diary
	15	The Blue Goose/Comedy – matinee				
					21	There'll Always Be an England/S. P. B. Mais
					26	Never a Dull Moment/Trevor Wignall
March	1	Nineteen Naughty One/Prince of Wales – bright and original				
	8	Max Miller/Palladium – unquestionably vulgar but he made me a fan			12	Through the Dark Night/J. L. Hudson
	15	New Faces/Apollo – Eric Maschwitz show	22	All This and Heaven Too/Dominion – disappointing		
	29	No Time for Comedy/Haymarket – by S. N. Behman				

Appendix B

		Theatre Visits		*Cinema Visits*		*Books Read*
April	1	Orchids and Onions/Comedy – too long!	12	Major Barbara/Odeon Leicester Square – Shaw; outstanding	4	Forty Years in the Limelight/W. H. Berry
	5	Wednesday After the War/New – a strange nondescript show	13	Arise, My Love/Paramount	11	Mayfair/Michael Arlen – an old favourite of mine
	29	George Black's Third Intimate Revue/Victoria Palace	19	Down Argentina Way/Regent	12	Drama/Desmond McCarthy
			20	The Prime Minister/Metropole – Disraeli biography		
	30	Under One Roof/St Martin's – another suburban family play	27	Vigilantes/Paramount	30	The Friends of the People/Alfred Neumann novel
May			3	Comrade X/Regent – riotously funny satire		
			4	Second Chorus/? – not even a second rate musical		
			10	City for Conquest/Warner	16	Busuch/John Paddy Carstairs – biography of his father Nelson Keys
			17	The Fighting 69th/Regent – James Cagney		
			22	Married But Single/Regent – previously banned by the LCC	23	Bismarck – biography
			25	Boom Town/Empire – oil prospecting epic	24	Up at the Villa/long Somerset Maugham short story

Culture Capture

		Theatre Visits		Cinema Visits		Books Read
June			28	Hudson's Bay/Regent – uninspiring	30	Bombers' Moon/Negley Farson
			31	Backstreet/Paramount – a mature film for mature minds		
			7	Kitty Foyle/Dominion – Ginger Rogers	5	The Amazing Summer/Sir Phillip Gibbs – contemporary history
			21	Love on the Dole/Paramount – a credit to the British film industry	12	English Saga/Arthur Bryant
			28	Rebecca and Virginia/Gaumont, Camden Town – two timely reissues for a four hour programme		
July	2	Blithe Spirit/Piccadilly – a witty sophisticated Noel Coward comedy				
	19	The New Ambassador's Revue/Ambassador's – a sprightly and attractive				
	22	Quiet Weekend/Wyndham's	23	The Lady Eve/Forum, Kentish Town		
	26	Lady Behave/His Majesty's – good to see a musical again	30	The Letter/Forum – from a Somerset Maugham story		

Appendix B

		Theatre Visits		*Cinema Visits*		*Books Read*
August	23	Fun and Games/Prince's – Frith Shepherd's new show of song and dance			11	*The English Wits*/?
	27	Squaring the Circle/Vaudeville	30	*The Death of Miss Jones*/King's Cross Cinema – a modern fairy tale – and *Target for Tonight*, at every cinema in London this week		
				Handy Andy's Private Secretary/Palace, Kentish Town – Mickey Rooney	12	*How Vainly Men*/R. J. Minney – an incessantly sordid book
September			13	*Atlantic Ferry*/Forum	15	*Notebook in Wartime*/Lord Elton
			19	*Dangerous Moonlight*/Forum – as original as the original sin		
			24	*Lady Hamilton*/Paramount –Korda's history of England		
			26	*Ziegfeld Girl*/? – James Stewart		
October		[11 October marriage of Anthony and Marjorie – then a week's honeymoon in Somerset]	4	*Adam Had Four Sons*/Regent – domestic drama	1	*The Perfect Place*/Martin Shove-Gore
			18	*Hold Back the Dawn*/Odeon, Swiss Cottage		
	25	*The Nutmeg Tree*/Lyric –a scintillating hodge podge				
	28	*Up and Doing*/Saville – an exuberant show				
	29	*Jupiter Laughs*/New – A. J. Cronin about doctors				

Culture Capture

	Theatre Visits		Cinema Visits		Books Read
				31	*Time Was Mine*/Derek Tagye
	30	*Distant Point*/Westminster – a Soviet play			
November	1	*Other People's Houses*/Ambassador's – domestic country house comedy	15	*Lady Be Good*/Regent – a lack of ideas in Hollywood	7	*Men Do Not Weep*/Beverley Nichols
				19	*Cholly Clover*/Reginald Pound
	20	*Love in a Mist*/St Martin's – a flimsy little comedy			
	22	*Get Ahead of This*/Hippodrome – by James Hadly Chase			
	26	*Ducks and Drakes*/Apollo – an affable but anaemic little comedy	29	*49th Parallel*/Odeon, Swiss Cottage – entirely failed to disappoint!	
December	4	*The Man Who Came to Dinner*/Savoy – stimulating display of dramatic fireworks			
	10	*The Morning Star*/Globe – Emlyn Williams' new and powerful piece of drama	13	*The Strawberry Blonde*/Odeon-Astoria, Finsbury Park	
	17	*Gangway*/Palladium – with Max Miller			
	18	*Old Acquaintance*/Apollo – by John Van Druten			
	20	*Rise Above It*/Comedy		22	*Cock a Doodle Do*/C. B. Cochran show
	23	*Warn That Man*/Garrick – Gordon Hacker excelled	26	*Tom, Dick and Harry*/King's Cross Cinema – charming little film	23	*Hanover Square*/Patrick Hamilton
Totals	**31**		**33**		**26**	

587

Appendix B

Recorded Culture Capture 1942

	Theatre Visits		Cinema Visits		Books Read
January		3	*The Birth of the Blues*/Paramount		
		10	*It Started with Eve*/King's Cross Cinema – Charles Laughton jitterbugging!		
		17	*Meet John Doe*/Regent – an impossible film	18	*Autobiography*/Frank Swinnerton
		21	*Here Comes Mr Jordan*/Regent		
		24	*Sullivan's Travels*/Paramount – moves and excites		
		29	*Unholy Partners*/Regent		
		31	*Hatters Castle*/Paramount – from the Cronin novel		
February	5 *Good Night, Children*/New – the first new production for six weeks	4	*Citizen Kane*/King's Cross Cinema – a work of art and a masterpiece		
	10 *On Approval*/Aldwych – revival of Lonsdale comedy	7	*Honky Tonk*/Regent – a western		
	18 *Jam Today*/St Martin's	14	*Sergeant York*/Regent – WW1 film; the Yanks haven't caught up with this war	16	*The Empty Room*/Charles Morgan
		25	*Appointment for Love*/King's Cross Cinema – Charles Boyer		

588

Culture Capture

		Theatre Visits		Cinema Visits		Books Read
March	4	*The Doctor's Dilemma*/Haymarket – Shaw revival	28	*Met in Bombay*/Plaza		
	17	*Blossom Time*/Lyric – charm and pathos of Schubert's life	7	*The Little Foxes*/King's Cross Cinema –psychological drama		
	26	*The Skylark*/Duchess – from New York stage	14	*Two Faced Woman*/Regent – Greta Garbo	15	*Hocus Pocus*/Noel Langley
			21	*The Shadow of the Thin Man*/Paramount – slick domestic detective comedy	27	*The Long Alert*/Sir Phillip Gibbs – a well told tale
			28	*You'll Never Get Rich*/Regent – Fred Astaire		
April	18	*Full Swing*/Palace – a blitz delayed 1940 show	11	*The Corsican Brothers*/King's Cross Cinema – Dumas vendetta story	10	*Not Such a Bad Life*/Sidney Dark
	23	*Scoop*/Vaudeville – a desultory little revue				
	25	*Watch on the Rhine*/Aldwych – New York's play of the Year				
May	2	*Fine and Dandy*/Saville –lives up to its title			5	*H. M. Pullalong*/John P. Marquand
	9	*Big Top*/His Majesty's – Cochran and Farjeon revue	15	*Johnny Eager*/Regent – slick gangster film		

Appendix B

		Theatre Visits		*Cinema Visits*		*Books Read*
June			30	*Next of Kin*/Paramount – about the worst!		
	6	*Sky High*/Phoenix – not my personal taste	13	*This Gun for Hire*/Regent – Alan Ladd western		
	17	*About Time*/Comedy – one damned revue after another!	19	*Woman of the Year*/Regent – comedy		
			20	*How Green Was My Valley*/King's Cross Cinema – superb film		
			27	*The Foreman Went to France*/Regent – the sort of war film I enjoy	29	*As the Days Go By*/Sir John Hommerton – weekly diary
July				[On holiday in Somerset, 11–26 July]	1	*London Front*/F. Tennyson Jesse and H. Harwood
	4	*Lifeline*/Duchess – this war will not produce a finer play				
	8	*Macbeth*/Piccadilly – John Gielgud				
	9	*Salt of the Earth*/Vaudeville – much promise and little fulfilment				
	31	*No Orchids for Miss Blandish*/Prince of Wales – dramatization of James Hadley Chase novel; matinee				
August	1	*Murder Without Crime*/Comedy – matinee	8	*Let the People Sing* and *Rosie Hart*/New Victoria –double feature		
	1	*Light and Shade*/Ambassador's – Herbert Farjeon intimate revue	12	*Unfinished Story*/Regent		
	13	*Flare Path*/Apollo – Terrence Rattigan	15	*Gold Rush* and *Uncensored*/New Victoria – double feature	11	*Victorian Grotesque*/Thomas Burke

Culture Capture

		Theatre Visits		Cinema Visits		Books Read
	16	*Escort*/Lyric – Patrick Hamilton; a services war play	22	*The Bride Came COD*/Regent – the flight from serious drama now complete		
			27	*Mrs Miniver*/Regent – the spirit of England in 1940	30	*Strictly Personal*/average Maugham short story
September	5	*Men in Shadow*/Vaudeville – Mary Haley Bell play	12	*The First of the Few*/Paramount – R. J. Mitchell biography	2	*One Pair of Feet*/Monica Dickens
	16	*Belle of New York*/Coliseum – 44 year old classic				
	17	*Claudia*/St Martin's – comedy classic				
	18	*A Man with Red Hair*/Ambassador's – Ben Levy revival	26	*Young Mr Pitt*/King's Cross Cinema	19	*War in the Strand*/Hector Bolitho
					30	*Marriage Bureau*/Mary Oliver and Mary Benedettes
October	3	*Waltz Without End*/Cambridge – Eric Maschwitz's Chopin biography			1	*Enter Three Witches*/D. L. Murray
	8	*The Duke in Darkness*/St James's – escape drama				
	17	*The Importance of Being Earnest*/Phoenix – John Gielgud				
	21	*The Little Foxes*/Piccadilly – Lilian Hellman				

Appendix B

		Theatre Visits		Cinema Visits		Books Read
	24	Dubarry Was a Lady/His Majesty's			28	All Our Tomorrows/?
	29	Murder from Memory/Ambassador's	31	My Girl Sal/Paramount – nostalgic nineties		
November	11	Best Bib and Tucker/Palladium – George Black offering	5	Tortilla Flat/Regent – an unusual film		
	14	Home and Beauty/Playhouse – Maugham revival	7	The Great Mr Handel/Paramount – biography	19	St George and the Dragon/?
	21	Let's Face It/Hippodrome – George Black for Bobby Howes' return	5		20	Express and Admirable/James Agate
					24	Table for Two/T. A. Layton
					27	Plague Year/Anthony Weymouth – diary '40–'41
December	10	It Happened in September/St James's – by Beverley Baxter	5	The Big Shot/Regent – Bogart gangster film	2	A Narrow Street/Elliot Paul – delectable
	15	The House of Jeffrey's/Playhouse – homicidal maniac play again	12	San Francisco/Regent – 1936 reissue		
	16	The Petrified Forest/Globe – Robert Sherwood play				
	23	Arsenic and Old Lace/Strand				
	29	The Romance of David Garrick/St James's			31	Preludes and Studies/Alan Dent – dramatic criticisms
Totals	39		35		21	

Culture Capture

Recorded Culture Capture 1943

	Theatre Visits		Cinema Visits		Books Read
January		2	*The Pied Piper*/Odeon, Swiss Cottage	1	*And So To Bath*/Cecil Roberts
		7	*In Which We Serve*/Regent – Noel Coward	8	*A Village in Piccadilly*/Robert Henrey
		16	*The Major and the Minor*/Odeon, Islington – Ginger Rogers	13	*I Would Live the Same Life Over*/Robert Lindsay
		30	*Talk of the Town*/Regent – comedy	18	*I Lived Another Year*/Eric Baume
				22	*Here's Richness*/James Agate
				26	*Shake the Bottle*/W. Buchanan Taylor
February				1	*Londoner's Life* – diary
				3	*Hotel Splendide*/Ludwig Bemelmans
				4	*Life with Topsy*/Denis Mackaul – diary
				9	*Ego 5*/James Agate
	11	*A Month in the Country*/St James's		14	*Pubs and the People* – mass observation
	17	*Old Chelsea*/Prince's – Richard Tauber			

Appendix B

		Theatre Visits		Cinema Visits		Books Read
			25	Man and Superman/?	19	Channel Packet/?
					23	Evenings in Albany/?
			27	Algiers/London Pavilion	24	Theatrical Cavalcade/Ernest Short
March	4	The Merry Widow/His Majesty's			2	The Years of Endurance/Arthur Bryant
	10	What Every Woman Knows/Lyric – one damned revival after another!			5	George Augustus Sala/Strauss – biography
	11	Brighton Rock/Garrick –Richard Attenborough	13	Random Harvest/Regent – a love story		
	20	Heartbreak House/Cambridge – Shaw revival	16	The Magnificent Ambersons/Astoria – too intelligent for the average film goer	22	Next Please/Macrae
	23	Strike a New Note/Prince of Wales			24	World's End/Upton Sinclair
	25	A Bit of Fluff/Ambassador				
	27	It's Foolish But It's Fun/Coliseum – matinee				
	27	Hedda Gabler/Westminster				
	31	La Di Da Di Da/Victoria Palace – Lupino Lane				
April	1	Sleeping Out/Piccadilly – unfunny, I was bored			4	The Scene is Changed/Ashley Duke

594

Culture Capture

	Theatre Visits		Cinema Visits		Books Read
		3	Junior Miss/Comedy – American comedy	9	The Square of Shaftesbury Avenue/Cornell
		8	Love For Love/Phoenix	13	Wild is the Rover – American civil war story
		28	Yankee Doodle Dandy/Regent	14	Mr Bowling Buys a Newspaper/Donald Henderson
				20	Panorama 1900–48/Harold Herd
				22	Between Two Worlds/Upton Sinclair
May	1	This Happy Breed/Haymarket – Noel Coward play			
	6	Present Laughter/Haymarket – Noel Coward satire	8	Keeper of the House/Regent	
			15	Tales of Manhattan/Regent	20	Dragon's Teeth/Upton Sinclair
	25	Shadow and Substance/Duke of York's – New York success			
	27	Magic Carpet/Prince's – rapturous reception			
June	2	Case 27 VC/Comedy – abortive venture			4	John Barrymore/Alma Power Waters – biography
	3	Hi Di Hi/Palace – all laughs			
	5	The Imaginary Invalid/Westminster			

595

Appendix B

	Theatre Visits		Cinema Visits		Books Read
	8	*The Moon is Down*/Whitehall – John Steinbeck play			
	9	*Living Room*/Garrick			
	11	*The Russians*/Playhouse – war drama			
	12	*Ambassador's Revue*/Ambassador's			
	17	*The Lisbon Story*/Hippodrome – George Black play with music		22	*Honest Injun*/John Paddy Carstairs
	30	*The Fur Coat*/Comedy – amusing		24	*The Thirties*/Malcolm Muggeridge
July	1	*The King Was Bold*/Piccadilly – a rollicking romp		12	*Arnold Bennett's Journal – Vols 2 and 3*
	3	*The Master Builder*/Westminster – Ibsen's greatest play		13	*Marion Alive/?*
			14	*The Life and Death of Colonel Blimp*/Odeon, Leicester Square – sound, solid and satisfying	
				[Holiday in Somerset, 24 July–9 August]	
	21	*Lottie Dundas*/Vaudeville			
	22	*It's Time to Dance*/Winter Garden			
August	11	*Blow Your Own Trumpet*/Playhouse – by Peter Ustinov		10	*Craven House*/Patrick Hamilton – a remarkably clever book revival edition

Culture Capture

	Theatre Visits		Cinema Visits		Books Read
	12 Mr Bolfrey/Westminster			11	Arnold Bennett's Journal – Vol 1
	14 War and Peace/Phoenix – in three hours!				
	18 Sunny River/Piccadilly – American musical	24	The Man in Grey/King's Cross Cinema	27	Farwell My Youth/Arnold Bax
	26 Flying Colours/Lyric – excellent revue			29	Off the Record/Charles Graves
September	1 Pink String and Sealing Wax/Duke of York's			4	Daylight on Saturday/new Priestley novel
	11 The Wingless Victory/Phoenix – Maxwell Anderson	9	Clive of India/Regent – 1934 film	16	Arnold Bennett's Journal for 1929
				17	Strange Street/Beverley Baxter
	23 My Sister Eileen/Savoy – crazy American comedy			22	A Psychologist's Wartime Diary/Arthur Weymouth
	25 Something in the Air/Palace – the Hulberts			24	The Career of Philip Hagen/John Hammond
October	1 The Time To Dance/Winter Garden			2	Self Selected Essays/J. B. Priestley
	5 Landslide/Westminster – by adolescents for adolescents	12	King's Row/Regent – a film to see!		
	15 Acacia Avenue/Vaudeville – suburban life				

Appendix B

	Theatre Visits		Cinema Visits		Books Read
	16	She Follows Me About/Garrick – new Ben Travers farce			
	19	The Dark River/Whitehall – disappointing Rodney Ackland play			
	28	The Admirable Crichton/His Majesty's – revival			
	30	The Love Racket/Victoria Palace – Lupino musical comedy			
November	4	Panama Hattie/Piccadilly – appalling rubbish	2	Journey Into Fear/Astoria – Orson Welles	9	Holy Matrimony/King's Cross Cinema
			6	Heaven Can Wait/King's Cross Cinema – Lubitsch film worth waiting for		
	10	Arc de Triomphe/Phoenix – Ivor Novello show	13	Gentleman Jim/Regent – slickly produced	11	Travel in England/Thomas Burke
	16	The Ideal Husband/Westminster – Robert Donat	18	The Adventures of Tartu/Regent		
	17	Ten Little Niggers/St James's – Agatha Christie	20	For Whom the Bells Toll/Carlton	22	Arnold Bennett's Letters
	24	This Time It's Love/Comedy – I was petrified with boredom for two hours	27	Holy Matrimony/King's Cross Cinema	29	Late Joys at the Players' Theatre
December	2	Look Who's Here/Palladium	4	The Lamp Still Burns/King's Cross Cinema	7	The Fancy?
					10	The Saturday Book

Culture Capture

Theatre Visits	Cinema Visits	Books Read
15 *There Shall be No Night*/Aldwych – moving drama		12 *All Change Here*/J. W. Drawbell
		18 *Born Under Satan*/McDonald MacLean – Hazlett biography
		22 *Other Things Than War*/Sir John Hammerton
24 *While the Sun Shines*/Globe – Terrence Rattigan		28 *These Were the Actors* – a newspaper cuttings book
Total 56	**22**	**50**

Appendix B

Recorded Culture Capture 1944

	Theatre Visits		Cinema Visits		Books Read
January				1	*Time with a Gift of Tears*/Clifford Bax
				6	*No Complaints*/O. B. Clarence
				10	*Taste and Fashion from the French Revolution until Today*/J. Laver
				15	*All Change Here*/J. W. Drawbell
				17	*In the Meantime*/Howard Spring
				29	*Ho! Or How It Strikes Me!?*
	26	*The Druids' Reef*/St Martin's – Emlyn Williams		11	*The Days We Knew*/J. W. Booth
	27	*The Cradle Song*/Apollo – Sierra Brothers		25	*The Isthmus Years*/Barbara Cartland – attractive book
February	2	*The Gay Fillies*/Cambridge – a flop		27	*The Small Back Room*/Nigel Balchin
	3	*A Soldier For Christmas*/Wyndham's – Reginald Beckwith	15	*Jane Eyre*/Paramount	
	18	*Sweeter and Lower*/Ambassador's – new revue		2	*American Drama and Stage*/Boyd Martin
March	4	*Hamlet*/Old Vic – Robert Helpmann	2	*This is the Army*/Regent – Irving Berlin; glittering	5	*Once in Vienna*/Vicky Baum
	15	*This Was A Woman*/Comedy	11	*The Lodger*/Dominion	

600

Culture Capture

	Theatre Visits		Cinema Visits		Books Read
	22 Murder for a Valentine/Lyric Vernon Sylvane			7	Mean Sensuous Man/Stephen McKennon
	28 One Room/Apollo	25	Phantom of the Opera/Paramount		
	29 Uncle Harry/Garrick				
	31 Something for the Boys/Coliseum – American musical comedy – the type I can't abide!				
April		1	The Song of Bernadette/New Gallery	5	Prisoner at the Bar/Anthony Ellis
	12 Meet Me at Victoria/Victoria Palace – Lupino Lane show	15	Madame Curie/Regent	11	I Hate Tomorrow!?
	18 Guilty/Lyric, Hammersmith – reopened after some years			13	The World of Yesterday/ Stephen Zweig – autobiography
	21 Jill Darling/Winter Garden				
	22 The Rest is Silence/Prince of Wales' – elaborate thriller			27	Shake It Again/W. Buchanan Taylor
May	4 How Are They At Home/Apollo	6	The Heavenly Body/Regent	1	Wide is the Gate/Upton Sinclair
	11 Crimson Heaven/Lyric – Eric Linklater – I was bored!			19	Pleasure Beach/Frank Tisley
	25 The Quaker Girl/Coliseum – revival	27	Escape to Happiness/Angel – Leslie Howard		

Appendix B

		Theatre Visits		Cinema Visits		Books Read
June					1	*On the Danger List*/Georges Simenon
	7	*The Last of Summer*/Phoenix – I was not impressed	9	*The Half Way House*/Regent	2	*Sing High, Sing Low*/Osbert Sitwell
	14	*Zero Hour*/Lyric			8	*The Turning Point*/Klaus Mann
	15	*The Last of Mrs Cheney*/Savoy – a scintillating evening				
	17	*The Gypsy Princess*/Prince's – musical comedy			22	*The Critic and the Drama*/?
					28	*While London Burns* – I can't get on with this
July			7	*The Tawny Piper*/Plaza, Camden town	13	*Inside story*/?
			8	*The Way Ahead*/Paramount – dreary monotony		
			15	*Mayerling*/Astoria – French film; worth seeing	18	*So Far*/?
			29	*This Happy Breed*/Dominion – Noel Coward	22	*Great Days*/?
					29	*The Turn of the Screw*/Henry James – short story

Culture Capture

		Theatre Visits		*Cinema Visits*		*Books Read*
August	1	*Is Your Honeymoon Really Necessary?*/Duke of York's – the first premier for 7 weeks	2			*Berlin Hotel*/Vicky Baum
	10	*Keep Going*/Palace – inferior little revue	12	*Un Carnet Du Bal*/Carlton, T C Rd – 'the outstanding French film of the decade'		*Keep the Vanman Waiting*/Adam de Hegedus
			25			*Rebel in Fleet Street* – journalist's memoirs
	30	*Tomorrow the World*/Aldwych – American importation	31			*Impressions*/S. G. Bergmann
September	8	*The Banbury Nose*/Wyndham's	1	*A Canterbury Tale*/Rialto – Eric Portman	6	*Red Letter Nights*/?
	15	*Arms and the Man*/New – Old Vic Company			13	*So Little Time*/J. P. Marquand
	16	*Richard III*/New – Old Vic Company	23	*Going My Way*/Odeon, Swiss Cottage		
	27	*Jane Clegg*/Lyric, Hammersmith – really worth it!				
	28	*Bird in Hand*/St Martin's – fair to middling				

Appendix B

		Theatre Visits	**Cinema Visits**	**Books Read**
October	3	*Happy and Glorious*/Palladium – George Black's success		
	4	*No Medals*/Vaudeville – too much of a women's play		
	5	*Scandal in Barchester*/Lyric		
	7	*Jenny Jones*/Hippodrome – needs pulling together		
	10	*Happy Few*/Cambridge – by Paul Anthony		
	11	*The Circle*/Haymarket		
	12	*Peer Gynt*/New – Old Vic Rep Company		15 *Rosie Todmarsh*/Adrian Allington
	18	*Daughter Janice*/Apollo	19 *Double Indemnity*/Plaza, Camden Town – a near perfect crime film	16 *Home Front*/J. L. Hodson
	15			20 *Hard Facts*/?
	16			31 *Off the Record*/?
November	2	*Private Lives*/Apollo – revival ; I never saw the original		1 *Katherine*/Hams Habe
	8	*Residents Only*/St James's – a bad flop	11 *Champagne Charlie*/Regent	16 *Dark Nights*/Thomas Burke
				21 *The Tree in the Yard*/Betty Smith
	23	*The Magistrate*/St James's		

Culture Capture

	Theatre Visits		**Cinema Visits**		**Books Read**
December	6	*Strike It Again*/Prince of Wales'	1	*Henry V*/Carlton – a picture that does credit to Shakespeare	3	The Trojan Brothers/Pamela Hansford Johnson
					11	*English Diaries and Journals*/Kate O'Brien
	16	*Another Love Story*/Phoenix – comedy			14	*The Road back to Paris*/?
	20	*Love in Idleness*/Lyric			20	*From the Life*/Phyllis Bottome
	23	*The Glass Slipper*/St James's – Robert Donat				
Totals	**45**		**19**		**44**	

Appendix B

Recorded Culture Capture 1945

		Theatre Visits		*Cinema Visits*		*Books Read*
January	4	See How They Run/Comedy – I yawned!	17	Laura/Odeon, Swiss Cottage – mystery film	7	Dr Philligo/C. E. Vulliamy
	20	Uncle Vanya/New – Old Vic Rep Company			22	Britain's Brains Trust/Howard Thomas
	25	A Midsummer's Night Dream/Haymarket – John Gielgud	31	The Impatient Years/King's Cross Cinema		
February	7	Emma/St James's – Jane Austen adaption	2	Summer Storm/Astoria – adaption of Chekhov story	1	Night and Day/J. W. Drawbell
	14	Laura/St Martin's	3	Waterloo Road/Paramount – London life cameo	12	Things Past/Michael Sadlier
	22	Madame Louise/Strand – farce	10	Frenchman's Creek/Paramount	20	Memories of Happy Days/Julian Green – diary
March	1	Three Waltzes/Prince's – romantic and sensual play	3	The Woman at the Window/Paramount	2	One More Shake/W. Buchanan Taylor
	8	Gay Rosalinda/Palace – triumphant revival	9	Kipps/Metropolis, Victoria	15	Now I Lay Me Down to Sleep/Ludwig Bemelmans
	14	Great Day/Playhouse – a women's play	16	Wilson/Paramount – inaccurate but a grand film	20	Ego 6/James Agate – criticisms
	22	The Assassin/Savoy	17	The Constant Nymph/Regent		
	29	The Gaietier/Winter Garden				
	31	Appointment With Death/Piccadilly – Agatha Christie tale				

Culture Capture

	Theatre Visits		Cinema Visits		Books Read
April					
	10	Lady from Edinburgh/Playhouse – delightful comedy	2	A Song to Remember/King's Cross Cinema – a picture to forget	
	11	The Shop at Sly Corner/St Martin's – good thriller	5	Hanover Square/Dominion – from the Patrick Hamilton novel	10 Books and Myself/Sir John Hommerton – autobiography
	12	The Wind of Heaven/St James's – pretentious Emlyn Williams play	14	None But the Lonely Heart/Paramount	
	18	The Duchess of Malfi/Haymarket – John Gielgud			
	25	Perchance to Dream/Hippodrome – Ivor Novello musical	28	The Keys of the Kingdom/King's Cross Cinema – A. J. Cronin	
May					
	15	The Gay Pavilion/Piccadilly – 'the first peace production'		[Victory in Europe celebrations, 10 May]	14 It Always Rains on Sunday – East End life
	16	The Skin of Our Teeth/Phoenix – an extraordinary Thornton Wilder play			19 The North Wind of Love Book 1/Compton Mackenzie
	17	The Night and the Music/Coliseum – mammoth revue but boring	26	Tonight and Every Night/King's Cross Cinema – the Windmill story	25 English Social History/G. M. Trevelyan
June					
	6	Jacobowsky and the Colonel/Piccadilly – I have no time for comedy of this sort	2	Under the Clock/Regent – Hollywood boy meets girl story	9 The World is Square/Hermione Gingold – autobiography, all 57 pages of it
			14	The Picture of Dorian Gray/Regent	10 Trumpet Voluntary/G. B. Stern

Appendix B

	Theatre Visits		*Cinema Visits*		*Books Read*
20	Chicken Every Sunday/Savoy – superior American comedy	16	Czarina/Paramount		
21	Sweet Yesterday/Adelphi – new musical romance			27	The Aesthetic Adventure – art history
				27	Saki Short Stories – unable to get on with them
July					
3	Two Hands/Lyric – plastic surgery drama!		[General Election, 5 July]		
		6	They Were Sisters/King's Cross Cinema – far from exciting	9	A Cockney on Main Street/Herbert Hodge
		7	Experiment Perilous/Regent – ponderous period piece		
12	The Cure for Love/Westminster – Lancashire comedy	11	The Fifth Chair/King's Cross Cinema – burlesque		
		14	The Way to the Stars/Paramount	24	Time Must Stop/Aldous Huxley novel
18	The First Gentleman/New – not a great play	21	To Have and Have Not/Regent – spy rehash	25	Our Hearts Were Young and Gay/Cornelia Otis Skinner – gleeful reading
			[General Election count and announcement of Labour victory, 26 July]	31	Men in Suits/the new Priestley novel

608

Culture Capture

	Theatre Visits		Cinema Visits		Books Read
August					
1	Kiss and Tell/Phoenix – inane American comedy	4	I'll Be Your Sweetheart/King's Cross Cinema	3	Daly's/S. Forbes Wilson
7	For Crying Out Loud/Stoll		[Surrender of Japan, 15 August; Somerset holiday, 11–21 August, but in London for VJ celebrations]	12	The North Wind of Love Book 2/Compton Mackenzie
22	Sigh No More/Piccadilly – Noel Coward revue	25	The Affairs of Susan/Paramount	23	The Razor's Edge/Somerset Maugham
30	The Hasty Heart/Aldwych – the finest war play to date			29	Long, Long Ago/Alexander Woolcott
September					
5	Young Mrs Barrington/Winter Garden – the problem of post-war mental readjustment	1	Blood on the Sun/King's Cross Cinema – anti-Jap propaganda	3	Transient Joys/James Agate
6	Merrie England/Prince's – revival by Jack Waller	6	I Live on Grosvenor Square/Regent – Anglo-American friendships	14	Forever Amber – American best seller
13	Big Boy/Saville – I'd have done better to stay at home	15	Mr Skeffington/Regent – a fascinating film		
19	A Bell for Adam/Phoenix – should not fail in London	22	A Bell for Adam/Paramount – film adaption		
26	Henry V Part 1/New – Old Vic Company	23	Roughly Speaking/Warner, Leicester Square – diverting comedy		

Appendix B

		Theatre Visits		*Cinema Visits*		*Books Read*
October	3	*Henry V Part 2*/New – Old Vic Company	6	*Weekend at the Waldorf*/Regent – sophisticated hotel story		
	11	*Fine Feathers*/Prince of Wales – Jack Buchanan revue	13	*Dead of Night*/Dominion – thriller	14	*Restaurant Roundabout*/T. A. Layton
	18	*Oedipus* and *The Critic*/New – Old Vic Company; the perfect balance	17	*Perfect Strangers*/Regent – disappointing	20	*The Foolish Decade*/Robert Henrey
	25	*Follow the Girls*/His Majesty's – with Arthur Askey	24	*The Ferryman Reel*/Sadler's Wells – James Bridie	22	*The Next Horizon*/Douglas Reed
			27	*Johnny Frenchman*/Paramount – dull; lacking interest		
November			3	*Conflict*/Astoria – another 'perfect crime' film	4	*Charles Dickens*/Una Pope Hennessy – biography
			10	*The Seventh Veil*/Paramount – pseudo psychological drama		
			15	*The Lost Weekend*/Paramount – a really adult film		
			17	*The Valley of Desire*/Regent – disappointing	18	*London Belongs to Me*/Norman Collins novel
	22	*Under the Counter*/Phoenix – inconsequential comedy				
	24	*The Sacred Flame*/Westminster – a revival				

	Theatre Visits	Cinema Visits		Books Read	
December		1	*The Southerner*/Metropole – vivid little masterpiece of Southern life		
		3	*Early Films to 1913*/Lyric – London Film Society	8	*Pride in the Morning/?*
				11	*A Showman Looks On*/C. B. Cochran – autobiography
				12	*Wanderings in London*/E. V. Lucas
				22	*The Incredible City*/Robert Henrey
				27	*No Man Is An Island*/Francis Williams
				30	*English Diaries and Journals*/Kate O'Brien
Totals	41	40		37	

BIBLIOGRAPHY

BOOKS

Addison, Paul, *The Road to 1945: British Politics and the Second World War* (London: Jonathan Cape, 1975)
Aston, Mark, *The Cinemas of Camden* (London: London Borough of Camden, 1997)
Berwick Sayers, W. C., *Croydon and the Second World War* (Croydon: Croydon Corporation, 1949)
Butler, David and Butler, Gareth, *British Political Facts 1900–1985* 6th edition (Basingstoke: Macmillan, 1986)
Calder, Angus, *The People's War: Britain, 1939–1945* (London: Jonathan Cape, 1969)
Collier, Basil, *The Defence of the United Kingdom* (London: HMSO, 1957)
Dear, I. C. B. (ed.), *The Oxford Companion to the Second World War* (Oxford: Oxford University Press, 1995)
Gardiner, Juliet, *The Blitz: The British Under Attack* (London: Harper Press, 2010)
Gardiner, Juliet, *The Thirties: An Intimate History* (London: Harper Press, 2010)
Gardiner, Juliet, *Wartime: Britain, 1939–1945* (London: Headline 2004)
Hennessy, Peter, *Never Again: Britain 1945–1951* (London: Vintage, 1993)
Hickin, William, *Fire Force: A Short Organisational History and Directory of the National Fire Service of 1941 to 1948* (London: WHF Publications, 2013)
Jackson, W. Eric, *Achievement: A Short History of the London County Council* (London: Longmans, Green and Co., 1965)
Jones, H. A., *The War in the Air: Being the Story of the Part Played in the Great War by the Royal Air Force, Vol. 5* (Oxford: Clarendon Press, 1935)
Kynaston, David, *Austerity Britain, 1945–1951* (London: Bloomsbury, 2007)
Kynaston, David, *Family Britain, 1951–1957* (London: Bloomsbury, 2009)
Madge, C. and Harrison, T., *Britain by Mass Observation* (London: Muller, 1937)
Martland, Peter, *Lord Haw Haw: The English Voice of Nazi Germany* (Richmond: The National Archives, 2003)
Newbery, C. Allen, *Wartime St Pancras: a London borough defends itself*, originally compiled 1945, transcribed by Robin Woolven, edited by F. Peter Woodford (London: Camden History Society, 2006)
O'Brien, T. H., *Civil Defence* (London: HMSO, 1955)
Pile, Frederick, *Ack-Ack: Britain's Defence against Air Attack during the Second World War* (London: Harrap, 1949)
Plomer, William (ed.), *Kilvert's Diary: Selections from the Diary of Rev. Francis Kilvert, 1 January 1870–19 August 1871* (London: Jonathan Cape, 1938)
Pugh, Martin, *Hurrah for the Blackshirts! Fascists and Fascism in Britain between the Wars* (London: Jonathan Cape, 2005)
Ramsey, Winston G. *The Blitz: Then and Now*, 3 vols (London: Battle of Britain Prints International, 1987–1990)
Saunders, Ann (ed.), *The London County Council Bomb Damage Maps 1939–1945*,

Bibliography

with introduction by Robin Woolven (London: London Topographical Society, 2005)
Sheppard, Martin, *Primrose Hill, A History* (Lancaster: Carnegie, 2013)
Taylor, A.J.P., *English History 1914–1945* (Oxford: Clarendon Press, 1965)
Titmuss, R. M., *Problems of Social Policy* (London: HMSO, 1950)
Walkowitz, Judith R., *Nights Out: Life in Cosmopolitan London* (New Haven, CT and London: Yale University Press, 2012)
Waller, Maureen, *London 1945: Life in the Debris of War* (London: John Murray, 2004)
Ward, Laurence, *The London County Council Bomb Damage Maps, 1939–1945* (London: Thames & Hudson, 2015)
White, Jerry, *London in the Twentieth Century: A City and Its People* (London: Viking, 2001)
Young, Ken, *Local Politics and the Rise of Party: The London Municipal Society and the Conservative Intervention in Local Elections, 1894–1963* (Leicester: Leicester University Press, 1975)
Ziegler, Philip, *London at War 1939–1945* (London: Sinclair-Stevenson, 1995)

ARTICLES

Woolven, Robin, 'Camden's Vestry and Town Halls: Vestries, Councils and Ratepayers', *Camden History Review*, no. 39 (2015), pp. 8–15
Woolven, Robin, 'The Fall of John Sperni, Mayor of St Pancras 1937–38', *Camden History Review*, no. 35 (2011), pp. 9–14
Woolven, Robin, 'The London Experience of Regional Government 1938–1945', *London Journal*, vol. 25:2 (2002), pp. 59–78
Woolven, Robin, 'London's Debris Clearance and Repair Organisation 1939–45', in M. Clapson and P. Larkham (eds), *The Blitz and Its Legacy* (Farnham: Ashgate, 2013), pp. 61–72
Woolven, Robin, 'The Middlesex Bomb Damage Maps 1940–1945', *London Topographical Review*, vol. 30 (2010), pp. 132–210
Woolven, Robin, 'A Tendency to Deprave or Corrupt in Chalk Farm?' A Camden Resident and *Oh! Calcutta!* at the Round House, July 1970, *Camden History Review*, no. 38 (2014), pp. 21–26

INDEX

Abdication crisis 166–7 *see also* Edward VIII
Abyssinia *see* Italy
actors, actresses, impresarios and musicians (stage and film)
  Sir Thomas Beecham 103
  Jack Buchanan 36, 123, 333
  Maurice Chevalier 47
  Charles B. Cochran 37, 97, 149, 177, 353, 411
  Cecily Courtneidge (Mrs Jack Hulbert) 33, 597
  Noel Coward 97, 122, 149, 291, 365, 501
  Marlene Dietrich 75
  Bud Flanagan 264
  John Gielgud 253, 262, 286
  Bobby Howes 58
  Walter Kraus 84,
  Beatrice Lillie 264
  John McCormack 31
  Ivor Novello 78, 264
  Laurence Olivier 451
  George Robey 98, 124, 444
  Richard Tauber 39
Adam (de Hegedus) 30, 36, 48, 53, 62, 75, 77, 83, 85, 101, 140 n27, 205 n10, 286, 293, 511, 603
Admiralty Citadel 418
air raids, Pre-Blitz 293, 304–9
  Major Blitz raids 1940–41
  7/8 September 309–10
  15/16 October 326
  29/30 December 337, 341, 353
  19 March 351–2
  16/17 April 355–6
  19/20 April 356
  10/11 May 358–60
  Baedeker raids 1942 396
  'Hit and run' nuisance raids 1942–43 417, 424–6, 434

Mini Blitz 1944 443–4, 446–7 *see also* V-1 and V-2
Air Raid Precautions 210, 1944 reductions 473
  blackout 228 n1, 259, 261, 263, 265, 329, 369, 377, 408, relaxation 465, dim out 466
  Control Room duties (AH) 357, 363–5, 373, as Plotting Officer 393, 408, 410, 416, 454, 465, 468, 478, North Centre closed 393 n8
  gas masks 217, 254, 257, 262–4, 268, 284, 288 n25, 345 n9, AH's service respirator 217, 247
  HQ Camden High St 336, 350, 368–9, 382, 473
  sandbags 222 n38, 238, 257–8
  sirens/alerts (significant entries only) 255–6, 293, 422, 452, Senate House klaxon 463, London Alert statistics 486
  trench shelters 9, 216 n26, 220, 264, 266, 291, 332, 367 n34
Air Raid Shelters used and AH's experiences of shelter life in:
  Friends' House 326, 346, bunks 334, Christmas 335, New Year 337, damage 355, 362, bedding and diaries retrieved 387, 393
  Royal Hotel, Bedford Way 319–23
  Rashleigh House basement 448
  Bidborough St 457
  St Pancras Church Crypt xxiv, xxv, 311, 316–18, return to crypt 323
  Sinclair House basement 293, 302, 304, 306, 309, 311, 456
  Tube stations as shelter 315, 320, 455, 473
  Albany St barracks 171, 175, 224, 344, 352

Index

Albert Hall   53, 102, 342 n2, 454,
  Promenade concerts suspended 458
Alby (Holmes)   267, 501
Aldershot Military Tattoo   189
Alfred Place   268 n59, 355
all-in wrestling   132
allotments   280 n8, 281, 394, 409, 461–2
Anschluss   205 n11
Anti-Aircraft barrage balloons   257, 309, 484
Anti-Aircraft gunnery   220, 244, 256, 284, 313 n56, 314–15, 332, 341, 350, 355 n19, 416, 420, 424, 433, 448, 454 n20
Anti-Aircraft searchlights   244, 254, 287, 305, 307, 311, 489
Anti-Nazi propaganda   209, 234
Anti-Semitism   84, 138, 208, 211, 217, 221, 229, 244, 246, 276, 281, 290, 307, 374, 417
Athenia   256
Atomic Bomb   498
Attlee, Clement MP   288 n24, 352 n14, 430 n24, 492, as PM 497, announces V-J Day 500
Australia House   179–80, 197, 359, 456 n22
Austria   107, 204–5, 486
authors and playwrights *see* Appendix B for complete list of authors of books, films and plays
  James Agate   10 13, 125, 149, 156, 206, 229, 287, 347, 416
  Herbert Banyard   232
  Vernon Bartlett   96
  Arnold Bennett   10, 13, 347, 574
  Clifford Bax   77
  Charles Dickens   123, 561, 574
  Monica Dickens   574, 591
  St John Ervine   99
  John Evelyn   13 n20, 217, 347, 378, 393
  John Gunther   179
  Rev Francis Kilvert   13 n19, 15, 345, 347–8
  Compton Mackenzie   10, 253
  A. G. Macdonell   229 n5
  Somerset Maugham   10, 241,361
  Margaret Mitchell   286
  Oswald Mosley   83, 106

  Samuel Pepys   13 n20, 347, 378, 393
  J. B. Priestley   52, 125, 449 n9
  Franz von Rintelin   201
  William Shakespeare   54, 104, 123–4, 160, 407, 451
  G. B. Shaw   166, 167 n19, 422
  Hugh Walpole   10
  Evelyn Waugh   57, 327
  H. G. Wells   10, 162

Baden Powell, Lord Robert (Chief Scout)   32 n10, 33 n11, 42 n26, 43, 78 n14, death 342
Bainbridge, Cyril (St Pancras ARP Controller)   408 n21
Baldwin, Stanley   9, 27, 167 n20, 168, 204
Ball, Sir Girling   239 n26
Bangle Farm, Nunney   378, 389, 414, 427–8, 455, 464, 501
Bank Holiday – wartime cancellations   288, 299, 335, 384
Barts hospital   238–40
bars *see* pubs, bars and hotels
Bath   251
Baxter, Mrs   181, 182–3, 186, 205, 230, 235, 237 (death of Mr B), 191
BBC (British Broadcasting Corporation   149
  AH seeks job   306
  wartime operation   256
  Wodehouse ban   436
Bedford Row   321, 359
Bedford Square   325, 359
Beethoven symphonies   230, 242
Beit, Sir Alfred MP   127, 130, 188, 208–9, 221, 222, 231, defeated 496 n13
Belgium   248, 266, 288–91, surrender 290 322 n62, 1945 472, 477
Bell, John   179, 196, 246, 282, 345, marries 372, 395, 443, 503
Belsize Park   283, damage 322, 346, 448, 482
Berwick St   169, 306, 307 n50, 328
Bethnal Green disaster   420 n10
Beveridge Plan for Social Insurance   410 n24, 467
Bevin, Ernest MP   188 n18, 449, 500
Birkenhead St   434

616

Index

Blackpool 192
Blitz 1940–41 *see* air raids
Bloomsbury Squares 187, 218, *see also* Brunswick, Gordon, Russell, Tavistock Squares
books read *see* annual culture appendices, AH total 1933–39 282
Boat Race night 37, 55, 100, 126, 154, 180, 206, 234 at Henley 283
Bolsheviks (AH's perceptions) 99, 364, 376, 398, 400, 427, 441, 471, 486, 492, 499, *see also* Russia

Boot's *see* libraries, lending
Box Hill 236, 395, 491
boxing (AH watching) 78
Brains Trust BBC programme 384, 406, 432, 457, 468
Brighton Rock 420
British Museum 230, 317, 360
British Restaurants 411 n25, 412
British Union of Fascists (BUF) 4 n7, 7–8, 72, 79, 115, 116, 123, 136 (Rallies) Olympia xxiii, 106, Marble Arch 111–12, Earls Court 248 (Islington Branch) 110
see also newspapers, *Blackshirt*
Brown, Ford Madox 213
Brunswick Sq 188, 244, 311 n54, 319
Buckingham Palace 73, 129, 158 n12, 186–7, 314, 489–90, 500
Budget measures 155, wartime 263, 296, 353, 395, 422, 485
Bulgaria 353–4
Bunny *see* Kaye, Bunny
'Burglary' 373, 382
buses, London, strikes 162, 183, 188, 449, army crews 449, from provinces 328–9, internal lights 357, 490, clear windows 498
Bush House 142, 152, 324, 456

Café de Paris 350 n11
Cambridge 213
Camden High St 101 n13, 328, 344, 375, 424
camping under canvas 22, 126, 243–4, 248, 270, 294, 302, 322, camouflaging tent 287–8

Canadian forces 277, 305 n47, 363, 370, 372, 395, 403 n16, 483, 495
Carnarvon 225
Carreras factory NW1 322
Casablanca 106
Catford, school incident 417
Cenotaph 47, 61, 79, 115, 138, 195, 267 *see also* Remembrance Day
Chamberlain, Neville MP 4 n7, 204, 216, 225, 233, 3 Sept broadcast 254, 268, resigns 288, death 330
Chamberlain, Tiny 126, 137, 138, 140, 151, 163, 164
Chelsea 116, 432
'Cherub' 33, 38, 68, 87, 127, 160
Chester 212
Chilterns 100, 135, 154, 211
Churchill, Winston distrusted by AH 276 n3, 396, becomes PM 288, at St Pancras Stn 361, 364, 383, sick in Cairo 436, seen at Mornington Crescent 494, resigns 491, 497, on VE Day 488, shouts for on VJ Day crowd 500
cinemas (only the first and significant entries indexed but *see also* multiple entries in Annex B)
  Academy 530
  Alhambra 530
  Angel, Islington 581
  Astoria, Finsbury Park 587
  Bedford Kinema 130
  Britannia 162
  Camden Hippodrome 101 n13
  Capitol 51
  Comic 577
  Embassy, Torrington Place 355
  Euston Cinema 343, 518
  Forum Kentish Town 544
  Gaumont, Camden Town 364
  Globe 515
  Hippodrome 36
  King's Cross Kinema 371
  Leicester Square Theatre 52
  London Pavilion 31
  Lyceum 182
  Majestic 527
  Metropole 584
  Movietone New Theatre 187
  New Gallery 514

617

New Victoria 590
Odeon Haverstock Hill 562
Odeon Islington 304
Odeon Leicester Square 427
Odeon Swiss Cottage 566
Palace, Kentish Hill 526, 193
Paramount 568, 416
Phoenix 558
Piccadilly 552
Picture Playhouse
Prince Edward 123,
Rialto 39, 55,
Tatler 35
Tivoli 53
Trocadero, Elephant & Castle 31
Warner 584
circus performance 176
CIS (Chartered Institute of Secretaries, examinations 39–40, result 42, subscriptions 87, 388, 412, 437
Clacton (cruise) 131
clothing coupons 362, 375–7, 392, 419, 441, stolen 445, replacements 447, 493, 502 – loss by AH replacement
Cockneys 108, 111, 124–5, 269
Colbourne, Bill 141, 144, 146, 149, 170, and Lilian 188, 192, 207, 210, 230, 241
Communists and AH's perceptions of 72, 75–7, 82, 96 n3, 106, 108, 110 n24, 142 n31, 159, 179, 195, 216, 246, 290, 294, 343, 364, 370, 376, 396, 400, 403–4, 435, 437, 467, 471, 477, 480, 485, 487, 492, 497
conscription measures 238, 261, 276, 281, 288, 290, 344, 383, 407, 464, 472, 484
Conservative Party, local ward matters 183, 186, 209, 229, 247, 268
Conway Hall 68
Co-op hikes 11, 34–5, 44–5, 47, 61–2, 80
Corner House (Oxford St) 36, 40, 46, 56, 67–8, 76, 115, 163, 372, 400, (Coventry St) 50, 60, 169, 370, 381, (Marble Arch) 95, (Angel) 122
Coronation (1937) 184, decorations 186
Cotswolds 109, 160
Courageous, HMS 263

Covent Garden Opera House 12,17, 397
Coventry 330
Cox, Stan 12, 34, 37, 40, *see also* Maud Cox in Heap (girlfriends)
Cromer St 219, 324, 326
Croydon, airport 230, cinema incident 442
Crystal Palace Fire 165–6
Cumberland Market 332 n76, 352
Cutner, Dr (GP) 252, 255, 257, 266, 292, 405, 423–4, 426
Czecho-Slovakia 9, 216–7, 219, 233, 480, 484, 486

dances 35–6, 42, 46–8, 50, 56, 62–3, 68, 77, 82, 87, 95–7, 104, 123, 142, 152–3, 162, 165, 177, 179, 188, 197, 203, 207, 214, 219, 222, 224, 231, 250, 269, 282, 372, 379, 388, 407, 411, 433–4, AH learns 45
Danzig 246 n33, 253
Defence Regulations 290 n28, 490
democracy (AH's views) 107, 139, 211, 225, 244, 262, 286–7, 290, 330, 359, 396, 471, 492
Derby (horserace) 7, 39, 76, at Newmarket 425, 453, 493
dogs after Nigger 215–16, 220
Doodlebug *see* V-1
Douglas, Lord Alfred 482
Dunstable 135

Earl's Court 178, 221, 248
East End 163
Eden, Anthony Foreign Secretary 139, War Minister 204, 294, 419 n8
Edward VIII as Prince of Wales 53, proclaimed King 149, serious incident witnessed 158, King's speech 152, and Mrs Simpson 166–7, Abdication crisis 166–7
Eileen (AH's mistress) 295–7, 302, 305, 317, ends affair 319, her letters 296, 298–9, 300–2, 307, 312–3, 331
Elections, General (1929) xvii
(1931) 46
(1935) 142
(1945) as poll clerk 494, the count 496, result local 486 n13, national 497

Index

(1979) 508
Elections, LCC 99
Elections, Borough 193–4, 195
electric iron 480
Elkonians 37 n21, 40, 58
Ellis, Mrs 375–7, 380–1, 401–2, 421
Empire State Building 498
Employment Exchanges *see* Labour Exchange
Epsom 61
Euston Rd 1, 84, 87, 189, 223, 257, 259, 314, 316, 318, 322, 326–7, 334, 337, 343–4, 348, 356, 358, 411, 417, 430, 466, 469, 490
evacuation 229 n1, 336, 34, 458, returning 486
Eversholt St 70 n3, 311, 327

Fincham, Alderman R. 211
Finland (invaded) 268
Fire Guard/Fire Watching and registering – AH volunteers 233, 341, 343, 364, 374, Marjorie 447
Fire Services, AFS 233, 265, 278, 282, 343, National Fire service NFS 423
Fitzrovia damage 355, 358, 453
Flying Bombs *see* V-1
food parcels from Somerset 411, 419, 430, 436, 472
Foundling site (Coram's Field) 32, 40, 57, 164, 244, 345
France 292–3, Free French HQ 358
Frensham Ponds 73, 76, 81, 107
furniture – setting up home 394, 406–8.413–5, 421, 429, 438, 442, 448

gas masks *see* Air Raid Precautions
General Elections *see* Elections
George V HMS 397
George V Silver Jubilee 128–9, Radio speech 144, death 149, lying in state 149–150, funeral procession 150
George VI, proclaimed King 168, Coronation 184, speeches 185, 269, 335
Germany 11, 27, 73, 96, 122, 153, 201 n1, 204–5, 209, 216–9, 225, 235–6, 246 n33, 253, 256, 266, 284, 288, 291–3, 353, 356, Hess 360, 363–4, 383, 398, 407, 429–31, 459, 480–1, surrender 486–8
Gilwell Scout Centre viii, xvi, 22, 41, 229
Gone with the Wind 286–7
Gordon Square 327
Gowers, Sir Ernest (Regional Commissioner) 436
Gower St 318, 355, 358
grandmother (maternal) in hospital 21, 31, danger list 97, dies 115, 116, 120, tombstone 153
Gray's Inn Rd (No 139) xi, xviii, 2, moving from 53, return and leave again 53, 58–60
Greece 249, 329, 354, 357, 471, 477
Green Park 126, 128, 150 n2, 258, 286
Greenshirts / Green Band (antifascists) 110–11
Greenwich 354
Guildford 47, 56
Guilford St 316, 321, 324, 359

Haden Guest, David 82
Hampstead Heath, AH's numerous walks thereon not indexed 262, 368, 394 Ken Wood 88, 132, 161, 236, 280, 308 *see also* Parliament Hill sandpits 222, 258, 348
Hampstead Rd area damage 310, 317–18, 322, 344, 352
Handel St, drill hall 244, 323, 447
Harrington Square, No 20 xi, xxi, xxvi, found 103, moved in 104, 119, outlook from 180, moved out 182, damaged xxvi, 310
Harris, Mrs 202–3, 205
Harrow 209
Hastings 160
Haverstock Hill damage 356
Haw Haw *see* Lord Haw Haw, 'the Italian Haw Haw 208 n18, 512
Hayes, Kent 462–3
Heap, Anthony (AH the diarist)
  early life 2–3
  school 3
  Diaries – reasons for keeping 13, 15–16 (quoting Kilvert) 347–8, resumes after illness 255, safe storage xxxiii, 381 wanting them

619

Index

to be read 1, 15–16, writing by candlelight, 393 sourcing the books 380, 408, 443–4
work at PR's 3, questioned on his politics 290, sacked 297
CIS examinations 3, 42, result 46
further education courses 3, 25, 27, 36 n18, 44
job interviews 20, 57, 78, 161, 303, 306, 313
finances and savings 31–2, 61, 65, 145–6, 163, 172, 197, 256, 271, 277, 353, 364, 388, 438, 445, 474, 502, Post war credits 353 n15, 438, 445, 474, 502
pay rises (PR's) 56, 100, 119, 125, 206 (Council) 349, 364, 380, 400, 414, 429, 438
girlfriends
    Maud 40, 44, 47, 49, 58, 62
    Beatrice/Trixie 54, 57, 62, 67, 95, 153, 512
    Lilian 76, 80, 81, 87–90, 95, 98, 100, 106–8, 115, 118, 124, 131
    Joan 350–1
    Josephine 178
    Glynis 214, 215
    Irene 231
    Norah 74, 322, 320, 328, 336, 343, 348, AH proposes 349–51, 512
    Marjorie, meets 360, proposes 366, marries 378–9, decision on children 493
    see also Heap, Marjorie
    the 1971 'other woman' 507
health (AH) stature 19, eyesight and spectacles 61–2, 143, 155, 213, 265–6, 416, dental problems 45, 117, 122, 384, boils 61–2, 143, 155, 213, 265–6, 416, testes 74–5, circumcision 153, 237–8, 240, 270, peritonitis 252, 261, 270, 381, 405, 423, 464, rupture 5, 423, 430, 438, rupture appliance 440–1, 469, 474, 488, 503, falling hair 133, 136–7, 143, 265, vomiting 241, 267, 363, 371
medical fitness and examinations 235, 266, 292, 297–8, 344, 380–1, 438
Army medical and grade 381

spectacles 61, 123, 143, 155, 265–6, 268
liability for military service 293
self-criticism 64
loses ring 158–9
theatre going 1, multiple theatre days 193, 284, 401, totals, 1931–1984, 1928–1939 271, see also multiple theatre attendances listed in Appendix B
Rover Scouting see Rovers (Holborn) see also Kandersteg
politics 7–9 see also BUF, Conservatives and Elections, Borough
police interest in family's politics 290–1
sacked from PR's 317
affair with Eileen see Eileen
unemployment, see Labour Exchanges
nostalgia bouts 230, 406, 414, 450, 468, 473, 487
St Pancras Council job:
Wardens' pay rounds 324, 326–7, 329, 334, 352–3, 369
paying staff at ARP depots and First Aid Posts:
    Bartholomew Rd 367
    Highgate hospital 357, 360, 389
    Inverness St 328, 334
    Malet Place/Street 321, 329, 349
    dispute with employee 349
    Old William Ellis School 370
    Veterinary College 389
rent collection at council estates:
    Brookfield 461
    Camelot 351
    Ferdinand Place 385, dispute with tenant 403–5
    Flaxman Terrace 325
    Montague Tibbles House 343
    Somers Town 348
hiking and holidays
    Chilterns 100, 135, 154–5
    Cotswolds 109, 160
    Epping Forest 305, 395, 463
    Kent 111,
    Hertfordshire 242
    Lake District 192
    North Downs 156

Index

South Downs 208, 235
Peak District 249
Snowdonia 212
Surrey Hills 47, 74, 76, 123, 126–8
holiday camps: Kent (Kingsdown) 213, Somerset (Brean Sands) 291
Marjorie *see* Heap, Marjorie
wedding plans 374, wedding 378, AH's mother-in-law 378, 396, 400, death 508
AH on married life 398, discusses children 493, *see* Heap, Anthony Charles
AH's death 508
Heap, Anthony Charles (son of AH) xxxiv, 3, 4, 19, 505, 509
Heap, Emily (AH's mother), 47, health 112–14, 118, 164–5, dental problems 117, 145, 417, report to *Evening Standard* 158, her politics 290–1, entertaining 196, politics 298, questioned on her politics 290, work as ARP Warden 254, catering at HQ 369, at Russell Square 473, resigns 491, other jobs 85, 133, 137, 155
Heap, Fred (AH's father) 2, 63 suicide xx, 66, goods removed 69, Coroner's inquest 70, funeral 71, disposal of belongings 73, 98, grave 74, 88
Heap, Marjorie, meets 360, courting 361–6 , moods of depression 367–71, 393, AH proposes 366, marriage and honeymoon 378, hair colouring 385, dental problems 417, job problems 389–91 Land Army 402, 406, 'preserving mania' 406, Fire Guard duties 418, 421, 423, 432, 447, 452, later mental problems 505–7, death 509
Heatley, Marjorie *see* Heap, Marjorie
Heatley, Charles 371–3, 396–7 399, 411,472, 479, 483–4, 499, 501, 511, his girlfriends Audrey/Lois 371, 501, 511, Jill 399
Hess, Rudolf, arrival in Scotland 360
Highbury Place N5 (No 27) 53–4, 58

Hitler, Adolf 27, 73, 122 n3, 179, 204–5 (Munich) 216, 218–19 n 29, 230, 233 n14, 239, 249, 253, 258, (Poland) 262–3, 292, 334, 356 n23, 451, 460, (death) 485–6, *see also* Germany
Hobson, John 196, 203, 250, 264, drunk 282, 291, marries 295, conscripted 327, 354, 387, 411, in North Africa 401, 426, 429, home 440, Italy 441, France 460, Belgium and Holland 468, on leave 485 Germany 496, 503
Hog's Back 73, 97, 395
Holland 266–7, 322 n62, 342, 467–8, 381, 503
Home Guard, AH encounters 294, 367
Homeopathic Hospital 252–5, 311, 331, 333, 423, 426, 438, 464, 503
homes of AH *see* Gray's Inn Rd, Highbury Place, Penryn St, Harrington Sq, Sinclair House, Queen Alexandria Mansions and Rashleigh House
Hore-Belisha, Leslie MP 235 n19, 276, 416
hotels *see also* pubs, clubs and bars
  Bedford Head 232, 324, showing lights 422
  Brighton Hall 344
  Bonnington 232
  Charing Cross 194
  Cumberland 378, 482
  Grosvenor 152
  Imperial 319
  Langham 318
  Midland 374
  Regent Palace 456
  Royal 62, 188 as a shelter 319, 322, dance at 425
  Russell 46, 71, 355
  Savoy 331,
  Shaftesbury 130, 221, 312
  Ship 354
  Strand Palace 331
  Swan 363
House of Commons 203, damaged 360
Hume, Dr B. 238
Hyde Park 20, 50, 67, 108, 111, 131, 284, 325, 363, 373, 399, 459

ice cream   470, 477, 488, substitute 420
Identity Cards demanded   294
Ilford weekend   134
Impressionist reproductions bought   426, 429, 431
Imps (Conservative *Junior Imperial League*)   189, 190, 209, 211
Incendiary bombs   318, 333, 336 n78, 337, 341 n1, 344, 355 n18, 358 n25, 399, 444, 447–8
Income Tax   155, 256, 263, 287, 296, 353, 374, 395, PAYE 422, 470, 485
inflation/rising prices   x, 271, 492
Influenza epidemic   435
Islington   293, 321, 338, 389, 445, 447, 457
Italy, invasion of Abyssinia 138–9, 330, of Albania 236, enters war 291, anti-Italian demonstration 291, allies invade 429, surrender 431, Germans into Rome 431, withdrawal 451, Italian shops attacked 292–3, *see also* Mussolini

Japan, declares war 383, sinks *HMS Prince of Wales* and *Repulse* 383, Singapore surrenders 391, Atomic bombs 498, surrender 499
'Joshua' Reynolds   32, 56, 66–7, 122, 160–1, 242, 512
Jugoslavia   114, 353–4, 486

Kandersteg Rover Jamboree 42–4, film of 126
Kaye, Bunny   41, 62, 95, 137, 141, 167, 176
Kent, Duke of wedding   116, death 403
Kentish Town   137, 139, 304, 308, 318, 320, 323, 326, 361, 365, 418, 445, 452, 469
Kew Gardens   157, 370, 426, 453, 495
King's Cross Station   351,
Kingsway tram tunnel   35 n13
'Koko' (Rover leader)   114–15, 140, 164

Labour Exchanges
   Barnsbury (Penton St)   293, 298
   Snow Hill   298, 299–302, 303, 306–7, 313–14

Lake District   192
landmines   326, 355 n18, 356, 358, 360
League of Nations   43, 122 n3, 138 n25, 139, 153, 246 n33
libraries, circulating
   Mudies   63, 190 n24, 191, 193,
   Boots, joins   191, 193, 206, 308, 388, 415
Life and Death of Colonel Blimp   427
Lisbon   106
Little Italy   354
Lloyd George, Earl David – death   483
London
   bridges: Hungerford Bridge   453, temporary   389 n3, 418,
   Vauxhall 150, Waterloo   124, 286, 359, 389 n3, 418, film 582
   City of London damage   309–10, 312–3, 336–7, 341–2, 356, 359–60, 383
   street decorations and floodlighting   116, 127–8, 130, 185–7, 490, 501 n7
   Tower of London pageant   131
'Lord Haw Haw' (William Joyce)   5 n7, 278, 279 n6
Lyons (Cafés)   41, 70, 76, 81–3, 85, 97, 100, 111, 239, 258, 313, 336, 419, Head Office seeking job 160
Lyons Corner House   36, *see also* Corner Houses

MacLavey/McLavey Mrs & Mrs ('Mrs M')   25, 171, 175, 177, 213, Bernie   155, 158, 164, 176, 179, 191, 217, 223, 409
McOrmie, Ginger   69, 79, 83, 109, 126, 155
Macnaghten (Police) House   244, 260
Malaya Club   154, 163, 170, 193, 203, 206, New Malaya 247, 248, 264, 282, 283, 289, 427
Malet Street/Place   321, 329, 349, 358, 465
Mall   126, 150–1, 184, 489–90
Maples furniture depository   344, 355–6
Margate   60, 136, 190
Mary Ward Centre   217, 231, 246, 327
Milk Bars   178, 179

Index

Ministry of Information 276, Senate House klaxon 463
Morocco 409, 436 n24
Morrison, Herbert MP 99 n8, 203, 288, Home Secretary 435 n23, 452 n15, 500
Mosley, Sir Oswald *The Greater Britain* 83, 86 229 n3, 248, arrested 290 released 435–6 *see also* BUF meetings and rallies
Mount Pleasant Post Office damage 425 n14, operating 430, 447
Mrs Miniver 404, 591
Munich crisis 216–19, 225
Municipal Reform Party 99 n8, *see* Conservative Party local
Mussolini, Benito 4 n6, 27, 179, 218, 239 n25, 253, 428, 431 n18, death 485

National Fire Service (NFS) 399 n12, 423
National Register 222, 261 n46, 262
National Service Handbook 233 n16
National Temperance Hospital 112–15, 344
Newbery, C Allen, Councillor 210, 377 n45, 450, 457, 647
Nigger (family dog) daily references not indexed, losing 180, 183, housing 180, 183, 189, loss and death 201–2, puppy replacements for Nigger (Bob) 215, Fox terrier 216, 220
newspapers and periodicals:
  Blackshirt 5 n7, 72, 73, 79, 83, 111, 179
  Chicago Daily News 179
  Clarion 99
  Daily Express 57, 68, 129 n14, 131, 229, 416, 433, 436
  Daily Mail 102, 128–9 n14, 229, 489
  Daily News 21
  Daily Sketch 22, 447
  Daily Telegraph (seeking job) 94, 137, 152, 237, 354
  Daily Worker 179, 343, 404
  Evening News 7 n8, 102, 105–6, 139
  Evening Standard 70, 158, 346, 433
  Everybody's 468
  Hampstead & Highgate Express 482
  Holborn Guardian 71
  Illustrated London News 192
  Morning Post 139
  News Chronicle 179
  Popular Educator 72, 137
  St Pancras Chronicle 221
  St Pancras Gazette 206, 208, 235–7, 245
  Star 346
  Sunday Graphic 412
  Sunday Times 143, 287
  Theatre World 30, 106, 238
  Times 139 (footnote references omitted)
  Westminster Gazette 21
North Africa 400, 408 n22, 409
Northampton Polytechnic 12, 48, 55, 83, 85
Numerology 145
Nunney, Somerset 379 n47, 400, 501

Oddenino's 433–4
Olympia xxiii, 105–6, 176
Open Air Theatre 73, 211, 245
Opera House, Covent Garden 12, 17, 372, 397, 508
overtime (AH) 4, 130, 183, 326, 329–30, 353, 377, 429–30, 469–70, 472, 477
Oxford Street damage:
  Bourne & Hollingsworth 316
  D. H. Evans 316
  John Lewis xxvii, 316, 318
  Littlewoods 356
  see also Peter Robinson's *and* Selfridges
Oxford (the) *see* Lyons Corner House
Oxford (city visit) 207, 213

Paddington station 16, 109, 150, 154, 160, 194, 380, 396, 464, 499, 501
Pancras Square, NW! 355
pantomime 63, 87, 121, 144, 171, 196, 223, 269, 336, 472
Paris (AH visits) 37–8, riots 96
Parliament Hill 166, 218 n28, 232, 236, 251, 257, 262, 264, 279,–80, 295, 299, 304, 308, 322, 352, 361, 363–9, 375–6, 394, 409, 429, 444, 462–3, *see also* allotments

623

Index

Penryn St, No 11, NW1 xi, xix, 3, 8, 59, 60, bugs 81, 101–2, landlord problems 102, moved out 104
Peter Robinson's xvi, 237, AH returns to 254, 259, McOrmie dismissed 126, 155, Reeve scandal 152, 155, staff halved 259, AH sacked 297, PR's damaged xxvi, 317, 330, 356
Petticoat Lane Market 124
Piccadilly Circus celebrations 56, 64, 100, 126, 130, 171–2, 206
Pioneer Corps debris clearance 325, 331 n75,
Poland 262, 275 n1, 441
Police (Metropolitan) 217
Police War Reserve 233–4, 234–5, 237–49, 246, 259, 260
Pop, Aunt 31, 34 to USA 47, subsequent communications 113, 164, 179, 232, 245, 265, 275, 283, 351, 382, 425, 446, 449
Portelet Rambling Club 163, 169–70, 196, 200, 202, 205, 210
Post War Credits 353, 438, 445, 474, 502
Power, Dr (surgeon) 252
Priestley, J. B. 10, 125, pink propaganda 449
Primrose Hill 125, 159, 166, 218 n28, war 'desecration' 220–1, 262, 266, 275, 280, 308, 332, 394, 461, 482
Prisoners of War Fund 425
Promenade Concerts, Queens Hall 59 n13, 242, 360 n29, 454, 458
prostitution – Tunis 429, London 468
pubs, clubs and bars
 Abbey Tavern 369
 Bird in Hand 79
 Blue Posts 163, 207, 219, 221, 269, bombed 318–19
 Bricklayers Arms 269, 276, 278, 424, 427, 444
 Bull and Bush 304, 321, 332
 Camden 234, 237, 246
 Chandos 424
 Dolphin 501
 Duke of York's 427
 Euston Tavern 327, 349, 358, 363, 367, 372, 378, 397–8, 201, 410, 443, 479, 493

 Fitzroy 276 n2, 284–6, 289, 363, 368, 370–3, 397, 399, 427, 444, 479
 Freemasons Arms 405
 George 285, 379, 405, 424, 442, 444
 Green Man 169
 Green Parrot Club 268–9, 276, 282, 289, 295, 304, 349, 363, 370
 Haverstock Arms 285, 384, 405, 424
 Horse Shoe 83, 86, 96, 115, 122–3, 142–3, 152, 154, 162, 170, 178–9, 182, 194, 196, 203, 206–7, 234, 241, 247, 262–4, 266, 284, 289, 293, 295, 299, 302, 307, damage 333, 363, 370, 373, 396, 399, 444
 Jack Straw's Castle 96
 Kentish Arms 343, 389, 433
 Load of Hay 384, 405, 424
 Malaya Club 142, 154, 163, 203, 206, 247–8, 282–3, 289, 427
 Marquis of Granby 241, 343,
 Mitre 268
 Museum Tavern 231
 Queen's 130
 Plumbers Arms 432
 Rising Sun 283, 297
 Robin Hood 219, 221–2, 234, 237, 250, 262–4, 266–9, 276, 278, bombed 312
 Rose & Crown 238, 244–9, 287
 St James' Tavern 433
 Skinners Arms 471
 Spaniards 361, 402
 Tartan Dive 371, 399, 479
 Tunnel Club 442 n2, 444
 Venetian Club 169
 Wheatsheaf 264, 276, 370, 396
 White Hart 248, 289
 see also under hotels
Putney raid 435

Queen Alexandra Mansions Flat 93 xii, xxxi, learned of flat 375, viewed 376, moved in 377–8, moved out 421 438, bought flat 505
Queens Hall *see* Promenade Concerts

racism 8, 139 *see also* Anti-Semitism
radio/wireless sets 121, 376, 380–1, 384, 401

624

Index

RAF (Royal Air Force) Fighters 304 n44, Bombers 256, 304 n36, 371, 398, 431, 444, 451, 484

Rashleigh House, Thanet St, flat 61 xii, xxxii, learned of flat 420, moved in 421, burglary 445, left 505

Ration Books 398 n11, 422, 493

rationing (sugar, bacon, butter) 277, 289 cheese 352, 481, jam 351, meat 284, 332–3, milk 332, soup 391, tea 294, 'points' system for tinned food 382 (August 1945) 502, *see also* clothing coupons

Reader, Ralph 11, 34, 40–1, 94, 96, 121, 138, 139, 144, 148, 202 n6, 337, 468, 479, Gang Show 114, 116, 131, 139–140, 158, film 182, on radio 202

Redfern, Bill, ARIBA 193, 196, 201, 203, 236, 287

Red Lion Street/Square 267, 312, 321, 356, 359

refugees, in shelters 322 n62, 328–9, payments to 329

Regent's Park 30, 33, 80, 158. 187 n17, 215, 218 n28, 220, 260, 275, 295, shelter 302, 307, 332 n76, 352, 367 n34, 453 n16, 458 n26, 459–61, 466

Reith, Sir John 276

Remembrance / Armistice Day 115, 141, 164, 193, 221, 267, *see also* Cenotaph

restaurants and cafes
 ABC 40, 328
 Chaffie's 230, 250
 Bodega's 86, 130, 170, 370
 Kardomah 488
 Milk Bars 178, 180, 435, 488
 New Oxford St bar 94
 see also Lyons

Richard I statue damage 324

Richmond 157

Reynolds, 'Joshua' 32, 56, 67, 71, 122, 137, 160, 242

Roland House Panto 32 n10, 52, 95, 219, 230–1

Rolls Razor 158, 161–2

Ron 142, 146, 149–50, 152–4, 162–3, 169–70, 197, 203, 226, 231, 247, 264, 271, 276, 282–6, 339, 346–8, 396, 398, 405, 414, 427, 439, 442, 444, 474, 493–4, 503, 512

Royal Free Hospital 457

Rover Scouting AH at xvi, 55, 140–41, German Scouts 72–3, 110, AH Holborn Secretary 79 84, 128, Treasurer 113, London District Council 84, 128, resigns 163–4

Rumania 233, 262, 294, 353

Russell Square 184, 319, 325, 359, 455, 463

Russia (Soviet Union) 76, 159, 216–17, 262, 264, 268, 284, 290, 294, 363–4, 383, 396, 3987, 400, 403, 427, 441–2, 471, 477, invades Poland 480, 485–6, 492, 497, 499, *see also* Bolsheviks

St Pancras Church xxiv, xxv, 183, 321, 343, *see also* Air Raid Shelters, the Crypt

St Pancras Control Room (AH's night duties) *see* Air Raid Precautions

St Pancras Station/Goods Yard 316, 319 damage, Churchill visit 361

St Pancras Town Hall opening 189, 217, AH seeks job 303, 306, 31, 3, starts work 315, damage 316, temporary windows 361, decorated for parade 376, Savings for Warships Week 392

St Paul's Cathedral 128–9, 232, 312, 324, 337, 383, 490

Salisbury 210

salvage – iron railings and tramlines 391, paper 392

Salvation Army, restaurant 354, shelter 456

Sandwich House 419

School – Mrs Kemp's 3, St Clement Danes 41, sports day 79, 211, 262, 248

seasonal observations
 Spring 125, 224, 232, 281, 285, 391, 394, 396, 421, 439, 449, 453
 Summer 128, 133, 187, 439, 464
 Autumn 406
 Winter 20, 143, 151, 223, 264, 278–9, 332, 353, 396

Second Front 403, 437, D-Day 451

625

Index

Selfridge, Gordon   127, 184 n14
Selfridges, Oxford St   127, 184, 186–7, damaged   317, 356, 471 n41
Sheppard, PC Fred and family   30, 61, 69, 71, 112, 115–6, 117, 169, 254, 283, 351, 375, 392, 446, 512, Christmas with 117, 114–15
shortages in wartime   bacon 491, beer 373, 389, 491–2, 502, cigarettes 361, 492, clothing 427, coal 390, 478–9, coffee 495, fruit 391, fuel 479, 490 12, 502, furniture 396, gas 313, housing 482, jam 351, matches 373, meat 342, oranges 357, paper 287, potatoes 477, toothpaste 344, razor blades 344, 357, 422, 436, safety razors 447, shaving soap 344, shoes 425, soap 344, 357, soup 363, 391, 491, 502, wines and spirits 389, 433, *see also* Clothing Coupons
Sinclair House, Hastings St, Flat 19   xi, xii, finds 180, moves in 182, viewed flat 25 345, moves to flat 25   347, outlook 347, 'burglary' 372, 382, AH leaves 377
skiing, skating and tobogganing   68, 223, 279
Smart, Phil and Kath   219, 223, 243, 246, 248, 261–3, 269, 270–1, 287, 315, 332, 339, 367, 398, conscripted 405, 501, 512
smoking
   cigarettes   40, 75, 108, 165, 168, 175, cutting down 288, 303, 332, 342, 442
   pipe 168–9, 175, 472, 478
   cigars 55, 86, 97, 169, 171, 175, 178, 197, 227
Snowdonia   212
Soleby, Mrs   103–4, 113, 175
Somerset, honeymoon, summer holidays
SOS Society   59
Southend   156–7, 189
Sperni, John (senior)   183 n10, 186, 195, 205, 207–8, 211, 222, 229, 248, 254, 290 n18, 298
Sperni, John (junior)   208, 211, 'the Italian Haw Haw' 208 n17
Stanhope St   322, 461
Stratford on Avon   109–10, 160

Stonehenge   211
Summertime   219, 281, 328, Double Summertime 357, 394, 462, 465
Swaffer, Hannen   79, 266, 523
Swedish Drill   62, 124, 151, 189, 231
Swiss Cottage   281, 332
Switzerland *see* Kandersteg
Syria   492

Tavistock Place   319 n27, 231, 305, 327, 355, 479–80
Tavistock Square   xxix, 98, 244, 305, 325, 327, 336 n77, 359
Territorial Army   123, 235 n19, 238, 244
Thames Bridges
   temporary bridge 389, 418
   new Waterloo Bridge 418 n6
Thames House   203 n8
Thames, River   20, 131, 310
theatres in London, total pre-war visits   268, wartime management   256, closures 258, re-openings 261, 269, Sunday Opening Bill 352–3, closures during V-weapon offensives
theatres, London (only the first and significant mentions are indexed but *see also* multiple entries in Annex B)
   Adelphi   136, 177, 516
   Aldwych   41, 456, 514
   Ambassador's   516
   Apollo   31, 517
   Cambridge   87, 330, 517
   City Literary Institute (amateur)   246
   Coliseum   36, 518
   Comedy   10, 124, 514
   Court   514
   Cripplegate Theatre   515
   Criterion   56, 64, 67, 518
   Daly's   515
   Dominion   53, 78, 259, 514
   Drury Lane   30, 39, 234, 328, 330–1, 455, 514
   Duchess   284, 359, 517
   Duke of York's   277, 291, 515
   Embassy, Swiss Cottage   332, 562
   Fortune   514
   Gaiety   20, 40, 517
   Garrick   21, 111, 514

Index

Globe 78, 124, 515
Haymarket 32, 105, 523
His Majesty's xxii, 54, 97, 171, 518
Lyceum 45, 63, 515
Lyric 518, 524
Lyric, Hammersmith 515
New 523
New Gallery 526
Old Vic 30, 32, 34, 100, 526
Palace 129, 520, 529
Palladium 2, 218, 516
Pavilion 517 burned 326
Phoenix 149, 519
Piccadilly 30, 33, 456, V-1 514, 517
Playhouse 60, 525
Prince Edward 515, 524
Prince of Wales 523, 525
Princes 87, 196, 319, 602
Queen's 318, 515, 523
Regent's Park Open Air Theatre 73, 211, 532, 568
Royalty 514, 523
Rudolph Steiner Hall 576
St James's 126, 440, 516, 525
St Martin's 124, 188 n19, 351 n13, 514
Sadler's Wells 32, 45, 104, 131, 520
Saville 58, 98, 195, 323, 328, 520
Savoy 20, 59, 516
Scala (amateur) 11, 61, 114–15, 140–2
Strand 128, 295, 328, 515
Shaftesbury 84, 356, 515
Streatham Hill Theatre 549
Vaudeville 36, 514
Victoria Palace 222 n36, 519, 564
Westminster 422, 524
Whitehall 35–6, 44, 52, 519
Winter Garden 455, 526, 596
Wyndham's 109, 342, 515
Théâtres in Paris, Casino de Paris 38, Folies Bergère 38, Opéra 38
Theobalds Rd xxx, 248, 356, 359
Tilbury 37–8, 41, 44, 205–6
Toscanini, Arturo 242
Tottenham Court Road xxviii, 36–7, 46, 51, 83 n19, 180, 207 n13, 283 n14, 318–9, 325, 333, 342, 355, 358, 394, 407, 416, 453 n18, V-1, Howland St 456, 482–3
Thompson, Bonar 108, 112, 216

Trafalgar Square demonstrations 77, 98, floodlit 489

Underground (Tube) routine journeys not indexed 17, 87 (floodgates), 267, 294, 320, 327, 347, as shelters 319 n57, 320, Bethnal Green 420 n10, 448, 455, 473
United Nations Restaurant (St Giles High St) 427, 445
Unemployment Exchanges *see* Labour Exchanges
United States enters war after Pearl Harbour 383, troops in London 433, 442, 446, 449, Military Police 445, 453, 468, 495, troops leaving 483, 498, Shaftesbury Ave Club 419, behaviour of soldier and local girls 419, 430, 433, 483, murder trial 470 n40
University College, Gower St 318, 355
Utility Goods – suits 391, 392 n6, 418, 'austerity suit' 425, women's garments 429, furniture 396, 422

vacuum cleaner 491
Venereal disease, publicity 420
Venetian Club 169
Victory celebrations
  VE Day 486–9
  VJ Day 499–501
V-1 flying bomb, offensive opens 452–4, 'pilotless planes' 452–4, V- weapon and casualty statistics 454, 458, 462, 465, 'local' incidents:
  Aldwych 456
  Bethnal Green 452
  Bishops Gardens 461
  Camden Town (Rochester Place, Torbay and Hawley Roads 457–8
  Chancery Lane 464
  Clements Inn 453
  Colville Place 453
  Conduit St 459
  Copenhagen St 459
  Crowndale Rd 462
  Denmark Park Hill 461
  Gaumont, Holloway 463
  Howland St/Tot Ct Rd 456
  Hungerford Bridge 453

Index

Ibex House EC3   453
Kentish Town   452, 469
King Henry's Rd   470
Moorgate   459
Ossulston St   457
Parliament Hill   463
Pentonville Rd   455
Regent's Park   453, 458, 459, 466
Royal Free Hospital   457
Russell Sq   455
St Pancras Goods Yard
Shelton St   455
Stanhope St   461
Staples Inn   464
V-2 long-range rocket, offensive opens 465, rocket statistics and casualties 485, 'local' incidents:
Archway   469
Chiswick   465
City Rd   470
Duke St   471
Finchley Rd   481
Kentish Town   469
Marble Arch   481
Tavistock Place   479–80
Primrose Hill   482
Smithfield Market   481
Warwick Court   470
Whitfield Tabernacle   482–3

Wallace Collection   110, 114, 317, 355
Wanstead Flats/Forest Gate   71, 115, 144
War (1914–18) *see* Cenotaph, Remembrance Day and Ypres League
War (1939–1945) approach of Czech crisis 216, Danzig corridor 246 n33, Poland 253, 258, declaration of war and alarm 254, 'Phoney War' 228 n1, first bomb on UK 265, German invasion of Holland, Belgium and France 288–90, Denmark and Norway 286–8, withdrawal of BEF from Belgium then France at Dunkirk 291 n29, removal of place names (anti-invasion) 292, first bombs on London (Croydon and Edmonton) 304 n44, Blitz opens 309–10, firestorm on City 336, withdrawal from Crete 362, Dieppe raid 403, El Alamein victory 408, Allies land in Morocco 409, Allies in Sicily 427, then Italian mainland 430, D-Day 451, Operation Market Garden (Arnhem) 467, German Ardennes offensive 472, Allies' Rhine crossings 483, capture of Berlin 486, German surrender 486, Atomic bomb 498, Japanese surrender 499, *see also* Belgium, France, Germany, Italy, Japan, Poland, United States and Air Raid Precautions *and* Air Raid Shelters

weather:
 floods   420 n24 (Tube floodgates) 267 n56
 fog   47, 52, 63, 67, 93, 152, 170–1, 194, 196–7, 223, 231, 277, 333, 377
 frost   30–2, 143–4, 450, 477
 snow   17, 21, 33–6, 98, 143, 155, 223–4, 279–80, 341, 389–80
Welwyn Garden City   285, 297, 302–3, 307
Wembley, Empire Pool   132
West Hampstead Station   444
White, Jack (bandleader)   283
White, Mrs   203, 221, 229–30
Whitehall   129, 258, 324, 446, 488–9, 500
Whitestone Pond   322, 369, 402
Whistler, Rex   461
Whyte, Dr (GP)   69 n 2, 75, 153–5, 237–9
William Ellis School   444
Windsor Great Park   35, 44, 80, 149–51, 186
Wodehouse P. G., BBC ban   436
Wolff & Hollander   333
women – in uniform   285, as dust collectors and bus conductors   373
Working Men's College   329
Wrestling, Lines Club   132

YMCA – Young Men's Christian Association   22, 30, 37, 44, 56, Swedish drill 62 n14, AH resigns 287, damage 318–19
York Way   352, 459
Youth Hostels   6, Chilterns 100, 135, 154–5, Cotswolds 109, 160, Euston

628

Index

(YWCA) 63, Kent 111, Lake District 192, Surrey and Sussex 76, 123, 126–7 ((Bentley Cottage) 74 (Godstone) 127, Ridgeway 47, 128, Peak District 249, Snowdonia 212

Ypres League 8, 140, 157, 232

YWCA – Young Women's Christian Association 63, 86, 99, 123

Zelger, Mrs 69–70, 73, 103, 113, 231, 254, 377

Zoo (London) 332 n76, 367, 377

LONDON RECORD SOCIETY

President: The Rt. Hon. The Lord Mayor of London

Chairman: Professor Caroline M. Barron, MA, PhD, FRHistS
Hon. Secretary: Dr Helen Bradley
Hon. Treasurer: Dr David Lewis
Hon. General Editors: Dr Robin Eagles, Dr Hannes Kleineke, Professor Jerry White

The London Record Society was founded in December 1964 to publish transcripts, abstracts and lists of the primary sources for this history of London, and generally to stimulate interest in archives relating to London. Membership is open to any individual or institution; the annual subscription is £18 (US $22) for individuals and £23 (US $35) for institutions. Prospective members should apply to the Hon. Membership Secretary, Dr Penny Tucker, Hewton Farmhouse, Bere Alston, Yelverton, Devon, PL20 7BW (email londonrecordsoc@btinternet.com).

The following volumes have already been published:

1. *London Possessory Assizes: a Calendar*, edited by Helena M. Chew (1965)
2. *London Inhabitants within the Walls, 1695*, with an introduction by D. V. Glass (1966)
3. *London Consistory Court Wills, 1492–1547*, edited by Ida Darlington (1967)
4. *Scriveners' Company Common Paper, 1357–1628, with a Continuation to 1678*, edited by Francis W. Steer (1968)
5. *London Radicalism, 1830–1843: a Selection from the Papers of Francis Place*, edited by D. J. Rowe (1970)
6. *The London Eyre of 1244*, edited by Helena M. Chew and Martin Weinbaum (1970)
7. *The Cartulary of Holy Trinity Aldgate*, edited by Gerald A. J. Hodgett (1971)
8. *The Port and Trade of Early Elizabethan London: Documents*, edited by Brian Dietz (1972)
9. *The Spanish Company*, edited by Pauline Croft (1973)

10. *London Assize of Nuisance, 1301–1431: a Calendar*, edited by Helena M. Chew and William Kellaway (1973)
11. *Two Calvinistic Methodist Chapels, 1748–1811: the London Tabernacle and Spa Fields Chapel*, edited by Edwin Welch (1975)
12. *The London Eyre of 1276*, edited by Martin Weinbaum (1976)
13. *The Church in London, 1375–1392*, edited by A. K. McHardy (1977)
14. *Committees for the Repeal of the Test and Corporation Acts: Minutes, 1786–90 and 1827–8*, edited by Thomas W. Davis (1978)
15. *Joshua Johnson's Letterbook, 1771–4: Letters from a Merchant in London to his Partners in Maryland*, edited by Jacob M. Price (1979)
16. *London and Middlesex Chantry Certificate, 1548*, edited by C. J. Kitching (1980)
17. *London Politics, 1713–1717: Minutes of a Whig Club, 1714–17*, edited by H. Horwitz; *London Pollbooks, 1713*, edited by W. A. Speck and W. A. Gray (1981)
18. *Parish Fraternity Register: Fraternity of the Holy Trinity and SS. Fabian and Sebastian in the Parish of St. Botolph without Aldersgate*, edited by Patricia Basing (1982)
19. *Trinity House of Deptford: Transactions, 1609–35*, edited by G. G. Harris (1983).
20. *Chamber Accounts of the Sixteenth Century*, edited by Betty R. Masters (1984)
21. *The Letters of John Paige, London Merchant, 1648–58*, edited by George F. Steckley (1984)
22. *A Survey of Documentary Sources for Property Holding in London before the Great Fire*, by Derek Keene and Vanessa Harding (1985)
23. *The Commissions for Building Fifty New Churches*, edited by M. H. Port (1986)
24. *Richard Hutton's Complaints Book*, edited by Timothy V. Hitchcock (1987)
25. *Westminster Abbey Charters, 1066–c.1214*, edited by Emma Mason (1988)
26. *London Viewers and their Certificates, 1508–1558*, edited by Janet S. Loengard (1989)
27. *The Overseas Trade of London: Exchequer Customs Accounts, 1480–1*, edited by H. S. Cobb (1990)
28. *Justice in Eighteenth-Century Hackney: the Justicing Notebook of Henry Norris and the Hackney Petty Sessions Book*, edited by Ruth Paley (1991)
29. *Two Tudor Subsidy Assessment Rolls for the City of London: 1541 and 1582*, edited by R. G. Lang (1993)
30. *London Debating Societies, 1776–1799*, compiled and introduced by Donna T. Andrew (1994)
31. *London Bridge: Selected Accounts and Rentals, 1381–1538*, edited by Vanessa Harding and Laura Wright (1995)

32. *London Consistory Court Depositions, 1586–1611: List and Indexes*, by Loreen L. Giese (1997)
33. *Chelsea Settlement and Bastardy Examinations, 1733–66*, edited by Tim Hitchcock and John Black (1999)
34. *The Church Records of St Andrew Hubbard Eastcheap, c.1450–c.1570*, edited by Clive Burgess (1999)
35. *Calendar of Exchequer Equity Pleadings, 1685–6 and 1784–5*, edited by Henry Horwitz and Jessica Cooke (2000)
36. *The Letters of William Freeman, London Merchant, 1678–1685*, edited by David Hancock (2002)
37. *Unpublished London Diaries: a Checklist of Unpublished Diaries by Londoners and Visitors, with a Select Bibliography of Published Diaries*, compiled by Heather Creaton (2003)
38. *The English Fur Trade in the Later Middle Ages*, by Elspeth M. Veale (2003; reprinted from 1966 edition)
39. *The Bede Roll of the Fraternity of St Nicholas*, edited by N. W. and V. A. James (2 vols., 2004)
40. *The Estate and Household Accounts of William Worsley, Dean of St Paul's Cathedral, 1479–1497*, edited by Hannes Kleineke and Stephanie R. Hovland (2004)
41. *A Woman in Wartime London: the Diary of Kathleen Tipper, 1941–1945*, edited by Patricia and Robert Malcolmson (2006)
42. *Prisoners' Letters to the Bank of England 1783–1827*, edited by Deirdre Palk (2007)
43. *The Apprenticeship of a Mountaineer: Edward Whymper's London Diary, 1855–1859*, edited by Ian Smith (2008)
44. *The Pinners' and Wiresellers' Book, 1462–1511*, edited by Barbara Megson (2009)
45. *London Inhabitants Outside the Walls, 1695*, edited by Patrick Wallis (2010)
46. *The Views of the Hosts of Alien Merchants, 1440–1444*, edited by Helen Bradley (2012)
47. *The Great Wardrobe Accounts of Henry VII and Henry VIII*, edited by Maria Hayward (2012)
48. *Summary Justice in the City: A Selection of Cases Heard at the Guildhall Justice Room, 1752–1781*, edited by Greg T. Smith (2013)
49. *The Diaries of John Wilkes, 1770–1797*, edited by Robin Eagles (2014)
50. *A Free-Spirited Woman: The London Diaries of Gladys Langford, 1936–1940*, edited by Patricia and Robert Malcolmson (2014)
51. *The Angels' Voice: A Magazine for Young Men in Brixton, London, 1910–1913*, edited by Alan Argent (2016)

Previously published titles in the series are available from Boydell and Brewer; please contact them for further details, or see their website, www.boydellandbrewer.com